Christian Musings

Christian Musings

by

H. W. Moore

MINISTRY OF GOD'S LOVE
BOSTON, MASSACHUSETTS

Ministry of God's Love
112 Shawmut Avenue
Boston, Massachusetts 02118
617 357-8145

Printed in the United States of America

12 11 10 09 08   5 4 3 2 1

ISBN 978-1-930566-73-6

Library of Congress Control Number: 2009923246

Book design and layout by
D. & F. Scott Publishing, Inc.
North Richland Hills, Texas

With eternal gratitude to God for leading me to His wonderful inerrant Word and drawing me to His Son, my Lord and Savior Christ Jesus, I dedicate this book to:

The Memory

of

Dr. Pamela J. Whitney

A most blessed disciple of our Lord and Savior Christ Jesus who was the first to read and appreciate these writings, and the first to tell me that I was saved.

Contents

Foreword by Joe Fitzgerald xi

Acknowledgments xiii

My Testimony xv

Why These Essays? xix

1. How Do I Know that God Is Really the Author of the Bible? . . . 1

2. What Is a Born-Again Christian? 41

3. Repentance 47

4. The Professor and the Possessor 56

5. Have You Checked Your Temperature Lately? 74

6. Candy Cane Faith 77

7. Many Are Called, but Few Are Chosen—A Challenge
   to Serious Faith 84

8. Is It True Faith? 100

9. Counterfeit Faith 102

10. The Certainty of a Saving Faith 108

11. A Conversation Between a Soul and Its Body 114

12. The Temple of God 120

13. A Biographical Sketch of Sin 123

14. The Consequences of Sin 152

15. The Covering of Sin 156

16. Confession of Sin 160

17. Sin Unto Death 171

18. God Provided the Law so Sin Would Increase 181

19. Disobeying the Ten Commandments Can Never
    Condemn Anyone to Hell 186

20. Hell . . . What Is It . . . Where Is It?—And Some
    Other Observations 189

21. Good and Evil and the Paradox of Free Will vs. Predestination 204

Contents

22. Free Will—Is It Humanity's Bane or Benefit, and
    What Can We Do about It! 210
23. Mankind's Sovereign Will 217
24. The Great Dilemma 222
25. Are You an Overcomer? 225
26. The Watchman 230
27. Jesus, the Early Years 233
28. The Father's Drawing 255
29. About My Father's Business 262
30. Loving Jesus 267
31. What's in a Name? 278
32. Christ Jesus 283
33. In Christ 284
34. The Numerous Other Roles of Our Blessed Mediator 287
35. Without Me You Can Do Nothing! 295
36. Christian R & R 300
37. Come Let us Reason Together 306
38. And We know 309
39. Do You Know Truth? 316
40. Biblical Myths 325
41. The Belt and Suspenders Philosophy 350
42. Benefit of a Doubt 357
43. What Do You Mean by "If"? 362
44. The Heart 394
45. How Do Your Attitudes Be? 401
46. The Spirit Connection 409
47. Ye Are the Salt of the Earth 413
48. Nothing but Leaves 420
49. The Bema Seat Blues 427
50. Belief Without Salvation 438
51. Making a Case for Salvation 451
52. The Price of Salvation 463
53. Can Salvation Be Lost? 467
54. How to Loose Your Salvation 474
55. Work out Your Salvation 484

Contents

56. Salvation 486
57. The Foolishness of God Is Wiser than Man 488
58. Spiritual Stumbling 539
59. Is It Stumbling or Foolishness? 551
60. Pride 557
61. Satan 562
62. Self-Love 565
63. Why Did Satan Do It? 570
64. Sincerity 590
65. A Lesson in Humility from Job 601
66. Forgiveness 619
67. Gratitude and Forgiveness 625
68. The Lord's Prayer 630
69. The Power of Prayer 640
70. Some Thoughts on Prayer 645
71. Prayer 648
72. Does Prayer Accomplish Anything? 656
73. Peace 662
74. Love 666
75. The Fifth Love 668
76. The Third Commandment 672
77. The Three Thieves 674
78. The Bulls of Bashan 679
79. Was It Murder He Wrote? 687
80. The Crucifixion—The Rest of the Story 693
81. Walking Out the Door 697
82. Transcendent Love 699
83. In Defense of Jacob 701
84. The Mark of Cain 729
85. Role Models 734
86. The Samaritan Woman at the Well 768
87. The Parables of the Mustard Seed and of Leaven 776
88. The Parable of the Talents 784
89. The Parable of the Ten Virgins 793
90. The Marriage of the Lamb 801

Contents

91. Putting Words in God's Mouth 805
92. Cat and Dog Theology 818
93. The Lord Is Throwing a Party and We Are All Invited! 821
94. The Master Tailor. 826
95. Meditation 831
96. Lent 834
97. Oh Death, Where Is Thy Sting? 838
A Prayer for the Country 841

Foreword
A Project Finished Right on Time!

Bill Moore is my friend, and I really need no other reason than that to celebrate the publication of *Christian Musings,* the culmination of what has now become his life's work, late in a life already distinguished by achievements that made him one of this region's most respected civil engineers.

As a friend I have great affection for him.

But I also celebrate as one who writes for a living, one whose own faith is buoyed by the inspired writing of others, especially hymn writers, which is why I have great admiration for my friend, too, because of the clear devotion and obvious commitment he has brought to this project.

More than prolific, Bill is passionate, a wonderful quality immediately apparent to the reader.

He often notes, as he did again in the prefacing pages, that most of his life was lived outside of the faith that now defines him, as if those were years of wasted time and lost opportunities.

I would respectfully disagree with my friend on that, instead seeing in his journey a perfect example of how, as promised, the Lord makes everything beautiful "in *His* time," not our time. Indeed, if you want to make God laugh, tell Him your plans! He tells us, through the prophet Jeremiah, *"I know the plans I have for you,"* which is why this book, coming at this particular stage of Bill's life, seems to me to have been written precisely right on time.

Consider this: The thirst he now has for Scripture might have been partially quenched with the passage of time, had Bill spent the fullness of his life immersed in its passages.

Instead, armed with intellectual skills that have been honed in the fires of commercial success, and driven by the spiritual hunger of a new-born believer, he began to scrutinize the Bible, to absorb and contemplate it, and then to write with an engineer's   eye and a ' servant's heart, to say nothing of "a fire in my bones" not unlike the one Jeremiah described.

For me—and perhaps for you, too, as you pour through these pages—his finished work conjures up an image of the psalmist who wrote, *"As the deer panteth after the water brooks, so panteth* my *soul after thee, O Lord; my soul thirsteth for God."*

There is intensity in these pages.

Some chapters will be easier to read than others.

Some conclusions will be easier to concur with than others.

And that's OK, exactly how it should be.

Good writing isn't meant to simply entertain us; it's also meant to inform, provoke, challenge, and inspire us, all of which Bill does with the singular purpose of sharing with his readers what's been placed upon his heart.

It's his hope, and the hope of those of us who hold him in the highest esteem, that *something* in his writings will touch your heart, too. Speaking through the prophet Isaiah, the Lord vowed that His Word would *not* return to Him void, but rather would accomplish what He intended in the place to which He sent it, which, in this case, means your hands.

May you, too, be richly blessed by it.

Joe Fitzgerald
January 31, 2008
Boston

Acknowledgments

There are four most gracious women who are responsible for this collection of thoughts having become a book.

Cindy Fitzgerald. It was her patience, long suffering, never complaining, and dedication over many years that converted every word from pencil to type. Cindy credits her early exposure to this work as having softened her heart, allowing the Holy Spirit to bring her and her husband Michael to the faith.

Harriet Thompson. Her many hours of patient listening and reading my earliest writings, long before she met our Lord, was a needed encouragement.

Marie McKee. It was because of her intense appreciation of these papers, and her insistence that their purpose would be far better served as a single bound volume.

Jennie Jones. She most graciously proofread every page for spelling, punctuation, and typos.

I am also greatly indebted to the many of God's disciples to whom He gave much wisdom and discernment for the interpretation and articulations of the many subtle messages that enrich God's Word. First there was Dr. Chuck Missler, my earliest mentor, who also led my son Hal to the faith. Additionally there are many other inspired men such as Charles Spurgeon, Donald Barnhouse, Henry Ironsides, Dave Hunt, J. Vernon McGee, John Brice, Edward Young, Sidlow Baxter and John MacArthur who have guided my Christian walk. God led me very early to the writings of these great men, as a way of filling my heart with a hunger for His Word. I believe this was to more rapidly advance in me the understanding of Scripture so as to compensate for my very late-in-life recognition of the truth of Jesus' work on the cross. The privilege of being able to learn from these and many others of God's chosen as I seek His wisdom and discernment, has been among the greatest of all of the many privileges with which He has blessed me. I pray that I have not diminished the high standard of faithful Scripture interpretation they have set.

My Testimony

How can I tell you how Jesus first came into my life?

In retrospect, I realize that He was with me always, guiding me, protecting me and waiting hopefully for me to acknowledge Him, and to hear His gentle knock at the door of my heart. He's been with me since the day I was born. However it was only in the December of my life that I realized this.

From a human perspective, you could say, that after sixty-eight years of this one-sided patient and loving relationship, God decided it was time to really get my attention. On November 19, 1994 I was diagnosed with stage 4 terminal cancer. The biopsy report said that it was the most aggressive and rapidly growing type.

The chief oncologist at Dana Faber as well as those at Mass General and Tufts Medical Center, all in Boston, MA told me and my family that it was too far advanced and too late for any kind of treatment. They estimated that I had six months, maybe twelve at the most to live.

Rather than just wait to die, I chose to investigate alternatives and to self-treat through diet, nutrition, minerals, supplements, and every other possible modality that conventional medicine calls quackery, but which I now know can cure, rather than simply treat symptoms of degenerative diseases.

For most of the next eighteen months, the cancer continued to grow and spread to other areas causing considerable inconveniences, bleeding, pain, and much sleep deprivation. However, a very strange thing was also happening. Because of these efforts, I was actually able to go to work feeling stronger and healthier most days. Of course I didn't know it then, but this was Jesus setting up the stage for the main event. However, toward the end of the ordeal, when the cancer had nearly filled my bladder causing kidney failure, I went back to the oncologist who originally discovered the cancer, and he removed enough of it to be able to insert a stint into one of my kidneys.

To make a long story short..... three months later, when he went back for the periodic stint replacement, he found, to his utter astonishment, not a trace of cancer, anywhere, and except for some scar tissue, all areas where the cancer had been, were normal in size and appearance, as if the cancer had never occurred. I am *still* cancer free in 2007. I can now say PRAISE GOD, but I was unable to at the time.

You might ask what does this gory cancer story have to do with my testimony. The importance is two-fold. First, it provides a peek into how our Lord might choose to work in any of us, and second, it establishes the foundation for a second ministry to which He has led me.

During this entire ordeal, it never entered my mind to pray or to beg God for mercy, or even think about where I was going when my life was over. I *always* knew that there was a Creator God. But I didn't believe that He got involved in any of my problems, that it was only my own initiative, my own strength and my own effort that could achieve anything. Self-reliance was my *real* god and had been all my life. Surely, it was this *self*-effort that had caused my healing.

For the next two to three months, I strutted around proud as a peacock of *my* achievement, and how I had done better than the best minds in medicine! I felt completely full of myself. I alone had delayed death and became younger, stronger and healthier than I had been ten years earlier. I was ready to re-conquer the earth!

I don't know how it happened. It was not a thunderous, or in anyway memorable event. As I look back, it can probably be best expressed as a feeling of sorts that someone was tapping on my shoulder, beckoning me to turn around.

Again to shorten the story, it was Jesus who turned me around, and straightened me out. I finally got it into my head that it was not me, but He who guided me through that painful maze, and that it was He, who, at the end of it, and with one masterful stroke, had removed the cancer and restored my health.

Pride was soon replaced by humility, gratitude and faith as my Savior finally penetrated my heart. That's when I knew that my life was His, that He had extended it for a purpose, and that He was to be in charge of it from then on, forever.

Somehow He led me to the Bible and to the teachings of several great Bible scholars. Between these, and the result of His love, directed through me, I developed an insatiable hunger for His Word, and a compelling need to share its great wonders with others through my own writings. He also made certain that I not waste the blessing of the cancer ordeal, but instead that I should continue to study healing methods so that I could help every hurting person He would send to me.

This study period went on for about three years, for He had put it into my heart, that if I was to be an effective servant, I must really *know* my Lord, *know* His word and *know* how to deal with what He expected of me.

During this whole period, I never even thought to venture out into the Christian world. I don't believe that I had ever met a real Christian.

I know that Jesus wanted me to first become well grounded in faith, and to have a firm foundation in His Word before I ought to be exposed to all of the false and deceptive teaching, and apostasy which dominate much of what today is called Christianity. Then about six years ago He removed me from my cocoon, and eventually led me into a Christian body.

I see now how my dear Jesus purchased me with His love and with His blood. He purchased me twice. First, my body, then, my soul. Now my service to Him, as He has ordained it, is also two-fold. It is to help others physically as well as spiritually. God calls each of us, as He has called me, for specific purposes. It took a while, but I finally realized that the cancer had been a blessing, because of all that necessarily flowed from the ordeal. Were I to suffer the very worst portion of that ordeal continually for the rest of my life, I would consider it of little consequence as compared with what Jesus did for me *after* He removed the cancer.

I must tell you, I am among the most blessed persons to have ever live. Not only has He, my Lord, extended my life, saved my soul, and given me a purpose, but he has also allowed me to continue working in my life-long profession as an engineer, and to continue sharing this extended life with my loving family and with some very dear brothers and sisters in the faith. He has also given me the blessed opportunity to teach His word and to compose these essays that follow. How many more blessings could possibly be packed into such a low and unworthy soul?

In essence: My life is His, and *He is* my life.

Much, much more could be said about what my blessed Lord has done in my life. Some small portion can be found in what this volume is all about, and also on a website called www.christianmusings.com. On this website can also be found several papers related to my physical journey, along with some of my opinions on how healing and health can be achieved.

May God bless you, the reader, as much as He has blessed me!

Preface
Why These Essays

First, I must say, there is nothing profound to be discovered here, and I'm sure that any Bible scholar would find these to be the work of an amateur, which they most certainly are. However, I pray that in the simplicity of these essays the reader may find some of God's truths more easily understood than might be derived from more scholarly works.

As noted in "My Testimony," I became a believer in Jesus as Lord and Savior by first having determined that the Holy Bible was without any doubt, authored by God Himself, that it is His inerrant word as it has been preserved in the original Greek and Hebrew. It has been given to us that we may know Him, His purpose and what He expects from us. To be aware of this and to not seek, with great zeal and perseverance, to know and to share all that the Holy Spirit is willing to reveal, would be a very sad and inadequate response to this great blessing.

From the beginning, as I read and studied, He revealed the most wonderful truths, precious pearls of wisdom, and priceless insights, which I wanted to shout out and to share with all who would listen. But, I realized that my ability as a speaker was sadly limited. What passed through my lips was never as compelling as it was while it sat in my heart.

Making essays out of these musings became my response to this difficulty. My writing skill barely exceeded my speaking ability but, limited as it is, that seemed to be the forum God has given me to use. The Holy Spirit continues to prompt me to write and share in this manner all that He chooses to allow me to discover. What follows is a selection of those essays which, I pray, He has chosen and which He is offering as my legacy to my four children and four grandchildren, and all others who may in some way benefit.

—1—
How Do I Know that God Is Really the Author of the Bible?

Believers in the Holy Bible claim that it was authored by God Himself, and that it contains within itself absolute proof of that authorship! This truth I was finally blessed to have discovered, even though it was late in my twilight years, and I pray that the Holy Spirit will choose for me here the appropriate words that someday, somewhere will lead someone to recognize and make this great truth his or her own. This book reveals not only history of the past, present and future, but does so with 100 percent proven accuracy. At the same time it has the capacity to give sustaining comfort, solace, and peace to even the most troubled, confused, and fearful souls if they believe and have faith in Jesus and in His resurrection. Once you realize that God, the Creator of the universe and of all that is life, actually authored the Bible, you realize that it cannot be anything but truth. Yet today, it seems to be fashionable to seek answers almost anywhere else except from this unique and most precious book, or at best to pick and choose from it only that which is pleasant, comfortable, or logical and which fits our own personal preferences. The problem is that only a small remnant seem able to believe the whole Word as expressed in it. While this current widespread lack of belief is a source of sorrow to the true believer, it is not at all a surprise because the book itself makes clear that this would, in fact, be exactly so at this point in history. It predicts that hearts would grow cold and that many false prophets would rise distorting the Word, as well as that many false religions will become popular, religions that sound wonderful and promise much, but which, in the end, can not deliver any-thing but eternal separation from God.

Among the many verifiable proofs of its divine authorship are the hundreds of prophecies, all of which have been fulfilled with com-plete accuracy and precision, while others can be seen today in the very process of fulfillment. It is this, along with many other proofs of authorship, that has caused many, such as myself, to believe, and through belief to find faith as well as solid answers to life's continu-ous concerns and questions. It is a sampling of these proofs, that I will here attempt to present.

This book, the Bible, is not a compilation of myths, allegories, and contrived history as many wish to view it. It is also far more than an accurate reporting of history—past, present, and future—as archaeol-ogy and unfolding events are slowly recognizing it to be. No archae-ological find has ever disproved its historical accuracy. In fact, archeology continues to discover and verify places and events believed by most to be myth. The Bible is also the unique means through which inner peace and eternal life can be obtained for those who accept it for what it truly is, the Word of God. For those who believe, it is a window through which many aspects of the mind of the Lord are revealed and by means of which communications with Him can be established. This is the *only* book, two volumes of it, that God ever wrote and had pub-lished for distribution for mankind. Its message, its guidance, its direc-tives, and its promise are unlike those of any other religion, cult, belief, custom, superstition, agency, or government. It is the Word of God Himself! How can I say this with such confidence? Because I have studied it well, examined the evidence, and found undeniable proof of its authorship. I did not seek this proof or even wish it to be. I exam-ined it as a matter of extraneous interest related to a totally separate topic with which I was dealing. As the evidence mounted and grew so compelling and undeniable, my former interest faded and God's Word became the primary focus of my life.

Most of us including myself, until I discovered the truth, obtain much of our "wisdom" and "knowledge" from thirty-second sound bytes from talking heads reading on the TV or radio. We hear ten or fifteen minutes of selected, carefully sculptured "news" or "documentary" between equal or greater amounts of commercials, and we tend to think of ourselves as "informed." If we read at all, it's usually fiction or a skimming of a newspaper or a magazine that we feel tells us all we need to or want to know. To many, sport coverage is what is really important! When a special such as "The Search for the Real Jesus" comes along on TV or in Time magazine, we tend to believe that a truth is being told and that we now *really* have the last word, certainly at least on this particularly thorny and enigmatic issue. How many ever stop to consider that what we conclude from this or any other program is exactly what the producer and his controller intended us to conclude and that we were skillfully and scientifically led to that conclusion? Who today researches and digs out facts the hard way in order to find the *whole* truth instead of the selected portions through which any totally contrary conclusions can be imposed on even the best minds? What is the truth? Does it even matter anymore, as long as the market is up, the economy looks good, my job is secure, and I have the material things I want?

Where God and religion are concerned, many "good" people believe that through good work and a virtuous life, one can *earn* one's way into heaven, or some other elevated state. Unfortunately, this is purely human logic and the human sense of "fairness," and is anything but biblical truth. The Lord Himself says in Isaiah 55:8, *"For my thoughts are not your thoughts so neither are your ways my ways . . ."* In the following paragraph, I've tried to express a few thoughts and questions that have passed through my mind at various times in my life prior to finding the truth. I believe that some are surely familiar and generally consistent with the beliefs of many whom I pray might read and benefit from this paper.

"How can a fair and just God (assuming that there even is one) want to punish anyone who has led a decent life? I'm sure that I've earned my place in heaven (if there is such a place) because on balance I've done pretty well! I've resisted sin, I've even gone to church, I give to the poor, and I am generally attentive to the rules of decency. I try to be a good person. So, I've earned some decent treatment in the hereafter if there is such a place, so how can God deny me? He can't condemn me if I've adhered to most of His laws as best I can, and on balance, have

done more good than bad. Hey, if I want to get serious about this thing, there are many religions around. I can choose any one of them. They are all pretty much the same; they believe in the same God; they all get you to the same place; they just take different routes, that's all. Why should one way be any better than another should? Look at the ecumenical thing, all religions accepting the validity of each other and all seeking ways to merge into one big happy family. Even the Pope has admitted that his isn't the only way, so what's the big deal?"

Well, the big deal is that there are many gods, but only one real true God, and He is the Author, the God of the Bible who cannot be allegorized, synthesized, or compromised. The ancient Greeks had tens of thousands of gods, as do many eastern religions today. Most profess to some chief god and many (I guess the pope included) even believe that He is the same one almighty god in whom all religions believe. Some even believe that Jesus was a god, one of several who have come to earth and passed through history. The Bible clearly states many times that there is but one God, and Jesus is and always was part of that triune Godhead. There are *no* other gods, only pretenders and objects imagined by man to have some mystical qualities. Some may, in fact, have limited supernatural powers, but they are derived not from God but from Satan through his agents. The God of the Bible is the one true and *only* God, the Creator. There are no other gods, nor can any so called god that is not the God of the Bible, and is not believed in the context of the Bible, be considered the one true God. Surely this is an affront to everyone who sincerely believes in another god, or who believes that their god is the same, or as good as the God in the Bible. It should, however, become evident to anyone who undertakes a serious study of the Bible, that here is something different, something special, something profound. It is the true and undeniable Word of God. I pray that this paper will be a good introduction and stimulus for that study.

What appears above in the italicized paragraph is not at all unlike something that I might have reasoned, up until I discovered the truth of God's Word. To anyone who relates to, or agrees with any part of these thoughts, I must inform you that it is wrong, dead wrong! Dead like eternity dead! It does not work; it does not, cannot lead to salvation! There is only one door to salvation and that door is through Jesus Christ. I hated to come to this conclusion! I fought to avoid it. However, I just couldn't rationalize my way out of it no matter how hard I tried. This door opens only to those who believe in Him as God, as our Savior, who physically died on the cross, was raised from the dead and ascended to Heaven so that we might have eternal life. His physical death was the death and forgiveness of all sin of those who believe and who put their trust and faith in Him. That's what the book says, clearly and simply, in God's own words. When you finally realize that He did write the book, you can't believe anything else. I pray that what I've written below will convince you, or at least get you on the road to knowing the true Authorship of the Scripture. Once you recognize this truth, a saving faith may not be far away.

The Lord gave us the law, the Ten Commandments, to show us what He *wanted* of us, *not* what He *expected* of us. He knew we couldn't possibly go through life totally unblemished, that no human could score 100 percent, and nothing less than 100 percent adherence could qualify for admission to heaven. The idea that a good deed can cancel a bad deed is strictly a human contrivance as is the idea that enough good deeds will save the soul on the day of judgment, or that sincerity of belief, whatever it is, is good enough. That's not the way it works! God has deemed that only He has the power to remove sin. We are not endowed in any way with that privilege or authority, not even a priest or the pope. He chose the cross, the shedding of innocent blood on the cross, as the means to that end. He chose this way even before the world began. He told us so quite clearly and eloquently in Isaiah 53, several hundred years before He did it. This may make no sense to you and may seem as a strange or even stupid way for God to solve a problem or get a point across. However, if you will check out 1 Corinthians 1:18, 21, 25, 27 and 28 along with Isaiah 29:14, you will see that the Lord has already anticipated your response and told you why you find His procedure foolish.

For the ancients, He symbolized and previewed this event through the shedding of innocent blood of animals. The salvation of those who lived by faith was thus assured, but it had to be later ratified and validated on the cross, because this was the only way God chose to provide for salvation. Thus, even in ancient times it was their faith, not their work, or their adherence to the law, or even the sacrifice of animals, that saved. It has always been faith, that saved, as the lives of Noah, Abraham, David and others so clearly reveal. It is the same today. It is by faith and faith alone, faith in Jesus and the resurrection, that saves (Ephesians 2:8). The ancients had only the Old Testament that is the Torah, the Writings and the Prophets. They didn't know of Jesus by name, yet He appeared one way or another on every page. The distinction of Father, Son, and the Holy Spirit, the triune Godhead, is also there. Although quiet subtle in its expression, it is readily discerned when viewed from our now available hindsight. Today, if we choose to know, we are greatly blessed by the good news in the New Testament, by our knowledge concerning the actual life of Jesus, His crucifixion, death, and resurrection. The ancients had only the many predictions by the prophets and in the psalms, of His coming and His gift of salvation (Psalms 22, Isaiah 53, etc.). It was the temporary symbolic substitution for the cross, represented by innocent blood of sacrificial animals, that anticipatorily removed sin, but which removal, by necessity, had to be later affirmed on the cross. We on the other hand, have direct evidence and benefit of this most glorious event, documented and proven more surely than any event in all history.

What seems to be so sorely missed is the understanding, recognition, and *full absorption* of what really happened on the cross and why? That one act of love by the Creator of the universe opened the gate of heaven for all time and for all faithful believers, past, present and future. He paid for all sins of all ages of history from Adam to the end of the world. His dying word was *tetalistai*, which means in Greek, "paid in full," as well as what is normally found in English translations, "it is finished." Full means exactly what it means, completely fulfilled, no room or need for anymore, all that is necessary or even possible, enough, just plain full, complete, entirely sufficient. Can it be any clearer? So how can anyone conceive of earning or paying for any part of his or her way into heaven, when He already said that He "paid in full" all that was required or even possible to pay? Jesus made this very clear in His own words, as did Paul and other apostles and even the Prophets (Isaiah 53, 1 Corinthians 15:3, etc.). There is no doubt or ambiguity or cloudiness of this fact in the Scripture. Jesus did it *all* on the cross. To try to add to it or to modify the message in any way is to presume that His act was insufficient, which, of course, is another way of saying that one doesn't believe that Jesus was who He claimed to be, or that God is less than omnipotent and truthful. This glorious completed act of redemption by way of the cross is the fundamental precept of true Christianity. Any belief that includes any intercessory on our behalf, any belief that requires or allows any form of adding to or taking away from the *sufficiency* of what our Lord did on the cross is not Christianity, because it fails to be scriptural and, therefore, consistent with God's Word!

The fact that through His grace and His sacrifice alone are we saved, and the fact that we are also thus freed from the law, does not provide us a license to sin. But sin we will, we know we will, God knows we will. Because we are human and yet in the corrupted flesh, we are incapable of total abstinence from sin. But because we know and believe the who, how, and why of the cross, we believers will struggle mightily not to sin as our token of thanks for salvation. Therefore, it is love and gratitude that causes the Christian to avoid temptation and sin, and not any hope for the reward of salvation. Through faith, salvation is already ours, the hope has been fulfilled; through good works and a virtuous life we give grateful thanks for that salvation and demonstrate to others and ourselves the sincerity of our faith. Leading a "Christian" life does not by itself make one a Christian. Only faith and commitment to Jesus and unconditional love of God, makes a Christian. The "Christian" life necessarily follows.

If one reflects on what I hope I have meaningfully articulated above, it should become evident that Christianity—pure true unadulterated Christianity—is not a religion, in the more commonly applied sense. It is a faith and a belief centered around the literal Word of God as expressed in the Scriptures. It is an eternal fellowship with Jesus that, while in the flesh, we express in prayer, in communication with Him, and in love and obedience as we "eat our daily bread" through a study of the Scriptures and attempt to walk the Christian walk. True Christianity doesn't necessarily need a church edifice nor does it adhere to any rituals. In fact, the "church" is by definition the whole of the Christian body of faithful individual Christians, also called the Body of Christ. It requires no trappings, costumes, altars, vessels, or cathedrals, only the Word of God written in the Scriptures and in the heart. Believers may gather anywhere at any time. The more formalized this gathering of the faithful becomes the more at risk it becomes of succumbing to form over function and thus compromising worship for ritual.

The Pharisees, at the time Jesus walked among them, were extremely religious people. They devoted their lives to their religion and lived it as dutifully as they could. They fasted faithfully, gave to the poor, memorized the Torah, prayed "religiously" and were extremely devoted. However, this "sincerity" was sadly misdirected as they were so entangled in the web of their 613 rituals that they failed to find time or inclination to "faithfully" worship their God. Jesus was critical of them for this reason. Because of the many distractions that their religious rituals demanded, they even failed to recognize Him as the fulfillment of more than three hundred prophecies that foretold His coming to the very day, prophecies that in their roles as spiritual leaders they should have known and understood. It is this web of rituals, that has also entangled, confused, diluted, and confounded many of the various religions that today call themselves Christian. Unless they are able to free themselves from these diverse entanglements and return to the simple basics of the Scriptures and to the gospel, they continue to fail to avail themselves of our Lord's glorious promise. Today it seems endemic throughout many denominations to dilute the faith through many rituals and "church" activities, while at the same time deluding themselves by believing that these "works" are appropriate and necessary adjuncts to true faith. Works are noble and welcomed, but not when they compromise attendance to the first (primary) love (Revelation 2:4).

What a shame. Here we have the greatest book ever written, a book that alone changed the world, a document given to us by the Creator, that provides with simple, yet profound clarity, an understanding of the origin, the purpose and the destiny of all creation. Yet, too many today, perhaps I should say to most, it has no more value or credibility, and far less interest than a book on Greek mythology. Some even view it with disdain or even contempt, while many choose to avoid it, perhaps through fear, because of its message of accountability, its insistence that we are created for a purpose and are, therefore, accountable for our actions.

What a shame that this disinterest, or disdain, or fear or whatever it is, is depriving so many from sharing the greatest blessing ever offered to mankind. However, the Lord does not impose it on anyone. That would violate our sovereign right to choose, a right that He will not violate. However, once you choose to understand, once you sincerely choose to understand and to study His works, once you set aside animosities, suspicions and fears of His word, He will, through the Holy Spirit, happily guide you to a marvelous understanding of Him and of your, as well as His, purpose. What is so beautiful about the process is that the book was designed or tailored to fit the interest, capacity, limitation, and need of every individual. A great observer once noted that the Bible and its message is simple enough or, let's say shallow enough, for a baby to wade in, and yet deep enough for an elephant to swim in. For some, belief, faith, and trust in the Word come quickly, easily, and profoundly. For others, like myself, the doubting Thomases who must feel, taste, smell, and kick the tires before being convinced, it is all there for them as well. For you see, the book provides its own many proofs that it is what it says it is. But God won't press them into your face; you must seek and examine them for yourself. The more you study God's Word, the more astounding it is, and more irrefutable it becomes. One could write many volumes describing the many proofs of the divine origin of the Scriptures, but it would be nothing more than the summary or rewording of the hundreds of books already available by true scholars of the Word.

There are at least three distinct ways, that the Scriptures prove themselves to have divine origin from outside time and space. The first, which is the easiest to discern, although not necessarily so until considerable study has ensued, is the inerrant fulfillment of the thousands of prophesies, predicted events, that occurred exactly how and when God, through the words of the prophets, said they would. The second is the astounding integrated nature of the Scriptures. These are sixty-six books penned by forty writers over a period of perhaps 1700 years, yet when examined as a whole, the variety of writing styles notwithstanding, it is evident that it is the work of a single author. The third is in the codes, that pervade and interconnect and provide an amplified meaning to every book. These are macrocodes, microcodes, slightly hidden codes, and equidistant letter codes. Below is but a sampling of each of these categories of evidence of divine authorship.

Fulfillment of Prophecies

There are literally thousands of prophecies in both the Old as well as in the New Testament. These have such unerring accuracy that it should be all but impossible for even the most tightly closed mind, when truly confronted with the facts, not to at least wonder what is going on here. In desperation, those who feel they must refute the biblical facts will call into question the timing of some of these prophecies. They tend to assert that some biblical entries must have been inserted after the fact in order to "stack the deck" and present false evidence so as to "prove" what in human terms would be totally impossible. Yes, these prophecies are totally impossible from a humanistic perspective and, therefore, if viewed in the time sequence reported in the Bible, must be, in fact, divinely inspired by the one true God of the universe.

Of course, our Lord, who knows the beginning through to the end of all things, covered this base beautifully leaving no wiggle room, only squirming space for the doubters when, in around 270 to 300 B.C. He inspired seventy rabbis in Alexandria to translate the entire book, which we call the Old Testament, from Hebrew into Greek. By that time, Hebrew had become a "dead" language much like Latin is now. At that time, because of the multiple authorities, that had controlled the Israeli people from the Assyrians to the Babylonians to the Greeks, the Hebrew language, especially under the Greeks, ceased to be spoken or written except by scholars and the religious hierarchy. Thus there was the need for a translation to Greek, which by then was the universal language of that part of the world. From this, we have handed down to us after that date, which was more than a hundred years after the writings of the last prophet

Malachi, two independent and parallel historical records of the Old Testament, each preserved and copied with meticulous accuracy and precision, and each narrating the same Word with the same consistency and precision. As if that were not enough, we have today the Dead Sea Scrolls, which are known to be more than two thousand years old, validating many parts of the Hebrew Old Testament. The most prominent and awesome of these is the whole book of Isaiah. Careful comparison of this scroll with the current Old Testament indicates a 99.9+ percent constancy while the differences being only a few slight letterforms, but *nothing*, that has any bearing to its message. Thus, whatever else may be said, one must admit to the absolute antiquity of Old Testament books and the prophecies included therein. This bit of logic and evidence may not convince the skeptic regarding prophecies made and fulfilled prior to 300 B.C.; however, for those prophecies made before that date and fulfilled well after that date, it would seem quiet difficult to simply dismiss them as chance. This will be evident from the following few of the more than three hundred Old Testament predictions relating to the coming of Jesus, the Messiah.

In listing these, I must assume that the reader is reasonably familiar with the New Testament narration of the birth, life, death, and resurrection of Jesus. Therefore the following will concentrate mostly on the Old Testament prophecies of these events. Included also here are the approximate dates when these events and/or prophecies occurred.

1. Jacob, the grandson of Abraham, before he died, called all his twelve sons together and prophesied the future of each of them. Through Judah, he foretold that the Messiah would be born, and that through his line the power of civil authority over the Hebrews would continue until the Messiah arrived (Genesis 49:10, 1689 B.C.). *"The scepter shall not depart from Judah nor a lawgiver from between his feet until Shiloh, and unto Him shall the gathering of the people be."* Shiloh is well recognized as an Old Testament name for the coming Messiah. The term "scepter" refers to both the tribal identity and the right to enforce Mosaic laws especially to adjudicate capital offenses. Throughout their

history this control had never been taken away, even during the Babylonian captivity. Then in 6 or 7 A.D., a Roman procurator named Caponius was appointed by Caesar Augustus to govern the area. With this, the legal power of the religious rulers, that is the Sanhedrin, became restricted and they lost the power of the adjudication, that is, the scepter departed. This happens to be why, later, they had to appeal to Pontius Pilate to crucify Jesus, because they had not this power. Recognizing that the scepter had been removed, the Sanhedrin panicked, believing that God had broken this promise, this messianic prophecy that He made through Jacob (Babylonian Talmud chapter 4 folio 37). This is because they saw no Messiah, the king from the line of David who was to assume power and free them from the Romans. While they didn't know it, and even after being faced with the evidence refused to believe it, this prophecy had been fulfilled; God's promise was not broken, because in Nazareth there was a young boy growing up who was the fulfillment of that prophecy. If we are to believe that God keeps His promises, and how else can it be, then there *had* to be a Messiah somewhere! Only Jesus had all of the credentials for that role, which He, in fact, claimed in no uncertain terms. Unless you believe that God breaks His promises, and that Jesus lied, then there is but one conclusion to be reached.

2. The Lord told David that a descendant of his would be the Messiah and rule forever on his, David's, throne. In 2 Samuel 7:12–13 (1000 B.C.) "*. . . and when thy days be fulfilled, and thou shalt sleep with thy fathers, I will set up thy seed after thee, which shall proceed out of thy bowels, and I will establish his kingdom He shall build a house for my name, and I will stablish the house of his kingdom forever.*" This is a unilateral covenant by God to David that from him would come the Messiah, the king who would reign forever. Technically, this prophecy is yet to be fully fulfilled, because there is yet to be a ruling king of the house of David that would rule forever. In order to rule forever, He must be the Messiah, not a mere human. Of course, in the New

Testament, in Luke 1:32, the angel Gabriel told Mary that her virgin birth would bring forth the son of God who would sit on the throne of David forever. Also we know from Matthew 1 that the genealogy of Mary establishes her bloodline directly from David, and from Luke we see the genealogy of Joseph, the stepfather of Jesus, having also the legal lineage directly from David. An omnipotent God who makes promises surely keeps them; you can count on it! This prophecy regarding the throne will certainly be fulfilled in the end times, and it is Jesus who will sit on that throne. The problem here is that the Old Testament speaks of two comings of the Messiah. The Jews well knew this at the time of Jesus. They knew, or could have known, because the Scripture is clear on this, that one would be king the other a suffering servant. We'll deal more with this later. What they didn't know was that there were not two Messiahs, but one who would come twice! Somehow, probably through wishful thinking, they expected the "king" to come first to rescue them from the oppression of the Romans, and, therefore, never considered that there could only be one Messiah who would and did come first as the suffering one, and that much later He would *return* as king. This also, they should have known because the Lord says in Hosea 5:15, "*I will go and return to my place, till they acknowledge their offense and seek my face: in their affliction they will seek me early.*" In order to return to His place, He must have left it, He was here but they didn't recognize Him. That was their "offense" (singular). When they acknowledge it, He will return (the second coming). If to the skeptic, this partial fulfillment seems somewhat convoluted and less than convincing, please read on.

3. The virgin birth of the Messiah was foretold several times in both the Old and the New Testament (Isaiah 7:14, 735 B.C.). "*Therefore the Lord Himself shall give you a sign; behold, a virgin shall conceive and bear a son, and shall call his name Emmanuel.*" Emmanuel translates to "The God With Us." This is not God's first reference to the virgin birth. In Genesis 3:15 God speaks to

Satan in the Garden of Eden and says "*. . . and I will put enmity between thee and the woman and between thy seed and her seed . . .*" This, of course, makes no sense in terms of what we know biologically. Women have no seed, only men. Therefore, in order to make sense as a message from God which He expects us to understand, it is referring to some woman, somewhere, sometime, with her own seed. Because this is biologically impossible in earthly terms, this seed must be of supernatural origin. It is hers, but not given to her by man but through the intervention of God, just as Gabriel had revealed to Mary and to Joseph.

4. The Messiah's birth was foretold to take place in Bethlehem (Micah 5:2, 700 B.C.). "*But thou Bethlehem Ephrathah, though thou be little among the thousands of Judah, yet out of thee shall come forth unto me that is to be ruler in Israel; whose goings forth have been from of old, from everlasting.*" Wow! This is a tight little prophecy. Here God specifies just which Bethlehem He will come from and that HE will rule Israel, and that He has been around, as only God could be, *forever*. Of course we all know that Jesus was born in Bethlehem and claimed to be God the preexistent one when He said, as recorded in John 8:58 "*. . . before Abraham was, I Am!*" Here He was referring to Exodus 3:14 (1450 B.C.) "*And God said to Moses, I AM THAT I AM.*" And He said; "*Thus shalt thou say unto the children of Israel, I Am hath sent me unto you.*" This occurred at the burning bush where Moses first encountered God. From that time on, this was one of God's names, the "I am." That is why Jesus said ". . . before Abraham was, I am." The Hebrew leadership knew that He was calling Himself God and claiming to be the God of the burning bush. This explains why they tried to stone him. Claiming to be God was a crime requiring stoning to death. In John 18:5 when they came after Him to put Him on trial and asked of Him, He replied, "I am." Hearing this, they all "fell to the ground." They were shocked at His claim to be God. It was this for that they claimed the legal right to have Him executed. (Note the English translation reads, "I am He." The He is not in the original Greek

14

but was added for grammatical correctness, thus obscuring the profound impact and meaning of His response.)

5. The very manner in which the Messiah would present Himself to the world was predicted more than five hundred years before Jesus declared Himself. Even the exact date of His coming was also predicted! (Zechariah 9:9 487) *"Rejoice greatly, O daughter of Zion; shout O daughter of Jerusalem; behold thy King cometh unto thee: He is just and having salvation; lowly and riding upon an ass, and upon a colt the foal of an ass."* Of course, in Matthew 24:4–5 the event as it takes place is described exactly as predicted. What is most intriguing about this, however, is that the exact date of the event was also predicted in Daniel 9:25 (538 B.C.) where the angel Gabriel tells Daniel *"Know therefore and understand, that from the going forth of the commandment to restore and build Jerusalem, unto the Messiah, the Prince, shall be seven weeks, and threescore and two weeks . . ."* To understand this, one must recognize two things, first the word weeks is translated from the Hebrew *shabuim,* which also means sevens. Throughout both Scriptures, seven seems to symbolize completion, just as in our musical scale, there are seven notes with the eight being the same as the first or a new beginning of notes an octave higher or lower. Here Gabriel is speaking of 7 plus 62 sevens of years or 69 sevens of years. The other thing is that the biblical year is always 360 days as it was in every recorded culture on earth until 701 B.C. when something happened to the earth's orbit that changed the year to its present length. All known cultures confronted and dealt with that change after that date. Thus 69 sevens of years amounted to 69 times 7 times 360 or 173,880 days. We know that the date of the command to rebuild Jerusalem was given by Artaxerxes Longimanus on March 14, 445 B.C. If we move forward 173,880 days by our calendar we come to April 6, 32 A.D. or the 10th of Nisan on the Hebrew religious calendar, the very day that Jesus proclaimed Himself King! This is arrived at as follows:

445 B.C.–32 A.D.(476 X 365)*	=	173740
March–April 6	=	24
Leap years	=	116
Total	=	173880

*(note there is no zero A.D.)

Thus, we have fulfillment of two prophecies regarding the same subject by two different prophets about fifty-one years apart, living in different countries. How nicely this expresses the integrated nature of these sixty-six books by forty different writers! Daniel, taken captive as a boy by Nebuchadnezzar spent his entire life as a captive in Babylon, first by the Chaldeans and then by Cyrus and the Persians. Zechariah, however, was in Jerusalem as part of the returned remnant from seventy years in captivity after Cyrus released them. Boy! This book is sure full of coincidences!

6. Details concerning the betrayal of Jesus by Judas Iscariot were foretold with eerie accuracy (Zechariah 11:12, 13, 487 B.C.). *"And I said unto them, If ye think good, give me my price; and if not, forbear. So they weighed for my price, thirty pieces of silver. And the Lord said unto me, Cast it unto the potter: a goodly price that I was prized at of them. And I took the thirty pieces of silver, and cast them to the potter in the house of the Lord."* Here we have a preview more than five hundred years in advance of what appears to be thoughts of Judas Iscariot as he bargained to betray Jesus and then later as the full impact of his awful deed finally dawned on him. The actual event is described in Matthew 26:14 where he tells of Judas going to the chief priest and offering to betray Jesus for thirty pieces of silver. Jesus had earlier predicted that Judas would betray Him to the priests, for they had long sought to catch him under the right condition in order to have Him killed. Then in Matthew 27:3–8 we read that Judas later realized that he had "betrayed innocent blood" and tried to return the money to the priests but they wouldn't take it, so he threw it on the temple floor and left. Then the priests had a

problem, because they couldn't return the tainted money to the treasury. So they cleverly decided to prepay for an ongoing obligation. One of their expenses was to provide for burial plots for indigents, and so they bought a burial field with the money, a field belonging to the potter, thus unknowingly fulfilling Zechariah's five-hundred-year old prophecy, where Judas is predicted to sell his soul for thirty pieces of silver, but then it's the potter who is to get the money in the end. This is a pretty tough one to have been contrived.

7. Jesus' words, thoughts, and pains as He hung nailed to the cross are expressed in awesome clarity and detail in a psalm written more than 1000 years earlier and many hundreds of years before crucifixion was invented (Psalms 22–1, 6–8, 14–18 980 B.C.). *"My God, my God, why hast thou forsaken me?" "... But I am a worm, and no man, a reproach of men, despised of the people. All they that see me laugh me to scorn, they shoot out the lip, they shake the head, saying, He trusted on the Lord that He would deliver him: let him deliver him, seeing he delighted in him ..." "I am poured out like water and all my bones are out of joint: my heart is like wax; it is melted in the midst of my bowels. My strength is dried up like a potsherd; and my tongue cleaveth to my jaws, and thou has brought me into the dust of death ..." "For dogs have compassed me: the assembly of the wicked have inclosed me: they pierced my hands and my feet. I may tell all my bones: they look and stare upon me. They part my garments among them, and cast lots upon my vesture."*

Here we have excerpts of an incredibly graphic first person description of someone suffering and dying on the cross. Some of the details are identical to those described in Mark 16:34. Here Jesus utters the exact same words that begin Psalms 22 *"My God, My God, why hath thou forsaken me?"* This was the fourth of the last seven utterances of the physical Man, Jesus, after six hours of excruciating physical suffering as He appealed to the heavenly triune Godhead of which His spiritual self was and always had been an integrated part. It was the cry of the human manifestation of God, having taken into Himself all the sins of the world, thus being made sin, and thus necessarily, but temporarily abandoned by God until these sins had been *Tetelistai, Paid In Full*. It is the only time recorded in the Scriptures that He called upon God and not the Father. He was calling for God, the whole Godhead, in a way, calling on Himself as well, in His role as the flesh and blood suffering Messiah. The rest of the above quotes from the Psalm unmistakably describe what someone who was nailed to a cross, as was Jesus, might feel and say or think.

In pondering this strange utterance of our Lord, *"My God, My God why hath thou forsaken me?"* it is also interesting to note that being hung on a tree (here the wooden cross) was an accursed thing as noted in Deuteronomy 21:22, 23 *"... and if a man have committed a sin worthy of death, and he be put to death, and thou hang him from a tree ... for he that is hanged is accursed of God."* Thus, God as judge turned His face away from Jesus and had to forsake Him, the accursed on the tree, in order that an eternity of wrath against the sins of the world, now manifest in Him, could be stilled, forgiven, and justice satisfied. As He was nailed to the cross He became a violation of God's law and became accursed. It was God, the Father, who put God the Son through a temporary spiritual death, and thereby made atonement for our sins, as only He could.

It should be of considerable significance as a point of evidence regarding the supernatural nature of this prophecy, to realize that crucifixion was "invented" by the Persians between 300 and 400 B.C. at least six hundred years *after* this Psalm was composed. Crucifixion was later "perfected" by the Romans and employed extensively after 100 B.C. This historically verifiable fact leaves the question as to whom, but God Himself, could have painted such a graphic and accurate picture of this hellish form of torture, six hundred years before such a scene could ever have entered any human mind.

8.   The most profound and explicit of all Old Testament prophecies attesting to the coming and purpose of the suffering Messiah is here recorded from the New King James version for easier understanding.

9.   Isaiah 52:13–15, 53:1–12, 690 B.C.)

"Behold, my servant shall deal prudently, he shall be exalted and extolled and be very high. As many were astonished at thee. His visage was so marred more than any man, and His form more than the sons of men: so shall He sprinkle many nations; the kings shall shut their mouths at him: for that which had not been told them, shall they see, and that which they had not heard they shall consider."

"Who hath believed our report? And to whom is the arm of the Lord revealed? For he shall grow up before him as a tender plant, and as a root out of a dry ground. He has no form nor comeliness; and when we shall see him, there is no beauty that we should desire him.

"He is despised and rejected of men: a man of sorrows, and acquainted with grief: and we hid, as it were, our faces from him: he was despised, and we esteemed him not.

Surely he hath borne our griefs, and carried our sorrows; yet we did esteem him stricken, smitten of God, and afflicted.

But he was wounded for our transgressions, he was bruised for our iniquities: the chastisement of our peace was upon him; and with his stripe* we are healed.

All we like sheep have gone astray: we have turned every one to his own way; and the Lord hath laid on him the iniquity of us all.

He was oppressed, and he was afflicted, yet he opened not his mouth: is brought as a lamb to the slaughter, and as a sheep before her shearers is dumb, so he opened not his mouth.

He was taken from prison and from judgment: and who shall declare his generation? For he was cut off out of the land of the living; for the transgression of my people was he stricken.

And he made his grave with the wicked, and with the rich in his death: because he had done no violence, neither was any deceit in his mouth."

"Yet it pleased the Lord to bruise him: he hath put him to grief: when thou shalt make his soul an offering for sin, he shall see his seed, he shall prolong his days, and the pleasure of the Lord shall prosper in his hand.

He shall see of the travail of his soul, and shall be satisfied: by his knowledge shall my righteous servant justify many; for he shall bear their iniquities.

Therefore will I divide him a portion with the great, and he shall divide the spoil with the strong; because he hath poured out his soul unto death: and he was numbered with the transgressors: and he bare the sin of many, and made intercession for the transgressors."

A careful reading of this reveals a translational error. Stripe is singular not plural. This changes the perspective from which to interpret this verse. Man inflicted many stripes, but it was but one stripe through which "we are healed;" that is the stripe that the Father inflicted through that terrible spiritual separation from him that the Father imposed while Jesus was the embodiment of all past, present and future sin of all redeemed souls.

Here we have the Christian's Old Testament "Holy of Holies," the Lord's suffering servant prophecy. It is a prophetic narrative of the events relating to Jesus as they occurred some 723 years later, and are recorded a number of times in the New Testament. Most importantly, it tells us also about Him, His suffering and Why! "His visage was marred more than any man, and His form more than the sons of men" Note Isaiah 50:6, *"I gave my back to the smiters and my checks to them that plucked off the hair: I hid not my face from shame and splintering."* We have here further evidence of the unspeakable physical cruelty and torture our Lord endured. From these passages and facial etching that the extreme pain of God's wrath must have imposed, it is evident why neither Mary nor the disciples on the road to Emmaus, nor the Apostles in the upper room could recognize Him at first. In the New Testament, we find only that He was beaten, spit on, a crown of thorns pressed painfully on His head, and that He was crucified. These Old Testament observations attest to a far more extensive sadistic torture, as well as a spiritual torture, which was infinitely greater than we are capable of understanding.

Even before the ordeal, "He had no form nor comeliness; and when we see Him there is no beauty that we should desire Him." Here is another insight lacking in the New Testament. Physically, He was nothing special, a simple non-descript man, just what on reflection one would expect our God /man suffering servant to look like. Handsomeness or beauty could be seductive and influencing. He was here strictly for the merit of His message and His self-sacrifice, not to participate in a beauty contest or to seduce through looks and charm.

"He was despised and rejected of men and we esteemed him not. Surely he has borne our grieves and carried our sorrows: yet we did esteem (judge) Him stricken smitten of God and afflicted." "Stricken smitten of God and afflicted." Here appears to be another expression of the Father's wrath against this personification of sin, which Jesus became while on the cross. The New Testament repeatedly relates how the leadership detested Him, tried to stone Him, push Him off a cliff, and finally had Him tortured and killed. He certainly bore the grief of many as He expended His spiritual energy healing hundreds, perhaps thousands, during His brief three years of ministry. He wept over the death of Lazarus as He also did over Jerusalem as they failed to recognize His coming. In spite of all His incredible works, they chose to judge Him who was sinless to be tortured without mercy and crucified. "He was oppressed, and He was afflicted yet He opened not His mouth: he was brought as a lamb to the slaughter, and as a sheep before its shearers is silent, he opened not his mouth." This is consistent with the first-hand account at His trials—he made no defense but remained silent. "He made his grave with the wicked, and with the rich in his death." Actually, He died on the cross between two criminals and was buried in the tomb of Joseph, a rich man. All these details came to be, *just as God said they would*, through His Authored prophesies!

"But he was wounded for our transgressions, he was bruised for our iniquities . . . and with his stripe are we healed . . . we are like sheep have gone astray; we have turned every one to his own way; and the Lord *has laid* on *him the iniquities* of us all . . . for he was cut off from the land of the living (killed) for the transgressions of my people was he stricken . . . by his knowledge shall my righteous servant justify many for *he shall bear their iniquities* . . . and he was numbered with the transgressors; and he bares the sins of many, and made intercession for the transgressors." Here we have it, repeated and rephrased to be certain that it is understood. We have here the why, the purpose of His coming, as well as the prediction of His suffering, and of His death!

Socrates said to Plato something to the effect, "Perhaps a just God can forgive sin, but I don't see how." Here is how He could! It is a pity that the old boy couldn't have been around a few hundred years later so he could see how our "just God" did it! Nothing speaks more eloquently of the power of the intellect of the great philosopher than this profound question. Socrates obviously could see clearly God's dilemma. A just God cannot ignore sin and He can't forgive it without compromising the true meaning of His justice. In order for justice to be served, *sin must be paid for.* Yet, even the most virtuous of humans commit sins innumerable times in a lifetime, far more than any commensurate amount of punishment or payment could ever extinguish. Besides what kind of being or soul would be the result of any just form of punishment? Would it be of a type or quality even then, worthy of eternal life with God? Could ten years or any amount of punishment in prison or anywhere else result in a fully repented man ready for life in a perfected society such as heaven? No! It required a loving God to pour out His divine blood, and to suffer away the sins of those who return His love, who believe and have faith in His resurrection.

God gave us laws, the Commandments, not because He hoped or thought we could keep them, but instead to show us how impossible it is for us to live up to His requirements without His grace and mercy. We all rationalize that we do a pretty good job of what we choose to believe and of trying to live by these requirements. However, from God's viewpoint we all hang over the burning fire of hell, suspended on a ten-link chain (the Ten Commandments). It only takes one broken link to send us to the pit, unless . . . In thinking about this issue we must realize that we are dealing with God's definition of justice, not our limited often perverted form of human justice. All of this, or something like it, is what I believe Socrates perceived when he made that profound observation. Just as Socrates couldn't see the answer, neither could any other human; only God had the answer. Many choose to say there is no such thing as sin, there is only good karma or bad karma, or everything is relative, subjective, and situational, or there is no meaning to anything—nihilism, no God, no objective truth. They rationalize anything to avoid the real truth, to face the reality of God, of sin, of good and evil, of ultimate accountability. All of this sin and salvation stuff is abhorrent to many and is to be avoided at all cost. So they do. So did I. What a shame.

But here in Isaiah 53, we have revealed for us the answer to the dilemma, that Socrates thought was an insurmountable problem. How could a just God forgive sin? While from the human perspective, at least in a mind capable of seeing the whole significance and difficulty of the issue, this was a serious dilemma. Not to God, however, because He knew from before the beginning of time exactly what He would do at the appropriate time and He revealed it to Isaiah, as well as to a number of other prophets, though in somewhat more subtle forms. He came to earth as Jesus, one aspect of the Triune Godhead, to pay, as only He, the Perfect One, could pay by collecting unto Himself all of the world's sins and forgiving them in the only possible *just* way, by Himself suffering them away on the cross. He was thereby our "Kinsman Redeemer, our unblemished sacrificial Lamb of God." The entire Old Testament speaks of Jesus in many ways. However, these two names symbolize Him most surely in His role on the cross.

To begin to understand this we must first look back to the early Israeli culture as God ordained in anticipation of this event. Being a relative, a kinsmen carried with it strong obligations. Widows, orphans and any other relatives falling on bad times could expect assistance from the nearest kin, if he was capable of such assistance. This was considered a moral obligation of the strong, to help the weak or less fortunate. This person who took on the obligation, this relative, was called the kinsmen redeemer. He was also the avenger of blood. That is, it was also his obligation to punish the wrong doer, if there was one, who caused his kin harm. For instance, if his kin was a widow as a result of murder, it was the kinsmen redeemer's obligation to chase down the murderer and slay him. Thus, the kinsmen redeemer is a foreshadowing of our blessed Kinsmen Redeemer.

Of course, we all know about the custom of the sacrificing of an unblemished lamb as a means of atonement for sins. This ritual had been practiced since at least Abel. Thus, in retrospect, it should not be a great surprise or difficult leap to see this also as a clue to God's answer to Socrates finally played out on the cross as the grand crescendo and finale of this five-thousand-year symbolic orchestration. As *our* Kinsmen Redeemer, He had to be born of a woman; He had to be a blood relative to us, which He was as man. He also had to be the perfect, unblemished, spotless "lamb" in order to be worthy of sacrifice to God for our sins. Thus also, he had to *be* God Himself, for only God is capable of being totally unblemished, perfect, free from sin, and otherwise qualified for such an awesome assignment having eternal consequences! By His physical death on the cross, as well as His spiritual separation from the Godhead, this spotless lamb, this Kinsman Redeemer, our God, provided of Himself the *only* way that the just and almighty God could cleanse away the sins of His own sons and daughters. Like it or not, believe it or not, understand it or not, this was/is God's way, the only way for us to be cleansed, redeemed of sin, and thereby made suitable for life eternal with Him. We have His word for it!

As noted, there are hundreds of other prophecies related to the coming of the Messiah. However, these eight should suffice to get the point across, that only through God could such accuracy of events have been foretold. If the reader hasn't been at least stirred a little by these and concluded that there is something quite powerful here, then he or she hasn't read this carefully, or, I haven't articulated the facts adequately, or . . . I'm greatly saddened by the third possibility. This is because I'm certain that only through faith, which in turn is so intimately tied to a total belief in the Scriptures, can eternal life be obtained. Before I forge ahead to the next aspects of the Scriptures, that also prove their supernatural origin, it comes to mind that I should include here a few more prophetic evidences of supernatural authorship that are quite current and, therefore, even more difficult to dismiss. This is also because I suspect that to the doubters most set in their doubts, the prophecies of the Messiah may be, at least initially, somehow disconcerting and less than convincing of the supernatural authorship of the Bible, because they represent things that are of the distant past and that also seem too astounding to be real. For many, as certainly in my own case, a broader base of proven scriptural inerrancy is needed before this astounding yet vital element can be digested and wholly assimilated.

10. Rebirth of Israel

The prophets foretold the final return of the Jews to the Land, that God promised them through His unilateral covenant with Abraham. Being a unilateral and unconditional covenant by God alone, it did not depend on anything that Abraham or Jews did or did not do. They, therefore, could not, and God would not break it. While they broke other covenants and were thus punished and temporarily removed from the land, nevertheless, at some point, toward the end of time, they were ordained to return and never again be removed. God reaffirmed, reminded and / or rephrased and clarified this several times through several prophets. Some of these are as follows:

a) Genesis 12:1–3, "*Get thee out of thy country, and from thy kindred, and from thy father's house, unto a land that I will show thee: and I will make of thee a great nation, and I will bless thee, and make thy name great; and thou shalt be a blessing: and I will bless them that bless thee, and curse them that curseth thee: and in thee shall all families of the earth be blessed.*" (These are the seven famous "I wills" in the covenant to Abraham.)

b) Genesis 12:7, "*Unto thy seed will I give this land.*" Genesis 13:14, 15, "*And the Lord said onto Abram lift up now thine eyes, and look from the place where thou art, northward and southward, and eastward and westward: for all the land which thou seest, to thee will I give it, and to thy seed forever.*" In Genesis 15:9–19, the Lord takes special care to make note of the fact that this is His unilateral binding promise by demonstrating so through the enactment of a strange-to-us covenant ritual in common practices at that time.

c)   Deuteronomy 30:3, 5 *"that then the Lord thy God will turn thy captivity and have compassion upon thee, and will return and gather thee from all the nations, whither the Lord thy God hath scattered thee . . . and the Lord thy God will bring thee into the land which thy fathers possessed, and thou shalt possess it . . ."* The Jews were never scattered to "all the nations" until 70 A.D. after the destruction of the temple and of Jerusalem by the Romans. This prophecy was fulfilled on May 14, 1948, 1878 years later!

d)   Ezekiel 36:19, 24, 28 *"and I scattered them (Israel) among the heathen, and they were dispersed through the countries . . . For I will take you from among the heathen and gather you out of all countries, and will bring you into your own land . . . and ye shall dwell in the land that I gave your fathers . . ."* Boy! Can it get any more specific than that! Yes, it can!

e)   Ezekiel 37:21, 22, 25, *". . . Behold, I will take the children of Israel from among the heathen, whither they be gone, and will gather them on every side and bring them into their own land, and I will make them one nation in the land upon the mountain of Israel; and one king shall be king to them all, and they shall be no more two nations, neither shall they be divided into two kingdoms any more at all . . . and they shall dwell in the land that I have given unto Jacob, my servant, wherein your fathers have dwelt, and they shall dwell therein even they, and their children, and their children's children forever, and my servant David shall be their prince forever."*

f)   Isaiah 11:10–12, *"And in that day there shall be a root of Jesse, which shall stand for the ensign of the people; to it shall the Gentiles seek: and his rest shall be glorious. And it shall come to pass in that day, that the Lord shall set his hand again the second time to recover the remnant of his people, which shall be left, from Assyria, and from Egypt, and from Pathros, and from Cush and from Elam, and from Shinar and from Hamath, and from the islands of the sea. And he shall set up an ensign for the nations, and shall assemble the outcasts of Israel and gather together the dispersed of Judah from the four corners of the earth."* Need more be said on this point? The Jews *are* back in the Promised Land as a single nation, though not yet under the eternal kingdom from the line of David. The only thing that could possibly nail down the undeniable accuracy of this would be if the Lord had given us in advance a firm date for the fulfillment of this back-to-land promise. As a matter of fact, He DID!

g) Ezekiel 4:5, 6, *"For I have laid upon thee the years of their iniquity, according to the number of days, three hundred and ninety days: so shalt thou bear the iniquity of the house of Israel, and when thou hast accomplished them, lie again on the right side, and thou shalt bear the iniquity of the house of Judah forty days: I have appointed thee each day for a year."* That's 390 plus 40 or 430 years that Judah/ Israel are to be punished. However, they were already in captivity for seventy years of punishment leaving 360 years yet remaining. But after their seventy years they still failed to obey the Lord and continued transgressing greatly. Thus, applying Leviticus 26:18, 21 *"And if ye will not yet for all of this hearken unto me, then I will punish you seven times more for your sins . . . and if ye walk contrary unto me, and will not hearken unto me, I will bring seven times more plagues upon you according to your sins."* Well, they didn't hearken and so the Lord implemented His seven times rule, which resulted in 360 times 7, or 2520 years of punishment just as He said He would!

From 2 Kings 25:1, Jeremiah 52:4 and Haggai 2:10 we learn of both the beginning date and the end date of the first seventy years of the "servitude of the Nations." This is the same seventy-year prophecy previously described. Thus this, the date of the beginning of this later period of punishment, can be determined to have begun on July 23, 537 B.C. Adding 2520 years to this date allowing for leap years and calendar changes, we reach May 14, 1948, the very date that David Ben Gurion declared on international radio using Ezekiel as his authority, a reestablished Israel as the Jewish homeland. This is obviously an over-simplified summary of the basis and calculation of this prophetic statement. It is not without controversy and challenge regarding the calendar calculations and starting date. However, using any reasonable set of assumptions the result is close, certainly within a year of the above date. My belief is that the Lord does not approximate or estimate His messages. He is clear, precise, and accurate. Any divergent conclusions by man are nothing more than inadequacy of man's understanding. This prophecy was fulfilled exactly as stated.

11. Restoration of the Hebrew Language

Who ever heard of a "dead" language being resurrected? Never in the history of the world has this happened, until recently. Yet God thought it to be good that His 'pure" original language be restored to His people and so decreed it in prophecy more than 2500 years ago. Zephaniah 3:9 (635 B.C.), *"For then will I turn to the people a pure language that they may all call upon the name of the Lord to serve Him with one consent."* With the restoration of Israel also came the restoration of Hebrew as the national language. One could rightly and logically say that that was only natural. Here was *suddenly* (in *one day* as predicted in Isaiah 66:8) a new nation composed of people "gathered from the four corners of the earth," from seventy different countries, having diverse customs and languages. Surely a common language was needed, but why Hebrew, a dead language, one, that began dying after the Babylon captivity in 606 B.C., and was clearly dead after Alexander declared that all conquered people were to speak only Greek. That is why the Septuagint, the Greek translation, was written around 300 B.C., because no one except scholars and religious leaders knew Hebrew. It was as dead as Latin is today. Logic might have suggested the adaptation of a more universal language, common to the majority perhaps. Instead, what had never before happened, this dead language was restored, as was the 1878 years "dead" nation of Israel, all per God's plan as He revealed it thousands of years ago.

The prophecy speaks of a "pure" language. Many scholars believe that Hebrew was the original language God gave Adam. It consists of twenty-two letters, five of which have a slightly different form if they are the last letter of a word. Therefore, the language is self-parsing. It is also extremely efficient. While the written English is said to contain close to 75 percent redundancy, mainly because of grammatical rules, Hebrew, which contains no vowels is the least redundant, and, therefore, might be considered "pure" in the context of this prophecy.

12. Astounding Fertility of Israel

A very sparsely inhabited desert-like, arid wasteland before 1948, Israel is now a veritable agricultural "Eden," as God said it would be when He would again gather His people into their Promised Land. Consider the following:

Isaiah 27:6, *"He shall cause them that come of Jacob to take root: Israel shall blossom and bud and fill the face of the world with fruit."*

Joel 2:23, *"Be glad then, ye children of Zion, and rejoice in the Lord your God: for he hath given you the former rain moderately, and he will cause to come down for you the rain, the former rain and the latter rain in the first month."*

Isaiah 35:7, *"And the parched ground shall become a pool, and the thirsty land springs of water . . ."*

Here we have the three prophecies suggesting a restoration of fertility and rain resulting in abundance of crops. After the total dispersions of the people in 70 A.D., the land became progressively arid and desert-like, in which condition it continued until recent times. The returning Jews transformed this deserted desolate dry land into the most agriculturally efficient land on earth (really God did it through them but most don't yet understand this). This is according to a U.N. survey. For example, Israel now is the third largest producer of fruits in the world, supplying more than 90 percent of the citrus fruit consumed by all of Europe. It is a country smaller than Orange county California. A large part of this is a result of the fulfillment of the rain prophecy in Joel 2:23, because annual rainfall has "strangely" increased by 10 percent every decade for the whole of the last century. What does that tell you about the kind of planner our God is? He started a hundred years ago to prepare the ground for what He told us more than 2500 years ago He would do, and it's done just as He said it would be done!

13. Rebuilding the Temple

The likelihood that the temple in Jerusalem, which was destroyed in 70 A.D., would ever be rebuilt is today as absurd as was a belief for 1800 years that the Jews would ever again be a single nation in their "promised land." Nevertheless, there are many references in the Scriptures, that predict the rebuilding of the Temple in the end times. In order to not belabor this, I'll simply refer to some of them, that the curious may wish to confirm. This prediction occurs in Isaiah 2:2, Ezekiel 43, Revelation 11:1, 2. The fact is that plans are underway for this event. At this moment more than five hundred priests are in training to officiate in the Temple, and more than seventy-five of the objects needed in the Temple, such as priestly garments, curtains and vessels, have been made in anticipation of this event. Great world-wide efforts were made to find the shellfish, no longer native in this area, from which were extracted the original purple dyes for coloring the vestures. However, one "insurmountable" problem developed when they tried to prepare the required anointing oil. The only tree from which this oil came was the afarsmon. The only grove of these trees in the world was outside of Jerusalem, and these were burned and totally destroyed by the Romans along with Jerusalem in 70 A.D. Well, it seems as though that ends it! God surely cannot deliver on this one! Just as He "broke" His promises of a Messiah before the "Scepter departed," you'd think that here He missed another one! Hold on! a) Dr. Joseph Patrick of Hebrew University found a two-thousand-year-old clay flask full of anointing oil buried near the Dead Sea! Scientists confirmed its age and composition. It has precisely the ingredients necessary as described in Exodus 30:25, 26! (This was made known by the Associated Press, February 16, 1989.)

Can you imagine the long range planning of this guy, our God? He got some group of people more than two thousand years ago before the trees were destroyed, to extract some extra oil, put it in a flask and bury it like a time capsule. Then He guards it for two thousand years, this fragile, little clay bottle, and then at the right time, directs someone to it, just so He can be known as a promise keeper. He promised us salvation if only we believe in Him and have faith in Him through Jesus Christ, our Kinsmen Redeemer!

Well, the Temple hasn't been rebuilt yet, and there are a number of very serious issues, seemingly impossible issues, preventing it. But a God, who can with unerring precision and accuracy predict all the above and also bury, and at the right time retrieve, a two-thousand -year-old cache of extinct and essential oil out of the desert, obviously can do anything! Keep watching the 11 o'clock news. One of these days you may witness the ground breaking!

14   The Bible has but One Author

Although penned by forty writers more than thousands of years, these sixty-six books are a single integrated text, wholly authored by God Himself. No simple reading or rereading of it will necessarily reveal this. Yet, through careful study by a mind not fearful that it all might be true, and not doubting that there is a loving God who actually would provide such a wonderful expression of His plan and purpose, this soon becomes evident. Such a mind should readily recognize His intimate involvement in this intricate tapestry of expression to which the writers provided only their hand where He provided the whole of its design. The Lord Himself spoke of this integration of His word through Isaiah in 28:12, 13 when He said, *"This is the rest wherewith ye may cause the weary to rest; and this is the refreshing; yet they would not hear. But the Word of the Lord was unto them precept upon precept, precept upon precept; line upon line, line upon line; here a little, and there a little ..."* That certainly does describe the Scriptures. There are no specific chapters or doctrine as one might expect in an instructional manual. There is no specific and complete section on, say marriage, or baptism, or sin or Satan or worship. These doctrines are truly scattered throughout the Bible, a little here, a little there, precept upon precept. Separate specific doctrinal sections if they existed could well have been claimed to be by individual "experts" on specific subjects. However, to have His whole message, conveying the entire broad spectrum of information in such scattered yet intimately integrated and coherent form, presents a very strong case for a single author.

My great mentor Chuck Missler, has a precious analogy for explaining this biblical quality. He likens the Bible to a hologram in even more ways than this. A hologram is a photograph taken using a laser light of some specific frequency. When the picture is developed and viewed in normal light it is not coherent; it looks like a mistake; "it has no form or comeliness that should be desired." It can be made coherent and understandable as a three dimensional representation of the photographed scene, only when viewed by a laser light of the exact same frequency. Actually, any light, other than that by means of which the picture was created, will produce either a false image or have no coherency at all. To the natural man viewing it in natural light, the Bible may seem to be foolishness, incoherent nonsense, or simply a nice fairytale. However, when viewed by the light provided by the Holy Spirit who wrote it, it becomes without doubt the true word of God in all its magnificent glory, accuracy and divine wisdom. The other quality of the hologram is that if you cut off a piece, the entire picture, or message remains intact, only having lost some of its resolution or clarity. Thus it is also with the Bible; remove a page and you have lost none of its message, because the message is "a little bit here, a little bit there" "percept percept upon percept."

Already in the previous section we have witnessed a number of evidences of this textural integration as the messages from the variety of writers, especially the prophets, compliment and build on each other to more fully and richly express God's Word. This is even more explicitly evident in the New Testament where its writers had the benefit of the whole of the Old Testament as hindsight from which to draw fuller meanings of God's earlier words. Even more profound from their perspective was the detailed fulfillment of the ultimate prophecy, the coming of the Messiah! In retrospect, it seems that the Old Testament was in some ways like a textbook on some highly complex subject where the student finds it impossible by himself to fathom all of the deep theories and concepts. Only after a great teacher joins the class and begins to explain and link together the more subtle aspects, does the light of full understanding brighten and the mysteries become revealed. In this case, the great teacher was God Himself, who came not only as the teacher of the Scriptures, but also as its author, its chief subject, and ultimately the living, dying, resurrected and ascended manifestation of its purpose!

Even so, there remain many tantalizing, seemingly random or even abstract and pointless verses and chapters. Yet, through love of the Word and divine inspiration, the meaning of many of these has been revealed over the centuries. Eventually all of them will be understood, for there is nothing in the Bible, this Word of God, not one word, that does not have important meaning and that will not eventually be understood. How do I know this? Because in Matthew 5:18 our Lord says, *"For verily I say unto you, Till heaven and earth pass, one jot or one tittle shall in no wise pass from the law, till all be fulfilled."* The Hebrew scholars interpret further that when the Messiah comes, He will even interpret the spaces between the letters.

One example of the seemingly pointless chapters in the Old Testament beyond its passing historical interest is chapters one and two of the book of Numbers. Here, the population of each of the thirteen tribes (counting the "Half Tribes" of Ephraim and Manasses) is listed along with detailed directions as to how they are to be arranged as they camped. With the Levites forming a square, the other tribes were to form rectangles, three tribes each emanating in a specific order from the four sides of the Levite camp. If one plots this prescribed pattern of encampment, one would find it formed the pattern of a cross, with the smaller group camped to the east, the largest group to the west forming the foot, and two equal groups forming the arms to the north and south! Thus, this seemingly pointless, and even boring section in the Old testament is, in fact, a very subtle yet profound message to the more discerning, and then to all of us, that the Creator of the universe planned the event on the cross even before the beginning of time, that event that took place nearly two thousand years ago on Mt. Moriah.

Another very provocative example of the Holy Spirit's authorship of the Bible and of its integrated character can be found buried here with the surface of Genesis 5 in the descendants of Adam through Noah.

Below is a list of the direct line of descendants from Adam to Noah. To the right of each name is its original root meaning. Some, such as Seth and Noah are given in the Bible text. A Hebrew root dictionary is needed in order to ascertain most of the others.

Adam	Man
Seth	Appointed
Enos	Mortal (frail, incurable)
Cainan	Sorrow
Mahalaleel	Blessed God
Jared	Shall come down
Enoch	Teaching (teacher)
Methuselah	His death shall bring
Lamech	Despairing (from which we get Lamentations)
Noah	Comfort (to bring relief)

Now let's put that into a sentence.

"Man (is) appointed mortal sorrow;(but) the Blessed God shall come down teaching (that) his death shall bring despairing comfort."

WOW! That is a one-sentence summary of the whole history and purpose of mankind! Through the original sin, that opening of Pandora's Box in the Garden of Eden, man was appointed mortal (subject to death) sorrow, but God (Jesus) shall come down teaching, that His death (crucifixion) shall bring the despairing comfort (salvation and eternal life). End of Story. (We have Dr. Chuck Missler to thank for having pointed out this, and the preceding pearl hidden in Scripture.)

Here is one more of the many strange and interesting examples of how the Bible is so beautifully integrated, and how Old Testament events, teachings, and predictions are intimately related to, or predictive of, the New Testament events. In Numbers 21:5–9, we find that the people sinned by speaking against God. In return, He sent "fiery serpents among the people" and many died. Acknowledging that they had sinned and that this was their punishment, they begged

Moses to pray to the Lord for forgiveness and relief. The Lord told Moses to make a brass image of a "fiery serpent" and put it on a pole after which anyone who beheld this brass serpent would not die from a serpent's bite. Now we go to John 3:14, 15 and find Jesus saying ". . . *And as Moses lifted up the serpent in the wilderness, even so must the Son of man be lifted up; that whosoever believeth in him should not perish, but have eternal life.*" Of what was brass the symbol? It was a levitical symbol of judgment, a metal associated with fire. The serpent is the symbol of sin throughout the Scriptures. Thus, we have the symbol of sin and judgment placed on a wooden pole and endowed by God with the power to negate the serpent's deadly bite and certain death to those who viewed it and believed in its power. What a strange way to cure a snakebite! Yet later, our Lord chose to place Himself on a wooden pole and become the summation of all sin and judgment, and, thereby, its cure and its atonement, for all who would see and believe in Him. They also would be spared the ultimate death and receive eternal life. Why else would the brazen serpent have been used by God in this strange manner, and to record it for future generations, except to provide it as a preview of more important things to come for those blessed with understanding of God's Word? (2 Corinthians 5:21) *"For He made Him to be sin for us, who knew no sin; that we might be made the righteousness of God in Him."* The story of Abraham and his intended sacrifice of his son on the very spot where the Lord did sacrifice His own, is again, nothing more than a deliberately recorded preview of this same event for the same reason. These Old Testament pearls, of which there are many, are there to prove that there was a single, supernatural author of the entire Scriptures. As our understanding of the Scriptures continues to increase, and strangely that is still happening, we will find many more of these gems. I believe that such discovery will not be complete until Jesus Christ is clearly evident on every page of even the Old Testament. Why am I so certain of this? Because as one searches, the more of His presence is found in every chapter. Furthermore, Jesus Himself is reported in Hebrews 10:7 to have observed, ". . . *in the volume of the book it is written of me* . . ." What book? The Old Testament, which was the only book, because the New Testament did not yet exist. Of course, the New Testament is all about Him most explicitly.

Looking back from the perspective of what we know now from the New Testament, many things become quite clear, which in the context of the earlier times were not as easily discernable. In these respects, the New Testament is as a "Rosetta Stone" by means of which much can be deciphered. This is even more accurately and eloquently stated in the clever observation that the "New Testament is in the Old Testament concealed, while the Old Testament is in the New Testament revealed." At first, this may seem to be nothing more than a cute, witty, little ditty; however, it is in fact most astute and accurate. Everywhere in the Old Testament are found (concealed) references to Jesus, His purpose, His identity and His message. The cross formed by the tribes in the wilderness and the prophecy of his coming in the Genealogy of Moses are but two examples. Yet, many of these are difficult to discern until viewed (revealed) in retrospect from the vantage point of the New Testament. In one sense, there is surprisingly little new information in the New Testament. A great deal of what it contains was long ago provided, if not somewhat hidden in the Old Testament. For instance, there are more than eight hundred allusions to the Old Testament in the 404 verses of the book of Revelation. In this case it can be said that the book of Revelation cannot be well understood by itself without a good understanding of these eight hundred Old Testament verses in their original context. Likewise, many aspects of the Old Testament such as Isaiah 52 and 53, Psalm 22, etc. seem somewhat abstract and lacking in content, until viewed from the perspective only available from the New Testament, and the fulfilling events that they so vividly anticipate.

One could fill many volumes with examples of how various books in each Testament relate to each other in a manner clearly characteristic of a single Authorship. Similarly, it could be demonstrated just how the Old Testament and the New Testament combine, interrelate, and actually explain and fully compliment each other, thus, further strengthening this contention. However, to a large degree, the previously described and fulfilled prophecies already venture effectively in this direction providing strong evidence to support the subject of this paper. Therefore, we'll travel on to the next and last segment of this effort, the Bible Codes.

15   Bible Codes

Throughout this paper I have sought to prove to the skeptical observer that the Bible was authored by God Himself through the hands of various writers over a long period of time. Evidence of this is absolute if one only examines it carefully and with a mind not demanding that it not be so. For that mind will not accept this, however, let's offer the following challenge. That is, to construct a genealogy with the following characteristics:

- ➤ The total number of words must be divisible evenly by 7.
- ➤ The total number of letters must be divisible evenly by 7.
- ➤ The total number of consonants must be divisible evenly by 7.
- ➤ The total number of words beginning with a vowel must be divisible evenly by 7.
- ➤ The total number of words beginning with a consonant must be divisible evenly by 7.
- ➤ The total number of words, that occur in one form, must be divisible evenly by 7.
- ➤ The total number of words, that occur in only one form, must be divisible evenly by 7.
- ➤ The total number of nouns must be divisible evenly by 7.
- ➤ The total number of names must be divisible evenly by 7.
- ➤ The total number of males must be divisible evenly by 7.
- ➤ The total number of generations must be divisible evenly by 7.

If you can do this, then you have duplicated what Matthew did in writing the genealogy of Christ in the original Greek in Matthew 1:1–17

That's not all. Matthew was equally clever to have written his whole gospel in such a manner that he used 42 (7 x 6) words unique to his work. These words contain 128 (7 x 18) letters. They are to Matthew unique in that no other writer used them, and thus they are not found in any of the other Gospels. How could he do this unless he wrote the Gospel last? It just happens, however, that the number of words and letters making up these works, that are unique to Mark, are also all divisible by 7. So he too must have written his gospel last in order to know what Matthew had written. Or else, they sat together working out this clever yet seemingly pointless game. Well, it's even a little more involved than that, because a unique collection of words always divisible by 7 is also found in the books of Luke, John, James, Peter, Jude. Thus, each Gospel has a certain number of words that are not used in any of the other Gospels and in each case that number is a multiple of seven. What a time they all must have had getting together to contrive this little bit of word play, each agreeing not to use certain words so that each could have a set of words unique to his particular individual work. They must have burned out a dozen computer and word processors each, trying to get this to work out with even sevens! Or, could this be the work of the Holy Spirit supernaturally guiding this bit of word play so that it might be discovered many hundreds of years later for the benefit of the "doubting Thomases" who need to see such things before they can believe?

This hepatic structure is found extensively and quiet openly throughout both the Old and New Testaments, many hundreds of times in every book. Seven is consistently used to signify complete-ness. The preceding, which are only two of many examples, come from the legacy of a man named Ivan Pavin (1855–1942). He left Russia, then Germany, and settled here receiving his Ph.D. from Harvard after which he received Jesus and spent the next fifty years studying the Scriptures and especially this hepatic coding. He left us 43,000 pages of notes regarding this one aspect of God's Word.

Pavin, however, was not the first to notice the less obvious numerical coding to be found in the Bible. Reference to such codes goes back hundreds of years at least to the twelfth century when Rabbi Nachmanidis referred to them and saw them as providing a powerful reason to guard the integrity and perfection of every letter in the biblical text. That it has been so guarded is evident from the fact that the decoding of the current texts reveals relevant informa-tion, that would be impossible had these texts been modified. Of course, as we have seen, the Dead Sea Scrolls have confirmed that the integrity of the original Scriptures has survived the thousands of years of repeat copying.

With the advent of super computers, much has been done to unravel some of the coded evidence of divine authorship. "The Mysterious Bible Codes" by Grant Jeffrey (World Publishing) is but one of many that report on this fascinating subject. The following taken from pages 33 and 34 of that book is but one smaller bit of evidence, that I believe further proves the divine Authorship of the Scriptures:

Rabbi Bachya and the Codes

Six hundred years ago, Rabbi Bachya, a European rabbi, wrote a book in which he described his discovery of a pattern of letters that formed meaningful words encoded in the Torah at equally spaced intervals. When he examined the Hebrew letters, beginning in Genesis 1:1, he noticed that if he began with the last letter in the first word of the Bible, beginnings, and skipped every forty-nine letters, the word Torah was spelled out. In other words, every fiftieth letter of text spelled the word Torah.

Rabbi Bachya also found that the opening verse of Exodus contained the word Torah, also spelled out at the same fifty-letter interval, beginning with the first appearance of the letter yod. When he examined the opening verse of Leviticus, however, he could not find the encoded word Torah. Instead he discovered the Hebrew word HaShem, which means "the Name" (of God), spelled out every eighth letter, beginning with the first letter yod.

When the rabbi examined the initial verses of Numbers and Deuteronomy, the fourth and fifth books of the Bible, again he found that the word Torah was encoded. In the book of Numbers, Torah was spelled out in reverse at a fifty-letter interval and in Deuteronomy, to his surprise Torah was spelled out in reverse order at a forty-ninth-letter interval, beginning with the fifth verse.

Dr. Daniel Michelson calculated that, based on a letter-frequency analysis, the odds are more than 3 million to 1 against the word Torah being encoded by chance, beginning with the first word of Genesis. Therefore, the odds that the word Torah would appear in ELS code at the very beginning of each of the four books of Moses simply by chance are astronomical.

∽

The examples of a single authorship described in section14 above, such as the message continued in the genealogy of Noah, and the cross that Israeli's camp formed in the wilderness, are but two of the dozens of similar hidden pearls, or examples of hidden messages, attesting to the Bible's supernatural origin.

If you have waded through all of the above to reach this ending, I am grateful for your perseverance. If you were in any way edified or received a desire to pursue further the truth of the Bible, and in particular of the gospel, I thank God for His blessing and guidance to have allowed me to choose whatever the words they were that caused that desire. If you have that desire, please get started before it fades away. There is nothing more vital or of higher priority than knowing the true God and what He is eager for you to know. Just sit down with His book knowing that it is His Word; as you read, ask Him to explain it. He is ready, willing and eager to do so, but He won't unless you sincerely ask.

Don't delay. Do it now! Tomorrow may be too late!

—2—

What is a Born-Again Christian?

Even though I'm now somewhat beyond the allotted three-score and ten, I'm only a new three-and-a-half-year-old born-again Christian. Thus, in spite of my very young age, or perhaps because of the exuberance that is characteristic of that age, I am most eager to share my wonderful discoveries along with the knowledge and belief that transforms the soul, spirit and heart, and thereby clears the path to eternal life. What I have learned is the foundation and purpose of all creation, and how, through faith and love, anyone can become saved into eternal life with our Creator.

First where did the term, the idea, "born-again" come from, and what does it mean? In the Gospel of John 3:3 Jesus tells Nicodemus that ". . . *except a man be born-again he cannot see the kingdom of God.*" Nicodemus, a wealthy old Pharisee and "ruler of Jews," had apparently become a secret convert to Jesus, but had some questions that needed answering. In this instance he came to Jesus to seek the answers. In response to these words from Jesus he asked, " How can a man be born-again, when he is old? Can he enter the womb and be born?" Jesus then repeated the essence of his first statement and added in part "that which is born of the flesh is flesh; and that which is born of the spirit is spirit." This means born of the Holy Spirit. In the original Greek, the word "again," is *anothen,* which also, and more appropriately, translates "from above." Thus the English translation would be a more accurate message if it were to say "born again from above." Nevertheless, the Lord adds the necessary clarity when he speaks of being born of the Spirit. Thus a born-again Christian is one who has received in him the Holy Spirit, which is in effect a spiritual birth independent of the original physical birth. This is the first and only birth of the spirit, which in essence is until then dead, unborn. The Holy Spirit sparks it into life. This occurs only through the acknowledgement of the power of the Cross and belief and faith in the resurrection and in the deity of Jesus Christ.

Now, I suppose, unless you are a born from above Christian, this dogmatic one-way-only-to-heaven view may be offensive to you. I know that we live in a secular world of relativism where your right is as good as mine and nothing is absolute. Of course, you are free to believe as you will; God gave you that sovereign choice. As a true Christian I have no right to be your judge or to twist your arm. My only right, no my obligation, is to love you and pray for you and if you choose to let me, to tell you about my faith. This matter of judgment in the Christian context is often confusing and misunderstood. Christians have no right to judge others, or even each other, in the sense of the Greek *krino,* meaning to judge, decide, and by implication to try, condemn, punish, avenge, etc., or even in the sense of Hebrew *shophat* to pronounce sentence, condemn, punish. They do, however have the right to judge in the sense of the Greek *anakrino,* to judge so as to examine, determine, and discern. Because true Christians are admonished to avoid sin and sinful situations, it is necessary that they make this latter form of judgment, or discernment, but not the kind that leads to a lack of love, condemnation or attempt to punish or avenge. That form of judgment belongs only to God, and under certain conditions, the courts to which He has ordained that authority.

Furthermore, born from above Christians do not consider themselves better than anyone else. For to believe so would first be incorrect, but would also be a form of pride, a sin that if left uncorrected would be a cause to question the very validity of their faith. Born-again Christians are probably even more acutely aware of their own many weaknesses and deficiencies, and especially of their sinful natures. Thus they have no basis for feeling superior or better than anyone else. What they do feel, however, is that they are most fortunate to have been blessed with the Grace of Faith. This is never something of which to be proud, but only of which to be most grateful. Anyone expressing any signs of superiority, of betterness or of pride because of their faith, has taken a very wrong path away from the true Christian Walk.

What really happens when one is born again, or born from above? I know that I have already described this, but it is so important that I must say it again. The instant one acknowledges as a deep and permanent commitment, the truth of the Gospel, and wholeheartedly, without reservation, accepts Jesus as one's Savior, one receives a new heart and an awakening of the spirit, through the actions of the Holy Spirit. Thus one receives a spiritual heart, or it could be said, a new internal control center, never before experienced. This born from above individual is never again the same, because this new control center, manned by the Holy Spirit, directs the host along a higher plane in terms of thoughts, values, priorities and emotions. He or she still has the same old sinful soul and body, however, with the new spiritual control center, his or her whole existence takes on a new perspective. One becomes progressively more discerning of sin and never again feels comfortable in its presence or in any sinful thought or action. Unfortunately, the natural sinful nature has not changed; the change is in the attitude towards it, how one chooses to deal with it, and the manner of one's attempt to reduce and hopefully eliminate it from one's life.

This new heart, this spiritual control center, must always be kept clean. But how can it be kept clean when our natural self is repeatedly dirtying it with sin? Only the spiritually clean, the sinless, may enter heaven, because it is impossible for sin to enter heaven, much less reside there. When Jesus died on the cross it was a universal, forever payment and cleansing of all sins of all believers who are born from above Christians. This is the key to *everything*! The instant one became born from above, all sins were washed away and thus the one and only qualification for entry into heaven has been attained. This is probably the only true instance where believing something actually makes it so. The very instant that a person truly believes that Jesus died in order to purge our sins, they are purged! If one's faith in Jesus is a genuine, true, saving faith, one's life is forever changed. While one may yet sin occasionally, these too are forgiven as long as one chooses to:

1. Cultivate and maintain an awareness and sensitivity to sin,

2. Strive at all times to avoid sin, and

3. When a sin nevertheless slips in, be aware of it, admit it, be sincerely sorry for having committed the sin, confess it to the Lord, and resolve to avoid it in the future.

As long as this process is sincerely applied, the soul remains clean and acceptable to God. As one can see, this is a moment-by-moment, day-by-day process, because our mortal selves cannot at all times refrain from sin. This is especially true for the truly faithful Christians, because as we proceed along the Walk our sensitivity to sin increases and we, therefore, recognize as sins, actions and thoughts that would have previously been dismissed as normal, natural and wholly defendable. While they may be all those things, we now notice that they are also sins to be recognized, admitted to, and removed from our lives.

The born from above Christians are aware of the power of prayer, and so communicate with the Lord more and more frequently as they progress along the Christian Walk. Having each handed back to the Lord his/her free will and asked that He henceforth guide their lives, the true Christians now place their total reliance on the Lord, and, therefore, must seek through prayer, the guidance they need in order to continue their earthly lives. Along with their reliance on prayer, believers are also dependent on the written Word of the Lord as their daily bread. Thus the Scripture also becomes a vital aspect of their lives, one for which they develop an insatiable hunger that requires daily satisfaction. Through the Scriptures, believers continue to learn more of God's ways and desires and purpose, which further add to their ability to understand and better live the way He wants us to.

Through careful and loving study of the Scriptures, the born from above Christians, (I'll henceforth call them True Christians.) learn many truths, that seem to be hidden, ignored, or despised by most of the world. They see clearly from their studies that this book, The Holy Bible, the combined Old and New Testament, is a single integrated inerrant message authored by the Holy Spirit from outside of time and space. Soon it becomes the sole source of all relevant knowledge and the guiding light by which they choose to continue their journey through life. True Christians see themselves not as citizens of any place on earth, but only as sojourners, here for a while on their way home.

True Christians, as their faith matures, seek to approach their ultimate goals not to hate or hold grudges, to always be forgiving, to speak no ill of others and to avoid sinful situations and temptations. This is but a sampling of the full Christian's Walk. The true Christians have no hate in them; they hold no animosities towards anyone or any group. Because of their careful and inspired reading of the Scriptures, they learn many truths that seem to escape most others. They recognize the proof of the authorship of the Bible. This proof is discovered in many places, the most obvious being the accuracy of the prophecies or little excerpts from history written long before the event occurred. From these for instance, they realize that the Lord still has an unfulfilled destiny for the Jews. This is partly evidenced by the return of these people to the promised land on the exact day, May 14, 1948, that, through Daniel, 2500 years earlier that the Lord said it would occur. They know that the Jews did not kill Jesus, that this was preordained as evidenced in Psalm 22, Isaiah 53 and in several other places in the Old Testament. The true Christians know that they, through their own sins and not the Jews, were responsible for His physical death. For even before the beginning of the world, He chose the shedding of His own blood, the blood of His innocent, incarnate manifestation, Jesus, as the means by which sin could be forgiven. Thus it was a handful, probably not more than a dozen Jewish leaders and high priests who instigated the crucifixion through the authority of the Romans, unknowingly fulfilling prophecy.

As did Jesus, the true believers shun ritual and formalized religion. Jesus was, in fact, against religion, because no matter its good initial intentions, religion by its nature grows ever more rituals, and these subordinate faith, love and worship, the real and only expressions the Lord wants from us. True Christians will, of course, do good works, that is, good deeds, and will strive to obey the commandments. They will do these, however, out of love for the Lord, not out of obligation or as perceived requirements for salvation. Salvation is a free gift given to all true Christians. Jesus gave this gift on the Cross. His last words were *Telelestai,* "It is finished" (John 19:30), better translated from the Greek as "Paid in full." These last words were the most profound words ever spoken.

They were the culmination and summation of the entire Scripture and of his brief three-year ministry. They express the whole purpose of His First Coming, that is, to take away the sins of the world, to provide all humankind the means through which heaven is obtainable. His time on the cross did that. When that time was at an end, as he died, his mortal life finished, it was at that moment that our sins, the sins of those who believe were "paid in full."

I have tried here to summarize the beliefs and qualities of a true born again Christian. I sincerely and totally believe as I have written. However, I must confess that I am some distances from the qualities here described. Three score and ten years make for very deep ruts that are difficult to climb out of. Nevertheless, I have worked myself out far enough to at least see the path I want to travel, and I will, with the help of the Lord, surely get there, not for the sake of salvation, for that is already mine through faith in Jesus. What I seek is perfection of my Walk, and this out of gratitude and love, and the belief that it is right.

If you like what you have read, confess to the Lord; accept Jesus as your Savior. That's the cue for the Holy Spirit to implant your new heart, take over your spiritual control center, and change your life. It's never too late nor is anyone too wicked. If He would accept me, He will accept anyone.

—3—

Repentance

Let us examine this simple word that has become all but totally obsolete and stripped of its biblical relevance or importance in the modernized, enlightened realm of "Christian teachings." Webster's definition of the word is somewhat consistent with its biblical meaning. The dictionary defines the word "repent" as "to feel sorry or self-reproachful for what one has done or failed to do, be conscience-stricken, or contrite." The word is translated "repent" from three slight variations of the Greek word "metamorphos." Collectively these mean, "to care afterwards, regret, transform, metamorphos, change, transfigure, think differently or afterwards, compunction for guilt, reformation." Why am I making so much ado about a word rarely even mentioned, let alone preached about from most pulpits? Because it is one of the three most important words in the entire lexicon dealing with salvation! These vital prerequisites to salvation are repentance, belief and faith, and each requires our in-depth understanding of what they mean and how they must be applied if eternal security is to be secured. Wait a minute you say, "Doesn't Ephesians 2:8 say that we are saved by grace through faith?" And then you say, "doesn't Romans 10:9 say that if we confess with our mouths the Lord Jesus, and believe in our hearts that God has raised Him from the dead, that we are saved?" To these scriptural references I say, absolutely, that is what they say and therefore most certainly their sincere application provides assurance of salvation. Then you ask, "Then what is the big deal about repentance? If belief and faith do it for us then why belabor this point about repentance when no one else does?" I'm glad you asked!

At the very beginning of the New Testament, in Matthew 3:2, right after Jesus' genealogy and the issues surrounding His birth are dealt with, we have John the Baptist entering the scene with a resounding voice saying *"Repent ye: for the Kingdom of Heaven is at hand."* Then in Mark 6:12 after Jesus had instructed the disciples, he tells us that *"and they went out, and preached that men should repent."* Then we find in Luke 13:3 Jesus is quoted saying *"I tell you, nay: but except ye repent, ye shall all likewise perish."* Jesus repeats this again in verse 5.

In Acts 2:38 we read, *"Then Peter said unto them, Repent, and be baptized every one of you in the name of Jesus Christ for the remission of sins and ye shall receive the gift of the Holy Ghost."* In Acts 3:19 Peter again says, *"Repent ye therefore, and be converted, that your sins may be blotted out . . ."* In Acts 17:30 Peter says ". . . *And the times of this ignorance God winked at, but now commandeth all men everywhere to repent."* In Acts 26:20 Paul is on trial in front of a king describing the details of his ministry. His principal message as he described it, is that he preached to both Jews and Gentiles ". . . *that they should repent and turn to God, and do works meet with repentance."* In Luke 24:47 Jesus says, *"And that repentance and remission of sins should be preached in His name among all nations beginning in Jerusalem."* Finally in 2 Peter 3:9 we are assured that our Lord ". . . *is long suffering to us-ward, not willing that any should perish, but that all should come to repentance."*

Lets first look at this last notation, where, through Peter, the Holy Spirit has told us that God doesn't want any to perish, ". . . *but that all should come to repentance."* This indicates that there are two kinds of people, those who perish, and those who repent. From this we can only conclude that repentance must be very closely related to redemption, because, it's equally true that all who do not repent are the ones who perish! Could it be any clearer? Without repentance, there is no salvation! Look back at Mark 1:15 where Jesus says ". . . *repent ye, and believe the Gospel."* After that we are told that Jesus instructed the disciples and they went across the countryside *"preaching that man should repent."* From this we can see that "repent" was the key, the primary message. It is not that faith and belief were not essential to salvation, but that repentance was somehow a guiding principal or perhaps a prerequisite essential for salvation. The validity of this premise seems to be confirmed in Luke 13:3, when Jesus says that unless you repent you will perish. Again, a lack of repentance is an assurance of eternal damnation, which is very clearly just what perish means!

In Acts 2:38, Peter tells his audience to repent and be baptized in Jesus' name so their sins would be forgiven and that they could then receive the Holy Spirit. Let's examine this a little more closely. We know that water baptism doesn't save souls and is not an essential ingredient of salvation. It's a graphical, physical, public expression of ones commitment to, and fellowship or association with, Jesus, in His death and resurrection. Anyone can go through this simply as a ritual, and have no saving faith whatsoever. We also know that the Holy Spirit takes up residency in the heart the instant one becomes redeemed. Notice that in this verse Peter says nothing about "belief" or 'faith." This verse might be interpreted in several ways. However, if it is taken literally, from a salvation perspective, Peter is directing his audience to simply, "repent." What results from the proper application of this word alone, is the remissions of sins, and the receipt of the Holy Spirit! Effectually, repentance is given as a formula for salvation without any mention of belief or faith! Therefore, it appears that we can conclude that repentance, in its full context, is a state of the mind and heart that all by itself provides salvation. This again is strongly implied in Luke 24:47, as quoted above, where Jesus instructs His disciples quite simply that they are to preach "repentance and the remission of sins" throughout the world.

Let's look at just one more of these verses regarding the matter of repentance, in Acts 3:19 we are urged to, *"Repent ye therefore and be converted that your sins may be blotted out."* However, in Acts 16:31, the Holy Sprit tells us to ". . . *Believe on the Lord Jesus Christ and thou shalt be saved . . ."* and Romans 10:9 we are told *"That if thou shalt confess with thy mouth the Lord Jesus, and shalt believe in thine heart that God hath raised Him from the dead, thou shalt be saved."* In Ephesians 2:8 we are assured that we are *"saved by grace through faith."* From these verses we find that salvation comes through belief alone, and faith alone, and repentance alone! Could this mean that there are three alternative ways to salvation, faith, belief and repentance? Hardly! Then what is going on? I may be alone in this thought, but there is something profound here to be chewed, swallowed and digested!

For those earnestly seeking salvation, and for those who believe they have it, but are willing to examine its legitimacy, this should be an important question for which to find a solid answer. It should also serve to raise the question as to why this word repentance sits on the back shelf of almost every church assembly and evangelical out-reach group, hidden and drawing dust rather than being taught, as it was in the early church. Shouldn't it be a major and frequent theme being preached from every pulpit? What is the cause of the near universal avoidance of the word within the so-called Christian church? It cannot be its lack of importance. The quotations noted cry out otherwise! Is it ignorance of Scripture among those who "spread the word"? Is it fear of emptying pews if its meaning is seriously preached? Perhaps it is the manifestation of prophecies regarding these end times when false teachers with deceitful tongues would preach only pleasant cheerful messages, and deliberately avoid those that could lead souls to repentance. Paul, in 2 Timothy 4:3–4 sums up the point perfectly when he says, *"For the time will come when they will not endure sound doctrine; but after their own lusts shall they heap to themselves teachers, having itching ears; and they shall turn away their ears from the truth, and shall be turned unto fables."* To varying degrees each of these reasons has tragically contributed to repentance languishing, abandoned on the back shelf of Christian doctrinal teaching and preaching. A graphic example of why the faint of hearts who may know better, yet fail to focus on the subject may be found in the study of the Old Testament prophets who bravely expressed the vital importance of what this word means. Most were killed for their bravery in this respect. Look at Jeremiah for instance, God commanded him to prophesize and preach repentance continually for forty years, but first He warned him that he would not convince anyone, and would suffer greatly for his obedience. Because of his preaching of repentance, he was beaten, imprisoned, left to suffer in a cesspool and exiled to Egypt. His friends and even his own brothers conspired to kill him for no reason other than for his message of repentance, a word they didn't want to hear.

Belief and faith are seemingly innocuous concepts that can easily be absorbed in the mind but sometimes never reach the heart where they must exist for the soul to find salvation. Repentance on the other hand, requires a turning, a humbling, and an unvarnished recognition of a hopelessly sinful nature that can only be corrected by a Redeemer, our blessed Lord and Savior Christ Jesus. That demands a commitment too big for many, and provides the real test, that separates the possessor of the saving faith from the mere professor of an ineffectual faith.

On this basis, it is essential that we come to a true understanding of just what repentance means in the context of Christian belief, for how else can we apply this obviously essential element of salvation?

1. Repentance is a conscious, serious, life-altering change; it is a change of mind about what sin really is, and having great sorrow for having lived a life of sin. But mere sorrow of mind no matter how sincere is not repentance. It must be a Godly sorrow. In 2 Corinthians 7:10 we are told *"For Godly sorrow worketh repentance to salvation not to be repented of; but the sorrow of the world worketh death."* Worldly sorrow for sins is quite common, but it has no effective relationship to repentance that leads to salvation. The natural human conscience can be very sensitive to sin, and the resulting regrets and desires to repent from them can be very sincere, but that is not Godly repentance. Absent a truly Godly sorrow there is no genuine repentance. Godly repentance must be accompanied by a resolve, and a holy longing and desire that with Gods strength we can escape from its clutches. Real repentance is not only accompanied by a fear of God's wrath, but also by the sweetness of His love, as we grow in knowledge of who He is.

2. Repentance is a profound sense of shame for having lived in sin, and a longing to avoid it forever. And as Spurgeon says, that "sorrow for sin is a perpetual rain, a sweet soft shower which to a gracious man, last all his life long." He also observes that it is a "sorrow which is associated with a believing faith, for Godly sorrow must be one that makes the heart that feels it yield itself to Christ. Yielding itself to Christ, it must believe in Christ. For if I do not believe in Christ, it is certain that I have not yielded

51

myself to Him." We must therefore conclude also that if one has not yielded to Christ, then one is not an effectual believer in Christ! How grievous it is, or should be, for a redeemed soul to sin, realizing that it is by ones own election to do so, and knowing that each sin is against the One who has been our Redeemer of sins. To the extent that we continue to do so with a Godly shame and firm resolve to no longer do so, are we not spitting in His face and admitting that our repentance, belief and faith are nothing but a sham?

3. Repentance is recognition of our own hopeless sinful nature, a nature from which we realize that only Christ Jesus can rescue us. Today there seems to be much preaching on the remedy for all sins, that is, that by believing, we are saved. However the true nature of what it is that we are to be saved from is often ignored. Spurgeon reminds us that "it will never do for men to be led to think that they are healed before we know that we are sick unto death, or to imagine that they are clothed before they see themselves to be naked, or to be taught to trust in Christ before they are aware that they have anything for which they need to trust Him."

4. Repentance is a turning around, a change of ones whole being regarding sin, along with a keenly focused turning toward Jesus, believing in, and choosing to live in obedience to Jesus as our Lord and Savior. Isn't this the change of ones whole being that Jesus meant when He said to Nicodemus ". . . *except a man be born-again, he cannot see the kingdom of God*?" It's being born again as a whole new spiritual being. Above all things, we must remember (although Calvinists would not agree) that repentance, as with faith, is of our own volition, but after its first spark, God's grace will fertilize and water it to make it grow strong. Serious prayer, praise of our Lord, and gratitude for His love, guidance and mercy will cause the "Son-shine" energy needed for more rapid and stronger growth. From this, we must conclude that repentance is an essential ingredient in providing redemption. If so, just where is it in this chain of events? Is it something that happens before or after believing, or when we receive the grace through faith spoken of in Ephesians 2:8? I

believe that Spurgeon gave an astute answer to that question when he responded, "Which spoke in a wheel moves first when the wheel starts." In other words they are simultaneous! But the fact is, it is even more profound that that!

Repentance, belief and faith are simply three words, the meanings of which are bound in unity, as are the Father, Son and the Holy Spirit! Not one of these exists without the other two. Without repentance, there is no forgiveness of sins. Without repentance there is no valid belief; without repentance there is no saving faith; and without repentance there is no justification, no sanctification, and no promise of a heavenly home! This is a profound and essential truth that I didn't realize until I reached this point in my journey regarding the meaning of repentance. Consider this, as a way of recapitulation of what has been presented above.

1. Scripture tells us several times that if we believe in Jesus we are saved.

2. Scripture tells us several times that it is grace through faith that saves us.

3. Scripture tells us several times it is through repentance, we are saved.

Now back to the earlier question; does that mean there are three paths to salvation? Again, certainly not! Well, if it doesn't mean that, then it can only mean that the three are an integrated whole, without which salvation is impossible! Implicit in the word "faith," there must exist belief and repentance. In the word "belief" there must be "faith" and "repentance," and in "repentance" must also be found both "belief" and "faith!" If this is true, and I believe the evidence is compelling that it is, I ask again, why do we almost hardly ever hear the word repentance coming from the pulpits or from evangelical leaders? I'm already given the sad painful answer. But please suffer my repetition for a moment, while I summarize with, what I pray, will be more effective and complete. We don't hear the word repentance because:

1. Perhaps, collectively we don't want to hear it, or to "face up to it," anymore than they did in Old Testament times. We prefer

ignorance to any cramping of our lifestyle, as has all of humanity throughout the ages. The words "faith" and "belief" are seemingly innocuous and don't, as commonly understood; cause much of a threat to ones lifestyle.

2.   Some of those who preach and teach "the Word" fail to understand the essential nature of repentance as a requirement for salvation. How can they, or why should they when the "soft" definitions of "belief" and "faith" seem to be all that are necessary.

3.   Others may fear what dwelling on it would do to the pew population and the "box office receipts." They prefer to compromise the saving of souls to the loss of pew warmers and check writers. This type is exemplified in the highly popular very wealthy mega churches where they have abandoned the preaching for genuine belief or faith for the sake of mammon and ego. Many of these also fall into category 4 below.

4.   The pulpits and airways seem to be filling up with non-believers who deliberately and knowingly preach what pleases but does not save. These are the false teachers spoken of by Jesus, and are also described in the Epistles as those who would proliferate in these end times, deliberately preaching false doctrines.

Dear soul if you think that you are riding a heaven-bound wagon, I beg you to stop, get off, and look at the wheels. Count the spokes, and if you don't see one that is called repentance, stay off that wagon because, it will never deliver you to the heavenly realm. The modern usage of the words "believe" and "faith" has stripped them of much of their vital roots, and thereby weakens and deprives them of the fuller depth of meaning they had in the early days of Christianity when the New Testament was written. From the verses quoted, it should be evident that this greater depth of meaning included a greater sense of resolve of persevering commitment and at least the essence of the meaning of that word "repent." How else can one explain the independent ways to salvation that the several verses herein quoted seems to establish? Given the comparative weakness and even superficiality of the words "belief" and "faith" as they are used today, isn't it a tragic thing for the seeking soul to be introduced to Christianity through these words absent the introduction of the word "repentance" as well? I pray that those who find the above disturbing, non-scriptural, even offensive, before they condemn the premise of the essay, will prayerfully re-examine God's Word in this context so as to make a solid scriptural based conclusion regarding this matter of the position and importance of repentance in the process of salvation.

—4—

The Professor and the Possessor

D o you posses that faith that accepts God's grace of salvation and eternal life? Or do you merely profess to possess? Are you sure? How do you know? In the final analysis, there is nothing in this mortal life more important than the *possession* of salvation. And it is only through possession of a true and saving faith that God's amazing grace and eternal life can be obtained. The stakes are infinite and, therefore, too great to rely on anything less than the whole and true word of God, through which to determine whether you possess or merely profess the real born-again Christian faith.

In one sense, the first question is a silly one. Who would profess to possess, if they didn't believe they posses what they profess? However, I doubt that you believe that everyone who is a professor is actually a possessor. Surely, some are mistaken or deceived, or simply ignorant of what constitutes a saving faith. But that's not you or me! We are both surely possessors of that saving faith! Would it in any way disturb your complacency or certainty to learn that Christian polls indicate that as many as ninety-one percent of those who call themselves "born-again" Christians, that is those who profess to possess, do not believe fully, if at all, in the basics of what Scripture tells us is fundamental to being a true "born-again" Christian? That is basics, such as the virgin birth; that Jesus died so that our sins could be forgiven; that we are saved by grace through faith alone; that Jesus is the *only* way to eternal life? And they didn't even ask whether or not confession, repentance and obedience were significant elements! Does it concern you, as it does me, that a similar percentage of those who "come to Christ" as a result of many evangelical efforts, such as the Billy Graham crusades, were found a year later to be expressing little or no resemblances to what one might consider evidence of being "born-again"? In fact, many were found to be embracing false religions or no belief at all! Yet I suspect that many believed, and continue to believe, that they were saved by that one act of profession!

The parable of the sower (Matthew 13) comes powerfully to mind when I hear of such disturbing evidences. So, also does Matthew 20:16 and 22:14, where Jesus tells us that many are called, but few are chosen. It seems quite evident that it is far more frequent for someone to recognize a calling than it is to *validly* conclude that one has been chosen. By chosen it means to be a possessor of the saving faith. On the other hand, could that "calling" have been somehow misunderstood, by the many? Could it be that through insufficient knowledge of Scripture, or wishful thinking they jumped to that comfortable but false conclusion? Could the "calling" of the "many" thereby become construed in such a way as to lead one to become a professor, but not one of the "few" who actually become possessors? The above noted statistics certainly suggest that there must be something of that tragic nature afoot in the so-called Christian Community.

Perhaps at this point you are still absolutely certain that you possess salvation and find this message not relevant to your spiritual condition. If so, then you must surely believe that you are one of the less than ten percent of the professors who actually possess the saving faith and are thereby in the born-again status. If you are, then I would ask you to consider the following. When was the last time you chose to ". . . *work out your own salvation with fear and trembling*"? In Philippians 2:12 the Holy Spirit tells us we must do that. It doesn't say to do but once, or more than once. However, if we take seriously our need for salvation, we may sense that this is something to be repeated occasionally, if not for any other reason than to reset our course more accurately. Also have you been periodically applying 2 Corinthians 13:5 where we are told "*Examine yourselves, whether ye be in the faith, prove your own selves . . .*" This also seems to suggest periodic reappraisal of our spiritual condition. But why would the Holy Spirit urge this examination if a saving faith was so easy and obvious? Jesus said in John 8:31 ". . . *if ye continue in my Word then are ye my disciples indeed.*" Here, as well as elsewhere where His words are recorded, some truly believed and put their trust in Him, thus becoming possessors, while others simply acquiesced to the truth of His words but were not rooted in a saving faith. They were the original "empty" professors. We know that to be His disciples we must possess that saving faith through which we become born-again. But you can be a disciple only if you "continue in the Word." That sounds like an on-going process of study and application of the Word. That means the whole Scripture. The following, taken from "Life and Habit" (London: Jonathan Cape 1923, page 112) is an excellent commentary expressing the same message regarding the empty professor, that is the visible church, and the possessor, here depicted as the invisible church.

> *"The general sense of our Lord's teaching here would seem to be what the Theologians have sought to sum up for us in the doctrine of the visible and invisible church. To belong to the former, to be brought up in its atmosphere, to be played upon day after day by its gracious influences is in itself an immense advantage which ought to predispose one to become a member of the real church (called invisible, because only God knows with accuracy who belongs to it), i.e.: to the body, not merely of traditionalists and conformists and outward adherents, but of genuine believers of those who have accepted God's offers of salvation, and have put on the Lord Jesus Christ, and are learning to grow up into His mind and ways. Apart from that, membership in the outward church is not nearly enough."*

In that same vein, consider 2 Timothy 2:15 ". . . *Study to show thyself approved unto God* . . ." I don't believe that you want to be "disapproved" of God. This verse again requires study of the Word. Do you, and have you seriously studied God's Word, or simply read portions of it? We are admonished by Scripture to study and to know God's Word. One vital reason is because, as Scripture tell us over and over again, that in these end times there will be many false witnesses (1 Corinthians 15:15), false brethren (Galatians 2:4) false prophets, (Matthew 7:15), false Christ's (Matthew 24:24), false accusers (2 Timothy 3:13), false teachers (2 Peter 2:1) etc. We are also told to ". . . *take heed that no man deceive you.*" (Matthew 24:4) and many other warnings regarding doctrinal deceit. Some of the largest "Christian" churches in the country are deceiving hundreds of thousands of "seekers" through blatantly false doctrine, because their followers don't know Scripture and, therefore, cannot discern truth from cleverly masked falsehood. Imagine how many more are deceived and led to false or inadequate belief by the more subtle deceivers who fill the airways, the literature, the podiums and the pulpits. Many teach comforting, easy-does-it, but effectively damning doctrines and directives for achieving salvation. They spew platitudes including the niceties of Christian life, but fail to tell it like it is, when it comes to teaching how to become, and what it means to be, a possessor of faith.

The path to salvation is not a cakewalk, contrary to many commonly held views in the Christian community. Until the Holy Spirit has settled in the new heart of a redeemed person who has fully given himself to Christ Jesus, it is never easy, comfortable nor convenient to give up the old ways. Even then, it is a moment-by-moment commitment. Faith, confession, repentance and obedience are inexorably woven into the fabric of the possessor of salvation. A professed faith absent any one of these components is not a saving faith.

While we are at this issue of assurance as to possession of a saving faith, let us look at a few more "inferences" about this, that the Holy Spirit has given us. In Colossians 1:23, we are told that we are saved *"If ye continue in the faith grounded and settled and be not moved away from the hope of the Gospel."* In 1 Corinthians 15:1, 2, Paul says *". . . I declare unto you the Gospel which I preached unto you, which also ye have received and wherein ye stand; by which also ye are saved, if ye keep in memory what I preached unto you, unless ye have believed in vain."* Believed in vain? That means to believe in a way other than that which leads to possession of a saving faith. This is the same message as in the parable of the sower. Also Hebrews 3:6 says, *"but Christ as a Son over His own house; whose house we are, if we hold fast the confidence and the rejoicing of the hope firm onto the end."* There is no doubt that this means that faith and its evidences must continue through to the end, in spite of all the adversities that will necessarily come along to test us as we proceed through life to the end. In 2 Timothy 2:15 the Holy Spirit through Paul tells us to *"Study to show thyself approved unto God."* Is that rhetoric to be ignored? I think not! Study what? His Word of course! In John 8:31 Jesus says *". . . If ye continue in My Word, then are ye my disciples indeed."* To continue in His Word is to know His Word and to then continue to learn more and more of His Word, and to live His Word. Clearly He is telling us here that this is the mark of a disciple, one who is redeemed, and one who is a possessor. We are told in 2 Peter 1:10 *"Wherefore the rather, brethren, give diligence to make your calling and election sure . . ."* Have you made it sure? Are you sure it's sure?

This reminds me of the tragic case of Charles Templeton. (See his autobiography or my essay "How to Loose Your Salvation.") This was a man who, for more than twenty years, professed the Christian faith. During the 1950s and 1960s he evangelized to millions all over the U.S., Canada, and Europe, on his own, and with Billy Graham. It is said that early on he was more popular and effective than Billy Graham. Yet, after twenty years of solidly professing the faith and compellingly preaching it, he suddenly renounced it and even claimed there was no God! He spent the rest of his life "preaching atheism." Did he ever possess what he so powerfully professed, literally to the whole world? Of course, only God knows what was in his heart, but the evidence is certainly very disturbing, not only in terms of his soul, but also for the many he may have misguided into believing they possess what they may only profess.

Can all of the above noted admonitions be in order to periodically reconfirm that you haven't lost that saving faith you believed you had? Of course not! If we ever had it, we can never lose it. The crux of all of this may be summarized by one word, EVIDENCE! Evidence of the possession of a saving faith is expressed by conviction, repentance, a changed life, forward movement in faith, increased love and fellowship toward and with brethren, perseverance, etc, etc. Everything in Scripture is for our learning and appropriate application. Therefore, it makes sense that because our hearts are hopelessly wicked and *deceitful*, none of us should rely on the absolute certainty of our own conclusions as to whether we possess salvation until we have thoroughly and prayerfully purged our souls of any possible reason to doubt. That is why we are so many times urged to "check it out," to reconfirm the evidence. If that were not so, why would the Holy Spirit insert so many of these expressions that call us repeatedly to self-examination? To be a fruitful self examiner it must involve much prayer, conviction and confession in a spirit of true humility, without any pride of faith, for it is such pride that can so often be found in the heart of an empty professor, that impedes his or her from becoming a possessor.

Do you ever feel that you are backsliding in your zeal for the Lord? If it tends to become prolonged, do you ever become concerned? Does the possibility ever enter your heart that your salvation may not have been real? Perhaps you haven't felt this, but I have, and even that great nineteenth century English pastor Charles Spurgeon had those moments of doubt and despair. In one of his sermons he spoke of times when even he was unsure, and when he felt the need to "examine" his faith, to again "work out" the truth of his salvation. In his sermon called "The Bite of Iniquity," he tells how he knelt down in anguish, and said, *"O'Lord I long to have this point decided, am I thine or am I not? If so why am I thus? Why is it that these confessions and these warrings are carried on in my spirit? Show me wherefore thou contendest with me, and why my sin contends with me. O'Lord show me where I am vile!"* Near the end of another one of his sermons, where he is describing the triumphal entry of Jesus into heaven with His raptured and resurrected, Spurgeon pauses to ask his audience *"Shall thy voice help to swell the everlasting chorus? Sometimes, I fear it shall not. There are times when the awful question comes—what if my name should be left out when He reads the muster-roll? Brethren, does not that thought trouble you? Will you be there—shall you see this pomp? Will you behold him triumph over sin, death and hell at last?"*

Can you answer Spurgeon's question with absolute assurance? It seems that many of us, both possessors as well as professors do sometimes tend to backslide down that slippery slope toward perdition. However, those who possess are always stopped and caught on the Rock, the rock that is Jesus. With His loving hands He catches us and guides us back up and out of our pit, ever closer to our ultimate eternal destiny. For Charles Templeton, He didn't do that. Spurgeon tells us how he viewed those times to be *". . . of essential benefit to us. We have grown strong by these grieves; the rite of iniquity has made us wiser, more cautious, more patient, more humble, more affectionate, and made us more firm in our belief in our Savior afterwards, than we had ever been before."*

By now, you are either angry with me, disgusted, or I pray, concerned enough to "examine" and "work out" your faith. Remember, there is strong evidence that a vast majority of those who comfortably profess their faith do not possess it. Why is this? How could this tragic condition have developed? I doubt that this great disparity in number between those who profess vs. those who possess was always the case in the Christian community. Surely there were always more professors, than possessors, but it is difficult to believe that it was ever 10 to 1. The answer however, as with most things, can be found in the Bible. Scripture tells us in 2 Timothy 3:1–5 *"this know also, that in the last days perilous times shall come. For men shall be lovers of their own selves, covetous, boasters, proud, blasphemers, disobedient to parents, unthankful, unholy, without natural affection, trucebreakers, false accusers, incontinent, fierce, despisers of those that are good, traitors, heady, high-minded, lovers of pleasures more than lovers of God: having a form of godliness, but denying the power thereof; from such turn away."* (Emphasis mine) And in verse 7 *"ever learning, and never able to come to the knowledge of the truth."*

After all this, perhaps you might want to take stock in yourself, to see how much possession there is in your profession. On balance, do you believe that you are a better Christian today than you were a year ago? If you are a possessor, you must be a better Christian, because in Philippians 1:6, the Holy Spirit tells us, "being confident of this very thing, that He which hath begun a good work in you will perform it until the day of Jesus Christ." In whom does He do this good work? He works in those who are born-again (born of the spirit) those who *possess* the saving faith. His purpose is to make His adopted children more and more Jesus-like. Can God ever fail to do what He has said He would do? Can His promised effort in you be so negligible as to go unnoticed year after year? Silly questions. If you can't feel His working inside or see evidence of it on the outside, maybe it is time for an in-depth examination of the basis of your profession.

How can you do this? You can't! Not without the preparatory work of the Holy Spirit. Before you can examine yourself in any meaningful manner you must be humble enough to recognize the potential need. Any pride of faith you feel must be eliminated from your soul, and you must be truly ready to "examine" and "work out your salvation." With life eternal at stake, is there any reason to not seek that reassurance?

There are many great Christian writers who have addressed this concern. One who characterizes the nature of saving faith most beautifully, and has identified the principal Scripture verses, that provided God's words in this regard, was Jonathan Edwards. In "A Treaties Concerning the Religious Affection" written by Edwards around 1746, we find what he called "holy affections" or a zeal for holy things and for God. Edwards also noted that whereas the principal evidence of life is motion, so the principal evidence of a possessor of a saving faith is holy practice, that true salvation *always* produces a continuing change in the nature of the convert. Therefore, whenever profession does not accompany *repentance* and a *confession of conversion*, it means that the person is not a possessor, that is, he is not a redeemed Christian. Thus he further notes that *"Assurance is never to be enjoyed on the basis of a past experience. "There is need of present and continuing work of the Holy Spirit . . ."* THIS IS THE ESSENCE OF WHAT THIS PAPER IS ALL ABOUT!

Edwards set down eleven evidences of a possessor of a true born-again Christian faith as it can be discerned from the Scriptures. These are presented as questions and are here simply listed for further study along with the relevant scriptural verses from where they are derived. (They are not multiple choice)

1. Do you enjoy fellowship with Christ and the Father? (1 John 1:2, 3)

2. Are you sensitive to sin? (1 John 1:8–10, Romans 7:14–25)

3. Do you obey God's Word? (1 John 2:3–5)

4. Do you reject this evil world? (1 John 2:15–17, 5:19); John 17:14–16; 2 Corinthians 4:4)

5. Do you eagerly await Christ's return? (1 John 3:2, 3; 1 Corinthians 15:49, Titus 2:11–13, Phil 3:20,21)

6. Do you see decreasing patterns of sin in your life? (1 John 3:4–10, Romans 6:14, 17,18)

7. Do you love other Christians? (1 John 2:9–11, 3:10, 16, John 13:35; 1 Peter 1:22, John 8:44)

8. Do you experience answered prayer? (1 John 3:22–24, 5:13–15, Psalm 37:3–7)

9. Do you experience the ministry of the Holy Spirit illuminating Scriptures? (1 John 4:13, 2:27, 1 Corinthians 2:10, 12, Galatians 4:6, 5:22–23, Ephesians 5:19)

10. Can you discern between spiritual truth and error? (1 John 4:1–6, 5:1, Romans 4:25, Acts 17:11)

11. Have you suffered rejection because of your faith? (1 John 3:13, 1 Peter 2:20, 4:4, 5:13, Philippians 1:28, 1 Corinthians 4:13)

It is evident that these questions and scriptural references can be helpful in assessing the reality of ones own salvation and eternal security. However, they are all suggestive of an on-going process, a day-to-day moment-by-moment continuing condition of the heart. It must be acknowledged that *none* of these questions can be answered yes in a completed sense, but only in terms of whether there is an "upward" movement, a progression no matter however small, in the "yes" direction. In order to understand the full meaning and importance of these questions, one must be well versed in Scripture and really *know* what God expects of His own. How can you know you are His own unless you also know what He expects of His own, and are in the continuing process of attempting to achieve it?

By now many who have read this far will believe that I have beaten this subject to death, and should get off of it. Those who need the message the most may well be the ones who feel this the strongest. But please bear with me a little longer. Give this old fool a couple more minutes and a few additional drops of patience. Even if you don't believe that you need to hear more, perhaps there is someone you know who does, and with whom you might want to share even these last observations. Please know that all that I write here, as well as my other papers, come from a heart that grieves for the unsaved, and especially for those who have been led to believe they are saved, but are not.

Let's go back to page 55 and to the Barna poll, which tells us in effect, that there is about a 10:1 ratio of those "Christians" who believe they are born-again, that is, who profess the saving faith, but that in all likelihood do not possess it, as compared to those who more likely do possess the grace of salvation. As noted earlier, this distinguishes the visible church from the invisible church.

One of the difficulties with speaking or writing in this manner, about the issue of salvation, is the inevitable accusation of judgment. "Who are you to say who is saved and who is not?" Sooner or later their question, in its accusatory form, enters the discussion, quickly ending any further meaningful dialogue. For the record, let it be known that where salvation is concerned, I do not judge, for Scripture tells us that no man can so judge, because salvation is of the heart and only God knows what is in the heart. Could it be that this also applies to each of us regarding our own hearts? If only God can judge what's in the heart, how can we be certain that we know our own hearts?

The Barna poll tells nothing more than Scripture has been telling us for nearly two thousand years. That is, that in these end times there would be many more professors than possessors of God's saving grace. Genuine truth can only be found in Scripture. Science and philosophy provide much information and sometimes stumble upon a true fact, but Scripture is THE truth and nothing but the truth. It is not about the factual truths such as $10 \times 10 = 100$, but truths involving the soul and spirit, salvation and eternity. If one had never heard of such a poll, or even listened to a sermon or lecture, or read any written word other than Scripture, one could, if the reading was Spirit led, know with absolute certainty that the professors of today many times outnumber possessors of saving faith. This warning is a primary theme of the entire New Testament. You cannot find one epistle, that does not, in one way or another, warn of the coming apostasy, of false teachers, and false prophets purveying false doctrine, false gospels, and false Jesuses. How could it be otherwise when Scripture tells us that these would, if it were possible, even fool the elect? Preaching of a half Gospel can be as damaging as a false gospel.

Repeated exposure to pleasant half gospel truths can make one feel good and believe that one has really heard the Word, and therefore knows enough to understand the process of salvation. What is the result? Profession without possession! Like any half-truth, it is deceit, and therefore, a lie as sinful as any lie. It seems evident that the single most pervasive cause of the great disparity between possessor and the mere professor is the widespread scriptural ignorance, that prevents the mere professor from becoming a possessor. How many really know Scripture? How many simply accept what they hear from the pulpit, on radio, and TV and from fellow "Christians," and accept it as truth without ever going to the Scripture to prove that those things be so? Who bothers to do as the Bereans did as told in Acts 17:11? How can you even begin to live the Truth if you don't even know what it really is? Anything learned regarding faith, grace, salvation, Jesus, and Christianity should be regarded as merely hearsay until it is clearly verified in Scripture. Limiting your knowledge of Scripture to what you hear or read from man has a strong likelihood of being terminally and eternally fatal!

If it is needed to express the primary theme even more clearly, one needs only to go to chapter two and three of the book of Revelation. Here Christ Jesus Himself, in His seven letters to the seven churches spells out in sequential order, the entire history of the Christian church from the beginning through the end times in which we now live. The end time's church is the church of Laodicea. This is the only church about which Jesus has absolutely nothing good to say. In every other church, that is throughout all the church ages until the present age, Jesus had some redeeming quality to mention, but not about the church of our present age. This age is characterized as the church of Laodicea, which means "Rule of the People." The name itself may be viewed as prophetic because one might interpret this definition as "democracy." It is through a democratic process that biblical scholars suggest that the antichrist will achieve his power. He will be "elected" as world ruler by the "democratic" process. In considering this age of "Rule of the People" one is reminded of the awful period referred to in the Old Testament as the time of the Judges when "everyone was doing what was right in their own eyes."

Jesus speaks of this end time church as "lukewarm" in the faith. The church claims to be "rich" and to have need of nothing." But Jesus calls this church, ignorant of the fact that it is ". . . wretched and miserable, and poor and blind, and naked." What an indictment! Are you part of this "lukewarmness" of the church or are you zealous in the faith? Are you personally as ignorant of the status of the church as Jesus says we are? Of course not! If you thought you were, you know that you would immediately set out to learn about that of which you were ignorant. The trouble is, we are all victims of the unknown ignorance! We simply cannot know that about which we have no knowledge that it even exists! Again the truth is the Scripture. But who prayerfully studies Scripture, under the guidance of the Holy Spirit, sufficiently to discover that which they don't even know exists? How many limit their entire biblical education to the twenty to thirty minutes weekly sermon they hear? Perhaps they choose also to hear "evangelists preaching the Word on the radio or TV and, therefore, consider themselves biblically educated and in need of nothing more in the way of what is required to be adequately knowledgeable Christians. But remember, this is the end times period about which Scripture speaks more than of any other time in history! This is the time of the lukewarm church of which Jesus speaks no good! It is the time of most rampant apostasy, of ignorance, of false teachers and false prophets. It is the time when Jesus has been cast out of the church, just as we see Him cast out of the schools, out of government, out of the media, and to the extent possible, through regulatorial edicts, out of our lives. Jesus Himself says in Revelation 3:20 "Behold, I stand at the door and knock; if any man hear my voice, and open the door I will come in to him and will sup with him and he with me." What a sad and terrible indictment of our age! Our dear Lord and Savior, the Creator of the universe, still as humble as when He walked the earth, is relegated, through the rebellious nature of man, to stand outside of what is supposed to be His church, knocking and asking to be let in! Notice, however, that now He is not speaking to the church, He has condemned it! He is speaking to a remnant of potential possessors, pleading that He might save individual souls from eternal suffering, and to deliver them to eternal life and companionship with Him! If these passages do not portray to you exactly the times in which we live, and do not, at the same time bring tears along with a sense of guilt and wanting to love and obey our most wonderful Lord and Savior, I wonder then if the full meaning of these precious verses are fully understood.

In verse 19, Jesus prefaces His knocking at the door by declaring that "as many as I love, I rebuke, and chasten, be zealous therefore and repent." Dear God, this is your whole message summarized in five precious words! If only the whole of the visible church could but apprehend these words in their full meaning all professors would become possessors! BE ZEALOUS THEREFORE AND REPENT! Be zealous, not lukewarm! Oh how the world hates the zealot, especially when he has zeal for Jesus and the Gospel. Lukewarm is the order of the day, sayeth Satan! But God says repent! How often does one ever hear this unfashionable, frightening, inconvenient, and distasteful word, *repent*, uttered from the pulpit or anywhere else, let alone spoken zealously in its true spiritual context? Between hardly ever and never! That might tend to heat up the spirit and take away the "lukewarmness"! Satan will seek to prevent this at all costs!

Why is there such a "lukewarmness" that our Lord and Savior will not tolerate any part of this modern day church, but says that He will "spew it out of my mouth"? There are many reasons that have been put forth over the years. But for the purpose of this essay, we'll elaborate on but one, which should be sufficient.

First, back again to the Barna poll. In order to make the poll meaningful, Barna had to initially establish what he calls the biblical World view by which those being polled were to respond. He defined this in terms, that all biblical Christians could call the essence of what the Christian faith is all about. His criteria were as follows:

A.   Absolute moral truth exits.

B.   That such truth is defined in the Bible.

C.   That there must be firm belief in six specific religious views, which are as follows:

  1.   That Jesus Christ lived a sinless life;

2.   That God is the all-powerful and all-knowing Creator of the universe, and

3.   That He still rules today;

4.   That salvation is a gift from God and cannot be earned;

5.   That Satan is real;

6.   That a Christian has a responsibility to share the faith in Christ with other people;

7.   That the Bible is accurate in all its teaching.

As noted previously, it was a random poll of those who *claimed* to be born-again Christians, that is professors of the faith. Of the total, only 9 percent were willing to agree with the Christian World view as herein above defined. Does that make the 91 percent who did not agree, not born-again Christians? Not necessarily, for once again, only God can judge the heart. But it certainly suggests that there are a great many who, out of ignorance, are falsely believing they are possessors of a saving faith. However, what appears to be most relevant to the question as to why there is such a small acceptance of this biblical World View, why this "lukewarmness" of belief in this particular church age, may be found in a parallel poll. Barna also polled 601 pastors nationwide representing a random cross section of Protestant churches. From this he reports that only half of the pastors believed in the biblical worldview! As Barna pointed out, "You can't give people what you don't have." This obviously shows up in the people who attend the churches, that have non-believing or not fully believing pastors. Another interesting finding was that 55 percent of the pastors who did not have the biblical worldview were seminary trained, while the 45 percent who did have the biblical worldview did not attend a seminary. Satan is a master at infiltrating institutions and the Christian seminaries seem to be no exception.

But the disease is even much worse than that! Many of the churches manned by pastors, who have a biblical worldview, tend to preach only the part of the Gospel truths, that are pleasant and pleasing to hear, avoiding those parts, that are not. In the best of churches, Jesus as Savior is preached. Believe and you are saved is preached, believing that His shed blood washes away our sins is preached, and describing the many pleasant attributes of Christian living is preached. But what about His Lordship? What about a contrite humble heart? What about conviction, confession, and genuine repentance? What about real commitment of one's life to Jesus, by doing that which is right, not as the world views it, but as it is in God's eyes, even though it may be inconvenient, difficult, and require much self discipline and personal denial? Are these essentials of a qualifying faith, the mark of a true possessor, ever subjects of today's sermons? Not that you would notice! And what about some structured and mandatory study of Scripture or some evidence of scriptural literacy as a condition of membership, or at least for its office holders? Not on your life! Why would a pastor dare, even if he thought it appropriate, suggest such a thing? Such an edict today, in this "lukewarm" Laodicean church age would either empty the church or quickly put the pastor out to pasture! Who would dare to set a course that would raise the temperature, increase scriptural literacy, preach the whole Gospel and replace apathy with zeal? Silly question! All of these conditions and more were considered minimal requirements in preaching in the Philadelphia church, which prevailed from about 1600 to 1900 A.D.

In the Philadelphian church age, the primary goal of the church was to bring souls to Christ, not to lure them into false complacency or to provide parishioners with amusements, entertainment and gushy Gospels. These were the days reflective of Whitehall, Wesley, Spurgeon and others who preached several times a day in churches and halls filled with thousands and often tens of thousands who were well versed in Scripture and yet were eager to hear the more learned pastors preach the whole, unvarnished Word of God. In our "lukewarm" church age, the order of the day is to fill the pews by whatever means is expedient. "Let's get them and we'll deal with their salvation later," seems to be the motto. This may well begin as a sincere and laudable strategy for bringing in the "under churched" and somewhere along the way a soul may actually be saved. But evidence seems to indicate that for the most part, only that which brings them in, keeps them in. Thus it is usually the "lite," not too long, no sweat Gospel, along with perhaps modern music, comforts and entertainment facilities, which bring them and keep them in. But if lite turns to heavy, and entertainment is replaced by calls for serious worship and scriptural study, as it must for these who are to become possessors of a saving faith, how many souls can be saved? Will it be more than in a smaller no frills church, that "tells it all" and "tells it like it is," a church, that preaches the whole Word of God? I really don't know! But what I do know is that there will be many many more un-possessing professors resulting from the Christian lite, seeker-friendly churches then there will be from fundamental, strong, bibli-cally-based churches! And that is one of the great tragedies of this age. Those large seeker-friendly churches "graduate" professors by the droves. They have been fed spiritual "doughnuts," a taste good substance with absolutely no "redeeming" nutritional benefits! They feel full, but all they have ingested were empty calories. They feel they have possession, but all they have is a satiated appetite, absent any spiritual nutrition, because they have eaten little if any of God's whole food Gospel, nor have they drunk from the true spiritually nutritious living water. More than likely, they don't even know what these are. Yet, they have become professors! And who can persuade them otherwise, once they believe they possess! For most, it will be Jesus when they come before Him and He says, "I never knew you, depart from Me." (Matthew 7:23)

By the way, this metaphor, regarding spiritual food, the need for it, and where to get it, occurs many times in the Bible. Jesus Himself said, as recorded in Matthew 4:4 ". . . *man shall not live by bread alone but by every word that proceedeth out of the mouth of God.*" Note the *every*! Where do you find that idea? Jeremiah said in chapter 15 verse 16 "*Thy words were found, and I did eat them; and thy word was unto me the joy and rejoicing of mine heart.*" It sounds like Scripture is ter-rific food for the heart! It even tastes good, because David found God's word "sweeter than honey," as he tells us in Psalm 19:10. At the last supper when Jesus told the disciples to eat His flesh and drink His blood it is evident that He was speaking not of actual physical flesh and blood, but rather the spiritual food of His Word. From the Gospel of John chapter 1:1, we know that Jesus is the Word, the Word that was made flesh, and so it's the Word we study and eat for

71

spiritual nutrients. Scripture is like a vast menu of spiritual food, but not from which we can pick and choose only what we want. We must eat the *whole* word, every thing on the menus, if we are to be properly nourished. It's the perfect food, a precisely balanced diet, through which it is possible to live *forever*. If you claim to be a Christian and have not a hunger, a desire and a taste for the Word of God, and find that some parts taste so bad you cannot bring yourself to eat them, then perhaps something is wrong, and you better examine your heart and see if you really do belong to God.

Is there even the very remote chance that you may be one of the non-possessing professors? I beg you to meditate long and seriously on that matter and consider all of the above scriptural references before you seek an answer. Examine your faith, and your life, adjust as needed your behavior, so as to get acquainted with our Lord, and pray that you will never hear those terrible words of Matthew 7:23, but instead, that you will hear, "Well done my good and faithful servant." May God bless you and I thank you for persevering to the end of what must have seemed to some, to have been an endless verbal beating.

P.S.

After struggling through almost sixteen pages, trying to articulate a message that lies so heavy on my heart, I was blessed and rightly humbled as I read the following. This is the closing paragraph of one of Charles Spurgeon's many extraordinary sermons. Here, this great herald of God's Word has succinctly and masterfully summarized much of my message, as well as his own. It was delivered sometime in the mid-1800s when he was yet a young pastor, preaching several times a day to thousands of eager seekers, speaking to standing-room-only audiences. His was a time within the age of the "Church of Philadelphia," when the majority of the population knew the Scripture and when the preaching of the Whole Word of God was in vogue, both strong and *undiluted*. This sermon was titled "Thus saith the Lord," a phrase, that occurs about five hundred times in Scripture. It was, of course, focused on the literal Word of God regarding various matters, and how important it is to abide by them. This was one of his milder sermons, yet, right-on in terms of what I have been trying to express regarding the difference between possession and mere profession.

> *Now, to close, let me say to you, my hearers, have any of you a hope in Heaven which will not stand the test of "Thus saith the Lord?" What are you resting upon? Are you resting upon something which you felt when excited at a prayer-meeting or under a sermon? Remember, you will not have that excitement to bear you up in death, and the religion of excitement will not suffice in the Day of Judgment. Are you building upon your own works? Are you depending upon your own feelings? Do you rely upon the sacraments? Are you placing your trust upon the word of man? If so, remember that when God shakes all things he will shake these false foundations; but Oh! To build upon the Word of my Lord and Master; trust your soul to Jesus. Hating sin and clinging to the great sin-bearer you shall find in him a rock a refuge which can never fail you; but I do conjure you, as the Lord liveth, search and try yourselves by the Word of God. No doubt there are many among us who are not built upon the Rock of Ages, and we may, many of us be deceived, by a mere name to live. Do, then, since the test-day must come—since you must be weighed in the balances—weigh yourselves now, my hearers; and let none of us go down to the chambers of destruction believing ourselves to be heirs of heaven, being all the while enemies to the Most High God. May the Lord exalt his own Word, and give us a sure inheritance in the blessings which it brings. Amen.*

—5—

Have You Checked Your Temperature Lately?

What on earth does your temperature have to do with Christian faith, you ask. As born-again Christians we know that belief in Jesus and His message, along with the purpose and meaning of His life, death, resurrection and ascension, are both the essence and substance of our faith. With that firmly in hand and in our hearts, it was our Lord Jesus Himself who admonished us to check our temperature. Perhaps, you may have missed this as I did even after numerous readings of the New Testament. Until recently I did not personally relate to the message. It seems to be directed to a specific group from the ancient past, and certainly not to me.

The particular message to which I am referring may be found in Revelation 3:14–22, which is the last of seven epistles that our Lord Jesus dictated to John. It was directed to the church of Laodicea whom the Lord saw as neither hot nor cold, but of lukewarm temperature, worthy only of being spewed out of His mouth. This lukewarmness was the result of the influence of comforts and riches, that they viewed as attesting to the adequacy of their spiritual condition. While they saw themselves as well off, comfortable and sufficiently religious, our Lord saw them as "wretched, miserable and poor, blind and naked" in terms of their faith and condition of their immortal souls. Surely they prayed, attended services, even gave to the poor etc., but perhaps did so in a perfunctory, duty-like obligatory manner without much heart or zeal or spiritual sincerity, being only "lukewarm" in these attributes and in their faith in Jesus. As we all know, the Scriptures in its entirety, was written for the learning and edification of all of us, past, present and future. This letter to the Laodiceans was written to us. The appropriateness of His message to them is every bit as relevant to us today. They too were a Christian church, a church that, to the Lord, had obviously fallen away, cooled off perhaps even unknowingly in its collective opinion. As a result of their relative physical comforts and prosperity, they apparently felt less need for the spiritual "heart" that our Lord demands of those who would be His own. It is not difficult to notice that we too live in times and in a place of relative prosperity and comfort, which can promote some of the same feelings of sufficiency and temptations toward a lukewarmness of faith. It seems to be human nature to drift away, soften or cool off from a true and hot spiritually relevant faith, the more prosperous and comfortable we become in terms of earthly riches.

There have been many commentaries written regarding these seven letters to the seven churches as found in Revelation 2 and 3. They make a compelling case, that illustrates that these, in the order written, symbolically represent seven stages or periods of time in the history of the church from its beginning to the end times. As faithful Christians we take the Scriptures very seriously and the proven accuracy of the prophets literally. Therefore, I believe that most of us readily conclude that we are now living somewhere in, or very near the end times. In this context it is not difficult to see that the Lord's description of the church at Laodicea represents very well much of the present day Christian church. Of course, each of us likes to believe that we individually belong not to the church of Laodicea, but instead to churches like Philadelphia or at least Smyrna. However, before we firm up that sort of conclusion, it would be best to check our collective and individual temperatures in order to be sure that we haven't slipped into the comfortable and insidious "lukewarm" waters of Laodicea

Clearly the Lord's "report card" to each of the seven churches is as relevant now as it was then. No doubt these individual qualities of which the Lord made note in each of the churches, was meant to be edifying to all the churches and to us today. Note that He ends each letter with "He that has an ear, let him hear what the spirit says to the churches" (plural). Surely even today there are to be found remnants of Ephesus or Smyrna or any of the others, even though our present day church is most typified by Laodicea.

What I find most beautiful and heartening are the closing words of this last letter, verses 20–22, *"Behold I stand at the door, and knock: if any man hear my voice, and open the door, I will come in to him, and will sup with him, and he with me. To him that overcometh will I grant to sit with me in my throne, even as I also overcame, and am set down with my Father in his throne."* Wow! Where in the *world* can you get a better offer than that!

Interestingly, and I believe prophetically, our Lord didn't give the church any direction by which it could correct itself as He did for the other six churches. Instead He chose to offer salvation only to individuals of the church body. This may seem to suggest that the church had drifted too far from the faith to be worth saving, so He chose to "spew" it out of His mouth and instead to offer His fellowship and salvation only to the remnant individuals capable of hearing His "knock." It would seem that this situation is eminently current in most of the denominational churches, at least in this country.

If you have that fire in your belly for worldly achievement, please consider redirecting that heat to raise your spiritual temperature to the boiling point. While you are doing that, don't walk, run to the door and let Jesus in while He is yet knocking.

—6—

Candy Cane Faith

What is faith in the *true* Christian sense? It is the deep-rooted belief or trust in the Gospel, that tells us that Jesus lived, died, was buried and on the third day rose again from the dead (1 Corinthians 15:4). For the most of the world this is a ludicrous statement that a dead and rotting body could ever come back to life, let alone "ascend into heaven." For many others, however, it is absolutely true, and on that basis they choose to call themselves Christians, but what is the basis of their faith? How important in their lives and how much reliance do they place on the absolute truth, validity and eternal value of this seemingly absurd statement? Can it be verified; must it be verified before it can become a faith of lasting substance, an ever-reliable *saving* faith? Can a blind faith, a faith without evidence, be a saving faith?

It seems evident that for those choosing to call themselves Christian, these are only a few of the questions that should be answered before one can comfortably settle down into the "peace that passeth all understanding," a peace based on a faith that cannot be negated or diminished by the very worst that Satan and the world can use to attack it. This is a peace to which only a genuine Christian can aspire. Such faith must be based entirely on facts. Those facts can all be found in Scripture if one sincerely seeks.

Even the slightest amount of blind faith will be like leaven or cancer and eventually will contaminate the whole loaf, that is, weaken the faith structure, that faith in Jesus on which we must lean if our faith be real. Any amount of blind faith is a faith always in danger of faltering, of becoming doubt ridden and failing when under attack through our many natural weaknesses. It cannot, it will not, prevail over persecution and torture as has been perpetrated on Christians in the past, is being inflicted now in many parts of the world, and will be dealt out here in the not too distant future.

Belief that this cannot happen, and that pain and suffering and extreme tragedies will somehow be less severe for the Christian, is but one of the evidences of the scriptural illiteracy, or of a refusal to believe what Scripture says. It may also be evidence of a seduction of the mind by the evil webs spun by the false prophets, and even by genuine hearts, but ones who choose to reveal only the sunny side of Christianity.

We are all born ignorant and in total darkness as to the existence of any saving faith. The only real and effective light that exists, and that can eliminate this ignorance, is the light provided by the Holy Spirit as He illuminates and makes coherent the truths found in the Holy Bible, which *is* the inspired Word of God. It is only through Him that this truth is able to pierce every heart. All the lifetime studies of the Bible, all thought and research by great minds composing their doctoral theses on scriptural meaning, and by PhD's and doctors of theology writing, their books are of no redeeming spiritual benefit unless the Holy Spirit guides the efforts. They avail nothing by way of salvation. They are but "hay and stubble" as are all such good works, even those provided by the most virtuous of mankind, unless conceived and carried out in true faith in the Gospel of Jesus Christ.

The world calls such faith a crutch, a support for the weak, for those who can't "cut it" in the "real world." The mature Christian will freely admit that they are right, but for reasons and ways different from those that the world believes. But "crutch" isn't quite the correct analogy for Christian faith that is faith in Jesus. Perhaps a "staff" or a "walking cane" would be a better choice, because they are far from being invalids as a "crutch" might suggest. Christians do *walk*, ". . . they shall walk, and not faint" (Isaiah 40:31), *"For we walk by faith"* (2 Corinthians 5:7), *"and narrow is the way . . ."* we walk (Matthew 7:14), *"and your feet shod with the preparation of the Gospel of peace . . ."* (Ephesians 6:15) so that they can stand firm in faith. On the other hand, Jesus said in, (John 15:5) *"I am the vine, ye are the branches, he that abideth in Me, and I in him, the same bringeth forth much fruit, for without Me ye can do nothing."* By this He meant that without faith in Him nothing we do has spiritual merit. So Christians are those who are helpless and useless in terms of spiritual fruitfulness, and for providing good works of lasting value, unless Christ is in their hearts, and they are willing to trust in His trustworthiness, to depend on and lean on the "cane" of faith as they walk through this treacherous stumbling block filled earthly life. The ever supporting "staff" or "cane" of faith that steadies his or her walk is, in fact, the hallmark of every true Christian. Shepherd's always carried a staff. It was not only used to control their sheep, but it also supported them and helped them as they navigated the rough and hilly terrain on which they lived. Today, not many of us tend sheep, but many find a staff or cane a helpful implement where walking is difficult. No one can walk through this life and on into eternal life without the support of the "cane" called faith in Christ Jesus as their Lord and Savior.

For the large part of nearly seventy years I also believed "faith" or "religion" was nothing but a "crutch." While I loathed Communism, I agreed with Lenin "religion was an opiate of the masses." I believed that "religion" was truly but a crutch on which those who were weak or simply lazy, those without gumption, ambition, fortitude or strength to stand on their own feet, found it necessary to lean. Any religion would do as long as it could serve as an excuse for their own inadequacy. This was a despicable state, making one unworthy of even being called a man! I was what I believed, the epitome of self-reliance. I had trained myself from youth to need nothing from anyone, certainly not a religious crutch or a cane, or anything or anyone else to lean on or depend on in any way under any circumstances. Even after doctors from three prestigious medical institutions each pronounced the same verdict, that I had an untreatable stage four terminal cancer, and that I should go home and get my affairs in order because I had only six to twelve months to live, I found no reason to seek a crutch. Being abandoned by conventional medicine, (I now thank God for that) I proceeded to study alternative treatments with great intensity and to apply every protocol and modality of self treatment alluded to in the vast maze of literature on the subject of cancer. Nevertheless, the cancer grew, along with the pain and localized debilitation, even though through my efforts, my energy and overall health seemed to improve. During this period, I never prayed, not even once (why bother?). This was my problem, and it was up to me to solve it. After eighteen months of ever worsening and painful manifestations of the problem, that spread to several organs of my body, the beast suddenly left me completely, from every part of my body, and has not returned in these, now well over eight years.

Of course I knew that *I* had prevailed over the beast. It certainly wasn't the doctors, because they had nothing to offer in spite of their vast learning and experience. To them it was hopeless. But through *my* determination, *my* perseverance, *my* study, and *my* effort *I* had healed myself! Looking back now, how ashamed I am of my pride, my conceit, my arrogance, my self-righteousness and false self-reliance, and my gross ignorance of God's truth! I had done *nothing* but follow a divine procedure my heavenly Father had laid out for me before the beginning of time! Though I didn't know it, He had always been with me, guiding me, protecting me, teaching me valuable lessons and preparing me for His purpose, perhaps even to write this paper. In other papers I have written more fully the saga of my affliction, and the path toward health and healing along which He led me. Today, through our Lord's blessed mercy and His love, I need no cane for physical support, for He has blessed me with greater health, strength and youthful energy than I had ten years ago. But I desperately need and try during every waking moment, to hold fast to, and to lean heavily on, my cane of faith, my faith in Him who healed me and for whose purpose I am here to serve. I find that whenever I fail to use it for support with every decision regarding every step I take, I risk a spiritual stumble. It's only through a continued moment-by-moment remembrance of how weak and useless I am without Him on whom I lean in faith, that I am ever able to make any real forward progress in my Christian purpose.

Perhaps now you are wondering if I am ever going to tell you the point suggested by the title of this paper. Scripture in general and our Lord Jesus in particular, used many grammatical devises such as similitudes, analogies, idioms, metaphors, and parables as teaching aids. It came to me that the "cane" or "walking stick" would be a good analogy for expressing Christian faith, in that a true faith in

Jesus is what must be leaned on. It is what steadies and keeps a Christian from falling and helps him or her back on his or her feet when they do fall as they travel the difficult terrains of life. But for the "cane" to represent true Christian faith, it must be made of something, that is strong, unbendable, unbreakable and insoluble. It must not bend in the heat of lust and passion. It must not break under stress, pain or great sorrows. And it must not dissolve in the unrelenting tides of temptation and the ever-eroding weakness of our corrupt nature. For the sake of an analogy, *shittim*, or acacia wood, will suffice. It is the wood of the burning bush, which burned, but was not consumed. It was the wood of Moses' shepherd staff, the rod that he carried through the wilderness, the rod, that God empowered to turn into a serpent, and through which He administered the plagues in Egypt, and it was the rod, that struck the rock, that brought forth the water. It was this wood of which the Ark of the Covenant and the tabernacle were made, all chosen by God Himself.

However, Christian faith comes in varying strengths and durabilities, as do materials from which one may make a cane. Perhaps the very opposite in quality from acacia wood could be a candy cane, one made simply of sugar. Hard rock candy can be easily fashioned into a cane and made to look quite strong and sturdy. However, it cannot help but crumble when leaned on too heavily, it must break when even moderately stressed, and it will melt away during a storm. So sugar candy is not a good material from which to make a strong, durable, all weather, all conditions, dependable cane, if one is seeking to have a cane be representative of a true Christian faith. Yet, very sadly, isn't "candy cane" faith the kind of Christian faith that is most prevalent today? Isn't it this type of faith of which Jesus spoke in the parable of the sower in Matthew 13, the kind that fails under temptation and stress? It should not come as a surprise that such weak faith is more the norm than the exception during these final days. We live in a fat, complacent, easy-does-it, quick fix, society, addicted to comfort, pleasure, convenience, and yes, to sugar. Many who call themselves Christians, practice their faith quite consistent with this type of overall lifestyle, and why not, for most "came to the faith" guided by preaching and witnessing quite consistent with their environment.

Don't most sermons from pulpits as well as Christian radio and TV even when consistent with Scripture, convey Christian "lite" messages, a "gushy Gospel," absent from any teaching other than the pleasantries and rewards side of Christian faith? How much reference, let alone serious "discussions," is there of Hell, or evil spirits or Satan or the many difficulties of Christian life, and the fact that a true acceptance of Jesus and His gift *assures* one of greater pain and suffering, and most likely fewer earthly rewards in this life than would likely occur otherwise? Most pastors, evangelists, and witnessing disciples, even those who know the truth and are redeemed, are so in fears of alienating or "turning off" the fragile seeker or losing portions of their flock, that they avoid revealing the more difficult and unpleasant aspects of the true and whole commitment on which salvation depends, and that Scripture makes very clear when understood in its whole context beyond the over simplified "believe and be saved" message.

A "believer" who has not learned and absorbed the greater aspects relating to the conditions associated with God's "free" gift of salvation, is in grave danger of being misled into a sense of eternal security when none exists. As in the parable of the sower, many will believe they are saved because of the early but only superficial expressions of what they will believe is adequate faith. This fear of "spooking" the seeker, or the novice believer, that causes those hoping to "spread the Word and bring many to the faith" to do a potentially fatal disservice to the initiate. By revealing only the touchy-feely comfortable and idealistic aspects of His Word, the seeker is "lured" into a false understanding of the faith and is thereby providing a fatal and "damnable" disservice. By presenting only the easy, the pleasant and rewarding aspects of real Christianity, they serve the seeker no better than a used car salesman, who directs focus only on the visible attribute of the vehicle, or the insurance salesman who fails to reveal the "fine print" of the policy. While our Lord would prefer that "none should perish" (2 Peter 3:9), He takes no solace in filled pews, if the hearts in the pews are not filled with Him. God is more like the Marine general who seeks "a few good men" rather than like the sports promoter, whose main interest is in filling the stadium.

Jesus spoke of hell and Satan, and evil spirits, much more than He ever spoke of heaven or any earthly niceties of Christian faith. In fact, He spoke far more of the difficulties and dangers along with the pains and persecutions that would assuredly afflict those who followed and believed in Him. Knowing that we are to try to pattern our lives after His, to seek to emulate Him, doesn't it make sense that we should also pattern our ministering, our witnessing and our discipleship after Him and His teachings?

A candy coated Gospel cannot help but increase the odds of a candy cane faith, a weak and dissolvable faith that cannot save. Add to this the many false prophets, that contaminate many pulpits, much of the airwaves and all the book stores, and we have exposed only a few facets of the many faceted cause of the high recidivism rate of the would be believers. Oh, where are you Charlie Spurgeon, or you Donald Gray Barnhouse, or you Chuck Smith, or you Henry Allen Ironside, now when we really need you who were willing to tell the whole Truth, and to tell it like it is!

—7—

Many are Called, but Few Are Chosen—A Challenge to Serious Faith

What is the procedure by which salvation is achieved? Of course we know salvation is a free gift, given by the grace of God through faith. However, what must precede this momentous event whereby salvation takes place? Because God would have none perish but all be saved (2 Peter 3:9), He calls out to all mankind to first *recognize* that He exists, second to *know* His Word, and third to respond and thereby to *accept* His divine gift of salvation. Thus He calls everyone who is willing to come to Him through this three-layered veil, which He gladly peels away if we, through our own free will, become receptive to these callings. Few will deny that there is an invisible force or power somewhere in the universe, that calls out to be recognized. The awesome rolling out of the universe with its sun, moon and stars, and the exquisitely woven tapestry of life around us, all call out and irrefutably expose the infinite glory, power, knowledge and wisdom of a Master Planner, our Creator God. That our eyes can see, our minds comprehend and our souls appreciate the immensity of this creation, and the omnipotence and omniscience of the Creator, is what we might say is the first calling, the peeling away of the first veil. In providing us with this capacity, He has called us all first to recognize His existence. Some choose to reject even this first calling, that is, to admit that there is a creator, for to admit this would be to accept the fact that the created have a responsibility or accountability to the Creator. But those who do acknowledge this first calling find that regardless of all its grandeur, power and incredible complexity, His creation reveals to us little about His nature and nothing about

His, or our purpose. This by itself leaves it open for the fertile mind to conjure up any number of theories and fantasies and false religions regarding what or who God is, or who we are, and what life is all about. These too often become terminally serious obstacles to further progress toward the *real and the whole* truth.

Thus it was, in our Creators infinite wisdom that He, through His Spirit as Author, commissioned some forty writers more than thousands of years to pen His book, wherein He reveals Himself, His ways and His purpose as the only One and true God. It is this book, the Holy bible, that we can refer to as the second calling. Here is the ultimate answer book. It answers the how, when, and why, of His creation. It provides explicit instructions on the very best way to live. It gives us insight as to His nature, His methods, His purpose, and His plan for our eternal destiny.

These two callings can rightly be referred as outward or external callings. They call on ones intellect, and on ones capability to understand in the physical and mental sense to whatever extent one chooses to let ones mind examine and accept this information.

Much of the world, however, dismisses its supernatural origin and regards His book as merely a quaint history of a minor ancient tribe put forth in a mythological setting that was later embellished through the advent and workings of a great spiritual teacher of that tribe whom some of His friends tried to deify. Nevertheless, the Holy Bible is many times over the most read, most studied, most debated book, yet much of the world has never understood or accepted its supernatural origin as the inspired Word of God. Others have recognized its origin, yet have been inclined to only pick and choose and believe only certain portions while dismissing other parts as merely figurative, allegorical or otherwise questionable in their accuracy. It's as if God, the source of all truth and love, would choose to weave fiction, deception, lies, and irrelevance into His precious book, the one and *only* source book for those recognizing the existence of, and seeking to attain eternal life. Thus it might be said of this second calling, that it is *to* the Word but not really into it.

Finally, there is the third calling. It is the inner calling, the calling through which God draws His own, the remnant, the ones who are born again and who become His eternal sons and daughters. This I believe is the calling Jesus refers to in Matthew 20:16, 22:14) wherein He says, ". . . *for many be called, but few chosen.*" It's the calling through which spring forth many who call themselves Christians, some truly, many falsely. It is the calling, that is either effectual or ineffectual depending on the richness of the soil (the heart) of the one called. This is the essence of the message repeated over and over again by the Holy Spirit somewhat subtly throughout the Old Testament, and most specifically in many epistles, parables and other direct quotes of Jesus in the Gospels, all found in the New Testament. To those who will study diligently, they clearly illustrate and identify the differences between the true and the false Christians. As here defined, the true Christian is one who has been redeemed while the false Christian is one who has not, but may believe he or she has.

The parable of the Sower, or of the Four Soils (Matthew 13:1–15, Mark 4:1–20, Luke 8:4–15) is a prime example of this message, and the key to an understanding of the several other parables, that provide variations on the same message. The seed (the Word) is sown many places, that is throughout the world. In some places it falls on deaf ears, that is onto the trodden path where there is hard soil; that is a hard heart or spirit that is easily, and sometimes even preferably, deceived and seduced by Satan and his tempting ways. Scripture tells us this seed was trodden down and the birds of the air devoured it. Jesus explains that these ". . . *are they that hear, then comes the devil and takes away the Word out of their hearts lest they should believe and be saved.*" Here we see clearly one category of those called but not chosen. These heard the truth but only superficially and were therefore easy prey for Satan and his birds (evil spirits) who turned these minds and hearts to false gods, that is to whatever false beliefs or religions are represented by the individual evil spirits who plucked out the seed. Religion, not atheism, is Satan's best weapon. For behind every false faith or religion there is an evil spirit, an agent of Satan promoting, guiding, orchestrating and recruiting; Satan cares not what you believe as long as it isn't in salvation by grace through faith in the sufficiency of the blood of Christ Jesus.

Next the parable speaks of the Word falling on stony ground. These are the people "*. . . who when they have heard the Word, immediately receive it with gladness and have no root in themselves, and so endure but for a time; afterward, when affliction or persecution ariseth for the Word's sake, immediately they are offended.*" (Mark) or "*. . . have no root, which for a while believe, and in time of temptation fall away.*" (Luke) Here again we find another example of those who are called but not chosen. Doesn't this sound like the reported 80 to 90 percent of those who answer the altar call or some other inducement, voice acceptance of Jesus into their hearts, and "after a time" are never again heard from or seen in any faith-expressing context? Perhaps they continue to call themselves Christians, but are more likely false Christians. The Holy Spirit never really entered their hearts, because their actions were not symbolic of real faith but mere expressions of superficial emotions. But how long is "for a time"? Is it a few days, months, or even years? It's likely that it is until they are tested by severe trials and temptations. On a short-term basis it is difficult for mortal man to discern the differences between a strong emotion and real faith, especially in himself. This part of the parable is telling us that we should not rely entirely on that initial blush of "belief" that first manifests from an exposure to the truth, but should be ever watchful of its strength in times of adversity and temptation. If someone has made a profession of faith and then falls away, it is very likely that the person was not saved in the first place. This we learn can be the case from 1 John 2:19 "*They went out from us, but they were not of us; for if they had been of us; they would no doubt have continued with us; but they went out, that they might be made manifest that they were not all of us.*" Yet many will maintain the façade of Christianity without having its inward substances, all the time fooling themselves. In 2 Corinthians 13:5 Paul warns us to "*Examine yourselves, whether ye be in the faith; prove your own selves.*"

Now let us revisit the "root" analogy for a moment in order to glean a little more from it ". . . they have no root, (faith) which for a while believe and in time of temptation, fall away." A tree without roots is structurally unstable. It cannot stand against much wind (temptation) before it will fall away (topple over). Also a tree without root (faith) is not well nourished, no matter how deep, rich and well watered the soil. If it is not so nourished, it cannot bear fruit and will fall away by being cursed, cut down, as it was in the parable of the fig tree (Matthew 21:19) Just as the shallow weak-rooted tree cannot withstand the winds of nature, neither can the man poorly rooted in faith, resist the sultry tempting whispers of Satan or the turbulent waters of adversity. A true saving faith is a faith, that commits, resists, and perseveres to the end!

The third category who received the calling, Jesus described as "they which when they have heard go forth and are choked by cares and riches and pleasures of this life, and bring no fruit to perfection." (Luke) or "to maturity" (NIV) or "becometh unfruitful" (Mark). Matthew reports it most simply "some fell away among the thorns; and the thorns sprang up and chocked them." This perhaps is the most prevalent of the called but not chosen. It is the nominal Christian of the visible (flesh and blood) church rather than of the invisible (spiritual) church in which are *only* the regenerated. These nominal Christians you might say, are the worlds "weed garden type." They are found everywhere, often in the visible church doing good Christian type works. But, for the most part, because of the poor soil and lack of sufficient "Son Light" the world has captured their hearts either through success, pleasure, temptations or stressful circumstances. They find little solace in His Word or in prayer which, if expressed at all, is often rote, perfunctory or half-hearted, and they find obedience subjective and prone to rationalizations rather than as a vital, absolute defined requirement. Real joy and peace that "passeth all understanding" is not in them because they have not received the Holy Spirit. In these examples Jesus is clearly warning us that some would only *seem* to receive the Word (the Gospel) but would not become among the chosen. Paying lip service, and often going through all the right motions, saying the right things, and using the appropriate words may fool even the elect, for only God knows the heart. That possibility should send chills down the spine of everyone who believes he believes, and should cause one to reflect with the utmost care and concern as to the true basis of ones own belief that one is saved. Again 2 Corinthians 15:15 comes to mind. Consider

Mark 7:6–7 Where Jesus says, *"this people honoreth me with their lips, but their heart is far from me. Howbeit in vain do they worship me, teaching for doctrines and commandments of men."* Henry Allen (H. A.) Ironsides had an insightful commentary on this point. He observes that, "It is always a great mistake for those who profess to be servants of God to observe forms and ceremonial rites and traditions that have no scriptural basis. Such traditions may seem innocent enough to begin with, but little by little they will usurp the place of the Word of God over the consciences of those who follow them; this is most dangerous."

Perhaps most numerous and most tragic of all, are those belonging to so-called Christian faiths that are not Christian faiths at all; they either deny the sufficiency of Jesus on the cross as the sole means of salvation, or they have chosen to add to or remove something from the whole and only Word of God, the Holy Bible. These may be very moral, devout, sincere, and faithful to preachings. However those attributes do not make a redeemed Christian unless they are attributed to Jesus and Him alone and to His infallible Word, *and His sufficiency*. This then in total, is the principal category, perhaps referred to by our Lord in Matthew 7:22 and in Luke 13:25, where on the day of our Lord, the judgment day, as they stand complacent and confident of their salvation, they will instead hear our Lord say "I never knew you." Nothing on this earth, in Heaven or Hell could be more devastating than to hear those too-late-to-do-anything-about-it words. Yet, many will, for again we know that many are called but few are chosen.

Now we come to the fourth part of the parable, representing what we all want to be, where the seed (the Word) falls into deep rich soil of the "honest and good heart." There it will bring forth fruit in great quantities. In this analogy of the seed, we can also visualize the life giving water (God, Jesus) adding enrichment and life to the soil where strong, deep nurturing roots give unyielding support to the soul and also properly feed it. One might call into this picture the bright rays of the sun (God Jesus the Son as the light and energy source of the world). To the well-watered deep-rooted soul in the rich soil, the sun is a blessed friend for it provides the energy, essential for life and growth. However, as noted in Matthew 13:6 where the Word falls on the stony soil, where there was not an "honest and good heart" the sun scorched the soul and it withered away. In the end, the sun will also "scorch" the unregenerate heart unto death. Similarly, when "choked" and shadowed by the weeds, the soul cannot receive enough "Son" and also dies. It is this rich well-watered soil where the Word is fully received and where that glorious, healing, nurturing, light of the Son bathed soul, that regeneration (salvation) will bloom. These are the born-again Christians, those who are called *and chosen*.

Notice that in all three Gospels, at the end of this parable, Jesus issues His highest-level alert, "He who hath ears to hear, let him hear." Notice also that this is how Jesus ends each of His seven Epistles to the seven churches in Revelation 2 and 3. From this we must recognize that this is a message of utmost importance, which if we have an ear, and most of us do, we must listen intensely and fully apprehend the message for it is profound. Therefore we must chew it well, swallow and digest, and thoroughly assimilate it into our souls. For to fully understand the difference between the saved and unsaved is a matter of *eternal* life or death.

The message in the parable can be summarized as simply a clarification or explanation of our Lords statement that "many are called and few are chosen." There must be a *true conversion* of the heart, not just a decision for Christ. This is the key to understanding many of the other parables, that express the difference between true conversion and false faith. The message of Wheat and Tares (Matthew13:36–43) the Wedding Feast (Matthew 22), the Ten Virgins (Matthew 25:1–13. the Great Supper (Luke 14:15–24), the Net (Matthew 13:47–50) and the Sheep with the Goats (Matthew 25:32, 33) each expresses the difference between the saved and the unsaved.

The principal problem expressed in these parables is a faulty root system, (faith) and the lack of an honest and good heart, (the new heart). This prevents the nourishing of the soul and fostering of real saving faith. Without this, the heat of the sun soon betrays any falseness of faith because the false facade collapses. In real life, the sun's rays are the tribulations, temptations and persecutions to which one is almost certain to be subjected. Without these trials, these tests, one cannot know the sufficiency of ones roots, (faith) to be certain that one is redeemed. Many will deny this and say that their commitment to Jesus was sufficient and that their salvation is a certainty. But faith by its very nature and definition must be tested before it can even be called by that name. To conclude that one has a saving faith without having been severely and successfully tested perhaps over and over again is profoundly dangerous and self-deceiving. Scripture tells us in many places that a true believer must be subject to testing of his faith. In 2 Corinthians 13:5, Paul urges, *"Examine yourselves whether ye be in the faith . . ."* Why would He urge this if saving faith was so easy and obvious? In Colossians 1:23 we are told that we are saved *"if ye continue in faith grounded and settled, and be not moved away from the hope of the Gospel . . ."* In 1 Corinthians 15:1, 2, Paul says, *". . . I declare unto you the Gospel which I preached unto you, which also ye have received, and wherein ye stand; by which also ye are saved, if ye keep in memory what I preached unto you unless ye have believed in vain."* Believed in *vain*, means believed without benefit of salvation, or without benefit of a true and saving faith. This is the same message as in the parable of the Sower. Hebrews 3:6 says, *"but Christ as a Son over His own house; whose house are we if we hold fast the confidence and the rejoicing of the hope firm unto the end."* There is no doubt that this means that faith and its evidences continue through to the end in spite of all the adversities that will necessarily come along to test us as we proceed through life to the end. Matthew 7:21 *"Not every one that saith unto the me Lord, Lord, shall enter into the kingdom of heaven, but he that doeth the will of my father which is in heaven."* Jesus says here that only the ones who do the will of the Father, that is *obey*, are saved. Jesus then proceeds to hammer this home in Matthew 7:24, where He says *"Therefore, whosoever heareth these sayings of mine, and doeth them, I will liken him unto a wise man, which built his house (his faith) upon a rock; and the rain descended, and the floods came, and the winds blew, and beat upon that house; and it fell not (tribulation did not undermine faith); for it was founded upon rock. And every one that heareth these sayings of mine, and doeth (obey) them not, shall be likened unto a foolish man, which built his house upon the sand and the rain descended, and the floods came, and the winds blew, (weakness of faith, trial, tribulations, temptations) and beat upon that house, and it fell; and great was the fall of it."*

Throughout the Scriptures Jesus is the rock. Here we are to build our lives, our faith, on the rock, that means to *hear* and *obey* Him. That is the principal theme of the entire Bible. *Hear* and *obey*, *believe* and *obey*. The Greek word for *obeying not*, *apitheho*, also means *believing not*. Those who do *not obey* are *not believers*! How else can you interpret all of the admonitions to perseverance and obedience without accepting the fact that they are all time dependant components of the evidence of a saving faith? You cannot obey once and call it obedience. Obedience by definition is an on-going condition. Hearing His Words and doing them is not a one shot deal. It must be on-going in order to be meaningful and effectual.

This mandatory call to obedience does not mean that any subsequent sin will result in a forfeiture of our inheritance. We are by nature infected incurably by a propensity to sin. However once saved, we can never lose our salvation. Obedience, and therefore true belief, must for starters, be accompanied by:

A. Full acknowledgment of our sinful nature,

B. Recognition of the true vileness of every one of our sins, even little "white ones"

C. The necessity of removing from our lives all *on-going sin*,

D. Praying for the strength to refrain from sin.

E. Struggling moment by moment to eliminate sin from our lives.

No matter how much we try, we are bound to sin at times. However, those who are redeemed will, as part of their obedience (belief, faith), be extremely sensitive to sin. They will recognize it, acknowledge it, hate it, confess it, repent of it, and renew their resolve to not repeat it. These then are some of the evidences of a true saving faith.

For most of 1900 years, the Christian "church" has had what must be called an obsession with legalism. It has been true of the Roman Catholic as well as the Eastern Orthodox churches. This is legalism in the sense of the many rituals and procedure, that are mandated and preached of as conditions of salvation. It is also this legalism that has caused these and many other "Christian" religions to drift away from the principal truth, that it is the sufficiency of Christ

Jesus, and from the whole teachings of the Scripture, and thus into serious apostasy. As a result, those who chose to follow the true biblical teachings were branded heretics and were slaughtered by the millions by the "church" in the "name" of Christianity. Finally, with the reformation, beginning in the sixteenth century, a glimmer of light began to shine and to develop a sufficient following in the west so as to make a small dent in this highly distorted and corrupt religious structure.

It was Luther who rediscovered Habakkuk 2:4 "*. . . but the just shall live by his faith.*" It further became clear that the books of Romans, Galatians, and Hebrews are a trilogy, that expands and explains that profound truth. Romans tells us who are the *just*; Galatians shows us how the just shall *live*; and Hebrews reveals what *faith* really is. The centerpiece of the reformation was Ephesians 2:8, 9, which finally restored some of what the early church had known and lived; that we are saved by grace alone through faith, and not by anything we can do, not rituals, works or any other applications of legalisms. However, it has become evident that, in many respects the pendulum has swung too far the other way, in that there seems to be considerable confusion regarding the theological basis of our salvation, with its fervent calling to *obedience* as evidenced where there is a more complete understanding of *whole* Scripture. Many have become so fearful of the pitfalls of legalism as a heresy, that they fail in their personal walk to recognize this call to obedience. Obedience is faith in Action! Faith equals obedience! They find it difficult to distinguish between obedience and legalism. We are not called to legalism but to holiness and *obedience*; not to works as obligations or payment, but to *works of obedience* as loving gifts to our Lord and Savior. What is obedience? Again, it is *faith in action*! It's a continuous forward expression of our quest for holiness. It is attempting with all our hearts to live the Ten Commandments as evidence of our saving faith. (They are commands, not suggestions.) It is trying to live them as Jesus refined their meanings in His sermon on the mount. We are to live by this *law of Jesus* through love, respect and gratitude to Him. Of course, we cannot possibly live it fully. No one ever could except for Jesus. God never intended that we could. The law was

93

given to identify what would be a goal, a state of perfection. Those who are His children are to strive to be like Jesus. The unsaved obey out of fear, but fear can never do anything but restrain. But for the true believer, the motive is love. Love, the love commitment incorporated in a saving faith, constrains, compels, and brings one into holiness.

So, how can one know that he or she is really walking the narrow path, the path of the saved? Evidence of salvation may manifest in many ways. What greater testimony is there to the power of saving grace then the hopeless addict who has sunk to the lowest depth of depravity due to alcohol, drugs, illicit and deviant sex, kleptomania, etc, who finally gets on his knees, confesses to Jesus and is thereby healed? Many of the "great men of God," such as John Wesley, have found salvation only after having reached such depths. Yet even in this realm of clear-cut miracles, recidivism, or falling away, still occurs. How many miracles did it take to bring the children of Israel to a sustaining faith? Though they witnessed the miracle of the plagues, the Passover, the parting of the Red sea, the manna, the delivery of the Ten Commandments, the healing by merely looking at the brass serpent, water from the rock etc, etc . . . they believed for a while but still failed to sustain a belief, and thus wandered unsaved for forty years and died never reaching the "promised land." So will the unbelieving and false believers of this age, and all generations, fail to reach the "promised land." How many miracles did it take our Lord Jesus to perform in the three years of His ministry to convince the Pharisees who were of all people, the most biblically, learned and seemingly obedient to the Word? These couldn't believe even while witnessing miracles. Obviously it would have taken more than the many thousands He performed, for they never did believe. Miracles just don't do it, as Scripture makes so very clear. Only true sustaining faith can bring about the acceptance of saving grace. But that faith must be in the real Jesus, the one conceived by the Holy Spirit, born of the virgin Mary, who died on the cross, was buried, rose again, and ascended into heaven to sit at the right hand of the Father. That faith must be in that Jesus the Eternal One, who is our Lord and Savior as well as the Creator of everything (John 1:1–10.) In the so-called, but false "Christian faiths," there are many Jesuses. There is the Jesus who depends on Mary to help Him save souls; or the Jesus who is a great teacher and man of God but not really God; or the Jesus who is one of several who comes to earth periodically to teach; or perhaps He is God, but He has changed His views; after all, we live in different times than when He was here, and surely the real Jesus does not expect us to live now by the old fashioned rules He put out for a previous era. In this context it is well to remember 1 Timothy 4:1 where the Spirit clearly says that in later times some will abandon the faith and follow deceiving spirits and things taught by demons. These times have arrived!

How much falling away from the faith, from the apparent evidence of salvation must one witness or experience before it must be concluded that one never was saved at all. Who knows? Only God knows. We cannot ever be certain, but surely we should become alarmed, and not remain complacent as to the certainty of salvation if, after some time, the falling away is not reversed. It was Calvin who said, "we are saved by grace through faith, but faith is never alone." Thus I believe that there must be a continuing evidence that our Lord is working in us (Philippians 1:6) before there can be a certainty of salvation. Again, it is *obedience*. Obedience is a necessary condition existing in those who are justified, although it is not the basis or prerequisite of justification. True faith will by necessity yield the fruit of obedience. When no growing evidence of obedience follows a confession of faith it must be concluded that there never was a true faith and thus no salvation. How long? How much testing? Only God knows. Many cast their lot with the thief on the cross who obviously had no time of testing, yet was surely saved. But he had the Son of God next to him in the flesh, the God Himself who knew his heart and personally revealed its sincerity to us. Who among us can claim that same perceptive quality regarding his own heart, much less the heart of another?

Careful and loving study of Scripture can reveal a number of ways in which one may discern in himself whether or not one is a real or counterfeit Christian. Actually love is the principal litmus test. First a Christian must know and profess that Jesus was sent from God the

Father and is our Lord and Savior according to the Scriptures (1 John 4:14, 15, 5:1–5) Second, a Christian must love above all our Lord and Savior Jesus Christ (1 John 4:2), for this love is a commandment. But genuine love begins in the will, not in the emotion. This love manifests also in righteousness and in fellowship, faith, trust and commitment to Him. Of course, we know that He cannot make us love Him no matter how much He commands it. Being able to love Him is a fruit of our salvation, not its cause. Third, a Christian must love his/her fellow Christian in spite of any differences. (1 John 4:7) This love manifests in caring, compassion, cooperation and fellowship. These then are the essence of true Christianity, however, as with the essence of anything, there is much more to be known in order to understand its richness and fullness and its intimate application in ones life.

There are many great Christian writers who have addressed this concern. One who characterizes the nature of saving faith most beautifully, and has identified the principal Scripture verses, that provided God's words in this regard, was Jonathan Edwards. In "A Treaties Concerning the Religious Affection" written by Edwards around 1746, we find what he called "holy affections" or a zeal for holy things and for God. Edwards also noted that whereas the principal evidence of life is motion, so the principal evidence of a saving faith is holy practice; true salvation always produces a continuing change in the nature of the convert. Therefore, whenever *holiness of life* does not accompany a *confession of conversion*, it means that the person is not a redeemed Christian. Thus he further notes that "Assurance is never to be enjoyed on the basis of a past experience. "There is need of present and continuing work of the holy Spirit . . ."

Edwards set down eleven evidences of a true born-again Christian as can be learned from the Scriptures. These are presented as questions and are here simply listed for further study along with the relevant scriptural verses from where they are derived.

1.   Do you enjoy fellowship with Christ and the Father? (1 John 1:2, 3)

2.   Are you sensitive to sin? (1 John 1:8–10, Romans 7:14–25)

3.   Do you obey God's Word? (1 John 2:3–5)

4. Do you reject this evil world? (1 John 2:15–17, 5:19; 2 Corinthians 4:4)

5. Do you eagerly await Christ's return? (1 John 3:2; 1 Corinthians 15:52, Titus 2:11–13, Philippians 3:20, 21)

6. Do you see decreasing patterns of sin in your life? (1 John 3:4–10, Romans 6:14, 17, 18)

7. Do you love other Christians? (1 John 2:9–11, 3:10, 16, John 13:35; 1 Peter 1:22)

8. Do you experience answered prayer? (1 John 3:22–24, 5:13–15, Psalm 37:3–7)

9. Do you experience the ministry of the Holy Spirit illuminating Scriptures? (1 John 4:13, 2:27; 1 Corinthians 2:10, 12, Galatians 4:6, 5:22–23, Ephesians 5:18)

10. Can you discern between spiritual truth and error? (1 John 4:1–6; Acts 17:11)

11. Have you suffered rejection because of your faith? (1 John 3:13, 1 Peter 2:20, 4:4, Philippians 1:28; 1 Corinthians 4:13)

It is evident that these questions and scriptural references can be helpful in assessing the reality of ones own salvation and eternal security. However, they are all suggestive of an on-going process, a day-to-day moment-by-moment continuing condition of the heart. It must be acknowledged that *none* of these questions can be answered yes in a completed sense, but only in terms of whether there is an "upward" movement, a progression no matter however small, in the "yes" direction.

Also there is another major point, that is often overlooked or under appreciated. John speaks of our Lord and Savior. The Savior aspect of Jesus is easy to accept and understand, and it is gratifying to embrace. Through His death and resurrection, He became our Savior, but in our acceptance of the grace of salvation through faith in Him, He also became our Lord. In so doing He purchased us and we agreed to be His. Thus, He, as our Lord, and because in that manner we belong to Him, we are obligated to *obey* Him. The sacred currency of the heavenly realm is a coin with Jesus our *Savior* on one side and Jesus our Lord on the other. It is the Lord side of the coin that is most difficult to accept. However, this is and will be the currency of our Spiritual economy now and throughout eternity. But in that economy as in any other, there are no one sided coins. There are no transactions possible for the Spirit led Christian other than by means of Jesus Christ our *Lord* as well as our Savior. Our proper relationship with Him is one of reverence, worship, and obedience.

Of particular concern in the context of this paper are questions three and ten of Edwards' eleven points. Do you obey God's word, and can you discern between spiritual truth and error. More than one hundred and fifty years ago in some of his sermons the great Pastor Charles Spurgeon lamented over the lack of spiritual knowledge among the "brethren." At that time, the Bible was taught in the schools, and Scripture was recited daily in every Christian home. What would he say today regarding biblical understanding, when Scripture illiteracy is pandemic, and where false doctrine is spewed from not only books, journals, radio, and television, but even from many of the Christian Pulpits. But who even notices when it is so cleverly cloaked in pious scriptural references, expressed in faulty but persuasive and logical, worldly reasoning. When it is thereby made to sound authentic, it is accepted by all but the well-informed literate few who can detect the falsehood because they have earnestly studied the word and are capable of sufficient discernment. Subtle deception is both a science and an art, that has grown exceedingly well in modern times and in every aspect of society. The Christian body has in no way been spared its deadly fruits. Under these conditions, how can one even hope to recognize the difference between Spiritual truth and error, and even obey God's word, unless one is *very strongly* grounded in scriptural knowledge. ONE CANNOT! The widespread apostasy within the so-called "Christian" body as it pertains to ecumenicalism, and acceptance of perverted sexual behavior are but two of the more obvious examples of the many evidences of a crumbling spiritual structure. Most of this can be traced to biblical illiteracy in concert with the compelling nature of false teachers and false doctrines. How simple it was for Satan to twist a couple of words, which then compelled Eve to violate God's command. Satan has since had six thousand years to hone his skills of seduction and deception on countless generations. It's doubtful that many of us are less gullible than Eve, and the only additional defense we have is prayer and God's Holy Word, with which to resist Satan's fatal influence. Under these circumstances, if we are serious Christians, seriously seeking, or hoping to confirm our salvation, how can we justify doing less than acquiring a strong *working* knowledge of His book?

In summary, there is a vast eternal, and uncrossable gulf between those who are saved and the unsaved. The greatest of all tragedies is that many who won't make it are among those who believe they will. They heard the call, sought the Word, but took one of the many wrong paths through apathy, ignorance or the following of false teachers. There is only one path to eternal life. It is available to all who accept God's grace of salvation through faith in Jesus as our Lord and our Savior. But that faith must grow to be genuine, lasting, uncompromising and unconditional. It must manifest as a wholly committed love and obedience to Him and to His commandments. Nothing less can be assured of being a saving faith. The powers of the earth are continually striving to confuse, undermine, discredit, and twist God's Word to make it say what is comfortable, pleasing, easy and subject to any interpretation, that is convenient for the occasion. Saving faith must contain love, obedience, prayer, and perseverance under all circumstances, well as well as bad. Again, and I am not ashamed to repeat it over and over again . . . 2 Corinthians 13:5 *"Examine yourselves whether ye be in faith; prove your own selves . . ."* Finally, as Jesus Himself said at least nine times in the Scripture, "He that has an ear let him hear."

—8—

Is It True Faith?

One problem that I see in this issue is the specter of contrivance. Satan's deceptiveness is so cleverly disguised, that a vain, weak or false faith on the part of a newcomer may be mistaken for a saving faith. Thus, the great paradox; is the faith one has a false faith masquerading as saving faith through Satan's extremely clever and supernatural devices, or is it a false faith from fear of hell, having no substance in the heart; or is it true saving faith being undermined with equal cleverness by Satan through the instruments of doubt and delusion? How can one know? Certainly searching within the mind is not enough because that is the very forum wherein both the natural man and Satan perform their most insidious work. Furthermore, how reliable is the feeling of the heart in this matter? How effective can Satan be in this realm? I don't know. Perhaps the very articulation of this attempt to understand is itself the work of Satan at his best, casting doubt and confusion. However, can the matter be set aside or dismissed on this basis without risks that the heartfelt faith is in fact a most cleverly construed counterfeit? The only solution to this dilemma that I see is prayer time. Prayer for guidance, walking the Christian walk as faithfully as possible, and always examining it critically along the way. Through God's grace, the truth may be revealed. Or could it be that this cross of doubt and uncertainty is precisely what the Lord intended that one carry until that precious goal of a saving faith, does in fact manifest through one's unrelenting walking the walk that carries this very burden?

Perhaps this cross of uncertainty is necessary in order to keep us from growing complacent in our faith and lax in our attentiveness to our commitment to Him. I am a "late bloomer" as it pertains to having come to the belief that Jesus is God, and all that goes with that belief. Perhaps, with time, this concern will be reconciled for me personally. For others, I pray that my concern with the matter will either comfort or alert those who are yet seeking or who are also new to the faith.

—9—

Counterfeit Faith

The world today is filled with the many false teachers Jesus, Jude and the Apostles warned us about. They predicted that these end times would be the age of deceit. Those deceivers would concoct carefully designed false religion along with twisted and counterfeit precepts and doctrines claiming the authority of the Holy Bible. As is now very evident, they even fashion counterfeit gospels and many a counterfeit Jesus, as well as other seemingly attractive gods.

They fill receptive trusting, but biblically ignorant hearts with wheelbarrows full of legitimate looking, but worthless counterfeit nuggets of fool's gold that they are told will set them right with God. Those who actual chose and want to have the Christian faith are no less deceived by these agents of spiritual death. Unless those who choose Jesus and seek to know who He really is through His Autobiography, they are very susceptible to these peddlers of counterfeit Jesuses, and this can only lead to a counterfeit faith.

Satan has had thousands of years of experience observing man and perfecting ways to deceive even the more discerning. Right after the success of his very first deception, that of Eve, he trained his hordes of demons, with their impressive but limited supernatural powers, to become counterfeit gods, to carry out his evil mission of leading people away from the true God by giving them gods whose messages were more to their liking. Thus the world was given idols, many varieties, through which the demons minister. These remain effective today in their evolved forms fashioned to better satisfy "modern man." To the aspiring Christian, there has been given a great variety of counterfeit Jesuses by means of which the false teachers tragically mislead gullible souls. A Jesus who was not of a virgin birth; a Jesus who didn't actually rise from the dead; a Jesus who isn't God; a Jesus who paid only a portion of the price for our sins; a Jesus who is but one of a number of deities; a Jesus who provides one of several ways to heaven; and a Jesus who is actually the brother of Satan, thus providing the Ying to counterbalance the Yang as the two opposing forces who maintain equilibrium in this world of the flesh. Have I omitted any? There are more counterfeit Jesuses available to believe in than old Howard Johnson had as kinds of ice cream with his twenty-eight flavors. There is a Jesus who has just the right flavor for every pleasant, fashionable but perverted belief system Satan could devise, and to which fallen man might be attracted too. Take your pick; one is as good as the other. Follow any of them; they will each take you to the same place, Hell. Some of these more modern Jesuses are wonderfully packaged and promoted in the best style Madison Avenue can provide. See their promoters on TV; hear them on the radio, and from many pulpits.

Perhaps the most insidious of all hell assuring Jesuses is the half-Jesus. This is the Jesus represented most effectively from within what is euphemistically called the evangelical Christian church, regardless of its denomination. Here we find the real Jesus, but rarely is more than half of Him presented. Only the part we learn about of Him, is, He who was the Good Shepherd, the One who turned the other cheek, who loved children, and who gave wonderful advice to live by. This half-Jesus healed the sick, and did many wonderful acts of charity. He explained what forgiveness should be and how love was the greatest of virtues. He even demonstrated how a thief, a professional sinner could be saved moments before death by a simple confession of faith. How wonderful, wise, and loving this Son of God is depicted, and all of it is true. But what about the other half of Him the half that most pastors and evangelicals avoid mentioning because, while it might convict them, and lead them to a saving faith, the resulting call to serious accountability would offend and send people away, emptying the pews. What about the Jesus who demands repentance, obedience and compliance with his Word? The whole of Scripture was provided for our learning and guidance not just the pleasant parts. What about the Jesus who will sit in stern judgment and send all non-believers into the eternal lake of fire. What about the Jesus who will, in the last days descend from heaven, and is spoken of by Isaiah in chapter 63 verses 1–4, as having waged war at Bozrah killing millions? He left the battle with His vesture badly stained with their blood (Revelation 19:11–13). He isn't all Mr. Nice Guy from the human perspective. And who ever hears about Him as Judge and Executioner of those who refuse the divine and just offer He made on the cross?

The true Jesus is both Lord and Savior. He cannot be one and not also be the other. He must be both to every saved soul. A half-Jesus is no Jesus, if you claim to worship Jesus but only know of His Savior part, you may be dealing with a counterfeits, and your profession of faith may not include the possession of a saving faith. Really know whom you believe in, who you worship. Study His word carefully so you can discern with absolute assurance, the real from the counterfeit. Learn of and accept the Lord portion of Jesus in your life.

After World War I the German currency, the Reich mark was so inflated as to be nearly worthless. It has been said that it took a wheel barrel full of this paper currency just to buy a loaf of bread, providing there was a baker who had bread and was willing to exchange it for that nearly worthless paper. One might say, for the sake of comparison, the worth of one mark was equal in value to that of a single mustard seed. It's not likely that anyone would bother to counterfeit such useless money, but suppose someone did and that that wheel barrel was full of authentic looking, but nevertheless counterfeit money. Would it have still been acceptable to the baker? Probably, because he would not know the difference nor suspect that it was not the real thing. How many of us can tell the difference between carefully crafted counterfeit, twenty-dollar bill and a real one? Many such counterfeits have circulated for quite a while escaping detection, even passing through bank screening only to be detected at a central bank or at the treasury.

So what is the point of this? It is simply an attempt to demonstrate by analogy how a professor of a redeeming faith, unknowingly to him or herself or even to others might not be a possessor of that faith. Let us say that person has a "wheel barrel" full of faith, instead of Reich marks, and he or she comes to our divine Heavenly Father, the Great Baker who dispense the bread of life, that precious grace of salvation. He examines that wheelbarrow full of faith, and sees that every "banknote" is a counterfeit. Will the seeker receive the bread of eternal life? Certainly not! Now suppose another comes to Him with a convicted and repented heart and has a wheel barrel completely empty, except for one tiny bit of genuine faith, but only as big as a "mustard seed." What happens? Why the divine Baker will, with great pleasure, give him what he seeks, that divine bread of life! What a wonderful God we have! At the point of God's acknowledgement of the reality of ones faith, it is not the size but rather the genuineness that matters initially, because with the aid of the Holy Spirit, that faith will surely grow and become all God wants it to be. The great danger is that that speck of faith might also be counterfeit, which means of course no bread! But will the seeker know this? Probably not! Because he or she has presented a counterfeit faith to our Creator believing that it's genuine. They most likely don't even know about the existence of counterfeit faiths and even if they do, are they sufficiently versed in God's truth about the matter to recognize the more "perfect" counterfeits? They have most likely been fed by those who themselves cannot recognize the counterfeit nature of their beliefs. This has led many down the sterile trail of false belief, to a counterfeit faith, so genuinely looking that only God can discern the difference. Being absent true scriptural knowledge they have no reason to question what they were led to believe. So they are stuck with it right down to the tragic end. The longer they continue to hear "Christian lite" sermons or half-gospels that seem to validate and never challenge their belief, the more deep-rooted such a false belief becomes. After a while, only anger and indignation will be the greeting to anyone who seeks to set them straight. For them, to study the Bible and see what Christian "heavy," that is Christian truth, might be all about, is an absurd waste of time, because they believe already they know all they need to know. Haven't those who "converted" them, told them. So? Haven't their "handlers" kept them fed with what they claim to be the bread of life? The truth is that, instead of the genuine bread of life, it is the leaven-loaded loaf of apostasy, that will puff up the soul unto death.

Does anyone wonder about the genuineness of one's faith? Probably many do, and those who do, will be the least likely to have a counterfeit faith. For they probably have searched the Scripture, prayed for evidence, and sought with eagerness, the precious relationship with our Lord and Savior. I believe that it is many of those who are absolutely sure they have it, never questioning it, and who go about their lives without ever even thinking about it, may be in the greatest danger. They are those who claim that Scripture commands us to know we are saved and therefore we are wrong to ever even question it. To be certain of our salvation is indeed a command. But it should come about as a result deep introspective prayer, and genuine knowledge of His Word. Certainly some may rightly know, and know immediately when it occurs. How blessed they are! But perhaps a word of caution is appropriate here. As has been expounded on ad nauseam, here and in several of my other essays, Satan's diabolical cleverness as a deceiver can produce counterfeits so near perfect that even the most astute can be fooled. Combine his abilities with the human heart, which is ". . . *deceitful above all things, and desperately wicked*" (Jeremiah 17:9) and you have all the ingredients needed for an incredibly convincing yet false conclusion regarding the most urgent and important of all possible matters. I don't believe that it's any violation of God's command to occasionally feel that we need to stop and re-examine the sincerely and legitimacy of our faith. Even the highly blessed and exceedingly fruitful of Christ's disciples, Charles Hadden Spurgeon admitted that he even found it necessary to occasionally question and reassure himself as to the genuine of his faith.

As the theme of many of these essays indicate, my heart aches for those who don't know Jesus, for those who are unsaved but believed they are saved. However, my more specific focus of concern is for the many who profess the Christian faith, but do not possess the grace of salvation, because they don't even know what they don't know regarding that which would allow them to recognize the clear evidence of a saving faith. Because of this, for many reasons described above, they spend their lives in "blissful" ignorance presuming they do belong to Jesus. How do I know? Who am I to judge another's faith? Of course, I cannot judge another's faith, only God can. But evidence abounds to even the half-discerning eye, that such is the case with a large majority of professing Christians. This particular comment is sparked by a recent Barna poll of people calling themselves born-again Christians. The poll indicates that of those who responded, only 17 percent believe that salvation is by grace without works; only 25 percent pray, attend church, and read the Bible; only 37 percent are convinced that Jesus did not sin, and only 24 percent are certain that Satan is a real spiritual being. David Kinnanmau who directed the most recent poll said, *"Americans hold few convictions about their faith. For instance, even among those who disagree about orthodox views, many do so while hedging their bets. Most Americans have one foot in the biblical camp and one foot outside. They say they are committed, but to what? They are spiritually active, but to what end? The spiritual profile of American Christianity is not unlike a lukewarm church that the Bible warns about."* (Barna Annual Tracking Study .org (May 21, 2007).

What does the result of the poll reek with? A wide spread abject ignorance or rejection of biblical truth. Would your response to the poll have been included in these percentages? I pray not! Can there be a mustard sized seed amount of genuine faith in the hearts of very many of these professing Christians? I pray so, but I fear many will be shocked and terrified on judgment day.

Once again, I pray that if the reader considers himself or herself to be a redeemed Christian, each will take heed to what I have tried to communicate and will also choose to examine their individual beliefs in the context of the poll. How tragic it would be to complete one's life believing one is saved, where one's faith is a cleverly disguised worthless counterfeit, that cannot affect redemption.

—10—

The Certainty of a Saving Faith

For the last three years I have been a believer in Jesus Christ. I know that He died for my sins, and that it is through belief in His resurrection and faith in Him as our Savior, that one is saved and given everlasting life in heaven. The Bible is clear in the fact that *"For by grace are you saved through faith; and that not of yourselves; it is the gift of God; not of works, lest any man should boast."* (Ephesians 2:8, 9) It is also clear that good deeds and a virtuous life do not save, although anyone who has saving faith will seek and develop these qualities as part of their Christian walk, as evidence of their faith and as an expression of their love of Jesus. Paul speaks of faith, that is vain, or not a saving faith, and Jesus noted that many are called but few are chosen.

These two observations are the root cause of all of my concern and continued preoccupation with this issue. I know that I was called but I don't yet know that my faith is not a "vain faith" and I can only conjecture as to the discernable nature of such a faith. My commitment to Jesus was not a momentous, memorable event. It resulted from a critical yet comprehensive examination of the evidence, which led to the only possible and logical conclusion, that He was / is who He said He was. This was an intellectual conclusion for sure, but as a spiritual one, I'm not yet certain, and I don't know how to become certain. Because of the great portion of each day that I spend in prayer, reading the Bible and other religious materials, listening to Bible teaching tapes, discussing the subject, writing these papers, thinking about the matter and trying to mold my life more and more as I believe Jesus would have it be, I suppose I could conclude that mine is a saving faith, if only my heart would tell me so and if my spirit would speak of the matter. But these, for the most part are silent. Only my soul seems troubled and eager for an assurance. I say these things here, when in reality, I don't even know what my heart and spirit feel like, nor is it likely that I would recognize their involvement if it were to happen.

According to the Scriptures, when I accepted Christ as my savior and committed my life to Him, I was born again, that is my old sinful self died, I was given a new heart and became a new man in the spirit, saved to eternal life in heaven. However, the Scripture also notes that the old flesh remains and continues to desire its sinful ways, thus causing the continuous struggle within, a struggle that I know very well. I know that there is nothing that I can actually do, that Jesus did it all on the cross, that He was made sin, the sin of all mankind, past, present and future, and that sin was thereby purged from all who truly believe in Him. Only perfect, sinless believers can be admitted to heaven. No one is capable of completing a mortal life without committing sin, no matter how hard one tries. Thus no one can enter heaven without those sins being purged and forgiven. Jesus' death on the cross was the only way that this could occur. Thus a true faithful believer in Jesus is cleansed and eligible to join Him in heaven.

This all seems much too easy and too wonderful to be true, yet it is true, that is, providing the professed faith is, in fact, true saving faith. But how does one know? How can one distinguish the true faith from vain faith? In order to add a perspective to these questions, I'm reminded of something that I recently heard regarding the Evangelical "crusades" where a speaker inspires many in the audience who are "called to the alter," where they commit to Jesus and are thus "saved." Apparently research into this phenomenon has indicated that as few as 15 percent or less of those so inspired indicate discernable retention of that commitment. Thus it would seem that these inspirations and so-called commitments are but shallow emotional flames and superficially erasable thoughts having never penetrated to the hearts. What of the remaining 85 percent? What is the likely percentage of those who remain "committed," five, ten, or twenty years later? Of all these, which were actually saved? The answer seems obvious, yet from an earthly human perspective how can one know if anyone was saved? Only God can know.

How do we achieve saving faith? Clearly it is only through the grace of God. What is the manner of its manifestations? Is it sudden, complete and forever sustaining or is it a slowly growing flower, planted as a seed by God's grace and left for us to nurture? The Scriptures indicate that it happens when it happens and it is then complete and forever. Perhaps also there is a period of preparation before this blessed event can take place. Perhaps before the Lord can plant this seed of saving faith, one must first awaken the spirit, clear away all the weeds of ignorance and doubt, soften the sin hardened soil of the soul and then enrich it with a recognition of the existence of the Lord Jesus and of His resurrection. It is clear to me that my soul went through this clearing, softening and enriching process. However, I've heard nothing from my spirit, at least nothing that I have been able to recognize as such.

To add further focus to a difficult nature of my dilemma, I'm reminded of a true story, that I believe illustrates the vulnerability of even a most powerful enduring faith. There is a man of exceedingly strong faith and a genuine love for Jesus who is a great Bible teacher and to whom I am indebted for nearly everything I know about the Scriptures and of the Christian walk. In knowing Him, one cannot otherwise conclude but that after judgment day He will surly spend eternity in the company of Moses, and Abraham and the great prophets, discussing their lives and times, and getting briefed on the many wonders that His beloved Scriptures did not fully explain. I have listened to hundreds of hours of his taped lectures on every one of the Old and the New Testament books, and have read his several books on the Scriptures. In the lectures he has been most generous in revealing some of his personal life and the manner of his forty years of Christian walk He was educated at the U.S. Naval Academy and had a very impressive and successful career as an engineer and as CEO and chairman of the Board of several large high tech corporations. In the course of that career he amassed a large fortune and for some period he and his family lived with great wealth and all that it could provide. Suddenly, all of this was gone and replaced with a series of personal tragedies not unlike those, that tested Job of the Old Testament. Not only did he lose his wealth, but he also went deep into bankruptcy and even his best friends abandoned him. After losing his home and everything except a few personal possessions, he and his family moved into an apartment, where, due to a severe earthquake, he even lost his few remaining possessions. He admits that for some period during these trials he seriously considered taking his own life in order for his family to collect on a very large insurance policy. It is now evident that this period was both a test of his faith and a clear message from God, not unlike that that Jesus sent to the Ephesians in Revelation, chapter two, which in effect told the church to return to your first love or else! As a result, he is now, and has been for several years, a full time teacher and minister of God's Word, giving comfort as well as knowledge and hope of salvation to millions throughout the world. The grand purpose of this ordeal was to call him to a full time ministry of God's Word.

The point of this story is that this man of great love and faith in Jesus, truly one of the saved by any means of human measurement or definition, actually considered the taking of his life, which is probably the only unpardonable of all sins, because it occurs at the moment beyond which confession, regret and prayer, and therefore forgiveness, are impossible. Certainly until that time when he considered suicide, he believed that through his faith he was saved, and I'm sure that if anyone has the right to that belief he should have had it. However, had he taken his life, clearly it would have been a reason to have at least wondered about His Salvation.

Could I pass such a test of my faith? Might I someday be subjected to an even more rigorous task? Will I pass or fail? How can I know? Charles Spurgeon goes so far as to say that a faith not tested is no faith at all. I find this a little too severe, but who am I at this point in my walk to know much of anything when compared to this incredible man of God?

It is my current conclusion that few, if any, can be certain of their faith until their faith has survived severe testing, such as Job experienced, or until the end of our mortal lives when we see evidences of having persevered to the end. We can only hope and pray and seek an ever strengthening of our faith and to have the armor of God's Word to protect us during those inevitable tests that will surely come.

Why is it that a person's accomplishments are seldom acknowledged until that person has passed way? Perhaps it is because only then can one be certain of the appropriateness of that acknowledgment. One can never know what can happen, what transgressors may occur that might negate or render invalid and premature any intended adulation. Had Hitler died shortly after he had restored the devastated, defeated, post World War I Germany, history would have ranked him as a great and noble man, perhaps a George Washington or Simon Bolivar. However, his subsequent acts negated these outstanding accomplishments and made him one of history's worst villains. So it is I believe that in many cases one must reserve one's judgment as to the effectiveness of ones faith until the end. At this point of my life, I believe that only the Lord knows with certainty whether or not my belief and faith commitment is, in fact, a saving faith. If it is, nothing will negate it. If it isn't, then one can only pray that the grace of a true saving faith will at some point manifest. In either case, prayer, continued learning of the Word, walking the Christian walk, and continually examining one's life and one's professed faith are the least and probably the only things that can be done.

Where has all this taken me, and where do I now think I'm going? Putting all of the evidence together regarding my self-analysis, I must, with something less than absolute conviction, conclude that at this moment I am saved. I also conclude that this condition and the quality of my faith require a daily reality check. I suspect that in this realm, complacency is one of Satan's most effective weapons. Vigilance, prayer, and large well digested portions of "our daily bread," as a continuous way of life is what I see at this time as probably the best way of confirming this condition.

By the way, after completing, the above, I read for the nth time the passage about vain faith and now view it in a less ominous context, which I pray, isn't simply the rationalization of a desperate soul. It may well be related to Paul's admonitions to guard against heresy, that is, false doctrine, those not wholly in accordance with the Scriptures. These abound everywhere especially today. Paul admonishes us further to check the Scriptures daily and check all things against the infallible truth of the Holy Bible. Even the slight, seemingly negligible deviations can lead to a false or vain faith. I pray that this is what he meant because I believe it is something that I can deal with, rather than some ethereal or spiritual deficiency that I cannot identify, or comprehend.

There are many who call God their Father who will rail against my uncertainty as to my saving faith. This is because Scripture seems to require that we have full assurance of our salvation. I don't disagree in the slightest, but I know that it is the existence in the *heart* of a true saving faith, that is, the single most important thing in anyone's life. It's not number one on a list of whatever. It must be the stand alone, ultimate priority of everyone's life who has any sense of the two choices we have for our place in eternity. To be quick to conclude out of wishful thinking, to be complacent, cavalier, or presumptive about the matter should be completely out of the question. I pray to become sure of the adequacy of my faith. But I will not presume that I have it until I find the evidence in me, that demands that assurance. I pray also that your assurance of a saving faith is based on substantiated fact.

—11—
A Conversation Between a Soul and Its Body

Greetings friend. This is your soul speaking through our mind. It has been a while since we had a conversation. Remember our first? That was when we were fighting the beast, the cancer that was killing you. Until that time, I thought that only I had cognitive power and that you were simply the biological machine assigned to carry me around. Then I had heard that direct mind soul body conversation could, under some circumstances, be useful in the fight and, by George, I think it was! During that period, we conversed a great deal. Of course, I did all of the talking but most certainly I am sure that you were listening. Of course, God was too and certainly it was only through Him that you were able to hear me and to do what needed to be done.

Remember how I tried to recruit and direct your energies while we lay on the table with the radiation beam being focused on and bombarding the beast within you? I visualized your white blood cells as being thousands of little pac men surrounding the beast, and I urged you to have them put up their shields to protect themselves just as the beam attacked the beast so that radiation damage to your good cells would be minimized. Each time, as soon as the bombing ceased, I urged you to mobilize the medics and ambulances to get at and treat the good cells that the shields had failed to protect and to then send in the dozers, loaders and garbage trucks to haul off, as soon as possible, the dead parts of the beast as well as the less fortunate good cells. With Gods help, you did a great job because the beast died, the damage to your good cells was minimal and the immune system survived,

114

it would seem completely in tact, and, in fact, even stronger due to enhancements that we provided to it.

As we look back, it is evident that we didn't need the thirty-six radiation bombardments because the cancer vacated your entire system even before the sixth bombing. Had I been more perceptive, I would have noticed that the beast was already on its way down the drain even before this madness started. You probably knew this, but I wasn't sharp enough to figure that out until sometime later.

During, this period, and for years after, we have had many other conversations regarding our common effort to get well and stay well. Remember how we conversed, almost always while we were lying on the floor forcing mind over matter to hold in a two-quart coffee enema? There were the times I told you what a splendid job you did during the needless radiation war, and then about all of the good things that I was sending you and doing to you, the diet, the juices, the green powders, the supplements, the enzymes, the phytonutrients, the anoxidants, the microwater, the ozone, the trace minerals and on and on, as well as the photo luminescence, the full spectrum light, the laser therapy, the sauna, the A.T.P. inductor, the electrical acupulse machine the magnetic mattress pad the acupuncture the hypothermia machines, the rebounder and on and on and on. Sometimes you were less than happy and let me know it with stomach growls or some other minor rebellious acts. However, for the most part, you seem to benefit from some, and perhaps many, of these efforts because I felt that much of the time you were stronger, younger and healthier than you were ten years ago, long before the beast invaded your loins.

How well I remember the day that the doctors told us that our case was hopeless, that nothing, could be done except to get ready to die in six to twelve months. Neither of us panicked nor became sad nor frightened nor resigned to this fate. We only saw the challenge and never even considered the odds against us. I immediately stopped feeding you junk food and instead filled you with only good stuff and subjected you to many dozens of protocols of which only a few have here been hinted at. Remember the Vitae Elixxor that we put on your groin as a poultice and that burned so that it blistered your skin, or the Dr. Suns Soup that tasted so awful that dinner became a dreaded time? Silly to ask; how could you ever forget? How about the hypothermia machine with six-inch thumb sized steel rod up the rectum and the steel plate on the groin with sparking, burning, excruciating microwaves flowing in between trying to burn the beast, or the gnawing 714x injections that had to be slowly pushed into the lymph nodes of the groin continuously over the longest five minutes imaginable. How about the acupulse where we put an electrode under each foot or in each hand and sat for an hour or more several times a week letting a variety of pulsating electrical currents surge through you from one extremity to the other.

We had quite a time of it, didn't we? It was a memorable experience. What do you mean "had" you say, when I'm still subjecting you to many of these things? Don't forget that as "astounded" as the doctor was that the beast was gone, he pointed out that there is more than an 80 percent chance that it will be back within five years. Well, we went from no chance with six to twelve months of life to a possible 20 percent chance to have five years or more, of which we have already had more than three here in 1998. So don't complain about all of the stuff I'm making you do. It's all geared toward ever further improving these odds.

Any time you get complacent, just remember the months of monumental pain and bleeding as the beast grew and spread, choking the urethra and invading the bladder until the ureters plugged causing the kidneys to fail. It wasn't much fun either pushing that catheter; the sixteen-inch plastic tube, up the urethra into the bladder those many hundreds of times when the beast wouldn't let you remove urine naturally. Need I remind you how we had to do this fifteen to eighteen times each night and for months how the only sleep we had were those ten to twenty minute intervals in between? It's diabolical how the beast commandeered so much of your blood and then used large clots to plug up the bladder even before it had grown big enough to do the plugging itself. As if that wasn't bad enough, the clots plugged the catheter, too, making it necessary to remove it, clean it and reinsert it as many as ten times in order to affect a single drainage of your bladder. In case I haven't mentioned it before, I was very proud of how well you handled all of this, especially the many months of sleep deprivation and the awful pain. You, nevertheless, got up every morning and never let me down by going to work as usual, as well as performing all of our many domestic duties. Without questions, it was only possible through Divine intervention and inspiration as manifest in our frame of mind and the many seemingly hokey protocols that I subjected on you.

Here is the bottom line of all of this that you should know about. One of these days you and I are going to part company. You're going back to the dust from which you came and I'm going to heaven without you for a while. Later will come that great day of rapture! You'll be instantly reconstituted to who you were in your prime but then you will be incorruptible and eternal. Then we will again be joined as one body, soul and spirit. On that blessed day we will stand before Jesus to receive our heavenly assignments as part of the Body of Christ. Had the beast separated us as predicted, I'm afraid that our fate on judgment day would have been one extreme tragedy. However, as you know, after eighteen months of our combined effort, when we were congratulating each other, our dear Lord made it clear exactly who really healed us. At that moment I became a saved soul and so you have been blessed to share with me all of the incredible future rewards that became ours as a result of His blessed grace through my faith in Jesus.

Looking back, it seems unfortunate that I couldn't have recognized much, much earlier in our life the profound truth, that now is so clear and so obvious once the evidence is examined with real and sincere objectivity. Why did we have to become an old man stricken with terminal cancer and then blessed with an "astounding," remission (as the doctor called it) before I could recognize the Truth? Think of what a more worthy life we might have had, how much more good we could have done, and the spiritual benefits that we might have imparted to our loved ones. But that borders on questioning God's perfect timing. What happened and when it happened was exactly when it should have happened.

What a shame! Throughout this ordeal, it never occurred to me to pray or to ask the Lord for help. I simply didn't believe. It was only after your bleeding, our pain (I feel pain too, you know) had stopped, and the cancer was long gone, did I feel the Lords touch, and His gentle knock. It was then that He opened our eyes and our ears so that we could grasp the Truth and the meaning of His Word. Whatever you do, dear body, and take this from someone who knows, don't ever regret or feel that you were victimized by what happened to us. That was the Lords wake up call! A call to change our life, to break the chains that held us in Satan's grip, and to begin to understand the Word in order that we would believe and find that saving faith. I regret nothing of that ordeal, and have only thankfulness and gratitude to the Lord for giving us this second chance, this extended life, and the opportunity to help others, both physically and spiritually, from our experience.

You and I each have a lot of work to do and a number of weaknesses to overcome. Our long life of unbelief and false belief had made our scorecard somewhat shameful. You have been far from the epitome of virtue and I haven't been the good leader that I though I was. God be praised, He knocked and I heard Him! Since then, our life has been much more difficult, but at the same time quite wonderful because for the first time, I am able to see clearly why we are here and what we must do. Our future is secure through my faith in Jesus, and we are here to prepare for the day of judgment; everything else is secondary. That sounds quite simple. However, after living a life full of the secondary and knowing not the primary, totally resetting priorities is no easy task. You may not see it this way, and just as dealing with the beast was most difficult for you, this is much more difficult for me, and absolutely impossible without the loving patient guidance of the Holy Spirit. Many of your stimuli and responses have contributed to our poor scorecard. However, you couldn't have gotten into too much mischief without my concurrence. On the other hand, I also have all of the issues of chastity, honesty, love, faith, charity, etc. to strengthen and perfect, as well as those of lust, greed, hate, vengeance, avarice, etc. to defeat and purge from me. It isn't easy, but neither was it easy getting rid of the cancer. However, just as the Lord saved us from that beast, He will guide us to the end and make clear what His purpose is for us, because He surely didn't extend our life without a reason.

What all of this means is that we both have to work hard and dedicate ourselves to accomplish that for which He extended our lives. We each have two jobs to do. Mine is first and foremost to thoroughly examine my faith to be sure that it is genuine saving faith. To do so, I must study and know His Word, worship Him and pray for His strength and guidance in all things. Yours is to stay healthy and to live long enough for us to achieve all He had purposed for us. My second task is to help you with yours and your secondary task is to help me with mine. I will help you by maintaining a discipline in food, drink and environment I choose for you as well as assuring adherence to the various health giving protocols that seem to have helped us so far. I also will keep an eye out for new ones whenever possible. You, on the other hand, can help by trying to redirect some of your energies and priorities away from the fleshly pleasure, comfort and satisfaction that lead to the sinful behavior that I must deal with. Praise the Lord that through His grace we are both saved to an eternal life in heaven, and not to the eternal lake of fire, where we would have gone had He not intervened to heal us and draw us to Him.

—12—

The Temple of God

Seven times in Scripture, the Holy Spirit tells us that we are the temple of God. But let not everyone blindly rejoice in this. Scripture also makes it very clear that only those who accept Jesus, as their Lord and Savior, and all that that implies in terms of repentance, obedience and evidential works, are temples indwelt by the Holy Spirit. All others have an empty place where the Holy Spirit would like to dwell, if the person would allow Him to. These persons are at risk of being occupied by other spirits who have stolen in by means of Satan's law of "squatter's rights." Only through the work of the Holy Spirit, authorized by the free will of the individual, can these usurping, evil squatters be evicted and replaced by Him who has the power to evict and to convict.

Prior to Pentecost, the temple of worship where God would dwell was made of stone or wood. With Pentecost, God decreed that henceforth each human body, whose soul gave itself to Christ Jesus, would become a temple, the place of personal worship, because with the acceptance of Jesus as Lord and Savior, that is where the Holy Spirit would take up residency. Remember, your body is not you. You are the soul / spirit that dwells in that body. When one says, "my body" it is on an inadvertent admission that the body is not the person speaking, otherwise why say, "my body" the same as one would say "my house" or "my car"? Aren't we simply all bags of bones and flesh where we must dwell until God takes us? Our bodies consist of nothing more than dust, water and air of a particular mix and shape into which the Creator breathed life. We are each tenants-at-will (His will) in these temporary homes, that He has loaned to us. But they are also temples. What are temples for? They are places of worship. Therefore, we who are saved each live in our own temple of worship, and worshiping our Creator is what we are expected to do there.

The old stone temple of worship needed much care and maintenance. The oil lamps needed to be kept full and burning, the shewbread needed to be replaced daily, the incense dish had to be kept full, and, of course, the place had to be kept clean. Our bodies as living temples need similar maintenance. We should keep God's spiritual light always burning and shining from within. We need daily spiritual bread even as our bodies need material nourishment. As the burning of incense in the stone temple symbolized worship, so must we in our souls maintain a burning thirst to seek and worship God. Keeping our body, our temple, our place of worship, clean is also of great importance

As organic temples, rather than the ones, made of stone, the cleaning and maintenance of each temple requires a different system of care. In these end times, the world dominated by you know who, is almost in complete control of all food supply, making it more and more difficult for us to obtain unadulterated, God-intended nourishing food with which to keep our temple healthy and clean from sickness. Because we dwell in God's temple, isn't it highly incumbent on us to do all we can to not only keep it spiritually clean and pure, but also physically healthy? We are stewards of His temples as well as tenants. Can anyone doubt that He expects us to treat it responsibly and lovingly as He treats us? So it seems appropriate that just as we seek His Word as the source of pure, wholesome, spiritual food for ourselves, we should also seek and apply all available knowledge regarding what our bodies need for their health in order to assure them full measure of useful lives.

Where food is concerned, the world's primary objective is to sell it for a profit. That's fine, but it has little, if any, interest in whether or not it nourishes. In order to sell well, its flavor and texture as well as its appearance must be pleasing, and its shelf life as extended as possible. Therefore, these are the primary "attributed" that all food producers try to put into their products. Major industries exist for the sole purpose of producing chemical additives to enhance taste, color, texture and shelf life. There is convincing evidence that many of these are harmful over the long term. Public knowledge of such things as these, along with the several health dangers associated with transfats, sugars, chemical sweeteners, white flour, etc. is slowly emerging as is the fact that many heavily consumed "foods" are not only void of any nutritional benefits, but are also slow-acting, serious poisons. However, the forces in control continue to confuse and deceive for the sake of their economic interests as the population grows ever more sick and ailing. If you really care for God's temple, as you should, you ought to become educated and knowledgeable of what is and what is not healthy. Read every label before you buy in order to know what is in the package, and then be very selective about what you feed your temple. By God's permissive will, I was told more than twelve years ago I had no more than twelve months to live, due to a metastasized cancer for which there was no treatment. Through God's directive will, He guided me through the maze of conflicting information about what I should eat and other things that I should do to restore His temple. Just as with Scripture, if you pray and seek with singleness of mind you can do the same for the temple that has been entrusted to you.

—13—

A Biographical Sketch of Sin

Ever since I discovered and began to study the Holy Bible and recognized that it was authored by our Creator God Himself, trying to understand the meaning, nature, cause and effect of sin has been an important component of my "Christian Musings." Three previous essays titled, "The Consequence of Sin," "Sin Unto Death," and "The Covering of Sin" express my earlier observations and beliefs regarding this provocative word. What follows here, I pray, is a look at sin from what might be a little closer to God's universal perspective, as we can determine it from His infallible Word. To represent one's self to be an authorized spokesperson for our Creator, is a privilege, which was given by Him only to the Prophets and the Apostles, and their revelations are accurately recorded in His Holy Bible. The only legitimate privilege anyone else has is to search, find and attempt to interpret from, and only from, this Book, as clear an understanding as possible, of what He would have us know. It is on that basis, and much prayed for perception, that I offer the following observations.

God tells us that on the sixth day of the week, during which He instituted all of creation, He made man, and made him in His own image out of *adamah*, the Hebrew word that means "ground," not "dust." Dust is *aphar,* which is similarly alluded to in other parts of the Scripture. Careful study of this portion of Scripture cannot help but engender an awe and unlimited respect for the exactness and precision of God's Holy Word. God created the heavens and earth. Created is the translated Hebrew word *bara* which means created out of nothing, something only God can do. When He speaks of having made man, He uses the word "formed" in Genesis 2:7. This is the translation of the Hebrew word *yatzar* which means, "to mold." Hence we often see God's use of the analogy of the potter molding the clay when He refers to man. While in Genesis 1:27, we find God telling us that He "created" man, in Genesis 2:7, God enlarges on this idea by revealing that He made or formed man from the very substance which He made from nothing.

Naming man Adam after the word for earth reflects man's material origin in that he is but an earthling made out of earth, or ground. This is important to remember in the context of so many religions, which portray man as being as God, or becoming able to achieve godhood, just as Satan believed he could. God, the Creator, obviously is infinitely above any part of His created image. What separates us from all other forms of life is that into the particular composite of earthly matter called man, He imparted His breath (*neshameh*), which is the spirit of eternal life. The Hebrew word for soul or spirit is *rauch*. This He gave to man, animals and even to false gods (demons). But *neshameh* caused man to become a living, immortal soul with the unique faculty of spiritual understanding. Animals were given only *rauch*, a soul or spirit of life, which is not immortal and cannot understand the spiritual aspects of life or of eternity. Angels are also created beings, who were given immortality, but in a different and less revealed manner. They were created as spirits with considerable power but not in the image of God. Their powers, however, great and presently far superior to man, have no future destiny greater than that which was originally given them. Man, however, being in the image of God, has the potential for being "above" the angels in the final dispensation of God's grand plan. Those who will achieve that potential are those, and only those, who accept, comply with, and obey God's Word as the whole of Scripture clearly prescribes. Thus one might fairly conclude that earthly life for man is a proving ground, a school, a one time only period of preparation and absorption of understanding, all predicated on, and evidenced by, a humble recognition and unconditional acceptance of God's goals as represented by God's own Word. This Word was manifested here on earth through the virgin birth, life, death and resurrection of Christ

Jesus. Not just believing, but *knowing* that Jesus is Lord and Savior, is the precondition which allows for admission into this school of preparation for Godly service.

Having said all of this, what about sin, and what does all of this have to do with it? To this I am persuaded to offer this somewhat simplistic overview, which may at least serve as an outline for a more comprehensive analysis, which is presently beyond my capacity and level of ability or understanding. This outline consists of five components, the definition, the origin, the impact, the progression and finally the disposition of sin.

1. *Definition of Sin*

Sin is simply defined as anything contrary to God's will. This is clearly an all inclusive definition which stands alone and is adequate as a starting point for those who seek to be "in His image" as He demands of all who would be His sons and daughters. What this means, what God considers contrary to His will, is clearly described in Scripture and available to all sincere seekers who avail themselves of it. However, this is not as easy as it may sound, because we are all inveterate sinners who find it almost impossible to avoid rationalizing, diminishing and excusing our own sins. Until we are able to remove those cataracts of the mind's eye, which deliberately cloud portions of God's Word, those portions, which we would rather not understand, all of our efforts in genuinely seeking God's truth will be fruitless. Only the truly humble heart which recognizes the depth of depravity within which its sin filled nature exists, and then enlists the power of the Holy Spirit to remove this glaze, can ever even hope to discover what God would have His own be able to understand. The result of this self deception and lack of Scriptural understanding is, that not only are there sins which we choose not to acknowledge, but that there are also sins which we don't even know are sins, and which we inadvertently commit daily. If we are serious in our desire to try to obey the command to be perfect as our Father is perfect, then we must seek to at least know as much as possible, the full spectrum of what sin is. The ancient Hebrews had been given this insight, and, therefore, had a special sacrifice for the sins they may have committed but didn't know that they were sins. This wasn't an empty ritual. This was a part of the God-ordained process of full coverage of their sins until Christ Jesus would come to wash them away with His blood. When Jesus gave the "Sermon on the Mount," He revealed to all who would take Him seriously, many of these "unknown" sins. For instance, He revealed that mere thoughts of doing sinful acts were as fully sinful as the acts themselves.

How awful is sin? It's simply a matter of personal judgment, as the world believes, that is, that portion of the world that even acknowledges that there is such a thing as sin. Limiting the first question to the Christian worldview, it seems even here, sin is often trivialized. Perhaps this is because it seems that it is so easily cleansed from our souls through simply believing that Jesus is Lord and Savior. First, sins are not cleansed from the soul by that simple belief, unless that belief has outgrown its place in the brain and has penetrated every fiber of the heart and soul, as evidenced by a changed life, which grows in reverence and obedience, and away from sin. Second, Jesus' substitutionary payment was not easy, but was the most painful ordeal of suffering ever possible to have been perpetuated; a pain worse than any human could possibly comprehend. It was a God-sized pain that only God Himself was capable of suffering and surviving. The more one studies Scripture and is given an understanding available only through the Holy Spirit, does it become possible to even begin to appreciate what God did to make it possible for us to be extricated from that unbearable burden. Psalms 22 and 69, along with Isaiah 52 and 53 express but a tiny portion of what Jesus suffered out of His love for those who would but accept Him as Lord and Savior.

Doesn't this tell us much about how God views sin? The whole of Scripture makes much ado about sin, how God views it, and what it has done to all of creation. Let's look at just one little phrase in the Book of Romans, chapter 7, verse 13. Here Paul is describing how law brought sin into focus. But at the end of this verse he says, *". . . that sin by commandment might become exceedingly sinful."* There doesn't seem to be anything very exciting there, or even suggestive of being worthy of extended thought. That is unless you are full to overflowing with the Holy Spirit, having been given the spirit of wisdom, discernment and articulation, as was the great man of God, Charles Hadden Spurgeon. He was able to derive from the two words "exceedingly sinful" an entire one hour sermon, filled with divine insights and understanding. Here is but a small portion of how he began that sermon:

> *Now, what I want to call your attention to is that Paul here calls sin "exceedingly sinful." Why didn't he say, "Exceedingly black," or "exceedingly horrible," or "exceedingly deadly"? Why, because there is nothing in the world so bad as sin. When he wanted to use the very worst word he could find, to call sin by, he called it by its own name, and reiterated it: "sin" "exceedingly sinful." For if you call sin black there is no moral excellency or deformity in black and white, Black is as good as white, and white is as good as black, and you have expressed nothing. If you call sin "deadly," yet death in itself hath no evil in it compared with sin. For plants to die is not a dreadful thing; rather it may be a part of the organization of nature that successive generations of vegetables should spring up, and in due time should form the root-soil for other generations to follow. If you call it "deadly" you have said but little. It you want a word; you must come home for it. Sin must be named after itself. If you want to describe it, you must call it "sinful." Sin is "exceedingly sinful."*

If we recognize that every sin represents rebellion against God, that its first introduction upset the very order of the universe, and that it is responsible for what has happened, and is going on in the world in terms of pain, suffering, disease, death, etc., it should be evident why God has put so much emphasis on its "wrongness." Isn't it right, therefore, that we should seek to better understand it and treat it with the same seriousness as God does, and has told us that we should as well?

2. Origin of Sin

There are several eminent Bible Scholars such as Barnhouse and Fruchtenbaum whom I value and respect most highly, who believe in a so-called "gap" theory based on Genesis, chapter one, verse two, which seems to suggest that there was something in existence before God created the heaven and earth. Verse two speaks of a darkness being on the face of the deep and that "the spirit moved upon the face of the water." I presently don't have a satisfactory explanation of this with which I am satisfied. However, these Scholars conclude that prior to the Genesis creation there was some form of substance, and that this was an earth-like place which was the abode of Satan, a place to which he was exiled and which was later destroyed, leaving this formless water mass. If that was the case, then his sin of envy must have occurred well before God created the universe. That such mightily spiritually blessed servants of God can believe this, tells me that it may be my own deficiency of understanding that is the problem as I here try to advance my thoughts as to the origin of sin. I mentioned this other view so that the reader may know of it and seek, if he or she chooses to, just what that is all about.

At any rate, Scripture tells us that the first sin was committed by Adam. Eve, of course, ate the forbidden fruit first. Adam was told directly by God not to eat from a particular tree or he would surely die. (Genesis 2:17). It was after that, that God made Eve, and there is no evidence that God repeated this to her. The fact that she distorted the message by claiming that God said not to even touch it, (Genesis 3:3) suggests that it may have been Adam who relayed that information, and may have even added the "no touch" for emphasis. While Eve was deceived, Adam knowingly, through violating God's direct word, willfully did sin, that is, he did what he knew was contrary to God's will. Here the origin of sin gets a bit sticky. Both Adam and Eve sinned by eating the fruit. But what about Satan who convinced them to ignore God's decree? Didn't he sin first through envy, and also by his lying and deceiving Eve? Yet the shame of Adam's and Eve's nakedness, the entry of death, the commencement of universal entropy, the groaning of the universe, the turning of vegetarians into carnivores, the development of thorns and thistles to plague man, the institution of labor pains in the woman, and the expulsion of Adam and Eve from that perfect environment of the Garden, were all the result of man's first sin, not Satan's. This makes it evident that the first act of man's disobedience, and not Satan's acts of rebellion, was the activating sin. Satan persuaded Eve to sin, to act contrary to

God's will. But was Satan acting contrary to God's will? Don't jump too quickly to a conclusion.

Before we enter that tangled web, let's first look back a little to see how this drama may have begun. God made man in a state of unconfirmed creature holiness, that is, he was created holy, but with the power of contrary choice. At that point, his holiness had not yet been confirmed. That is why he was given a choice, a choice to obey or disobey, and a choice to remain holy or to sin. It was his choice that confirmed him to unholiness. The angels were all holy, but yet unconfirmed when Satan rebelled. Those who followed Satan confirmed their wickedness, while those who didn't became confirmed to holiness and are no longer even capable of choosing sin. Those who followed Satan, no longer had the ability to choose holiness. By this line of reasoning it may be concluded that God also instituted for man some probationary period wherein, if he had retained his holiness, that is, avoided the fruit, he too would have gained perpetual holiness and lost any possibility to sin. He would have then been confirmed to eternal holiness. But once he sinned, his lack of holiness made it impossible for him not to continue sinning. Man, by his own efforts, cannot climb out, but remains in this state until God in His loving mercy initiates a change in him. This change, and the restoration to holiness, is offered to all of mankind who will become believers in Christ Jesus as Lord and Savior. Prior to Jesus' resurrection, this restoration to holiness was positionally available to all who believed in the God of Abraham, chose obedience and faith in Him, and obeyed the laws He had given them. It became effectual upon the completion of Jesus' work on the cross. Note that the lost angels have no Savior, no redeemer, for Jesus died in order to redeem only man, not angels or demons, or any other form of life. All genuinely saved believers became justified, and then are glorified as they ascend to heaven (Romans 8:30). In their glorified state, they no longer have any capacity to sin. They become forever holy. What a blessing we have in our Savior! And what a relief it will be to never again even be able to sin!

Now, back to who sinned first Satan or Adam? The preponderance of evidence, from my viewpoint, points to Adams' sin as having commenced the decline of all creation. However, it was most certainly Satan who sinned first. I don't believe that we can know just when Satan committed his first sin, but it did manifest here on earth as he toyed and manipulated this intellectually far inferior species God has just created. It seems, therefore, that we might rightly conclude that Satan's sins are of a different nature than man's sins, because he is of a totally different species, and in a different realm. The Greek word for sin is *hamartano* which means, "missing the mark, so as to not share in the prize." There is no prize waiting for the angel species, even the one's who proved their holiness. Their future is in serving the redeemed man. Sin by that definition is ascribed to man, and doesn't appear to be applicable to Satan or to the angels. Pride is certainly a sin in man's realm and was also a fault in Satan's heart. But somehow the effect seems to have been different, because Satan's sin didn't shake God's Genesis-recorded creation, as did Adam's sin. There is no God ordained formula for forgiveness, justification or sanctification for any beings other than humans. God made the earth and all living things for the benefit of man and man alone (Genesis 1:28–31).

God didn't orchestrate Satan's rebellion by His directive will, but by His *permissive* will He allowed it, as He well had to if His provision of free will was to be an authentic, sovereign characteristic of His created beings. It is by God's permissive will, that God allows Satan to exert influence on man. Having failed the test in the Garden, man's sinful nature was established, as was Satan's even earlier. It appears that it was God's will that Satan, who is the perfect prototype of evil, should become the "standard bearer" for the "dark" side, so that there would continue to be a genuine choice available to man even as God would continually strive to convince man to choose His way. There seems to be no doubt that man's mortal life is yet another probationary period God has given him in order to seek a remedy for the sin affliction, which Adam and Eve imposed on all mankind by their first sin. All of God's love, mercy, grace, blessings and eternal fellowship are freely offered subject only to making the right choice, which is Jesus.

To see just how deep and indelibly anchored in man's soul sin really is, consider what the Holy Spirit has revealed about this fact in the Book of Revelation. During the Millennium, Jesus Himself will personally and physically rule "with an iron rod." Yet the sinful nature will remain in the heart of man. This will become so pervasive that after Satan is allowed out of the abyss for a while, he will be able to recruit a vast army of men actually willing and eager to wage a massive war against Jesus! (Revelation 20:18).

3. Impact of Sin

It's impossible to apprehend the full impact of that first sin, let alone that of its later manifestations. A hint of this is found in Romans 8:22, where the Holy Spirit through Paul says, *"For we know that the whole creation groaneth and travaileth in pain together until now."* The word "groan" in Greek is *sustenazo* which means, "to experience a common calamity," that is, a calamity experienced by all. Groan is found twenty times in Scripture, but only this one time with that all encompassing meaning. That common calamity which affects the entire universe is sin, that first sin in the Garden of Eden when man exercised his free will and chose to go contrary to God's will by eating fruit of the tree of knowledge of good and evil. This put into the heart of man, and woman, the concept of having the power to decide for one's self what is and what is not in ones best interest apart from God's directive.

How could such a small infraction cause this terrible "common calamity" which was suddenly shared by all of creation? Seven times in Genesis, chapter 1, God speaks of His creation as being good. In fact, when He speaks of having created man, He says, "that was very good!" This obviously indicates that *everything* was good at the beginning. This offers no hint of any kind of impending calamity. Suddenly, however, all "very good" disappeared. The instant sin was committed, that is an act contrary to God's will, that perfect edifice God had created began to crumble, to deteriorate. Man, generally ignorant of how it happened, calls the condition entropy, the winding down of the universe, that all pervasive and continuing existence of chaos and disorder. Before sin, there was no death. Scripture clearly states that sin caused the advent of death. Therefore, all creatures had to have been vegetarians. The first recorded death was that of the animals which furnished the skins with which God first clothed Adam and Eve.

With the greatest of self restraint of which I am capable, I'll resist going into my usual tirade on the "billions and billions of years hypothesis that modern "science" insists is the only answer to the great size of the universe and to the "evolution" of man. God said He made all things in six days, clearly six of our twenty-four-hour days, not billions of years-days. If one carefully examines the Hebrew word for "day" as used in Genesis chapter one, and in Exodus chapter twenty, as well as many other places in Scripture, one cannot help but conclude that God meant twenty-four-hour days! Because various stars are billions of light years away from each other doesn't mean that it took billions of years for this to happen. This is only relevant if one accepts a single point of beginning, the idea of the big bang theory, that first there was nothing and then it exploded from one single point, outward for billions of years in order to reach the vast distances at which the stars are now observable. Why only a one point beginning? Couldn't God have created the various segments of the universe at many distant places all at the same time on the same day? Also, isn't it possible that *"in the beginning"* the speed of light was billions of times faster than it is now, so that any distance measured in light years could have delivered these stars to where they are much faster, like in twenty-four earth hours? I'm not claiming that those thoughts necessarily have any validity. I only know that what is called "science" today is wrong, and that God is right. He created everything in six twenty-four-hour days! Period! End of story! Anyone who tries to torture God's words in order to make them something other than what He said they were, twenty-four-earth-hour days, is accepting man's word over God's word. Why rationalize and try to accommodate to man's godless theories, when God made it clear as to the truth!

Man's theories, those that desperately try to eliminate God as the Creator and His precious truth as meaningless, are like what is called New England weather. Wait a few minutes and it will change. How many of the ever changing "scientific" theories on this and other matters must be advanced before sad, simple, gullible and brainwashed man finally realizes that this is nothing but a desperate game by those who deny God and will propose any explanation, no matter how absurd, as long as it doesn't require having to admit that there is a Creator God. If "science" would expend its time, energy and money in prayerful thought on *how* God created, rather than trying to prove that it was accidental and absent of God, perhaps *real* scientific progress could be made in this and related fields! The earth groans. We have earthquakes, volcanoes, hurricanes, typhoons, droughts, floods as evidence of its groaning. There are star collisions, super novas, dying stars, fragmented stars such as comets and meteors all attesting to the groaning and the continued groaning caused by that first sin, and I suspect that it is also because of the progression and growth of sin which we will discuss next.

4. The Progression of Sin

It was the musing about this aspect of sin that sparked my need to write this paper. Of course, as is too often evident, it was like putting an overdose of leaven into a measure of dough. This thought expanded well beyond its initially intended scope. What do I mean by the progression of sin? As I thought back through world history as our Lord recorded it, it became evident that mans sinful nature, his rebelliousness against God, has increased, become deeper seated, more matured, and ever more sophisticated, especially in these late end times.

At first there was but the one sin. But it, by itself, was enough to break the bond that had existed between the Spirit of God and the spirit in man. This severance was the spiritual death, the on-going penalty for the sin that remains in man, and will remain to the very end of existence of mortal man, except where God will intervene and restore that bond. God's intervention which is able to restore that bond was His coming to earth in the form of Christ Jesus and paying the penalty that God's justice demanded, through Jesus' suffering and death on the cross. But that restoration is effectual in only those persons who believe He did this, and who, on this basis, obey His ordinances. I believe Jesus tells us this when He offers to give us His peace, the peace which passeth all understanding (John 14:27, Philippians 4:7). The word for this particular peace in the Greek is *eirene*, the definition of which includes to "set at one again." I believe that this peace, the peace that accompanies salvation, is the reconnection of the Spirit of God with the spirit of man that had been severed by the original sin, and incapable of reconnection until Jesus did His work on the cross. Isn't evidence of the Spiritual reconnection manifest in the very presence of the Holy Sprit in the new heart of redeemed man?

Back again to the progression of sin. After that first sin, the next sin of which we are given evidence is Cain's choice of an offering contrary to God's will. It is evident that God must have instructed that first family on at least some of what later became the levitical laws. They apparently were told that they were to perform at least some form of worship associated with the sacrifice of animals. Abel apparently followed the rules, while Cain chose to "do it his own way" by instead, bringing to the altar the fruits of his toil, "works." We are told that God was displeased with Cain's offering because it was contrary to His will and His instructions. The next recorded sin seems to have been that Cain was "wroth" at God's response. The word "wroth" is a translation of the Hebrew word, *charah*, which means to blaze up in anger, jealousy, incensed, etc. He was mighty angry. Here in Genesis 4:7, God even tells Cain that this anger was sinful! Of course, the next sin was that of murder. How rapidly the cancer of sin spread and deepened. Only nine more generations after Adam, God found it necessary, because of the universal spreading of sin, to destroy the entire world and kill every breathing soul, except Noah and his family. That evil heart, that soul having a dormant or "dead" spirit no longer linked to God, fully expressed its evil nature to the point where God had had enough! Through Noah, who "walked with God" and was "perfect" in his generations, God in His loving mercy, offered mankind another chance to deal with his problem through the "covering of sin" procedure He gave Moses as recorded in the Book of Leviticus.

Another evidence we have of God's pre-Leviticus instructions as to how man was to worship Him and "cover" his sins, is found in

Genesis 8:20. Here we are told that as soon as he left the ark, *"And Noah builded an altar unto the Lord, and took of every clean beast, and of every clean fowl, and offered burnt offerings on the altar."* However it wasn't long before sin was evidenced again. The occasion recorded is when Noah fell into a drunken stupor and somehow in some unidentified way, a very serious sin occurred having to do with his son Ham, or perhaps Ham's son Canaan. Many commentaries suggest that Ham committed the sin because he is the one who reported Noah's nakedness to their brothers. But it was Canaan on whom God levied the resulting curse, not Ham. Most believe that the sin was homosexuality.

Scripture informs us that Ham begat Cush who begat Nimrod. This was the world's first dictator and founder of Babel, which was the future site of Babylon. He also built Nineveh and other Assyrian cities. The sinful nature of Babel is well known as we read of the Tower of Babel and, of course, it's outgrowth. The City of Babylon is consistently, more than any other place on earth, referred to both symbolically and literally as the very citadel of evil. Because his name seems to be associated with the verb, *marad* meaning to rebel, early tradition identified Nimrod with rebellion against God and his seeking of tyrannical power. With the Tower of Babel, he tried to unify the human race into one nation under his leadership. As "a mighty hunter before the lord" is seen as him having put himself before or ahead of the Lord as he founded two great empires, Babylon and Assyria, both of which were the major enemies of God's people. Based on what he accomplished, we might conclude that he was a mighty hunter of the souls of men, not of lions and deer. Some expositors, such as Alexander Hishop in the book "The Two Babylon's depicts Nimrod as the lawless one and a shadow, or type of the last world ruler, the antichrist. Thus we have in him a primary source of pagan religions and the institutionalizing of man's concerted sin filled rebellion against God, wholly apart from that segment of the human race God later designated as His "chosen" people.

God chose Abram, later to be called Abraham, as the one through whom He would develop this chosen people. By then, less than five hundred years after the flood, we find wickedness already spread throughout the populated world. Whatever Godly ways may have survived the flood through Noah had quickly vanished or had been severely perverted into a variety of idol worshipping religions. It would seem then that the world had been almost completely "given over to sin," hardly any different than how the world is today. It was through these chosen, as they multiplied out of Abraham, that God would reveal Himself and His plan of redemption to all the world. Abraham was of the sinful pagan culture from a Chaldean town called Ur, not far south of the point of beginning in Babylon. God didn't call him until he was seventy-five years old. The story of his wanderings for the next forty years or so reveals some of the highlights of God's work in him as He converted him from an idol worshipper to the epitome of Godly faith and obedience.

Jumping from Abraham down through the entire history of these people, up to the birth of Jesus, man's sinful nature is a major theme. Only two men of the Old Testament, whose lives have been described, appear to have nothing mentioned about them regarding their sinful nature. These are Joseph and Daniel. As a people, they were almost continuously reminded of God's love and power. They were also instructed most clearly and in great detail, as to God's purpose for them and His requirement of them. The entire biblical account may be characterized by the ups and downs of their obedience, or the tug of war of good vs. evil. Sin, deep rooted and wide spread, prevailed more than did the ways God had taught them. This is most evident from the time when the Tribes of Israel came to the easterly shore of the Red Sea to become the nation Israel, until Jesus came ushering in a whole new dispensation. We see sin and its consequences on both a personal as well as a corporate level, evidenced by the good or bad fortunes of not only the nation Israel, but the surrounding pagan nations as well.

Backing up to Abraham again, we see God's plan for the nation Israel unfold through his son Isaac producing Jacob who would father the twelve tribes from which the nation would grow. Sin and its painful consequences are evidenced in essentially every principal participant in this saga. As noted, of the many participants, only Joseph, the eleventh son of Jacob, escaped having any of his sins being revealed in the Scripture. The Old Testament depicts the brothers of Joseph as a despicable lot making one wonder why God would chose such a bunch from which to forge His own special nation. But the answer is quite evident. They, we, everyone, is hopelessly wicked and have hearts as described in Jeremiah 17:9. So, why should we be so surprised that God chose this motley lot? Where could He find any collection of twelve who were better? God has no problem working with what is available, as bad as it may be. That should give each of us great hope that we too can be used by God for His purpose!

Scripture tells us that they were in Egypt for 430 years, and it is silent as to their character and conduct after Joseph died until Moses was born. It's commonly believed that they were slaves during that 400 plus years. However, this was not the case. They became slaves considerably later under a completely different Egyptian dynasty, which had no cause to honor any of the commitments that the earlier dynasty had made to Joseph. Dr. Nolan Jones, in his "Chronology of the Old Testament," established with compelling evidence that the servitude could not have been more than 135 years before the birth of Moses and, therefore, was no more than a total of 215 years until the Exodus. With their patriarch Jacob gone, and Joseph, their benefactor and moral example also gone, it is reasonable to conclude that whatever ways of Godly worship and conduct the brothers may have known were soon lost in the subsequent generations. The idol worship and other pagan ways of the Egyptians most likely penetrate their culture quite deeply. This, no doubt, became even more pervasive when they became slaves and were thereby denied some, or perhaps all, of the last vestiges of their original heritage. Under the servitude it is known for example, that they were even forbidden the custom of circumcision. We also know from the narrative regarding the birth of Moses, that the Israelites were required to kill their male babies. This was to hold down their population, the number of which was seen as a threat to the then ruling dynasty. Can we see something like "poetic justice" or a "tit for tat" in that the tenth plague took the first-born male from every Egyptian household? We need only to look around us here today to see how effectively and quickly a society can descend into depravity when it is induced to accept ungodly ways. Look what has happened to our whole culture in just forty years since God was removed from the schools and the killing of pre-born human babies was legalized and encouraged. On the basis of all of this, it is evident that by the time of Exodus, while their racial identity seems to have been well preserved, there was bound to have been little or no remembrance of the God of Abraham nor of how or why He was to be worshipped and obeyed. So, except for their bloodline, we can conclude that there was little difference between these children of Israel and the Egyptians with whom they had so closely commingled for centuries.

All of this has been mentioned in order to put into proper perspective the reason for the low level of spiritual understanding and faith in our Creator God with which they left Egypt. The fact that so many, perhaps all of the families, adhered to the ritual of sacrificing a lamb and smearing the door frame with its blood was more likely motivated by a supernatural prompting from God rather than any residual of understanding of faith. The ten miracles, plagues conveyed through Moses, certainly must have impressed them and caused them to be more easily convinced to implement that instruction, but it hardly can be viewed as evidence of a genuine faith in God. They did obey Moses and moved out in accordance with his instructions, recognizing this once-in-a-lifetime opportunity. But their resolve quickly vanished when they reached the sea and saw Pharaoh coming with his army. That repeated vanishing of faith in God was evidenced over and over during their stay in the desert. It took them but three days to get out of Egypt, but it took nearly forty years to get Egypt out of them. The greatest sin, that of unbelief and also that of idol worship, remained in their hearts in spite of all of the miracles and love God quite personally and dramatically provided them. Look what happened at Mount Sinai. After Moses came down from the mountain and told the people all that God had instructed, they said, *"All that the Lord hath said will we do, and be obedient"* (Exodus 24:7). However, only a few days later, their leader Moses returned to the mountain and remained there for forty days. But long before his return, panic gripped them. God's

Word and their commitment to it were forgotten. Without Moses' physical presence to support their "faith," their resolve to be obedient faded away. Words, even from God, couldn't support them. They quickly reverted to their desire for a former comfort, that of a physical image, an idol, the golden calf that they had worshipped while in Egypt. Therefore they prevailed on Aaron to make for them a golden idol like that which they had worshipped in Egypt (Exodus 32). They were willing to worship God as just another god, but felt the need for an experiential physical god they could see and pray to. Aaron was a Godly man, yet he yielded to their demands for the sake of consensus. Isn't this the embryo of both the "user friendly church" and the ecumenical policies of today's "Christian religion?" The less there is of serious Bible study and genuine understanding of Scripture as the rock foundation of faith, the weaker and more vulnerable to false beliefs does the Christian body become. The golden calf of today is the pastor whose sermons are filled with pleasant, social advice seemingly derived from Bible verses but which are always pleasant feel-good platitudes. Never do we hear of our hopelessly sinful state curable only by our Redeemer. When, if ever, are such words as repentance or obedience to God's Word heard from a pulpit? Today's Christianity would better be called merely "churchanity" because, while Jesus is spoken of, more often than not, He is forced to share His throne with some form of modern day golden calf. This translates to blasphemy, apostasy, heresy, criminal negligence through willful ignorance, and in the end eternal damnation.

Scripture tells us that the forty years of wilderness wandering was punishment for their sin of lacking faith in His promise of protection and victory when they would cross into the Promised Land. It was only three months after their entry into the wilderness when Moses made that trip up to Mt. Sinai to receive the Ten Commandments (Exodus 19:1), and to teach them the laws, as well as what God had given them to know regarding what he would have of them. They were given not only the Ten Commandments, which made clear the basics of what God viewed as sin, but also how to worship and how to be spared the spiritual consequences of sin. This is when all of the processes and implements of worship dealing with blood sacrifice were specified. These artifacts included such items as the Arc of the Covenant, the Mercy Seat and the Tabernacle along with all of its accouterments. Having thus set up the theocratic government and all of its decreed privileges, obligations and behavioral codes, they were commanded to proceed on the eleventh day journey to Kadesh-barnea. It was from this location that they were to move on into the Promised Land. We all know how their lack of faith in God and His promises of protection and victory caused them to hesitate. This in turn resulted in God's punishment of forbidding their entry into the Land, but instead to spend forty years in wilderness wanderings until every single person over age twenty had died, all accept Joshua and Kaleb, the two who were trusting of God's protection. The wilderness wanderings reveal very little as to an increase on faith or reduction of sin. They repeatedly expressed a desire to return to Egypt, even to slavery. However, when they finally crossed under Joshua's leadership, there did seem to be a stronger faith consensus, at least for a while.

From there on throughout the entire Old Testament recording of the exploits of His chosen people, that 1450 year period from the time of Exodus to the coming of Jesus, we see precious little conformance to God's ways. God spoke to them through the prophets for more than 1000 years, teaching and prophesying His intensions, but seldom would they listen and even less often offer any semblance of obedience and resistance to sin. Then, for about four hundred years you might say He gave them over to Satan until once more He would reappear and offer His love and righteous ways through our blessed Lord and Savior Christ Jesus. Throughout those many centuries of knowing through the written word, all that God wanted of them, the ways of the world, Satan's ways, always seemed more attractive. Sin and punishment, as having a cause and effect linkage, never seemed to be recognized in the hearts of those who chose sin, and so the temptation to sin was seldom thwarted by forethought of any consequences, as long as the world had no objections. For the most part, rituals were observed, but sincere worship was scarce. As it was then, so it is today, but even more so today, during these end times, as the world moves toward, and revels in, unconstrained, unabashed sinfulness, that total departure from the true God. What did Jesus find when He brought His divine presence and holy message to the world? Sin prevailed everywhere, and even more so than it had in earlier times. His chosen people, through who by His earlier instructions through Moses and the prophets were to have evangelized their faith, failed completely to do so, and thus they sunk even deeper into apostasy. They had not only kept His teachings to themselves but during the four hundred years of God's "silence," after the last prophet, Malachi, they had actually added to and subtracted from His sacred instructions by formulating a perverted self centered self serving religion with no "redeeming" value. This is demonstrated by how Jesus attacked the ways of the Pharisees, the official and undisputed leaders and the purveyors of the legacy He had left them through the sacred Scripture. Here we could say that the powerful threads of sin had been cunningly woven into the whole fabric of their religious belief, that very belief with which God had so carefully clothed His people through His love. It was the power of these sinful threads that now held together the spiritually worthless temple rituals, along with the false doctrines, which they preached and by which they lived.

Jesus introduced a new dispensation and a different way of recognizing the "sinfulness of sin" with all of its horrible yet seductive disguises and consequences. He proved Himself to be the Messiah, the Son of God, and the One who would come to save the world and provide the way to eternal life through His power over sin. Jesus fulfilled *every* prophecy, which predicted His coming, and also demonstrated through His coming that He was the One. Yet that powerful thread of sin, which by then had permeated the souls of the Pharisee / Sanhedrin leadership of Israel, spread a veil over their eyes so that they could not or would not, acknowledge Him for who He was. Instead, they chose to kill Him rather than shed their prominence, leadership, and carnal comforts they enjoyed in their pious self-righteousness yet woefully sinful ways. Because of their denial of Him, these "chosen" people temporarily lost their exalted position as

God's earthly representatives. Instead Jesus trained His twelve "sowers" to go forth and plant His great truth throughout the world, the truth that was to grow and form the church of which Christ Jesus is the Head and the Rock foundation of assured salvation.

With Jesus' suffering, death and resurrection, a whole new spiritual enterprise, or dispensation, came into being. Sin, and how it could be dealt with, was, of course, the primary purpose and focus and His momentous achievement. Prior to this event, the souls of all of the faithful, who died from Adam on to the moment of Jesus' resurrection, were sent to a comfortable "way station" called Sheol, located near the center of the earth "next door" to where the condemned souls were sent to suffer. They were, of course, heaven bound, but could not yet go there, because their sins had not been cleansed away but merely covered. One could say Sheol was like Ellis Island to the millions of European immigrants who sought permanent residence here during the late nineteenth and early twentieth centuries. They were quarantined there until their health had been assessed and other conditions of entry into the USA had been satisfied.

From the very beginning when God killed the first living creature to ever die, in order to provide a "covering" for Adam's and for Eve's sinful nature, a shedding of innocent blood had been God's ordained way of dealing with man's sins. In the five books called the Books of Moses, God explained in minute detail how this was to be done in order to affect this temporary covering for those who had demonstrated their faith by their obedience and compliance to this and other rituals. Because there can be absolutely no sin whatsoever entering heaven, it was not possible for any saved soul to enter there, until those sins were removed. The covering only got them to Ellis Island, that is Sheol, but when the Lamb of God was sacrificed, Jesus' precious blood instantly and completely cleansed those souls. The covering that had allowed them to proceed to the way station was no longer needed. They were now clean and pure. It was at that moment when Jesus Himself left Sheol, after visiting there for three days and three nights, that He brought them out of Sheol and straight to heaven where they now reside, waiting for their incorruptible bodies which will be delivered to them by Jesus at the Rapture. There is no longer a need for covering of sins. Jesus paid in full for the sins of all of His faithful from the beginning of time to the end of time.

For a while the efforts of the "sowers," the Apostles whom Jesus has equipped and sent out, had great success in spreading His Gospel. The world was yet filled with sinful pagans, idol worshippers, but Christianity was making major inroads and spreading throughout the world. Satan-led persecution and execution sought to eliminate believers, but God allowed a remnant of His to remain and "re-seed" those purged areas. By around 330 A.D., Satan found agency for his most effective way to damage the church. That was to subtly subvert the church from within. Through the Roman Emperor Constantine, the previously underground, much persecuted but extremely faithful church was suddenly legalized and even made fashionable. Evidence seems to indicate that while it was underground, it was made up of groupings of people who were genuinely saved believers in Jesus as Lord and Savior. They devoted their lives to that faith and would rather die than forsake it, as many did. But now, under Constantine, they could walk freely professing their faith. However, this was not before the church became thoroughly impregnated with pagan rituals, customs and idols, no longer having any vestige of that purity it enjoyed previously. Finally, under a Caesar once removed after Constantine, this compromised "Christianity" became the state religion. The blasphemous sin-filled doctrines of the evolving "official" Christian church can easily be characterized by the lifestyles and decrees of the subsequent leaders of the church, the Popes. Anyone of these for many generations would casily have met the requirements for the position of antichrist, and they did, in fact, function to a large extent in that capacity as they persecuted and caused the execution of millions of the genuinely faithful, and even those who merely possessed Bibles.

We might consider here what Jesus, through Scripture calls the "Kingdom of God that is this present dispensation which is the church age. It is a manifestation of another people "set aside" by God, as were the Jews, until they rejected Christ Jesus. Therefore, we can say, this age has been and is, even more wickedly sinful than that previous age. Satan keeps learning, sharpening his skills and finding new ways to propagate sin and destroy souls.

The Pharisees, for the most part, were men of some integrity, deep learning of Scripture, and dedicated to what they believed was God's truth. Because they were wrong, because they projected God's Word into a Satan-inspired, twisted, tangled assembly of additional laws and rituals, which obscured the purity of God's way, does not negate what was probably in some perverted sense, their good intentions. As it is said "hell is paved with good intentions." So their good intentions did little to benefit their trusting flocks.

However, the hierarchy of the official "Christian Church," at least until Martin Luther, cannot be credited with even a modicum of those qualities. Satan finally had *his* church. His church for centuries totally controlled the kings of Europe and amassed physical wealth and power beyond anything previously imagined even by Greece, Egypt, Babylon, Assyria, or even Rome at its pinnacle.

Spiritually it was antithetical to the true church of our Lord Christ Jesus and it persecuted to the death any and all who were true believers, in every country into which its tentacles could reach. An understanding of its structure, its doctrines, its activities and its leaders can lead one to a justified conclusion that it could serve as a prototype and preview of reign of the Antichrist during the tribulation. It was rich in rituals and superstitions and destitute of any trace of Christian holiness. Later, evidence of this is profoundly expressed by Pope Leo X as he exclaimed to his cardinals, "what a profitable thing this myth about Jesus Christ has been to us." He was far, far from being the exception among the many popes who proceeded and followed him. Institutionalized sin reigned everywhere except where small underground remnants of the real church could be found. In essence, it was again the persecuting power of Rome of the second and third centuries and well beyond. What had changed was the leadership, Caesar to Pope, and unabashed paganism to a pseudo Christianity, masking an even great satanic influence.

What has been described was the status of the official "Christian Church," all the way to the time of Luther and beyond. The reformation under Luther brought back a great many of the biblical truths and a rejection of some of the heresies, which had become institutionalized. The result was the formation of the so-called Protestant churches. However, these various "denominations," while at first restoring Jesus to His rightful place, failed to address and correct a number of the other institutionalized heresies such as the allegorization of most of Revelation, as well as of certain critical parts of Genesis. Thus there remained in the "reformed churches" several easy points of entry for Satan to do to those "churches" what he had done to the organized "mother church" under Constantine and beyond. It took a while for Satan to establish himself fully in these new institutions, which collectively did contain large segments of the genuine church body. These early years of the reformation, until the beginning of the twentieth century, were the prophesized years symbolized by the church of Philadelphia as described in Revelation 3:7–13. This was probably the most prolific of all ages in terms of biblical understanding and the salvation of souls. It was the age when a large majority of the western world had Bibles and who read, effectively understood, and tried with sincerity to live the essential Christian doctrine. It was also the age of evangelism, where biblical truths were spread across the entire world.

However, at the same time, Satan was busy raising a new crop of apostates and conjuring up a number of pseudo-Christian cults and other deceiving belief systems. He was also burrowing his way into each of the denominational Christian churches, planting many seeds of diversions, divisions and confusion. These seeds soon germinated, and during the whole twentieth century, grew into the grotesque monster which most of them are today. The parable of the mustard seed is a graphic and accurate representative of what exists today, which may, in the abject ignorance, be called the "Christian Church." If the great late church fathers such as Luther, Spurgeon, Wesley, etc. could see even the best of the denominational church of today they would be sickened unto death as to what had become of the institutions in which unvarnished truths about repentance, obedience and the nature of sin had once been so effectively delivered to seeking souls.

The Christian church is for the greatest part perfectly typified by what Jesus said it would be in the end times before the rapture, when He described the church of Laodicea in Revelation 3:14–22. It's the church age about which Jesus had absolutely nothing good to say. He said to it, "*. . . I will spew thee out of my mouth . . .*" Of course, there remains a small remnant of saved believers scattered throughout the world. This will remain so; otherwise, there would be no living soul to rapture.

One could go on and on compiling mountains of evidence as to the terrible spiritual decay present today in what are called Christian churches. Except for a small, faithful remnant inside each gathering of professors of the faith, there is no spiritually effective difference between them and the world at large. Scripture tells us most clearly just what the end time condition of the world would be, and that is exactly how it is. Each of its facets, the economic, political, military, social and spiritual realms are in the final stages of preparation for the eagerly awaited coming world leader. He is called by many names, but it will surely be the one we call Antichrist, who will solve all the world's problems and bring peace and prosperity. That he will surely do, for about three and a half years, according to Scripture. We now live in a society in which sin in every form, has been standardized, legalized, enforced, and lovingly embraced in one way or another across the entire world. How much longer can the patience of our sin-hating God endure before He unleashes His wrath on such a world? Scripture says, not much longer!

5. The Final Disposition of Sin

As we have seen throughout the study of God's word, sin has been a dominant, debilitating and evil force, which began with Adam's first sin. But how could this possibly be? Our Creator God, who made it a point of emphasis, as He made the various components of His creation, that it was good. Would He also create sin, which He most surely hates? If we define sin, as we did earlier in this essay and as

Scripture defines it, as being anything that is contrary to God, the question has a chance of being answered, even at our lowly human intellectual level. Consider what darkness is. It isn't anything; we have simply given a name to the absence of light. What about cold? Cold, as with darkness, has no real meaning, but cold, like darkness is absolutely nothing; it is the absence of heat. It has been observed by others that sin can also be similarly characterized. It is the absence of God and godliness. From the human perspective it seems more complicated than that, because of the very many forms and degrees of intensity it can take. Heat is also measured in degrees upward from absolute zero, which is no heat, and light is also measured upward by intensity from the base of zero light; this is absolute darkness. Man exhibits degrees of absence from God as well. However, from God's perspective, when it comes to salvation, there are no degrees; it is digital; it is on or off; one is either living in accordance with God's will or is absent of godliness; there are no degrees. Degrees of ungodliness have meaning only in the positional placement of the ungodly soul in the lake of fire. No matter how rebellious and disbelieving of the idea one may be, the entire human race, without exception, *every person,* has an incurable sin nature. To use the above definition of sin, there is no one who is not absent from God. Sin, that propensity to keep rejecting the presence of God in our hearts, along with a heart already full of a lifetime of such rejection, is by definition a heart completely empty, completely lacking in God, or godliness. This fact is incredibly difficult to accept, and most of the world scoffs and snarls at the idea. Scripture, God's Holy and inerrant Word, offers a means of restoration, a way to bring heat where there is none, to bring light into where it doesn't exist, and to bring God into a heart absent of Him. He only asks that first we need to recognize that we are hopelessly empty, condemned sinners, without God within us, we are lost, and that our only hope is for a Savior. It's at the moment when we realize this that God's love and mercy begins to manifest. The heat comes on, and light begins to shine. God gave His blessed Son Christ Jesus for that very purpose, for He and only He is capable of eliminating that absence of God we call sin from our souls, and fill that void with God's Holy Spirit.

Lest anyone be led to carry this analogy too far, it should be recognized that thoughts, actions and behavior contrary to God's will are far from nothing in the context of life's purpose, and individual, as well as corporate destinies. Sin in the true sense is very real, and the consequences are both earth and life shattering. The purpose of the analogy was simply to illustrate the fact that God did not create sin. As far as the consequences of sin are concerned, the condition of the world, with all of its pain and suffering, is the consequence of the collective sins of all mankind from Noah to the present. Failure to understand and comprehend this fact is the result of one's inability to recognize the intricacies, complexities and subtleties of cause and effect, as well as to accept the fact that we all have a sin nature and all contribute to that collective consequence. Therefore, to varying degrees, we are all guilty of the causes and we are all victims of the effects. It is convenient and seemingly self-cleansing to blame God for the terrible macro conditions of the world, just as it is to find blame in each other for the painful micro circumstances in our daily lives. As long as we persist in blaming God for these ills, of which He is not guilty, we can never have that close relationship with Him that we want to have, and that He wants to have with us. It is wrong that God should suffer the wrath of His creation for not preventing or correcting the conditions which man himself has created. God offered a perfect solution through Jesus, and if he had been universally accepted, it would have ended all pain and suffering. Instead, only a few always but a remnant, have accepted the offer. Unfortunately, because of its limited acceptance, it could not provide that universal solution. Therefore, even those who have accepted do not escape the all-encompassing earthly consequences of sin. Their great and unique reward comes upon leaving this world and spending a blissful eternity with Him in the heavenlies. Also, as we shall see in time, God will end the mess man has made, and there will then be a world free of sin and its terrible consequences. There is much more to be said on this matter of blaming God for all the bad in the world. As I got on this track I realized that the topic is too extensive to be developed any further in the context of this paper. God willing, it will be the subject of a separate essay.

Having now, I pray, established the fact that God didn't create sin and that sin, having begun with Adam's choice to reject God's way, we should now see just how God planned from the beginning to finally dispose of sin, that is, to be forever rid of His absence from the human heart. For six thousand years, God has patiently, and sometimes not so patiently as we have seen, allowed rebellion from Him (sinfulness) to continue. Can any thinking person believe that He would allow this to continue forever, that He would not one day say ENOUGH, and simply end all rebellion? Scripture makes it clear that He will call a halt, and that the countdown to that moment is now in process. In order to totally eliminate sin, He has chosen to literally destroy and replace heaven and earth. That should tell us much regarding how pervasive and deep-rooted sin has become. His first choice was a worldwide flood to remove this blight. Now Scripture tells us He will end it with an all-consuming fire. The Old Testament prophets alluded to His plan quite precisely. However, it was through Jesus' revelation of Himself in the Book of Revelation where we see most clearly the unfolding of His final resolution of the problem.

Here it is in a "nut shell." As we look around us we would have to be blind not to see that the world is drifting at an ever-accelerating rate away from the God of the Holy Bible. Scripture tells us in Luke 21:24 that God will allow this to continue, "*. . . until the times of the gentiles be fulfilled.*" Perhaps this is when apostasy will be so firmly established, and drifting away from God so advanced, that there will be an end to conversions to Christ. Then the Rapture will occur. In the Rapture, Jesus will empty the earth of every believer. With the concurrent removal of the Holy Spirit, who will have until then restrained the advancement of the anti-god forces, the preparation for the coming world leader, Antichrist, will now proceed very rapidly. Also this worldwide pressure cooker of pent up sinfulness will explode allowing mans' godless sin filled nature to come to full bloom. Into this will enter Antichrist with his incredible Satan-given political, economic, managerial and "religious" skills. Because of this, and through the "democratic" process, he will gain control of the world power and will rule for seven years. For three and one half of those years he will provide peace and prosperity. He will continue to bring about such great signs and wonders that he will find it possible to declare himself to be god and have the world believe him. He will place his image in the Holy of Holies in the Jewish temples in Jerusalem. This act will commence what is called the great tribulation, during which about three-fourths of the world population will be destroyed as well as most of the earth's livable environments.

During this period to the very end of the tribulation, God will offer several opportunities to be cleansed of sin for those who are willing to come to Jesus. These will be many millions, but most will be executed by Antichrist and his agents. So while God will allow godlessness to flourish all in accordance with man's free will, His mercy will prevail for all who choose to renounce rebellion from him through Jesus. At the end of the reign of the antichrist, he will be cast into the lake of fire, while Jesus, now having returned to earth and sitting on David's throne, will judge the "sheep and the goats" (Matthew 25:32). These will be those people who are alive at the end of the tribulation. Those who were loyal to antichrist will be cast into hell, while those who survived, who were believers along with those who served God's purpose by helping saved souls, will remain to repopulate the temporarily rehabilitated earth. Thus sin will have been dealt with most severely.

However, even after this, while Christ Jesus in the physical person, reigns here on earth for the next thousand years, sin will yet be present. There will be those who will for the most part, secretly want to rebel, but out of fear will not. I suppose that that is why, at the end of this thousand years God will allow Satan to again express himself on earth. Satan will somehow draw each and every one of these rebellious hearts to him. Using them, he will form a great army, which will again seek to attack Jerusalem in order to overthrow King Christ Jesus. The battle will end almost before it began, because Jesus will have simply spoken, and "fire came down from God out of heaven and devoured them" (Revelation 20:9).

From this we can conclude that all forms of unbelief, rejection, rebellion, sin, will have been stamped from the universe. All that now remains of humanity is sin-free and will spend eternity with the Triune Godhead, the Father, the Son, and the Holy Spirit in the New Jerusalem, the new city on the new earth under the heavens (Revelation 21). Satan, Antichrist, the false Prophet, and all who rebelled, having failed to recognize and accept the Savior, will have his her own place in the lake of fire which is in the outer darkness. That is how God will finally dispose of all sin and have a holy people unto Himself forever. Godlessness had so permeated the entire earth that it was like the natural human heart, totally and desperately wicked. Just as He gives every redeemed man a new heart, so also He will provide a new heaven and earth.

Well, there you have it. It's probably far too long and boring to retain the attention of most, and much too short to be anywhere near a comprehensive study, which such a complex subject deserves. Nevertheless, in the "immortal" words of Pontius Pilate when he etched on the cross "Jesus of Nazareth King of the Jews," which expressed the acrostic "YHWH," the name of God. "I have written what I have written."

—14—

The Consequences of Sin

Every redeemed Christian knows that by grace through faith in the completed work of Jesus on the cross, that one has been forgiven of all sin and now has eternal life, and a home waiting for him or her in heaven. Everyone who has ever lived was an incorrigible sinner, hopelessly in debt in his sins, and by divine judgment destined for hell for lack of any ability to pay his debt. But for those who truly believe in the redemptive power of the cross, Jesus has fully paid the debt, leaving the believer judiciously sinless and therefore a bona fide member of the Body of Christ.

But what about the earthly consequences of those forgiven sins? They remain. They demand to be reckoned with. They did not disappear from the physical world, as did the sins themselves from the spiritual realm. As we look around the world in general, we can see almost everywhere the ever-worsening condition of humanity. What we are actually seeing is the accumulative compounded consequences of about 4500 years of the sins of all mankind since Noah. That is what we might call the ambient macro atmosphere in which we all live. Now, let's look more closely at each of your own micro atmospheres over which we have some, but limited control. That is where we live as individuals, in our town, family, job, church, etc. Here we can examine our individual lives and see the many consequences of our own unfortunate actions that we may choose to call indiscretions, transgressions, mistakes or what you will, but in fact, they are simply sins, and we live in the additionally polluted atmosphere of their consequences.

When you committed to Jesus and were redeemed, you know that all your sins were forgiven. You know because Scripture told you so. You know because of the Gospel's truth contained in God's Word. Perhaps you never thought about it, but the consequence of your past sins still remain in your life. Not only that, but so it will be with the consequence of the sins you have yet to commit. These sins are no less vile to God and no less causes of undesired consequence simply because they are committed by a saved soul, than were those you committed before being saved. If, as a young Christian, you haven't yet grown sufficiently to bring out some meaningful amount of control over your sinful nature through your love for Jesus, and in gratitude for all He has done, perhaps this additional insight may add some incentive. Very likely those sins, which you yet have difficulty constraining, you can now see will also have hurting earthly consequences even though they can no longer condemn your soul.

If you haven't thought much about this perhaps, you are wondering how these consequences can seriously manifest in your personal life. Let's look at a lie. Everyone lies. Whether it is a full-fledged, deliberately articulated untruth, a half-truth, an omission of truth where a true statement was appropriate, a non-verbal deception, or a truth stated in such a way as to knowingly lead to a false conclusion, it is a lie in the context of sin. Most of us "get away" with these sins, or believe we do often enough to feel justified in continuing them, for what we rationalize at the moment to be for the "greater good." But as sins, they have earthly personal consequences. The obvious consequence is when one is caught, and is branded a liar, judged unreliable and untrustworthy, and all of the resulting ramifications, such as loss of stature, of esteem, and of opportunity. It is not being believed when telling the truth. It is not being believed when it is vital to you that you be believed. How many truths cancel the image of being a liar in the mind of the one having been lied too? Seventy, or seventy times seventy? Probably no amount of truth can ever erase the stigma from the minds of the victims, and we must therefore continue indefinitely bearing the consequences of those sins. Consider theft, or sexual "transgressions," or any other form of sin, and substitute it for "liar" in the above scenarios. You can be sure that there will be adverse consequences, that may plague you for the rest of your life.

I believe that the most tragic and painful consequences are not necessarily those, that merely effect our reputation and our dealings with others. These may in time fade away or be lost through a changed location of one sort or another. The worst kind are those with ramifications that affect our loved ones, that warp their lives, and for which we and they never stop paying. Here, the consequences are compounded because they are levied on the innocent as well as on the guilty. Although certainly not limited to any one type of sin, the consequences of sexual sin, both in and out of marriage, are probably the most graphic in terms of how cause and effect are clearly evidenced, with effect being essentially synonymous with what we are here referring to as consequences. The pain and payment as a consequence is not confined to only the sinner, but also to parents and friends and especially to any children involved. Here, the consequence cannot only last the sinner's lifetime, but also the lifetime of the innocent offspring, and even beyond to subsequent generations. This is very evident when we examine the "macro atmosphere."

So what can be done? For the redeemed sinner, acknowledgment, prayer, conviction, confession, and repentance are always the most important first steps. Next, admission and a request for forgiveness from the victim, if possible, are appropriate, if not essential. While these may provide some relief of guilt for the sinner's conscience, it more than likely will not eliminate much if any of the earthly consequence. Payment will continue, perhaps softened, but not abated.

Perhaps the most valuable thing here is the lesson to be learned. If you are truly born-again, especially early in your redemption, you realize the incredible love and sacrifice our Lord provided in order that you may have eternal life in heaven. For this, you are exceedingly grateful, and out of that gratitude you want to be all that He wants you to be. Yet, you are still caught in sin, which you are yet unable to remove from your life. Surely this will happen over time, because once you are His son or daughter He will never cease His beneficial work in you. But in the meantime you are yet piling up sins, that you know you could avoid, if only you had sufficient strength to resist them. Maybe now that you know that there are earthly consequences to even forgiven sins, you may, in this, find additional motivation that will help you to amend your ways so as not to pile on any more conse-quences. I pray so, and may God bless you in your increased efforts.

Please note, that although I haven't cited chapter and verse in making the above observation, Scripture is replete with confirming evidence that this is true. The recorded aspects of the lives of nearly every character in both the Old and New Testament well attest to this. On a personal note, what I've described as the consequence of sin, I find very poignantly expressed in my own walk, and which, it seems, that I've been appointed to contend with every day of my life, for the rest of my life.

—15—

The Covering of Sins

Scripture has several interesting and provocative verses regarding this subject that are worthy of examination in order that they maybe be understood, rather than simply "covered over." Proverbs 10:12 observes that "hatred stirreth up strife, but love covereth sins." Psalm 32:1 tells us that "blessed is he whose transgression is forgiven, whose sin is covered." In Psalm 85:2 we are told ". . . thou (God) hast covered all their sin." Also, in the New Testament we find sins covered, as in 1 Peter 4:8 where we read ". . . and above all things have fervent love among yourselves; for love shall cover a multitude of sins." Also James tells us in chapter 5:20, "brethren if any of you do err from the truth and one convert him, let him know that he which converteth the sinner from the error of his way shall save a soul from death, and shall hide a multitude of sins."

The three Old Testament references are fairly easy to understand, because they predate Jesus and the redemption He provided. Prior to this, all sins were merely "covered" because our Lord had not yet shed His blood through which they could be washed away. All of the animal sacrifices and other God-ordained rituals administered for the purpose of dealing with sin did not cause forgiveness of sins, but merely "covered" them over and provided in effect a salvation "credit slip" which was to be redeemed when the Redeemer came.

However, the New Testament references require a deeper insight to explain them because the Redeemer has come, and all sins have been washed from the souls of genuine believers. Both Peter and James are speaking to "brethren" and therefore to saved souls. So the question to be answered is what sins are being covered, and why should they be "covered" or "hidden"? In the case of James 5:19, 20 we have a powerful example of what is called the "sin unto death." A brethren who has backslidden into chronic sin is very likely engaging in a sin unto death as referred to in 1 John 5:16. This, of course, is not spiritual death, but simply premature physical death. James is telling us that if another brother can convert the backslider, that is prevail on him to end his sinful way, he can save him from that premature death. If this effort is successful, it "shall hide a multitude of sins." At this point it seems appropriate to ask, whose sins, what does it mean to "hide" them, and what is the purpose and benefit of hiding them?

Whose sins? While there are some who believe otherwise, it is my contention that it is the converters sins, which may be "hidden," and not the one who has been converted. Should the one whose sins were so vile, and protracted, but was saved from God's just intervention which would have resulted in a premature death, be rewarded by having them also "hidden?" The sinner was amply blessed. I believe that it was the "converter" the brethren who saved him from the sin unto death punishment, who receives the benefits of this "hiding of sin, whatever that means.

What does it mean to "hide" sins, and what is the purpose and benefit, are questions, which it seems necessary to answer together, in conjunction with related questions, such as: from whom or from what are these sins being hidden or covered over, and how is this achieved? Surely nothing is hidden from God. Therefore, because He is of necessity involved in this process, the term "hidden and covered over" is probably more allegorized than literal. Furthermore, we are here dealing with "brethren," those whose sins have already been spiritually forgiven. Therefore, whatever is going on has nothing to do with eternal security, but is instead strictly of an earthly physical nature. Once we recognize this, and the fact that there are earthly, that is physical, emotional consequences of sin, the pieces to the puzzle come together quite rapidly.

The central message here, I believe, is that if one intercedes and rescues a brother from a sin unto death, he may be rewarded by having a "multitude" of his sins hidden, that is covered over in such a way that some of their earthly consequences may be diminished, softened, or removed. I believe that 1 Peter 4:8 is telling us that same thing regarding similar benefits which "fervent love" can achieve in the lives of brethren. What is fervent love? It would seem in this context that it is a love, which sacrifices, which goes well beyond normal limits to help a brother or sister to stay the course, to live the God-ordained life, which will preclude the condition, which could result in sin unto death. What a wonderful gift this is, that through God's love in us, and our sincere unselfish application thereof, God may choose to "cover," that is soften or to eliminate the deserving earthly consequences of our sins. Can you see the thrilling beauty of this? He is offering us a way to obtain the very opposite of the consequence of a sin unto death!

If you haven't thought much about the consequence of sin in our daily lives, reading my essay titled "The Consequences of Sins" should be quite helpful as might also be "Sin unto Death," which I wrote earlier. These might be useful in evaluating the merits of what is stated here. It should be an axiom in every believer's life to accept no alleged truths unless they are clearly validated by careful study of the Scriptures. Although there is much scriptural evidence of the earthly consequences of forgiven sins, and several references to sin unto death, as well as the concept of "covering or hiding sin" I have found no concrete Scripture basis for combining these in the manner described above, although I believe that there is ample evidence from which to conclude so by the many Scripture inferences. If you disagree, great! But don't just leave it at that. Search out the truth for yourself. The consequence of these scripturally offered clues is far too great to be dismissed and to simply trust it to luck. Surely some serious prayer for wisdom and discernment in these matters might provide much for your benefit in terms of how you might improve the quality of your remaining earthly existence. Please let me know if the

Holy Spirit provides you with clearer answers than I have been offered and have here shared.

—16—

Confession of Sin

Everyone professing to be a Christian knows that "by grace you are saved through faith; and that not of yourselves; it is a gift of God, not of works lest any man boast." (Ephesians 2:8) But there can be no "faith" through which to be saved, unless there is an acknowledgement that there is a need to be "saved," and an understanding of what it is you need to be saved. A drowning man shouts for help, knowing that he can't save himself, because he can already feel the water filling his lungs; and so it is with the soul. Every soul is drowning in a sea of sin, and will surely die, unless saved. But unlike the unmistakable sensation of suffocation afforded by water entering the lungs, the deadly suffocation of the soul through sin can seldom be felt. It is discerned by only a few, and of these there is only a remnant who call with *sincerity* on the only One who can save them, our Lord and Savior Jesus Christ. In order to be saved by the grace through faith, the faith must be a saving faith. This is a faith which first acknowledges that it cannot be a saving faith unless it has the prerequisite admission and confession of sin, and the recognition of the hopelessly sinful nature of the soul.

Proverbs 28:13 tells us that "He that covereth his sins shall not prosper; but whoso confesseth them shall have mercy." That confession must be all encompassing, unqualified and sincerely felt and believed by the mind, soul and spirit if it is to lead to a true saving faith. Belief and confession by the mind alone is not enough and can only lead to a fictitious faith and thwarted salvation. All *would-be-saved* Christians should look carefully into their hearts and examine the true nature of their "confessions" and their forsaking of their sins. It can do much in the way of establishing in their own hearts whether or not their "faith" is genuine.

The great English pastor of the nineteenth century, Charles Spurgeon, preached a wonderful sermon titled "Confession of Sin," using seven scriptural verses, each of which included the words "I have sinned" as illustrative of how differently, and with what degree of sincerity this admission by various people has been expressed. The following will be an attempt to summarize, paraphrase, comment, and most often quote his brilliant, inspired insights on the subject.

1.   In Exodus 9:27 Pharaoh says, "I have sinned." This first case is one of a hardened sinner who when under great stress will confess, "I have sinned." This is like the "fox hole believer in battle." He confesses passionately while the battle rages, but soon forgets his "faith" once back where it is safe. Spurgeon observed:

> How many of the same sort of confessions, too, have we seen in times of cholera and fever and pestilence? Then our churches have been crammed with hearers, who, because so many funerals have passed their door, or so many died in the street, could not refrain from going up to God's house to confess their sins. And under that visitation, when one, two and three have been lying dead in the house, or next door, how many have thought they would really turn to God! But, alas! When the pestilence had done its work, conviction ceased; and when the bell had tolled the last time for a death caused by cholera, their hearts ceased to beat with penitence, and their tears did flow no more.

Since September 2002 a far more timely and relevant analogy for this type of "believer," would be the "9–11 believer." Praying was suddenly in great fashion, even in the media. Churches were filled, even politicians switched from preying to praying. How long did this sudden piety last? About as long as the media could attract viewers by its coverage of the event, and until the sitcoms could get back on schedule.

2.   In Numbers 22:34 Balaam says, "I have sinned." Here is a perfect example of the double-minded man referred to in James 1:8 "a double-minded man is unstable in all his ways." It seems evident that Balaam tried to serve the Lord and felt deeply in his confession, yet he was worldly-minded and he loved the wages of unrighteousness.

He was truly a prophet through whom God spoke, but while he stead-fastly refused to curse the Hebrews as Balak, King of Moab hired him to do, he nevertheless instructed the king on how to entice their young men to sin and thus to hopefully incur God's wrath on the whole nation. He offered sacrifice to God, but did so on a pagan alter. Spurgeon, in his precious way, puts this double-mindedness into personal perspective:

> This man seemed to have the voice of an angel at one time, and yet the very soul of a devil in his bowels. He was a terrible char-acter; he was a man of two things, a man who went all the way with two things to great extent. I know the Scripture says, "No man can serve two masters." Now this is often misunderstood. Some read it, "No man can *serve* two masters." Yes he can; he can serve three or four. The way to read it is this: " No man can serve two *masters*." They cannot both be masters. He can serve two, but they cannot both be his masters. A man can serve two who are his masters or twenty either; he may live for twenty different purposes, but he cannot live for more than one master purpose; there can only be one master purpose in his soul. But Balaam labored to serve two; it was like the people of whom it was said, "They feared the Lord and served other gods." Or like Rufus, who was a loaf of the same leaven; for you know our old king Rufus painted God on one side of his shield, and the devil on the other, and had underneath the motto: "Ready for both; catch who can." There are many such, who are ready for both. They meet a minister, and how pious and holy they are; on the Sabbath they are the most respectable and upright people in the world, as you would think; indeed they affect a drawl-ing in their speech which they think to be eminently religious. But on a weekday, if you want to find the greatest roughs and cheats, they are some of those men who are so sanctimonious in their piety. Now, rest assured, my hearers, that no confession of sin can be genuineness, unless it is a whole hearted one. It is of no use for you to say, "I have sinned," and then keep on sinning. "I have sinned," say you, and it is fair, fair face you show; but alas! Alas! For the sin you will go away and commit. Some men seem to be born with two characters. I remarked when in the library at Trinity College, Cambridge, I saw a very fine statue of Lord Byron. The librarian said to me, "Stand here sir." I looked and I said, "What a fine intellectual countenance! What a grand genius he was!" "Come here," he said, "to the other side." "Ah, what a demon!" There stands the man that could defy the deity." He seemed to have such a scowl and such a dreadful leer in his face; even as Mil-ton would have painted Satan when he said—"Better to reign in

hell than serve in heaven." I turned away and said to the librarian, "Do you think the artist designed this?" "Yes," he said, "he wished to picture the two characters; the great, the grand, the almost super human genius that he possessed, and yet the enormous mass of sin that was in his soul."

3.   In 1 Samuel 15:24, Saul says, "I have sinned." Saul is the classic example of the insincere man. While Balaam could seem to be sincere in two things Saul was not sincere in anything. His sincerity floated along with his circumstances, there was no sincerity in him. Over and over he expressed love for David only to then plot and vigorously seek to kill him. He molded lying excuses for his every sinful act, whenever it served him to do so. Spurgeon very skillfully connects this type of man with the Christian assembly, by the following:

> How many such we have in every Christian assembly; men who are easily molded! Say what you please to them, they always agree with you. They have affectionate dispositions, very likely a tender conscience; but then the conscience is so remarkably tender, that when touched it seems to give, and you are afraid to probe deeper; it heals as soon as it is wounded. There are some men who seem to have India-rubber hearts. If you do but touch them, there is an impression made at once; but then it is of no use, it soon restores itself to the original character.

> O sirs, too many of you have done the same; you have bowed your heads in church, and said, "We have erred and strayed from thy ways." And you did not mean what you said. You have come to your minister, you have said, "I repent of my sins." You did not then feel you were a sinner. You only said it to please him. And now you attend the house of God: no one more impressible than you; the tear will run down your check in a moment, but yet, notwithstanding all that, the tear is dried as quickly as it is brought forth, and you remain to all intents and purposes the same as you were before. To say, "I have sinned." in an unmeaning manner, is worse than worthless, for it is a mockery of God thus to confess with insincerity of heart.

> Balaam was the great bad man, great in all that he did; Saul was little in everything, except in stature—little in his good and little in his vice; and he was too much of a fool to be desperately bad though too wicked to be at anytime good.

4.   In Joshua 7:20, Acan says, "I have sinned." Here we have what Spurgeon calls, the case of the doubtful penitent. While he and all the

people had been instructed to take no spoil from Jericho, the temptation to keep some gold and silver and a garment was too much for him. Because of this single bit of disobedience, the whole tribe was condemned to defeat in their next battle. When God informed Joshua that there was leaven in the loaf, he sought out the culprit, and of course found Acan and the loot. Because Acan confessed, and because Joshua spoke kindly to him, some believe that even though he was stoned to death his soul may well have been saved. Other expositors are certain that his soul perished as well. But who knows. The saving quality of his confession cannot be verified through any available evidence, because he had no opportunity to provide a "track record." Thus it is, as with the thief on the cross, only God knows the condition of the heart.

Spurgeon has the following very unsettling observation to contribute to the matter, one that should give all of us serious concern.

> Ah! Dear friends, it has been my lot to stand by many a deathbed, and to see many such a repentance as this. I have seen the man, when worn to a skeleton, sustained by pillows in his bed, and he has said, when I have talked to him of judgment to come, 'Sir, I feel I have been guilty, but Christ is good; I trust in him. And I have said within myself. I believe the man's soul is safe." But I have always come away with the melancholy reflection that I had no proof of it beyond his own words; for it needs proof in acts and in future life, in order to sustain any firm conviction of a man's salvation. You know the great fact, that a physician once kept a record of a thousand persons who thought they were dying and whom he thought were penitents; he wrote their names down in a book as those who, if they died would go to heaven. They did not die, they lived, and he says that out of the whole thousand he had not three persons who turned out well afterward, but they returned to their sins again, and were as bad as ever. Ah! Dear friends, I hope none of you will have such a death-bed repentance as that; I hope your minister or your parents will not have to stand by your bedside, and then go away and say, "Poor fellow! I hope he is saved. But alas! Death-bed repentances are such flimsy things, such poor, such trivial grounds of hope that I am afraid, after all his soul may be lost." O! To die with an abundant entrance leaving a testimony behind that we have departed this life in peace! That is a far happier way than to die in doubtful manner, lying sick, hovering between two worlds, and neither ourselves nor yet our friends knowing to which of the two worlds

we are going. May God grant us grace to give in our lives evidences of true conversion, that our case may not be doubtful.

5.   In Matthew 27:4, Judas says, "I have sinned." Here we have the repentance of despair. We all know his story only too well. Judas, the thief and traitor, who betrayed our Lord for thirty pieces of silver. Later he repented and brought again the thirty pieces of silver to the chief priests and elders, saying, "I have sinned in that I have betrayed innocent blood," and cast down the pieces in the temple and went . . . and hanged himself." Spurgeon has this to say:

> Here is the worst kind of repentance of all; in fact, I know
> not that I am justified in calling it repentance; it must be called
> remorse of conscience. But Judas did confess his sin, and then
> went and hanged himself. O! That dreadful, that terrible, that hid-
> eous confession of despair.

Those of us who love Jesus, as did Spurgeon, have no compassion for Judas. He has been branded the epitome of villainy, the personification of evil, and without doubt is now (we hope) agonizing in one of the hottest spots in hell. But as I was writing this, it came to me very strongly, that I should not end my reporting of the matter without offering at least a summary of some other observations that suddenly leaped into my heart.

We all piously pay lip service to the premise that we are not to judge who is saved and who is not. For only God knows what is in the heart, and it is what is in the heart that determines whether or not one is saved. Yet does anyone doubt that the souls of Hitler, Stalin and Lenin were condemned to hell, or that all the Apostles are in Heaven? We do make judgments of this sort, when it seems so obvious. But is it always so obvious that we should *ever* reserve that right to ourselves? Read 2 Kings 21:1–18. Here we learn of the reign of Manasseh, reported to be one of the most sinful of all the kings in Judah. Verse 2 says, ". . . he did that which was evil in the sight of the Lord, after the abomination of the heathen. He rebuilt all the high places and alters to Baal which his father, the good king Hezekiah did destroy; he worshiped all the idols and served them; he used enchantments and set up graven images; he seduced his people to do more evil than even the nations which the Lord destroyed; and moreover he shed innocent blood very much, till he had filled Jerusalem from one end to another besides his sin wherewith he made Judah to sin . . ." It is also understood that he is the one who had Isaiah sawed in two. How bad can you get? Surely this man must be in hell! Can't we safely make that judgment? Well, if 2 Kings is all that we know about Manasseh, maybe so. But when we read 2 Chronicles 33 we find that ". . . when he was in affliction he besought the Lord his God, and humbled himself greatly before the God of his fathers and prayed unto him . . . then Manasseh knew that the Lord was God!" From the rest of the narrative, we are led to conclude that he was forgiven, and is therefore probably now in heaven.

All we know of Judas is that he did confess his guilt, gave back the blood money and hung himself. We do not know the timing of these events. This could have been before or after the crucifixion or the ascension. Nor do *we* know what was in his heart as he died. We do know, however, from John 13:27 that "Satan entered into him" as he sat at the last supper. But did Satan stay there? I doubt it. If he had, would Judas have returned the money and confessed his guilt while Satan was still in him? Also remember that at the time of Jesus' betrayal, it is doubtful that Judas did know who Jesus really was; none of them did. Even though Peter stated that Jesus was the Son of God, it seems very unlikely that he really believed this, or how could he have denied him as he did? How could all of the others have run for their lives? Suddenly Jesus' weak submissive nature, as He was arrested and carried away, must have undermined whatever confidence in Him they might have had. They evidenced no sense of His divine nature at that moment. Only after the resurrection did they know with certainty who He was. Perhaps that's when Judas also found out and began suffering that profound remorse. Remember it was only four days after the betrayal that He was walking among them. I do not believe that we are told enough in the Scriptures to be able to make this judgment of him simply by his actions. Because it happened to be the betrayal of our Lord, we tend to react almost entirely with our emotions and not with our minds. We see the consequences of his betrayal, and are outraged. Remove the identity of the betrayed and examine the act itself. How many millions under Hitler and Stalin and Mao betrayed their friends and kin in a similar manner and with similar consequences for the betrayed? Surely such betrayal is an awful sin, expressive of a weak, despicable soul, but nevertheless, it is not an unforgivable sin of a truly contrite heart. When we are inclined to judge, we ought to remember Manasseh. Had the Scriptures ended its recording of his life with 2 Kings 21, our judgment of his status would have been much different than it is having read 2 Chronicles 33.

This is no way intended to be a defense of Judas but merely a call to temperance in our willingness to hastily judge the actions of others, as indications of what is in the heart. Jesus on the cross said, "forgive them Father, for they know not what they do." Could He have included Judas in this request?

Probably not, because in John 17:12 Jesus refers to Judas, as the "son of perdition." This word perdition in the Greek is derived from *apollumi* meaning destroyed fully. Perhaps than, he was one of those in Romans 1:28 whom "God gave over to a reprobate (castaway, worthless) mind," and therefore is surely in hell.

6.   In Job 7:20, Job says, "I have sinned." Spurgeon calls this " the repentance of the spirit" In reading Job we find it difficult to discern a sinful nature of any kind. Yet when God was through with His seventy-seven questions, which incidentally contained numerous scientific facts not re-discovered by science until recent centuries, we find Job confessing that he had sinned. It seemed to have been one of presumption or perhaps complacency. At any rate, it would seem that Job was fully exonerated and surely saved. Here is what Spurgeon had to say about Job.

> And now I come into daylight. I have been taking you through dark and dreary confessions; I shall detain you there no longer, but bring you out to the two good confessions, which I have read to you. The first, is that of Job in the seventh chapter at the twentieth verse: "I have sinned; what shall I do unto thee, O thou preserver of men?" This is the *repentance of the saint*. Job was a saint, but he sinned. This is the repentance of the man who is a child of God already, an acceptable repentance before God.

David was a specimen of this kind of repentance, and I would have you carefully study his penitential Psalms, the language of which is ever full of weeping humility and earnest penitence.

7.   In Luke 15:18, The Prodigal says, "I have sinned." Spurgeon calls this the blessed confession. Until I read Spurgeon's commentary on this, I didn't appreciate the full significance and meaning of this parable. So rather than insert my own blather, I'll simply share with you the full text of this portion of his impassioned sermon:

Here is that which proves a man to be a regenerate character—"Father I have sinned." Let me picture the scene. There is the prodigal; he has run away from a good home and a kind father, and he has spent all of his money with harlots, and now he has none left. He goes to his old companions, and asks them for relief. They laugh him to scorn. "O," says he, "you have drunk my wine many a day; I have always stood paymaster to you in all your revelries; will you not help me?" "Get you gone," they say; and he is turned out of doors. He goes to all his friends with whom he had associated, but no man gives him anything. At last a certain citizen of the country said, "You want something to do, do you? Well, go and feed my swine." The poor prodigal, the son of a rich landowner, who had a great future of his own, has to go out to feed swine; and he a Jew, too! The worst employment (to his mind), to which he could be put. See him there, in squalid rags, feeding swine; and what are his wages? Why, so little that he "would fain have filled his belly with the husks that the swine did eat, but no man gave to him." Look, there he is, with the fellow-commoners of the sty, in all his mire and filthiness. Suddenly a thought, put there by the good Holy Spirit, strikes his mind. "How is it," says he, "that in my father's house there is bread enough to spare, and I perish with hunger? I will arise and go to my father, and say unto him, father I have sinned against heaven and before thee, and am no more worthy to be called thy son; make me one of thy hired servants." Off he goes, He begins his way from town to town. Sometimes he gets a lift on a coach perhaps, but at other times he goes trudging his way up barren hills and down desolate valleys all alone. And now at last he comes to the hill outside the village, and sees his father's house down below. There it is; the old poplar tree against it, and there are the stacks round which he and his brother used to run and play; and at the sight of the old homestead all the feelings and associations of his former life rush upon him, and tears run down his cheeks, and he is almost ready to run away again. He says, "I wonder whether father's dead. I dare say mother broke her heart when I went away, I always was her favorite. And if they are either of them alive, they will never see me again; they will shut the door in my face. What am I to do? I cannot go back, I am afraid to go forward." And while he was thus deliberating his father had been walking on the housetop looking out for his son; and though he could not see his father his father could see him. Well, the father comes down the stairs with all his might, runs up to him, and whilst he is thinking of running away, his fathers arms are round his neck, and he falls kissing him, like a loving father indeed, and then the son begins, "—Father, I have sinned against heaven and in thy sight, and am no more worthy to be called thy son," and he was going to say, "make me as one of thy hired servants." But his father put his hand on his mouth. "No more of that," he says; "I forgive you all; you shall not say anything about being my servant, I will have none of that. Come along, he says, "come in, poor prodigal. "Ho," said he to the servants, "bring hither the best robe, and put it on him, and put shoes on his poor bleeding feet; and bring hither the fatted calf and kill it; and let us eat and be merry." O, what a precious reception for one of the chief sinners! Good Matthew Henry says, "His father saw him, there were eyes of mercy; he ran to meet him, there were legs of mercy; he put his arms round his neck; there were arms of mercy; he kissed him; there were kisses of mercy; he said to him—there were words of mercy, wonders of mercy—all mercy. O, what a God of mercy He is.

Now, prodigal, you do the same. Has God put it into your heart? There are many who have been running away a long time now. Does God say, "return?" O, I bid you return then, for as surely as ever thou dost return he will take thee in. There never was a poor sinner yet who came to Christ, whom Christ turned away. If he turns you away, you will be the first. O, if you could but try Him. Ah, sir, I am so black, so filthy, so vile." Well, come along with you—you cannot be blacker than the prodigal. Come to your Father's house, and as surely as he is God He will keep His word.—"Him that cometh unto me I will no wise cast out.

Charles Haddon Spurgeon was one of the most, if not the most fruitful and respected pastors of the nineteenth century. He filled to overflowing every church in which he spoke, several times a day. It is recorded that he sometimes spoke out of doors to as many as twenty thousand at one time. He apparently wrote out all, or most, of his sermons, and they have been preserved in many huge volumes. I have read more than six thousand pages of them and have many more thousands yet to read, God willing. Each one is a testimony to a past era, when God's Word was preached unabashed, uncensored, in its entirety, and without fear of offending tender sensibilities with such words as repent, obey and hell. He filled the churches even with his occasional "hell, fire and brimstone" messages. His was an era when the *whole* truth of the Scriptures was preached, not just the touchy-feely inoffensive parts, which seem today to be the only parts which Pastors perceive are able to draw and hold people in church. This sermon was by no means one of these, but it was one, I believe worthy of being heard again, because so much of it is as applicable today as it was when given 150 years ago. In its timelessness as a useful spiritual message, nothing has changes except the calendar.

—17—

Sin Unto Death

What is a sin unto death? One of the most disturbing and difficult to understand verses in the Scripture is 1 John 5:16 where the Holy Spirit tells us "If any man see his brother sin a sin which is not unto death he shall ask and he shall give him life for them that they sin not unto death. There is a sin unto death; I do not say that he shall pray for it. All unrighteousness is sin, and there is a sin unto death." What can this mean? John doesn't tell us, but instead leaves us hanging with more questions than answers. We are to ask to pray to God for those whose sins are *not* unto death, but he doesn't recommend praying for those who sin unto death. Then he drops it by simply stating again that there is a sin unto death but never tells us what it is. Clearly the Holy Spirit is here challenging us, if we care enough to search His word, to seek the answer so that we may become certain that we do not stumble unknowingly into this terrible predicament.

To the serious Christian reader of the Scriptures, this verse should evoke a heavy concern and a vital need for a solid, satisfactory explanation. The first thought that might enter the mind is that this verse seeks to negate, or somewhat limit the meaning of Ephesians 2:8, 9 and thereby seem to confirm the contention that, indeed, under certain conditions, salvation can be lost. But the context of 1 John makes it clear that he is writing to born again Christians, as is Paul when he speaks of them as "brethren." So here is a clear indication that there is, or are, sins that can cause death. Yet again, from Ephesians 2:8, 9, John 10:28, 29 etc., we know how we have been saved and have certainty of our irrevocable salvation. Therefore, this "sin unto death" cannot be addressing the death of a soul, but the death of a body.

So with a great sigh of relief from having resolved that point, we still find ourselves confused, and rightfully very concerned as to what kind of sin can it be which can cause physical death. Could one stumble into such a sin and not know it? We know that once we are of the faith, when we acknowledge our sins, confess them, repent, and pray for forgiveness with a contrite heart, the sins are forgiven. Scriptures assures us that when we do this, all sins are forgiven, not just some but all sins. But what is this sin unto death? Is it a sin for which we are forgiven but for which we are nevertheless punished by physical death? Scripture tells us that that is exactly what can and does happen, and in fact a prayerful search of the Word of God finds several examples of such punishment and also reveals the types of conditions we must avoid in order to not suffer this fate. Please know that this is no abstract, remote or academic issue. It is a very real and serious situation relevant to all born again Christians who seek to live in faith, and hope to continue living in health throughout a full measure of life.

Scripture gives us several specific examples, which appear to be of these types of sins. While Scripture does not actually and individually call them "sins unto death," the message is clear that that is exactly what they are. The first one noticed, which seems to fit the definition, is found in Leviticus10 regarding Nadah and Abihu. These were brothers and priests, two of the sons of Aaron. Here the Scripture tells us that they willfully disobeyed the Lord's specific and well-understood instructions regarding the burning of incense. This was a deliberate sin, surely a sin unto death in that our Lord struck them dead for this disobedience. Then in Joshua 6, 7 there was Achan. Here was another intended and direct act of disobedience, where God tells Joshua and the people to destroy, and take no spoils from their battle with the Amorites. But Achan, one of the soldiers, couldn't resist keeping some captured silver and a garment. For this sin against God, Achan and his whole family were killed and Israel was caused by God to lose a battle. God says what He means, and means what He says, including punishment for "sins unto death." A third example is Uzzeh in 2 Samuel 6. This sin unto death was for the touching of the Arc of the Covenant by any of the "chosen people," except authorized levitical priests. It did not apply to pagans. Everyone knew that this was forbidden and even though Uzzeh acted instinctively to steady the Arc as the wagon carrying it swayed to where he must have thought it would fall off. Nevertheless, he knew better and died instantly for that one unfortunate act. A fourth example is the story of Ananias and Sapphira found in Acts 5:1–11, a story we all know well. They had promised to sell all their goods and give everything to the Christian community, which they had joined. Instead, they secretly held back some of their wealth. For this they were struck dead. Their sin unto death was not holding back, but lying about it both to the church and to God.

Perhaps these four examples seem pretty remote and totally irrelevant to present day circumstances. Maybe you even believe that God has mellowed and is no longer the same God, that harsh God of older times. Scripture assures us that there is but one same God yesterday, today and forever. In these latter times, He may be speaking in a little different tone of voicc, but He is the same never changing God. This, and what comes next is relevant, very current and very disturbing. If you don't find it so before you reach the end of this paper, then you have missed the point, or what is more likely I have failed to clearly articulate the importance of this issue.

While the purpose of John's epistle is to assure believers that they are in fact possessors of eternal life, it is also evident that the purpose of 1 John 5:16, 17 is to warn believers that there are specific sins which cause dire consequences expressed as severe chastisement and which can lead to "premature" death, just as in older times, even though not always as dramatically or with such finality. If the believer becomes guilty of the sin of presuming upon the grace of God to justify some sinful act, God, even today, may set in motion, through His grace, a whole series of corrective measures of various degrees of severity which as noted, can even lead to physical death!

There is no reason to believe that the people in the four examples listed above were not saved. But their sins were particularly reprehensible to God because they were in each case, a leaven that would, if not quickly purged, pollute the whole body of God's people, whether they are an Old Testament Hebrew tribe or a modern day Christian body. It would seem that perhaps God is especially concerned with sins, which can contaminate the church body, as compared with more private sins, which have little effect beyond the individual. Could this be the criterion, which defines "sin unto death"?

In terms of Old Testament vs. New Testament nothing has changed. There is sin unto death, and God holds the Christian body responsible for its own policing, that is, "correcting, rebuking and encouraging" our brothers and sisters in the body, (2 Timothy 4:2). We don't know how much each of these exampled ancients knew when they so sinned. However, we must believe that our loving merciful God must have given them fair warning so that they could have known what they were doing. But perhaps, today, through the teachings of Jesus Himself and the Holy Spirit through John and Paul, and the universal availability of His written word, we must be held even more accountable for our actions and their consequences. Ignorance of His Word thus can be extremely dangerous, even for the redeemed.

There are two very explicit and compelling New Testament examples of what seems to illustrate a sin unto death. The first is found in 1 Corinthians 11:27–30 having to do with partaking in communion unworthily. Here we read in the NIV, "*Therefore whoever eats the bread or drinks the cup of the Lord in an unworthily manner will be guilty of sinning against the body and blood of the Lord. A man ought to examine himself before he eats the bread or drinks the cup. For anyone who eats and drinks without recognizing the body of the Lord, eats and drinks judgment on himself. That is why many among you are weak and sick and many of you have fallen asleep.*" In the eyes of our Lord, communion is a serious and sacred matter. It is public testimony by the believer that he or she has accepted Jesus Christ as Lord and is saved. He or she is also attesting to the fact there is no unconfessed sin in his or her heart. Thus, anyone living in sin, or one who has not forsaken his sinful condition prior to communion, and knows he or she will continue in that state after communion, will be committing the sin unto death by partaking of the bread and wine. Verse 30 describes this death as what might be considered a slow-motion death, wherein "many among you are weak and sick and a number of you have fallen asleep." This tells us that there is a deliberate act of punishment, which God extracts from those who commit the "sin unto death!"

Is there any reason to believe that there aren't brothers and sisters in the Christian body today who are suffering afflictions precisely because they maintain an on-going sin as they partake in communion? Barnhouse sharpens the point where he offers two otherwise seemingly innocuous examples of this form of sin. He tells of a man juggling his books as he prepares his tax returns, stopping his work to attend church and take communion, after which he goes back to continue what is a sinful act. He also cites the neighborhood gossiper who stops her phone conversation in order to attend church and receive communion, with every intention of going back to the sinful conversation. When conditions such as these exist, when the believer may be living a willful act not to God's liking and intends to continue it after taking communion, he or she is engaging in a public lie and must be dealt with by God, first because it is blasphemous, and second because it undermines the integrity and image of the Christian body. One might say here in regards to 1 Corinthians 11:27–30, "He that hath an ear to hear, let him hear what the Spirit saith unto the sinner."

The second New Testament example of a sin unto death which is obviously of relevance to us today is found in 1 Corinthians 5 where the Holy Spirit tells us of a Christian who was guilty of fornication, and the church was directed to expel the wicked man from among them, to hand this man over to Satan, so that his sinful nature might be destroyed and his spirit saved on the day of the Lord. This they finally did because of Paul's insistence. However, prior to his epistle, they had done nothing. Perhaps it is best here to let the eloquence and spiritual insight of Dr. Barnhouse explain:

> "*Unfortunately, the church had adopted an easy tolerance of its members and had not disciplined this man when he publicly sinned in such a way that dishonor was brought on the name of Christ through his actions. In his letter to the church, Paul empathetically pointed out that the church must take official action in the matter. The man had committed a sin that was a sin unto death and the church should have prayed to God to remove this man from their midst, by death, if necessary. This is the significance of delivering the man to Satan for the destruction of the flesh so that his spirit might be saved in the day of the Lord Jesus*" (1 Corinthians 5:5).

When the epistle was read to the church at its Sunday morning service, quite possibly the sinning member was there and was shocked to hear himself referred to. Realizing the enormity of this sin, he cried out to God in true repentance, and forsook his sin at once putting away the woman he unlawfully held. Thus, in the second letter to the Corinthians, we see that Paul urged the church to forgive the man. He had repented and had submitted to their discipline. "For such a one this punishment by the majority is enough so you should rather turn to forgive and comfort him or he may be overwhelmed by excessive sorrow. So I beg you to reaffirm your love for him" (2 Corinthians 2:5–8).

Therefore, if one has committed a sin that is worthy of the strongest chastisement from God, he can always flee to God's grace and the chastisement will be removed through the same grace.

Again we are indebted to Barnhouse for the third example which is an astute observation regarding the "sin unto death," this time in James 5:20. Here we read in the King James version "Brethren, if any of you do err from the truth, and one convert him, let him know that he which converteth the sinner from error of his ways shall save *a soul from death* and shall hide a multitude of sins." Where the Scripture says "save a soul from death" Barnhouse said, "save him from chastisement of an *early death*." As James says, "shall save a soul from death," it sounds like bringing someone to salvation. Strangely, many noted expositors and teachers have erroneously, I believe, made the assumption that that is what James is saying. Yet it is evident that James is speaking to the saved about one who is already saved unto eternal life, for he is speaking to brethren about a brother. Therefore it can't be a soul that is to be saved as we think of eternal salvation, because the soul of the saved cannot be unsaved in order for brethren to re-save it. For this to be otherwise would be a renunciation of eternal security, one of the cornerstones of the Christian faith. Furthermore, neither a brother nor anyone else can "save" a soul, only God can do this. It's also been suggested that James doesn't mean brother in Christ when he is speaking to the "brethren." This is doubtful. The Holy Spirit does not engage and inspire His scribes to write sloppy or erroneous Scripture. Also, note that the error from which the brother is being saved is an error from the *truth*, not from any failing or lack of faith. While seeking truth is an important goal, it is only by grace through faith in the truth of the Gospel, which saves an immortal soul.

Finally, the confusion ends when one discovers the double definition of the word soul. According to Strong's concordance the Greek word for soul, "psyche," can have different meanings. It can mean "mere vitality, even of plants." It can also mean the "rational and immortal soul." The Greek word *pneuma* also means "rational and immortal soul" as well as "spirit." Thus it is evident once more, that context and translation must be examined carefully whenever there seems to be a question of meaning of any particular Scripture verse. Therefore in summary, because a "brethren" cannot "save" a rational and immortal soul, it is evident that James is referring to the "mere vitality" of physical life of a man who has departed from the truth and is thereby living in a manner, which includes a sin unto death. In that case a brother can save him through scriptural truth, if he or she is willing to hear it and repent.

There is yet, I believe, one more allusion to the sin unto death. It is found in the Gospel John 15:2 "Every branch in me that beareth not fruit He taketh away . . ." Verse 6 also alludes to a similar fate. There are various opinions as to the meaning of these verses. However, a careful reading indicates that these are saved persons who have not been fruitful, so God takes them away as with sin unto death. This is yet so, "—as by fire." (1 Corinthians 3:15) Here is another example of the redeemed who loses his rewards but not his salvation. If the above interpretation of these verses is correct, and I believe it is, we each have another and very disturbing way to qualify for the sin unto death punishment simply by being unfruitful. I am persuaded that this does not apply to all unfruitful believers, but perhaps only to those who are given much, from whom much is expected, yet they chose to ignore opportunities to be fruitful. Everyone who receives eternal life also is blessed with some spiritual gift by means of which they can, in gratitude, glorify God. If they choose to waste these gifts, that is, not apply them to His service, to His greater Glory, then they are like fruitless vines, to be cut off and burned. Clearly, it is not the soul that is cut off, for that being, a living branch of Christ is saved. But the body, being deliberately fruitless, having forsaken its divine calling is cut off early because it has committed the sin unto death.

Other than the quotes from Barnhouse, I have yet to find anywhere in my studies a serious discussion or concern for this issue of the sin unto death. Yet the Holy Spirit has provided ample evidence that this is a very serious issue, which may be affecting the health and longevity of many Christian lives, perhaps even some of us, and those around us. This is no trivial matter, even though the Holy Spirit has chosen to present it in this most subtle manner, rather than hitting us over the head with a very explicit doctrinal statement. I pray that whoever reads this paper, will not treat its message lightly, but will be very serious in examining Scripture to see if it be so, and then using it for the benefit of our brothers and sisters in Christ as the Holy Spirit leads you.

Since writing this two years ago, I have observed three instances of what I believe to be examples of "sin unto death." The first two are brethren who each in his or her own and different way appear to be living an on-going sin. Each partakes in communion "religiously." In each of these dear persons it can be seen that he or she is slowly growing "weak and sick" just as it was foretold to be in 1 Corinthians 11:27–30. Certainly neither I nor any other individual is qualified to conclude that this is an absolute example of such a cause and effect. It is the obligation of the church body to attempt such a determination and to save them from further pain. However, in these days of the "lukewarm" church this will never happen. Someone's sensitivities might be offended.

The third example is an extreme case of which I have no doubt was a "sin unto death." I knew this incredible disciple of our Lord for more than four years. I loved and respected her more than anyone I have ever known. Just to be with her for a few minutes was enough to realize that in her precious heart the Holy Spirit reigned supreme and actually radiated from her very being. She was an extremely prolific and fruitful disciple of the Lord, bringing a great many souls to the foot of the cross. I saw for myself on many occasions, and with great awe, how the Holy Spirit, through her, drew to Jesus nearly every one to whom she directed her discipleship. I also personally witnessed how intensely and mercilessly Satan continually attacked her, as one would expect, given her incredible fruitfulness. A detailed narrative of this incessant attack as I witnessed it would probably be of value as a demonstration of his many assorted evil powers. I may write this one day if so directed by the Holy Spirit, when and if my grief ever wanes sufficiently to allow me to deal with those awful memories.

She withstood these attacks valiantly up to the last eighteen months of her life. As I look back I can see more clearly the cracks that were forming in her defenses. But at the time, because of my youthfulness in the faith and the esteem in which I held her, I could not then see what was coming. At first there was a trickling element of pride, then a tiny measure of hypocrisy, combined with a weakened intensity of purpose, and a growing interest in the things of the world, which had not been previously in evidence. When I finally could see what was happening inside her, I strove to express my concerns, but it was too late. Satan had finally surrounded her with false and apostate teachers and "friends," and had torn away her resistance to worldly ways. Around then, I wrote for her the paper entitled "Spiritual Stumbling," but she refused to read it, even though she had always valued my papers. She had always been in great physical health, being able to climb mountains and jog for miles. As a Naturopathic Doctor, she also knew how to eat and live healthy. In her practice, she cured hundreds of "incurables" and had lectured as well as taught in England, India, New Zealand and other parts of the world on these matters. Then she became sick, sick unto death and died just two months before her fifty-first birthday. In her twelve short years as a redeemed Christian, I believe that she earned more crowns than I or than ten more like me could ever earn in many lifetimes. As her fruitfulness waned and apostasy took over, however, I am certain that our dear Lord simply chose to take her home before she lost them all.

Finally, when I say here with great conviction, that this was a "sin unto death" and that He took her lovingly and with compassion lest she lose any more of her crowns, I say it with just reason. I say it after nearly two years of almost unbearable grief and tearful prayers of petition to the Father to give me the wisdom and assurance to understand why He would take her home, this exquisite fruitful disciple in the very prime of her life. What's written here is the result of those prayers. The boundless gratitude I feel for this understanding cannot be described in words. It has allowed me to deal with the grief and to actually *thank* Him for taking away the most precious person to have ever entered my life, other than my own family.

I pray that this paper may serve as a source of scriptural insight from which one can learn and be of benefit to others when the potential seems to exist, that is, when there is a recognizable "sin unto death" taking place.

—18—

God Provided the Law so Sin Would Increase

Romans, chapter 5 verse 20 expresses a concept quite difficult to understand when first read, or even after some amount of rereading and contemplation. The King James Version says, *"More-over the law entered that offense might abound, but when sin abounded grace did much more abound."* The NIV expresses the same thing but in words more common to the present day terminology. *"The law was added so that trespass might increase but where sin increased grace increased all the more . . ."* Does that mean that people chose to sin more because God, through Moses, provided them with a set of laws which identified and listed what was sinful? That seems to be what the Holy Spirit, through Paul, is telling us. But there is something wrong with that picture. The God I know is love, truth and righteousness. He is not a God who would give His law for the purpose of making His creation increase their sinfulness.

Perhaps a brief look back at man's origin and history up to the giving of the law will help to establish a basis for understanding the true meaning of this troubling verse.

We know from Scripture that Adam and Eve were made perfect, or sinless. However, even as with the angels, God gave them a free will and ability to choose their own thought and actions. It was through their choices that they disobeyed God regarding one and only one condition He imposed on them. Given everything in the world that they might consider doing, this was the only one choice, which He asked them not to make. The moment they made that one transgression, they realized that it was a huge mistake, because they suddenly saw themselves stripped of the glorious cloak of perfection with which God had clothed them. Here was the first sin, the going against God's will, and the feeling of guilt, which necessarily accompanied it. How do we know that? Because among their first thoughts was to cover themselves with fig leaves and to hide from God. The whole universe "groaned" and continues to groan (earthquakes, volcanoes, etc.) as a result of what that sin did (Romans 8:22). It activated a great curse on all of creation. Entropy, that is the winding down, and eventual death of all existence was the physical result. Their immediate moral and spiritual death through the severing of the spiritual linkage between God and man was the additional price that all mankind was to pay for that one sin.

In Genesis 1 God tells us that His creation was "good," when He created it. That would mean perfect from our perspective. Life was made to be eternal, no death, no winding down, only eternal perfection in every sense. But now, sin had permeated every aspect of creation, even to the very DNA of Adam and Eve, so that their offspring throughout history would have a built-in propensity for sin, and but for God's selective grace, they would also inherit the inevitability of death. But God in His divine mercy and foreknowledge also put in each soul a conscience, that is an internal sense of what is right and what is wrong. The first two people, in hiding themselves from God, revealed the first inkling of that sense. Cain also demonstrated guilt when he avoided God's question to him as to where was his brother Abel. He further exposed the fact that the internal sense of right and wrong was present in others when he pleaded with God to protect him from the people who would know of his transgressions and seek to punish him (Genesis 4:14).

And so we can see that all through the biblical period, down to the giving of the law through Moses, God had endowed man with the knowledge of His omnipresence, as well as a clear sense of right and wrong, through that facility we call conscience. This was to guide him spiritually in his thoughts and actions. In effect, one could say that the basic precepts of the law, as articulated to Moses, were already in the hearts of man from the very beginning. But as it was then, and probably is even more so today, through his innate propensity to sin, man chose more often than not to override that internal directive. Eventually this override would sear or dull the conscience making it, to varying degrees, and sometimes permanently, quite insensitive to its calling. And so without the actual formality of law, the "desperately wicked heart" (Jeremiah 17:9) could, with seeming impunity, rationalize almost any of its wicked ways.

But until the law came, was such a violation of that internal sense a sin? Could sin be imputed based solely on one's violation of that internal conscience? From God's perspective, I believe the answer is yes. This is because man is judged from two perspectives, both related to what he does with the amount of light he is given. He is judged by both his faith and by his works. By God's grace mankind is saved to eternal life in heaven through faith alone. It is his works, that is what he does with the light and with the spiritual gifts he is given, which determine his position in heaven, as these will be judged by Jesus as soon as the soul enters heaven. For those who are not saved, they too will be judged similarly regarding their works by Jesus from the Great White Throne at the end of the tribulation. The quality of their works will determine their relative positions in the lake of fire. God put this procedure in place long before the law was given.

The great patriarchs of the Old Testament such as Enoch, Noah, Job, Moses, Abraham, Jacob, and Joseph, each in his own way are examples of men of both faith and law-filled consciences, all prior to the formalized giving of the law. Certainly each one, with the possible exception of Enoch, did sin. They all admitted their transgressions and sought forgiveness.

So now why does Scripture tell us that the law was given so that sin might increase? It must be remembered that before the law, although the conscience was there as a guide regarding right and wrong, sin as such was unrecognized. The horrible nature of every sin as a damning transgression against God, and what could be done about it, was not yet fully understood. It took the law to bring this out and into the minds and hearts of those willing to accept this revelation. Putting the law "on paper" so to speak caused an end to the mystery and too much of the rationalizing which a weaker conscience could hide behind.

Now, "the law served to give to sin a specific character of transgression, thus deepening the sense of guilt and unworthiness" (H. H. Ironsides lectures on Romans pg. 87). What increased was the recognizing or awareness of sin. Suddenly sin seemed to be everywhere. Things of a seemingly minor nature, ignored by the imperfect conscience, were now identified as serious sins.

Some commentators conclude that because of man's depraved nature, the identifying of sin caused him to rail against such an imposition on his freedom of choice, and that this in turn, caused him to defy the law and to sin even more. Perhaps this is true in some cases, but I prefer the idea that the law simply intensified the sense of wrong, which had been suppressed by the conscience. I like Matthew Henry's commentary as the best expression of what God meant by the subject verse:

> *The moral laws showed that many thoughts, tempers, words, and actions, were sinful, thus transgressions were multiplied. This was not making sin to abound the more, but exposing the sinfulness of it, just as letting a clearer light shine into a room, exposes the dust and filth which were there before, but were not seen. The sin of Adam, and the effect of corruption in us, is the abounding of that offense which appeared with the entrance of the law. And the terrors of the law make gospel comforts sweeter. Thus God the Holy Spirit has delivered to us a most important truth, full of consolation, suited to our need as sinners. Whatever one may have above another every man is a sinner against God, stands condemned by the law, and needs pardon. A righteousness that is to justify cannot be made up of a mixture of sin and holiness. There can be no title to an eternal reward without a pure and spotless righteousness: let us look for it, even to the righteousness of Christ.*

Remember this, when God gave the law, He gave it along with a sacrificial system, which when properly adhered to, covered man's sins. Then Christ, to fulfill the law and end the sacrificial system, sacrificed Himself so that all who believed, past, present and future would, through faith, have their sins completely forgiven. This is the blessed grace, which increases ever more and can save even the very worst of sinners. Thus, we all have the opportunity to be delivered from the guilt of sin, although not from our nature to sin. That old sin nature remains with each of us to the end of our mortal lives. But now those who are saved have the indwelling Holy Spirit to hold that evil nature captive, to keep the conscience increasingly sensitized against sin, and to give spiritual strength to overcome the temptations of the world.

—19—

Disobeying the Ten Commandments Can Never Condemn Anyone to Hell

Of course Scripture calls us to obey the Ten Commandments, but that is not a prerequisite, or in any way a condition of salvation. No one will ever come before the judgment seat and hear Jesus say, "depart from me for I never knew you," (Matthew 7:23) simply because he or she has sinned through any or all of the Ten Commandments once, or a thousand times. The fact is that everyone who ever lived has disobeyed these commandments.

There is but ONE sin that will send anyone to hell, and all who commit it do surely go to eternal hell. That is the sin of unbelief, the sin of not acknowledging that Christ Jesus alone is our Lord and Savior. It is the sin of not repenting and trusting Him to having, through His blood, totally cleansed us of our sins, and to have thereby opened for us the door to heaven. Having professed a genuine faith, that is, a saving faith, all past, present and future sins have been forgiven and can never be used against us in the spiritual realm. Nevertheless, one must hasten to realize and assert that the by-product of that redemption is a changed life, one dedicated to the Lord's will which is revealed only by the Holy Spirit and from the study of His Word. The Ten Commandments amplified by the Sermon on the Mount will then become the guiding light of one's life. This message is called the beatitudes. Just as the word indicates, those are the *be-attitudes*. They summarize the attitudes that must be in us. It is our attitude, the substance of our inner beings, more than our actions, which are involved.

Failure to accept His gift of salvation through faith (Ephesians 2:8, 9) totally negates any and all attributes or good works, which one may live by, no matter how impressive and wonderful they appear from a worldly perspective. Scripture calls them but hay and stubble which will be burned and be of no value at that moment of judgment which everyone must face one day.

There are but two ways to heaven. The one described above, and the other, through a life of absolute righteousness, that is, never to have sinned, even once. For there are absolutely no sins allowed in heaven. The fate of the unbeliever is as a person suspended over hell by a ten-link chain, each link representing one of the Ten Commandments as embellished by Jesus. This person hangs there his or her entire life until the chain breaks that is until one sin is committed. How many links must break before the descent begins? Only one, and only once! There is no repair kit available, so that descent begins once that very first sin is committed, and continues on into hell at life's end, unless a rescue is affected. There is but one Rescuer for the falling soul, and He responds only to the cry of true repentance, which generates true faith, which in turn brings about the blessed grace of salvation. This halts the fall forever and immediately cleanses the sinner, guaranteeing him or her a place in heaven, which has already been prepared.

Where are you in this process? Are you sure? There is nothing more critical, more vital or of more monumental importance in this life than establishing, while you can, what your eternal destiny will be. This is not a place for ignorance, complacency, assumption, presumption or guesswork. It's not an issue which can be settled with absolute assurance, except through a genuine understanding of what Scripture says, not by what some pastor, preacher, or teacher says. For that is second hand information. It dare not be relied on, but must be confirmed as did the Bereans in Acts 17:11. The issue of salvation is too important to place any reliance on fallible man, no matter who he is. There are too many false prophets and false teachers, those telling only half-truths, and also many who mean well but don't know what they are talking about. Satan the great counterfeiter and liar, clouds the minds and intentions of well-meaning but poorly informed souls into believing they are doing God's work when in fact they have been manipulated to his perverted purpose, which is to keep one from a saving faith. His greatest triumph is when he can create a belief in people's hearts that they are saved when, in fact, they are not.

Search the Scripture! For that is the only reliable source of truth! Then dedicate your life to that truth!

Scripture makes it very clear that God doesn't judge you on how wicked or evil you have been, or how much damage you have caused. Total forgiveness of all sins occurs when there is, in your heart, a genuine acknowledgement of your hopelessly sinful nature, after which you confess all sins, and resolve to repent into an absolute belief, that only through the blood of Jesus are your sins forgiven, and that He is now your eternal Lord and Savior.

The assurance of your salvation can be well evidenced by a changed life a life, of gratitude, motivated service and your ever-growing likeness to Jesus.

—20—

Hell . . . What Is It . . . Where Is It?—And Some Other Observations

Do you ever think of, or concern yourself with hell? Probably not. Polls indicate that a majority believes that there is such a place, but only one percent believes they will go there. Wouldn't it be something if truth could be formulated by a majority opinion? In today's perverted society, it often appears that that truth is formed by consensus; at least that's how many political, social, economic, and even religious decisions are made. Whoever controls the dissemination of information (the media) controls popular opinion. I believe it was Kissinger who said that perception is more important than reality in the affairs of man. In the short term, and as the world moves today, this observation is probably more right than wrong. But the topic here, that is understanding what and where Hell is, is neither a short term nor trivial issue, but one of eternal consequence. Jesus spoke of hell many more times than He did of heaven. Yet, how often have you heard a pulpit message regarding this very real place, which Scripture tells us, is one of only two possible places our immortal souls, will spend eternity? Probably never! It's likely that you heard more about it from fiction novels than anywhere else. Although it is tempting to do so, this paper will not discuss the issue of what souls go where, and how this destination is determined, but instead, will simply report on my studies as I have sought to understand what hell is, along with the several different circumstances and places mentioned in Scripture which have been rather unfortunately mistranslated as "hell" and sometimes the "grave."

189

For instance, the occurrence and definitions of the words "grave" and "hell" in the Scripture are as follows:

Grave: This word appears sixty-nine times in the Old Testament of which forty-seven times it means sepulcher and twenty-two times it means Sheol. It occurs five times in the New Testament, four times meaning sepulcher and once it means Hades. The grave as we think of it is a burial place, but in the Hebrew culture the dead were placed in sepulchers or tombs located above ground in stone structures or caves, natural or carved. The grave is obviously the repository of bodies absent their souls, which have gone elsewhere.

Hell: This word occurs thirty-one times in the Old Testament and means Sheol *every time*. It occurs twenty-two times in the New Testament of which eleven times it means Gehenna, ten times it means Hades and once in 2 Peter 2:4, it means Tartaros.

From this it is evident, as stated above, the King James Version, and for the most part, other translations as well, seem to have been quite careless in their translations of these two very serious and concerning words. But now we have several other words to contend with if we are to gain some understanding of what Scripture is really saying to us about this after death place or places where I would sadly suggest, many more than one percent are destined to inhabit forever. The words grave and hell have led us back to the original Greek and Hebrew words Sheol, Gehenna, Hades and Tarteros. However, in order to better understand our subject, we must also look into some other related words and terms Scripture uses to express the meaning and location of what we broadly think of as Hell. These are, bottomless pit, outer darkness, lake of fire, and abyss.

Sheol and Hades

Sheol is the Old Testament Hebrew word defined as the world of the dead. It is the equivalent of the New Testament Greek word Hades, which is defined as the place or state of departed souls, the receptacle of disembodied souls or spirits, a dark and dismal place. The word originated as the name of the Greek God of the lower regions called

Hades or Pluto. Prior to its use as a biblical term and Jesus' clarification of its biblical meaning, the word had only a negative connotation. Sheol is first mentioned in Genesis 37:35 where Jacob is lamenting the apparent death of Joseph and says, "I will go down into the grave unto my son." This is a strange statement if we try to understand it in terms of the actual meaning of the word grave. How could he go meaningfully "unto" his son in a grave? But it's meaning becomes clear and appropriate when we understand that he is talking about the place where the living, but disembodied souls go. We get a similar perspective in 2 Samuel 12:23 where David matter-of-factly says of his dead son that he will one day go to him even though his son can no longer come back to him. It would make no sense if the two fathers were talking of going to their dead son's graves. The place they believe they would ultimately go is called Sheol, which appears fifty-three times in the Old Testament and was evidently known about by the various scriptural writers, as well as the general populous. It was considered a real place and the place where one's immortal soul was taken when it departed the physical body. Almost everything we now know about Sheol-Hades is recorded in Luke 16:19–31 where Jesus confirms its existence and character by telling us of the rich man and Lazarus who both went there. Please read those passages and then see if you agree with the following observations, which can be gleaned from them.

1. Sheol appears to consist of two distinct places somehow separated by a deep chasm, or abyss. It is located somewhere near the center of the earth. The one side must indeed be a dark and dismal place as the definition of Hades suggests, but the other side of the abyss surely must not be so unpleasant, and would seem from other clues, to be somewhat of a soul paradise.

2. The chasm separates the temporary residence of souls condemned to eternal punishment from those ultimately destined for heaven.

3. While there is no possible crossing of the chasm in either direction, there appears to be some limited relationship between the two sides.

4. Even though all who are there on either side are disembodied souls, we learn the following:

   a. There is communication across the abyss in both directions.

   b. Those on the condemned side have desires and feel physical pain and discomfort (heat and thirst, etc.).

   c. Both retain pre-physical death memories.

   d. Both love, show concern, and the condemned even express regrets

   e. Both recognize individuals, even across the abyss.

   f. Both know their fate and the condemned are resigned to it, and know that it is fair and just.

5. Sheol is neither heaven nor hell, and it's not the grave, but it is a real place. It possibly is, and surely was, a "way station" for all souls, saved and unsaved immediately after physical death. Notice in Luke 23:43 that Jesus tells the thief on the cross "today you shall be with me in paradise." We assume He meant heaven, but He couldn't have, because He didn't go that day to heaven. Paradise as He meant it is not heaven. It's the Greek word *paradisos,* which means park or Eden (place of future happiness) while Heaven is *ouranos* which means "Heaven as the abode of God," I submit that when Jesus said this, He was speaking of the good side of Sheol as He was when in Matthew 12–40 He said He would be "three days and three nights in the heart of the earth." The Greek for heart is *kardia*, which can also mean "middle."

What rejoicing there must have been in Sheol at our Savior's arrival and as He declared His victory over death! Could it be that His visit there was to personally deliver to those saved and patiently waiting souls the goods news, that the great day had finally come, that His resurrection as the "first fruit" would finally open the gates of heaven for their ascension as well? Until He died on the cross, all previous blood sacrifice, from Adams coat of skin to the last sacrifice in the temple, had been anticipatory of this final and ultimate *effectual* sacrifice of Jesus, this perfect Lamb of God. Through faith they had been saved, as the book of Hebrews tells us, but they could not be justified or sanctified so as to be qualified to enter heaven until Jesus had completed His work on the cross and had risen from the dead. Thus it seems that all saved souls, from the time of Adam to the thief, resided on the paradise side of Sheol, waiting for Jesus and His resurrection. The paradise side of Sheol is now empty. This is because Jesus, having paid the price with His blood, all of the covered sins became forgiven sins. Therefore, all of the souls in paradise were now qualified for heaven, and Jesus took them there as He ascended to His eternal glory.

Gehenna

Gehenna was originally the name of a place in the Hinnon valley, south of Jerusalem. It was sort of a garbage dump, where wastes and dead animals were burned. scripturally to those at the time, it served as a graphic metaphor or example of the "lake of fire," which is the true hell as we think of it, the place of everlasting punishment. This is the ultimate destination of the unsaved souls temporarily held in Sheol. Gehenna is spoken of eleven times in the New Testament, each time by Jesus Himself. The Old Testament does not appear to refer to any equivalent place. This is probably because it didn't exist yet. Scripture tells us in Revelation 20:11, 12 that there will be but one resurrection of the damned, and that will occur at the end of the millennium. As noted previously, every time the word hell is used in the Old Testament, it means Sheol. It would seem therefore that knowledge of Gehenna as the final abode of the condemned souls is another one of the "mysteries" which God chose to conceal from the ancients and to reveal only in the New Testament.

Topologically, Gehenna seems to be far away from Sheol. While Sheol is in the belly of the earth, Gehenna is in the outer darkness (Mark 8:12; 22:13; 25:30). At least twenty-three times, Jesus speaks of the hell fire, the unquenchable fire, the everlasting fire, the eternal fire, the furnace fire, and in Revelation, the lake of fire, all as the eternal residence of the unsaved and of Satan.

Bottomless Pit

This place is referred to seven times, all in Revelation. It's also referred to as the abyss. In Revelation 9:11 we are informed that the king of the bottomless pit is Abaddon (destroying angel) in Hebrew, and he is called Apollyon (a destroyer, Satan) in Greek. As noted, Sheol is reported to be in the heart, or somewhere near the center of the earth. The fact that there is a chasm between the two parts of Sheol indicates that there is some additional and substantial depth further toward the center of the earth than the location where Sheol is to be found. While it isn't definitively stated here, it is evident that the chasm of Sheol is in fact the "bottomless pit," which exists at the very center of the earth, as we shall see below. Also, how else could it be bottomless, unless, by definition, it was at the point where every direction away from its center is up! Revelation indicates that the bottomless pit will be the abode of Satan, and his evil spirits during the millennium. How appropriate it is that it be the very bottom of the Sheol abyss.

In Revelation 20:3, we find Jesus saying, through the writings of John, that Satan will be cast into the bottomless pit and sealed there for a thousand years. After that, his final home will be the lake of fire (Revelation 20:10) as it will be for all false prophets (Revelation 19:20) and all those whose names are not found in the book of life. So like Sheol, the bottomless pit is a *temporary* place. It has to be, because one day there will be a new heaven and new earth (Revelation 21:1). So these places will be gone!

Tartaros

As previously noted, the word Hell in 2 Peter 2:4 is the English translation of the Greek word *Tartaros*, which means the deepest abyss of Hades, to incarnate in eternal torment, cast down to Hell." This indicates that Tartaros is another name for the "bottomless pit" and here it very clearly puts it in the Hades or Sheol abyss! Note again that it was certain of the "angles who sinned" who went there, not man. It is likely that the fallen angels who have been already condemned to Tartaros are those who fathered the Nephilim as recorded in Genesis 6.

To summarize, we have Sheol/Hades as the temporary abode of all souls, at least up to the time of the resurrection. The bottomless pit is also a temporary place below Sheol, which only Satan and his evil angels and spirits can inhabit. It is not at any time a place inhabited by human souls. It's only, figuratively speaking, the "shelves or plateaus" on either side of the abyss, which leads to the bottomless pit, where souls are stored. Then there is Gehenna, the lake of fire in the outer darkness, where all unsaved souls, as well as Satan and his angels and spirits will spend eternity. This place is eternal and, therefore, will remain as is, even after the new heaven and earth exist.

Other Observations

Searching the Scripture regarding the above discussions about Hell brought to mind two very strange passages, and seemed to stimulate an insight or at least some very plausible conjectures as to their meanings. The first is in Matthew 11:11 where Jesus tells us that no one ever born of woman was greater than John the Baptist, yet he that is least in Heaven is greater than John. The second is in Jude 9, where we learn that Michael, the archangel, contended with the devil disputing about the body of Moses.

1.   Regarding John the Baptist, who could it be that was the very least in Heaven yet be greater than John, if there were never anyone born of woman greater than John? This indicates that John was among the number one greatest persons who ever lived. That puts him at least equal with Abraham, Moses, and David and even as great as Enoch and Elijah. These two must have been somehow very special to have been raptured directly to Heaven. So who is in Heaven, or rather who was in Heaven at the time Jesus made this announcement? God was, but He surely wasn't the least in Heaven. The angels were, and are above all humans, although that wouldn't always be the case. (1 Corinthians 6:3) We could stop here and simply conclude that He was speaking of the angels in heaven, but the context of His

statement suggests that He is speaking of others "born of women." Therefore, perhaps the least in Heaven who was born of women, were simply Enoch and Elijah and perhaps others who were raptured but about whom we have no knowledge. This may seem too simple an answer, but I do believe that it was just that simple, subject to something else that follows.

2.   Why were the archangel Michael and Satan arguing over the body of Moses? (Jude 9) Why are we told this? Why is it told so much later, and only in Jude, the next to last of the sixty-six books of the Bible? It seems totally devoid of relevant context with anything anywhere in the Bible. However, we know that all things are in Scripture for our learning. But what is to be learned from this? Of course, where it says that Michael dared not rail (pass judgment) against Satan, but had to leave it to the Lord to rebuke him, it is telling us that we too must respect even evil principalities and powers including the devil, and let our Lord deal with them. But what about this body business? Perhaps some light can be shed here if we look at some other seemingly unrelated verses. In Deuteronomy 34:6 we find that our Lord Himself buried Moses and that no one ever found his grave, except Michael and Satan. In Matthew 17:3 we find Moses and Elijah at the transfigurations obviously having a conversation, perhaps a strategy-planning meeting. Why does the Holy Spirit choose to tell us these things? Then in Revelation 11:3–12 Jesus, through John, tells us that during the tribulation, He will send two witnesses from Heaven to Jerusalem to prophesy for forty-two months. These men will have special powers. One will "have power to shut the heavens," that it rain or not rain as he wills it, and the other will have the power to turn water into blood and to smite the earth with all plagues as often as he wills it. Where have we heard about these powers before? Elijah in 1 Kings 17:1 was given the power to prevent rain for forty-two months and then caused it to rain (James 5:17, 18), and who had already been given the power to turn water into blood and to smite the earth to bring on plagues? Moses of course, in Exodus 7:10!

Now let's take these little, seemingly incidental and unrelated verses, and somehow try to connect them to form a significant and hopefully edifying message. Why is Satan so concerned over Moses' body, and what is Michael trying to do? Could it be that we are being clued to the fact that God is not yet through with Moses, and Satan knows it? Is he therefore trying to do something with the body, which he believes could thwart God's plan? Clearly, much of Scripture in one context is an account of the many ways Satan has tried to thwart God's plan. From the temptation of Eve to the killing of male Hebrew babies by Pharaoh and later by Herod, to Haman in the book of Esther, to the temptation of Jesus, Satan never missed an opportunity to try to do so. Could it be also that Michael is there to recover the body, perhaps to restore him to life, after which Moses would be transfigured directly to Heaven? It seems from Michael's comment that it required a direct intervention by God to rebuke and hold back Satan so that Michael could do his job. By itself, this verse would not warrant this conjecture, but when we see Moses appear with Elijah at the transfiguration obviously with himself having hyper dimensional powers to physically appear and disappear (Matthew 17:3), we should begin to wonder. Later in Revelation 11, there we find the two men, very likely Elijah and Moses, sent by God to Jerusalem where they will prophesy for forty-two months during the tribulation, will be murdered and then after three and half days will be brought back to life and raptured back to Heaven. Putting this together, we can reasonably conclude that Moses was raptured to Heaven and was therefore another one of those in Heaven "greater than John" (the Baptist)

But now there is a serious question to be answered or perhaps it's a dilemma to be solved. From this study it seems clear that prior to the cross, the souls of all who died went to Sheol, both saved and unsaved. This is because no one could ascend into Heaven until he or she had received the cleansing power of the cross, which didn't occur until Jesus died. We are told in John 3:3 that one must be born again in order to ascend to Heaven, this being a creative act of the Holy Spirit conditioned on faith in Jesus crucified. So how did Enoch and Elijah and Moses, certainly each of them sinners, qualify to be raptured, thereby preempting the only way Scripture provides for this journey? The likely answer is that in His sovereign will God does as He will, including making exceptions to His rules. Scripture offers several examples. Take the case regarding His rule that the first born in a family is to have stewardship after the father passes away. The stories of Isaac, Jacob, Judah, Ephraim etc, violate this rule per God's intervention. Then consider the fact that "it is appointed unto men once to die" (Hebrews 9:27), yet Scripture sites at least six examples of people who died and who were brought back to life to die again later. God promises, His love, His justice, His mercy, His covenants, His grace and His laws are all inviolate, and part of, or representative of His divine nature. But His divine sovereignty allows Him to intervene and to carry out His plan as He chooses. Perhaps prior to the cross, these three men, Enoch, Elijah and Moses, were the only humans in Heaven, having been so chosen for His divine purpose after having been justified and sanctified by some special dispensation, perhaps by Jesus Himself, something of which we have no knowledge.

To summarize this perhaps confusing effort, please consider the following points, some of which stand as scriptually based facts while the others may be conjecture, but which I believe have considerable scriptural support.

1. The translations of the words "grave and Hell" are poorly translated from both Hebrew and Greek.

2. Sheol / Hades is a place toward the center of the earth where all souls saved and unsaved were sent prior to the cross.

3. The saved and unsaved souls were in two vastly different environments within Sheol/Hades, and were separated by an abyss, which extended to the center of the earth.

4. Many characteristics of physical life are retained by the soul such as seeing, being able to hear, converse, feel pain, express concern and love, understanding ones circumstances, remembering the past life etc.

5. The bottomless pit is at the center of the earth, the very bottom of Sheol/ Hades abyss.

6. The bottomless pit is not an abode of souls; only Satan and his angels and evil spirits are assigned there.

7. Sheol/Hades and the bottomless pit are temporary places, because one day the present earth will be no more and there will be a new heaven and new earth. (Revelation 21).

8. The outer darkness is where the lake of fire, also known as Gehenna and Tartaros may be found. This is the real and eternal Hell.

9. Enoch, Elijah and probably Moses were transfigured (raptured) to Heaven and therefore must have been rendered sinless and sanctified through faith by some dispensation different from that allotted to all the rest of mankind (grace through faith in the blood of Christ on the cross).

10. Because John the Baptist died prior to the cross, he was not yet purified by it, thereby causing him, for the time being, to have a lesser status than those that were already in Heaven

This ends this little search for understanding, which I pray will be of some interest to the reader. Perhaps you won't agree with all or any of my conclusions, but praise the Lord if this provokes or inspires you to begin your own search of the Scripture, and to develop a passion for His Word.

P.S.

Seven months have gone by since I wrote the above. Since then I have remained less than satisfied that the explanation given regarding John the Baptist as Jesus described him in Matthew 11:11. There may yet be some validity regarding the conjecture as to the presence of Elisha, Enoch and Moses in heaven. However, I now realize that those observations are not at all relevant to John the Baptist, nor to his stature or fate. Perhaps I should have instead revised this portion of the paper. However, I have chosen to leave it because to me, it is a very humbling testimony to my sin of presumption, to my choosing to present an answer to a scriptural question without having applied sufficient patience and diligence in seeking the Holy Spirit's revealing grace. I thought I had done so when I wrote the above, yet deep down, as I reflect on it, I knew that I had expressed more conjecture than exegesis and had not researched Scripture as thoroughly as I should have. For at that time, I reasoned that this was one of those mysteries that would not be fully explained here, but only in the coming realm. What follows, I believe is a better answer as to the question invoked by Matthew 11:11. In this whole matter, however, I believe that I have been doubly blessed, first by the increment of Spiritual growth this humbling has caused. This in itself is two-fold, in that I was not only presumptive in that I too quickly settled for a non-biblical answer, but also because a fully biblical answer was embarrassingly available, "for those with ears to hear . . ." (Matthew 11:15) And second, is that the Holy Spirit did, in His perfect timing, choose to guide me to the real answer which I believe can be learned from the following.

Let us again read Matthew 11:11 "Verily I say unto you, among them that are born of women there hath not risen a greater than John the Baptist: notwithstanding, he that is least in the kingdom of heaven is greater than he." Notice that Jesus is saying that he who is least in the kingdom of heaven is greater than he. Then in verse 12, "And from the days of John the Baptist until now the kingdom of heaven suffereth violence, and the violent take it by force." Jesus says that the *kingdom of heaven* suffers violence. That is *not* heaven He is speaking of, but the *kingdom of heaven*, something totally different. In straight reading of Scripture, how many pick up the distinction? I surely didn't, not once, until now! What is the difference? All the difference in the world! Read the parables! At least nine of them start out with the *kingdom of heaven* is like . . . It is like the mustard seed; the leaven; the wheat and tares; the pearl; the net; the unforgiving servant; the laborer in the vineyard; the ten virgins; the talents; etc. What a wide assortment of seemingly unrelated allegories Jesus uses to describe the *kingdom of heaven*. Every time, until now, as I have read them, I wondered how these earthly, and some of them unpleasant, circumstances could possibly describe the *kingdom of heaven*. This is because I continued to equate the *kingdom of heaven* with heaven itself. But this is not so, and Scripture makes it very clear, if we but read it carefully and prayerfully. When we do, the Holy Spirit will, in His good time, connect the dots for us as He has promised in James 1:5–7. Here are the *dots:*

1.   We begin our treasure hunt, the hunt for the dots, or clues, in Matthew 18:1–4. "At the same time came the disciples unto Jesus, saying, who is the greatest in the *kingdom of heaven*? And Jesus called a little child unto him, and set him in the midst of them, and said, Verily I say unto you, except ye be converted, and become as little children, ye shall not enter into the *kingdom of heaven.*

Whosoever therefore shall humble himself as this little child, the same is greatest in the *kingdom of heaven.*

Here is perhaps our first solid clue. "Except ye be first converted and become as little children, ye shall not enter the *kingdom of heaven."* He is not saying one is to become childish, but instead innocent, trusting and humble as a little child. (Trusting in Him and His Word) The more solid, the stronger these qualities, the greater position we'll have in the *kingdom of heaven*, whatever that is.

2.   The second dot or clue in evidence is found in Matthew 13:10–17

> "And the disciples came, and said unto him, Why speakest thou unto them in parables? He answered and said unto them, because it is given unto you to know the mysteries of the kingdom of heaven, but to them it is not given.
>
> For whosoever hath, to him shall be given and he shall have more abundance: but whosoever hath not, from him shall be taken away even that he hath.
>
> Therefore speak I to them in parables: because they seeing see not; and hearing they hear not, neither do they understand.
>
> And in them is fulfilled the prophecy of Isaiah, which saith,
> By hearing ye shall hear, and shall not understand;
> And seeing ye shall see, and shall not perceive;
> For this people's heart is waxed gross,
> And their ears are dull of hearing,
> And their eyes they have closed;
> Lest at any time they should see with their eyes,
> And hear with their ears, and should understand with their heart, and should be converted, and I should heal them.
> But blessed are your eyes, for they see; and your ears, for they hear.

> For verily I say unto you, That many prophets and righteous men have desired to see those thing which ye see, and have not seen them; and to hear those things which ye hear, and have not heard them."

There is much here worthy of contemplation and discussion. However, we will limit it only to that which is relevant to the John the Baptist issue. Here Jesus tells the disciples, and us, that the parables reveal the mysteries of the *kingdom of heaven*. Clearly the parables do not describe heaven in any sense that Scripture leads us to believe. Therefore the *kingdom of heaven* is obviously somewhere or something else. In verse 17 He speaks, in the past tense of the many prophets and righteous men (and women) who have desired to see and hear about these things regarding the *kingdom of heaven*, but because they remained as mysteries until His revelation of them, these people were not privileged to know or experience them.

3.   As we near the finish of the chase, we find a third clue in Luke 16:16 "the law and the prophets were until John; since that time the kingdom of God is preached, and every man presseth into it." Here we find that John the Baptist was of the old dispensation the last of the prophets, which in effect closes the Old Testament period. This ushers in the new dispensation as presented by Jesus, who is God, in-the-flesh and who now reveals the mystery here-to-for kept secret from everyone else, even from John the Baptist. Here we are told that this mystery of the *kingdom of God* is now preached and every man presseth into it. (Greek word *biazo* = crowding oneself, force, vital activity through thought or idea) NOTE: the *kingdom of heaven* and the *kingdom of God* seem to be one and the same, as evidenced by Matthew 13:31 vs. Luke 13:20.

Thus we now see that the *kingdom* is not necessarily a place, or only a place, but a concept and idea or doctrine which is preached and which many now seek to acquire.

4.   And now we come to the final dot, the last clue that perhaps brings closure to the quest, as well as clarity to the dot-lined picture we seek. In Luke 17:20, 21 we read, "And when he was demanded of

the Pharisees, when the *kingdom of God* should come he answered then and said, The *kingdom of God* cometh not with observation;

Neither shall they say, Lo here! Or lo there! For, behold the *kingdom of God* is within you.

Here Jesus tells us that the *kingdom of God / heaven* is within you! That is those who choose to accept His message, and believe in Him. It is a message of love and grace, and faith, which creates the re-birth! It is the overriding theme of the New Testament, summarized and fulfilled in every redeemed heart! It is also the place where all of the redeemed dwell in spirit even here on earth, even amidst all the pain and suffering, evil and tribulation. The lowliest of those who have this blessed grace of the new dispensation, those who become joint heirs with Jesus to rule from heaven are hereby each and everyone, greater than John. For John, being of the old dispensation, surely being saved as are all the faithful of the old, will not rule from heaven, but rather will rule, here on earth, when Jesus assumes the throne of David, here on earth. So, it is not a question of who is in heaven, where the greatness of John is being compared, but rather who belongs to the *kingdom of heaven*. It is they who are born-again by grace through faith that are in the *kingdom of heaven* and the *kingdom of heaven* is *in* them. For they, by their status as adopted children of God, and thus joint heirs with Jesus, are above all who were saved before, including John, as Luke 16:16 tells us. "The law and the prophets *were* until John."

I pray that those who read the original paper and accepted my answer to the Mathew 11:11 issues, will accept my apologies for misleading them. Perhaps in a way it may be a blessing to you by alerting you again to the fact that all of man's words regarding Scripture should be confirmed as taught in Acts 17:11.

—21—

Good and Evil and the Paradox of Free Will vs. Predestination

The Holy Spirit, among other things, is a love essence of God, and when called upon through our embracing Jesus as our Lord and Savior, He enters the heart, sensitizes the human spirit and stimulates a higher consciousness of Himself within us. Thus the human spirit becomes capable of establishing communication with God, and obtains an enhanced ability to understand God's purpose and will. Achieving this, the conscience can now more accurately interpret, articulate and communicate God's will through the soul to the mind and body. In this way, the physical being receives the necessary guidance, strength and resolve to conduct itself as God would have it be. If this were the only force, the entire earth could simply be an expanded Eden without pain or suffering or any of the physical, mental and spiritual difficulties that now plague the earth

Why isn't this the way things are? Surely it would seem that this is the way that God would want it to be. As the supreme and ultimate all encompassing power, He could have it any way that He would choose to have it. Why then is there evil along with all of the associated human tragedies that have always plagued mankind? I don't know, and I doubt that anyone really knows, because I don't believe that God has told anyone in a good, solid, fully understandable way. He has, however, included a few clues in the Scriptures. An explanation that satisfies me, at least for the moment, and based on what I have read, observed and reasoned, is as follows. Satan, the angel who would be God, was banished to earth from heaven. He became and is the manifestation of all evil, the antithesis of God, though in a comparatively puny way, because he is himself only a created being. It would seem that he is the epitome of a free will and an insatiable ego gone astray. Although banished from heaven, he retained all of his angelic powers, powers that from a human viewpoint are incredibly God-like obviously, but compared to Gods', are quite limited.

In the meantime, God made man in His own image. Think about that —in His own image. I don't believe that that means what I used to think that it meant, or what many people believe that it means. Look in a mirror and you will see your image. That image is a reflection, the playing of light and shadows; it has no substance; it is nothing. Modify the surface topography of the reflector, and the image becomes grotesque, distorted, or disappears. As that essentially nothingness image is to each of us as flesh and blood, so are we as compared to God.

Nevertheless, this "image" of God was created and endowed with many and complex characteristics including free will. Herein lay the ultimate paradox and a topic for debate that might well never be reconciled to any mutual satisfaction. Can there be free will if there is predestination? If God knows everything, and he does, then all of our actions and their results are known to Him before they happen, and were thus, it would seem, predetermined or known from the beginning of time. If it is already known by God exactly what we will do, our every act, and how everything will end, then free will would seem to be a farce and we, therefore, have no choices; they have already been made for us, and we are merely following a prepared script which we didn't write and which we can't change. I understand that St. Augustine wrestled with this problem for many years and finally satisfied himself that free will and predestination do coexist. Although I have yet to read his work on this subject, I have found reason to believe this also. At the risk of being embarrassed in the future if I find his or another explanation to be superior, I, nevertheless, feel compelled to record my current views on this matter.

We do have control of our actions; we have free will. He gave this to us almost unconditionally to do with it as we see fit, to the very limits of human capability. It was given as an amoral quality, being neither good nor evil. Stockpiled also within our psyche after the fall, were the means, the potential, and the propensities for good and for evil. It would seem that perhaps these propensities are attached to the boundaries of the soul. That for good is at the spirit/soul boundary, and that for evil is at the soul/flesh boundary. In between, within the soul is the conscience, that internal judgment seat that must continually arbitrate between these two competing factions and render personal judgment on one's actions. Under unencumbered free will conditions, when our spiritual side scores a point or wins a round, we feel good and have a "clear conscience." When evil wins a round we feel a "troubled conscience." However, we do not live in a balanced, unencumbered, free will environment, as world conditions clearly illustrate. Because we live in the world of the flesh, that propensity for evil, which resides at the soul/flesh interface, is closer and more accessible to the external world than is the more internal force for good. Satan, the prince of this earthly, external world, the would-be god of all creation, the hater of God the creator, has as his mission the seduction and destruction of God's creation, man. To this end, he proceeds to insinuate himself into the flesh, stimulating these evil propensities such as pride, lust, avarice, hate, etc., and causing them to grow and engulf the soul, subdue the conscience, and subordinate, or eliminate the Holy Spirit-directed propensities for good.

Try as he may, however, Satan can never pierce the veil that surrounds the God-given, noble qualities inherent in man. He may cause them to be totally subordinated, and may banish them from the consciousness, but he can never destroy them. Thanks to the teachings of Jesus, no matter how low one may have sunk, there is always hope for redemption and forgiveness as soon as we accept Him as our Savior. Unlike Satan, He will not impose himself but waits to be asked into our lives. Only then is it possible to break Satan's grip. Satan's grip on our soul through our flesh can be, and often is, overpowering and seemingly impossible to overcome. The pleasures of the flesh are often irresistible and addictive as well as cunningly deceptive, because Satan knows our weaknesses better than we do. Once he has penetrated a soul and taken command, he builds within it a whole new set of values and a new "morality" fashioned after his likeness. The individual so afflicted is no longer able to exercise free will, even though for a while, he may think that he is "liberated." The great deceiver has instilled an illusion of freedom as he proceeds to enslave that soul in the morass of selfishness and evil, masquerading as enlightened modernity. The enslaved individual is not aware of his condition. Through Satan's deceptive powers the person may feel just and moral and a pillar of enlightenment. After a while, as it often happens, uncomfortable feelings, feelings of some kind of spiritual void or lack of satisfaction or fulfillment, may enter the soul. Perhaps this is that imprisoned higher self, kicking the walls of its confinement and begging to be released. Perhaps also, it is the Lord knocking at the soul with His offer of salvation. Those who respond through sincere prayer, regardless of their sinful status, will find God. At that moment, Satan will reluctantly pack up and leave. The prayer will unleash a powerful antibiotic, completely eliminating Satan's viral grip, and bring forth from captivity those nobler qualities so abhorrent to Satan.

Although the power of the Lord is infinitely greater then his, Satan will, nevertheless, lurk in the shadows waiting for another opportunity to reinfect the soul. As with so many diseases, the host remains susceptible and can easily have a relapse. Only through constant vigil, as provided by prayer and faith in Jesus, can the soul's immunity be maintained. Whenever Satan looses a soul, he is mightily enraged and leaves a permanent cloud of evil virus and temptations surrounding his former host. These are always ready and able to penetrate any void or exploit any weakness, which might regain for him, that soul.

The existence of Satan and his ability to subvert souls and enlist them in his army of evil and destruction is the cause of the pain and suffering and all of the wrongs in the world. A subverted soul lives for its own gratification and pleasures. These take many forms that inevitably inflict pain and suffering on others, the lust for and attainment of power being the most evident and destructive. Stalin, Mao and Hitler are but three of this century's most prominent of his legions of dedicated agents. These three alone are responsible for the tragic deaths of more than one hundred million innocent souls along with the pain and suffering and illness of hundreds of millions more. These are the result of man's free will and Satan's exploitation of his more base capabilities. If God is so good, how can He allow all of this suffering to continue? For those whose priorities are in the here and now, a satisfactory explanation may be impossible. However, those who have studied the Bible and believe in Jesus may find some value in the following.

The earth just might be a quality control and testing center for souls. Making a soul that has the qualities necessary for everlasting life in heaven is not a simple matter, even for God. Making the stars, the earth, and everything on the earth was easy for God, but making a good, reliable, everlasting soul is not that easy. Look at the angels. One would think that they would be perfection itself. Yet a third of them "went bad" and revolted. Instead of destroying them, He simply banished them to earth for a while before issuing a final sentence. During this while, as Satan, the ringleader of the pack of mutineers, schemes to get back to heaven and displace Him, God has found a use for them in this center for quality control we call earth.

In order to be sure, even for God, this test is necessary. How does He test these created souls for the necessary qualities? Simply put, He gives them free will and sends them out into the devil's world of temptations and observes their conduct. In order to pass the test, the soul doesn't have to be a bastion of strength and infallibility. He didn't make it that way. If He had, man's free will wouldn't be all that free. Man had to be vulnerable and capable of choosing freely between God and Satan. Through the clear, crisp, beautiful message of Jesus, we know that in order to pass the test, we need only to seek Him and put our unconditional faith and trust in Him. I say "only" not because it is easy, but because it is all that we need to do. It is not easy. It is extremely difficult. Satan, in his own mind isn't here as a quality control tester. He has a different agenda. He is here to build a mountain of captured souls so high that he can climb back to heaven over it. It is difficult for us because it is difficult not to live of the flesh and not to succumb to all of the temptations of the flesh, even without Satan's involvement. God, of course, knows this and He willingly forgives all sins, as long as we believe in His Son and, as a consequence, sincerely, with all of our ability, work to avoid sin. In the final analysis, the only thing He wants is a total, unconditional faith in Him and, of course, all that that implies. Perhaps it is because of the partial mutiny of His first creation, that He has chosen this route as the means for obtaining for heaven, only those souls that can endure this test of temptations, pain and suffering and still stay loyal to His Word.

—22—

Free Will—Is It Humanity's Bane or Benefit, and What Can We Do about It!

In the beginning, God had a desire for something He didn't have and couldn't create. So in His infinite wisdom and power, He set about creating the means by which He could obtain that which He couldn't create. First, He arranged for a brief alteration in His eternal timeless expanse wherein time and matter would come into existence. Then out of the matter He created life, including mankind, which He chose to make in His own image. In doing so, He endowed mankind with a few of His own attributes, the principal ones being the ability to reason, to comprehend and to make choices on his own, that is to have free will. Free will as defined by Augustine is "the ability to make voluntary decisions free from external constraint or coercion."

Prior to this, God had created angels. Even though they had the power of choice, they were not made in His image, nor did they possess the power or qualities to provide Him with that which He was seeking. As we know, and of course as He knew from before the beginning of time, there was one angel who would rebel, taking with him a third of all the other angels. Naturally, He also knew that this would happen in that it had always been part of His plan. But now, there are two wills in existence, God's and Satan's. The wills of the rebel angels were in unison with Satan's as were the wills of the others in unison with God's will.

With the advent of created man, the potential for a third will came into existence. At first, man's will also remained in unison with

God's will. But God, in His divine wisdom and in accordance with His divine plan, gave man a list of do's, and also a single don't, thus giving him this simple, elementary, but very essential opportunity to use his free will, to either stay with the do's or to apply his free will and do the don't. Of course, we all know that through the influence of Satan, he did do the don't, and thus another will contrary to God's will came into being. However, the one don't, as soon as it was eaten by Adam, not only exploded into a myriad of other don'ts we call sins, but it also shook the very foundations of the entire universe, initiating entropy, decay, and death.

Here we should pause for a moment to examine a very important related precept. Today, if we really think about it, we must acknowledge that in our fallen human state, doing the don'ts, that is to engage in sin, is a very attractive, compelling alternative to not sinning, that is, to living God's way. The condition of the world reveals ample proof of that. The temptation to sin is obviously caused by this attractiveness and our desire to have or experience its perceived benefits. Man does not lust after ugliness but only after that which is attractive and pleasure producing. He steals because he recognizes the attractiveness of obtaining his wants in ways easier than working for them. He lies because at the moment of choice, the lie is more attractive than the truth, because it seems to achieve what truth cannot.

These and many more examples of that attractiveness of sin express how all of the world functions. But, we know Satan became the father of all lies and of all evil. We tend to think of Satan, if we think of him at all, as a significant adversary of God, a challenge to His omnipotence. We think correctly in terms of some kind of a real and evil spiritual force behind the scenes engaging in a power struggle between God and Satan. This is because we know from Daniel 10:13–20 and other scriptural references, that there is a power struggle going on between principalities and powers, and that Satan does have behind the scene power over earthly governments and other organizations. However, we also know, or should know, that Satan can do *nothing* beyond that which God allows him to do. It is no more of a bona fide power struggle than it is the wrestling match on the living room floor between a father and his four-year old son. Satan in all his evilness and power is allowed to exist because God has chosen it to be so as part of His divine plan. Satan exists in part to provide the yang to go with the ying, the darkness to go with the light, and the wrong to go with the right, all to provide the genuine choices that made free will legitimate and not a sham. Thus, we must realize that Satan is merely a tool, or unpleasant agent in the implementation of God's grand plan. It does not seem, however, that it is for us to know the whole of God's plan where Satan is concerned, but from what Scripture does reveal we can see that he is a real part of it, if nothing but a pawn.

Getting back to Adam, we see that he, of course, became the father of all the other free wills, which then proceeded to populate the earth, each a different will, but all contrary to the will of God. In his fallen state, hopelessly infected with this sin virus, it was impossible for man to have a will *not* contrary to God's will. With all of this having taken place, and in seeing the depravity that exists today through the only lenses available to natural man, one could conclude that God blew it. His plan somehow went out of control. But those who see through lenses provided by the Holy Spirit, know differently, because through their lenses, God's word, the Scriptures, reveals clearly to them the wondrous and perfect choreographing of God's plan as it has been taking place.

But now what did all of this do for God in terms of His desire to obtain that which He couldn't directly create, and just what was this illusive thing He wanted so much? From John 4:16, we know that God is love. But what good is love without a beloved? In fact, love cannot even manifest without a beloved. There must be a loved one to love. However, love can also be unrequited, that is it doesn't have to be returned by the beloved. Such a love, however, is a very lonely and extremely painful love. Love yearns to be returned by the one being loved. Surely God loved the angels and they loved Him. But they were not of His kind; they were not made in His own image, as was man. Perhaps this can in one way be likened to the love between a man and his pet, as compared with a genuine love between a man and his bride. I pray that the angels not be offended by this analogy.

It is applied only to illustrate the differences of love between diverse and like kinds.

Now, therefore, He had created the potentiality, the being, through whom he could get what He sought, a being made in His own image, you might also say potentially of His own kind, whom He could love. However, that wasn't enough, because of this yearning to also be loved by those after His own image. But even God in His omnipotence could not make anyone love Him. This is because love is a commitment given freely by a being having both the capability and the absolute, sovereign, free, unencumbered choice to love or not to love. So here at last we come to the answer to the question, as to why mankind had to be given free will, an unfettered right to make choices. It was so that man would be potentially qualified to provide to God that which He wanted but could not directly create. It was so that He could both love and be loved by beings of His own image or kind, so He could have an eternal loving family relationship in heaven. How wonderful it is, that that is His desire, and that we are thereby so blessed as to have the privilege of being part of His eternal family!

But the fulfillment of this desire cost God far, far, far more than we can ever comprehend. Because once He allowed sin and Satan and all these other diverse wills to exist, and we see that He had to for the reason given above, we also see that a wholly new and different process had to be initiated to counter the problems and clean up the wreckage which this free will caused. Scripture calls it salvation, which leads to justification and then to sanctification. Because God could not take into heaven any sin, and since free will and temptation made certain that all would sin, this additional incredible process, which is the unqualified expression of God's perfect love was made necessary before God could actually acquire a mutually loving family and eventually bring it home to eternal bliss.

Now let's see what this all cost God. For starters, God has had to suffer the on-going painful indignity of seeing those created in His own image in constant rebellion against Him. Through their free wills, nearly all of humanity chose and choose even today, to chase after and worship false gods and many so sadly choose to deny that He even exists. Even after having chosen a particular man, Abraham, through whom he generated a whole race to which He many times personally revealed Himself, His love and His omnipotence, the choice to do evil remained in every one of them as it has in all other people. Even more painful to our God must be to see the long suffering of all humanity from the accumulative and compounding consequences of all of the individual choices throughout history, which were, and continue to be, made contrary to God's will. While it is sometimes tempting for the redeemed, and is universally popular for the natural man, to blame God for humanity's predicament, God never does, nor could He, initiate pain or evil. But as difficult as it is for the natural man to understand, God has to allow this to happen in order to preserve the un-coerced freedom of choice regardless of the consequences. That is not to say that He doesn't intervene in many ways. Scripture is full of examples, but it is difficult to find evidence of His intervention in choices, however, it is most common to see evidences of His divine hand in many of the consequences. Also, He does put forth for our consideration many evidences of what He prefers us to choose, but He then leaves it to us to make the final choice.

However, in the redeemed, those in whom the Holy Spirit dwells, those who have fulfilled His desire for a mutually loving family, He retains an on-going fellowship through which He does, in fact, strongly influence the heart to live by His will. This is because the former will of the redeemed has served its purpose and is no longer needed or wanted in His divine plan. His will remains sovereign. Now, in order to redeem man from sin, He, Jesus, the Son person of the triune Godhead, had to enter His own creation in order to save from sin that portion of His likeness which He chose to be His eternal family. Not only did He have to enter it, but He also had to suffer physically and spiritually and then die at the hands of those He had created in His image! This, of course, was followed by His resurrection. But His death was the only way He could cleanse the sins of the elect in order to make them eligible for heaven. Another price He paid for this act of love is that He now sits in heaven as both God and man, having visible proof of this incredible sacrifice as evidenced by His pierced hands, feet and side, for we know that when He returns these will still be there (Zechariah 12:10, 13:6, and Revelation 5:6). We also know that even the earth, and the stars and the whole universe groan from the pain of the original and subsequent sin (Romans 8:22).

So as we see the terrible consequences wrought to all creation by this quality called free will, we can also see the necessity of it as a means by which God has achieved His purpose. For we know that those who are of the spirit and possess that love, are the embodiments of that purpose. Because He foretold all that would happen, we also know that the times of universal suffering are nearing the end; from His word we know the signs of those times, and can now see that we are actually in the times of those signs.

Those who are His chosen, who see by the light of the Holy Spirit, see the folly and the burdens associated with ownership of free will, this independent personal will. Having completed its principal purpose at the moment, we become born again, that is to have become part of His eternal family, having made the love commitment, and having had our sins forgiven and forgotten, there is no longer any good purpose or need for a free will. It has, in fact, become the bane of our lives. It is poisonous to the soul. It is a point of entry for Satan and for all of our former thoughts, emotions, and desires, which are contrary to God's will. Therefore, it is to our great benefit to give back to God our free will, to beg Him to take it and to pray that He will. In doing so, we should pray that He live every moment through us so that it is now His will, and only His will which governs us. This is not easy to do, because our old selves are yet very strong and want mightily to retain their independence and self-determination as to what to choose, and the desire to sin yet remains strong in our loins. But as children of God, we no longer need, nor should we want, anything contrary to His will, so His will should always be our goal and our only choice. As the love for Him, which He so much wanted and for which He paid such a high price, grows in our hearts, His will in us must also grow evermore beautiful, joyous and easier to follow. At the same time, as He continues His blessed work in us, the old self should become ever more repugnant and easier to subordinate. So ask God to take back your free will, pray that He will do so, and then try to live every day, moment by moment, as if He has taken it!

—23—

Mankind's Sovereign Will

Perhaps God's most profound gift to mankind is the God-like quality of sovereign free will. What does that mean? It means that we have absolute sovereignty over our will, our ability to choose our thoughts and our actions, sovereignty that God cannot, because He will not, compromise. Does God intervene in our lives? Yes, and so does the devil, his cohorts and a goodly portion of the rest of mankind in one way or another. Then how can one possibly believe that we have sovereignty of will, of choice, when this intervention is so evident?

All intervention is through persuasion. Neither God nor man can take away what God has unconditionally given us, our right to choose our own beliefs, thoughts and actions. Persuasions, which may influence our choices, take on many forms, from loving guidance to prolonged sadistic torture and death. History is full of evidence regarding those who *chose* to believe in Jesus and were tortured without mercy as a means of persuading them to choose otherwise, but who nevertheless chose to die for their faith. Those less firm in their chosen belief were persuaded to make another choice. Parents choose to raise their children to live under a particular system of values and beliefs. They apply these through persuasion, example, instruction, indoctrination, reward and punishment. The child, however, chooses, as he or she will, to accept or reject these values and beliefs. They usually will also revise these as they enter the world and are further influenced by their peers and by many confusing and contradicting forces, which they encounter over the course of their lives. However, they never lose their capacity to choose, and always do so as a result of some composite of all of the persuasive forces by which they choose to be influenced.

217

Although God does influence our lives, so does the devil. God certainly intervenes in our lives and in the fate of nations, as evidenced especially throughout the Old Testament. God intervenes through both punishment and rewards, but never as a direct assault on our free will. Revelation. 3:20 tells us that He may knock on the door of our soul, but He will not enter unless we choose to let Him in. Ephesians 2:8, 9 tells us "For by grace are you saved through faith; and that not of yourselves it is a gift of God, not of works, lest any man should boast." God gives (offers) us the grace of salvation, however, we must choose to accept it before it can actually be received and become the means through which we are born again. As born again Christians, we seek and obtain a unique affiliation with the Lord. Our faith, which is a choice, requires that we seek and live His way. In that capacity we ask Him to guide our choices and to intervene in our lives through our prayers. We ask Him to make choices for us and to take over our wills as well as our lives. This He will do at and only at our specific request, because He will not override our sovereign right to choose our own direction. Again, when God intervenes by punishing or rewarding, and thus in effect altering events related to individuals, groups or even nations, it does not mean that He is thus usurping anyone's free will. Individual choice is still absolute in that one may choose to view these events as natural or manmade, coincidences, or God inspired, and to respond to them as one chooses.

The whole purpose of man's physical life is to grow to believe, love, and obey the Lord, have faith in Him and to thus become prepared to share the wonders and delights of eternal companionship with Him. There are a few things that God cannot do. Among them is that He cannot make us love Him. This is the key to the whole issue. Love, true unconditional love, is not an emotion, but a choice commitment. How sincere or worthy could that love be if it was derived in any manner other than from a sovereign ability to make that choice? Would God find any value in a love or faith that resulted from a stacked deck, that is from a source less than totally free to make that choice? An absolute free will is the only source from which such a commitment could originate.

The premise of man's free will is also challenged when the idea of predestination is considered in this context. It would seem that the awesome accuracy of biblical prophecy would suggest that God directs everything and therefore even our individual thoughts and actions have already been choreographed well in advance of our commencing them. How else could He know what will happen centuries before it happens unless He has already planned and orchestrated it? The answer is quite clear. He knows what will happen before it happens because He is outside of time and in multiple higher dimensions that are beyond our powers of comprehension. From there He sees the future as easily as the past and present. For Him it's not necessary to cause something to happen in order to know that it will happen, because past and present and future have no significance from outside of time, which in fact we now know to be a physical dimension which did not always exist, but was instead part of creation. A weak and limited analogy that may provide some insight into this phenomenon is the passing parade. A spectator standing at the curb will remember portions of the parade which have already passed, and is seeing that which is in front of him at the present. However, he has no way to know what is coming but which is not yet in view. He will not know that until it reaches his position, his present time. However, to a reporter in a helicopter overhead, viewing a parade from this higher dimension, if you will, sees the entire parade from beginning to end, and can therefore report to the spectator exactly what he can expect to see later, all the way to the end, if he has a radio and is tuned in to the right station. God is our reporter and the Scriptures are our radio. If we are tuned into the right wavelength, through which to hear the Word that is if we have the Holy Spirit, we also can know the nature of the whole parade. Therefore, what may seem to be preordained and thus already decided for us, leaving no room for choice through this sovereignty of will, is nothing more than evidence of the power of the Lord to see into the future and to thereby know in advance what choices we will make when that future becomes our present.

Nothing that the Lord does interferes with our free will. He may have influence over events along the way and thus limit our available range or type of choices, but not the freedom to truly make our own choices. This sovereign power of mankind and the choices resulting there from are in many ways the major sources of both the agony and the ecstasy of our mortal lives as well as the determining factors as to where our souls will spend eternity.

As a postscript, I believe that much of the Old Testament narrative depicting the Israelites ups and downs through the ages, there devotion and their transgressions, and God's response to them, can easily be viewed as a saga of man's sovereignty of choice and God's restraint from violating that sovereignty. To those who haven't studied carefully the entire message, and especially to non-believers, the stories might seem very strange in the context of an omnipotent God. Without the concept that God irrevocably ordained this sovereignty of free will and, therefore, that He has allowed man to proceed through the ages disobeying, ignoring, perverting and modifying His stated ordinances, and even denying that He exists, one could easily conclude that God is neither all powerful nor all knowing. Certainly, however, He has adequately demonstrated His omnipotent capabilities, by His creation as well as in performing miracles, showing His wrath, rewarding and punishing individuals as well as whole nations, while He has also proven Himself to be a God of infinite love through Jesus Christ. Yet man seems always to have been able to go on his independent way, free to choose as he will, with seeming impunity here on earth. As a result, pain, suffering, poverty, starvation disease, torture, murders and all forms of evil proliferate. I believe that all of this is caused by fallen man's free will expressed against his own kind. It is the compound aggregate result of all pride, envy, deceit, lust, covertness, anger, lies, ignorance, and lack of love for God and his fellow man. We, of course, know that our God is omnipotent and could stop this or anything else if He so chose. Then why doesn't He?

I believe He will, and quiet soon. In His book where He has written all of the history, there is a part where He tells us about future history. He told us of, and described the many events, which would precede the end of His patience. Many of these events have happened while others are at this moment taking shape with astounding accuracy. If you are concerned with what is really happening, and going to happen in the world, turn off CNN and curl up in your best chair and read the Scripture. CNN only has a curbside, curb level view of the passing parade. The Scriptures will, if you enlist the interpretive power of the Holy Spirit, show you the whole parade, all the way to where the fat lady sings.

—24—
The Great Dilemma

The preeminent philosopher, Socrates, is recorded to have said, "Perhaps God can forgive sin, but I don't see how." How many throughout the history of the world, absent the knowledge imparted by God through the Scripture, were capable of such an intellectually astute question? That there is such a thing as sin, and that God alone is its assessor and forgiver is a profound thought, absent the benefit of Scripture. In order to have conceived of such a dilemma is evidence that Socrates was fully aware of, and understood the impeccable nature of God's righteousness and His uncompromising, perfect justice. He must also have recognized the absolutely indelible nature of sin, and how impossible it was for man in any way to erase such blemishes from his soul. Thus it must follow, that because such a question was worthy of being asked, Socrates must have realized that some eternal purpose needed to be served by that forgiveness, or cleansing, by God.

What seems likely however is that regardless of his great intellect, he may have lacked an understanding of another one of God's qualities, which is love, a fully committed love for all of His creation, especially mankind. It is doubtful that even this would have allowed him to solve the dilemma. However, it would at least have armed him with all he needed. If only he had been privy to, and had been able to read, a series of scrolls already in existence in a small city barely 850 miles from his home in Athens. For you see, having lived from 470 B.C. to about 399 B.C. he was a contemporary of the prophet Malachi who wrote the last book of the Old Testament around 430 B.C. Thus, had the systems of communications been better, he might have had access to the entire early recordings of God's Word and all of the information needed to answer this most challenging question. With his great intellect, perhaps comparable to that of the Apostle Paul, what an effective expositor of God's Old Testament truths he would have made!

For reason known only to God, and in accordance to His divine purpose, He chose to reveal Himself most clearly to only one small area in between the Dead Sea and the Sea of Galilee. It was also the tribe from which was to come the Redeemer, the one who would give life to the answer Socrates so solemnly sought. Had he been able to read those scrolls which were in the Hebrews possession, no doubt he would have soon recognized that these were indeed Gods inspired messages which clearly spelled out with inerrant accuracy not only the answer to his dilemma, but to all of history. Here was history long lost to his culture and to all surrounding cultures, their history then being nothing more than traditions and mythology laced with vague and confusing smatterings of formerly known truths no longer discernable in a coherent framework. How astounded he would have been to learn from these parchments, not only history past, but history present and future, as only the immutable "Logos" could have revealed it. How joyous would have been his heart and the hearts of his fellow thinkers, such as Plato and Aristotle who followed, as they recognized that here was that great, and heretofore elusive "Logos," that awesome and controlling "principal of the universe" which they had so ardently and vainly searched for from within their own intellect.

It is likely that he would have also soon discovered the great truth, which was fully known only to a few of that tribe of Gods "chosen people." Only through the likes of such great personages as Enoch, Noah, Abraham, Moses and David does it seem that sufficient amounts of the whole great truth of sin and its true means of forgiveness had been yet revealed. In Malachi, God ended the "preview of these things." Yet everything needed, from which the great dilemma could be solved, had been revealed although not in a manner readily discernable by any but those with ready and willing hearts.

And so it is today, even after the actual physical personification of the "Logos," the incarnation of God Himself, and even after His completely animated and ultimate expression of almighty sanctified

223

love, and His crystal clear means for salvation secured, there are only a small remnant who seem capable of understanding and accepting the truth. Why? Because many cannot even accept the fact that sin actually exists. They, and even those who do realize the existence of sin, shrink from the idea that there is an accountability associated with it. To admit that sin exists, or that sin is somehow associated with accountability which leads to a need to seek forgiveness, necessitates that there must be a forgiver who in turn sets up conditions which may be fearfully contrary to one's chosen path.

How sad it is that the carnal nature of man rebels so violently against the concept of accountability, and that this nature needs to be subordinate to the way, which He, to whom we are accountable, has decreed. Throughout history it has been demonstrated that man will take almost any route, believe in the most absurd and ridiculous religions and rituals, in order to avoid accountability, to negate the indelible nature or even existence of sin, and to believe that if saving is even necessary, he can save himself through his own efforts and works. Because Scripture, the Holy Bible, is so clear and is the inerrant Word of God, pointing to the *only* way to salvation, natural man, always aided by the deceiving devices provide by Satan, will vigorously avoid, or seek to discredit it.

What a shame! I pray the reader is not so seduced, but has accepted God's way.

—25—

Are You an Overcomer?

A few months ago during our Sunday noontime Bible study at the beginning of the book of Revelation, a lady in attendance asked, "What is an 'overcomer'?" We tried as best as we could to answer "off the cuff" as it were. This was her first time there and she never came back. I've often wondered if it had been the inadequacy of our collective answer or, and I hope, some other reason which caused her not to return. I pray the following commentary will provide her and others with a clearer and more accurate answer to what was a very important question.

As I look back to the early chapters of Revelation to see where we might have been during that particular study, for the first time I noticed a peculiar thing. Jesus speaks of "overcoming" to each and every one of the seven churches!

To the church of Ephesus, He says, "*To him that overcometh will I give to eat of the tree of life, which is in the midst of the paradise of God.*"

To the church of Smyrna, He says, "*He that overcometh shall not be hurt of the second death.*"

To the church of Pergamos, He says, "*To him that overcometh will I give to eat of the hidden manna, and will give him a white stone, and in the stone a new name written, which no man knoweth saving he that receiveth it.*"

To the church of Thyatira, He says, "*And he that overcometh and keepeth my works unto the end, to him will I give power over the nations.*"

To the church of Sardis, He says, "*He that overcometh, the same shall be clothed in white raiment, and I will not blot out his name out of* the Book of Life, but I will confess his name before my Father, and before His angels."

To the church of Philadelphia, He says, *"Him that overcometh will I make a pillar in the temple of my God, and he shall go no more out: and I will write upon him the name of my God, and the name of the city of my God, which is new Jerusalem, which cometh down out of heaven from my God: and I will write upon him my new name."*

To the church of Laodicea, He says, *"To him that overcometh will I grant to sit with me in my throne, even as I also overcame, and am set down with my Father in His throne."*

Once more, and for the eighth time in Revelation 21, Jesus says in verse 7 that, *"He that overcometh shall inherit all things; and I will be his God, and he shall be my son."* These are all statements made to John directly from the throne room of heaven as Jesus reveals the seven aspects of the entire church age from Pentecost to the Rapture, and then describes those who are saved during the tribulation. From this it is evident that Jesus is making a big deal over this word "overcomer." If He is emphasizing it so much, it must be very important and something which we should seek to understand thoroughly.

The word expressed as "overcome," "overcomer," or "over-cometh" occurs a total of twenty-six times in the New Testament as *nikao,* meaning "to subdue, conquered, overcome, prevail, get the victory." All seven epistles to the seven individual churches were meant to be circulated among the actual churches that existed in Asia Minor at that time. While each was addressed to a specific church and expressed the predominate, God-seen characteristic of that church, the individual message nevertheless had value to each of the other churches as well. That is why Jesus ends each message with, ". . . what the Spirit says to the churches" (plural). This is probably of even greater relevance to the prophetic churches to which these letters were addressed. The letters are demonstrated to be prophetic of the seven church periods from about 30 A.D. through to the Rapture, which will instantly end the entire church age. While the letters describe characteristics specific to the church during each of the individual historical periods, each of the messages has some application to all the churches in all periods in history. Therefore, we may conclude that while Jesus individualized the "overcometh message" to each of the churches, the composite of these also has relevance to all of the churches.

Now let's see what they say in this context. He that overcometh will eat of the tree of life, shall not be hurt by the second death, will be given the hidden manna to eat, will receive a white stone with a secret name, will be given power over nations, will be clothed in a white raiment and not blotted out of the Book of Life; will be made a pillar in the temple and have the name of God and of the new Jerusalem written on him, along with God's new name; and finally, will sit with Jesus in His throne.

Viewed collectively, this seems to be a whole basketful of goodies, which God has prepared for those who overcome. They depict a glorious eternal life filled with wondrous gifts, positions and circumstances that will be available to all who overcome.

Then we have Revelation 21:7 which is just forty verses from the very end of not only Jesus' Revelation, but also of His entire written Word to the world. Here is a grand finale message to the overcomer. Jesus summarizes it all when He says, "He that overcometh shall inherit all things, and will I be his God and he shall be my son." (Remember all of this applies to daughters as well.) How can it get any better than this? ALL THINGS! BEING GOD'S SON! All the individual gifts to the overcomer described in the seven letters are here included in one grand promise!

But now, just what and who is an overcomer? In Romans 12:21, the Holy Spirit speaks through Paul and says, "Be not overcome of evil but overcome evil with good." Overcoming sin is also the underlying essence of the messages given us in the epistles of both Peter and John. Therefore, it is apparent that the important characteristic of an overcomer, in the biblical sense, is to have overcome or to have been victorious over sin. But how can one do this when we know from Jeremiah 17:9 that ". . . the heart is deceitful above all things and desperately wicked; who can know it?" There is no way, by ourselves, that we can overcome sin when we are so hopelessly wicked. We need help, big help; help of a supernatural quality.

How blessed are we who recognize where this help can be found, and who are willing to trust and obey Him who can provide the strength and the way to become an overcomer. Look at what Jesus told His apostles and therefore us as well, in John 16:33: "*. . . in this world ye shall have tribulations, but be of good cheer, I have overcome the world*." Also, look back at Revelation 3:21 where Jesus again speaks of His having overcome.

Here we have the ultimate overcomer, the only person ever to have lived a perfect life of obedience to God, a genuinely sinless life. By being both God and a sinless man, He was made sin, the equivalent of the sum total of all sins perpetrated by all of mankind past, present and future. His suffering and death on the cross, along with His resurrection from the dead and ascension back to heaven, is the sublime achievement of the very first and greatest of all overcomers. He and He alone, because He was the only One who could, overcame the power and authority of sin, of hell, of death, and of Satan himself. He did this just for us, and out of His incredible love for us. Now, through Him and in no other way, is the power to overcome these things available to those who trust and obey to those who genuinely accept Him as their Lord and Savior *and all that this means*.

In order to become a genuine overcomer, one must become totally committed by yielding one's self to God and become controlled by the Holy Spirit. 1 John 5:4 assures us "*For whatsoever is born of God* (by His Spirit in us) *overcometh the world, even our faith. Who is he that overcometh the world, but he that believes* (trusts, relies on the fact) *that Jesus is the Son of God*."

Therefore, once you have truly accepted Him and are born again, you are an overcomer. You have overcome all past sins for they have been forgiven. Through the indwelling of the Holy Spirit, you have overcome the power of sin and have received an ever-growing strength and sensitivity of conscience to resist, moment by moment, the temptations of sin. To these has been added the blessing of having overcome the "second death;" "that is, your immortal soul as well as a new incorruptible body will spend a glorious eternity in heaven as one of the sons or daughters of God.

With so much at stake, who in his right mind would want to wait for even one second to get on his way to becoming an overcomer? If you don't know the way, just ask Jesus. He is waiting most eagerly to show you the way. You may not have heard Him, for He is very gentle, but He has been knocking continuously at the door of your heart during your whole life, waiting for you to accept His offer to make you an overcomer (Revelation 3:20, 21, 22).

FOR GOD'S SAKE AND YOUR OWN, ANSWER HIM!

—26—

The Watchman

In Ezekiel 33, our Lord tells us of one of His ordained instructions, that of the watchman. In the context of the time in which it was written, there was often imminent physical danger from both killer beasts and armed enemies who would attack wherever there was weakness. Therefore, people gathered together and built cities and surrounded them with walls on which they would assign sentinels, or watchman, to provide advance warning so that the gates could be closed and the able could arm and be ready to defend the City. Here God provides instruction and reveals the risks associated with the job of the watchman in a much broader context. In His description of the watchman on the rampart, He says that when the watchman sees danger approaching and blows the warning trumpet in a timely and appropriate manner, those who heed not the warning have only themselves to blame. But if he fails to warn the people, their blood is on his hands, and God says that it is the watchman's blood, which He will require.

Then God uses the watchman as an analogy in verse 7–9 where He says, "Now for you son of man, I have appointed you a watchman for the house of Israel, so you will hear a message from my mouth and give them warning from Me. When I say to the wicked, O wicked man, you will surely die, and you do not speak to warn the wicked from his way, that wicked man shall die in his iniquity, but his blood I will require from your hand. But if you, on your part, warn a wicked man to turn from his way, and he does not turn from his way, he will die in his iniquity, but you have delivered your life."

Although found in the Old Testament and directed toward Israel, it is equally directed to you and me, and all who know or should know His word and are His disciples. For He said in Romans

15:4, "For whatsoever things were written aforetime were written for our learning that we through patience and comfort of the Scriptures might have hope." Also, in 2 Timothy 3:16 the Holy Spirit tells us that "All Scripture is given by inspirations of God and is profitable for doctrine, for reproof, for correction and instruction in righteousness . . ." Furthermore, in 2 Timothy 4:2–5 we are exhorted to ". . . preach the Word; be instant in season; reprove, rebuke, exhort with all long-suffering and doctrine. For the time will come when they will not endure sound doctrine; but after their own lusts shall they heap to themselves teachers, having itching ears; and they shall turn away their ears from the truth, and shall be turned into fables. But watch thou in all things, endure afflictions, do the work of an evangelist, make full proof of thy ministry."

The above verses need little or no explanation; they are self evident as New Testament affirmations of the watchman message. However, their application is less simple than that of the watchman in the tower charged to warn of approaching physical enemies. Here we are dealing with the more subtle, less evident attacking of principalities and powers, and the great deceiver, as well as of man's own weakness, ignorance, and innate wicked nature. But how can we perform the duties of the watchman, which Scripture demands of us, unless we *know* Scripture, unless we *study* earnestly His Word with the divine guidance of the Holy Spirit who has promised to reveal all things to those who truly seek to know. If you consider yourself born-again, you have the obligation to be a "watchman." Do you know the Scripture well enough to fulfill that mandate? If not, why not?

Do you think your responsibility as a bride of Christ ended when you said, "I do."? Bible study, learning and conveying as much as possible of God's Word, seems to be the most neglected and ignored aspects of the "Christian marriage." With so many false prophets and false gospels being preached today, how do you even know for sure that you are married to the right Jesus? There are many, many counterfeit Jesuses around today, counterfeits that look and sound so real that only the biblically literate can tell the difference. You become so only through studying His Word, the whole Word of God, not just the portions that please you and make you feel good, or what others tell you about.

When Jacob found Rachel, she became his only true love. Her father Laban extracted seven years of servitude from him as payment for his right to marry Rachel. However, it wasn't until the morning after his marriage that he discovered that he had been tricked into marrying Rachel's older sister Leah. He then worked another seven years in order to marry his true love. There are "tricksters" around today in the pulpits, on TV and radio, as well as in books, magazines and street corners, far more clever and far better equipped than Laban to fool you into marrying any one of a multitude of false Jesuses. Thorough knowledge of Scripture is your only solid defense. Does it disturb you to think that perhaps it could be on that fateful day when you kneel before the judgment seat, confident that you are the Judge's bride, that He may look at you and say, "depart from me. I never knew you."? Don't take any chances; know His *whole Word*, so that you will *know Him*, and know who He is *not*. Then surely He will know you!

—27—

Jesus, the Early Years

It would seem that we know very little about Jesus from His birth to the beginning of His ministry at age thirty. Perhaps from the viewpoint of His purpose for entering the world that He Himself created, this may seem of little relevance. However, for those of us for whom He came, those who have accepted Him as our Lord and Savior, we cannot help but crave to know all there is to know about our Blessed Redeemer. Hebrew 10:7 quotes Isaiah 4:7 authenticating that the first volume of the book, that is, the Old Testament, is written of Him. And indeed it is, if we read it through the eyeglasses that the Holy Spirit gives to those who are of the faith. However, without the benefit of the revelations provided by the New Testament, a clear recognition of this fact is difficult. That is why it is said that the New Testament is in the Old Testament concealed, while the Old Testament is in the New Testament revealed. The Old Testament contains many prophecies and allusions that are difficult or even impossible to understand, as they stand alone. The New Testament illuminates and brings to understanding all that seems to have been hidden, or left obscure in that first blessed Word of God. In the Old Testament there are many prophecies and promises that were not yet fulfilled at the time of the completion of that portion of God's Word. Therefore, for more than four hundred years, God seemed to have stopped speaking to His people, and provided no evidence that He would ever keep His promises or cause a fulfillment of His prophecies. The advent of Jesus was the fulfillment of more than three hundred prophecies. However, for several reasons the vast majority of those who should have recognized this, did not. The Old Testament predicted, from the very beginning, of a Messiah, an Anointed one from

God, the Son of God. He would be both a suffering servant and the King of Kings, who would rule the world from David's throne. Unfortunately the common belief was that there would be two individual Messiahs rather than One, who would come twice.

Because they had already been continuously under the yoke of foreign rulers for about seven hundred years, they seemed blinded to the coming first of the suffering servant Messiah, and could only look for and hope for the One who would remove this yoke and conquer the world for them. Although Jesus met every prerequisite to identify Himself as the Messiah, including fulfillment of every relevant prophecy, His conduct during His three and a half year ministry showed them no evidence of having the kind of kingly nature that they expect of a conquering king. Therefore He was rejected by Hebrew officialdom. However, because of His great following, because of His sermons, His miracles, and healings, the leadership decided to kill Him before He so inspired the people that the wrath of Rome would crack down on them. In doing so they were unknowing agents of God's pre-ordained plan for the suffering Servant and Savior.

Thus through Old Testament prophecies and covenants as they have been explained in the New Testament, we know a great deal about who Jesus was / is and why He came, and what His role is and will be to the end of this world. Do we find Him in the Old Testament as a living, breathing, functioning and influencing manifestation of an earthly presence prior to becoming the Son of Man? Yes, we do! Who walked with Enoch, and with Noah? Jesus did! Was He not with Abraham at his tent near Sodom? Did He not wrestle with Jacob at Jabbok? Was He not the warrior who fought the battle of Jericho, to name a few more of His "stage performances" here on earth in the flesh long before He became the Son of Man?

In Psalm 2 we find Him, along with the Father and the Holy Spirit, looking down from heaven talking to each other about the final days and Jesus' end times' role. In Psalm 22, seven hundred years before they would take place, we are given the details of His intimate thoughts and observations He would experience on the cross. In Isaiah 52 and 53 we are given previews of other details of His earthly sufferings and exactly why He had to, that is chose to, allow Himself to be so treated.

From the New Testament we know much about His birth in Bethlehem, after which the family returned to Nazareth, then fled to Egypt, and later returned to dwell permanently in Nazareth. We next get the snapshot of Him at age twelve in the Temple, and finally Scripture is full of details of His three and a half year's ministry from age thirty until His death and resurrection. The last we learn about Jesus is in the book of Revelation where He "reveals" His post-resurrection Self, and the whole saga of His end times plan.

But again, what about those early years? If you are like me, you probably didn't think too deeply about it. Knowing what was available from the Gospels, the vague picture I chose to settle on was that of a normal boy happily growing up helping His dad in the carpenter shop. I saw Him as certainly being different, that is being especially saintly and super intelligent, but also I saw Him as being loved by His parents, respected by their neighbors, and looked up to as the older brother by His siblings. This would have been seen by others as a very happy, pious, strongly religious and honorable pillar of the community, blessed with an outstanding first-born Son. Is that at all representative of your image of our Savior's early years? If it is, get ready for a reality check, because if you stop to really think about it, with but a very little divine guidance, a much different picture will begin to emerge. A powerful clue from which one might develop some compelling questions regarding this idealized image of His early years can be found in John 8:41. Here the Pharisees reveal to us that they were certain that Jesus was "born of fornication." Wouldn't this "brand" have been public knowledge since His birth and had probably influenced the attitudes toward Him among the town folk where He grew up? Is there anything else in Scripture, which may shed some real light on those years? Yes, I believe there is, but it appears to be so concealed and obscure that it has, for the most part, remained unnoticed, or at least, not sufficiently examined until now. It is Psalm 69 where a considerable amount of light is shed on those early years. It was Dr. Chuck Missler, my original biblical mentor and a world class Bible teacher, from whom I learned of the inner meaning of this Psalm.

However, before we jump directly into the text, I believe it is necessary to step back for just a moment. Because of its esoteric nature, this Psalm deserves an introduction, a setting of the stage, in order that it be better understood and appreciated. Without this I believe that much of the substance, tone and impact of its message cannot be appreciated. So please stay with me as I try to briefly establish the background and circumstances under which it probably was Authored. This setting I'll try to present is less a figment of my imagination then it is of a loving emotion-filled attempt to put form and color to a duly recorded real life situation through which our Lord and Savoir suffered, and with which I can strongly identify as a part of my own "early years."

Picture if you will this little village of Nazareth during the earliest part of the first century A.D. Here was a typical all Jewish society steeped in well-established tradition, and a belief system strongly influenced by the Sanhedrin, the ruling religious authority of that day. According to them, that "aberration" that was rumored to have occurred two or three years earlier, had by then been completely discredited by these authorities who contrived a far more believable scenario than that rumored to have occurred in Bethlehem. The people were told that it was a myth, that there were no supernatural events. The star, the shepherds, the Magi, the virgin birth, all could be explained naturally. And especially this absurdity of a "virgin birth" which was merely a stupid effort to cover up the fact that this promiscuous girl had allowed herself to be seduced by a Roman soldier, and then claimed that "God did it." To add even greater shame to this brazen, reprehensible act, it happened while she was betrothed to this saintly man, Joseph, who rather than having her stoned to death, as she should have been, and as was their law, he accepted her as his wife and even took in this illegitimate son of hers! Illegitimacy was a rare thing in that culture. Because she was already espoused to Joseph, this was considered adultery, and rarely was a child born of such a union, because the potential mother was stoned to death before such a birth could be possible.

However, under the then current Roman law, the Jews did not have their former authority for capital punishment. Nevertheless, stoning to death was still widely practiced. Of course, we know that she was under God's protection. But from a secular perspective, she may have been spared because of their respect for Joseph. Nevertheless, she was thus known as a despicable scarlet woman, and He was her equally despicable bastard son. No amount of repentance pious living or prayer could ever erase that fact from their eyes, nor bring about a softening of attitudes toward either of them.

After giving birth to Jesus in Bethlehem, the family returned to Nazareth but soon, because of Herod's decree, they fled to Egypt where they remained for some time, several months to a year or more, until Herod died. It is likely the local folks in Nazareth may have believed that they left in order to get away from the intense ridicule and hate that Mary and the little toddler, Jesus, were by then being subjected to. When they returned, however, the community hadn't had a change of heart. In their eyes, Mary was still a scarlet woman, and her Son was even more despised, being the illegitimate son of a Roman! Drunks made up dirty songs about Mary and her Son, and whenever they passed the gate, the elders, the leaders of the village who congregated there, made them the topic of their scathing remarks and sordid conversation. Having been merely ostracized by the community would have been a blessing compared to their daily menu of slanders, curses, jokes, and perhaps even an occasional stone being thrown at them.

But let us picture some of the other aspects of this Boy's life as He grew into adolescence, teens and manhood. All we know directly from the Gospels is found in Luke 2:46, 50 where we learn that by age twelve He was already a Bible scholar and had a firm, accurate understanding of just who His real Father was. How He must have suffered from the taunts and threats and attacks by the neighborhood bullies. Here was the ideal kid to pick on! Well, almost anyway, remember He is the Son of God incarnate, and even then had qualities unlike any child who ever lived! When they mocked Him and cursed Him for His perceived faulty lineage and strangeness, when they spit on Him, even hit Him and tore His clothes, what could He do? He couldn't get angry or strike back, although He probably was strong enough. He couldn't swear or spit back. No such responses were in Him. His response was hurt, sorrow, pity, tears, and prayers for them so that the Father would forgive them because they didn't know what they were doing. When they hurt Him, He probably only asked why they did this without any cause. When they hit Him, He turned the other cheek. When they tore off His clothes, He offered them as gifts. Eventually this response may have generated some guilt so they may have backed off. But there was a never-ending supply of new bullies to keep up the attack. Although He never argued or fought back because of the attacks on Himself, in later years, when they blasphemed His real Father God, there would be scathing outpourings of petitions to the Father to punish those who were so wicked. Could there ever have been any joy and happiness for this little boy? Certainly not out in the neighborhood where only bullying and hatred could be found. Throughout His life these cursed things were with Him. Perhaps in the very early years He already knew He was different. He knew there was something about Him, something in Him that caused Him to see and feel everything differently than anyone else. No doubt His mother and Joseph had told Him the truth, but He also knew that the perceived absurdity of the fact could not be uttered without causing an amplification of the already painful situation, especially for His mother.

And what about His family? By then, Jesus probably had several half brothers and sisters; we know of six at least. These, of course, were children of His mother and Joseph, not of His Father. What was family life like for Him? Scripture assures us that there is no doubt that Mary and Joseph knew who He really was. But who would believe them? They had long since given up telling the truth, because no one anywhere would believe them, not even their other children, not until His resurrection! Mary and Joseph who knew the truth were His only refuge. But even there, it was not all that it should have been, because to treat Him much differently would have been to show partiality and that would have made it worse for Him. The others would have seen it as favoritism toward the weirdo, and the one who wasn't even a whole brother! They must also have had reservations about Mary if they believed the "party line" which they probably did. Otherwise they would have believed in His deity. What about Him? Externally, He was most evidently quite different from every one else and growing more so every day. He prayed a great deal of the time, was a passionate student of the Bible, which at some point He must have realized He had written! He even wore sackcloth as an expression of humbleness before His Father to whom He prayed so often. He shed many, many tears as a result of His loneliness, His treatment by the world, and by His family, as well as because of what He early on perceived was to be His life and His fate. No doubt Mary and Joseph told Him in confidence quite early just who He was. But being who He was, most certainly His intimacy with the Father, while in prayer, told Him a great deal more about Himself and what He was on earth to accomplish. As He matured, some of His prayers became precatory, as He felt even more indignant over the blasphemous conduct and the blatant lack of respect and reverence for the Father, His Father. By then it would seem He was fully and painfully aware of the whole picture and His involvement in it.

There is no doubt that our blessed Lord's entire life was one of pain and sorrow. Due to condemnation without cause, it was that way from His very beginning as a child. Before His incarnation, as He sat in heaven from eternity past, He knew even before He created the universe, exactly what He would suffer not only on the cross and during His ministry, but also throughout His entire life, even during these early years. But, nevertheless, He gladly chose to suffer all of this just for that precious few who would truly believe on Him. Doesn't this add in your heart an additional dimension of gratitude and understanding as to the quality and intensity of His love for us?

Now let us go to Psalm 69 and see if this preparatory picture I have tried to present is distorted, or is a reasonable likeness of our Lord's early years as the psalmist recorded them. As we read and examine each verse, we should remain aware that the order of verse does not necessarily progress chronologically with the thoughts or events as they may have taken place. We find this throughout many of the prophetic books such as in Isaiah, Jeremiah, Daniel, and Revelation. In this Psalm, I believe we see Jesus' thoughts as He looks forward and also as He at times looks back from different points in His early life. We will find some verses where He looks back to events past and also to events future, which at that moment have not yet been made clear to Him. Also in reading the first few verses it may seem difficult to accept the fact that the Psalm is speaking of Jesus' early years. But patience here is sure to reward the reader as subsequent verses begin to point most compellingly to that conclusion.

Psalm 69

Verses 1–3 *"Save me, O God; for the waters are come in unto my soul. I sink in deep mire, where there is no standing: I am come into deep waters, where the floods over flow me. I am weary of my crying: my throat is dried: mine eyes fail while I wait for my God."*

The person speaking to His God is overwhelmed with sorrow and troubles. It's as if He is about to drown. He is in deep mire, like quicksand. It's not even possible to swim and He can't find a spot to stand on as He feels Himself sinking deeper and deeper. This is obviously an analogy describing a person who is suffering with great stress, resulting from some prolonged conditions from which relief seems impossible. The Author of these verses is a person who has cried so much and so long that His throat is very dry and His eyes so swollen that He can barely see. He is speaking to God, His God, pleading to be rescued, waiting with confidence that eventually God will rescue Him. This must be a young boy, because such tears would never come from a grown man, certainly to this degree, if at all, no matter how frightened or painful the circumstances.

Verse 4 *"They that hate Me without cause are more than the hairs of mine head: they that would destroy me, being mine enemies wrongfully, are mighty: then I restored that which I took not away."*

Verse four tells us that there is no valid reason why they hate Him so, and those who do are large in number, probably the whole town or region. Our dear Lord Jesus during His ministry quotes this verse in John 15:25, about Himself as it relates to His ministry! But as a child, why should this have been? We already know, based on our preparatory musing regarding His childhood. It is John 15:25 that tells us *"But this cometh to pass, that the word might be fulfilled that is written in their law, they hated Me without a cause."* Psalm 69 is prophecy fulfilled, one thousand years later, but with a fulfillment of even more hate, and hate of a much longer duration, a hate that Jesus endured from His blessed birth to His atoning death on the cross. Let us wring a little more out of this. Romans 3:24 says *"being justified freely by His grace through the redemption that is in Christ Jesus:"* What is justified freely? It's the same as justified without a cause, without any basis or merit. They hated Him without cause so that we could be justified without cause. His darkness gave us light, His suffering and death gives us peace and eternal life.

They would have killed Him if it had been possible under Roman law. They were enemies without cause. The last phrase of this verse suggests that perhaps they sometimes extracted something from Him, in some perverted way, considering it as payment for something that He didn't owe. This would certainly be consistent with advice He gave in His sermon on the mount (Luke 6:29) *"if they taketh away thy cloak forbid them not to take thy coats also."*

Verse 5 *"O God, thou knowest my foolishness; and my sins are not hid from thee."*

How could this possibly apply to Jesus? He was holy undefiled and sinless every moment of His life, right? Well, not quite. In the last hours of His life He had been made sin. He contained the summation of any and all sins ever committed or to be committed by every human being for which He died! This of course occurred only hours before He died. However, as He grew toward manhood, the Father was revealing more and more about the fullness of who He was, His purpose and His mission of taking on the sins of the entire world. Knowing that this was the state in which His earthly life would end, must have weighed increasingly more heavily on Him as the years following it having been revealed to Him. We know that the night before it happened He perspired blood, so horrible was the thought of it. The word "foolish" is a translation of the Hebrew word *evyit* (*ev-cel*) that can also mean perverse. This is one of those sentence structures so common, especially in the Psalms, called "comparative or synonymous parallelism" where the same thing is said twice, each in a different way. Here foolishness or perversion is expressed as the

241

equivalent of sin. Notice He calls them "my" sins. He had no sins of His own doing, but at the recording of these thoughts, He had conceptually accepted them as His, as He had to in order to deal with them as had been preordained.

Verse 6 and 7 *"Let not them that wait on thee, O Lord God of hosts, be ashamed for my sake: let not those that seek thee be confounded for my sake, O God of Israel. Because for thy sake I have borne reproach; shame hath covered my face."*

Here is that "illegitimate" child and His sufferings from that image being revealed. In verse seven, He reminds the Father that He has borne all those years of reproach (rebuke, shame, disgrace Hebrew word *cherpah*) for the Father's sake as the One ordained to so suffer. He realized the necessity of it, for how else could it be. The people would never believe the truth, it was too preposterous. Thus, He had to pay the physical consequences for their local carnal unbelief, just as He would later pay for the spiritual violations of God's word for all the world. Jesus here is not blaming the Father, merely explaining why in verse six He asks the Father, again in synonymous parallelism, to let not those who put their trust in you be ashamed or stumble in their faith because of what they perceive of Him. In other words, He asks that no one lessen their faith in the Father because of the perceived problems of the son. Notice that in the King James Version, first God is God of hosts, that's the military powerful aspect of God, then it's the God of Israel, the creator God. What else could this be alluding to, but that vicious, unwarranted ostracism He and His mother suffered throughout His early years?

Verse 8 *"I am become a stranger unto my brethren, and an alien unto my mother's children."*

The theme that He was hated without cause as articulated in verse four is again pointedly expressed here. Notice it's *"my mother's children."* Who else but a person in such a genealogical condition as was Jesus would express His family status this way? This is carefully worded to express the fact that they were not His Father's children nor was their father His father. Again, it is synonymous parallelism with the essence of the second part of the eighth verse the same as the first part of the verse, but with a little added punch. Alien is a little stronger and distancing than stranger, and mother's children also adds distance not sensed in "brethren." This was not a happy household for Him. This Boy had at least four half brothers and two half sisters. They knew who their father was. But Jesus was not one of them in this respect, and they knew it. Regardless of Mary's and Joseph's attempts to dissuade them, it is likely that the "street" knowledge of Jesus' origin, along with His strange demeanor and ways, caused them to treat Him as an alien. This God-is-My-Father thing that their parents may have originally mentioned was way too difficult to swallow, given the "vast" majority of contrary belief so deeply imbedded in, and professed by, the world around them. That stigma, along with His "strangeness," followed Him all of His precious life. Clearly He was an outcast wherever He went, even within His family. How greatly this must have hurt Him is vividly expressed one way or another between the lines in every verse of this Psalm.

Verse 9 *"For the zeal of thine house hath eaten me up; and the reproaches of them that reproached thee are fallen upon me."*

The zeal of thine house. That would be the zealous priests and Pharisees functioning in apostasy and with reproach against God. (Reproach: disgrace, rebuke, shame, blaspheme, rail, upbraid, defame). This hurt Him deeply. How could they possibly blaspheme and rail against His Father, the Almighty God, their Creator from whom good things come. He took this very personally, knowing by then that He and the Father were one, although not necessarily yet knowing the fullness of His integral relationship within the Godhead. The blaspheming of the Father by this point in His life hurt Him very deeply, adding another unbearable layer of anguish to His troubled soul. Just how strongly He felt about the world's attitude about His Fathers will become clear in subsequent verses. Look at John 2:17 where it tells us *"and His disciples remembered that it was written, the zeal of thine house hath eaten me up."* They remembered Jesus' words as He spoke them during His ministry, and knew well from where He had quoted, for this was among singing Psalms, a hymn which they well recognized, for they had probably sung it many times. Now the Apostles saw that it had been a specific prediction of one of His great burdens He carried throughout His life. The strength of that zeal did not begin with His ministry, but had been instituted by the "official" verdict that publicly established His so-called tarnished parenthood at the very beginning of His life.

Verse 10, 11 *"When I wept, and chastened my soul with fasting, that was to my reproach. I made sackcloth also my garment; and I became a proverb to them.*

Weeping was not an acceptable male characteristic. But Jesus' sensitivities, because of who He was, were no doubt set at a very young age. There is no reason to believe under the circumstances, that weeping wasn't a big part of His life as verse 3 also tells us. He fasted and put on sackcloth, these being expressions of devotion, humbleness and submission, as part of His prayerful honoring of His Father God. These were pretty weird goings on for a young kid, or anyone at any age, who was not a temple priest. It is difficult to imagine His siblings not poking fun at Him, accusing Him of play acting, ridiculing, and reproaching Him at almost every opportunity. Is there any doubt that this ridicule continued one way or another over the whole thirty years before He began His ministry? How especially cruel and hurtful this mocking and zinging must have been to this highly sensitive misunderstood boy as He grew to Manhood. There was not even the slightest bit of spite, anger, hate, or any other possible imperfection or sin in Him. There was only pain and sadness as He here expressed it. What explanation could He use? "I am the son of God." Hardly! What defense of Himself could He use? As the ultimate of righteousness, purity and sinlessness, He had none of our earthly, naturally human defenses and offenses that any of us would surely have used to protect ourselves. "Chastened" is not in the original text, but seems an appropriate fill-in to make the thought into a sentence. It means to punish, make right, to correct; to justify, judge, reason, rebuke, prove, etc. He became a proverb to them. A proverb is an enigmatic or fictitious expression. He must have frequently dressed in sackcloth, which empathized His weirdness to both His siblings and the public. They made sport, or made fun of Him, or He became a by-word, as the NIV and NLV and NASV respectively have translated the word "proverb." Sackcloth, a harsh uncomfortable material, was used as a garment primarily by the priests during times of extreme bereavement. It symbolized humbleness, grief and total submission to God. What a weird Kid He was, going around in such ridiculous attire. This must have only further infuriated all who were around Him, except Mary and Joseph, who probably tried to tone Him down to "go along in order to get along." Clearly this was never Jesus' way, neither as a Child or ever after.

Verse 12 They *that sit in the gate speak against me; and I was the song of the drunkards*.

They that sat at the gate were the leaders, the mayor and city council of that day. The gate was "City Hall" of those days. Picture Jesus, this obviously strange as well as "evilly mongrelized" Kid, walking in and out of the city gate on errands for Joseph or Mary, and sometimes with Mary. These people would never miss an opportunity to mock, ridicule, swear or otherwise verbally degrade Him. Even the gatherings of drunks would join in on this sport, making up dirty songs about Him and probably also His mother. Who would dispute them? He was fair game for everyone. The base nature of much of humanity seems to need some kind of "whipping boys" and our dear Jesus was perfect for that role. If you are old enough, as I am, and lived in a very small rural town as I did, you may remember such attitudes, as I do. Where I moved to and grew up, you were not accepted socially, or any other way, but were automatically disliked and viewed with suspicion unless your family had lived there at least three generations. If you were Italian, Jewish, or spoke with an accent, you remained a total outcast. If you made any waves, or economically competed with a "towney" you might come home one night and find a pile of ashes where your home had been. For a person of color, it was best to never pass through, let alone consider staying. If I can remember such an environment such a short time ago, think of what our dear Jesus must have suffered, in a far more bigoted society, due to His great uniqueness. We probably have only a small hint of this recorded here.

Why did He have to endure all of this regarding His alleged illegitimacy? So that You and I could be made legitimate sons and daughters of His Father. Our Savior began this payment for our sins, even as a Child!

Verse 13 *"But as for me, my prayer is unto thee, O Lord, in an acceptable time: O God, in the multitude of thy mercy hear me, in the truth of thy salvation."*

Paul quotes this verse in 2 Corinthians 6:2. The Gospels tell us that He prayed much, but seldom tell us what He prayed. Here is what He prayed, as the Psalmist continues. How nicely this all fits together! The word salvation comes from the Hebrew *yasha* which can also be translated as "deliverance," "liberty" or "safety." One of these choices may have been more appropriate here in as much as what we see as salvation is something our Lord and Savior provided, but surely didn't need. Carnal safety or liberty from the bondage of the environment are perhaps more appropriate expressions of what He was dealing with.

Verse 14 and 15 *"Deliver me out of the mire, and let me not sink: let me be delivered from them that hate me, and out of the deep waters. Let not the waterflood overflow me, neither let the deep swallow me up, and let not the pit shut her mouth upon me."*

This echoes the opening phrases of this Psalm, but also amplifies the dark shadow being cast by the analogy. Here we see Jesus, perhaps as He begins to understand the role He must play, and the horrible conditions He is to face. He is first praying deliverance from the mire and to not sink or be overwhelmed by it. The mire here is the painful filth of those who hate Him, for they have no cause. This circumstance then expands to "deep waters," and is immediately followed by the image of being "swallowed up" within these deep waters. Here we have a thought preview of what Jesus articulated in Matthew 12:40 when Jesus gives His detractors the "sign of Jonah." From this verse, here in Psalm 69, we may be seeing the early part of Jesus' understanding of what was coming. First it is likened to Jonah's predicament in the depths of the sea. Then He sees this profound extension of the being-swallowed-up image transferred to the "pit." He prays that His Father God will not let the pit close its mouth on Him. That this appears to be the early part of the Father's revelation to Him of His divine destiny seems to be evidenced by the fact that he doesn't quite yet have the whole picture, or else He would not have had the concern that the pit would close up around Him and prevent His return. Could this be a "premonition" of that day when He would descend in to the deep, the belly of the earth, to Sheol? Could He, as a youth, already have had a foreboding sense of that coming event, but not yet having a complete understanding of the purpose or outcome, and, therefore, felt a vulnerability and need to petition His Father for assurance of rescue?

He most likely had already read the story of Jonah and realized that somehow Jonah was a proto-type for what He was to face. Jonah 2:1–6 tells us that Jonah actually died physically, and that his soul descended to Sheol before he was resurrected and cast out on the beach. This young Boy Jesus was being given the knowledge that His would be a similar journey, but He hadn't yet the fullness of the revelation that would have assured His rescue and divine eternal future.

Verse 16 through 19 *"Hear me O Lord; for thy loving-kindness is good: turn unto me according to the multitudes of thy tender mercies. And hide not thy face from thy servant; for I am in trouble: hear me speedily. Draw nigh unto my soul, and redeem it: deliver me because of mine enemies. Thou hast known my reproach, and my shame, and my dishonor: mine adversaries are all before thee."*

Here we may be receiving some insight as to His thoughts as His awareness grew of what was coming. In verse 19 His adversaries are all around Him. Was it simply the hating neighborhood, or could it have been also the "bulls of Bashan" even at this early age? We know that the demons knew Him, from Mark 5:6–17 and they feared Him when He was a grown Man/God with powers over them. But we see in Psalm 22 when He is seemingly powerless and dying on the cross, they become brave and *"they gaped upon me with their mouths, as a ravening and a roaring lion."* Might they have also have recognized Him when He was but a child? Could these hating, evil demon-spirits have been threatening Him even then, when He was equally helpless against them? We read of a great deal of pain and suffering and fears throughout these early verses of this Psalm. It was perhaps something more than man alone could cause.

In verse 16 He prays to the Father for His loving kindness and tender mercies. He prays that the Father not turn His face, that is, not fail to see all He is suffering. In verse 18 he asks that His soul be "redeemed" and delivered from His enemies. The word "redeemed" as used here is the Hebrew word *gaal* which can also mean "revenge" as well as "redeem," "purchase," "ransomed," etc. The more common word in Hebrew which is translated as redeemed is *padah* which is limited to "ransom," "redeem" or "deliver," with no connotations as to vengeances. Therefore, could this petition to the Father be more on the idea of avenging, along with redeeming? The word "deliver" in verse 18 is the same Hebrew word used here also as "redeem." However, in verse 14 where He asks to be delivered from the mire, the Hebrew word for "delivered" is *natsal* which means firstly, to be "snatched away." How I wish that I could read and think in Hebrew and Greek so that I could more fully savor and apprehend the full, complete meaning of every nuance of God's Holy Word, and not miss even a "jot or tittle" of His glorious message!

Verse 19 also seems to confirm the existence of the illegitimacy label with which He had been branded and carried throughout His life. He reminds His Father that He knows of His "reproach and shame and dishonor." What else could it be? This sinless perfect Boy could not have had a speck of reproach, shame or dishonor anywhere in Him. These were perceived imperfections in the minds of those who bought the lie. This petition is surely that of the younger Jesus rather than during His ministry years, when He certainly had at least the recognized stature of a great teacher and healer.

Verse 20 and 21 *"Reproach hath broken my heart; and I am full of heaviness: and I looked for some to take pity, but there was none; and for comforters, but I found none. They gave me also gall for my meat; and in my thirst they gave me vinegar to drink."*

Again the same theme. The reproach has broken His heart; He is full of heaviness. This continuing life of humiliation, shame, disgrace and rebuke is wearing on this very young Man because it never ends but continues day after day with every encounter with every person, except Mary and Joseph. (Reproach is the translation of the Hebrew word *cherpah* which can mean "shame," disgrace," rebuke," etc.) He seeks pity, but there is none. Perhaps not even His mother had the pity He sought because she knew that this was but a tiny "blip" in His glorious eternity, and that He was foreordained to suffer as the Savior she knew Him to be. Perhaps at this stage of His young physical life, this did not yet have the great significance that it would have later.

What could it mean, gall to eat and vinegar to drink? This seems to echo of the only other place where we read of this in Scripture, that is, in Matthew 27:34 when Jesus is on the cross and it says, *"they gave him vinegar to drink mingled with gall, and when he tasted thereof He would not drink."* Is Jesus now able to look into the future and recognize this to be something He will experience at the end, or did this also occur somehow as part of the abuse He suffered at the hands of His neighbors, or even His siblings? It may be of interest to note that "gall" translated from the Hebrew is "poison," "hemlock," "venom." It kills. When translated from the Greek as in Matthew 27:34, the word can also mean an "anodyne" that is, a pain reliever. But here as He speaks of it from the Hebrew, it surely was poison. Were there two such events, or only the one on the cross? Probably this is a recording of a vision regarding His future.

Verses 22–25 *"Let their table become a snare before them; and that which should have been for their welfare, let it become a trap. Let their eyes be darkened that they see not; and make their loins continually to shake. Pour out thine indignation upon them, and let thy wrathful anger take hold of them. Let their habitation be desolate; and let none dwell in their tents."*

These verses are imprecatory as are many of David's Psalms. Here Jesus is asking the Father to punish, to pour out His indignation on those who torture Him. This appears to some extent to be the eruption of the pent up indignation He had felt as noted in verse nine. It is a response to His indignation having to do with how the world railed against both Him and His Father without cause. Missler recalls that C. S. Lewis called these verses "a refinement of malice." Lewis, however, did not recognize that it was Jesus who was speaking through David. Paul, in Romans 11:9, 10 quoted these words of verse 22 as he condemned the Jews who would not hear, see and obey. Are we shocked that our gentle, humble, forgiving, loving Jesus would speak such words? Why should we be? This was a righteous wrath and condemnation against those who blasphemed His Father and condemned Him for the message that by now, He knew would be His mission to reveal. This message would include the acknowledgment of who He was. He was merely calling down the judgment that was just, and would one day be decreed just, as He requested it. In verse 20 and 21 and beyond, Jesus may be foreseeing His hours on the cross, as He certainly did when He spoke from the cross in Psalm 22. Verse 25 curses them to empty desolate homes. This verse is quoted by Peter in Acts 1:20 as applying to Judas Iscariot. Here the words seem to have a broader context. However, because all of Scripture is the inerrant Word of God, we should accept the fact that if Peter applied this as he did, then here in Psalm 69 it is a prophetic announcement of this curse on Judas. These later verses in this Psalm suggest that at this time during His youth, He was beginning to get an even clearer picture of His coming ministry and final earthly fate. That He should have by then known of Judas and his foul deed, is more than likely, and that when He thought these words, Judas was among those He had in mind.

Verse 26 For *they persecute him who thou hast smitten; and they talk to the grief of those whom thou has wounded."*

From here on, it is clear that the Boy Jesus is seeing ahead to the end of His earthly life, and is addressing certain of those future events. In saying "they persecute him whom thou hast smitten," Jesus is indicating that He is well aware of what had been prophesized of Him in Isaiah 53, where God the Father with a single stripe would inflict that ultimate complete and final punishment for the sins of the world. Notice that He speaks in the past tense, as if it had already happened. This could cause confusion in the context of this "early years" chronology of Jesus were it not for the fact that we see God often speaking in this manner. As One who sees the past, present and future from outside of time, these time categories have no relevance. All things were foreknown, and from the moment God thought them into being they were to Him all past tense. He sits on high simply watching as "time catches up," as it will when Revelation 22 becomes the "here and now." It's all a done deal, according to His "timeless" time. These allusions to gall, vinegar, being smitten by God, the zeal of the Temple, etc. make it clear, to me at least, that Jesus is seeing with increasing clarity what was ahead for Him during, and at the end of His glorious ministry.

Notice that verse 26 is not another example of synonymous parallelism, but instead is called antithetic parallelism. In the first part of the verse, "they *persecute* him (Jesus) who thou hast smitten." In the second half, "they *talk to grief* those whom thou has wounded." In other words, they justified and amplified God's action toward the innocent Jesus by adding their own persecution of Him, and they grieve (feel pain and sorrow) for those others whom God justly punished by wounding, (Killing, slaying, profaning) and who deserve such treatment.

Verse 27 and 28 "*Add iniquity unto their iniquity: and let them not come into thy righteousness. Let them be blotted out of the book of the living, and not be written with the righteous.*"

Again young Jesus is seeing the future and what has already been ordained and recorded elsewhere, that God will punish the faithless, and they will not be named in the Book of Life. This indeed is a scathing charge and punishment for which the young Jesus is petitioning. He has seen and heard all that has gone on around Him, and by now also sees all of the future horrible iniquities of which mankind will be guilty. With His reference to the book of the living, we can see that at this point our young Jesus knows much of what we might call "advanced eschatology." This is the only place I find in the Bible where the "book of the living" is mentioned. We don't see it again until Philippians 4:3 where it is called the "book of life." Then finally, the term appears seven times in Revelation. Bible scholars attach considerable significance to the first time a word or idea appears in the Bible. They call it the "principal of first mention," and they seek to extract from it its underlying significance, believing that this will help to better explain its subsequent usage. Isn't it appropriate that our blessed Lord Jesus would have first used it in His youthful lamentations?

Verse 29, 30 and 31 But *I am poor and sorrowful: let thy salvation, O God, set me up on high. I will praise the name of God with a song, and will magnify him with thanksgiving. This also shall please the Lord better than an ox or bullock that hath horns and hoofs.*

The young Jesus is yet lamenting over His poor and sorrowful state, and is asking His Father for salvation and to be set up on high. Here the Hebrew word for salvation is a different one than translated as salvation in verse 13. There its definition expressed "liberty" and "safety." Here the Hebrew word translated as salvation leans more toward "victory" and "deliverance." This is consistent with the next part of this verse 29 where He asks God to set Him on high. Being "set on high" seems to be a fairly exclusive term for Jesus' ultimate position at the right hand of the Father, the position "on high" which He temporarily left to fulfill His earthly mission. Here it almost seems that He is asking to skip what the next few years will bring, and be brought home now. Next Jesus is expressing what most pleases His and our Father God, namely praise and thanksgiving, rather than symbolic works such as animal sacrifice, provided by hollow hearted so-called worshipers.

Verse 32 and 33 *"The humble shall see this, and be glad: and your heart shall live that seek God. For the Lord hearth the poor, and despiseth not his prisoners.*

Perhaps now, having come to full knowledge as to His earthly purpose, His thoughts move toward that purpose, and the emphasis He will place on humbleness along with the advantages of the poor who are most likely to see, and to seek God. It seems as though He may be already rehearsing, or perhaps planning out His Sermon on the Mount! Then He mentions as part of this collection of thoughts, that God does not hate the prisoners, that is, the in venerate sinners who are prisoners of their sins, but loves them and would want *"that all should come to repentance."* (2 Peter 3:9).

Verse 34 *"Let the heaven and earth praise him, the seas, and every thing that moveth therein."*

This continues Jesus' expressions of love and praise for His Father where He calls on the heavens and the earth and the seas and all things to praise Him. This clearly is a vision He sees which will be realized in the very end times with the new heaven and earth.

Verse 35 and 36 *"For God will save Zion, and will build the cities of Judah: that they may dwell there, and have it in possession. The seed also of his servants shall inherit it: and they that love his name shall dwell therein."*

It now seems with these last three verses that Jesus has fully matured into the Man /God who will now enter His ministry. Here He is seeing and predicting, as a sort of sneak preview of what He will later reveal to John from His seat in heaven, as described in the book of Revelation. God saves the remnant Jews, "they that love His name" and His covenant promises to them will be fulfilled. For He will restore these cities when He returns to earth to sit on the throne of David as their sovereign King. How fitting that this Psalm, which depicts the early years of Jesus' life, should end with this reference to the end times prophecy. This symbolized His having reached full maturity of body, mind and spirit, for only then would He have known all things such as this.

Perhaps as you have labored through this, you may have concluded that I have been too passionate, too repetitive, too verbose, and that I may have projected somewhat beyond what the Psalmist actually had intended. Too passionate? Perhaps, but this was a deeply moving and passionate involvement for me. I felt as if I could put myself where He was as a boy, could actually feel His pain and I shed my own tears along with Him. Too repetitive and too verbose? Probably. But I claim justification by the "rule of synonymous parallelism." If the Psalmist can claim this right in order to better express His point, may I not also claim it in order to express my views on the Psalm? To me this Psalm is so very important and revealing, that in writing about it, I chose to forego any attempt toward conciseness or word efficiency. Too much projection? Perhaps, but as I projected myself completely into His home and His little town, I could actually see Him and feel the great suffering of this precious Boy. I could hear the wagging snake-like tongues yapping at Him; I could see and feel what I believe He felt as the bullies and His siblings ridiculed Him. I felt that I could understand His confusion, His fears, and the strange goings on within His soul and mind as the fullness of His precious being manifested itself. One may believe that I stretched the Psalmist's words too far, but the fact is that this paper only scratches the surface of what was in my heart and mind as I was there and walked with Him through town, ate dinner with His family, prayed with Him, and wished to God that I could have actually been there to be His one friend who understood and loved Him, and who would have fought off both the bullies and the "Bulls of Bashan," offering my life for His, if I could have. Instead, He gave His life for me, for all believers, that we might spend eternity with Him. He did it all! All He asks in return is that we believe on Him, and that we express out gratitude for all He did with the love, which can only come from a repentant heart, and with obedience to His Holy Word. This can only come through His strength working in a redeemed soul.

—28—

The Father's Drawing

In John 6:44, we find that none come to Jesus unless the Father draws them. This means that every saved soul, at some point was drawn by God the Father, toward Jesus, and toward that faith through which His grace of salvation is given. What does drawing mean in this context? I believe it is simply opening up opportunities by various and sundry ways for man to find Jesus and His saving grace. Prior to Jesus' earthly ministry, death and resurrection, that was the same drawing and the same faith through which the Old Testament saints were saved. We can see this clearly from John 1:1 and 14 when we realize what he is saying when we read that *"in the beginning was the Word, and the Word was with God, and the Word was God."* Then in verse 14 we discover that *The Word was made flesh and dwelt among us . . ."* Thus Jesus was always there and active in the Spirit as the Word toward whom the Father could draw all souls. While Jesus had not yet appeared in the mortal flesh, He had been made known in terms of expressions of Himself toward which the Father could draw all who would choose to see the light.

Since at the time of Calvin, there has been the question, does the Father draw everyone or only a select few? If He draws only the few and they are all saved, His drawing must be irresistible. However, if He draws everyone, and because everyone is not saved, then His drawing is not irresistible and so man must have the power to resist that drawing, and therefore some choose to not be saved. Most certainly, it is the latter, for several reasons, the discussion of which is beyond the intent of this writing.

From this, we may reasonably ask how can it be that the Father's drawings are not always successful? Surely our omnipotent sovereign

God has the power to do anything and everything. The answer is that He has chosen to give man a form of what can be called sovereignty over his own will, which by definition God has chosen not to violate. Thus man has the choice to follow or to ignore God's drawing. This sovereign will is self evident in our daily lives, especially in those who don't know God, and those who even deny His very existence. Many take issue with this idea of the sovereignty of man's will because it seems inconceivable that God would give up any part of His own absolute authority, yet strong clear examples of this abound throughout Scripture as to limits of interference God has imposed on Himself where man's choices are involved. Here again is an issue beyond the scope of our subject.

If man has that sovereignty of choice, doesn't that negate the concept that the Father draws all who come to Jesus? Couldn't some come directly to Jesus of their own free will without being drawn? Certainly not, because the inerrant Word of God tell us so. Mans natural heart, being deceitful above all things and desperately wicked, is incapable of this. Unless through God's drawing, a ray of light of truth penetrates his natural darkness, there can be no coming to Jesus. God's drawing in no way negates or diminishes mans free will or right to choose. God uses many ways to draw people without overriding their sovereign will. He uses His already drawn sons and daughters as examples to open pathways for His drawing. Their witnessing and their prayer can soften hearts and remove barriers to His drawing. God uses teachers, pastors, missionaries, and other evangelicals as well as Bible expositors to convey His Word and thus effectuate drawing. Both tragedies and triumphs provide opportunities to change attitudes and open the ways for the Father to draw those who might chose to come to Jesus.

If one has the faith that saves, that is has felt, acknowledged, and fully accepted the Father's drawing to Jesus, and all that that entails, then there must be evidence of it in that person's repentant nature, love, obedience and gratitude. Unless each of these manifest and proceed to grow in both mind and heart, one should most carefully and critically examine that faith to see if it be genuine, and if it was the Father and not another power who did the drawing. The extent of that examination should deal with all four of these evidences and should be in the context of the whole word of God, not just a few popular, attractive, and non-challenging verses. Perhaps the following can provide an outline guide for that evidence, at least as I see that it ought to be.

1. Repentance

Scripture assures us that without repentance there is no salvation. Repentance is the spiritual, mental, emotional, and physical turning away from the worldly ways and toward our Lord and Savior Christ Jesus. That turning, if genuine, is surely the effectualization of the Father's drawing. It must however be considered a work-in-process of a total change of focus, a change of priorities, and a change of attitudes as well as behavior toward sin, sin being everything that is contrary to God's will. To know fully what is and is not of God, one must determine it from Scripture, not merely from the opinions of others or from one's own intuition, feelings, or very likely deceitful rationalizations. There is another essay available called "Repentance" that is a detailed study of the word meaning which should be helpful in finding relevant scriptural references to this.

2. Love

Love is an essential component of every saved soul. 1 Corinthians 13 is completely devoted to explaining Christian love and all of its many essential manifestations. The beginning verses tell us that in effect that without love, we are nothing. The final verse tells is "*and now abideth in faith, hope and love, these three; but the greatest of these is love.*" These words, and the entire chapter, provide a wonderful insight into the very nature of our Lord. We know from other parts of Scripture that God *is* love. Therefore, we have here a detailed description of just what that means. Read the chapter, everywhere substituting Jesus in place of love, or charity, and see how perfectly it applies! Now substitution your own name if you wish to read a morbidly hilarious joke! That substitution should make clear how far away any of us are in terms of having that perfect love. Genuine Godly love is a commitment and one of action. Words and emotions are not love, no matter how well expressed and how passionately they are presented. Godly thoughts followed by Godly actions are the only valid expressions of Godly love. Our loving God implants this love to all He effectually draws.

3. Obedience

Obedience to God's will can only come from knowing God's will. This is found with certainty only in God's Word. Jesus said, if you love me, you will obey me. Therefore love and obedience are inexorably linked together. I don't see how they can exist separately, nor can genuine godly love and obedience exist anywhere but in a repentant heart. As noted above, Paul claimed love to be the greatest virtue above faith and hope. With love conditioned on obedience, it is evident why this is so. Obedience may be considered the action aspect of love, the part requiring, faith, energy, effort, commitment, work, suffering for Him, and perseverance.

4. Gratitude

Gratitude is what joins the Holy Spirit in the new heart of every justified (saved) soul. Gratitude for having been rescued is what motivates all godly thoughts, feelings and actions of the saved soul. There is another essay called "Gratitude" that deals extensively with this.

There is one thing more that I believe must be understood. The saving faith *"cometh by hearing, and hearing by the word of God."* Romans 10:17 It's not through the eyes, but through the ears that salvation manifests. Surely God infuses grace into the soul by other means, but it is hearing, hearing the Gospel that brings about belief and trust in Jesus as Lord and Savior. Recognize that when we read, we do see the words, but the seeing does not directly register in the brain. The seen word is translated into an inner voice that "hears" the word and thus conveys it to the brain. Many think that it is necessary to have dreams, visions, experience, and revelations as evidences of salvation. But life giving faith never results from these evidences. They may legitimately occur through God's grace as perhaps "drawing" mechanisms, but they do not result in or cause a saving faith. Only the knowledge and acceptance of the truth of the Gospel brings about salvation.

I'm reminded here, as I often am, of poor Charles Templeton, a confirmed "worldly" man, who according to his biography had a vision one night that totally changed his life, causing him to become an evangelist. He and Billy Graham often traveled together in their earlier evangelizing in Europe, Canada and here. It is said that he surpassed Graham in popularity and evangelical effectiveness. For twenty years he did this until he finally renounced his faith becoming an atheist. He preached atheism on the radio, and in his writing until his death. I suspect that the "vision" was from "another" who also has such powers to "draw" and that it was not from God. We must be very cautious in relying in such supernatural expressions and trust only in the Gospel and the rest of the Word of God, because that is the *only* way to truth and to salvation.

Now let me tell you a few of the ways that God drew me. Today, I realize that His gentle persuasive ways were seeking to draw me all my life, but I refused to acknowledge it. Once while pheasant hunting, my companion who was walking next to me, stumbled, striking my forehead with the barrel of his shot gun. At that very instant, he accidentally pulled the trigger. Had he been six inches farther from me, I would have been dead. Instead, only a bad bump and burn resulted. I know now that God was both protecting and drawing me at that time by trying to show me that accidents don't just happen to those He is drawing without a purpose. There is always a divine purpose if we will only look for it. In this case, it may have been only something for me to remember later as part of the evidence I needed in order to know of His continued presence in my life. At the time however I could not recognize His protection or His drawing. My only response was to curse His name.

Then there was the time in 1948 when traveling downhill at about seventy miles per hour, I crossed a patch of black ice causing the car to spin around, roll over three times, and slide a considerable distance knocking down twelve concrete guardrails. The convertible coupe was beyond towing. The pieces had to be loaded into a truck, but I crawled out from under the wreckage and walked away with only a long cut along my right eyebrow, a fractured nose, multiple lacerations and many bruises. Had the cut been even one sixteenth of an inch lower, I would have lost my right eye.

However, such a truly miraculous event failed to draw me or move me even the slightest way toward Jesus. Once again, to me, it was just dumb luck, bad luck that it happened, good luck that I got off so easily. I could no way hear or see or feel His presence and I now realize that once again His divine hand was on me rescuing me from my own fatal foolishness. Finally, but far from the only other drawing I have experienced, began in January 1995 when I was told that I had stage four severely metastasized cancer for which there was no treatment, and that it would surely end my life within six to twelve months. I realize now that my ever-loving persevering Father was again patiently, and perhaps this time not so gently, trying to draw me toward Jesus this one last time. Over the next eighteen months He guided me through a maze of protocols and procedures that conventional medicine calls quackery. At the end of that period, I felt ten years younger, stronger and healthier, and the cancer had disappears from every part of my body and has never returned. But even then I could not see, hear, or feel His drawing. Those eighteen months were filled with severe challenges and much pain, yet I never even once called out to Him, or prayed. At the end, my pride of "self-achievement" clouded everything else, for a little while. Now, once again I see clearly that His eternal love and persistent drawing was at work and had from the beginning been molding, conditioning, and preparing me for that moment that only He knew would come. It seems to me that His process was like Jesus' "water of life" continually falling one drop at a time on the hard calluses of denial and indifferences that covered my soul. A few months after having been healed, after sixty-nine years of this drawing, that is continuous dripping of Jesus' life giving water, laced with His own blood and tears, finally broke through those horrible calluses and began to bathe my soul. The drawing was completed! I finally got the message, and by His grace through my faith, He brought me into His family! Who having experienced such love and drawing, could have room for anything else in his heart but love and eternal gratitude!

For those who might be interested in some details concerning my cancer ordeal, I've written an essay called "My Story" which is readily available.

There is some kind of a "miracle" story associated with every soul that has been redeemed. This has to be true, because given the fallen nature of all mankind, a miracle, that is some supernatural event, or series of such events, must be involved. Natural man has an irresistible propensity to sin, and any number of ways to rationalize away any belief in the spiritual consequences. We live in a world filled with many diabolically tempting pleasurable sins. We have been given the free will to choose to either indulge in these sinful pleasures or else to run from them. Many do run from them to some extent by embracing one of the worlds many religions where they believe themselves to be safe and thereby perhaps even able to work their way into some eternal good place. But it isn't the Creator God who draws in those directions. There is another force that draws, a very cleaver but evil force that God allows to function as part of His guarantee to man that he has a genuine choice. It's the choice between eternal heaven or hell. It seems evident by simple observation, and made certain in Scripture, that in these last days, man will turn more and more towards these alternatives and less and less toward Him, until on the day that the polarization will be complete,. Then God will call His own to heaven and give temporary earthly reign to Antichrist. Dear reader, I pray that if you have not felt God's genuine drawing, that you will see, hear and feel more carefully to find it, and to let it draw you to Christ Jesus and to the eternal life with Him that He promises all believers.

—29—

About My Father's Business

Scripture tell us precious little about the youthful years of Jesus. But there is one very revealing insight given us in Luke, chapter 2, where he tells us about one particular event which occurred when Jesus was twelve years old, verse 40 tells us that "the child grew and was strong in the spirit, filled with wisdom, and the grace of God was upon him." When His earthly parents Mary and Joseph found him missing from the caravan in which they were returning home after attending the feast of Passover, they returned to Jerusalem and found Him in the temple "sitting in the midst of the doctors, both hearing them and asking them questions, and all that heard Him were astonished at His understanding and answers" (verses 46, 47). When his parents questioned Him as to why He stayed behind, His response was ". . . knowest ye not that I must be about my Father's business? (verse 49).

Here we read of this child Jesus growing "strong in spiritual wisdom" and astonishing the elders and priests by His great wisdom regarding the very knowledge of which they were the most learned of all men. This, of course, was about Scripture, the Word of God. Although He never ceased being God when He was born as a human baby, He could not have known of Himself nor could He have consciously been aware of the wisdom of all creation. God had ordained Him to be born and to grow up to be as a human man having human limitations, physically and mentally as He grew toward manhood. It is evident that by age twelve He had learned much and was at least beginning to recognize His specialness. The fact that He referred to God as His Father is indicative of this growing evolving spiritual knowledge. The Hebrews never referred to God as Father. It was a name for God, coined in heaven and used exclusively by Jesus every time He spoke to, or referred to Him. Only once did He refer to Him as God. This was when He hung on the cross and the wrath of God was purging Him of the sins of the world, which He had taken upon Himself. Psalm 89 verse 26 speaks of God as the Father, but it is God Himself referring to Jesus who would call Him Father. Elsewhere God refers to Himself as Father, Father of the national Israel, not of any individual. Thus, the Jews probably didn't even catch the significance of this when He spoke of the business of His Father. Later they would understand, and would try to kill Him for "blasphemy." By the time He was thirty and had begun His ministry, He knew full well of His position as part of the Godhead, that He was truly God incarnate. By then He also knew what His mission was, and every detail of how He would carry it out.

How fascinating it is to study Scripture and see how He fulfilled more than three hundred prophecies during His short earthly life. And why not? It was He who wrote the book. It is largely about Himself, although that is difficult to discern in the Old Testament without the aide of the Holy Spirit interpreting it through the New Testament. In earthly terms, one could say He first wrote the book, then the movie script, after which He became the producer and director and main actor, playing His role precisely as He had written it.

What was the Father's business that He was about? At this point He was in the temple learning and teaching. Later He would also be healing, casting out demons, setting example, and declaring His Sonship as the Son of God the Father. All of this would be in complete obedience to the Father and in close communication with Him in prayer. Finally, He would fulfill His main purpose on earth by providing the ultimate expression of His supernatural love as He paid in full the price of past, present and future sins of all who would believe and obey His Word.

Are you a Christian? Do you consider yourself born-again? Are you sure? If you are, you have the exclusive right to call God your Father because you have been born into His family as His son or daughter. Having received this most precious of all possible gifts, your heart must be filled with eagerness to do all you possibly can for Him out of gratitude and love. With Jesus as our example, is it not both appropriate and essential that we too be about our Father's business? If we are truly sincere about our faith and devotion to Him, as we must be if we are of His family, how can we not see this as the priority of our lives?

If you are of His family, the Holy Spirit resides in your new heart and is available to guide and to assist you in all spiritual matters. This includes the means and the direction by which you are able to be about your Father's business. With your new heart and the indwelling of the Holy Spirit came one or more spiritual gifts that are to be used for this purpose. In 1 Corinthians 12, Paul mentions nine such gifts, and indicates that there are many more to draw from in our quest to be about our Father's business. Every genuine Christian has at least one such gift. It may even be one or more that you had long before you were "officially" saved, because remember, God knew before the beginning of time, precisely who and when they would be saved, and on that basis may have chosen to endow in advance various individuals with particular gifts that would be already available and somewhat perfected prior to an application to His business. Writing, teaching, preaching, giving, organizing, leading, etc. would be such gifts which the redeemed might have had long before the heart would or could choose to use them for His glorification.

While every redeemed soul has one or more spiritual gifts which he or she is required to use to His glory, being about His business involves much more. It includes worshipping prayers not just petitioning prayers. Jesus as God Himself, while He was also man, did much worshipping and praying to the Father. Jesus attended to the sick and needy. We cannot do the miracles He did, but we can bring comfort and support to those sick and in need. Perhaps you have had a deadly sickness from which God rescued you. Have you wondered why? It could be the basis of a spiritual gift that will now allow you to be credible to others who are similarly afflicted. Through your experience, and perhaps unique knowledge, it may be possible for you to be especially helpful to them. Through your entry into their lives as a possible agent of physical healing, you may be given opportunities to turn souls to Christ as well.

What business was this twelve-year old Jesus about in the temple? It was the studying, along with sharing and teaching the Scripture. Through out Scripture we are told to do this. Its faithful pursuit can in itself be a strong indication of a saved soul. Read John 8:31 where Jesus said, "If ye continue in my word then you are my disciples indeed." Who is a disciple? You are if you are born-again. What is His Word? It is the Bible. What does it mean to continue in His word? It is to live in accordance with what the Bible teaches. But this is impossible to do unless you "continue in His Word" by studying and knowing His Word, the Whole Word, not just what you get from hearsay or a twenty-minute sermon once a week. Here twelve-year old Jesus was giving us an example to follow. Studying Scripture is being about the Father's business. This is but one of many verses where we are admonished to know His Word. Being about our Father's business is what James was talking about in James1:23 when he said, "But be doers of the word and not hearers only: In chapter 2 verse 20 he says, "Faith without work is dead, and in verse 24 ". . . by works a man is justified and not by faith only." He also says in verse 18 of the same chapter ". . . I will show you my faith by my works." Wherever "works" are mentioned in this context, we could rightly substitute "my Father's business." Spiritually meaningful works are by definition the Father's business, which is also that which glorifies His name.

Just as James observed, faith without works is dead, so even more are works without faith, faith in Jesus and in His shed blood. Scripture repeatedly reminds us that there is no salvation without the shedding of innocent blood, and *only* that blood shed by Jesus on the cross. As we are led to do works intended to glorify Him, we must look carefully at what these works are, and especially what is motivating them. Works derived from faith and love, and those that serve and glorify God are beneficial works. But unless we know Scripture, how are we to know with certainty which of the less than self-evident works accomplish this? However, motivation is the primary factor in determining the spiritual value of ones works, and love laced with gratitude is the essential element of that motivation.

As Paul tells us in 1 Corinthians 13, without love there is nothing we can do that pleases God or has any spiritual value. If the sense of duty, repayment, seeking credit, reputation, or any reason for our works other than a grateful love is in our hearts, the works are dead. It is through the loving study of His Word, and continual prayer for wisdom, discernment, knowledge, and understanding, that the Holy Spirit will reveal what nature of works He has planned for us. But again, no matter how much good works we may do, without God's love in our hearts it profits us nothing.

If you are His disciple, that is His son or daughter, you must not be spiritually complacent, lazy or negligent in your Christian walk, but eager and active in pursuit of His business. I pray you will examine yourself, find the spiritual gifts you surely have, and use them faithfully in love and in a sincere effort to emulate Jesus and thereby be about your Father's business.

—30—

Loving Jesus

Jesus, in Matthew 22:37, asks us to love Him with our whole heart and soul and mind. Finally, in my old age, having discovered who He is, what He did, and how my future is in His hands, that doesn't seem to be an unreasonable requirement or prerequisite to salvation. Paul said that we are saved through grace by faith alone. But as John Calvin said, "Faith is never alone." By its very nature, faith in Jesus incorporates the Gospel in its entirety. This means that love of Jesus and living by His word to the full extent of our limited capabilities is what the Christian walk is all about.

As the absolute pinnacle of omniscience, omnipotence and omnipresence, there isn't much that God doesn't know or can't do. Three things that He cannot do, of course, are that He can't learn, He can't lie, and He can't make you *love* Him. He gave us the God-like faculty of free will that provides us sovereignty over the many choices in our lives. Among these is the choice of whether or not to love Him. God cannot, by the nature of His choice in the manner of our creation, make us love Him. After giving us all we need to know about Him in the Scriptures, He left it for us to choose, and by that choice, to seal our destiny, which is to be either with or without Him. We are saved by faith in Him, but because faith and love in this case are so inexorably entwined, it is not possible to have a genuine one without the other.

At this very moment, just as I wrote this last sentence, it came to me as a revelation! I just expressed what I believe and, what I pray is the element that has been missing from my faith! I have accepted Jesus as my Savior for about three years. I firmly believe in the resurrection and I spend several hours each day reading the Bible, praying, listening to biblical teaching tapes, thinking, writing, and trying hard to understand my mission in Christ. Because of all this, it would seem that I am "saved." Every Christian that I talk to says that I am saved. But I don't *feel* saved, and suddenly, as I write this, I believe that I know why.

I feel that I am one of those of whom Paul spoke in 1 Corinthians 15:2, who believe in vain. That sentence flowed onto the paper, assisted by more than my very limited and failing mind, just as did the gnawing compulsion to write this paper in the first place. My problem, I just realized, is that I have failed to bring enough love for Jesus into my faith! It now seems clear to me, just as I have sensed and feared, that my faith *is* shallow and in vain. I know that Jesus is deserving of my love. At this moment, I don't know where I'm going with this, but I trust that the Holy Spirit will continue to guide me along this paper trail that I feel compelled to create, and that through these efforts I will find the fertile soil in which this love can begin to grow strong.

Why should I love Jesus when clearly much of the world hates Him and always has? What did He do, and who is He that He deserves such love? First of all, who was/is He? This I *know*. Jesus is God the Almighty as well as the Son of God. God is the Father, the Son and the Holy Spirit that operate as separate personages, even as they are a single Godhead. God is a singular plurality. This is a difficult concept to understand because we live in a three-and-a-half-dimension world (we only comprehend half of the time dimension, that is from the past to the present, but not into the future) while God is in at least ten dimensions (which the cutting edge of science now recognizes as existing, and a great biblical scholar, Moses Maimonides, made note of a thousand years ago). Careful analysis of the Old Testament reveals the plurality of God in a number of places. In Ecclesiastes 12:1, the English translation uses the world "Creator." However, in the original Hebrew the word Barrow for Creator is written in the plural. Genesis 1:26 says, "And God said let *us* make men in *our image* . . ." This plurality of God has been mostly obscured in the English translation, it would seem, because the plural noun is followed by a singular verb (i.e., the Gods is) and the translator chose to "correct" this "error" in grammar. The fact that Jesus is one of the plural singularities of the total Godhead, along with the Father and the Holy Spirit, is well, but subtly, documented in the Old Testament, and is revealed in the New Testament. All of this is most thoroughly discussed and documented by Chuck Missler in a set of tapes called "The Trinity."

However, for quick reference, a reading of Isaiah 53, Psalms 21 and the Hebrew meanings of the names of the lineage from Adam through Noah, should strongly suggest, even to a skeptic, that Jesus is written of at least several times and actually very many times in the Old Testament, and therefore is not some "newcomer" who first enters the scene only in the New Testament. Once this fact is understood, it becomes easier to recognize that the sixty-six books of the Holy Bible, written by forty authors over several thousand years, is an integrated message system dictated by the Holy Spirit from outside the time dimension. This then becomes compellingly more evident as one grows to recognize the precise fulfillment of hundreds of prophecies and the existence of the incredible coding system within the text, both open as well as hidden, which no humans, even with the largest most advanced computers, could possibly create. Finally, with this well understood, one is inexorably led to the only possible conclusion, that is that the Holy Bible in its original text is truly the Word, the Truth, the Absolute Truth, the rock foundation of all existence.

Now, back to love. Before there can be love, it seems to me that there must be some understanding of, and intimacy with, the person to be loved, perhaps even a sense of gratitude, awe or respect. The understanding of, as well as the gratitude, awe and respect for, are fairly easy to acquire in the case of Jesus, with even a cursory understanding of His life and deeds. The intimacy part, however, is more difficult and seems to be possible only after a familiarity develops as a result of delving deeply into these other elements, and of course recognizing whom He was/is.

In understanding Jesus, it must be recognized that He was both God and man. As God, the Son aspect of this divinely plural singularity, He chose to humble Himself and become subject to pain, suffering, temptation, and the limitations of the fleshly body of man. Thus, He could walk among us, His creation, as one *of* His creation, delivering directly and in human terms, His message of love and redemption. Existing outside of time and space, our Creator knew from before the beginning of time, everything that His effort would cause, every thought and every action that each of us would have, from Adam to the end of time. Even though He gave us free will and choice, from His perspective He could know everything that we would choose to do and think before it happened. He knew before time that, at this moment, I would be writing this and attempting to find my place in His universe. He also chose, before time, exactly where and what manners of intervention He would impose, including His brief journey into time and space as the man Jesus. Everything that He intended to do, including His birth as man through a virgin, His death by crucifixion, and His resurrection, were recorded hundreds of years in advance in the Old Testament. His message, the whole purpose of His coming, was then *restated* with greater clarity in the New Testament.

Why did the Lord choose to become man and to suffer for our sins? Wasn't this a convoluted, painful, impractical, unnecessary way to get His message to us, and to rid us of sin? As the omnipotent God, couldn't He have chosen some other, more sophisticated way to accomplish this? Given where the world had gone since then, the failure of any universal acceptance and acknowledgement of this effort, especially in recent time, and more importantly, the gross ghastly misunderstanding and perverted application of His message, one might easily conclude that His mission was a failure. Obviously, there is something wrong with that picture, these questions, and this conclusion. Nevertheless, it all seems reasonable from a secular sense, using human logic and reasoning.

It has been said that God acts in strange and mysterious ways, but that is only because we lack our Creator's intellect and His knowledge of the end from the beginning and all moves in between. He planned it all from before the beginning. He knew before creation that He would take on a human body and that's exactly what He did. He also knew exactly what the result would be. We know that He knew because He told us so very clearly in the Bible long before any of it happened. As one possible flicker of light that might be cast toward an answer to the question of why Jesus chose to become a man, I am reminded of a little analogy that Chuck Missler mentioned on one of his teaching tapes. It seems that when he was a small boy and wondering about the same question, he asked it of a wise old Christian. The man took him outside to where there was a busy ant colony, and as they were looking down on the activity, he said something like, "Do you see those ants down there? Now, if you really loved those ants and could do anything you wanted, like God can, what do you think you might do in order to tell them what you wanted them to know?" After discussing various options, it becomes evident that becoming an ant was the kindest, most loving way in which to accomplish this, even though the risks were probably the greatest.

For the skeptic, I don't have clear compelling answers to these questions. No one has, unless the Holy Spirit opens ones eyes as He did mine, you can never know. Because my eyes were opened, while investigating the available facts, I was able to find the compelling unmistakable evidence from which to form a rock solid belief in the Bible and in the Resurrection. I know that Jesus played out a necessary scenario in God's overall plan from His Godly, all-knowing perspective. That is the key to *everything*. The realization that the Old and New Testaments are collectively the impeccably accurate inspired Word of God and, as such, are the fundamental and absolute truth, every word without exception in the original Greek and Hebrew. Having reached this conclusion, the mystery to me is not what is in the Bible, and the advent of Jesus on earth, but why so many find it so difficult to see and to understand what to me is now so evident and so thoroughly proven. Of course, it is equally strange to me why it took me so long to realize this truth.

Jesus became man in order to take away and pay for all of our sins, in order that those who believe in Him would have everlasting salvation. To non-believers, this sounds not only bizarre, but also absurd and foolish. Admittedly, from a strictly human perspective, it might seem that if this needed to be done at all, there would be a better way than through His own pain, suffering, humiliation and physical death. Jesus the man even asked the Father three times, on the eve of his humiliation, whether there was any other way; but there wasn't. Because I know what I know about the truth of Jesus, and because His whole story was foretold hundreds of years earlier in the Old Testament, I have no problem accepting the fact that there is a logic, an imperative that necessitated this manner of action, even though it may be beyond my ability to so comprehend. In other words, I trust that the Lord's judgment and common sense are superior to my own.

Now let us examine the awesome nature of what happened, in the context of love. "For God so loved the world that He gave His only begotten Son; that whosoever believes in Him may not perish but have life everlasting" (John 3:16). Why is this His only begotten son? As God, He could have "begotten" any number of sons. After thinking about this, I have concluded something that I have not yet seen in any commentaries. God uses the vehicle of "Son-ship" to reveal Himself and walk among us because we are capable of relating to this as a specific, understandable, close relationship. But the original personage we now call Jesus was not a son in the sense of a normal father-son relationship. The Godly personage we call Jesus was/is God. He is and always was one of the Singular Plurality, one of the three Personages of the total singular God.

God could have simply "appeared" on earth in human, adult form, just as He did several other times, as recorded in the Old Testament. It would seem that He could have taken on the same tasks as teacher, prophet, healer, etc., starting as a man. Instead, He chose to be born and to grow into manhood in the normal mortal manner. This, of course, necessitated what has been called the "virgin" birth, with God, through the Holy Spirit, providing the father role in the "Immaculate Conception." Thus, God became the "Father," and the result of the conception, the "Son" Jesus. Now there existed on earth a human infant, growing into manhood, in which dwelled the spirit and soul of God.

But what does this have to do with love? A great deal, in my opinion, because to me it adds another dimension to His love and the sacrifice God committed on our behalf. With the Father, Son and Holy

Spirit being collectively one single God, God literally tore Himself apart and sent one part of *Himself*, whom we now call Jesus, to the earth and to incredible suffering. It wasn't a son in the human sense, a separate being, but God Himself who chose to perform this miraculous deed. That is God's love, unconditional love. It was *agape love*.

Then came thirty years of growth from infancy to the beginning of His ministry; a long and frustrating period for this transcendent God to contain Himself in time and space, and in so limiting fleshly form. This was *patient love*.

Then came what must have been, from His human aspect, a very disheartening three-and-a-half-year of ministry. Because, even with His awe-inspiring, incredible teaching, and thousands of healing miracles, He remained, for the most part, hated, hunted, stoned and not believed by the very leaders who claimed to be the ordained representatives and faithful followers of the same God. These were the "faithful" who failed to recognize Him even as He fulfilled the many prophecies foretold to be accomplished by Him whom they had waited hundreds of years to witness. It was these, perhaps no more than a dozen of the "spiritual leaders" who conspired and prevailed upon the Romans to have Him crucified. This, too, was patient, *selfless love and unrequited love*.

The climax of this love journey was His trial, torture and crucifixion, which, of course, He could have stopped at any time. The description of this event, as presented in the New Testament, lacks the detail, which is significant in any assessment of the actual love He felt, and the price He paid for our salvation. Consider one curious aspect of the recorded events after His resurrection. First, at the tomb, when Mary, who loved Him and worshipped Him and knew Him well, mistook Him for the gardener, until he spoke her name and thus she recognized His voice. Then, on the road to Emmaus, He met Cleopas and another disciple. The three walked and talked for seven miles and neither one recognized Him during this entire time. Later, at dinner, when He broke bread, they finally recognized Him, probably because of the nail holes in his wrists. Again, when He appeared in the room with ten of the apostles, they didn't recognize

Him until He displayed His wounds. One might conclude from this that He didn't look the same as He had when they knew Him before the crucifixion. Putting this observation in the context of Isaiah 50:6, God speaks "I have given my body to the strikers, my cheeks to them that *plucked* them; I have turned away my face from them that rebuked me, and spit upon me." It should be noted also that it was the Roman soldiers that beat Him. The highest level of this type of punishment given by Jewish law was "forty strokes minus one." The Romans had no such "humane" rules. Additionally, Isaiah 52:14 makes note that "As many were astounded at thee; His visage was marred more than any man, and His form more than the sons of men . . ." Read this and Isaiah 53 and it is evident that the prophet is describing Jesus and His incredible torture and disfigurement "more than any man," hundreds of years before Jesus was born! Psalm 22 also describes the crucifixion and the suffering in the words of Jesus as He hung on the cross, words written hundreds of years before His birth and hundreds of years before crucifixion was even invented!

Thus, we find that this process of intense torture, disfigurement and death on the cross, this ultimate love sacrifice which Jesus allowed and of which He knew since before the beginning of time, consisted of much more pain, torment and suffering than one might at first conclude, without benefit of the more remote and prophetic passages in the Old Testament. They not only beat Him severely, but they also plucked out His beard and "His visage was marred more than any man." This explains why He wasn't later recognized by even His closest friends! Knowing what was coming, He the man, prayed the night before, asking the Father three times if there was some other way. According to Luke 27:44, His emotional agony then was such that He sweat blood as He prayed. Remember that He could have, on His own, stopped this at any time. However, His consultations with the Father confirmed that there was no other way to provide salvation for His beloved mankind. He, therefore, proceeded to permit His own prolonged torture and execution. How does one describe such love? It is certainly beyond human capacity to understand, let alone emulate. Perhaps only the love of a parent for his or her children can begin to approach this.

Again one might ask if there wasn't some other way to "save" mankind that didn't involve such strain and pain on God's part. Obviously, in the human context, almost anyone can compose a dozen scenarios that would do the job. But none of them would, or certainly God would have chosen one. How about this as a seemingly simply way for Him to get the message out? God could come out of the clouds, say once every month or so, and shout to the whole world. He might say something like, "Hey, you turkeys, this is God and I am watching you! You had better behave or you'll all end up in the oven on Thanksgiving Day!" It would seem that this would certainly fill the churches and keep the jails empty. But that would, in essence, take away all choice and turn mankind into automatons. It would be like giving students the answer sheet along with the exam. The result would provide no evidence whatsoever as to the learning that the student had achieved. He gave us what we need to know Him and to love Him. He also gave us the answers, but everything is, and properly so, in the Textbook, and one has to study that Text in order to find them. Of course, He also gave us the choice, our free will. Thus, we can choose to learn the truth about Him and ourselves from the Textbook that He personally wrote and autographed, or we can choose to ignore it. He already paid the price of our salvation on the cross. All we have to do is believe in what the cross represents and have faith in Him who hung there and who ascended to heaven.

Unfortunately, many that do read the book will still not learn or believe. This is because of a chicken-and-egg type of dilemma. The Lord in the Person of the Holy Spirit is always available to anyone seeking the Truth of the Word. And only through His assistance can the Word be really understood. One must with sincerity ask for His help, consciously or unconsciously. Thus, it would seem that some level of belief or desire to believe must already be in place before the fullness of the Truth, which leads to faith and love, can manifest. One must have the egg before the chicken can hatch.

A most splendid analogy, which better explains the role of the Holy Spirit, is provided by Chuck Missler. The hologram is an unusual three-dimensional photograph that is created using a laser as a light source to activate ordinary photographic film. This type of photography provides several strange and unique qualities. One of these is that the resulting picture is a meaningless jumble of shapes when viewed in any light except the very laser light with which the photo was taken. Only when viewed with the same laser light will the picture image be coherent. The same is true for the Bible. Although forty authors put the ink on the paper, it was the "ghost" written by the Holy Spirit, and only through His light can it be read and really understood.

The Lord loves us all. He has made this very clear. However, He has rules, firm rules. You can be with Him forever or be turned away from Him forever. Your choice. He asks only that you believe in His resurrection, that you love Him, and that you put your complete faith and trust in Him. Think about it. That's all He wants. He's God. He can have whatever He wants. He wants you, but only if you want Him, and on His terms. It is entirely your choice. He made the first move, on the cross. The next move is yours. He won't choose you unless you choose Him. If you choose otherwise, you had better be certain of what it is that you are doing, because once the flesh dies there is no mind to change anymore, but there is an eternity which may be filled with regrets.

Well, looking back at what I have written, I seem to have flailed away in many directions trying to deal with this subject of loving Jesus. I think that I have made a strong case regarding His love for all of us, but what about my love for Him? Near the beginning of this, I noted my realization of my own deficiency, but did any of this enhance my state or better point my way? It may have. I could not hold back my tears as I made note of the evidence regarding the torture and mutilation that our dear Lord suffered on my behalf. That gets me to the question: "What is love?" Are gratitude, respect, awe, interest, concern, thirst for understanding of, desire for closeness to; are these all somehow related to love? Or might they collectively be manifestations of actual love, as He would have us feel? I don't know. But I sure hope so, because that seems to be where I am. He is on my mind, in the context of one or more of these forms, a great deal of the time.

I pray that with the help of the Holy Spirit my understanding and love of Jesus will mature, and the strength and fullness of my faith will be such as to remove all doubt from my mind. I also pray with equal sincerity that you too will find something here of value, something that will spark your interest and desire to seek the Lord and confirm your love for Him

—31—

What's in a Name?

Throughout history, and in most cultures, a person's name was one of the most prized possessions. Up until no more than two or three generations ago, even in this country, a man's name, his honor, and his word were immutable strands of the fabric of which his character and self worth were formed. In the old Roman and Greek cultures, and perhaps other cultures, the sons of wealthy and titled, as soon as they were weaned, were given over with essentially full authority, usually to educated slave governesses or governors who would rear, educate and disciple them until they reached the age of accountability. Only then, were they allowed to take the family name. This was formalized by an official, and legal adoption of the child into the family and celebrated much like a Bar Mitzvah. In more recent times, when an adult child drifted too far from his parental religion or tradition, so as to adversely reflect on the family name, he could in many cultures, be "disowned" or stripped of that valued family name and its lifelong benefits. Scripture is replete with many evidences of the importance of the family name. Essentially every person mentioned in Scripture had a name of some individual significance and often of inspired or prophetic origin. Even God Himself changed the names of some of those He called, as each rose to the occasion of His purpose, such as, Abram, to Abraham, (from high father to father of multitudes), Sari, to Sarah, (from diminutive to female noble, queen), Jacob to Israel (from supplanter to he will rule as god), Saul to Paul (from inquirer to little).

Scripture speaks very emphatically to us that God Himself attaches great value to *His* name. For example, in 1 Samuel 12:22 we are told that "God will not forsake His people for *His great name sake*." In

Psalm 23:3 we here, "He leadeth me in the paths of righteousness for *His name sake*." We see, *"For Thy name sake"* in Psalms 25, 106, 109 and 143. In Isaiah 48:9 our Lord says, ". . . My *name sake* will defer my anger." In Jeremiah 14:7 and again in verse 21 we find ". . . for *Thy name sake*." In Ezekiel 20:9 and again in verse 22, we see "I wrought for *My name sake*." And in Ezekiel 36:22 God says, for *"My Holy name sake*." This type of exhortation occurs as least twelve times in the Old Testament making it very clear how God feels about *His name*.

Therefore, it should be no surprise that the third Commandment, right after the two about not having any other gods and not making idols, attests to the importance to Him of *His* name. The third Commandment reads: "Thou shall not take the name of thy Lord God in

vain, for the Lord will not hold him guiltless that taketh His name in vain" (Exodus 20:7, Deuteronomy 5:11). Taking the Lord's name in vain; do we really know what that means? Of course, who doesn't? It simply means cursing or swearing and using His name Jesus and His title Christ as part of a vocabulary of profanities, whether it is disparagingly or in anger, hate, frustration, despair or just casual or habitual vulgarity. Surely, such utterances are sinful as are all things contrary to God's will. But is that what God had in mind when He carved that commandment on the stone tablets He gave to Moses? I think not, at least not the principal meaning.

The ancient Hebrews took this commandment most seriously, so much so that they would not even speak His name, under any circumstances, both out of great reverence and out of fear that somehow God would interpret it as having been spoken in vain. It has been said that in some of their writings, they would even leave a blank space instead of writing His name. Or as was more common, they substituted a tetragrammaton in the text instead of His name. However, by never speaking His name, its pronunciation was lost. All that is left are these four letter equivalents of His name, in Hebrew transliterated as JHVH, IHVH, JHWH, YHVH and YHWH. Adding vowels to these, they became pronounceable yielding the equivalent names such as Elohim, Yahweh, and Jehovah, etc. But we now know Him by His new name Jesus Christ, which is quite pronounceable, yet no less sacred.

In order to get a better understanding of what our Lord meant by the commandment, let us examine the Hebrew meaning of three key words, "take," "name" and "vain." The word "take" appears 587 times spelled out in the King James Version of the Old Testament of which there are thirty-five different Hebrew words that have been so translated. The applicable one here in Exodus 20:7 is *nasa*. It has a variety of related meanings with the first listed being "accept," with "take" being near the end of the list of related meanings such as, advance, arise, suffer to, extol, take. From this analysis and for reasons developed hereinafter it seems reasonable to conclude that this particular word *nasa* is used more because of its first and prime meaning, *"accept"* rather than in any other sense of the idea of taking. I believe this most closely relates to what our Lord intended, "Thou shalt not *accept* the name of thy Lord God in vain. At this point this subtlety may seem like nit picking, but read on, it may not be. The word "name" appears 741 times in the Old Testament, and all but twice it is translated from the Hebrew word, sham, which is defined as the idea of definite and conspicuous position, appreciation as a mark or memorial of *individuality, honor, authority, characters*

The word 'vain" appears eighty-six times in the King James Version of the Old Testament, and there are fifteen different Hebrew words that have been so translated. The applicable one here is *shav*. According to Strong's concordance, it means, "desolating, evil, ruin, guile, and idolatry, as false, deceptive, lying and lastly vain." From this it seems more in the context of the commandment to use "falsely or "deceptively" as the meaning of *shav*. Thus, we could perhaps more accurately translate the commandments. As "Thou shalt not accept the name of the thy Lord God deceptively." Tradition and long established mindsets are difficult to change or even to want to change. But the words "take" and "vain" simply do not, in our current understanding of their meaning, convey the full strength of the message God gave us on those tablets of stone. Those who thought and spoke in the original Hebrew better understood the fuller, more inclusive meaning of this commandment than we do strictly from the common English translation.

It is the unfortunate choice of the translators, along with the limiting capacity of the English language to convey the nuances, the subtle distinctions of certain words, which cause many of the difficulties associated with really understanding God's Word. Knowing that this would happen, our Lord took good care to carefully preserve, with great accuracy, the originally inspired writings of the Scripture in the original Hebrew and Greek language, where we could rediscover whatever meanings may have been lost and thereby enrich our knowledge of His Word and of how we could better live by His Commandments.

With all this in mind, let's see what profanity our Lord had in mind here that is beyond and more important than abusing His name by cursing. As part of God's plan for the redemption of mankind, God chose Abraham through whom to grow a people to represent Him, in His name. It was from these people that the "seed of the woman" would come to redeem the world. It is not that Abraham, or "His people" were any better than anyone else, or any other group. It was simply by His sovereign will that He chose this way to fulfill His plan. By accepting His name as His people, God promised them a special land and a good life, provided that they obeyed His commandments. It was their lack of obedience to His commandments, their lack of living as His people, by *His name*, which defiled His name and for which they, as a particular people, were repeatedly punished. The previously referenced scriptural verses attest to this and to this underlying theme regarding God's concern for *His name*.

What does this have to do with us in this present age? Everything, because nothing has changed, except that we now know God by another, most sacred and valued name, Jesus Christ. There is now an additional chosen people with a different purpose and a different destiny. They are called Christians because they have taken *His name*. This is what it is all about! He has, by His blood, provided eternal life in Heaven, for all who believe in Him and accept *His name* thereby calling themselves Christians. In order to legitimately and effectively *have* His name; they must be born-again into His family. To become *true* members of His family, with all benefits to be derived there from, they must be *adopted* into His family to become His sons and daughters, just as did the sons and daughters of the old cultures mentioned earlier. His prerequisites for this adoption are, true and lasting faith in Him and in the power of the cross, followed by a continuous, sincere and concerted attempt at obedience to *all* of His precept and commandments as Jesus embellished them in the Sermon on the Mount. To accept the authority, and ambassadorship of the family of Christ, requires love, commitment and obedience. It must not be used vacuously. Only by representing Him in a manner consistent with His Word and in accordance with His will, can they rightfully accept His name without doing so deceptively, or falsely.

If one believes that "take" is as good as "accept" and "vain" is as good as "falsely," that is fine. The only important thing is that one understands the deeper meaning of those words, if one has chosen to call ones self a Christian. It is a grave responsibility having eternal consequences. Those who accept Him, and assume His name, have become sons and daughters of God, and are thereby expected to honor His name by their thoughts, words, and actions. Whenever they violate the Father's Word, in *any* manner, they dishonor Him, and they dishonor *His name* as well as His family's name, which is called Christian. This is accepting His name falsely. This is taking His name in vain. This is violating the third Commandment.

—32—

Christ Jesus

In my thoughts and discussion I have now chosen to refer to my beloved Lord and Savior as Christ Jesus, rather than Jesus Christ, unless it is otherwise quite necessary. Christ means anointed, so it's either Jesus the anointed or the anointed Jesus. What is the difference? All my life, until I entered the Christian fellowship, essentially every time I heard His name mentioned, it was by someone using His holy name as a swear word. It was generally using His name as the most hateful of the many expressions of an angry, hate-filled person's vocabulary. I heard it this way many many thousands of times, no few of which came from my own lips. I very seldom hear His name used that way anymore. It is not because there are fewer hating hearts, but because I am rarely around them now. But even so, when I hear, or see His name Jesus Christ, even in the most loving reverent way, I feel, at the very least a slight twinge, a sickening feeling in my heart. It is clearly the result of my subconscious memories of that "early time" and that almost universally common derogatory use of His name. Sometimes it even causes me heart tears. They hurt all over my chest and tend to clog my throat. Calling my dear Lord, Christ Jesus feels and sounds delightful to my ear, and absent of that awful hate with which His precious name has come to be associated. If that has bothered you at all as it has me, try this, it might ease the problem for you as well.

—33—

In Christ

In studying God's Word, we see these terms "in Christ," "in the Lord" and "in Christ Jesus." But look as carefully as you can, you will never find the term "in Jesus" or "in Jesus Christ." Have you ever wondered why? Perhaps not, because it may have seemed trivial or irrelevant. But nothing in God's profound and inerrant Word is trivial or irrelevant, as this little observation may help to illustrate.

Jesus is the earthly name of our Lord. When spoken of as Jesus Christ while He lived, it meant that Jesus was the Christ *positionally*, and the One who would through His death and resurrection enter His full glory and power functionally. Christ which means the anointed one is the name of the office into which He was fully instituted *after* His resurrection and His anointing by the Father. This is when He acquired the full manifestation of Christ our Savior, both positionally and functionally. Peter reveals this, but in such subtle terms that, without further evidence, it could be easily missed, when in Acts 2:36 he says, *"Therefore let all the house of Israel know assuredly, that God hath made that same Jesus, whom ye have crucified, both Lord and Christ."* Notice God *made* Jesus Lord and Christ. The grammar suggests that He didn't have that status until God made it so. He did this on the cross and at the resurrection. That is why we find Abraham and Lazarus on the paradise side of Sheol in Luke 16. This is the same place where in Luke 23:43 Jesus tells the thief, *"Verily I say unto thee, today shalt thou be with me in paradise."* The thief was saved, just as was Abraham, but Jesus had not yet been given the power to raise them to heaven. After His three days and nights in the "belly of the earth" on the good side of Sheol where saved souls waited for Him, He was now able to redeem them, and take everyone who was there to heaven, through the power He now had as Christ and Savior.

We should remember that Scripture makes it clear that He deliberately limited His power as God during the time period when He chose to live on earth as man. Philippians 2:5–11 speaks of this great "kenosis."

> "Let this mind be in you, which was also in Christ Jesus: who, being in the form of God, thought it not robbery to be equal with God:
>
> but made himself of no reputation, and took upon him the form of a servant, and was made in the likeness of men:
>
> and being found in fashion as a man, he humbled himself, and became obedient unto death, even the death of the cross.

Consider this analogy. A person graduates from medical school and thereby achieves the positional title of Doctor. It must be considered positional until he or she takes the exams and becomes licensed to practice medicine. Only then can the title Doctor be considered functional. The doctor can not function as such without this additional credential. Likewise, Jesus could not function as Christ in whom we could reside, or as our Savior, who could open the way to heaven, until He obtained the credentials bestowed by the Father at the resurrection.

Jesus was a man and also the Son of God. *"For unto us a child is born, unto us a son is given"* (Isaiah 9:6). The child became the man, Jesus. As the only begotten Son of God, He was no less than equal to the Father in the triune Godhead, but for His earthly mission He shed as noted, most of His Godly powers. Yet, Scripture makes note of His "saving" or bringing eternal life to many even as He walked as man. By being the Christ *positionally*, He could make that commitment, as it had been made throughout the ages before, through the *covering* but not the *forgiving* of sins. That is why we find Abraham waiting in Sheol and not already in heaven. In these situations, He gave the promise of salvation through faith as it had been given to the saints of the Old Testament. He became the Christ affectually and the fulfillment of the promises of actual redemption. This was affect after the resurrection, not before.

Thus, as long as Jesus lived on earth no one could be "in Him." If they could have, they would have had to share the cross and the work of redemption. As God's only begotten Son, He alone was ordained from the beginning of time to become the Redeemer of all of that portion of mankind who would believe, confess, repent, and through faith, be saved. Jesus became fully functional as the Christ, the Savior, *after* the resurrection, and thereafter He was called the Christ Jesus, whenever one's ability to be in Him was expressed. Thus, when in 1 Corinthians 1:30 Paul says, *"But of Him are ye in Christ Jesus, who God is made unto us . . ."* he is saying that now we too can be in Christ or in Christ Jesus.

However, we may yet be confused and ask as to the difference between Jesus Christ and Christ Jesus. To this I suggest that Jesus Christ was the anointed, as it was the custom to anoint or consecrate kings and priests. It was usually an authenticating ritual which set apart certain persons. Jesus was one of these persons. However, as the Messiah, He became The Anointed One, the One and Only Christ Jesus, the One through sins could be forgiven, not just covered.

How wonderful is His Word, for He is the Word, He is our Creator, our Lord, and now through the cross and His shed blood, He is our Christ the Savior who can dwell in us and we in Him.

—34—

The Numerous Other Roles of Our Blessed Mediator

Scripture tells us in 1 Timothy 2:5, "There is one God and one mediator between God and men, the man Christ Jesus." Yet Christ is God equal in everyway with the Father and the Holy Spirit, who are One in the eternal Godhead. How all of this works, however, is not the purpose of this paper. Scripture assigns Jesus certain particular roles in the implementation of the divine program for the preparation of the new heaven and earth as alluded to in Revelation 21. Jesus is Lord and Savior to the redeemed. He is the intercessor who sits at the right hand of God the Father interceding for the redeemed against Satan, who by definition is the accuser. Christ Jesus is also the One who will officiate over the rapture, bringing all the redeemed to heaven. He is also the only one, in heaven or earth or under the earth, qualified to open the seven sealed scrolls, (Revelation 4) which brings forth the tribulation judgments.

But why is He the only one, not the Father, and not the Holy Spirit, of these three persons, all equally God within the triune Godhead, who is qualified to overcome sin and thereby open the scroll, setting in motion and implementing God's entire end time plan? This may seem ridiculous to natural man and his limited logic and understanding. Yet through careful study of the whole Word of Scripture under the tutelage of the Holy Spirit, it can be seen as the most logical and only way God's purposes could be achieved. Thus it becomes clear that in order to fulfill these purposes, God had to first become man and He had to do it the "hard" way by actually being born from the womb thereby going through the entire natural process of becoming man. He also had to be spiritually perfect in His manhood, an achievement that only His Godliness could make possible. He is the only such being that ever was or ever will be perfect. That He became both Man and God gave Him the essential qualities for this divine role as mediator between God and man and for all of the other work that must take place as part of God's end times plan. Because of this, He and only He, understands clearly both sides of all issues. Mediator in the Greek means, a go-between, an intercessor, a reconciler, or internunciator. Romans 8:34 and Hebrews 7:25 claim Christ Jesus as our intercessor. With Satan still having access to the throne room, he is the accuser of all mankind continually pointing out our sins and seeking the right to our souls. But our Lord and Savior sits on the right hand of God the Father to intercede on our behalf and mediates every case.

To illustrate that His unique quality as God and man makes this possible, as well as necessary, consider an earthly example of judicial mediation. Years past, civil disputes were most frequently brought before a judge and jury to be tried in court. However, in order to establish equitable results, as the quality of juries has degenerated in the ability to reason sensibly, and especially to understand even simple technical issues, attorneys on both sides of disputes have more and more feared the crazy verdicts which often result, such as the jury award of millions of dollars to a woman who spilled hot coffee on her lap at a fast food restaurant. Therefore many disputes never go to court, but instead are settled through a mutually acceptable mediator. For this to be satisfactory to both parties, the mediator must be a trustworthy person of known integrity and fairness. He must also be well versed as well as experienced in both the relevant law and both sides of the issues involved. When these qualities are embodied in the mediator, both parties are generally satisfied that justice will be well served. In heaven, all disputes are about sin. Could anyone be better qualified for this job than Christ Jesus, both God and Man, the one who was made sin so that there could be a way to reconcile the sin issue?

But in order also to be our Savior, it was not enough that our blessed Lord was and is both God and Man. As man He also had to die the most horrible death. Why? The limitations of human reason and vocabulary fall short of providing a fully satisfactory answer to the world. Only through the instruction of the Holy Spirit within the redeemed heart can a satisfactory answer be provided to this and to many other of our Lord's seemingly "illogical" or "foolish" activities. We say He had to die as Scripture tells us in Isaiah 53 in order to obtain forgiveness for our sins, that is, forgiveness for all those who would believe in Him. How could God die? He couldn't. But man could, and it had to be a perfect sinless man, who was also God, or else the effectiveness of that payment could not have been adequate to remove all sins, past, present and future from the souls of all who would believe.

God, from the beginning, ordained a temporary process involving the shedding of the blood of innocent, spotless animals. Only by this and sincere confession of sins could sin be covered. Prior to our Savior's death on the cross, the sins of the faithful and obedient believers had been merely covered through this process. These sacrifices were only symbolic of what Jesus would later provide on the cross. They achieved nothing that could open up heaven to the faithful and obedient. They only provided a temporary ritual through which a covering of their sins would occur in order that saved souls could be separated from the damned and kept on the paradise side of Sheol. This was until Christ Jesus had paid the full price for their sins and could thereby complete their redemption and bring them home to heaven. The plan for effective forgiveness had not yet been implemented and could not happen until our Lord Himself, this God/Man, the essence of perfect unblemished innocence, shed His blood. Scripture tells us that life is through the blood. He gave His blood, and thereby His life that we might have eternal life.

However, it was not the beating or the "stripes," or the nails, or the spear, or anything physical or mortal that He suffered or gave up that paid what had to be paid for our sins. Any man could have suffered these things and many martyrs have done so with even greater and prolonged suffering, many times over the centuries. It was with "His stripes, we are healed," according to the King James Version of Isaiah 53:5. However, careful examination of the original Hebrew finds this word to be singular, that is, it was only one stripe or wound that actually paid the price. Therefore, the Holy Spirit here is telling us that the man-inflicted lashes were not what did it. This makes the most sense given the magnitude of Jesus' accomplishment. To pay the price for the sins of that portion of the entire human race who would believe, obviously required infinitely more pain than any mortal men could inflict. It was this single wound, that horrible, though temporary separation from the Father which caused Him to cry out, "My God, My God why have you forsaken me?" He knew why. He knew at Gethsemane. That is why he actually sweat blood as He prayed to the Father. He knew what man was going to do to Him. That would be merely physical torture. But He Himself having to be made sin (2 Corinthians 5:21) was a condition totally abhorrent to God. Therefore, He had to be separated from the Godhead. He could not be both God and sin at the same time. That was the STRIPE of Isaiah 53:5. This was the first and only time in all eternity that there was an actual separation of the inseparable Triune Godhead, where the God/man Christ Jesus was not a whole and equal part of the Trinity. What unspeakable pain, beyond any human imagination, must this have been? It was this loving God of ours who literally ripped Himself apart and inflicted on Himself the ultimate and only pain sufficiently excruciating to, in fact, pay the whole penalty of the sins of all mankind. Only this magnitude of pain, a divine spiritual pain, which was beyond any possible mortal comprehension, was of sufficient awfulness to satisfy God's sense of justice, so that now sin could be removed from all who believe in Him. Thus, He redeemed us; He bought us; He bought us back from Satan's sin-slave auction through this incredible act of love.

The role of our Lord as our mediator is rapidly approaching its end. While no one knows the time or date of the Rapture, the world events of the past fifty years, and at the present time, are one by one precisely fulfilling each of the prophesies which Scripture tells us must come to pass before His second coming. At the time of the Rapture, Christ Jesus will no longer sit on the throne at the right hand of the Father, interceding and mediating for us. This is because as He calls up all of the redeemed to heaven, He will also cast out of heaven our accuser, Satan. The redeemed will no longer be on earth to need

His services in that capacity. He will now assume His other roles as so carefully described in Revelation chapter 4 and elsewhere.

During these past almost nine years since I first realized that Jesus was my Lord and Savior, I accepted that fact, and for the most part concentrated my studies of Scripture almost entirely in that limited context. That alone is incredible, that God so loved the world (you and me included) that He gave His only begotten son, that whosoever believes in Him should not perish but have eternal life (John 3:16). But now I have looked at what it cost Him as described above, and also how much more activity, or work in progress, or call it what you will, God has gone through, and will go through in order to achieve His total purpose and complete His plan.

What did creation cost him? Scripture tells us that it was but a thought that He breathed into existence. How much of Scripture does He devote to it? A few chapters in Genesis and a few verses scattered elsewhere within the book. But look at the space He allotted for His expressions of love and concern for His creation, and how it could be cleansed and redeemed from that fall which resulted from the first sin. The rest of the book alludes to, describes, explains, and predicts the whole process He chose through which He is dealing with and will deal with the sin problem as He finally restores the world to His liking. And Christ Jesus is the central and foremost performer as evidenced by His various assigned tasks, and the fact that the volume of the book is written about Him (Hebrews 10:7). Let us summarize some of the unique tasks, which He could accomplish only after having become man as well as God. This brief compilation can hardly be viewed as adequate to express even a tiny portion of our blessed Lord's attributes and commitments to His creation. It would be the height of arrogance and conceit to believe that anyone could do this. Perhaps, however, this will at least present some of the more basic scriptural revelations in such a way as to stimulate greater thought, love and eagerness to search His precious Word more thoroughly.

1. He taught in the temple, performed many miracles of healing, and demonstrated by His life exactly what perfected man should be. He spoke truths so profound and eternal that they have been

remembered and marveled at by all of mankind throughout the ages regardless of whether they be atheist or believers of any religions, Christian or otherwise. His short presence is recognized every day, consciously and unconsciously, through the calendar, which the whole world goes by, counting days and years from the date of His birth.

2. The ultimate demonstration of His love and God's divine plan was performed by His suffering and death on the Cross and subsequent resurrection, showing Himself as again alive for forty days before His publicly witnessed ascension into heaven. Here He showed Himself as having conquered death, becoming the "first fruits" of the resurrection and eternal life, available for all who would believe.

3. Having ascended to heaven, He initiated Pentecost, by sending the Comforter that is, the Holy Spirit, to permanently indwell in the hearts of believers. This of course, was a totally new phenomenon unique to the church age, which began at that time and will end with the rapture. It was Jesus' work here on earth through the Apostles, which resulted in the New Testament. And finally through this, those who want to, can find the answers to all of the questions the Old Testament left unanswered. This was made possible only through His earthly presence as God/man and by His teachings both before and after His resurrection.

4. Through having overcome both spiritual and physical death, He fulfilled the requirements as Savior of all who truly believe in Him through a genuinely repentant faith. The result of this faith of the redeemed, necessitated that He would also become their Lord, because true faith would lead inexorably to Him becoming both Lord as well as Savior, the Lord part exhibited through obedience, love and an associated lifetime of beneficial works accomplished in His name.

5. His blessed work now entered a new phase never before dealt with. He ascended to heaven to sit at the right hand of the Father, there to function as noted above, as our mediator /

intercessor in whose Name we pray to the Father both in praise and gratitude as well as to petition for our needs. This is His current role until the Father tells Jesus to go get them, at which time His task will be to descend to the clouds and call all the faithful saints, both living and dead, up to heaven.

6. Once He has brought the raptured saints to heaven, our Lord Christ Jesus initiates the end times activity, which is so clearly detailed in Revelation. His role as the Suffering Servant and the Lamb of God is over. Another of His blessed names now personifies His work. He is the Lion of Judah. He no longer sits on the throne. John sees Him as reported in Revelation 5 standing, taking the book from God the Father, the seven sealed book which no one "in heaven or on earth or under earth" is qualified to open, only this God/Man, Christ Jesus. This book contains the seven judgments, which are then about to fall on the earth. It is also the book which contains the details on how He will now proceed to deal with the earth, preparing it finally to be His "footstool," as we are told in Jesus' own words in Matthew 22:44. "The Lord said unto my Lord, sit thou on my right hand, til I make thine enemies thy footstool?" Notice how He has been *sitting, until*! His opening of this book and its seven seals unleashes the period known as the "time of our Lord" and also as the "great tribulation."

7. After this our Lord Christ Jesus takes on what seems to be His final role regarding this earth. He will judge the living and the dead and rule the earth, which will have been somewhat restored from the destruction caused by the tribulation. He will then rule the earth from "David's' throne" which is His throne as David's rightful heir, having been as Man, the royal descendant of David, as well as the Godly inheritor prophesied in Psalms 2 and many other places in Scripture.

8. Having completed His seventh and final role as King of the earth, during the millennium period, He is the Architect of the new heaven and new earth of Revelation 21, which will follow the destruction of the present earth at the end of the millen-

nium. There, of course, He will rule forever over both the angels and all of the redeemed saints, which, through faith survived and now take their places in this eternal realm.

—35—

Without Me You Can Do Nothing!

Have you ever wondered about this statement by our Lord and Savior as recorded in the Gospel according to John chapter15 verse 5? I certainly did when I first accepted Jesus as my Savior, but had not yet accepted Him as Lord, and all that such acceptance requires. My first thoughts were something like this. "Dear Jesus I understand what you are saying, that because You are the vine and I am a branch off of that vine, all that I am, all that I can do, must flow through you to me. But with those words, you were speaking to the Apostles, true believers, and special people of your choosing. I'm but a very recent believer, and, therefore, a newly grafted branch. I have spent a lifetime not being one of your branches, yet achieving things long before I even knew whom You were. Are you telling me I did nothing, that all my achievements amount to nothing? What about the many great men in history who never became branches, who were either atheist or worshipers of false gods. Many of them actually shaped history. Are you saying that their accomplishments were meaningless and only an illusion because they were not through you? Please explain, because it makes no sense to me."

If you are a believer, most likely you were not as dense as I was when you first believed. Therefore, you may not have needed an explanation, or if you did need one, by now you may have already been blessed with all you need for an answer. On the other hand, if you are a believer and it is not yet clear to you just what Jesus means by this, then the following is written for you as an expression of what I pray is a Spiritually led explanation. If you are not a believer then the question may have no relevance to you beyond a mere curiosity which may have been provoked by the title. I pray that for the believer, who is seeking clarification, this will be beneficial, and for the unbeliever I pray that he or she will read this to the end, so that it may stimulate an interest to know more about this "crazy, arrogant" assertion our Lord makes and about Himself. First of all, the Author, Jesus is in fact God Himself as every redeemed soul, and only the redeemed, know with certainty. In that same book, the writer John, at the very beginning identifies Jesus by these words: *"In the beginning was the Word, and the Word was with God, and the Word was God. The same was in the beginning with God. All things were made by him; and without him was not any thing made that was made, In Him was life; and the life was the light of men. And the light shineth in darkness; and the darkness comprehends it not."*

Being the Creator God Himself who is speaking, we need to conclude that He speaks with absolute authority and that, therefore, there is a compelling reason to believe His words. Clarification and full understanding of the exact meaning of the title statement can be satisfied by approaching it from two directions, depending on where one is in his or her theology or lack thereof. One direction is the purely solid Christian spiritual perspective and the other, for want of a better term might be called quasi-biblical / scientific physical perspective. That is from the perspective that one generally believes in a creator "force" or God, but not necessarily that Jesus is He.

The Christian sense of the message is very clear, and I am probably insulting the intelligence of the seasoned believer to even mention an explanation. In Christ's analogy of the vine and the branches, He is the vine who provides all spiritual sustenance to the redeemed Christian who is the branch. In that context, the believer, the branch, can do nothing spiritually valid or eternal, without the nourishment and the water of life provided by Jesus to the believer. All of a lifetime of generosity, honesty, service, and impeccable moral behavior, that isn't derived from a redeemed soul grafted to Jesus as his or her Lord and Savior, count for nothing. For it is only the fruit of the spirit that is in concert with the Holy Spirit, which has everlasting substance. Only the good deeds of the redeemed, which are derived out of love and gratitude for Jesus and for His sacrifice on our behalf, deeds done without desire for earthly gain, only these have eternal value. All else is "hay and stubble" to be burned and to become nothing. Jesus expands on this analogy both before and after the title statement in order to broaden His delivery of this fundamental truth.

John 15 1–6

Jesus the True Vine

1 I am the true vine, and my Father is the husbandman.

2 Every branch in me that beareth not fruit he taketh away: and every branch that beareth fruit, he purgeth it, that it may bring forth more fruit.

3 Now ye are clean through the word which I have spoken unto you.

4 Abide in me, and I in you. As the branch cannot bear fruit of itself, except it abide in the vine; no more can ye, except ye abide in me.

5 I am the vine, ye are the branches. He that abideth in me, and I in him, the same bringeth forth much fruit; for without me ye can do nothing.

6 If a man abide not in me, he is cast forth as a branch, and is withered; and men gather them, and cast them into the fire, and they are burned.

As with a great proportion of Jesus' teachings through the various media such as analogies, allegories, similitudes, and parables, the theme here is fruitfulness or lack thereof. A reasonable case may be made here that the fruitless vine being burned is simply a saved believer whose life is cut short for lack of fruitfulness and thus enters heaven absent any crowns. Or perhaps it is a category 2 person in the Parable of the Sower who may have gained a short lived pseudo attachment to the vine but had no real grafting or sustenance, and soon fell away, being effectually a non-believer. Disturbing thoughts, in either case.

Now to the quasi-biblical/scientific perspective of the title statement. This is a poor label for the idea that I am about to put forth, but at the moment I can't think of a more appropriate one. One could fall back on John 1:1–5 previously noted, and from this make the observation that if Jesus had not created all things there would be nothing nor anyone here to do anything. There wouldn't even be a here. Therefore, it is obvious that without Him no one could do anything, because there would be nothing and no one. But that is the wrong context, because the world long ago was set in motion and you and I are here. Now our free will enables us to do things with or without believing in Jesus, and seemingly without His involvement. However, consider this, and bear with me as I muddle through trying to make simple, a very complex idea.

In science class it is likely most of us learned about magnetic forces that opposite poles attract each other and like poles repulse each other. We also learned that all atoms contain a positively charged nucleus of any number of protons and a varying number of negatively charged electrons orbiting around the nucleus, like planets around the sun. If opposite polarities attract, why aren't all of the electrons pulled into the positively charged nucleus? One might say because the centrifugal force of their revolving motion keeps them apart. But the laws of entropy demand that this force must wind down, but it doesn't. Now an even more perplexing problem. The nucleus in the heavier elements contains many dozens of protons, all with positive charges yet tightly bound together. Why don't they repel each other and drift apart instead, as do all other polarized substances. This bond is so strong, with so much energy holding it together that when the nucleus is split through an externally applied force, there occurs what we call an atomic explosion. What causes that incredibly powerful bonding of the protons, when by all scientific principals they should be voluntarily pushing themselves apart and should never even have been joined in the first place? Scientists have pondered this for generations and have had many ever-changing theories. No one really knows, from an earthly perspective.

But consider this, in Colossians 1:17, we learn of Jesus that, "He is before all things, and in Him all things hold together." IN HIM ALL THINGS HOLD TOGETHER. So Who is adding the energy, which causes those electrons to continue spinning and never run down? And Who is exerting that tremendous force that holds the protons bound together in every multi proton atom in the entire universe? JESUS! The Bible says so. HE HOLDS ALL THINGS TOGETHER!

Every scientist in this secular society would scoff at this explanation because scientists, regardless of any flaws or absurdities in their theories cannot, because they will not, allow a supernatural explanation for anything. So they will go on seeking anything but scriptural answers, spending billions of dollars and wasting their lives chasing windmills, when the answers are right in Scripture!

Thus we have another explanation of how, even now without Jesus we can do nothing. Without Him continuing day-by-day, moment-by-moment, holding all things together, in fact, every atom in our bodies, none of us could even be, let alone do anything, literally. Jesus is the Creator of all that exists, and what exists He continues to maintain. If He didn't, all matter would immediately revert back to energy. It would cease to exist, as one day it will when He "lets go," and thereby destroys the heavens and the earth. But if you are one of the redeemed, one of those who has truly accepted Him as your Lord and Savior, have no fear! Because He has promised that He will create for you a new heaven and earth (Revelation 21).

—36—

Christian R & R

R and R is generally understood to mean rest and rehabilitation. It is commonly used to identify that break which soldiers are given to temporarily leave the area where fighting is taking place in order to somewhat restore their mental and physical health before returning to the war zone. R and R is also an enterprise vital to all Christians. But it is in the spiritual realm where rest and rehabilitation are most needed by Christians. While most of us seem to be oblivious to the fact, there is a deadly vicious and all encompassing spiritual war going on every moment of every day, and it has been so from the beginning of time. The reason that most are unaware of it is that the enemy operates in secrecy, and in such clever and deceptive ways that very few are even aware, much less understand, what is going on. I submit that it is only the Bible believing, Bible literate, genuine born-from-above Christian who is capable of understanding any significant portion of what is really happening out there. Even many who fully accept the notion that Satan is a real active personage, who is actually the present owner and ruler of the earth, find it difficult to understand how he directly affects our lives. Scripture tells us that his demon agents are the principalities and power, which govern from behind seats of power of every governmental, corporate and institutional entity on earth. God, through the Holy Spirit, acts as the Restrainer, limiting this otherwise nearly ubiquitous and totally evil supergoverment. During this very late portion of the end times we see Satan's strategies and their implementation become ever more clear and frightful as man's natural propensity to sin is increasingly nourished through progressively more compelling and universally accessible avenues. Sources available through the computer, along with the always-in-your face TV, theater, magazines, clubs, bars, video games etc., provide every manner of opportunity and seductive inducements to what Satan hopes will lead to full time sinning. These, along with governmental, legal, and educational institutions, are all working feverously and sometimes not even with subtlety, to remove God and promote godlessness wherever possible.

Is it any wonder then, that being in such a perpetual war zone, every genuine Christian needs R and R? But what kind of R and R can be effective under such circumstances?

Because this is a spiritual war, the rest and rehabilitation needs to be in large part of a spiritual nature. All redeemed Christians have the Holy Spirit dwelling in their hearts; therefore, Satan and his demons are powerless as far as being able to drag their souls away from God and into hell. They can, however, harass and make life miserable for them. The more fruitful and dedicated to Christ we become, the more temptations, stresses and other spiritual stumbling blocks Satan will use to impede him or her in their spiritual growth, and especially in their usefulness for the Lord, as well as in their witnessing to souls who might choose to be saved. Satan cannot take away one's salvation, and so it angers him to see a saved soul, especially one who is leading others to God. He wants all to perish, as he will one day. So the best he can do, from his perspective is to cause Christians to suffer and to tempt them into backsliding so as to discredit and diminish their effectiveness as witnesses.

Under these circumstances, rest and rehabilitation for a Christian must necessarily and always have worship, prayer and scriptural study as primary resources. Christian rest, as with the soldier's rest, must be at a safe place away from the battlefield. Thus, it must be away from the world, away from all of the satanic devices, which Satan uses to mislead, deceive, divert and tempt. That eliminates a great deal of what the world views as pleasures and amusements. Sorry, but if one is serious about his or her service to the Lord, that's the way it is! This doesn't mean that a good Christian cannot experience pleasure. It simply means that our pleasure should be among the many, which are at the same time pleasing to God. Those who live closely to God and continually seek to obey Him will find through prayer and careful attention to what the Holy Spirit tells them, exactly what the acceptable ways are. It's amazing how, if we let Him, the Holy Spirit can transform our desires, pleasures, joys and even our needs in ways we never thought possible, in ways perhaps strange to the world, but quite pleasing to Him and most satisfying to us.

In Matthew 11:28–30, Jesus tell us *"Come unto all ye that labor and are heavily laden, and I will give you rest. Take my yoke upon you, and learn of me; for I am meek and lowly in heart: and ye shall find rest unto your souls. For my yoke is easy and my burden is light."* There is an offer no one should refuse! It's God's offer of rest for all who will come to Him in faith. Literally, it says, "I will rest you." These three verses, when understood, tell us all we need to know and to do in order to find rest and not only survive, but also to thrive and prevail to the end in this increasingly ugly and tiring war. Jesus tells us to come to Him with our heavy burdens so that He can take the load off in order that we may rest through Him. What burdens do we have which He offers to rest us from? It's clear that He is speaking not to the believers but to sinners, and it is the burden of sin, which He is speaking of, although with the removal of sin, numerous other burdens are also lightened. Isaiah 1:4 and Psalm 38:4 use this concept of being laden, or burdened with iniquities. The "rest" He refers to is the rest of conscience and of salvation as can be found only in Christ Jesus. Then there is also the rest of the heart, which can calm the fears and anxieties under severely adverse circumstances. These two aspects of rest are the equivalent of the two forms of peace found in John 14:27, Romans 5:11 and Philemon 4:6, 7. Then Jesus tells us that He is meek and lowly in heart. What does that mean? How can the King of Kings, Lord of Lords be meek and lowly? Remember, His kingdom is not yet; He came the first time, when He wrote this, as a humble servant. The King role will come later when He comes again. Here is "The Son of Man," a person to whom one can talk to and readily relate to. The Christian role model is Jesus. Here He describes Himself as meek, lowly, and, therefore, that is what all Christians should be. Forget the worldly deceptive rubbish about self-esteem, which so many false teachers spew from the pulpits and the media. Self-esteem is a phrase right out of Satan's manual entitled "How to Neutralize Christians and Prevent Redemption."

Remember, meek doesn't mean weak. It is simply a lack of pride and having nothing to prove while being patient and without resentments. His lowliness was His chosen position as a servant, as should be ours. Even though He was God Himself, He *made himself of no reputation and took the form of a servant, and was made in the likenesses of men and being found in the fashion as a man. He humbled himself and became obedient unto death even the death on the cross."* (Philippians 2:7, 8).

Jesus also uses the analogy of a yoke. This word has several meanings, but I believe the one here intended as a symbol, is a wooden bar or frame by which two draft animals such as oxen are joined for working together. After offering rest, Jesus says, "take my yoke upon you, and learn of me." How does that work, rest in the yoke? The yoke has but one purpose and that is to fasten two workers together so they can share the burden that needs to be dealt with. This terminology causes many to shrink away from submitting to His yoke for fear that it may involve greater sacrifices then they are ready to make. Jesus is saying in effect "put on this My yoke which I want to share with you. My burden is light, yours is heavy, but yoked together, with My help, the two of us can do anything— no sweat and as a result you will get rest." I know that's a lot of paraphrasing, but might that be what the Creator of the Universe is offering? As long as we "stay in the yoke" with Him our burden will always be light, because He already paid the price and has lifted the burden of sin, the burden too great for anyone to carry. What's left is easy, as long as we are yoked with Him. For the yoke by design curbs a variant and independent will, and brings it under a single divine control which we gratefully accept. We have genuine rest, that spiritual rest along with that incredible "peace which passeth all understanding" When the world is out to get you, and it always is, only the genuine Christian has any real place of refuge and rest and that's in Jesus, and in His yoke, under His protection and control through our willing submission. How foolish can one be not to accept this incredible offer found in Matthew 11:28–30?

What is hereinabove is addressed to born-again Christians, and as such, they are already alive in that rest, and have been firmly yoked with Jesus since their re-birth. Jesus' invitation in Matthew chapter 11 is a call for the unsaved to become saved by the One and Only One who can save. Thus, the rest we seek as Christians is already ours, but we must continue to claim it if it is to rest and rehabilitate us in the here and now. It comes from the eternal security for His faithfulness, not yours. Yet the war continues, and battles rage with relentless and exhausting fury, and thus we grow weary even though we have His blessed spiritual rest. Rehabilitation is analogous to getting our batteries recharged, that is, getting renewed energy to continue the fight. His amazing grace, which accomplishes this, is always available through genuine deep felt worship and prayer, prayer of the intensity, passion and sincerity of a heart filled with love of God as David repeatedly expressed in his Psalms.

As noted, up to this point this has all been about true Spirit led born-again Christians. But what about the rest of humanity? Surely, they are in even greater need of R & R. But initially, that need is not the same R & R. That need is *Repentance and Redemption*. The dictionary definitions of repent is to turn from sin and dedicate oneself to the amendment of one's life; to feel regret or contrition; to change one's mind. From a biblical perspective that's a very light-footed dance around what repentance really means. Repentance is far more. It is a sea change, a transformation, a complete turn around and a focus on, and belief in, Christ Jesus as Lord and Savior. It results in a new attitude, and a new first order of priorities in one's life without which the other "R," redemption, can never be had. Redemption, the result of having been redeemed is what happens when one genuinely accepts Christ Jesus as Lord and Savior, and He thereby becomes the top priority in one's life. Any from of repentance that fails to result in redemption is not repentance in the true biblical Christian sense. But what does it mean to be redeemed? The dictionary tells us that redeem means to bring back, repurchase, liberate by purchase, ransom, release from blame or debt, to free from bondage of sin, remove the obligation of by payment, etc. When placed in the context of

Jesus being the One and only One who redeems, this is excellent as a biblical definition as well.

So now what? Every redeemed Christian has a "built in" full time access to Rest and Rehabilitation through the indwelling of the Holy Spirit and the "hot line" direct connection to the throne room of God through prayer, petition and worship. But that R & R is not available to the rest of humanity until they partake of this other R & R, Repentance and Redemption. Through Scripture, God answers all who are willing to study and accept His Word, acknowledging that He is *"not willing that any should perish, but that all should come to repentance"* (2 Peter 2:9). Repentance is a fundamental necessity and a theme word throughout Scripture. It is the essential first step toward redemption. One who is redeemed is with certainty heaven bound. One who is redeemed has automatically been qualified to have the first noted R & R as the blessed means by which one can get through this life with the always renewable strength to overcome whatever this world and Satan choose to inflict.

Do you have that blessed R and R, that rest and redemption which our Lord has promised to all who genuinely believe in Jesus? Do you feel His rest deep within your soul, the rest you can always call upon to calm the waters around you no matter how violent the storm? If not, look carefully into the meaning of repentance, apply it, believe in Him, and accept His yoke, and begin your eternal life as one of His. Then be assured, He will never deny you rest.

—37—

Come Let us Reason Together

What an incredible invitation this is as given to us in Isaiah 1:18! Here God, speaking through the great prophet Isaiah is beckoning His people to come to Him so that they can better know Him and reach a true understanding of what He expects of them. This offer is made in the context of a severe backsliding of the people of Israel, where their hollow prayers and meaningless sacrifices were repugnant to God. Can anyone today, who is at all conscious of the workings and the conditions of the so-called Christian Churches not recognize the similarity of that time with the present? With statistics regarding divorce, abortion, infidelity and many other measures of worldly ways no better within the "Christian body" than elsewhere in the world, isn't this highly suggestive of similar times and conditions within the ranks of "His" people? In verse 9 of the same chapter, God says that only because of the existence of a very small, and of course obedient remnant, they should have been treated to His wrath, as were Sodom and Gomorrah. Has God's wrath been similarly deferred on this nation by the presence of an ever shrinking "true" remnant which yet exits here? With the rampant biblical illiteracy in this country and the prophesized ever increasing proliferation of false prophets, false teachers, and false religions in these end times, the size of the present day, genuine remnant is ever shrinking and more difficult to find.

In Revelation chapters 2 and 3, Jesus reveals to John the true nature of the Christian Church as it was and is throughout the whole history of its existence. The typical church of our time, that is these end times, is characterized by the ancient church of Laodicea. Laodicea means, "ruled by the people." WOW! I thought that Jesus was the ruler of His church! No! Today the people rule, majority rules, democracy functions at its "finest" even in what is supposed to be God's church. We have market surveys to determine what the people want of the church. Salvation is no longer the issue; what Jesus taught is either ignored or twisted; it is all about attracting the unchurched, about filling the pews, as if that saves souls. It is about making them "feel good" and wanting to come back for more touchy feely advice about how to improve one's self esteem, and to live a more pleasant, seemingly "righteous life. That there must be conviction before a sinner can experience conversion is rarely if ever mentioned. At the rate certain words are disappearing from the pulpits and from bible studies, words such as repentance, humility and obedience, they may well eventually disappear entirely from the Christian vocabulary. While words, such as faith and belief and love remain in popular usage, the world has successfully hollowed them out and thus removed the true spiritual quality and meaning they once enjoyed, but now only survive in that "very small remnant."

In Isaiah chapter one, God is citing the repulsion and utter disdain with which He views their false, superficial, or at best half-hearted, motivation regarding worship, sacrifice and walking in His ways. In verse 6, He speaks of their "wounds and bruises, and putrefying sores" of their souls which they have done nothing about, trying to heal. He counsels' them to adopt His ways and to anoint their eyes with a spiritual "eye salve" that they might see the wrongness of their ways. There, after noting their vain, valueless and hated burnt offering and other formerly meaningful expressions of worship, along with examples of their sinful ways, does He offer those precious words of reconciliation, "come let us reason together."

To further illustrate this beautiful parallel between Isaiah and Revelation 3:14–22, let us further compare the two messages. Where in Isaiah 1:6, God speaks of an ointment to help heal the spiritual affliction, in Revelation, Jesus tells Laodicea to "anoint thine eyes with eye salve, that thou mayest see." History reveals that the City of Laodicea was noted for the manufacturing of a very effective eye salve. In Isaiah, God calls for repentance or His wrath would come, while in Revelation 3:19, God says, "As many as I love, I rebuke and chasten; be zealous therefore and repent." Where in Isaiah 1:13 God rejected the offering and the false worship, and therefore clearly left His place in the Holy of Holies in the Temple, in Revelation 3:20 God has left the "Church" and as He says, "Behold I stand at the door and knock, if any man hear my voice, and open the door I will come in to him, and I will sup with him and him with Me. How very similar in effect is this to God's invitation to "come let us reason together." Here again it is the small remnant with which He is seeking a true fellowship and eternal family relationship. God is the same yesterday, today and forever. He changes not. The God of the Old Testament is the very same God of the New Testament. He wants all of us to be His family. God is ". . . not willing that any should perish, but that all should come to repentance" (2 Peter 3:9). Have you heard His knock and His offer to reason with you? Can anyone in his or her right heart reject such an offer?

But how do we accept this offer to "come let us reason together" and how do we open our hearts so that He can enter? The way is very clear for those who sincerely wish to know it. First we must know that He exists and know of His presence. Then we must listen in order to hear "His Voice." Only then can we open the door of our hearts to let Him in. Primarily, it's the Word, the Holy Bible, through which God speaks to us most generously and convincingly. It's where His reasoning is revealed if one approaches these precious words in a true spirit of seeking to know Him, and what He wants of us. From this we begin to understand that it is Jesus who is the truth, the way, and the only way. And once we recognize this, and our hopeless state, we become ready to confess our sins, repent, believe in the salvation offered through the shed blood of Jesus, and accept Him as our Lord and Savior. Then we have opened that door, and can begin to reason with Him. From that moment on both here on earth and in eternity to come, He and we will both sup and reason together. We will "sup," that is eat and drink, and absorb the spiritual nourishment of His very presence in our hearts. Currently, through prayer and study of Scripture by the light of the Holy Spirit, His reasoning will be revealed, as will be our purpose in life, and how we should go about achieving it. Don't wait another moment. Begin that process NOW!

—38—

And We Know . . .

For many who have any knowledge of God's Word, except for John 3:16, Romans 8:28 is probably the most comforting verse in all Scripture. Pastor Dr. Reuben A. Torrey called it "a pillow for a tired heart." *"And we know that all things work together for good to them that love God, to them who are called according to His purposes."* The context of this verse makes it clear that this promise applies to all who are saved through faith in Jesus as Lord and Savior and who are thereby God's sons and daughters, for whom else can love God in a way consistent with Scripture?

The comforting comes from the "all things" which means that even during our darkest times of pain and suffering, sorrow, doubts, adversity and despair, somehow, these things are working for our good. During such times, this may be difficult to believe, but we must believe this because this is God's promise to each of His own. To doubt, is in effect, to call God a liar. A major test of faith of the saved soul is when that faith does not weaken or waiver under these extremely challenging and trying circumstances. I once heard, or read, of a Christian father whose son had just died. His prayer at the funeral, as I recall the story, was not of great lamenting on the tragedy, for he knew his son was safe in heaven. Instead, it was a prayer asking God to make clear the message that this tragedy was providing to the family so that it not be wasted. Here was a biblical, trusting, faithful and loving soul who knew and doubted not that God was in charge. Here this father was actually living and relying on the "all things" portion of this wonderful verse. In his grief he could not see the "work for the good" part, but in his unshaken faith he knew it was there somewhere and was simply asking God to reveal it. Surely this is an example of an unwavering faith in God under a most trying time.

When the Holy Spirit provided these words of comfort to us through Paul, it seems evident that the love on which He conditioned this promise was an agape love, a totally committed love, a love that could not help but reflect itself through its owner's words, deeds and way of life. This love serves as a major piece of evidence in determining whether or not one is saved. However, its intensity may vary with each individual. Because Jesus commanded us in Matthew 22:37 that we are to love God with all of our heart, soul and mind, each of us is severely challenged in our quest to qualify for eligibility regarding Romans 8:28. Such intensity of love for God does not happen instantly. It is a progressively growing commitment and dedication to Him that I believe God examines and tests. I believe that this is a very important precept. A vital measure of one's growth as a Christian is the ever-increasing love for God, our Creator God. The existence of that growing love is most likely the telling evidence of the existence of one's salvation! God knows we cannot instantly produce this love that requires all of our heart and soul and mind. He knows that no one can reach such a state within an entire lifetime. This will only, but surely, happen between here and heaven, when the soul finally leaves the confines of the corrupt body. Progress! Forward movement toward the commanded goal! That is what we are to be exhibiting through our thoughts, actions and deeds, and in every other way we conduct our lives. Too difficult? No it isn't. A snails pace will do. His love is patient and long suffering, and He has lots of time. Remember this; His love for us is infinite. But I believe that He does measure it out. Also remember that our hearts are "deceitful above all things and desperately wicked (Jeremiah 17:9). Where can there be God's love in such a place? There can not. We have no eternal love of our own. Any such love we acquire is His love, which He gives so that we can give it, back to Him, that is, to love Him and others.

Perhaps we are all born with a love valve for this special love. Due to our inherited sinful nature, that valve always comes closed. Only God can open that valve to let His love in. By His sovereign will, He has chosen not to even open it except under one condition.

That condition, under the present dispensation, is that we choose to believe and have faith in Christ Jesus. The greater that faith grows, the wider God's love-valve opens, and the more fully we are able to love God and also our brethren, as well as our enemies, as He so commands. Remember it's His love that He pours into His own sons and daughters who are to use it in accordance with His directions. If we are in the proper state to receive this love, we are also fully capable of using that love, as He requires us to. God adjusts the flow of His love to the exact rate we are able and willing to properly use it. We should pray, each of us, that we are capable of serving Him with a wide-open valve. As we all know, the word love is overused, and misused, bantered about in the world in every imaginable context. But there is no doubt that God has bestowed all of mankind with the capacity to love, but this love is not the same love with which God endows His children; this is a diffcrent love. It may feel, look, act and taste like the same love. In some cases it may seem to be even more intense and more committed, but it is, nevertheless, not the same love. For one thing, God's love, which He passes through His sons and daughters, is eternal; it transcends physical death. The love in the hearts of the redeemed is not extinguishable by physical death, but grows to a final all encompassing intensity the second the soul has shed thc limiting confinement of the physical body. The natural man's love ends when he dies. There may be temporary vestiges of it in the form of concern for those left behind, as there was with the rich man in Sheol as he called across the abyss to Abraham asking him to send to his living brothers a warning to repent so that they could avoid his fate. But ultimately, in the eternal lake of fire, there will be no love, only the pains of regret.

Perhaps this analogy may be useful in describing the difference between the love flowing in the hearts of the redeemed and the look-alike love that can fill the heart of the natural man. The Epistle of Jude verse 10 states: *"But these speak evil of those things which they know not; but what they know naturally, as brute beasts, in those things they corrupt themselves."*

Here Jude is describing apostate teachers of these end times. The first time he uses the word "know," it is the Greek word *eido* which speaks of mental reasoning and comprehension, deeper knowledge which can include a whole range of invisible (spiritual) things. It is the "know" that only the Holy Spirit can make real in one's heart! Jude says, the apostates, the unsaved, don't know of these things. These are above their level of comprehension. The second time he uses the work "know" he is describing the type of things they can understand. For this, Jude uses the Greek word *epistamai* which simply means to understand in the sense of a skill or handicraft, a knowledge of palpable things, an animal sense, the physical sense of feel, taste, hear and smell. The difference between the ability to comprehend the reality of the eternal nature and the limited ability to comprehend only the palpable, temporal things of this world separates what the believer can know and what the apostate is limited to understand. The "know" of Romans 8:28, as we would correctly expect, is *eido*! And so I believe it is with love. Just as only the born-again man can know (*eido*), so also only he has a new heart in which the Holy Spirit dwells. In the same way, just as the natural man only knows (*epistamai*) so also does he have only the old natural heart. It's through the indwelling Holy Spirit in the new heart that God infuses His unique love.

Having, I pray, identified which love it is and that it is a prerequisite "to all things for the good" let us now examine the other condition that must exist before this blessed promise can be claimed. The promise belongs to those who not only love God, but who are also called according to His purposes. This is not a requirement of the saved, which is unique to this verse. Everyone who is born-again is spiritually grafted into the body of Christ. What does that mean? Paul says it best in 1 Corinthians 12:12–26. It might also be said that each member of the Christian Body is like a single cell much like the cells of the human body of which there are a trillion or more. Each has a specific purpose or function within the body. One might say that God called each human cell, "according to His purpose" in order that collectively they would form a healthy living body. Paul's' analogy is most beautiful in its simplicity and relevance. He describes each component in more easily understood terms such as arms, legs, feet etc. with the head being our blessed Lord Himself. The subject verse tells

312

us that those who have been saved have been called for a purpose, His purpose. That means the called, the saved sons and daughters of God, each has a specific purpose within the Body of Christ. What is that purpose? Is it to fill a pew seat once a week, or to rest on one's laurels for having said the sinner's prayer and an occasional rote mumbling of the so-called Lord's Prayer? Anyone who has truly received the Holy Spirit knows and worships far, far better than that. If you don't, then quickly and with fear and trembling, examine your faith to see if it really exists in your heart. Do so with the Holy Bible in your face, and an urgent prayer in your heart, asking the Holy Spirit to point you to His truth, and to how you can really have that which you have not, but presumed you had.

Being called according to His purpose means exactly what it says. If you belong to Him, then He has a purpose for you. Your job is to ask through prayer, and in all sincerity and single-mindedness, to have Him explain that purpose. Single-mindedness means a singular, sincerity of petition, genuinely desiring to know His purpose, and absent of any fear, dread or misgiving regarding what that purpose might be. The prayer to know your purpose must be anchored in a sincere and *eager* desire to begin that purpose out of a profound gratitude for what He did for you on the cross. Whatever the purpose is, whatever you are called to do, is far beyond your ability to do it, guaranteed! But you must believe that it will never be through your strength or your ability that His purpose is to be accomplished. It will be 100 percent by Him through you! You may or may not already have the required attributes. But fear not, for if you already have them, it's because He foreknew everything and prepared you for His purpose in advance. If you believe you lack the necessary qualifications, know that He will provide them, and as much as they are needed, for His purpose. You bring nothing of yourself to this purpose except your love and your sustaining willingness. He will provide everything else.

Perhaps we should nail this down a little more firmly by considering one additional comment on this "who are called" requirement. This is no incidental or perfunctory requirement on which our Lord conditions His promises regarding "all things work for the good."

God's calling demands a response! If you believe that Romans 8:28 applies to you, and you are not seriously pursuing that for which you believe you have been called, or haven't even heard a call, it is on-your-knees time. God's calling demands a response and He will receive it one way or another, because His calling is His words, which will not be spoken ineffectually. This is made clear in Isaiah 55:11 where God spoke through Isaiah saying, *"so shall my word be that goeth forth out of my mouth; it shall not return unto me void but shall accomplish that which I please, and it shall prosper where I send it."* If He called you for a purpose, that purpose will be accomplished because He said so. The word void in the Hebrew is *rayjam* meaning, ineffectual, without cause, void. God says that will not happen. It is evident that this calling for God's purpose is the calling that places one into the Body of Christ and into that position as an eye, or hand, or foot, or whatever, as Paul so graphically depicts the Christian Body.

What is your condition in this context? Have you been called? Have you answered that call effectually? And are you pursuing that to which you were called? If your answer to these last two questions is a prayerfully attended to yes, then it indicates that you are qualified under this second prerequisite to receive the blessing offered by Romans 8:28. However, what if you haven't heard His call or what if you have heard His call, but for whatever reason you chose not to answer it, then it seems reasonable to conclude that in either case, at this point in time, He has not called you, and you have flunked this part two of the test. Because there is no such thing as God's words returning to Him void, that is, not having accomplished their mission, you didn't miss the call, and you didn't get a call, which you chose to ignore. You have not been called! To that I would, and you should too, prayerfully add YET!

I must carry this point a little further because it's much too important to let any discernable point be missed. As noted, in the beginning of this essay, Romans 8:28 applies to all genuine born-again believers, and only to them. Because it applies to all believers, then all believers must both love God and be called to His purpose. Therefore, one has to conclude that if there has been no calling, there is no salvation, YET!

If you have that love and calling, praise the Lord and seek always His wisdom, His discernment, His knowledge, His understanding, and all things He is willing to provide in order that you may do the very best to serve Him for whatever purpose He has called you. Nothing in your life can, or should, be more important.

—39—

Do You Know Truth?

Genuine truth is incapable of being conceived in the mind of man. Two times two is four, that is true, as are numerous facts. But these are not truth. No thought, action or deed originating on this earth is truth. Through his God given, but limited mind, man is capable of, and has made great strides in, discovering many things that are true. He has come to understand in the most superficial way, a few of the "physical laws" God chose to promulgate and employ in His act of creation of man and the universe. These collectively may be true facts, but they are not truth themselves.

Philosophers through the ages have sought truth, the logos, the controlling principal of the universe, but never found it, because it cannot be formulated in the human mind. They were wise enough to recognize that the collection of known facts and beliefs were not what they were seeking. They were seeking what they knew must exist, that is some sublime, all encompassing, eternal truth, which governs everything. They never found it.

Churchill is said to have once commentated on truth. He said that truth was such a rare thing that whenever it is found, it must immediately be surrounded by lies, lest it escape and bring down the entire man made facade we call reality. He was more right than he may have realized.

When Jesus appeared before Pontius Pilate, Pilate asked Him, "What is truth?" Then he turned around and left. What an incredible opportunity he had! Beyond that moment, no person ever had such an opportunity. Here was TRUTH standing before him, and he either didn't recognize it or he feared he might have to acknowledge it and the consequences, which would result.

It is Jesus and only Jesus who is the Truth, the logos, the Word. As Author of the Holy Bible, He could not express anything but the truth. Therefore, the Holy Scripture is His way of revealing to us, in accordance with His sovereign will, that portion of Truth, that part of Him, which He would have us know, and that we are capable of knowing. Scripture is the inerrant Word of God. Apart from this, there is no other earthly source of genuine truth. Of course, there are many true facts not specifically expressed in Scripture. We find them in mathematics, engineering, science, and every day life, but these, as previously noted, are but tiny superficial nibbles into the facts, which surround God's universal Truth.

Now to the meat of the matter! Do you know Truth? Do you know Christ Jesus? That's the same question. Jesus walked the earth as man two thousand years ago and so Truth was manifest among His apostles and others who came into His presences. While He is no longer among us as Man, He did not leave us absent of His presence in the Spirit or from the ability to know, that which is Truth. Before He came as Man, He authored part one of the Book of Truth. After He returned to heaven, He authored part two of that precious book. They stand as a single integrated message directly from Him and about Him. This book, provably written from outside of time and space, is His gift to us so that through it we might not only learn about Him, but also come to understand what He would have of those of us who are willing to trust Him and make Him our Lord and Savor. Without a genuine working knowledge of its contents, how can we ever know Him or what He would have of us? Are we willing to trust hearsay from others, or a thirty minute sermon once a week as our means of knowing what is essential for an assurance of eternal salvation? Is it enough to trust our conscience or our heart, which Scripture assures us, is "... *deceitful above all things, and desperately wicked* ..." (Jeremiah 17:9). On judgment day, ignorance will not be an excusable excuse. His book is not hidden or prohibited, at least not yet in this country. Therefore neither you nor I have any excuse for not studying that which He gave us for this exact purpose!

Well, you say, "that's all fine and good, but I have to work, and have a family as well as other responsibilities. I don't have enough time to even read, let alone study the Bible, and I sure don't have time to attend group Bible studies." To this response I would ask, how much time do you spend it front of the TV, reading magazines, reading sports pages, engaging in recreation and various forms of amusements or hobbies? These things of themselves are neither wicked nor good. They become wicked when they take away from God that which must be His if you are one of His sons or daughters. In John 2:15, the Holy Spirit *commands* us to "*Love not the world, neither the things that are in the world. If any man loves the world, the love of the Father is not in him*" you can't have it both ways.

What *must* be His is your number one priority, far above your number two and three priorities, which should be family and others. Scripture tells us that if we are His we are not of this world. The activities mentioned in the proceeding paragraph are all of this world. They are all very pleasant addictions carefully crafted to keep you focused anywhere but on Jesus and the Scripture, to keep you chained to the ways of the world. The true Christian must for a while be in the world, but must continually resist being of the world. If you are truly one of His sons or daughters, it should not be difficult to honor God and His way by weaning yourself from these addictions and to replace them with more praise, prayer and pursuit of truth, that is, biblical knowledge. That is the quality time which God wants to spend with you so that you can really get to know Him as your Father.

If you are raising a family and take parenting seriously, you know you must spend quality time with your children as well. And if you are concerned for their immortal souls, and of course you are, then you must do more for their spiritual development than dragging them to church on Sunday, letting (or forcing) them to attend that half hour Bible study provided by someone else, and setting yourself as an example of integrity and good works. Christian polls have shown that more than 80 percent of those who come from Christian homes abandon the "Christian faith" within a year after leaving home. Why? Could it be that that these homes expressed only the superficial aspects of Christianity and do not make worship, prayer, devotion and serious Bible study a strong and major part of family togetherness and self discipline? You are being no friend to your child's soul by allowing TV, video games, unnecessary computer conversation, theater and sports to occupy more time and priority than is given to worship and getting to know Jesus through Scripture and through prayer. Unless you have taken control of these things in your life as well as that of your family, then perhaps you should re-examine what you call your faith. Could it be that you are merely an ardent dabbler in the faith, typical of this end time's church of Laodicea, which God has said He will spew from His mouth (Revelation 3:16)?

Remember this! It is absolutely inescapable that one day every one of us will meet the Author of that divine book, which most of the world hates and many of us treat so casually. What will we say to Him? Nothing! Because nothing can be said which He doesn't already know. But as we stand before Him we will hear one of two, and only two, remarks from Him. He will acknowledge us through saying something like, ". . . *well done my good and faithful servant . . .*" (Matthew 25:21) or it will be something like ". . . *depart from me for I never knew you . . .*" (Luke 13:27). The one you hear will undoubtedly result to a larger degree from how serious you were in your pursuit of understanding and trust of Truth, and your obedience to Him. Obedience. That word deserves considerable elaborations, which we'll get to later. However, those who are serious about being Christians and promoting the Christian faith will soon discover all that is needed can be found in the Scripture.

Scripture tells us that an understanding of the Holy Word is only possible through the tutelage of the Holy Spirit, and that He dwells only in the redeemed heart. So how can one comprehended Scripture as here urged unless one is already born-again? And if one is born-again of what need is it to further pursue such learning? The second question is easy to answer. If you are truly born-again, you have accepted Jesus as your Lord and Savior and pledge your undying faith in Him. One of the compelling evidences of that faith is a love for Him and a burning desire to know Him, and to understand just what He would have of you, and how best you can express your appreciation for His gift of salvation. He authored the Bible for that very reason! The first question is more difficult, at least for me. In trying to answer it, which no doubt can be answered in several ways, it is clear in Scripture that prayers of the saved for the unsaved are often answered affirmatively. I believe that in these cases, the prayer is answered through a supernatural "drawing" of the individual toward seeking Truth (John 6:44). That person who is now a seeker will be led by the Holy Spirit to where Truth is revealed. The result is not automatic salvation. It is only exposure to the idea of, and potential for, salvation. God will not violate man's sovereign right to choose even though He is ". . . *not willing that any should perish, but that all should come to repentance.*" (2 Peter 3:10).

Jesus expressed most clearly four ways, in which that exposure might be received, in His parable of the Sower. The first way (Matthew 12:19) indicates that some will not understand and will return quickly to the devil's control. Next, others will hear, accept the truth, and rejoice, but at the first real test of faith, they will also retreat back to where they were. Still others will also accept truth, but with insufficient conviction to resist the continuous worldly temptation and troubles. They will also in effect remain of the world, although most may continue to profess to be Christians and never realize that theirs is not a saving faith. Only the fourth category in the parable are the saved. These are the ones who seek, find, repent, obey and really know Truth. Only these are the *saved*. "*. . . But He that receive the seed into good ground is he that heareth the Word and understand it, which also beareth fruit . . .*" (Matthew 13:23). Notice that the one who is saved "beareth fruit." One can therefore conclude that if bearing fruit is not part of one's Christian walk, then there should be cause for concern as to the efficacy of one's faith.

"Heareth the Word and understand it . . ." This is another phrase loaded with significance. The word is the Word of God, the God authored Holy Bible. It is not a single word, nor a few selected verses; it is the *whole* Bible that must be understood to the extent one is capable of so doing. That capability can be awesome if one is but willing to engage the power of the Holy Spirit who at all times stands ready and eager to assist the sincere heart. Sincere, dedicated Bible study should be an essential part of every real Christian life. How else can one go from simply hearing the Word to truly *understanding* it? Also how can one resist falling victim to the many false prophets and

false teachers of Scripture unless one is armed powerfully with the direct and entire Word of God?

If you believe this to be simply rhetoric, not to be taken seriously, consider this directly from our Lord Jesus as He came into Jerusalem riding a donkey. See Luke 19:37–44 as follows:

> *And when he was come nigh, even now at the descent of the mount of Olives, the whole multitude of the disciples began to rejoice and praise God with a loud voice for all the mighty works that they had seen; saying, Blessed be the King that cometh in the name of the Lord peace in heaven, and glory in the highest. And some of the Pharisees from among the multitude said unto him, Master, rebuke thy disciples. And he answered and said unto them, I tell you that, if these should hold their peace, the stones would immediately cry out. And when he was come near, he beheld the city and wept over it, saying, If thou hadst known, even thou, at least in this thy day, the things which belong unto thy peace! But now they are hid from thine eyes. For the days shall come upon thee, that thine enemies shall cast a trench about thee, and compass thee round, and keep thee in on every side, and shall lay thee even with the ground, and thy children within thee; and shall not leave in the one stone upon another, because thou knewest not the time of thy visitation.*

Here the people are declaring Him to be the Messiah, probably based more on the great works He had accomplished than on any knowledge of prophecy. However, the Pharisees the greatest Bible scholars of the day urged Him to stop the people from singing the songs of worship, and their acknowledgement that the Messiah had finally come. Jesus' response, that even the stones would cry out proclaiming the same thing, is telling them that even the whole earth knew of this prophecy and had been groaning and eagerly waiting for His coming. Then Jesus wept, because He knew, and told them, how horrible their future would now be ". . . *because thou knewest not the time of thy visitation . . .*" They could have known, and they should have known, because there are more than three hundred prophecies attesting to His coming. These prophecies describe Him fully, indicating where He would be born, how He would ride into the City on an ass, the exact day in which He would do this, and exactly why He had come. He held the entire Israeli race accountable for this ignorance. The price they have paid both individually and as a nation, for not knowing what He held them accountable to know is a great tragedy they still suffer to this day.

After this can one in good conscience, and for the sake of one's assurance of eternal salvation, sensibly reason that being weak in the knowledge of Scripture is not important? They had hand written scrolls, without designated chapters and verses, and very few copies of these. They had just one continuous roll of words for each book, which was exceedingly more difficult to study, than our very comfortable, easy to read and fully referenced and researched Scripture. Also we have the New Testament, Part II of God revealings which answer many of the questions left unanswered in Part I. If God could hold them so tragically accountable, both individually and as a nation, for not knowing Scripture, why should anyone believe that scriptural ignorance today can result in anything less tragic for any one of us?

Well, you say, "that was then this is now." Don't you know that the Holy Spirit through Paul in Romans 10:9, said, *"That if thou shall confess with thy mouth the Lord Jesus and shalt believe in thine heart that God hath raised Him from the dead, thou shall be saved?"* Yes, I know that, and I truly believe it. However, the efficacy of that proclamation is very much dependant of what one understands about the meaning of the words "confess" and "believe" and how they are applied. If the meaning of these two words was intuitively self evident and correctly applied, what need would there be for the rest of the Scripture? Judging by the proportionally very tiny remnant that attend Bible studies, it could be concluded that very many believe that there is no effective purpose for the rest of Scripture! It is not at all my purpose here to condemn those who chose not to participate in-group Bible study. Perhaps many study daily and diligently by themselves and are, thereby, well versed in the whole Word of God. If they are, then they know the meaning of "confess" and "believe" in the highest and only effective spiritual sense. They know that one must have a contrite heart, be submissive in servitude to the Lord, be filled with gratitude, and be bent on obedience and trust.

Lets' check out another famous pair of verses in the Gospel of John chapter 8 verse 31 and 32.

Do You Know Truth?

Then said Jesus to those Jews, which believed, on him, if ye con-
tinue in my word, then are ye my disciples indeed, and ye shall know
the truth, and the truth shall make you free.

Here He was speaking to believers who, IF THEY CON-
TINUED IN HIS WORD, would be His disciples, that is His followers, His faithful, born-again Saints. What does the verse say to
you? It tells me that one major evidence of being a genuine Christian is by continuing in His Word, which means to read, study, chew
and digest His precious Word, which for us must be nothing more
nor less than the blessed Scripture. All of it! Then He says that if
you do this, you will know the truth, and that the truth will make you
free. Verse 32 is very famous and is usually quoted out of context. It
even appears in stone, on the face of the U.N. headquarters building, which is one of the great citadels of those who are preparing the
world for the coming of their lord, the antichrist. Verse 32 has
Christian meaning only when preceded by verse 31.

Here Jesus is telling us that through continuing in a study of Scripture will you really know truth, that is know Him, and it is *this* Truth
which will set you free. Free from what? This great phrase has several
meanings. First, Truth—Jesus through His death and resurrection has
freed His disciples from eternal hell through the washing away of their
sins. Second, they are freed from the power of sin whereby sin can now
be resisted through the in dwelling of the Holy Spirit. Third, through
His legacy, the Scripture, He (Truth) can become known intimately,
and fourth, through His precious Word, combined with prayer, His
disciples can learn the truth of what His purpose is for them and how
they can live by His will. If you are a genuine Christian, you are one of
His disciples and so this all applies to *you*!

I could go on and on citing other similar, compelling examples of
why one *must* study Scripture. However, by now you probably have
more than exhausted your willingness to read on, so I'll close with this
summary of thoughts.

1.   The Holy Bible is God's inerrant Word. In its presently available
     Hebrew and Greek, it is provably so, in spite of all of those who
     attack, disparage, misquote and otherwise try with great clever-

ness to dismiss it as a mere work of fallible men and, therefore, not to be relied on or valued.

2. The infallible proof that it was Authored from outside time and space is available for all who need, want, and are willing to examine such proof. That the over and over copying of the Scripture makes errors inevitable, betrays a lack of a common sense fact, and a faith that if God chose to write this original, He would most certainly make sure that it retained its accuracy through the ages to this day, and provably, He did!

3. The Holy Bible was not meant to draw dust on a shelf. It has a divine purpose and everyone who professes to be a Christian is admonished to use it as the one great source of Truth. Over the centuries, millions have been tortured and killed and still are, for owning the Bible, for reading it, preaching it, or even discussing it. If you profess to be a Christian, doesn't this make you wonder why Satan and his followers have been so adamant about keeping it from people? Just because it doesn't yet evoke fatal hostility in this country doesn't mean that it should have less relevance here. The worldly diversions discussed above appear to be all that are needed at this time to keep most people out of the Bible. I pray that you are not of one those, and if you are that you will now see fit to reorder your priorities to conform with God's will. You'll be eternally glad and grateful that you did.

—40—

Biblical Myths

The Bible does not contain myths in the sense that the Word of God contains anything less than absolute truth. However, there are numerous places in Scripture, which lend themselves to misinterpretations and false conclusions, unless one pays close attention to context, expositional constancy, and translational accuracy, including the very grammar of the original language. Lack of attention to these matters has led to some commonly held beliefs, which are contrary to what the Bible really says. The following are a few of those I've been privileged to discover in the works of others whom the Holy Spirit has blessed with His tutorage.

Myth #1

Peter is the founding head of the Christian church.

This myth seems to be mostly limited to the dogma of the Roman Catholic Church and to those who believe in this precept. The basis for this belief comes from Matthew 16:18 where Jesus says to Peter, "... *That thou are Peter, and upon this rock I will build my church* ..." On the surface, this might suggest that Peter is the rock on which Jesus will build His church. But think for a moment. Does it make sense that God would build a church, a whole religious belief system, on a mere man, no matter how brilliant and honorable he might be? Or on any man, especially the "ready, fire, aim" impulsive Peter? Jesus is the Rock, Jesus is the head of the church; it is all about and by Jesus our Lord and Savior. There are many belief systems with some now-deceased humans as their founders and heads, such a Jehovah Witness, Mormons, Mohammedans, Christian Scientists, etc. But the head of Christianity is Christ Jesus, the eternal God who became Man in order to suffer and die for all mankind and who lives again throughout eternity as God/Man. No one less than God Himself could be the head of His own church. But that bit of logic was not enough for those who chose to conclude otherwise. However, the Greek words and grammar clearly and undisputedly attest to that fact. Substituting a couple of Greek words in the above quote, along with one aspect of its grammar, will totally clarify and nail down the fact of the matter. Jesus said, *"Thou are Peter* (that is *petros* = a little rock) *and upon this rock* (that is Petra = a huge rock) *I will build my church."* Obviously, Jesus is not speaking of the little rock or stone becoming a huge rock, because *petros* is a masculine noun and *petra* is feminine; and in Greek grammar, a masculine noun cannot be used to modify a feminine one or vice versa. Therefore, while Jesus is speaking to Peter, He is speaking of Himself as the one on whom He will build His church. Backing up to verse Matthew 16:15, Jesus asks the apostles who they believe He is. Then Peter (who has not yet been named Peter, but is still called Simon) answers for them by claiming Him to be "The Christ, the Son of the Living God." Jesus then tells Peter that the only way he could know this was that God the Father had told him. It is this marvelous, supernaturally derived confession, which precedes Simon's being honored with the name Peter, a "little rock." Perhaps it might be said that he became a "chip off the old rock." This symbolism might have been quite graphic to Peter and the other apostles if we can imagine them at the "coast of Caesarea Philippi" (verse 13). At that place, there is a gigantic rock escarpment with a stream flowing out of it. Can we not see Jesus pointing to a small rock in the stream and saying to Peter that he is that rock which is but broken, a chip off the tremendous rock cliff? Perhaps Jesus then pointed to the huge rock cliff for comparison and then to Himself when He said, ". . . *upon this rock I will build my church."* Surely He didn't mean He would build it on that physical rock. We know that the "Church" of which He spoke is the whole church body of saved souls, not any edifice at Caesarea or anywhere else. The "Rock" on which the church was, and will continue to be built until the moment of the Rapture, is Jesus Himself and no other. Finally, it should be noted that throughout both the Old and New Testaments, the rock has been used to symbolize Jesus. It is difficult to understand that such a myth should have ever been formed, and the whole of Catholicism centered on it, when surly there must have been many in those days who would have known the truth.

Myth #2

Because Peter was given the keys to the Kingdom; he now stands at the pearly gates of Heaven controlling who gets in.

First, there are no pearly gates to Heaven. The gates of pearl are only mentioned in Revelation 21:21 in reference to the twelve gates of the New Jerusalem. These gates will each be made of a single pearl. After the millennium reign of Jesus here on earth, the present Heaven and earth will pass away (Revelation 21). There will be a new earth on which the New Jerusalem will be established. Peter has nothing to do with this, other than the fact that the twelve foundations of the city will each have the name of one of the apostles.

This idea that Peter has the keys from Matthew 16:19 where Jesus tells him *"And I will give unto thee the keys of the Kingdom* of *heaven; and whatsoever shalt those bind on earth shall bind in heaven; and whatsoever than shall be loosed on earth shall be loosed in heaven."* First, it must be recognized that these are not keys to Heaven, but to the Kingdom of Heaven. The Kingdom of Heaven is the here and now on earth, and extends from its beginning at Pentecost to its ending with the Rapture. Keys are used for the unlocking and opening of doors. Prior to Pentecost, certain doors were locked and only Jesus had the keys to open them. Here Jesus gives these keys of authority to Peter. But what exists behind these doors, and for whom will they be opened? As the world-class, Spirit-led biblical scholar Dr. Arnold Fruchtenbaum has determined, the answers are found mainly in the book of Acts, chapters 2, 8 and 10. In Acts 2:1–4, we find the Holy Spirit entering the hearts of the apostles. Then we read in verse 38, after Peter had lectured about Jesus to a number of Jews, he said to them, *"... repent and be baptized every one of you in the name of Jesus*

Christ for the remission of sins, and ye shall receive the gift of the Holy Ghost." These other Jews were the very first in the kingdom of Heaven to receive the indwelling of the Holy Spirit. It was Peter alone, at that moment and by the authority of Jesus and through His gift of the keys, who opened the door to the Kingdom of Heaven to all Jews. After that, the door has remained open to the Jews, to all who would believe and repent.

Then in chapter 8, we find Philip preaching in Samaria where many believed and were baptized with water. But none did, nor could, receive the Holy Ghost yet. Only after Peter went there, accompanied by John, and prayed for them (verses 15–17), did they all receive the Holy Ghost. So here it was Peter who, using another one of the keys, opened the door of the Kingdom of Heaven to the Samaritans. Finally in chapter 10, we find a Roman Centurion, a Gentile, ". . . *a devout man, and one that feared God with all his house.*" (Verse 2). In praying to God, he had received a vision, which told him to seek out Peter. Because Peter was a Jew and had not yet understood that salvation was also for the Gentiles, God also gave Peter a vision through which he came to understand this. Thus it was Peter, when he visited the house of Cornelius the centurion and used the last of the keys, opened the door to the Gentiles and, at which time, ". . . *the Holy Ghost fell on all them which heard the word.*" Prior to this, we find Saul, later to be called Paul; an apostle who received the Holy Sprit directly from God as the other apostles had (Acts 9:17). However, when he tried to preach the Word (Acts 9:20–29), he convinced no one. Only after Peter had opened the door was it possible for Paul or anyone else to be effective among the Gentiles. Thus, only through the keys given to Peter was it possible for the three groups, Jews, Samaritans and Gentiles, which include everyone else on earth—to receive the Holy Spirit. Jesus said that after He left this earth, He would send the Comforter who is the Holy Spirit to be available to dwell in the hearts of all genuine believers. Jesus' method of initiating this blessing was through this special gift of the "keys" given to His chosen apostle, Peter. Only after these three keys were applied for the benefits of the three categories of mankind, was it possible for the rest of the apostles and the disciples to be effective in teaching the way to salvation.

Now, let's regard that other very strange gift that Jesus gave Peter as recorded in Matthew 16:19. Peter was given the power to "bind" and to "loose" whatever he chose here on earth, and this would be honored in Heaven. Apparently the rabbis could understand this power and others well versed in the Hebrew laws and traditions. It had nothing to do with binding and loosing Satan or anything of that nature. Rabbis used the power of binding and loosening in two ways: in the judicial and legislative senses. Legislatively, they could bind (prevent) or loose (permit certain things). The Pharisees, who by definition were also rabbis, took this authority as meaning to forbid (bind) what the law allowed, and permit (loose) what the law forbade. Judicially, to "bind" meant to be punished and to" loose" meant to excuse from punishment.

What Jesus gave to Peter and to all the apostles was a unique authority that was not transferable to anyone else. They had authority both legislatively and judicially to prohibit or allow (bind or loose) the then-current laws as they deemed appropriate, to Heaven. Until that event, none of these souls could ascend to Heaven because Jesus had not yet paid the price, which allowed for the cleaning away of their sins. That included the souls of all believers, all those who lived faithfully, who followed the Old Testament laws, and who had their sins course always under the guidance of the indwelling Holy Spirit. Neither the church nor anyone else since the passing away of the apostles has such power, even though the Catholic Church, through the Papacy, has unscripturally assumed many such powers. The church has only one binding or loosing power and that is to discipline or not discipline, and this is only through excommunication or restoration of church membership.

Myth #3

The saved will spend eternity in Heaven while the unsaved will spend eternity in Hell.

Hell in English is known as Hades in Greek and Sheol in Hebrew. Scripture tells us that Hell is in the belly or heart of the earth. In Matthew 12:40, Jesus tells us that He will spend three days and three nights there. In John 16:19, we learn that Hell has two compartments separated by an abyss, one for saved souls and the other for unsaved souls. When Jesus spoke to the thief from the cross, He told him in Luke 23:43 that he would, that very day, be with Him in the side of Hell with the saved souls, which He called paradise. On the third day when Jesus rose from the dead, He closed down the paradise compartment of Hell and brought all of the saved souls with Him covered through the God-ordained ritual of animal sacrifice. But their sins had not yet been forgiven and so they were waiting for His arrival and His divine cleansing of their previously covered sins. However, all unsaved souls remained on the tormenting side of Sheol and still wait there with all of the currently unsaved who go there when they die. So, as it stands today, all unsaved souls are in Hell, and all saved souls from all times are in Heaven. However, this is not a permanent condition. At the Rapture, all those living who are saved will be translated alive, directly to Heaven in their bodies, which will then become eternally incorruptible. All of the saints, whose souls are in Heaven and who died after Jesus rose from the dead up to the time of the Rapture, will also at that same moment receive their incorruptible bodies in Heaven. The "Old Testament Saints" whose souls are now in Heaven will receive their eternal bodies along with the tribulation saints, after the tribulation and before the millennium kingdom begins. All unsaved souls from all times will be resurrected, body and soul, and after the millennium and the white throne judgment, will be sent to their eternal abode in the lake of fire which is in the outer darkness.

Thus we see that Hell is not an eternal abode for anyone. The unsaved will spend eternity in the lake of fire, somewhere in the outer darkness. But what about the saved? Revelation 21 tells us of a new Heaven and new earth. During the millennium, Jesus will reign here on this present earth, which He will restore to a near-Eden quality right after the tribulation. However, after this, the present earth will "pass away" and a new one will be created. On this new earth, God will place a New Jerusalem where all of the redeemed will spend eternity. This will also be the eternal home of the entire Godhead, the Father, the Son, and the Holy Spirit. God will be seen and served by His chosen (Revelation 22:3, 4). Therefore, Scripture tells us that the redeemed will not spend eternity in Heaven, but in the New Jerusalem, which will be on an entirely new earth.

Myth #4

It was through His suffering at the hands of the Romans who severely beat Him and then placed Him on the cross to suffer further and to die, that Jesus paid the price for the sins of the world.

As we all know, Jesus was no ordinary man who suffered and died; nor could it be any man-conceived punishment that would allow for the accomplishment of what He completed on the cross. Much of this world has viewed this event as a great tragedy, but it was instead the greatest achievement ever to have taken place, even greater than God's creation of the universe. This man Jesus was also God, who greatly humbled Himself to become man and therefore to be a kinsman of man. Only in this personage as man could He become the Kinsmen Redeemer of all mankind, for no mere man could provide redemption from sin. He needed to be both sinless and to be God to have power over sin. The problem is, God's justice demanded eternal punishment for sin. However, God's love and mercy required some way to save man from this eternal punishment, while at the same time satisfying His demand for justice. The only way God's justice and mercy could be mutually satisfied was for a substitutionary punishment and death of someone qualified for the job. Only the sinless God/Man Jesus was qualified, but there was no earthly punishment painful enough to satisfy God's justice. No mere man could possibly absorb the type and magnitude of suffering required before the cleansing of the sins of the world could be achieved, and no man-inflicted punishment could be great enough for that purpose. Therefore, it was not the human aspect of Jesus that could satisfy justice. Only Jesus' godliness was capable of sustaining and surviving the ordeal, which God's justice demanded. It is from this perspective that we may conclude that the incredible brutality inflicted on the body of Jesus by men, was far and away not enough to accomplish the task of satisfying God's justice. Jesus took all the punishment man was capable of applying to Him in silence and with the manly dignity of a true martyr. History records many who have suffered martyrs' deaths, which were considerably more gruesome, painful and long lasting than what the God/Man Jesus suffered from other men. He always knew exactly what was to occur, and why. It was not about what Man was going to do to Him that caused Him to pray and sweat blood in Gethsemane. It was what God the Father would do which caused Him such great anguish.

It's far beyond our comprehension to grasp even a small measure of what transpired behind the scene on the cross. The slight inkling we do get is merely hinted at in Psalms 22, Isaiah 53, and Jesus' own words from the cross as recorded in the Gospels.

Isaiah 53, recorded seven hundred years before the event, tells us how and why Jesus suffered as He did. This chapter deserves many volumes of study and explanation, and many have been written. But for the purpose at hand, only the last part of verse 5 will be briefly discussed. Verse 5 tells us, *"But he was wounded for our transgressions, he was bruised for our iniquities; the chastisement of our peace was upon him, and with his stripes we are healed."*

With His stripes we are healed. This is where the myth comes in. The quote is from the King James Version (KJV), which is in error as to the use of the word "stripes." In the original Greek, the word is singular. It should read, "and with his stripe we are healed." Later translations have recorded it correctly, but the monumental significance of this seemingly slight difference does not seem to have been fully recognized. The corrected translation is not speaking of the stripes the Romans inflicted on Him, unless we take the ridiculous stand that there was a single, particular stripe that caused all of believing mankind to be healed of sin. No! This one stripe was the God-inflicted, real substitutionary punishment, the only sufficiently horrible punishment that could satisfy God's justice. Also in the Hebrew, the word for "stripe" can mean wound, hurt or bruise. Therefore, the word "stripe" need not be taken literally as a mark resulting from the application of a whip. Dropping down to verse 10, we read there, *"Yet it pleases the Lord to bruise him; he has put him to grief . . ."* In the original Hebrew, the word "pleased" can also mean, "inclined to." While the word "pleased" used here could denote "pleasure" to us, one cannot possibly justify a belief that God the Father found pleasure or was pleased to inflict a terrible pain on His Son. This was a momentous and horrible experience for both Father and Son, but out of their unconditional love for their creation, it had to be done. They were in unison as to the procedure and its result.

When I say it had to be done, I am only expressing the conviction that God is sovereign and makes whatever rules He pleases, both for His creation as well as for Himself. We must always remember that His ways are not our ways (Isaiah 55:8). His love, His mercy and His justice are not just words, which a fickle, capricious and whimsical god may or may not honor. Our God is a God of integrity and honor, One who is reliable and delights in keeping His promises. Of course, it was evident to Him from the beginning that mankind would falter and sin. God's love and purpose for mankind was to make for Himself an eternal family of those He made in His own image. Because of His unwavering and faultless demand for justice, He required that sin be punished. This punishment, by His decree, requires that the sinner spend eternity in the lake of fire, and no measure of repentance, suffering or compensatory goodness by man could ever remove even the slightest portion of sin, or reduce its consequences. Therefore, if God were ever to have His family, he had a God-sized dilemma to resolve. This He did most readily by proclaiming that His justice would be satisfied by the substitutionary suffering and death of God Himself, in the person of His Son, the God/Man Jesus.

But what was it that God the Father actually did to Jesus, which was so ultimately horrible that it could fully satisfy God's definition of justice and thereby propitiate all sin? We find the clue in one of Jesus' last utterances from the cross as recorded in Matthew 27:46 and foreshadowed in Psalm 22. Jesus cried out, *"My God, My God why hast thy forsaken me?"* There is great significance in this solemn

333

cry from the Son of God, far more than any mere human could ever comprehend. We can only point to it and cry for Him in His anguish, knowing that something far more painful was happening than we can ever appreciate. Throughout the Scriptures, Jesus had always called Him "Father," never "God." Because of the Son aspect of the triune Godhead, Jesus was equal in every way to the Father, and would, therefore, rightly refer to Him in a manner, which would never suggest that He were less than an equal. But here we can sense, from the change in salutation, a loss of equality, a separation, a rupture of the Godhead by the greatest and most painful of all supernatural forces. Jesus, for that moment or moments, was separated from the Godhead of which He had always been an integral part. This was the Hell, the lake of fire, the absence from the presence of God and all other forms of suffering all rolled into one unbearable pain that all of fallen Man was collectively doomed to suffer. Jesus suffered all of these and more, so that we who believe could be spared. It was this separation from the Father that the Father inflicted on His Son, which produced the ultimate and only acceptable suffering which could satisfy God's self-imposed decree that God's justice had to be served, and make sufficient payment for the sins of the whole world.

Myth #5

Just one more Peter story. Peter, in his irrational manner, put his foot in his mouth when at the transfiguration (Matthew 17, Mark 9, and Luke 9); he spoke rather ridiculously about making three tabernacles, one each for Jesus and His visitors, Moses and Elijah.

This is hardly in the category of a myth, but rather a widely misunderstood response by Peter to this very strange event. Because most biblical scholars and students of the Bible have chosen to view Peter as shallow-minded and impetuous, his participation in this event is not generally analyzed. As such, Peter's utterances here and elsewhere are taken as more amusing than meaningful. But the more his words and actions are seriously examined and studied; this view of him should change considerably. Just as Jacob's character has been falsely maligned through less than adequate examination of what Scripture really tells us about him (see my paper titled *In the Defense of Jacob*), so has inadequate scholarship underestimated the depth of Peter's character and purpose. Anyway, thanks to Dr. Fruchtenbaum's blessed insights and biblical knowledge, we again benefit from a deeper understanding of Scripture and of what Peter had in mind.

Just before this transfiguration event, Peter had had his highest moment when he told Jesus that he believed Him to be *"the Christ the Son of the living God"* (Matthew 16:16). Then after giving Peter the keys to the kingdom of God, Jesus foretold how He must suffer at the hands of His enemies and be killed. In response, Peter said, in effect, that he would fight to prevent it. Jesus severely rebuked Peter for saying this and for having yielded to things of Man rather than things of God. It is evident that this death thing was yet beyond the comprehension of any of the apostles. Next, Jesus spoke of the need for self denial (Matthew 16:24–26) and for taking up the cross with which to follow Him as being the way to salvation. After this, Jesus predicted that He would come *"in the glory of His Father"* (verse 27). Then He said, *"Verily I say unto you, there be some standing here, which shall not taste of death, till they see the Son of man coming in his kingdom."*

This verse is also very widely misunderstood, especially by those who don't want to understand but prefer to find ways to scoff at, and discredit, the true Word of God. They say that Jesus was predicting that His second coming would be soon, clearly within the generation of those standing there; yet it never happened. What Jesus predicted was just what did happen next, the transfiguration, that specific event which He described and which was witnessed by Peter, James and John.

Of the three descriptions of this event, Luke 9 is the most complete. (Incidentally, many scholars have concluded that the whole Gospel accordingly to Luke might more correctly be called the Gospel according to Peter, because they believe that the bulk of it came from Peter. This could explain why this and some other events, in which Peter was involved, are more detailed in Luke than elsewhere.) So now, what is this "tabernacles" business all about? What caused Peter to conclude that tabernacles (little dwellings) should be built for Jesus and His visiting friends? Did Peter think that they were going to camp there for a while and would need shelter? After all, they were on top of a high mountain where it was probably very cold, especially at night. Perhaps he was simply eager to prove himself to be an alert servant, anxious to please and to serve. As it turns out, a much more meaningful and learned reasoning seems to be behind his actions. Let us reconstruct the situation as Peter may have seen it:

> ➤ Peter knew that Jesus was God, the Son of God. Just prior to the transfiguration, Jesus had said that those then living, would see the kingdom of God. Who among us, prior to learning of the millennium kingdom, would not have assumed that Jesus was speaking of His predicted rule from the throne of David as had been predicted in so many scriptural passages?
>
> ➤ Jesus' transfiguration, His true state as God and the state in which He will exist throughout eternity, had taken place right before Peter's eyes.
>
> ➤ Did not the presence of two of the Old Testament's most revered saints, who had already "come down" to earth, indicate that they were the vanguard of all the returning saints to be participants in Jesus' reign?

Peter, from his viewpoint, had good cause to believe that Jesus had finally decided to assume His rightful place as the predicted ruling Messiah King. Having suddenly brought forth His elite vanguard from Heaven, Peter believed that this was the beginning of that time. We, in retrospect and with much hindsight from the New Testament, which Peter didn't have, can look on with all-knowing smugness, and simply smile at Peter's ignorance. But read on, and perhaps you'll find that Peter was quite biblically literate, even with comparatively less knowledge available to him than to us. What Peter knew, and which many people including me didn't realize, may be found in Zechariah 14, in which God through his prophet, has most graphically described portions of the tribulation period, as well as offered a glimpse of one aspect of the millennium period, when Jesus will rule as King on David's earthly throne. Verse 16 tells us that on that day, "*. . . it shall come to pass, that every one that is left of all the nations* *which came against Jerusalem, shall even go up from year to year to worship the King, the LORD of hosts, and to keep the feast of tabernacles.*" So it wasn't that foolish after all, that Peter offered to build the three tabernacles. It seemed to him consistent with Scripture, as he understood it. It was Peter's timing that was off. Luke 9:32 tells us that Peter and the other apostles were in a deep sleep when Jesus, Moses and Elijah were discussing Jesus' ". . . *decease, which he should accomplish at Jerusalem.*" None of the apostles had yet comprehended that Jesus must first fulfill the role of the Passover Lamb and die before the reign of His kingdom could take place. Peter dealt with what he saw and knew logically. I trust that this bit of insight will help us all to see Peter a little more clearly and respectfully.

Myth # 6

Jesus never said He was God.

This is a hot button for those who prefer to dismiss Scripture and, at the very least, to view Jesus as a mere man with some good ideas. The strength of their argument lies in the fact that there is no place in Scripture that one could point to where Jesus says, "I am God" in those words. Nevertheless, Scripture does most certainly allude to that admission quite a few times. These claims to be God and the Son of God were very clear to those hearing Jesus at the time and in the culture in which He spoke. It seems that a good way to clear this up is to quote His own words, explain their context, and then show how these words were understood by those who heard Him or heard the words would have indicted to them that He was claiming to be God.

First, however, we must understand the father-son relationships as it applied in the Hebrew culture at that time and earlier, as well as what the Old Testament says regarding the Son of God. An only son or a first-born son, who had reached maturity and was in good standing, was viewed as the father's equal or equivalent. While there may have been a hierarchal relationship functioning while the father lived, positionally, the son was equal to the father. Therefore, if God has a Son, the Son is also God. In Genesis 6 and Job 1 and 2 and elsewhere, the term "sons of God" is used. But it refers to angels who are the direct creations of God. Of these, there are many. But the "Son of God" is a singular, one-of-a-kind being not a created being but the One who is an integral part of the eternal triune Godhead.

In Psalm 2, we find the triune Godhead speaking among themselves with the Father saying in verses 6–7, *"Yet have I set my King upon my holy hill of Zion."* Then the Son says, I *will declare the decree: the Lord hath said unto me, Thou art my Son; this day have I begotten thee."*

"Begotten" in Hebrew can mean "brought forth" or "a declared pedigree." This has nothing to do with angels or any other created beings. It is the "God the Father" personage of the triune God declaring that God the Son will take on a specific time-related role in the Godhead's dealing with mankind. This role, of course, is amplified and detailed as the primary subject of the New Testament. Notice also Proverbs 30:4 as evidence of Old Testament reference of the singular Son of God. This verse first describes the powers of God and asks *". . . What is his name, and what is his son's name, if thou canst tell?"* Another such reference to the Son of God is Isaiah 9 verse 6, where we are told that:

> *For unto us a child is born, unto us a son is given: and the government shall be upon his shoulder: and his name shall be called Wonderful, Counselor, The mighty God, The everlasting Father, The Prince of Peace. Of the increase of His government and peace there shall be no end, upon the throne of David, and upon His kingdom, to order it, and to establish it with judgment and with justice from henceforth even for ever.*

Looking back at this and hundreds of other prophecies from the perspective of the New Testament, there is no doubt that these verses are speaking of Jesus the eternal Son of God. At any rate, these verses should make it clear that Old Testament Scripture establishes the fact that there is a singular, one-of-a-kind, genuine and eternal Son of God. Having determined this, where does Jesus claim that He, that is God, is the Son of God? Let us examine a few New Testament verses where, one way or another, Jesus alludes to that fact. We will only use His directly quoted words from which to make this case, not the statement of His followers.

1.   Right at the beginning, even before He began His ministry, Jesus claimed to be God. We find in Matthew chapter 4, after Jesus had fasted forty days and forty nights in the wilderness, that Satan came to tempt Him. After Satan's second temptation, Jesus responded by saying *It is written again, Thou shalt not tempt the Lord thy God.*" (Verse 7). Who is there is this wilderness scene? Only Jesus and Satan. Satan is tempting Jesus, and Jesus reminds him that Scripture commands that no one should tempt God. Who is Satan tempting? Jesus. Therefore it is crystal clear that Satan is here tempting God in violation of Scripture! Jesus is claiming to be God!

2.   As Jesus began His ministry, His first ministerial words were spoken in thc synagogue of Nazareth where He read from Isaiah 61:1, 2 the following:

> *"The Spirit of the Lord GOD is upon me; because the LORD hath anointed me to preach good tidings unto the meek; he hath sent me to bind up the broken- hearted, to proclaim liberty to the captives, and the opening of the prison to them that are bound; to proclaim the acceptable year of the Lord,—"*

Then He closed the book, sat down and told them, *"This day is this Scripture fulfilled in your ears"* (Luke 4:21). By saying that this prophecy had been fulfilled, Jesus made it evident that He was the one of whom it had been written. We may not comprehend the full impact of His assertion, but those who heard Him did, for the Scripture continues on to say, *"they were filled with wrath and sought to throw Him over a cliff as punishment for blasphemy."* He had proclaimed Himself to be the anointed one, which means the Messiah, the Christ, the One sent to fulfill this prophecy. What is particularly provocative, although we may not appreciate the significance to the extent that those who heard Jesus' responses did, is that He put a period where Isaiah had put a comma. The continuance of the Isaiah passage reads *". . . and the day of vengeance of our God . . ."* Thus by His admission, He was the One that Isaiah had written about and He had come at this time to fulfill the first part of the prophecy, as the Son of Man as He often called Himself, while the second, the vengeance part, was yet to be addressed sometime in the future when He would returns as the Avenger and Judge. From this one event, one cannot yet make the case that Jesus claimed to be God, but He was certainly claiming to be the One sent by God for this supernatural purpose.

3.   After lecturing on the Beatitudes and a number of other principles of the Kingdom of God, Jesus makes the following statement as recorded in Matthew 7:21–23.

> *Not every one that saith unto me, Lord, Lord, shall enter into the kingdom of heaven; but he that doeth the will of my Father which is in heaven. Many will say to me in that day, Lord, Lord have we not prophesied in thy name? and in thy name have cast out devils? And in thy name done many wonderful works? And then will I profess unto them, I never knew you: depart from me, ye that work iniquity.*

Notice the confident Godly authority with which He is speaking, as well as the clear future time frame of the events of which He speaks. He is speaking of those who professed to be among His chosen, and were not, because they didn't do the will of His Father. Notice that Jesus said "My Father," not "the Father" or "our Father." It was His Father, God, of whom He spoke as only the actual Son of that Father could so speak. Then He goes on to assert, ". . . *Many will say to me in that day* . . ." Which day? He was here on earth in His ministry for only about three-and-a-half years. "In that day," as all or most who heard Him would have known, referred to the Day of Judgment, the day He would return as alluded to in number One above, when all would come before Him as the divinely appointed Judge of all who ever lived. If you examine this passage carefully, it will take a mountain of rationalization to conclude anything other than here Jesus is speaking of Himself as the eternal Judge who will preside over the spiritual fate of all mankind. Who but God Himself could possibly be the eternal judge? This is a profound message that we should take seriously as we examine the quality of our faith and the works that accompany it.

4. In Matthew 16:15–17, we have a strong admission by Jesus that He is the Son of God. These verses read as follows:

> *He saith unto them, But whom say ye that I am? And Simon Peter answered and said, Thou art the Christ, the Son of the living God. And Jesus answered and said unto him, Blessed art thou, Simon Bar-jona: for flesh and blood hath not revealed unto thee, but my Father which is in heaven.*

When Jesus asks Peter to tell Him who it was that they believed Him to be, Peter readily replied that Jesus was the Son of the living God. Had it not been so in Jesus' own mind, He couldn't have responded as He did by saying that it could only be God the Father Himself who could have supernaturally revealed this to Peter. Notice again that Jesus referred to "*my* Father" as the one who told them this profound fact. So once again, Jesus is conveying the fact that He is the Son of God.

5. We find that in Matthew 23:37–39, Jesus is making an incredibly profound observation and prophecy, the full impact of which seems to be missed by many scholars. This passage reads as follows:

> *O Jerusalem, Jerusalem, thou that killest the prophets, and stonest them which are sent unto thee, how often would I have gathered thy children together, even as a hen gathereth her chickens under her wings, and ye would not! Behold, your house is left unto you desolate. For I say unto you, Ye shall not see me henceforth, till ye shall say, Blessed is he that cometh in the name of the Lord.*

First Jesus makes note of how, throughout the ages, these people of Israel stoned the prophets who were sent to them. Why? Scripture tells us that the main theme of what God told them through the prophets was essentially to repent, obey and worship Him as He had carefully directed them, or else! But they would not. Now here is the salient point regarding our subject. Jesus says, ". . . *how often would I have gathered thy children together, even as a hen gathereth her chickens under her wings, and ye would not!*" What is Jesus saying with that statement? He is claiming to be the eternal God who spoke to the prophets and who witnessed from Heaven all of their transgressions and unfaithfulness. Could He make it any more plain that He is claiming to be the eternal God? Then He prophesied their fate that their house, their temple, would be desolate, and it was destroyed forty years later in 70 A.D. Once again, Jesus alludes to His eternal existence when He tells them that they will not see Him again until they finally recognize Him for Who He is. By this statement, Jesus was speaking of His second coming at the end of the tribulation. Thus, He left the nation with the promise that He would one day return. If it were not presumed deity speaking, it would certainly be someone who considered Himself to have supernatural powers which included not only prophecy, but such control of His eternal existence that He could promise His own return from physical death at the particular moment when they would be willing to accept Him for Who He really is.

Dr. Chuck Missler has made a very astute observation regarding these passages. He observes that in these verses, Jesus reveals the purpose, the tragedy, and the triumph of all history. The purpose of all history is indicated by God's desire to gather His children together (Jerusalem being a synecdoche for, or used to represent, all of Israel); the tragedy of all history is revealed in His words, ". . . *and they would not*! *Behold your house is left unto you desolate"; and the triumph of all history is contained in His promise that He will return!

6.   There is a verse in chapter 8 of the Gospel according to John, which well relates our purpose here. After a rather heated exchange with the Pharisees regarding His parents and their lineage (John 8:56–58), we read, *"Your Father Abraham rejoiced to see my day, and he saw it and was glad. The Jews said unto Him thou art not yet fifty years old, and hast seen Abraham? Jesus said unto them, verily verily I say unto you, before Abraham was I am."* This is a powerful claim by Jesus as to His deity. He is claiming that 1500 years earlier, Abraham knew of His coming (His day) and rejoiced. We get a glimpse of this in Genesis 22 when Abraham is taking Isaac up Mt. Moriah to be sacrificed in accordance with God's directive. In response to Isaac's innocent question as to where the sacrificial lamb was, Abraham told him *"God will provide himself a lamb."* If Abraham had not seen the ram caught in the brush, there seems to be no doubt that Abraham would have carried out the

God-ordered sacrifice of Isaac. But of course, this never was God's intent. It was only to demonstrate to Abraham, and to all who would learn of this event, the absolute trust Abraham had in God. Abraham knew that God had promised that, through Isaac, a multitude of people would grow. Therefore, God had to somehow spare Isaac or restore him back to life, because Abraham knew that God would keep His promise. That is the great faith for which Abraham has been remembered and revered. He called the place Jehovah-jireh, which means, "in the mount of the lord it shall be seen." In so naming it, Abraham reveals an insight, a divine prediction that something great will one day occur and be seen there. It was on this mountain, at probably the same spot, where another Father really did sacrifice His only Son for the salvation of mankind. It is very likely that this first event on Mt. Moriah, and what God revealed to Abraham there, that Jesus may be referring to when He speaks of Abraham seeing the future event and being glad of what it signified. The big kicker here, however, is when He claimed to have existed before Abraham. This is so certain a claim of deity that those who listened to Jesus sought to stone Him to death for this horrible blasphemy.

7.   As quoted above, Jesus claimed, "*. . . before Abraham was, I am.*" The words "*I am*" were enough to accuse Jesus of claiming deity. He was claiming to be the "*I am*" of the burning bush of Exodus 3:14, when God answers Moses' question as to who was speaking to him by saying, "I AM, THAT I AM." From then on, God was known as the great I AM, but a name, which, out of fear, the Israelites never spoke but instead invented other ways of referring to God. Here Jesus is claiming to be the I AM. While this clear claim to deity can go completely unrecognized by the rest of the world, to the Jews it was unheard of blasphemy to the highest degree, even worthy of death. From our perspective, in the instance and under the circumstances of Luke 18:5 where the multitudes fell backwards to the ground upon His saying, I AM, these words are nothing special. But because of the strange response from those who heard this from Jesus, we are forced to conclude that He said something very provocative. Again, here is a most subtle claim of deity from our perspective, but clearly a most profound one in the minds of those who heard Him and understood.

8.   In John 6:40, we read *"And this is the will of Him that sent me, that every one which seeth the son, and believeth on Him, may have everlasting life; and I will raise him up at the last day."* Here Jesus is saying that everyone who believes on Him, Jesus Himself shall raise Him up to heaven to everlasting life on the last day, the day that a saved person physically dies. Who but God Himself has or could possibly have such power? It's His particular power as part of the Godhead! The Jews knew as He said these things who He claiming to be. They then murmured and later sought punishment by death for the blasphemy of claiming to be God and having come down from heaven. Over and over again Jesus states most clearly that those who believe in Him as the Son of God, that is His divine equality within the Godhead, He will raise up again the last day and give eternal life.

9.   In John chapter 9 we read of how Jesus healed the man who was born blind, a healing that all believed could only be done by someone direct from God. Later Jesus asked the man "dost thou believe on the Son of God." (John 9:35). The man didn't know who this could be so be he asked Jesus, "Who is he Lord that I might believe on Him (John 9:36) Then Jesus answered *"Thou hast both seen Him and it is he that talketh with the."* (John 9:37). That's about as clear as it can be that He considered Himself of the Deity as the Son of God.

10.   Just before Jesus performed the miracle of bring back to life, the four-day-dead Lazarus, Jesus said to Lazarus' sister Martha, *"I am the resurrection and the life, he that believeth in Me, though he was dead, yet shall he live, and whosoever liveth and believeth in me shall never die . . ."* (John 11:25, 26) Jesus said that He had the power to resurrect the dead and to give eternal life. Sounds like God to me. Who else could possibly have such authority and power?

11.   Jesus and the heavenly Father are one and same as the Triune Godhead, which includes the Holy Spirit. In John 12:45, Jesus says, *"And he that seeth me seeth Him that sent me."* That is pretty clear. If you've seen One you've seen the other, they are all One. In John 14:7, He adds, *"If ye had known me, ye should have known my Father also; and henceforth ye know Him and has seen Him."* Then in John

14:9–11, in answer to Philip's inquiry, Jesus says, "*. . . have I been so long time with you and yet hast thou not known me, Philip? He that hath seen me hath seen the Father and how sayest thou then, show us the Father? Believest thou not that I am in the Father, and Father in me? The words that I speak unto you I speak not of myself; but the Father that dwelleth in me, he doeth the works. Believe me that I am in the Father, and the Father in me, or else believe me for the very works' sake.*" Here again Jesus makes it clear, if you understand the fact, the significance, and the structure of the Triune Godhead, that Jesus is saying that He is an integral part of that Triune Being.

12. In Mark 2 we find Jesus preaching in the upper room of a house in Capernaum when some friends of a person sick with palsy cut a hole in the roof, and lower him down to present him to Jesus for healing. In verse five Jesus said to him. "*. . . Son thy sins be forgiven thee.*" The witnesses immediately recognizing the great significance of Jesus' statement and called it blasphemy, because they knew that only God himself has the power to forgive sins. Here Jesus was, by this statement, unmistakably claiming that power as only God Himself has the right to do. A similar situation is recorded in Luke 7:37–48 where a sin-filled woman comes to Jesus as He sat eating in the house of a Pharisee. She washed His feet with her tears and wiped them with her hair and anointed Him with expensive ointment. During the ensuing conversation Jesus gives the Pharisee a lesson in humility, and effective sincere worship culminating in His assertions to the woman in verse 48, "*Thy sins are forgiven.*" Again this decree was one that no human being had any authority to pronounce. Only God has such authority. Jesus was claiming that authority as the Incarnate God Himself!

13. During the time of Jesus' arrest and trials before the Sanhedrin and before Pilate, and while suffering their interrogations, there is additional evidence of Jesus' claim of deity. In Matthew 26:53, as Jesus was being apprehended, Peter took out his sword and struck one of the arresting officers and cut off his ear. Jesus immediately and miraculously restored the ear and told Peter to back off, saying, "*. . . thinkest thou that I cannot now pray to my Father, and he shall*

presently give me more than twelve legions of angels?" This may not be totally convicting evidence that He was claiming to be God, but it certainly attests to His belief that His relationship with God was so very close that, at His calling God would intervene on His behalf with such a compelling force as to send twelve legions of angels to take Him out of harm's way. Who but the actual Son of God could have such persuasive power available for the asking? Surely this was infinitely beyond any claims that the great men of God, such as Abraham, Moses or David, would have expressed.

14. In Matthew 26, the high priest Caiaphas cannot find any witness who can agree to the charge brought against Jesus, and Jesus refuses to speak in His own defense. Then the priest, in accordance with the authority of his position, says to Jesus, *"I adjure thee by the living God that thou tell us whether thou be the Christ, the Son of God."* "Adjure" is a translation from the Greek word *exorkizo* which means to extract an oath. In Leviticus 5:1 and 1 Kings 8:31, we find the basis for this demand and for Jesus' being obliged to speak and to speak truthfully. Therefore, Jesus testified under oath, in effect, in Matthew 26:64 saying, *"Thou hast said: nevertheless (better translated as "moreover") I say unto you hereafter, shall ye see the Son of man sitting at the right hand of power and coming in the clouds of heaven."* These words, neither in the King James Version in English nor in contemporary English, are able to convey the full meaning or impact of what Jesus said. But the priest found Jesus' reply very clear. Jesus had admitted to be God, the Son of God, and it was by this admission that they had, from their perspective, a blasphemy punishable by death. He not only agreed with their accusation, but also further confirmed it by identifying His exalted position in heaven. It was on this evidence that they could legally call for His execution. The admission of His deity comes from His first three words, *"Thou hast said."* In our way of speaking, this is hardly a convicting statement or admission. But notice that it is a direct response to the priest who was asking Him whether He was the Son of God. Several other times, Scripture records that Jesus responded to such questions in a similar manner and it is taken each time to be an affirmation of the truth that generated the question. If

you came in drenched and someone asked you if it were raining hard, you could very well answer "Man is it ever!" or "You said it!" These would be understood as affirmations, even though they were not direct answers to the question asked. So it was with Jesus' response to the big question. At the time Jesus makes this statement, Jesus is yet man even though He's God Himself. *"but made himself of no reputation, and took upon him the form of a servant, and was made in the likeness of men; and being found in fashion as a man, he humbled himself, and became obedient unto death, even the death of the cross. Wherefore God also hath highly exalted him, and given him a name which is above every name. that at the name of Jesus every knee should bow, of things in heaven, and things in earth, and things under the earth; and that every tongue should confess that Jesus Christ is Lord, to the glory of God the Father." (Philippians 2:7–11)* Jesus had temporarily relinquished the fullness of His godly power, which always had been His. Of the Triune Godhead, consisting of Spirit Father God, the Holy Spirit, and Jesus, He was the One to create, and will judge the physical space/time realm. This was not "given" in the sense of someone of higher authority having so provided. It was the "task assignment" given in unison by the Godhead, to Jesus. The equality and unity of the Triune God is expressed in quite subtle ways throughout Scripture as we read of the various tasks They/He have/has chosen to perform being attributed in a seeming random way to One or Another of the Trio. John in 6:25–27 again expresses this power as we read *"And when they found Him on the other side of the sea, they said unto Him, Rabbi, when camest thou hither? Jesus answered them and said, Verily, verily I say unto you, Ye seek, me not because ye saw the miracles, but because ye did eat of the loaves and were filled. Labor not for the meat which perisheth, but for that meat which endureth unto everlasting life, which the Son of man shall give unto you: for him hath God the Father sealed."* Notice He refers to Himself as Son of God and man Son of man. It is because that He is also the Son of man that He has the power of judgment over men.

15. In Matthew 28:18, 19, Jesus, after His resurrection and speaking for the last time before His ascension to Heaven said, *"All power is*

given unto me in heaven and in earth. Go therefore, and teach all nations, baptizing them in the name of the Father, and of the Son, and the Holy Ghost." No further comment or statement is necessary as to this admission of His deity. Parenthetically, however, it should be noted how meticulous is His statement of the facts regarding His power in Heaven and in earth. The more one studies God's book, the more astounding it is to discover the attention to detail it contains. The more one delves into the Bible, the more evident it becomes that the Bible has been supernaturally authored. Finding an apparent incorrectness in the Bible is a cause for excitement for the ardent student of His Word, because it provides an opportunity to search deeper into that particular passage. For those who know His Word to be inerrant, they also know that, through patience and perseverance, the Holy Spirit will guide them to a resolution of the issue. This is a most gratifying experience.

But here we see no error, only an observance of detailed accuracy. In having paid the full price on the cross, Jesus has redeemed and bought back the earth and all who believe in Him. The earth, since the fall, has belonged to the usurper Satan. We know this from Matthew 4 when Satan offered Jesus the whole world in exchange for His worship of him. Although Jesus had bought back the world through His blood, He was not yet ready to take authority of all that was on earth. Satan, the prince of the Air, was and is yet in subordinate authority. But *in* earth is a different matter. In the earth is Hell, Hades, Sheol or whatever you choose to call it. This is where condemned souls still exist and where we find the bottomless pit where some of the fallen angels are bound. With His resurrection, Jesus emptied the paradise side of Sheol where the Old Testament saints were waiting for Him. Therefore, we can see that His last words confirm what other parts of Scripture reveal, that in His position, Jesus has power over the entire universe, functionally however, He has not yet asserted His authority over the things *on* this earth. This He will do at His second coming, immediately after the tribulation.

There is much more evidence in Scripture that attests to Jesus' claim to deity, as well as to the fact of His deity. However, the above will be sufficient evidence to dispel the myth that "Jesus never said He was God."

The list of "biblical myths" could go on and on for there are many more. However, what have been here mentioned have I pray, been as informative and interesting to you as they have been to me as I searched them out. If they stimulated you to dig deeper and be more discerning as you study Scripture and the commentaries of others, I will consider myself to have been twice blessed!

—41—

The Belt and Suspenders Philosophy

For those who are perhaps too young to have heard this, it is an expression symbolizing excessive precaution. In earlier times it seems that many men wore suspenders. These are straps that hung over the shoulders and clamped on to the upper rim of their pants so as to hold them up. The belt around the waist of course accomplished the same thing. The expression to wear both belt and suspenders was used to describe to those who were excessively cautious in some area of activity, whether physical economic or otherwise. Those who seemed to exhibit such seemingly extreme precautions were often people who had experienced a failure of some sort even though they had applied precautions normally considered prudent. The Great Depression of the 1930s is an example of extensive economic failures where good prudent and seemingly safe placement of their assets proved to be inadequate. In these cases neither a 'belt nor suspenders" were adequate provisions to protect them from embarrassing, as well as tragic, "exposure" as they lost their pants! The result of this economic disaster, as well as any number and variety of debilitating circumstances led many to develop a "belt and suspenders" philosophy regarding the matters of importance in their lives.

Let's continue for a moment to use the Great Depression as an example regarding this "B and S" philosophy. It didn't take long, once a semblance of property returned for the next and subsequent generations to abandon such an "ultra-conservative" and "stifling" attitude. "It can't happen again" has become the nearly undisputed mantra. Who is silly enough to subscribe to such a belief? Very few, only some of the old coots who are still around and who lived and suffered through that period of history maintain that obsession. Could it be today that the millions in this country who are loosing their homes due to foreclosures, and the multitude of others in bankruptcy, might have been well advised to have applied some sort of economic "B and S" before they ventured into this high risk jungle. But who was there to warn them? No one to whom they would listen. Old coots have long ago lost their creditability. Time was when age symbolized wisdom. Today only the young know anything. The old are like John the Baptist, just weird voices in the wilderness crying out to repent before it's too late. Who wants to hear this when there are so many other very convincing voices offering more attractive choices? That of course, is reminiscent of poor Jeremiah, who was the Lord's true spokesman for more than forty years through the reigns of five kings of Judah, to the very end of the Davidic dynasty in 586 B.C. God told him at the very beginning that he would never convince anyone, yet he was to continue to the end, and preach repentance and a return to God or else they would be sent into slavery. But there were a host of false prophets teaching that this could not happen, that the old coot was a fool, that they were the true spokesmen for God. The people continued in the ways of words most pleasing to their ears and their desires. Jeremiah's teaching became so uncomfortable that some of the leaders, including his own brothers plotted to kill him. During this "end time" period, as far as the dynasty was concerned, the people did wear belts and suspenders in that they carried their idols with them to the temple so that they could worship them while they gave lip service to God. Needless to say, this type of "B and S" was not very beneficial.

The temptations of low interest rates, home equity loans, minimal down payments, and compelling arguments after arguments favoring more and more debt with little mention of potential consequences have led millions into bankruptcy and loss of their homes and other possessions. A belt and suspenders policy in which security was a higher priority would have meant a smaller home, a cheaper car, and perhaps no debt-financial vacation or other simply unaffordable pleasures. In our present society to say no to pleasures and desires, and to deny ones self-instant gratification, even to the compromise of essentials, has almost become a criminal state of mind. In this age of entitlements and so many governmental "guarantees" who needs such a stifling, punitive philosophy? Current events are confirming that everyone does.

With this serving as an analogy, might we not also apply it in the context of eternal spiritual security? Any and all aspects of physical life are as nothing of value compared to the need to prepare for our eternal condition and place of residence! If at all possible, shouldn't this be the area of activity where the "B and S" philosophy should be seriously applied? Let us look at the Gospel of John, chapter 10, and verses 27 through 29. Here Jesus says *"My sheep hear my voice, and I know them, and they follow me, And I give unto them eternal life; and they shall never perish, neither shall any man pluck them out of my hand. My Father, which gave them to me is greater than all; and no man is able to pluck them out of my Father's hand"* Now that is security! That is the ultimate expression by what is meant by the belt and suspenders analogy. Just one of these most powerful of all hands would be enough, but Jesus wants us to have the ultimate assurance of our salvation, *if* we are His sheep. He tells us we are in two hands, His and also the Fathers! But, notice these subtle qualifiers, "My sheep hear My voice" and "they follow me." In the context of the whole of Scripture these are fully loaded phrases. To "hear" and to know are synonymous with "to obey." The picture here is not of a sheep aimlessly and intermittently following the shepherd, drifting first one way than another, risking falling into a pit or being caught by a beast of prey. It is following Him very closely, close enough to hear His every word, and keeping our eyes on Him at all times while staying on the straight and narrow path He has blazed for His own. That is the condition that qualifies one to be in His and in the Father's Hand. But our fallen nature makes straying almost impossible to avoid. However, we can greatly minimize its effect if we assume a "belt and suspender policy in our daily lives where following Him is concerned.

First off, knowing God's inerrant Word is essential before effective following can take place. His sheep "hear" His voice, When, where, how? He does occasionally speak to His own. But I don't believe that He speaks personally often enough or in sufficient detail for that to be what He meant. The when, where and how are to be found in the Scripture, for God revealed there everything we need to know regarding what He wants of us. Do you know God's word well enough to say with full assurance that you know Him, that you know His voice and that you know all the ingredients that go into salvation, and finally that you have surely acquired them? Are you sure? Are you doubly sure, like "belt and suspenders sure?"

When I first became a believer, I read through the entire Bible three times. Then I began studying it more carefully. This led me to begin writing these essays. Then I began to study it even more intensely verse-by-verse and word-by-word, preparing for teaching His Word. I search for the true meanings in the Greek and Hebrew languages in which they were written. I collect the pearls from Scripture and try to share them in these essays. Through all of that, I've barely scratched the surface of real understanding. How do I know? Because hardly a day goes by that I don't discover something important that I have missed over and over again in my reading. Have you learned sufficiently the meaning of His Word, and are you dutifully applying it your daily living life, moment-by-moment the precepts of repentance, belief, faith, love and obedience as Scripture demands of His own? None of us do, or can, but when we have tried as hard as we can, and then give Him even more time, worship and love, then perhaps we have added the suspenders to the belt with which to can feel more secure.

Again I ask how sure are we that we are justified, redeemed, and saved. Do we believe we have applied the belt and suspenders philosophy in reaching that conclusion? Look carefully at these devises. We must make sure that they are strong. A belt made of hay and suspenders made of straw are bound to break, and our "pants" are sure to fall and causing us not only to stumble badly, but also to expose the fact that we haven't adequately prepared for our eternal future.

In that respect, think of yourself, standing before Jesus thus exposed, having nothing to offer except the dismal failure of not having earned any crowns made of materials any better then your belt and suspenders! But that is only if you make it to the Bema seat to receive your rewards! What if your belt and suspenders represent the truth of your repentance? If that truth is hay and straw, then it will not be the Bema seat you stand before, but the white throne of judgment before which you will stand naked and absent of that covering of salvation that you presumed you had. This won't be judgment that determines your place in the hierarchy of heaven, but instead it will be the judgment where you will be assigned the degree of heat you will be sentenced to endure in the lake of fire in the outer darkness. Why take any chances. Study Scripture; learn the true meaning of repentance, belief, faith, and obedience. Pray earnestly for assurance of the blessed free gift of grace that provides salvation through faith. Know you have it through a changed life, a life of humility, worship, and thus *"bring forth therefore fruit meet for repentance"* (Matthew 3:8)

Throughout many of these essays, I've repeated sung variations on the theme of this same song, the song of salvation assurance. Often I've applied scriptural verses to this end, which may be more applicable to the earning of crowns, then they are to the assurance of salvation. Where the verses could be similarly applicable, I chose to assume the "B and S" posture rather than "taking chances." The Apostle Paul expressed a great deal of concern about gaining and not losing his crowns, as well as assuring salvation. His concern gives us most of what we know about crowns, how to gain, and how to loose them. In 1 Corinthians 9:24–27, Paul tells us the following:

> *Know ye not that they which run in a race run all, but one receiveth the prize? So run, that ye may obtain. And every man that striveth for the mastery is temperate in all things. Now they do it to obtain a corruptible crown; but we an incorruptible. I therefore so run, not as uncertainly; so fight I, not as one that beateth the air: but I keep under my body, and bring it into subjection: lest that by any means, when I have preached to others, I myself should be a castaway.*

In this case, Paul is focusing strictly on crowns. He knows he is saved, yet he demonstrates here how very concerned he is about becoming a "castaway," that is of being rejected. This is not about loosing his salvation. He knows he can't lose that, but he fears that he will lose his crowns, if he strays at all from his God-ordained purpose! We should all share those fears with Paul, for ourselves. This is because we can, every one of us, enter a spiritual "Great Depression" and loose all of our savings, as did those who lost their earthly "gold" in the 1930s. To avoid this, Paul seems to have worked "B and S" frantically so as to not let that happen to him.

Perhaps you say to yourself, "I don't care about the crowns, I'll be happy just to get through the gate without any crowns." That is ok, and I suppose that this is the way it is for most folks. However, can we be that absolutely certain" of your salvation, that some deeper examination of the quality of our repentance is too foolish even to consider? Is now simply settling in to a comfortable lifestyle, and just "coasting to the end of our lives all that is needed? Many seem to think so, and perhaps a few may even be right.

However, a few scriptural references will set the tone for some additional observations regarding the putting on a "B" and "S" posture regarding salvation. *"And ye shall be hated of all men for my name's sake: but he that endureth to the end shall be saved."* (Matthew 10:22). *"But he that endureth to the end shall be saved."* (Matthew 24:13). The same words are repeated in Mark 13:13 when Jesus repeats Himself like this, know this is super-important! Paul, the likely writer of Hebrews continued this same theme where in Hebrews 3:16 he writes, *"But Christ as a son over his own house; whose house are we, if we hold fast in confidence and the rejoicing of the hope firm to the end."* (Hope in the Greek *elpis* means expectation, confidence, faith, hope). Hebrews 3:14 says, *"For we are made partakers of Christ if we hold the beginning of our confidence to the end."*

Each of these verses condition salvation on holding fast our commitment to Jesus continually to the end of life. This obviously doesn't mean that we lose our salvation if we coast or backslide. If we ever had it, nothing can remove it. The big question is did we ever really have it? The big question is, did we really have it? Because God knows the future, He knows what our life's process and ending will be like, even at the moment we claim to have accepted Jesus. He knows the depth and sincerity and reality of our commitment. If it is real, evidence of it will "continue to the end." In these verses, God appears to have imposed an additional condition of the evidence of salvation through the use of the "buts" and "ifs." To me this suggests that we simply never had salvation if we don't show a continuing evidence of it to the end of your mortal life. Relying on the presumption that we are saved because we "accepted Christ," and then not showing a continuous evidence of gratitude, repentance, faith, love, and obedience, must be considered evidence that the original commitment was faulty and ineffectual.

There is no more important an issue in our lives than that of eternal security. Therefore I wonder how anyone can do anything less than take a continued "B and S" stance regarding the assurance of salvation.

—42—

Benefit of a Doubt

How often and how loosely we use this common phrase as an excuse to end thought and to then proceed on a presumption, the validity of which we have chosen not to examine with any serious thought or concern. In this "modern" society where deep and genuine thought has been almost entirely replaced by "feelings" and "knee jerk" reactions, superficiality is the reigning queen of this present day "intellect." Sadly, this also describes what is called the "Christian church" because it is today difficult to distinguish any difference between the "church" and most any other modern social club. In Luke 18, Jesus asks rhetorically, ". . . when the Son of man cometh, shall He find faith on earth?" Of course, He knew. If He were to have answered His own question, I suspect His answer would have been something like "not so you would notice." Regarding feelings, Mark Twain observed more than a hundred years ago that "we all do no end of feelings, and we mistake it for thinking." How profoundly true this observation was and is even more so today. With that think-destroying power of television and other modern sources of spoon-fed intellectual pabulum our society is being fed, rare is the opportunity, desire or even real capacity of the average individual of today to actually engage in much of anything beyond superficial "small talk" conversation. Even when the rare opportunity for genuine thought and intellectually serious conversation presents itself, ensuing discussions are very often soon aborted due to the curse of relativism, which negates any affirmation of right or wrong. Also quite often, due to the abject ignorance of understanding of the subject by one or both participants in the conversation, very little edification results. On a general basis, how could it be otherwise, when nearly all information and educational sources are so controlled that what is available is only that which the controllers have chosen to disseminate Because of this severe distortion or omission of truth as provided by the media and the educational system, which are the average person's primary sources of information, any serious discussions that may occur is highly unlikely to lead to any truly accurate conclusions, but instead, more confusion.

In today's world, as it has always been, Scripture is the only consistently reliable source of genuine, unvarnished truth. While there may be lively discussions regarding interpretation on many issues among knowledgeable true believers, there should never be disagreement as to the fundamental doctrine around which a genuine saving faith is concerned. But how many who follow today's prescribed "rituals" through which one is alleged to obtain salvation, have sufficient scriptural knowledge to distinguish truth from falseness in this most serious of all matters? Isn't it most common to enter this realm through some prescribed ritualistic method, and then to give way to a presuming of salvation by simply giving one's self the "benefit of a doubt?" Lacking any challenge to the presumption from seemingly reliable sources from either the pulpit or from others whom one might presume to be acceptably credible sources, how is one to conclude anything else? But how much "benefit" can there be in a benefit of a doubt? It sounds to me like a very dangerous way to approach this most profoundly serious of all possible circumstances.

The greatest obstacle to discovering any truth is the presumption that one already has it. Knowing a few verses in the Bible does not, by itself qualify one to understand the way to salvation, nor should it give one any assurance that he or she possesses it!

As I ponder this issue, it occurs to me that an acronym may be a useful tool to bring out the essence of what this essay is about. Clever, catching phrases, image generating names and acronyms seem to be powerful and persuasive tools of the word meisters who engage in forming public opinion. Let's see if one here will tend to strengthen the intent of this message.

Benefit **O**f **A D**oubt B.O.A.D. Well, this isn't a real word, at least it's not in the dictionary, but its sound-alike, bode, is. Which

means "to be an omen of; portent: news that bodes evil for humanity." To my way of thinking that's not too far removed from what
may quite often be the result of having the benefit of a doubt. But
let's try what might be a relevant acronym. B.O.A.D.? **B**eware **O**f
Avoidable **D**eath. That seems to apply appropriately to what the
benefit of a doubt can do to the soul when there is no spiritual benefit in the doubt. D.O.U.B.T. also provides a very meaningful and
appropriate acrostic applicable in a similar vein. **D**anger **O**f
Unexamined **B**iblical **T**ruth. In the context of spiritual truth and the
way toward salvation, we must never assume that there is any benefit, but only the Danger of Unexamined Biblical Truth.

Please, dear professing Christians, neither I nor any other person but God Himself can judge whether or not you are redeemed, but
perhaps you can! You may if you will only BOAD, beware of avoidable death for your soul by seeking the Godly way that is through pre-
cluding DOUBT, the danger of unexamined biblical truth. How can
you justify giving yourself the benefit of a doubt regarding this most
profound of all matters? Learn not from here-say and the deceptive
easy-on-the-ears platitudes being spewed from so many pulpits and
TV / radio "evangelists" who care more for fame, fortune and filled
pews than they do for simply saving souls. Go into the Scripture! Discover the real truth direct from the truth source, from God Himself
as He provided it for you and me in the greatest of all books, the
supernaturally authored Holy Bible. If you consider yourself inadequate for the task, enroll in a small Christian Bible study group, one
that examines every verse and does not avoid the difficult passages.
Give no opinion offered, the "benefit of a doubt," even from the pastor or any other study leader. Think carefully and ask questions making sure that the answers satisfy, and are based on the scriptural
context of the verse in question. Seek additional sources of interpretations, but use only those whose credentials are well proven. There
are many older ones especially from the past two centuries, such as
Spurgeon, Wesley, Murry, Ironsides, Barnhouse, Baxter, Young,
McGee, etc., and even a few reliable ones today such as Missler, Mac-
Arthur, Hunt, Cloud, Ice, Fruchtenbaum, Gendron and a few others.
I have personally studied the works of each of these and can vouch

for their integrity as to biblical interpretation. They may vary in some details, but they are, in my opinion, in appropriate unison regarding important doctrinal issues. But if you choose to seek such sources, don't rely on my recommendations, but check their work against Scripture wherever a question, a doubt or a concern arises.

I pray for you, and I beg you, dear professors of the faith, look into the matter to which you may have given the benefit of a doubt. B.O.A.D. Beware of avoidable death of your soul, and preclude the D.O.U.B.T., the danger of unexamined biblical truth. Don't give your precious salvation up to simply a benefit of a doubt! Check it out with fear and trembling! Know you are saved through a thorough understanding of exactly how salvation is to be had, and just how it is evidenced in a changed life.

Salvation is a very simple thing to achieve. But the ingredients that go into it, and that provide evidence of its validity, are not that simple. Basically, it may boil down to simply an eleven-inch problem, the distance from the head to the heart. What could have been a saving faith if it reached the heart, very often never leaves the head. On the other hand, it may leave the head, but on its way down to the heart it may encounter difficulties, distractions and DOUBTS. Don't give those doubts the "benefit." Remove all doubts, distractions and difficulties through knowledge of God's Word so that the pathway to the heart may be cleared, and that intellectualized faith in the head may become the essential spiritual saving faith by the time it reaches the heart. Know this! This process has nothing to do with emotion, or feelings! They may be present during the process, but they have NOTHING to do with salvation! It's factual, knowledgeable, unrestrained commitment to Jesus as Lord, whom we are to obey, and Savior, who can save us because of His death on the cross, His resurrection, and His ascension to heaven. That spiritual passageway between mind and soul must be kept open at all times even after one has been redeemed. That's not easy. When it gets constricted, backsliding occurs. Doubts, distractions and difficulties are always there trying to close the passageway. They must be fought every day, often moment-by-moment through prayer and obedience, in order for the saved soul to be effectual in serving our Lord.

I pray that anyone who has accepted the fact of his or her salvation in any other way than through God's Word, seriously studied and considered, will stop giving it the benefit of a doubt, and proceed diligently to remove that doubt and seek the full assurance such a matter deserves. Keep in mind that presumption, assumption and ignorance in this matter are tantamount to ignoring the warning to BOAD, Beware Of Avoidable Death of the soul. Study Scripture seriously so that there will be NO DOUBT, so that there will be NO **D**anger **O**f **U**nexamined **B**iblical **T**ruth. Remember that faith is the absence of doubt.

Don't let your faith be damaged by doubt.

Note: The expression of the acrostic, D.O.U.B.T. came to Cindy as she typed the first draft of this paper. It is here incorporated because I believe the Holy Spirit led this dear sister in Christ to this thought that He wanted included.

—43—

What Do You Mean by "If?"

The English translation of the Hebrew and Greek writings can often be quite misleading. This is because of the subtleties of meanings of many words that fail to come across when translated. Where God's Word is involved this can be quite serious. If we are believers in His Word, than we ought also to be hungry for His Word, and to seek to know it thoroughly. We know it to be inerrant in the language in which it was originally written. But how faithfully expressive of the true meaning are the English translations on which we rely in order to know God's truth? They necessarily become mans interpretations of the word-by-word meanings. I prefer the KJV because I believe it to be, for the most part, the most reliable translation. Nevertheless, even there the limitations of the English language necessarily diminish the fullness, clarity and accuracy of what God gave us to know. For instance, as we all know, there are four distinctively separate meanings for what in the English is lumped into the single word love, and for just one of them, "brotherly love," there are six different words expressing subtle nuances of its meaning. In the Hebrew there are six different words to express love.

Now let us get to the subject. From our English language perspective the word "if" seems very simple to understand and of no need to be studied or even examined in any detail. Yet careful reading and interpretation of Scripture suggests that there are subtleties of meaning in the original Hebrew and Greek, that if not recognized, can lead to misunderstanding or not fully appreciating the meaning of God's inerrant word. In order to illustrate the point, consider the fact that there are ten different words in the Hebrew and twelve in the Greek that have been translated 'if." God's word in the original language is perfect and precise. Because He has chosen to convey His message utilizing such great care as to express it using, as applicable, these various nuances, it seems evident that we should at least, strive as best we can to comprehend the subtleties. Furthermore, this tiny word, in its many applications, could be considered one of the most important of all words in that it is so often a precedent to a statement that often imposes a disturbing limitation of the subject message, especially in Scripture.

The word "if" appears nine hundred and twenty-nine times in the Old Testament, and five hundred and eighty-two times in the New Testament. Utilizing what biblical scholars call "the principal of first mention," I have begun this quest for clarity by examining the verses where its various Hebrew or Greek expressions first occur. After that I intend to cite several verses where its intended meaning is often overlooked, yet is pivotal to understanding what God is telling us.

The very first "if" found in the English translation is in Genesis 4:7 where God spoke to Cain after expressing His displeasure of Cain's' sacrificial offering. Abel's offering had been one of faith, that is taking God at His word, but Cain's unbloody offering was a refusal of the ordained way. In spite of this, God by His divine grace, made a last appeal to Cain to even yet bring the required offering. God expressed this in Genesis 4:7 where He said *"If thou doest well,* (that is come back again with what I require) *shall thou not be accepted?" and if thou doest not well, sin lieth at the door." And unto thee shall be his desire, and thou shalt rule over Him."*

This is a verse rich in meaning. First we have evidence that our God is a God of the "second chances." Actually, He is the God of the "seventy times seven chances, (Matthew 18:22). Here God offers Cain the opportunity to please Him, and to wipe out the transgression by returning to obedience. We all need to heed this lesson! Second, we see the principal relating to the privilege given to the first-born. Had Cain repented, he would have ruled over Able because he was the eldest son. Third, we find here the first mention of the word sin, which in this instance is the Hebrew word *chattaah* meaning an offence against God, and implying a penalty. The word "if" in the Hebrew as used here is *im*. In the context of the verse in which it's found twice, it is clearly a conditional expression that could also mean "whether, although, oh that, hence, doubtless, nevertheless, verily, of a truth unless, where as, while, yet," and similar thoughts. The Hebrew word *im* is used 616 times, or 66 percent of the time "if" is translated from the Old Testament.

The next prevalent Hebrew word for "if," occurring 161 times, or more than 17 percent of the times is *kiy* and it occurs the very next time "if" is used, which is in Genesis 4:24. The meaning of *kiy* is more indicative of a casual relationship, rather than a conditional one as expressed by *im*. The word *kiy* can mean, "in as much, although, assuredly," etc. Here we find La'mech, the fifth generation descendant of Cain speaking to his wives regarding some young man he has just killed. He says to them *"If Cain shall be avenged seven fold, truly La'mech seventy and seven fold."* This verse is also rich in its implication. This suggests that the descendants of Cain maintained some knowledge of their ancestors, and here in particular a "hand-me-down" understanding of what may have been the last words God spoke to Cain. This would have been as noted in verse 15 when God put his mark on Cain as a badge of godly protection that carried a seven-fold punishment for anyone who would kill him. For some reason, La'mech seemed to believe that whoever might kill him would be punished seventy times more severely than whom ever might have succeeded in killing Cain. It is interesting, that this is the first mention of the number seventy in Scripture. We cannot know what La'mech knew that would cause him to expect this exact level of punishment, but it may be that there already was some tradition or inspired insight that put it in his head, because the number 70 does seem to have a later association with punishment. Judah was in captivity for seventy years. Tyre was laid low for seventy years. The seventy weeks of years as predicted in Daniel 9:24 have not been a "cakewalk" for God's chosen people either. But there also seems to be a universality about the number as well, for we find in Genesis 10, that the recorded decedents of Noah's three sons total seventy. Seventy of Jacobs' seed came down into Egypt at Joseph's request. (Genesis 46:27 and Exodus 1:5) Moses chose seventy elders (Numbers 11:16), and Jesus chose seventy disciples (Luke 10) etc.

The next mention of "if" in a translation of a different Hebrew word first occurs in Genesis 43:14 where the great drought had forced Jacob to send his ten oldest sons to Egypt to buy food. Of the twelve, Benjamin, the youngest had remained with his father, and of course Joseph had already been in Egypt for many years, now being second in command under the Pharaoh. They had returned with food, but soon it was used up and they needed to go again. But per Joseph's demand, they could not come back unless they brought Benjamin with them. This grieved Jacob greatly, but after understanding the whole situation which his sons had previously withheld until then, he agrees and says, "*. . . If it must be so now, do this . . .*" Here the word "if" is translated as the Hebrew word *asher.* The concordance indicates that it is used with "who, which, where, what, when, how," etc. but is "indeclinable" that is it seems to be what we could call an if "without choice." This seems to be why the "if" was chosen for this circumstance. Jacob had "no choice" as he used this word. Asher is used only eleven times in the Old Testament, as our word "if."

In Leviticus 26:41, 42, we find the Hebrew word *ou* translated as if. This is not only the first, but also the only mention of this word in all of Scripture. The concordance defines it "by way of alternative, or, also, otherwise then," etc. The verse reads "*And that I also have walked contrary unto them, and have brought them into the land of their enemies; if then their uncircumcised hearts be humbled, and they then accept of the punishment of their iniquity: Then will I remember my covenant with Jacob . . .*" There seems here to be a subtlety of meaning that renders neither *im,* a conditional "if," nor *kiy* a casual "if," appropriate for what God is conveying. This was not the normal "if you do this, then I will do that" kind of condition. This is more in the way of an action-reaction statement. It was automatic predictable and precise; no "ifs" of the usual meaning involved. Thus we have this unique word *ou,* which the translators have done their best to interpret. If we substitute the presumed meaning in place of this "if" the verse might read. and *that I also have walked contrary unto them, and have brought them into the land of their enemies; by the way of an alter-*

native, should their uncircumcised hearts. etc. It seems that God is not making the repentant posture a condition or a cause of His subsequent restoration of grace, but is reminding them of the fact that they always have this alternative available, and what He will do in response. This seems to be a precision of expressed thought far beyond what we as humans care to apply. But this is God speaking here, and He is always precise and inerrant. If He needed to create a new word for this singular application, because none of the other nine "ifs" would do it, so be it.

To briefly put this into a broader perspective, the last two chapters of Leviticus are what some call "Israel's Magna Carta." They spell out God's covenant with His people. It details their duties and obligations, all that God has promised in return, and what their fate would be if they failed to keep their part of the covenant. The word "if" is used thirty-one times in these two chapters with *im* being used all but this once.

We've now examined four of ten variations of the word "if." I've briefly examined the remaining six and find it difficult to see the benefit that might be derived from dealing with them here. Surely there are pearls to be discovered, but I fear that I have not yet been given sufficient insight with which to find them. Instead, let us now see what the New Testament "ifs" are all about.

Because Greek is known to be the most precise and comprehensive of all languages, it's no surprise that there should be so many variations of meaning of "if" as it is with so many other English words.

The first "if" we encounter is the Greek word "el" which also translates to, "for as much, whether, that." It is the most common, found 308 times in the New Testament. Its first mention is in Matthew 4:3. This is in the temptation of Jesus, when Satan says to Jesus *". . . If thou be the Son of God command that these stones be made bread."* Here we can see how comparatively limited our English language is compared to the Greek. As translated, we are justified in wondering whether or not Satan is certain as to whom he is talking. We could very well reason that Satan is saying, "this is a test, if you really are the Son of God, you'll have no problem turning these stones into bread. So now prove yourself!" But by the use of the word "el" Satan is not expressing any doubt. He knows to whom he is talking. He is saying "in as much as thou be . . ." In this particular case the context makes it evident that Satan knows to whom he speaks, so we are able to discern the intended meaning of "if." This however, is not always the case.

The second most common Greek word translated as "if" is *ean* which means, "in case that, provided, whensoever." It is used with other participles to denote indefiniteness or uncertainty." It occurs 258 times and is first used in Matthew 4:9 where we find Satan again tempting Jesus as he says ". . . *all these things will I give thee, if thou wilt fall down and worship me.*" There is no problem here. This is how we normally use the word "if."

All of the other ten variations of "ifs" amount to only 3 percent of the total number of "ifs." Perhaps their rarity will provide some interesting insights. The next one of first mention is the Greek word *kan* It can mean, "and also, so much as, at the least, though, yet." It first occurs in Matthew 21:21, where Jesus says, *Verily I say unto you, if ye have faith, and doubt not, ye shall not only do this which is done to the fig tree . . .*" Why didn't Jesus choose the more common "if" such as *el* or *ean*? Whenever the word verily begins one of our Lord's statements, be assured that He is saying something doubly important! By using the word *kan* here, Jesus is not expressing a conditional "if" but instead speaking to them as those who have the faith. Without this clear distinction, recognized only by searching out and finding this specific meaning of what has been translated "if," we would have to presume that Jesus is speaking to His Apostles in a way where their faith is yet in question. But by the use of *kan* we see that *so much as they do have faith and doubt not . . .* they can already do these things. The prerequisite faith has already occurred! The word *kan* is used only three more times in Scripture. In Mark 16:18 Jesus again chooses the word *kan* when after His resurrection He commissions the Apostles to go out into the world to preach the Gospel. Verse 18 records the last words our Savior spoke before His ascension according, to the Gospel of Mark. *"They shall take up serpents, and if they drink any deadly thing, it shall not hurt them, they shall lay hands on the sick, and they shall recover.*" Here again it's not a conditional or causative "if." The preceding verses established the validity of the believer to whom Jesus refers. Therefore He is saying *in so much as they do believe, drinking any deadly thing, it shall not hurt them* . . .

In Mark 5:28 where we are told of the woman who had an issue of blood for twelve years, who approached Jesus and said *"If I may touch but His clothes, I shall be whole."* This was absolute faith! No "if" in the usual sense. All of us who are really His would do well to put *kan* in our thoughts as we consider Jesus as our Lord and Savior. The last place this word occurs is in Luke 13:9 where Jesus is telling a parable about a fig tree. (This is not the same as Matthew 21:21) In verse 9 Jesus is responding to the keeper who has petitioned that the tree to not be cut down for yet another year. Jesus answered, *"and if it bear fruit, well: and if not, then after that thou shall cut it down."* This parable is, I believe, likening the unproductive fig tree to the fruitless redeemed believer. God expects fruitfulness from His own. Here it is suggested that He will wait patiently for three years for His own to begin bearing fruit. Then by His grace He will wait another year. But at some point "after that" He will cut him or her down as having been unfruitful, therefore useless to Him here on earth. Such a person, having been saved will go to heaven, but absent any crowns. There will be a very sad feeling of disgrace and regret as he or she face Jesus at the bema seat.

Let's look at both the "ifs" for there are two in this short sentence. The first is *kan* the last place it appears in Scripture. The other is *ean.* Thus Jesus is saying *so much as it bear fruit, well: and in case that it not, then after that thou shalt cut it down.* See how carefully the Holy Spirit has authored this Holy book! Even the "ifs" are most thoughtfully sculptured to a supernatural precision.

In 2 Timothy 2:25 we find "if" a translation of the Greek word *mepotel* (may-pot-el) which means, as closely as the English can express it: "not ever, also lest ever (or perhaps), not at all, whether or not." In verse 25 we have the Holy Spirit through Paul, near the end of his detailed instruction to the young Timothy telling him how to be strong in the faith when he is preaching to his congregation. *"In meekness instructing those that oppose themselves; if God perad-*

venture will give them repentance to the acknowledging of the truth" Because this word only occurs but once, we must interpret it as having a unique connotation here. Therefore it seems to be appropriate in the context of the chapter to say *whether or not God peradventure will give them repentance to acknowledging of the truth*. The next verse seems to require such an interpretations of "if" as it continues the argument thusly: "*. . . and that they may recover themselves out of the snare of the devil, who are taken captive by him at his will*. Saying, "that they may" rather than shall, precludes the "if" from being necessarily causative. In other words, it seems that the Holy Spirit is telling Timothy to preach the Word to everyone, not only *if* God gives them repentance, but whether or not He does so! This becomes quite a different message when we understand what this "if" really means.

Once again we have only looked at four of what are twelve variations of what has been translated from the Greek as "if." Also as I have examined the remaining eight, I find that it is beyond my present level of discernment to contribute meaningful value to any further discussion of the matter.

Before we move on to the main purpose of this essay, it seems that we need a foundation on which to build what follows regarding this pivotal word "if." That foundation centers on "obedience." All of Scripture might be expressed primarily as, the history of man's obedience and disobedience to God's will. From the beginning of creation God laid out His requirement of obedience. We see this in His instruction to Adam. It didn't take long for Adam to choose disobedience, and all of creation, from that moment on, has suffered the consequences of that one act. What followed was that God found it necessary to add additional requirements of obedience, to deal with mans now firmly established sin nature. The second man, Cain, chose to disobey at least two of these requirements. And so it continued with obedience being observed less and less until after 1656 years, the whole world was one seething cesspool of disobedience, so wicked that God chose to destroy all of unredeemable humanity, there being only one man and his family worthy of saving. Failure to be obedient ravaged even this second, first-family from whence we are all derived.

The proportion of disobedience to obedience has continued to increase in the behavior of all mankind. From that perspective, the whole of history to the present, from a corporate perspective, is recorded as times of modest ascendancy toward obedience being rewarded by God with peace and abundance, followed by even deeper descent into disobedience, eventually resulting in punishment. This seemingly never ending cycle continues in the history of nations. However, it will end, and soon, as God has said it would, not by flood as in the time of Noah, (Genesis 9:11) but by fire. (2 Peter 3:10, 11), Revelation 20:9, 21:1). Even so, within that corporate structure, God has always retained a small remnant of obedient souls to carry out His greater purpose. It is on this foundation of God's demand for obedience that we can find other important, or at least interesting "ifs" in Scripture.

The very first "if" in all of Scripture we have already touched on, that is when God, in Genesis 4:7, offers Cain another chance to repent of his disobedience. We can, if we see the full implications of this brief statement, a hugely revealing insight into God's divine character, which He will express repeatedly throughout history. Here our God first reveals most clearly His divine attributes of love, patience, forgiveness and a fatherly willingness to teach His creation about what is right and wrong. We see these attributes of our God manifest love and patience repeatedly expressed throughout all of Scripture to the very end of the book of Revelation. God's words to Cain ring true and relevant to every human being that ever has or ever will live. *"If thou doest well, shall thou not be accepted?"* It is all about obedience. If we do well, that is obeying God's word; won't we be accepted into God's eternal heavenly realm? Guaranteed! But, first, before we can "do well" we must know what "well" means. Jesus Himself, and then through His Apostles made that very clear for us if we but study, learn and then choose His way. This is in no way suggesting that "works" save. We know that only God's unwarranted grace through faith saves. However, out of a saving faith comes gratitude, and out of gratitude obedience must follow. It is obedience to His Word that is the evidence of gratitude and this also is evidence of a saving faith.

The next "if" of special interest to me is found in Genesis 28:20. Prior to this, in verses 12–15, God had spoken to Jacob very clearly in a dream in which He re-affirmed to him the Abrahamic covenant, and a wonderful promise that God would always be with Jacob. The covenant assured him that his seed would spread across the entire earth and be a blessing to all people. Then Jacob vowed saying *"If God will be with me and will keep me in this way . . . then shall the Lord be my God, and this stone which I have set for a pillar, shall be God's house; and all that thou shall give me I will surely give the tenth unto thee."* Many who have read this verse have assumed this to be Jacob's attempt to bargain with God, and for it to be just one more indication of the Jacob's evil, deceiving and scheming nature. He seems to be among the most vilified of all the major biblical characters. The favorite expression regarding him is that if God could forgive him, He can forgive anyone. I see Jacob quite differently and therefore several years ago I wrote an essay called "In Defense of Jacob" where I explain away, at least to my satisfaction, every negative claim that has been leveled against him.

Here we see a man in the process of coming to the faith, a genuine faith that would guide him the rest of his life. Jacob knew of the Abrahamic covenant because it had to have been a subject of much conversation both in his grandfather's house and often between his parents, Isaac and Rebekah. He also knew that even though Esau was the oldest, it was he whom God had ordained to be the one who was to be thus blessed. However, there is no indication that prior to this encounter; he had ever had any direct contact with God. He only knew the stories, which he most likely believed as head-knowledge only. Now at age seventy-seven he had this first encounter with our living God, who confirmed what he had heard all his life. What a life altering experience this was for him! Prior to this he had been a docile, obedient son even to the extent of participating in that charade his mother had orchestrated in order to prevent Isaac from confirming his blessing on Esau, because she knew from God's own decree to her that Jacob was the "chosen" one. Surely God would have used some more righteous way to affect His will, but nevertheless, by His permissive will, He allowed Rebekah to "do it her way," a way, by the way, that was not without punishment.

So now we see Jacob expressing this big "if" after hearing what God had said. This "if" is the Hebrew *im* a conditional "if" for which such words as "since" or "whereas" are equally applicable depending on context. The "since" or "whereas" interpretation of what Scripture actually says, is to me, the more accurate. There was no bargaining in Jacob's heart. What could he possibly be bargaining for? God had long ago made this covenant of which Jacob knew he would possess. Here God is merely confirming it to Jacob, in Person. There was nothing Jacob could ever do that could nullify it. He had it. It was already a done deal years earlier. Jacob's response was simply an expression of gratitude. He believed God, and in loving gratitude offered what he had, what God wants most, the willingness to be obedient to His will. (John 14:21) This situation is a prototype of what happens to every born-again Christian when he or she first comes to that saving faith. It is a deep heart-felt gratitude that wants to honor the Father and His Son our Savior with a life of obedience, this being the strongest possible expression of love. If you read carefully the available evidence of Jacob's life henceforth, you can see a strong faith, closeness to God, and a commendable on-going obedience for which he was richly rewarded.

They say that there is no greater gift a man can give than that he willingly sacrifices his life for his country. That may be the greatest sacrifice that one can actually give, but there is an infinitely greater sacrifice that one may be willing to offer, and that is the forfeiture of the salvation of ones soul. Of course the eternal security of all souls redeemed by faith precludes that possibility, yet the heart of the offerer may be completely sincere. This would seem to be the ultimate expression of man's God-given love for another. That is what we see in Exodus 32:32 where Moses says *"Yet now, if thou wilt forgive their sin; and if not, blot me, I pray thee, out of thy book which thou hast written."* The significance of this is almost beyond comprehension. What Moses is saying is that if God is going to condemn these people, the entire Hebrew race, to eternal damnation, then he implores God to do so also to him! This occurs very early after their exodus from

Egypt. The occasion is after Moses came down Mt. Sinai and saw the people worshipping a golden calf, and when he broke the stone tablets on which God had written the Ten Commandments. While Moses was on the mountain God told him what was going on and told him to get down there. Then God told him, in Exodus 32:10, *"Now therefore let me alone, that my wrath may wax hot against them, and that I may consume them; and I will make of thee a great nation."* However Moses delayed his departure long enough to point out to God that if he did this God would be defamed for having failed to do with "His" people what he had promised. To get the whole thrust of this, one should read Exodus 32:11–13. Because of this argument, and Moses' profound willingness to sacrifice his own salvation for the people, our Lord "repented." This repentance must not be considered a change of mind by God, or it would suggest that His omniscience is limited. Instead, this is in a sense, a sort of charade where our all-knowing God provides a test for Moses own benefit, of his faith in God and his commitment to the people for whom God has made him responsible.

Upon his return to the camp, and surveying the situation, Moses acted immediately putting to death three thousand of the instigators. God's response to Moses' "if" of verse 32 was to tell Moses that only those who sinned would he "blot out" of His book. But there is much more here well worth understanding, symbolically at least. God keeps books! The book first mentioned is the Book of Generations in Genesis 5:1. Then in Exodus 17:14 God tells Moses to *"write this for a memorial in a book . . ."* This had to do with the defeat of the Amalekites who plagued them when they first entered the wilderness area after leaving Mt. Sinai in Arabia. Perhaps this "book" is a reference, to the book of Exodus the second of the five books that Moses wrote. In Exodus 24:7 we read of the "book of covenant" wherein Moses had recorded what God had promised, and the manner of obedience with which the people had agreed to respond.

Again referring to Exodus 32:32 it is revealed that God keeps a book recording the names of all the people who are born. This may be the same book referred to in Revelation 3:5 where Jesus says, *". . . I will not blot out his name out of the book of life."* Then in Revelation 21:27 we find that there is a "Lambs Book of Life." The book of life seems to be the record of all who ever lived, and seems to be like a ledger where the names of the unredeemed sinners are erased, or blotted out as they die. The Lamb Book of Life however, I believe lists only the redeemed in Christ, those who will partake in the rapture and are His "Body of Christ." If this be true, then in the end, God's Book of Life will contain the names of everyone who makes it to heaven, including, not only the Body of Christ, but also all of the Old Testament saints, the tribulation saints, and those saved during the millennium.

In Numbers 14:15 we have another big "if" spoken by Moses after they had marched from Mt. Sinai and to the border of Canaan, the Promised Land. There they sent out twelve spies who came back telling of the wonderful land God had chosen for them, but also that it was inhabited by giants. Ten of the twelve expressed fear and spoke ill of proceeding, and only two, Joshua and Caleb had faith, and urged the invasion to proceed as God had directed. For this, the people tried to stone the two of them. I believe this spying excursion and its result was God's way, of demonstrating to them that their faith was only in their mouths, not their hearts. For two years, at and around Sinai, God, through Moses had sought to prepare them for this moment. They received all the laws, all the manner and means by which they were to worship, and how they were to live their lives as God's special people. They now had the Arc of the Covenant and the Tabernacle, which was God's physical living place among them from which He would be their Guide and Protector. Faith and obedience were all they needed to receive in this Promised Land all of the good that life in that rich land would provide. They were well versed in the covenants, that is, what God would do in exchange for their obedience, and what He would do when they disobeyed, because Moses had read it to them over and over and they had agreed to it. They were "head wise" all in agreement, but now, they failed the first real test!

Numbers 14:11–14 tells us how angry God was at this demonstration of disobedience and lack of faith. Again God threatened to exterminate them and use Moses as the "seed" of another new nation, but again Moses appealed to God's Holy name with that "if" in Numbers 14:15. Again in deference to Moses' plea, God "repented." However this time He said that they would wander the wilderness for thirty-eight more years until the very last of all of the men were dead who were more than twenty years old when they crossed out of Egypt. Thus only their next generation would receive that blessing. Joshua and Caleb were the only ones of that older generation to finally go and lead them into the Promised Land. Parenthetically, we have here an indication of age twenty as being the age of accountability at least at that time. It took only about forty days to get the Israel out of Egypt but it took forty years and an entire lost generation to get Egypt out of Israel. Even then, subsequent history seems to say that it has never really left them, nor is it out of us, in its symbolic meaning.

There is another lesson for us in this last episode, one that we should recognize as very applicable today. It is how God makes His case for the punishment of that generation. God cites how ten times during those first two years after leaving Egypt they had tempted Him through their disobedience, to render severe punishment. Next, He speaks of the continual murmuring against Him, which shows how little, or no faith they had. Then the final straw, the worst of their expressions of murmuring, when they said that they would have preferred to have died in Egypt or even in the wilderness rather than face the giants of Canaan. With this wish, they sealed their own fate, for that is what God gave them, death in the wilderness Our God today is the same God as the one who was there in the wilderness. Murmurings, disobedience lack of faith today are as bad or worse than they were then. This, our country, has been the most blessed nation in history, yet it has forsaken that blessing by treating it as an entitlement as did ancient Israel. Given that at the time of the gathering at the boarder of Canaan, they had had a close association with God, and His agent Moses for only two years after centuries of life under pagan rule, one can at least understand the difficulty of such a transition, but what is our excuse? If our God of the seventy times seven forgivenesses has been counting, and we can be sure He has, how many more slaps-in-the-face has He yet to forgive before we get what we deserve?

In the same vane as in the previous discussion, we find another most beautiful offer of corporate forgiveness, conditional on an "if."

It's a well-known, but painfully ignored standing offer to His people. We find it in the 2 Chronicles 7:14 where it says, *If my people, which are called by my name, shall humble themselves, and pray and seek my face, and turn from their wicked ways; then will I hear from heaven, and will forgive their sins, and will heal their land.*" The purpose and application of this conditional promise is clear. God wants, and rewards obedience! But notice, He expects it here from *His* people! He was speaking to His people Israel at the time, but God's Word is recorded and passed on as a truth for all times. Today there is another selected group who are also His people that is the invisible church, the true Body of Christ. I believe that God, with these words, is crying out to all of His people, Jew and Christian, to accept His offer. However, it seems that the prerequisites of obedience, as was imposed than, and is today, is just too much for sinful man to embrace, and so the offer remains unclaimed today as it has been throughout the centuries.

It is of interest to note that these words were spoken to Solomon at the very zenith of Israel's history when wealth, prosperity, and even godly worship were at their best. The Temple had just been dedicated and a seven-day period of feasting and worship had ended. God's earthly home had been finished and He had moved in! Why this "if" at this seemingly inappropriate time? It is because God knew that this moment of worship and obedience wouldn't last, and that all forms of idol worship and disobedience would again reign, even during Solomon's remaining tenure. Notice the subtle prophetic way in which God alludes to that eventuality. He says, "... *I will hear from heaven* ..." At the time God spoke these words, the Shekina (God) had taken up residency in the Holy of Holies of the Temple, but as evil again began to prevail, He would leave His place and return to heaven, so it is from there that He predicts that He will then listen for their cries.

Next let us look briefly into the book of Ezekiel. But first it should be noted that there were three sieges of Jerusalem by Nebuchadnezzar. The first took Daniel and his friends to Babylon. The second took Ezekiel and a few others while the third took the remainder into the seventy years of captivity. Here Ezekiel is ministering to Jews already in Babylon, but yet sometime before the final deportation. There is a series of four "ifs" in Ezekiel chapter, 14 that in combination provide a message of what I believe to be of great significance to us today, if we are willing to fully apprehend it, and apply it to help explain many of the confusing physical and spiritual issues that confound us in these end times.

In order to appreciate the context and even approach understanding the message of the "ifs" the whole chapter is here provided from the King James Version.

Ezekiel 14:1–23

"Then came certain of the elders of Israel unto me, and sat before me. And the word of the Lord came unto me saying, Son of man, these men have set up their idols in their heart, and put the stumbling block of their iniquity before their face; should I be inquired of at all by them? Therefore speak unto them, and say unto them. Thus saith the Lord God; Every man of the house of Israel that setteth up his idols in his heart, and putteth the stumbling block of his iniquity before his face, and cometh to the prophet; I the Lord will answer him that cometh, according to the multitude of his idols; that I may take the house of Israel in their own heart, because they are all estranged from me through their idols. Therefore say unto the house of Israel, thus saith the Lord God; Repent and turn yourselves from your idols and turn away your faces from all your abominations. For every one of the house of Israel, or of the stranger that sojourneth in Israel, which separateth himself from me, and setteth up his idols in his heart, and putteth the stumbling block of his iniquity before his face, and cometh to a prophet to inquire of him concerning me: I the Lord will answer him by myself: and I will set my face against that man, and will make him a sign and a proverb, and I will cut him off from the midst of my people, and ye shall know that I am the Lord. And if the prophet be deceived when he hath spoken a thing, I the Lord have deceived that prophet and I will stretch out my hand upon him, and will destroy him from the midst of my people Israel. And they shall bear the punishment of their iniquity: the punishment of the prophet shall be even as the punishment of him that seeketh unto him; that the house of Israel may go no more astray from me, neither be polluted any more with all their transgressions; but that they may be my people, and I may be their God, saith the Lord God. The word of the Lord came again to me, saying, Son of man, when the land sinneth against me by trespassing grievously; then will I stretch out mine hand upon it, and will break the staff of the bread thereof, and will send famine upon it, and will cut off man and beast from it: though these three men, Noah, Daniel, and Job were in it, they should deliver but their own souls by their righteousness saith the Lord God. If I cause noisome beasts to pass

377

through the land, and they spoil it, so that it be desolate, that no man may pass through because of the beasts: though these three men were in it, as I live, saith the Lord God, they shall deliver neither sons nor daughters; they only shall be delivered, but the land shall be desolate. Or if I bring a sword upon that land, and say, Sword go through the land; so that I cut off man and beast from it: through these three men were in it, as I live, saith the Lord God, they shall deliver neither sons nor daughters, but they only shall be delivered themselves. Or if I send a pestilence into that land, and pour out my fury upon it in blood, to cut off from it man and beast: through Noah, Daniel, and Job, were in it, as I live, saith the Lord God, they shall deliver neither son nor daughter; they shall but deliver their own souls by their righteousness. For thus saith the Lord God; how much more when I send my four sore judgments upon Jerusalem, the sword, and the famine, and the noisome beast, and the pestilence, to cut off from it man and beast? Yet, behold, therein shall be left a remnant that shall be brought forth, both sons and daughters; behold they shall come forth unto you, and ye shall see their way and their doings; and ye shall be comforted concerning the evil that I have brought upon Jerusalem even concerning all that I have brought upon it. And they shall comfort you, when ye see their ways and their doings: and ye shall know that I have not done without cause all that I have done in it, saith the Lord God."

If, as we proceed with this commentary, the thrust of the message remains unclear, try reading the previous chapter, because it does add some additional groundwork to help explain just where our Lord is coming from here. Basically, through Ezekiel, God is stating that Jerusalem is not going to be spared. Here, as with the other prophets, such as Jeremiah, Isaiah, Hosea, etc. God explains from several perspectives the how and why of His action.

The first "if" occurs in verse 9 where God accepts the responsibility for having deceived the deceiving prophet and then He says, He will "destroy him" from the midst of the people. What goes here? God will put a lie in his mouth, and then destroying him for being a false prophet? Is that any different then using Babylon to punish Judah and then punish Babylon for their actions against Judah? If you wish to understand this beyond what is written here, please study 2 Kings 22:13–23 and 2 Thessalonians 2:8–11. But why punish those persons who did what the false prophet told him to do? If we look carefully at these situations we see that God lets false prophets deal with those people who like them, are already in deep and prolonged irreversible disobedience. Perhaps the most relevant verses in all of Scripture for us today which depict this seemingly discordant view of our ever forgiving and merciful God who nevertheless must remain just, can be found in Romans 1:21–32.

Three times God gives the evildoers over to their own evil ways (verses 24, 26 and 28). In reading the listings of abominations to which their perpetrators are given over, one cannot help but shockingly realize that it is our nation, *our* own country being described! Even more disturbing however, is to realize that these verses also speak to much of what is today called Christianity and the Christian church! While the door to salvation always remain open to all who repent, in His foreknowledge God knows who have sunk into sin so deeply that they will never choose to extricate themselves no matter how persuasively they are righteously ministered to.

Righteous ministry has become a rare thing in the modern "Christian" church. As Jesus and the apostles predicted, false teachers have entered the church leading people away from the truth through half-truths, cleaver twistings of truth, and outright lies. Today we see the world tolerating, and even glorifying evil, while condemning biblical truth. That the "world" has entered, and is flourishing in the so-called Christian church, influencing a great many into false beliefs and eternal damnation, is becoming evident almost everywhere. However, truth is in the Scripture, and is available to everyone. Therefore, for those who claim to want it, there is no excuse for remaining ignorant of the truth that can save the soul. But man prefers the lie, and ignorance of truth, because it condones his lifestyle. God's inerrant vision of the future tells Him that certain people, and nations, will not repent, no matter how persuasive the truth may be presented to them. In these cases, God simply gives them over to their sinful nature and thus to Satan and eternal damnation. How painful this is for those who have learned the truth of Scripture and see this travesty thriving within their church, within their own families, and throughout their nation.

The other three "ifs" of Ezekiel 14 are found in verse 15, 17 and 19. They all express the same message that is that God is sovereign and will not be dissuaded from His righteous judgment. In order to make the point He uses the names of three of the most righteous men of all Scripture as examples of how even with their honorable presence and persuasive abilities being applied, His judgment cannot be changed. These men were saved, each from overwhelming earthly calamities and spiritual damnation because of their great faith. However, the intersession of even these holiest of men, had they been present, could not have averted God's judgment. This teaches us that no one can save anyone but himself, and then only by the grace of God. All of this is a way of expressing the fact that nothing could have saved Jerusalem. Just as the message of Romans chapter one is the message for nations such as ours, that God at some point will give them over to their sinful ways and extract His judgment, so here God has pronounced that unrepentant judgment on Jerusalem. Nothing can now save them. Notice they will not be saved from famine (verse 13), nor from the wild beasts (verse 15) nor from the sword (verse 17) nor from pestilence (verse 19). Again, even if Noah Daniel and Job were in the midst of all of this, God would not save Jerusalem, although they, the righteous souls would be saved. This is a strong referring to the fact that the ever-existing remnant the "invisible church" will always escape spiritual destruction.

Note the four "sore" judgments referenced here, famine, wild beasts, sword, and pestilence. They also appear in Revelation 6 and are what the present world has to look forward to in this rapidly approaching end period of the end times as described by Jesus and by the prophets. The condition of this country and of the world are well set for the implementation of these judgments as the world prepares to welcome in the reign of Antichrist.

Let's now pop over to the New Testament and to 1 Timothy 5:8 for a very sobering "if" message.

> *"But if any provide not for his own, and specially for those of his own house, he hath denied the faith, and is worse than an infidel."*

How in the world do we deal with this? Well, first off, "in the world" is not the place in which this needs to be dealt with. It is in the heart and mind of the redeemed soul where such matters are to be examined. Paul's two letters to Timothy contain among the most troublesome verse in all of Scripture in the context of current times. In these letters Paul outlines a number of today's difficult, and highly controversial precepts regarding the roles of women in the church, the essential qualifications for pastors, deacons, and other church officials, and numerous requirements for good Christian behavior, such as those regarding widows and other needy persons. We must however, remember that all Scripture is for our learning, and that it was all God-breathed, that is authored by God, not man. This verse as with all of Scripture, even the controversial ones, are inspired by God and were given to various men to record. Therefore we must take this one as seriously as we must all other verse in the Holy Bible.

The "if" here in the Greek is the word "ei" equivalently expressed as "for as much" or "whether." The word "denied" is *arneomai* in the Greek, and can also mean, "disavowed, rejected, contradict, abnegate, and refuse." The word "infidel" in the Greek is *apisttos* and can also mean "unbelieving, untrustworthy, and incredible." The meaning of this verse is quite evident. It is a despicable thing to not respond meaningfully to the needs of the needy, and especially the needs of one's own family. At first reading one might conclude that this behavior necessarily characterizes an unsaved soul. But the phrase, "worse than the infidel" or "unawares" seems to make it clear that it is believers about whom Paul is speaking. But are all of these really born-again believers, or are some only those professing to be believers, who have crept into the body of the church unaware? The presumption is that they are saved but who can be sure? Even Paul couldn't see into the hearts of those who claimed faith. The callused characteristics of a soul who would evade such responsibilities might well be considered evidence of an unsaved soul. I believe that a case can be made that Paul may have known that not all, if any of those he chastised were true believers. That he called them as worse than "unbelievers does not necessarily mean that he saw them as born-again believers, but perhaps believers in profession only. This point is strengthened, but not necessarily nailed down, by Paul's statement in Galatians 2:4 where he speaks of "*. . . false brethren unaware (secretly) brought in . . .*" We normally conclude that whenever an Apostle speaks of brethren it is a certainty that he speaks of redeemed Christians, but it seems likely that here he speaks of pretenders, professors, but not possessors of a saving faith. The Greek word meaning "false" as expressed in Galatians 2:4 is *pseudadelphos* which is translated as "a spurious brother, pretended associate, false brethren." It occurs only twice in Scripture. The other place is in 2 Corinthians 11:13, where Paul says *"For such are false apostles, deceitful workers, transforming themselves into the apostles of Christ."* Verse 14 and 15, of 2 Corinthians 11 are also important if we are to get the full meaning of the message. There Paul continues, *"And no marvel, for Satan himself is transformed into an angel of light. Therefore it is no great thing if his ministers also to be transformed as the ministers of righteousness; whose end shall be according to their works."* Dear God, how profoundly accurate are these words You so lovingly past through Paul's heart and into this epistle! We only need to see what, for the most part, is coming out of the seminaries, and hear what is being spewed out of many of the pulpits today to recognize the accuracy and significance of these verses. Nothing more than biblical illiteracy and the preaching of only the comfortable non-challenging verses are required to fill the pews where Satan's shepherds preach, and to thereby lead their unsuspecting flocks into eternal hell.

Let's look at just one more reference regarding this issue found in 1 Timothy 5:8. We find it in Matthew 15:4–6. *"For God commanded, saying, Honor thy father and mother: and he that curesth father or mother, let him die the death. But ye say, whosoever shall say to his father or his mother, It is a gift by whatsoever thou mightest be profited by me; And honor not his father or his mother, he shall be free. Thus have ye made the commandment of God of none effect by your tradition."* We hear this from the lips of Christ Jesus, as the Son of man condemning the ways of the Pharisees who also chose to avoid such family responsibilities. What is referred to here is the tradition involving what is called *corban* which deals with a gift or vow. This seems to have been a Pharasitical contrivance that allowed them to set aside their goods and wealth for either of two purposes: as dedication to the Temple, or in reserve for the performance of some other vow. If their wealth was in either category, they could claim *corban*, thereby evading accountability whenever any undesired obligations may have laid claim on them. From this came the practice where even when the caring for needy relatives was required, a Pharisee could declare exemptions under *corban* and therefore not be obligated to care for them because all of his assets were "tied up" and not available. This was the often-used excuse for not obeying the commandment to care for parents. That is what Jesus is condemning in these verses. How many today find similar or other excuses to shirk this responsibility, and who could if they would do the "right thing." Does this type of avoidance of difficult responsibilities happen among genuine born-again Christians? Probably, but who can know, because who can say who is a true "brethren?" Perhaps if we could only change our "knee-jerk philosophy" from "why should I," to "why shouldn't I," and then seek an honest answer from within, many such issues would depart from our society.

This essay could go on and on and become as lengthy as the Scripture itself if I were to touch on the many other significant "ifs" to be found in God's Word. Instead we'll end this part of those musings with just one more "if" message and that is to be found Romans 8:17 where the Holy Spirit prompts Paul to say in verse 16 and 17:

> *"The Spirit itself beareth witness with our spirit, that we are the children of God: and if children, then heirs; heirs of God, and joint-heirs with Christ, if so be that we suffer with him, that we may be also glorified together."*

The first "if" is a translation of the Greek word "el" which can mean "as much as." The second "if" is a translation of "el per" which can mean "if perhaps, if so be that, seeing though" The subtle difference between these two "ifs" is difficult to discern for us not schooled in Greek, but we know that it must be meaningful or it would not have been chosen. The word "heir" is translated from the Greek word *kleronomia* which means a "sharer by lot, getting an apportionment, an inheritor, heir possessor." From these, the translators chose "heir." But in this context it seems that the word "sharer" which is also the first of the listed choices, is a more appropriate translation here. That means that the saved soul is a sharer who receives something, some share of something, as a son or daughter of God. Surely it's eternal life, a heavenly home, an eternal career of some kind, and perhaps other blessings we cannot even imagine.

That second "if": "*. . . if so be that we suffer with Him . . .*" adds a new dimension to heir or sharer. There is something here very subtle yet I believe, very profound and essential to understand. Speaking of redeemed souls, Paul says in verse 16 that they are all children of God. With this fact in mind, Paul continues at the beginning of verse 17, to say that they are heirs (sharers) of God. But now there seems to be another category of the redeemed, and that is the "joint-heirs" (joint-sharers) with Christ! These are set aside under a different category, if they suffer with Christ! All Christians who take their faith seriously (can there be any who are really saved who don't?) will necessarily suffer for it. This is because the world hates Jesus and also all who genuinely believe in Him and live by His ways. Here however, we have another, and it seems unique category of suffering that qualifies one to a special relationship, as "joint-heir" with Christ. There is a very careful sculpturing of this verse. The Greek word *sumpascho,* translated as "suffer." means "experience pain jointly or of the same kind-suffer with." The word suffer or suffering occurs 167 times in the New Testament, and there are sixteen different Greek words for "suffer." This one is used only here and in 1 Corinthians 12:26b, which is regarding the joint sufferings of the members of the Body of Christ. This meaning must be considered to be a special form of suffering closely related to what Jesus suffered. We may conclude with some apparent justification that these "joint heirs" with Christ include the martyrs who died because of their faith, and perhaps those who spent long years of suffering in prison for the same reason. However, Jesus suffered in many ways from His early childhood to the final and ultimate suffering on the cross. At what point is ones suffering here on earth because of their faith, of a quantity or a quality sufficient to meet this particular criterion? Only God knows. But this verse seems to make it evident that such a criterion does exist, and will effect one's position in the eternal realm.

If this be so, what might we conclude about the nature of the other heavenly assignments that will be given to those who will populate the millennium as well as the rest of God's eternal kingdom?

We already know that by means of the good-works-crowns that the redeemed will have earned here on earth, and taken to heaven, they will be given various assignments within some form of heavenly social political structure. As "heirs with Christ" it seems likely that those so rewarded will occupy more elevated or separate places in this hierarchy. This last "if" gives me the "excuse" or the basis for delving into what follows.

In 1 Corinthians 12:27, Paul, speaking to redeemed believers, is saying, *"Now ye are the body of Christ, and members in particular."* In Romans 8:14 Paul again speaks of those who are led by the Spirit of God, as being the sons and daughters of God. Then, as we have seen in Romans 8:17, that these are also heirs, or some kind of "sharers" with God. Scripture speaks of heirs of salvation, heirs of the promise and heirs of the kingdom! Perhaps that is all that it means to be heirs of God, or maybe there is more. Again, it may depend on what crowns one brings to heaven.

Now let us bring into focus, several allusions to the categories of persons that will reside with the Lord in the heavenly places, keeping in mind the "if" of Romans 8:17 where appropriate. Scripture speaks of:

1. The church (Matthew 16:18)

2. The body of Christ (1 Corinthians 12:27)

3. The sons (and daughters) of God (Romans 8:14)

4. The heavenly positions of priests and kings (Revelation 1:6, and 5:10)

5. The heirs of God (Romans 8:17a)

6. The joint-heirs with Christ (Romans 8:17b)

7. The bride, the lamb's wife (Revelation 21:9)

After considerable study of the relevant portions of Scripture, it is my belief that all seven of these listed descriptions of redeemed souls relate to but are not all limited to the present dispensation, that is to the church age which began at Pentecost and will end with the rapture.

The *church* is first mentioned in Matthew 16:18 where Jesus says ". . . *upon this rock I will build My church* . . ." The Greek word for church is *ekklesia* and means a calling out, a religious congregation, an assembly. Therefore, the "church" is an assembly, a calling out of Jesus' own. What is called the Church today however, is not entirely Jesus' "called out assembly." Today we have the "visible church" consisting of all who call themselves Christians. The word Christian is greatly misused today. It is applied to nearly anyone who is favorably impressed with Jesus' earthly ministry. It is personalized by those who say the "magic words" of the sinner's prayer, then continue on with their lives as if nothing else was required. The label "Christian" is also claimed by those with no greater affinity to Jesus than to have been born into a family, the parents of which call themselves Christian. Within this "visible church" there is what is called the "invisible church." This is what Scripture usually calls the "remnant," that is the small segment of the visible church that is genuine "called out" assembly of Jesus' own. They are called invisible because salvation is of the soul and cannot always be discerned from outward appearances. There are also many who clearly do not belong to Jesus, but whose good works and lifestyles are more Christ-like than are those of genuine Christians. Only God, and sometimes those who are really His, know who are really His.

Only what is called the "invisible church" is what makes up the *Body of Christ*. It is well known by most within the "body" that each member has received a spiritual gift that he or she is expected to use with devotion befitting a true servant of our Lord. A spiritual gift is a special power given for the utilization of some attributes and talents which are to be used to advance our Lords purpose while we are yet here on earth, and to earn rewards that will effect our position in the eternal realm. Preaching, teaching, serving, giving, organizing, writing, etc. are examples of talents through which such spiritual empowerment will place one appropriately within that living functioning organism called "Body of Christ," the body of which Christ Jesus is the head.

The *sons and daughters, or children of God* are all who come to Christ Jesus in faith during this dispensation only. They are the same people that make up the body of Christ, and the invisible church.

There appears to be but one mention of the children of God in the Old Testament and that is in Deuteronomy 14:1 where God through Moses is instructing the people as to all of the "dos and don'ts" of His law. A quick reading of this verse might cause one to think that here also is a segment of people included in this category. However, the Hebrew word for "children" is *ben* and is defined as "son (a builder of the family name) in the widest sense (of literal and figurative relationship)." This can refer to "subject, nation, quality or condition," etc. Thus we cannot conclude that the phrase means saved souls but instead is speaking of those people as His nation, His special people. We know in the context of this verse that of these, surely not all, if even a few, were saved soul to whom God is speaking. Therefore, I believe that is reasonable to conclude that all "sons and daughters" or "children" of God are of the present dispensation. Of course there were, and will be others saved, but they do not fall under this classification of saved souls.

The reference to "sons" to "sons and daughters" and to "children" can be a bit confusing until one examines other English translations. Then it gets even more confusing because there is no consistency of use where these terms occur. The five translations of the many relevant verses that I have examined seem to be everywhere but in agreement. This is probably because of the latitude allowed in the Greek words being translated. Therefore, I believe it's safe to conclude that either "sons and daughters" or "children" is appropriate and "sons" alone should not be considered applicable in the subject context. Where spiritual issues are concerned, Christianity uniquely considers men and women equal before God, so this I believe is a very safe assumption.

The position of *kings and priests* in the eternal kingdom, and from whence they will come, seems less than absolutely clear, at least to me. Revelation 1:6 says *"and hath made us kings and priests unto God . . ."* This portion of Revelation I believe can be clearly seem as addressing the church. The "us" is the "church" who are made kings and priests. In Revelation 5:10 it seems to be the twenty-four elders who speak of having been made kings and priests who will reign on earth, presumably at least during the millennium and perhaps even later.

From studying Revelation, I believe that the twenty-four elders are of the "body of Christ," that is of the current dispensation. This is because they have "crowns of gold" (Revelation 4:4), and they ". . . *cast their crowns before the throne.*" (Revelation 4:10) These are of course spiritual crowns. I find no mention of crown in this context in the Old Testament. Scripture seems to limit such crowns to the "children of God" who earn them through good works in loving gratitude after they have been justified. Some Bible scholars maintain that the twenty-four elders are all, or at least half, Old Testament saints. One conjecture is that they are the twelve Apostles and the twelve sons of Israel. Another is that they are the twelve sons of Jacob along with other Old Testament "elders" such as Moses, Noah, Samuel, etc. Lacking any scriptural evidence to substantiate this, it seems to me fair to conclude that these are some very special people chosen for this honor out of the "Body of Christ." Indeed the twelve disciples may very well be among them, but not the sons of Israel.

Now let us see what else is revealed about the kings and priests in the eternal kingdom. Revelation 20:6 tells us something quite significant.

> *"Blessed and holy is he that hath part in the first resurrection; on such the second death hath no power, but they shall be priests of God and of Christ, and shall reign with him a thousand years."*

From this it seems evident that *all* redeemed souls will be priests of God, because the first resurrection, (there are only two) includes everyone who is saved to eternal life. This first resurrection includes all of the Old Testament saints, the raptured saints, and those saints who die during the tribulation, right up to the beginning of the millennium. The second resurrection consists of all the unsaved who ever lived and died by the end of the millennium at which time they too shall be raised, judged and each assigned to a God-chosen place in the lake of fire. Notice that the quoted verse says that they shall be priests but doesn't speak of kings. However, it says they "shall reign" with Him during the millennium. Effectually they will be kings because the word reign in the Greek is *basileno* which means to rule or reign in the sense of a king. Until studying this more carefully I believed as many Christians do, that only those of the Body of Christ would be kings and priests. However, from this we must conclude that all saved souls will be kings and priests during the millennium. That begs two questions; over whom will they be kings and priests, during the millennium, and what happens after the millennium? It must be those who survive the tribulation, along with their subsequent generations during the millennium. The sheep and goat judgment that Jesus tells us about in Matthew 25:31–46 shall occur sometime within the seventy-five days between the end of the great tribulation and the beginning of the millennium kingdom. (Daniel 12:11, 12) He speaks of gathering "all nations" and separating "them" into two groups, the "sheep and the goats." As one reads these verses, the "them" seems to indicate all the people from all the nations. However, in subsequent verses where Jesus describes the tribulation period behavior of the two groups, He is clearly referring to those who had opportunities to help or withhold help from His "brethren," that is those believers who were in danger of being caught by Antichrist's forces during the tribulation. It seems safe to assume that there will be many people, those in remote isolated regions throughout the world, who will have had no part of this scene, and that therefore they will not be participants of the "sheep and goat" judgment. They will obviously be among those who will continue to live and propagate during the millennium.

At the end of our Lords revelation concerning this judgment (verse 46 in Matthew 25), He says, *"and these shall go away into everlasting punishment; but the righteous into eternal life."* What can we glean from this beyond the obvious? First, He tells us that those who didn't assisted the brethren during the tribulation *"shall go away to eternal punishment."* The "shall go" does not necessarily means instantly. Those "goats," as well as the sheep, may continue to live out their natural lives before their respective punishments or rewards begin. Hasn't this always been the situation of both the saved and the unsaved? God knows all hearts and therefore knows from the beginning who will and who will not repent, yet He allows them all to live out their lives. This is beautifully symbolized by the wheat and tares parable in Matthew 13:36–43. Why wouldn't this be the case after the tribulation as well? Also it should be noted that the world population will greatly increase during that thousand years, until as we learn in Revelation 20:8 Satan will recruit an army as numerous as *"the sand of the sea"* to war against Jesus. Just imagine how many more souls loyal to Jesus there will be at that time. Souls that have been successfully guided by the "kings" and ministered to by the "priests" we are here discussing. How very strange and disturbing it is to realize that even with God Himself, that is, Christ Jesus physically, and of course spiritually, reigning here on earth, that the naturally wicked heart of man will continue to direct his choices even as it does today. This must be so, or else from whence would Satan draw his immense army? From this it seems evident that there will be many "troubled" mortals on earth during the millennium who will provide considerable "work" for the "kings and priests."

We have already identified the *Heirs of God* as mentioned in Romans 8:17a. As the children of God, these are also heirs or sharers of God. The sons and daughters of God become sharers of what He has chosen to offer from among His heavenly possessions as already described earlier.

Now we come to the sixth item on our list, the *Joint Heirs with Christ*. This too has already been discussed herein. The word heir, or sharer, here is the same as that of Romans 8:17a. The question begging an answer not offered in this earlier discussion is, what will be this unique or separate place in the heavenly hierarchy? I don't believe, as yet anyway, that Scripture gives us an answer, at least not directly, or with any assurance that we can perceive correctly. However, there may be pieces to the puzzle that, if positioned properly, may take form as to provide some portion of an answer. We will deal with this later. Whatever it means to be "joint sharers" with Christ, it seems clear that it applies to a group selected from within what are called the children of God.

Now finally we come to category seven *The Bride, the Lamb's Wife*. This of course is the Bride of Christ alluded to many times throughout the New Testament. Many conclude that the "bride of Christ" and the "body of Christ" are one and the same. However, there may be, and I believe that there is, a difference. Before attempting to identify what thus difference may be, we need to recall the importance of the earthly works of the redeemed souls, because these are what seem to provide heavenly rewards which one might consider being the basis on which heavenly positions are assigned. Notice what Jesus tells us in Revelation 22:12 *"And behold, I come quickly; and my reward is with me, to give every man according as his work shall be."* Elsewhere Scripture indicates that these "works" rewards are represented by "crowns" which may be considered "coins of the heavenly realm," that in a sense accompany one to heaven. There are crowns of rejoicing (1 Thessalonians 2:10); crowns of righteousness (2 Timothy 4:8); the crowns of life (James 1:12); the crowns of glory (1 Peter 5:4); the crown of glory and honor (Hebrews 2:9), and at least seven others woven in to the scriptural fabric. While there is no evidence, or even a thought that God discriminates in anyway regarding who He "draws" to Him and through faith justifies, and finally glorifies (Romans 8:30), Scripture makes it very clear that these crowns are rewards that have something important to do with what happens to those who manage to hold on to and bring their crowns to heaven. With this in mind we should be prepared to accept the idea that *there will not be a universal sameness or functional equality within the eternal society.* The mention of the twenty-four elders alone, I believe is evidence of this.

It seems clear that we can say with considerable certainty that the bride of Christ is drawn from, and only from, the body of Christ. While as yet I have found no concrete evidence that the bride is not the entire Body of Christ, there are enough clues to lead me to believe that the bride consists of only a select portion of the Body. Does it make any sense that the highest possible honor within the eternal spiritual realm would belong to that entire body? If so then, what is the benefit of any extraordinary dedication, obedience, service, and suffering? Also, what then are the purpose of crowns and rewards, and that particular "suffering with Christ?" Are they not the means and evidences of a hierarchy of elevated positions to be had in God's eternal service? Would it not be fitting that the most elevated position for man to attain in heaven, would be filled by those who most fully demonstrated their faith, obedience and fruitfulness, by those who "suffer with Him" in some specific way?

Revelation 19 tells us that the marriage of the Lamb takes place in heaven right after Babylon the great has fallen. That is near the very end of the tribulation. It seems to be before Jesus destroys the antichrist and rescues the Jewish remnant at Bozarh. Verse 9 says, *"Blessed are they which are called unto the marriage supper of the Lamb."* Are these wedding guests all the saved souls, other than the bride, or only some portion of them? I don't believe Scripture tells us, but it seems likely that it is all who have been redeemed up to that moment, that is both the Old and New Testament saints, and those saved during the tribulation. I don't believe it includes the remnant at Bozarh nor any other souls yet living "the first life." These are only the souls resurrected to eternal life and at the time are in their incorruptible bodies.

Revelation chapter 21 tells of a totally new heaven and earth. It also speaks of the New Jerusalem that will be the dwelling place of the Triune God and the bride of the Lamb. Chapter 22, verse 3 says the ". . . *but the throne of God and of the Lamb shall be in it; and his servants shall serve him."* Verse 5 speaks of these servants who will reign with Him forever, and ever. That ends the prophecy as it was given to John. It is revealed here that on this new earth, there will be a huge 1600-mile wide cube called the New Jerusalem in which God and the bride will dwell. Therein will also be servants who will rule with God forever. But do they live there? We don't know. The City has twelve gates that are always open, and presumably are there for some purpose consistent of that which gates are used, to allow travel in and out. Does everyone live in the New Jerusalem? I think not. It is my belief, lacking any evidence to the contrary that the major portion of saved souls will live outside of the city on this perfect new earth, and they are the ones over whom these servants of the Lord will reign forever and ever. This suggests some kind of worldwide social structure, and I believe that structure is in some way related to the fruitful works each redeemed soul performed while on this old earth. These translate into a certain number and type of crowns they "take" to heaven. All are pure and sinless, so all are eligible to pass in and out of the gates by means of some ordained order. It appears that the New Jerusalem will be the eternal home of God, the bride, and perhaps some of the other specially crowned people. Perhaps the angels who are now God servants will dwell there and also outside as they continue to serve Him, the bride and all other saved mankind who then dwell outside the walls. Of course these last thoughts are all conjecture, because Scripture does not appear to elaborate on these matters. Yet who cannot help but wonder and try to better understand the circumstances under which one will spend eternity? The clues are there but how to interpret them remains a mystery.

This ends this mini-marathon about "if." As is evident, I let that little word serve as a catalyst and excuse to both wander through, and delve into, a few of the many wonders of Scripture. I pray that it is informative and instructive as well as provocative, what ever it takes to grow in God's knowledge and into a greater love for Him and His Word.

—44—
The Heart

We all speak often of our hearts. "Have a heart; I don't have a heart for that; my heart isn't in it; you are breaking my heart, etc." What do we mean? When we say these things, we are not speaking of the blood pump in our chest, but of something else. For the purpose of this message, we will make use of the word "heart" as found in the translation from the Hebrew Old Testament book of Jeremiah, chapter 17, verse 9, because it is here that the Holy Spirit provides us with God's assessment of every human heart.

In this verse we are informed that "the heart is deceitful above all things, and desperately wicked; who can know it?" WOW! What a horrible indictment! Surely, there is something wrong here. This cannot be true of *my* heart. I'm basically a good person! Surely I am far better than many people I know. This can't be an absolute as it is written; there must be some varying degrees of deceitfulness and wickedness, from *almost* total wickedness like Hitler (after all, he did like dogs) to Mother Teresa who unselfishly served others all her life, and probably never knowingly hurt a soul. Sorry, Scripture makes no such exception. None of God's Word can be subject to private interpretation modification or watered down to leave anyone with an exception, which God Himself, in His own Words, has not clearly provided! Scripture provides NO possible exception regarding the condition of the heart. Escape, YES, exception, NONE!

Well, then let us analyze this horrible accusation to see if it actually means what it seems to say. What is the Holy Spirit talking about when He speaks of the "heart"? The Hebrew word used here is *leb,* pronounced as "labe," which is defined as, "feeling, will and the intellect." We know, or should know, that none of us "has" a

394

soul. The soul *IS* the person we are! The body is merely the bag of flesh and bones and blood which carries each of us souls around, giving us the ability to perform physical, earthly activities, and to articulate our words, thoughts and emotions. We can, to a surprising degree of applicability, use the computer as an analogy in order to understand this. The hardware, the physical, visible, dissectible parts of the computer, is like the body. The CD disc is like the brain. On it is stored all the information which gives the computer any useful function or purpose. That information is nothing but digitized, vibrational disturbances on the surface of the disc (brain) which give it a uniqueness of character and provides all of that which makes the computer a functioning device, a device that expresses and makes useful the information which its maker has programmed into it. That dimensionless, weightless and timeless "information" on the brain, is the mind, or we might say, the essence of the soul. The analogy is somewhat weakened by the fact that the soul has a certain divine maker, which a computer can never have, having been made by man's human hands. Among those divine qualities is that there is no erasure or obliteration possible of the soul as there is with that which has been given to the disc. The soul is immortal, and will, one day have an ageless, indestructible body to carry it around. The only issue is where it will spend eternity. I believe that from the above, we can correctly conclude that the "heart" is the summation of the characteristics, or the "character" of the soul.

Now, let us examine the word "wicked" as Scripture has defined it in the original Hebrew. The word is *anash,* which is pronounced aw-nash." There are a total of seventeen different Hebrew words, which translate into wicked, wickedness, or wickedly. The Old Testament uses most of them over and over again. Yet the word *anash* is used only *once* and only *here* in Jeremiah 17:9! The other sixteen versions of the word center around "morally wrong" as the definition. However, *anash* seems to have been most carefully and uniquely chosen to describe only the human heart. Strong's concordance defines *anash* as being "frail, feeble, desperately wicked, incurable, sick, and woeful." This word does not appear in any of the 460 other instances where "wicked" is used! How can one not revel in awe at the finely tuned precision and accuracy of the word choices our Lord has used in His authorship of this blessed, inerrant Volume! Therefore, the human heart, *every* human heart, which may be defined as the character of the soul, is "wicked, frail, incurable, sick and woeful." And catch this! The word desperately occurs nowhere else, but only here in the Old Testament, and is a translation of the *very same word* uniquely defining wicked! The same Hebrew word that is used in Jeremiah 17:9 for "wicked" is also used for "desperately"! How strange! And yet how singularly forceful in its effect in describing the awfulness of the human heart! Desperately wicked, therefore, is wickedly wicked or incurably incurable, etc. This reminds me of where Paul in Romans 7:13 calls sin ". . . exceedingly sinful." Sin is so bad that there are no adjectives adequate to describe it, therefore, he turned the word onto it itself in describing it. Here it seems that the Holy Spirit is doing the same thing as He describes the heart as being wicked, wickedly wicked.

Now, let's examine the word, "deceitful." This word in the form of deceit, deceitful, deceive, etc. occurs ninety times in the Old Testament and is used to translate ten different Hebrew words of that general meaning. However, the word translated "deceitful" in Jeremiah 17:9 is used only once, here and nowhere else! It is the Hebrew word *aqob*. pronounced "aw-kobe." It means fraudulent, crocked, deceitful, polluted. My oh my! Are you seeing the same picture of yourself as I am seeing of myself? Does it make any more sense to you when you read David's words in Psalm 51:10 where he asks "create in me a clean heart, O God." He doesn't ask God to clean his heart, or to repair it, or in any way to adjust or transform his heart. He knew several hundred years before God told Jeremiah, that the heart was "desperately wicked," that it was doubly feeble, so frail, so incurable and so polluted that only the Creator God could create a clean heart, and not a repaired, rebuilt or restored heart, but a New and Clean heart! David knew that with that natural heart alone, he had no chance for eternal life. Somehow he knew he had to have another heart, a new, clean one that only God can create. Perhaps that is why God called David a man after His own heart. Everyone who hopes for eternal life must make the same petition, as did David. But for that petition to be effective, it must come from a heart that knows that it is desperately and hopelessly wicked and has no other hope except through God's boundless grace and love, which He eagerly gives to anyone who will humble himself or herself recognizing their hopeless, hateful state, and *appropriately* seeking Jesus as Lord and Savior.

If we allow "heart" to be defined as the character of the soul and accept the truth of its incurable wickedness, then we might perceive a logistical problem in having a clean, new heart. Being born-again is another way of saying one has received a new heart, a new and different soul-character. But how can we have this new soul-character when the old soul-character remains, and it surely does remain because it continues to plague us? The explanation that I feel persuaded to offer may seem to be simplistic and perhaps even contrived. Nevertheless, I see the two hearts, that is, the two-soul characteristics residing in the soul at the same time, like two sides of a coin. The spiritual consequences of the sin nature are not cleansed from the soul at the instant the new heart, the new soul-character, is received. But the sin nature, that sin prone characteristic of the soul, remains until the moment it leaves the corrupt body. That sin nature stays behind along with the body, but unlike the body, it will not rise again because no sin or sin nature can enter heaven. But while we remain with our original hardware, our corruptible bodies, the two sides of the soul-character wage a continuing war for dominance. The one we favor, the one we yield to, is the one who will dominate our lives. However, this is a losing battle for the evil side, assuming that, in fact, we actually have that other "clean" side, because our love and gratitude towards our Lord and Savior will, because it must, inevitably put down, subordinate and eventually destroy the wicked side. So what is the "bottom line" in all of this? What is the message we are to receive from our Lord's Words given to Jeremiah? I believe it is this:

1. We are all, *every one* of us, hopelessly wicked whether we are willing to admit it or not!

2. Redemption, that is, relief from this hopeless state, which can only lead to eternal punishment, must begin with a "wholehearted" recognition of that hopeless sin-filled condition.

3.   With that recognition must come the realization that only through Jesus, the Redeemer, can we be extricated from that fate.

4.   With the realization, there must come faith that He *can* do it.

5.   That realization must be followed by a genuine faith that He *will* do it.

6.   This immediately turns into the fact that He *has* done it.

However, because of the incredibly deceitful nature of our hearts, as I hope I have convincingly reported here, we must, if we are to be certain that we haven't deceived ourselves, seek confirmation of that accomplishment. In order to gain a reasonable assurance of the fact of redemption, I believe that we must carefully search for evidence of it, because salvation is far, far too important to leave to chance, or presumption, or some superficial, and thereby false, evidence. At the minimum one must look for the following:

1.   Is there a conflict occurring within the "heart" as the two natures collide and compete? Here we are back to the two-sides of the coin analogy. If we are saved, especially during the early years following the event, there should be an inner conflict. This most likely is expressed by an increased sensitivity of the conscience. Sins which our old "heart" excused or rationalized, the new "heart" rebels against, using the sensitized conscience to cause the soul to seek relief by a growing avoidance of sin.

2.   The growing avoidance of sin must be sincere and not done in fear, but in gratitude to Jesus for what He did for us on the cross. Once one is able to understand, even a small portion of what Jesus willingly went through in order to deliver us from a deserved hell, it will be an overwhelming love, and profound gratitude which can not help but manifest in the soul, and express itself in every aspect of a saved soul's earthly life, in actions, behavior, thoughts, feelings, worship, and prayers.

3.   This manifestation is unlikely to "hit the soul running," but should be a continually moving, enlarging phenomenon as one grows and matures in the faith. As Jonathan Edwards once said, regarding a saved soul, "Life is evidenced by movement." If one is actually

alive in the faith, it cannot be a dead, motionless faith, or it is not a saving faith. It must move, that is, it must grow if it is to be recognized as a saving faith. An important and telling question one should ask, and ask often of one's self is, "Am I a better Christian today than I was a year ago?" Be very circumspect and honest. It may be the most important question one can ever ask oneself.

4. Those who are born-again become genuine components of the Body of Christ. Each component has one or more functions. Becoming born-again is not a retirement event. It's not an achievement, which allows one to rest on any laurels. The saved person did nothing to either deserve or to achieve this blessed condition. His or her involvement was nothing more than to sincerely believe. Jesus did every bit of the hard and painful pulling which brought the soul out of the ditch leading to hell and onto the straight road to eternity. The soul, who accepts the title Christian must live the name, must become an active, effective, loyal ambassador as His namesake. Anyone who cannot find these characteristics growing evermore dominate on the soul, to the extent that the old other "side-of-the-coin" is seen slowly fading, weakening and dying, should re-examine the sincerity of that initial vow by which one had assumed to have been given a born-again status.

5. Those who are His are called upon to bear fruit. Is there evidence of fruit or is the tree continually barren? Those who know a little Scripture know what Jesus does with trees that don't bear fruit and vine branches that fail to have grapes (Matthew 21:19–21 and John 15:5, 6). Reading and studying Scripture prayerfully, always seeking God's wisdom, is evidence of involvement and interest in what God so carefully, accurately and lovingly provides through His Holy Word, the Holy Bible. It's through it and what it reveals that gives us the wisdom and direction we need in order to do His will, to perform the function one is assigned as a member of the Body of Christ. How can one possibly serve Him, as He wants us to serve Him, if we go through life only guessing, applying questionable hearsay and a once-a-week twenty-minute sermon? He didn't write the book to sit on a coffee table or shelf. He wrote it to

be studied, mused on, digested, and assimilated into every aspect of our lives. Without having done this, or being in the process of doing so, how can we even pray to Him for guidance? He gave it all to us in advance in His book! His guidance is all there ready and willing to be revealed, if we but seek it sincerely.

As you can see, I never run out of ramblings. Having finally "come up for air" I see that I've exhausted all that I felt prompted to say about this topic, at least for now. So, I'll just stop here and pray that there is something of use to someone, as a way to perhaps see more clearly what Jeremiah was given to tell us.

—45—

How Do Your Attitudes Be?

Do any of us have the right attitude to be called genuine Christians? Jesus gave us a list of attitudes by which we will be blessed, if we hold to them. They are clearly spelled out in Matthew 5:3–11. This is in the first part of the Sermon on the Mount, where Jesus describes eight categories of blessed believers. These are commonly called the *beatitudes*, but one might also call them the *be*-attitudes, not the do-attitudes or the *attempted* attitudes, but attitudes which should *be* in every Christian's heart and daily life. Let's see what Jesus is telling us:

Verse 3 *"Blessed are the poor in spirit: for theirs is the kingdom of heaven."* This has to do with our attitude toward ourselves, in which we feel our need and admit that we are spiritually destitute without Jesus in our hearts. This means that we must be empty of ourselves before He can fill us with Himself. Here is the opposite of self-sufficiency and of being full of ourselves. God helps those who have come to the end of themselves, and we become rich in spirit *only* after the Holy Spirit has filled our hearts.

Verse 4 *"Blessed are they that mourn: for they shall be comforted."* 2 Corinthians 1:3–4 tells us that God is the Father of all comfort, and also Jesus can "bind up the brokenhearted," as we learn in Isaiah 61:1 and Luke 4:18. This is not about mourning at a funeral. It is about experiencing mourning and sorrow because of our own sins and for the unsaved, as well as for the poor and unfortunate of the world. Faith and trust in Jesus will comfort us because we well know that our prayers will be heard and that through them, as well as our fruitfulness in His name, some will be saved and benefited who otherwise might not have been.

Verse 5 *"Blessed are the meek: for they shall inherit the earth."* If our attitude is of meekness in the faith, we will be sons and daughters of the Father and "joint-heirs" with Jesus in the millennium and ever more. Meekness is not weakness! It is an attitude toward others that has nothing of ourselves to prove. It is a mind set that is teachable and will not defend itself when wrong. Meekness results from our priorities and focus on Jesus as our only source of strength (see Ephesians 4 and Titus 3).

"Blessed are they which do hunger and thirst after righteousness: for they shall be filled." This is an attitude toward God. It is a hunger and thirst for Him. How do we satisfy this hunger and thirst? It is through praise, prayer and pursuit of understanding of Him, His way and His purpose for us as found in His Holy Word. Here is one of the clues, which may help us to determine whether or not we are saved. Is our appetite mainly for Him or for worldly things? Put another way, what do we do when we have some spare time? Do we reach for the Bible, or for the TV clicker, or for the sport pages?

Verse 7 *"Blessed are the merciful: for they shall obtain mercy."* Here is our attitude toward others through a forgiving spirit. His mercy and forgiveness towards us must be reflected through us towards others, for we must remember, that we reap what we sow! Mercy is not tolerance of sin. It is God-like love in action!

Verse 8 *"Blessed are the pure of heart: for they shall see God."* This is about keeping our lives clean, seeking holiness as the only way to happiness in spite of the many worldly pleasures, which tempt us into other directions. There should be a singleness of purpose that is to serve and please Him, and to give all glory to Him. This is not absolute sinlessness, but of truth within, a singleness of heart and purpose. For this we need the new heart we are given when we are born-again. We must feed that new heart with prayer and His Word, and starve that old nature which will continue to tempt us back into worldly ways.

Verse 9 *"Blessed are the peacemakers: for they shall be called the children of God."* We are to try to bring peace between people and God, and also between peoples as well, where possible. God loves peace, and expects us to help promote it with love and kindness and through the wisdom derived from His Word, for He is the God of peace (Romans 14:19, 15:33). This has nothing to do with being a pacifist in the worldly sense. Peace based on sin, compromise, tolerances or ecumenicalism is not in any way God condoned peace. The ultimate peace, which we are to seek and where possible to promote, is that "peace of God which passeth all understanding, shall keep your hearts and minds through Christ Jesus" (Philippians 4:7).

Verse 10 through 12 *"Blessed are they which are persecuted for righteousness' sake: for theirs is the kingdom of heaven. Blessed are ye, when men shall revile you, and persecute you, and shall say all manner of evil against you falsely, for my sake. Rejoice, and be exceeding glad: for great is your reward in heaven: for so persecuted they the prophets which were before you."* We must recognize that all who are leading Godly lives will suffer persecution, unless we hide our faith under a basket, as one who is ashamed of the faith. Whether it is being ostracized, ridiculed or stoned, there will be persecution of those who lead sincere Godly lives and publicly express their faith. This is true across most of the world today, and has been since Stephen became the first martyr. It has not been so in this country, so we tend to not notice it. But in these end times, it is becoming more and more evident that the forces of darkness are gaining such power in this country that persecution of all genuine believers is not far in the future.

Here we have the eight attitudes Jesus described as being appropriately and necessary in the hearts of the saved. We think of an attitude as an outward expression of an inward condition. But our natural, deceitful nature is quite capable of hypocrisy, and in this sense, of expressing outwardly an image we wish to be known by, but which is not the same as what is in the heart. This human propensity to deceive is often expressed as to "put our best foot forward" or to appear more "Godly" than we really are. This is something we must always be on guard against. It is so easy and tempting to do this, and so destructive to our souls, that we should continually examine ourselves in this context. Is our outward projection of ourselves merely a contrived image, or is it the real person showing through? In the world, image and perception rather than reality have become the main themes of life, a pseudo reality around which people conduct their lives. Many never even stop to examine what is in their souls, but are quite happy if they can continue to receive benefit through the image each has created for himself or herself. Isn't this Hollywood or never-never land having become a national virtual reality?

In Matthew 23:13–29, Jesus gives us examples of this imagery and how dangerous it can be as He lists the eight woes against the scribes and Pharisees. Chuck Misler has observed that a careful comparison will show that they somewhat parallel the beatitudes, but in a very negative sense. Remember that the scribes and Pharisees, which Jesus so devastatingly rebukes and condemns, were both of the class, which was highly educated in Scripture. They were also very zealous and sincere regarding their religion. But as Jesus points out, in effect, that somewhere they "lost their first love." That the love of God was not in them, but instead the love of self as well as rules and rituals, many of them self-made and not of the Torah. Let us see what Jesus found as He looked both into their hearts and at their actions.

Verse 13 *"But woe unto you, scribes and Pharisees, hypocrites! For ye shut up the kingdom of heaven against men; for ye neither go in yourselves, neither suffer ye them that are entering to go in."* Notice here they are shutting up the kingdom of heaven not only to themselves, but also to others whom they influence. This is the opposite of those in Matthew 5:3, who are able to receive the kingdom of heaven. What a horrible indictment it is to be charged with influencing others into eternal damnation! There are many very notable "religious" personages around today which will one day have to answer to this same charge!

Verse 14 *"Woe unto you, scribes and Pharisees, hypocrites! For ye devour widows' houses, and for pretense make long prayer: therefore ye shall receive the greater damnation."* This is all show and no righteous substance. Instead of comforting and helping widows and orphans (examples of those who mourn of Matthew 5:4) they actually steal from them while saying long and empty prayers to impress others with their piety. We see variation on the same theme through some of the "tele-evangelists" and other false or half-truth teachers who are on the prowl today.

Verse 15 *"Woe unto you, scribes and Pharisees, hypocrites! For ye compass sea and land to make one proselyte; and when he is made ye make him twofold more the child of hell than yourselves.*" In Matthew 5:5 they hunger and thirst for righteousness, here they are greedy for gain, for the gold. They value earthly power and prestige more than any eternal kingdom. In bringing others to their evil ways they condemn their hapless proselytes. Another horrible indictment, reminiscent again of many of the false teachers and compromisers, will clog the airways, fill bookshelves and stand in pulpits.

Verse 23, 24 "*Woe unto you scribes and Pharisees, hypocrites! For ye pay tithe of mint and anise and cummin, and have omitted the weightier matters of the law, judgment, mercy, and faith: these ought ye to have done, and not to leave the other undone. Ye blind guides, which strain at a gnat and swallow a camel.*" Here Jesus accuses them of paying great attention to the small things, including the minor aspects of the 613 points of law, many which they themselves made up, while at the same time missing the main point of God's message. They were legalists and, therefore, their focus was on details while they miss the big picture, "the weightier matters," the great principals involved. Remember how they had no problem condemning an innocent Man-Jesus to death but dared not enter Pilate's' mansion, a gentile house, for fear of defiling themselves. In Matthew 5:7 they obtain mercy, here they reject the idea and show no mercy. Even in their tithing they are cheap and hypocritical, making offerings merely of inexpensive easily obtained herbs. Tithing is giving 10 percent of your income. This is what already belongs to God. If you choose to offer up a gift to Him, it must be something in addition to the 10 percent.

Verse 25–28

> "*Woe unto you, scribes and Pharisees, hypocrites! For ye make clean the outside of the cup and of the platter, but within they are full of extortion and excess. Thou blind Pharisees, cleanse first that which is within the cup and platter, that the outside of them may be clean also. Woe unto you, scribes and Pharisees, hypocrites! For ye are like unto whited sepulchers, which indeed appear beautiful outward, but are within full of dead men's bones, and of all uncleanness. Even so ye also outwardly appear righteous unto men, but within ye are full of hypocrisy and iniquity.*"

Here Jesus is using two idioms, the cup and the sepulcher, in order to illustrate that they strive to show their cleanness on the outside which the world can see, while they are filthy on the inside (something to which we must all be alert). Inner cleanliness is obviously the more important, but they strived for the opposite. In Matthew 5:8, 9, it is only the pure of heart and the peacemakers who are blessed. But the scribes and Pharisees seem to all have dirty hearts, as Jesus points out. There can be no Godly peace associated with a filthy heart.

Verse 29–35

"Woe unto you, scribes and Pharisees, hypocrites! Because ye build the tombs of the prophets and garnish the sepulchers of the righteous, and say If we had been in the days of our fathers, we would not have been partakers with them in the blood of the prophets. Wherefore ye be witnesses unto yourselves, that ye are the children of them which killed the prophets. Fill ye up then the measure of your fathers. Ye serpents, ye generation of vipers, how can ye escape the damnation of hell? Wherefore, behold I send unto you prophets, and wise men, and scribes: and some of them ye shall kill and crucify; and some of them shall ye scourge in your synagogues, and persecute them from city to city: that upon you may come all the righteous blood shed upon the earth, from the blood of righteous Abel unto the blood of Zechari'ah son of Berechi'ah, who ye slew between the temple and the altar."

Here again Jesus points out this hypocrisy when the scribes and Pharisees appear to adorn and respect the memories of the prophets whom their fathers killed and who they will also scourge, crucify and kill. He tells them that they will do this to those *He* sends (including Himself) Who is the sender of the prophets? Only God has that power and authority! Here Jesus in effect is disclosing Himself to be God, because it is *He* who is sending the prophets! In Matthew 5:10, 11 the persecuted receive the kingdom of heaven and they are to rejoice because they are in good company, that is the persecuted prophets before them. In the remaining verses of chapter 23, Jesus laments over their hypocrisy and longstanding unholy behavior, and predicts the dire consequences that will result. Notice that every woe, every accusation is characterized by their hypocrisy, that is pretending to be, or do, or believe the opposite of what was really in their hearts.

As previously noted, these were biblical scholars of the first order, in their day. Their lives were supposedly dedicated to studying, preaching, teaching and living what they understood to be what God had ordained through the Torah. They came from a long line of such agents of the law and were extremely proud of their heritage as sons of Abraham. In these woes, Jesus is showing them their total failure and the downright sinfulness of their representation of the Holy Word. Their shock at hearing these things is again against the messenger, and they appear to have learned nothing accept a hatred for the message and it's Deliverer. Jesus did not mince words; He was brutally clear and accurate in His condemnations. One might wonder what the reactions would be today if He were to personally address an assembly of many of the modern pastors, evangelists, and other church leaders. I suspect that the message and the reactions would be little different from these described above.

There is a great deal to learn from all of this for those of us who call ourselves Christians. The potential that we may have some level of hypocrisy regarding our faith and outward expressions of it, is always present and should be guarded against through frequent, deep into-the-heart self examination of our motives and purposes for which we do "good things." Remember, it is not what good we do, but what is in the heart, dictating the why of what we do, which causes it to be either gold, or hay and stubble. This is made clear in Matthew 6:1–4 when Jesus says,

> *"Take heed that ye do not your alms before men, to be seen of them: otherwise ye have no reward of your Father which is in heaven. Therefore when thou doest thine alms, do not sound a trumpet before thee, as the hypocrites do in the synagogues and in the streets, that they may have glory of men. Verily I say unto you, they have their reward. But when thou doest alms; let not thy left hand know what thy right hand doeth: that thine alms may be in secret; and thy Father which seeth in secret himself shall reward thee openly."*

Here Jesus is telling us to not advertise our good deeds. We should keep them as secret as possible so that any deserved credit will come from God alone. If we are credited and praised here on earth, there will be no added brownie points in heaven. So again this matter, as with all things, all boils down to what is in the heart. As Jesus said so many times, *"He who has ears let him hear what the Spirit says."* As far as I know, we all have ears.

—46—

The Spirit Connection

Scripture tells us that man was created as a body-soul-spirit being. Therefore, just as God the Creator is a triune God, so also did He create man a triplicate being. In Genesis 1:26, God said ". . . Let us make man in our image, after our likeness . . ." In this verse God reveals His more-than-one nature whereby He, in one of these natures, is speaking to the others of His own triune self. Throughout the Holy Bible there are many inferences, as well as very clear statements of His actual three-in-one being. He has identified these as the Father, Son and the Holy Spirit.

So Scripture tells us that at some point in eternity He / They chose to create man, a special being, in their image, who would be above even the angels in the structure of God's eternal realm. This occurred about six thousand years ago, as Scripture makes clear regardless of what the world and "science" would have one believe.

Adam, the created man, consisted of a body, soul (ego, intellect, will, emotions, psyche) and spirit (1 Thessalonians 5:23). The spirit of man is differentiated from the soul, because it is that part of man intended by God through which man could communicate *directly* with Him without need for any other audible or visual means. This communication with God could not in any way be achieved by the soul without this spirit connection. Genuine peace and fellowship with God is not possible for the soul without the spirit connection with God. Adam was originally created as a properly connected spiritual being, as was Eve. By close fellowship with the Creator, the spirit dominated the soul and the soul controlled the flesh, keeping it in submission and thereby maintaining the correct sinless relationship with God. The spirit connection, much like an umbilical cord, served to keep God as the primary source of all spiritual thoughts, nourishment and actions, as well as the recognition of their dependence on Him. However, our Sovereign God in His omniscient wisdom in accordance with His ultimate purpose, also imbued Adam and Eve with sovereign wills of their own, that is, an ability to make choices, an attribute which He had also given the angels. That ability to choose made possible that first sin.

Adam's sin caused a profound change. Not only was the spirit connection, that umbilical cord, broken, but also you might say his spirit died. That supernatural, immaculate and divine Spirit-to-spirit communication was no longer possible. The plug was pulled; the lights went out. Man was now spiritually detached from God, who until then had been both Father and Friend. To say that the "lights went out" is more literal than one might suspect. We find in Genesis 3:7 after their sin, Adam and Eve both discovered their nakedness. They suddenly realized that the divine light, that spirit filled glow of Godliness that had clothed them, was gone, "and they knew that they were naked; and they sowed fig leaves together and made themselves aprons." This was man's first religious act, an attempt to cover, that is, to hide his sins. We also find evidence of that divine spiritual glow in the face of Moses when he came down from the mountain after having been in the presence of the Lord for sometime in Exodus 34:35. We see this same glow of divine light shining from Jesus at the transfiguration in Matthew 17:2. Revelation also provides several examples of this as well.

With the breaking of that Spirit-to-spirit connection and man's spirit now functionally dead, he was no longer in the image of God, for he was no longer a triune being, but only a dual being having functionally only a body and soul. As Dr. Lloyd Nelson Jones puts it so well *"Soul power was not enough to the keep the lust against the body in check and tragically for man, it left him pridefully deceived into viewing himself as an independent creature not requiring any help beyond his own strength and mental abilities."* Sadly that has been man's condition continuously to this day. Once broken, that Spirit-to spirit connection could not be restored by anything which man could do. Therefore, after "the fall," all mankind has been born with this

410

condition, that is with a sin nature. Without a living Spirit-to-spirit connection, having only a soul and a body, mankind has been easy prey to the seducing spirits under Satan's control, thus adding fuel to man's now innate nature to sin, that is, to disobey God, and to seek distance from Him and His prescribed ways.

If you're genuinely a born-again Christian, you must be incredibly grateful to God for having provided through Christ Jesus, a way in which that Spirit-to-spirit connection could be restored! In making Himself actually born as Man, an absolutely sinless Man, then paying the entire price of sin by suffering and dying, after which He was resurrected from the dead, Jesus has now made it possible for mans spirit to also be resurrected from the dead. That Spirit-to-spirit connection is restored. Thus the lights are on again for those of a true faith in Jesus. He plugged our cord back into the socket providing access to that incredible power grid through which our lights will never again go out, even throughout eternity!

If you have received into your heart an absolute certainty of the Gospel message and have thereby put your faith and trust in Christ Jesus as your Savior, and have also made Him your Lord, you can believe that you are born-again, as Scripture says you must be in order to enter into eternal heaven. If this is a recent event, and you find that it is difficult to discern that restored Spirit-to-spirit connection, be patient, pray, study God's Word and persevere. Even though the connection has been restored, that is the plug is back in the socket making potentially available to you that full force of God's spiritual power, you may not experience much of it initially. Remember, that the sinful nature is still in you. That natural self, with the help of Satan and the world, are always struggling, and hoping to again pull the plug (which they can not do) or at least keep the power and its effectiveness as weak as possible. Nevertheless, take heart because once you are His, He has promised in Philippians 1:6, ". . . that He which has begun a good work in you will perform it until the day of Jesus Christ . . ."

However, and this is of *"eternal" importance*, if the light hasn't gone on, or you see no change in your life, its time to thoroughly "examine yourselves whether ye be in the faith, prove your own selves." (2 Corinthians 13:5). The minimal evidence of a saving faith should be a contrite, repentant and humble heart always seeking to be obedient to God's Word, as studying His Word becomes a major part of your daily nourishment. If these evidences are weak or lacking, and the natural self is still in effective control, then you had better, and quickly, check the plug; it may not have ever been plugged into the Holy Socket! Your faith may not be what you thought it was, and the Spirit-to-spirit connection may not have taken place. In any case, your best posture is on your knees praying to God, first praising Him for His incredible offer of salvation, then petitioning Him to validate the saving nature of your faith, to fully resurrect your spirit, and to turn up the voltage in order that you may recognize and have more and more of His divine light.

"Ye Are the Salt of the Earth"

Chapter 5 of the Gospel of Matthew begins as follows: *And seeing the multitudes, He went up into a mountain; and when He was set, his disciples came unto Him; and He opened His mouth, and taught them, saying,"*

From this, it is sometimes concluded that this was something He was teaching to the Apostles and perhaps the multitudes as well. However, after having described the nine categories of those whom He called blessed, and which are commonly referred to as the Beatitudes, He moved on to a few other "similitudes of the believer." This started with verse 13 which is the topic of this paper, and which in the King James Version is translated as follows:

"Ye are the salt of the earth; but if the salt have lost his savor, wherewith shall it be salted? It is thenceforth good for nothing but to be cast out, and to be trodden under foot of men."

Here it becomes evident that it is to the apostles only to whom He is speaking, at least here, because this is personal and specific to this select group and not to any multitude, for to many or to most of the multitude, this would not have been applicable.

But what does it mean to be "the salt of the earth"? This is a term I've heard many times. It has always applied to someone basically good natured, honest, hard working, and having a high measure of integrity. Perhaps the Apostles were all of these things, but they had to be far more than that, because that description lacks the vital element of Christian faith. All Christians should have these qualities, but there are many who are not in any way Christian, yet excel in this manner of behavior. Furthermore, how does salt get into this? It is spoken of as a similitude describing the Apostles, but how?

In order to find an answer, let's examine the qualities and purposes of salt from the earthly perspective. I count six physical characteristics or purposes of salt.

1. It's a preservative, that is, it prevents decay or corruption of many organic substances. It is found today, in nearly all processed foods to increase their shelf life, and to slow down or prevent bacterial growth as well as enzymatic degradation. Before refrigeration, canning and other forms of food preservation, adequate supplies of salt for this purpose alone were essential for survival.

2. Sprinkled appropriately on many foods, salt brings out their full flavor and results in a more tasty meal.

3. It causes thirst. Bars and restaurants serve salted nuts and potato chips or popcorn to induce thirst in order to sell more drinks.

4. It melts ice, thereby providing a means of restoring mobility to frozen objects and also to eliminate slipperiness of ice covered surfaces.

5. It is an essential mineral, which we cannot live without. Salt tablets are given to soldiers and athletes whenever profuse perspiration from rigorous activity is likely. Excessive perspiration without salt replacement can cause one to faint or even die, depending on the severity of its depletion. Our blood contains considerable salt. It is an essential outside coating for very cell. A healthy cell has potassium along the inside of the cell membranes and sodium along the outside. These two minerals form an electrical potential across the membrane, in effect giving life providing energy to the cell. This structure attests to its vitalness to life.

6. Salt was valued as much as gold in some cultures. From the earliest times up to quite recent history when vast underground deposits were discovered, salt has been a rare and much valued commodity in many parts of the world for the five reasons given above. Wars were fought over it, and vast trade routes across Europe and Asia were formed primarily to make it possible to transport it. The Chinese made little salt cakes and used them as

currency. Salt was, and is still, a major barter item in some primitive cultures. Roman soldiers were often paid in salt (*salarium* in Latin). From this we get the word salary. From this period we get the expression: "He is not worth his salt," that is, his pay or salary.

Well, of course, Jesus was not considering these attributes of salt in the physical sense, but rather in a spiritual way, given the context of the message. He had taught the Apostles many things, and would continue to do so even after His death and resurrection. These were all in preparation for their life long missions to serve Him, and to be what He now proclaimed them to be, "the salt of the earth." What did He mean by this? How were they to take on or utilize the characteristics of salt in the spiritual sense? Let's look at each of the five qualities of salt in the context of the Apostles' evolving inward characteristics as divinely implanted by their heavenly Teacher.

1. Salt Preserves

First they were given the Message of eternal spiritual preservation to spread across this corrupt and decaying world. The message that Jesus is the Savior, and that through faith in Him and in His shed blood, He would preserve them from corruption by giving them eternal life in heaven. Second, they themselves as salt of the earth were permanently preserved in an unyielding faith and potency as His messengers, persevering to the end. They devoted their entire lives to conveying the Good News of that eternally preserving condition we call salvation.

2. Salt Flavors

Having been so well taught by Jesus, and being filled with the Holy Spirit at Pentecost, they had the whole Word in their hearts. Therefore, as they preached the Gospel, they sprinkled it with the enhancing flavor of the words of Moses and the prophets, words that enriched and made the message more convincing and palatable to the Jews whom they evangelized. Isn't it also true today when we hear a pastor or Bible teacher enhance the flavor of a New Testament message by sprinkling it with Old Testament wisdom? How much more savory is it to see how our wonderful God prepared His two volume book as a single integrated message where His earlier delivered truths have lost none of the "savor," but simply add more supernatural flavor to all that is written in volume two.

3. Salt Creates Thirst

Just as their Master had done, did not the Apostles invoke a thirst for the Word and for the promises it included? Wherever they went, thirst for the message followed them, and through the gifts of the Holy Spirit they were able to provide quenching words and deeds, which brought salvation to many souls.

4. Salt Melts Ice

The heat and zealous passion of the Apostles, who were "the salt of the earth," did indeed melt ice-like frozen hearts. In doing so they restored motion to those who were frozen, dead in sin, and led them safely up out of the slippery morass to where Jesus stood waiting to offer them eternal warmth, safety and salvation.

5. Salt Is Essential to Life

"For life of the flesh is in the blood" (Leviticus 17:11) and salt is an essential ingredient of the life-providing properties of blood. From the very beginning of time, God ordained that the taking of life through the shedding of blood, innocent blood, was the only way to atone for sin. Jesus was the Lamb of God who willingly shed His precious blood unto death because it was the only means by which mankind could ever be totally purged of sin. It is only through faith in that sacrifice that one can receive eternal life.

6. Salt Has Intrinsic Value

Salt had an intrinsic value like gold, because it was so scarce and essential to life. Therefore, in calling the apostles the salt of the earth, Jesus was giving them a very strong compliment, which they could value in the strictly earthly sense. But in the context of Scripture, this had even greater spiritual value, because their saltiness would be like "gold, tried in the fire." Once they received the Holy Spirit and began ministering, they would, throughout the rest of their lives, be of the very greatest value in spreading the Gospel and bringing souls to Jesus for salvation. They along with Paul, an Apostle, who was specially tutored by Jesus, would write the entire New Testament, the final portion of God's written message to us, by far the most precious document ever written.

~

Notice how verse 13 continues ". . . *but if the salt have lost his savour, wherewith shall it be salted? It is thence forth good for nothing, but to be cast out, and to be trodden under the foot of man."*

To lose savor comes from the Greek word "moraine" meaning to become stupid or foolish. A reasonable interpretation of this portion of the verse could be that if the salt, that is the person so called, lost those qualities enumerated above, that is has become stupid or foolish in his application of them, of what use would he be? This situation is reminiscent of Jesus' parable of the sower, the second category (Matthew 13:20, 21) when the Word was received with joy and gladness, but because they were lacking sufficient roots, the message soon lost its savour. Also in the Gospel of John, chapter 15, Jesus uses the analogy of the vine to make a similar point. The branch which doesn't bare fruit is useless and, therefore, destroyed. It is also possible that even in this early point in His ministry, Jesus may have had in His mind the one "salt" who would loose "his savour," that is Judas, who would betray him

The Apostles, as salt of the earth, remained faithful adherents to each of the six properties of salt, as He foreknew that they would. They never wavered, but persevered with their mandate to the very end, when they too allowed their blood to be shed, rather than lose their savour by forsaking their faith and the cause for which Jesus had ordained them.

This calling by the physically living Man-Jesus was delivered personally and directly to the Apostles. But through His living Word, the Scripture, He was and is speaking to each and every one of His disciples. These are all the redeemed of God. Does this include you? Are you a disciple? Then you are called to be the "salt of the earth" and to follow as well as possible the example set by the Apostles.

One last point, and this is in regards to the value of salt as a barter item or as a commodity used as coinage. We are saved by grace through faith alone. With that having been secured, our most loving and generous Lord does not stop there in His generosity and offered opportunities. Having been saved, we most likely have intense gratitude, which we want to express. We can do this through our obedience, our fruitfulness, our prayers, our love, and our kindness towards others, along with our generosity with our time money and efforts toward the spreading of His Word. All of these expressions of gratitude, these evidences of faith, may be thought of as the coinage of the Kingdom. Through this coinage, which we send in advance, we can in effect, buy the rewards or crowns He makes available to His own. Jesus actually tells us to do this in Matthew 6:19 where He says:

> *"Lay not up for yourselves treasures upon the earth, where moth and rust doth corrupt and where thieves break through and steal, but lay up for yourselves treasures in heaven, where neither moth or rust corrupt, and where thieves do not break through or steal: for where your treasure is, there will be your heart also."*

Isn't it incredible that simply through our sincere acts of gratitude, which He Himself enables us to express through the indwelling power of the Holy Spirit, we are able to prepare ourselves to be more effective "kings and priests" in His heavenly realm? I urge you; take advantage of this small window of opportunity you have remaining to "buy" as many crowns as you can. The market remains open only just so long, and then closes forever, which for many of us may be sooner than we may think.

If you are one of the redeemed, you have received the greatest gift any human being could ever receive. You are richer than the wealthiest monarch, or even more so than all the monarchs of the world put together. If you have a full appreciation of what it means to be part of God's family, then your heart must be full of gratitude and eagerness to be all He would have you be. If you are one of His, as were the Apostles, He has a purpose for you as He did for them. Your free will allows you to choose to fulfill or ignore that purpose. Your decision in this matter may be a point of evidence regarding the actual validity of your presumption as to your saved status. I pray that you will pray earnestly for His guidance in this matter.

—48—
Nothing but Leaves
(Mark 11:13)

What a sad and trying time it had been for Jesus. Only yesterday He had rode into Jerusalem declaring Himself King amid crowds of followers who were all convinced that He was the Messiah. That is, all except the ruling hierarchy, the priestly class, and other biblical scholars of the day. They disbelieved even though He had done this on the exact day, which Daniel, more than seven hundred years earlier, had so predicted. The many exact biographical proofs of His claim were also undeniable, as evidenced by the prophecies of Isaiah, Micah, Jeremiah, Ezekiel, and others, with which they should have been well versed. Yet the ruling hierarchy hated Him and rejected His claim, primarily because acceptance of His legitimacy would have weakened their stature and authority. Therefore they sought to kill Him and be rid of the threat. This is why He wept. (Luke 19:41) For even though in His Godly foreknowledge, He knew that this would happen, when it finally became the here and now in His very earthly experience, His great love and sorrow engulfed His human countenance, bringing forth this divine expression of human emotion. His tears were not only because of this unwarranted hatred and rejection, but also because of the terrible and tragic consequence that it would bring to Israel and its people for the next two millennia. We too, who are His, have cause for many tears, because all around us is what seems to be an even greater rejection and hatred of His sacred Being. Were He here today, as the Lamb of God, and the world had its way, there is no doubt that He would be crucified again.

But now it's the next day, and He is walking with his apostles from Bethany back towards Jerusalem, when He sees in the distance the beautiful green fig tree. I suspect that He chose this particular route by divinely appointed foreknowledge so that He could provide this action parable as an instrument of learning for His followers, including us. The tree stood as a symbol of Israel, full of the outward expression of a great God-given religion, but it provided nothing but leaves. There was no fruit. It was totally barren "*. . . for the time of figs was not yet*" *(Mark 11:13)*. Notice in your Bible, the yet is italicized, meaning that it was not in the original manuscript, but was added by the translators to provide clarity. Nevertheless, with our Savior's earthly presence, Israel's time of great decision had come, and they blew it. Now there could be no fruitfulness. Perhaps the "yet" is in a way appropriate anyway as we learn from Daniel 9 and Revelation 7, where we are told that descendants of the twelve tribes will be the first fruits in the final days, just before His second coming, and the beginning of the millennium. But this will not be a renewed, corporate Israel as represented by the fig tree, because Jesus cursed the tree saying "*. . . no man eat fruit of thee hereafter forever*" *(verse 14)*. We are also told in verse 21, that the next morning as they again passed by, the cursed tree had withered away.

Thus the 144,000 who will come from the twelve tribes of Israel in Revelation 7 will not be a renewal of Israel, but will be supernaturally ordained individuals who are to evangelize the world during the seventieth week of Daniel (the tribulation), and they, along with the Jewish remnant who are saved, will all be believers in Jesus as Lord and Savior. We are told in Zechariah 11:10, that they will mourn for Him and shall look upon Him whom they have pierced, eager for His return.

One might wonder why Jesus would curse the tree for not having fruit when the time of the figs was not. It is my understanding that the fig tree bares fruit twice a year and that the first fruit appears before the leaves come. Apparently there weren't any of the first fruits, which could have been ripening as the leaves grew. Could it be stretching the intent of the parable too much to suggest that the tree, that is Israel, having rejected the Messiah, the first fruit of the resurrection, would, therefore, themselves remain a barren tree to be cut down? For it was cut down forty years later, as Jesus predicted, when the temple was destroyed and more than a million were killed during the Roman siege of Jerusalem. Then, there was a final "cutting" when in 131 A.D. Emperor Hadrian destroyed all of Jerusalem, totally dispersed the Jews, and even renamed the country, calling it Palestina from which later came the word Palestine.

Now let us see what else this parable contains which our Lord intended for our benefit. First, our Lord was hungry; He was most hungry for spiritual fruit, which He had every reason to expect from His chosen people. But as was the tree was found to be barren, so were His people Israel totally lacking in spiritual fruit.

He had very little time left, for it was now only two days before He would pay the ultimate price, that great sacrifice of Himself. For this He had been ordained from before the beginning of time. But Jesus lives! And yet He continues to be hungry for spiritual fruit from His own people, even today. Leaves however, contain no spiritual nourishment; only such fruit can satiate His appetite.

It was a fruit tree on which our Lord focused His attention. Christians are also His people, and as such, are also required to be His fruit tree. So during the present dispensation, Christians are to be His fruitful people. In this context, the fig tree here is like the vine in the Gospel of John chapter 15. Just as the unproductive vine is cut down and burned so is the barren fig tree caused to wither and die by His decree. So whether the analogy is a grape vine or a fig tree, if one is to be one of His, then fruitfulness is a basic requirement. In his epistle, for instance, James makes this very clear when he says in chapter 2 verse 20 that ". . . faith without works is dead." We may equate works with fruitfulness, although I perceive fruitfulness as the spiritually evident result of genuine obedience-driven works.

Notice that Jesus didn't curse any other trees which only bear leaves, but only the tree which was ordained to bare fruit and didn't. He had nothing to say about the elm or fir or pine, because they were not fruit bearing trees, nor did they pretend to be so. But Israel was such a pretender as are many today who knowingly, or out of ignorance, pretend to be Christians. They cloak themselves with many leaves that are the outward appearance of faith, but bear none of the fruit, which is the evidence of faith. Isn't it interesting, and also perhaps part of the same full tapestry of God's word, that fig leaves were what Adam and Eve used to try to cover their nakedness? It didn't work for them either. In the context of Israel, it was the Pharisees and scribes and other pious pretenders who had only leaves. In today's world, it is the vast numbers of professors of the faith who are spiritually fruitless that Jesus is analogizing through the fig tree. They follow the signs, but know nothing of the substance of faith. They have strong opinions, but not the faith, for their opinions are the result of hearsay and not from sound doctrine derived from the study of Scripture. There are those, like Mr. Talkative in Pilgrim Progress, who have much to talk about, but are absent of a contrite heart and genuine repentance. All of these produce only leaves. Regret for sinning is not repentance. Criminals seldom repent for their criminal behavior, but all regret the crime for which they were caught, because they were caught.

The great servant of God, Charles Spurgeon points out that where we see leaves, we have the right to expect fruit, as did Jesus. But because the fig, being a special tree where fruit precedes the leaves, he says, "... *so in a true Christian, fruit always takes the precedence of profession.*" He goes further to say, find anyone "... *who is a true servant of God, and before he united himself with the church, or attempted to engage in public prayer, or to identify himself with the people of God, he searched to see whether he had real repentance on account of sin, he desired to know whether he had sincere and genuine faith in the Lord Jesus Christ ...*" Here we have an expression of the way things are supposed to be regarding genuine Christian soul searching and conduct. Of course, Spurgeon was of the age (mid-1800s) of the Philadelphian church, that church about which Jesus had nothing bad to say (Revelation 3:7–13). Therefore this description, typical of genuine Christian procedures and values, was clearly in accordance with scriptural doctrine. Today as we sit smug and complacent in our "lukewarm" church of Laodicea, this expression of true Christianity exists in only a very small number of congregations, and probably most often in but a small remnant of the so-called Christian churches. As told to us by Jesus Himself, in Revelation 3:14–22, there is nothing good about this present day "church" and He will "spew" or vomit it out of His mouth. For us in this age He offers only one hope. In Revelation 3:20–21, having already damned the church, he offers salvation only to those individuals who will overcome the great apostasy, which the church of today represents. Thus there exists in some of the churches, which call themselves Christian, a remnant who will hear His calling and who will bear fruit among a vast forest of leaves, which is representative of the apostate church, the lukewarm church, and the whole of the visible church.

But how can one overcome in such an environment of half-truths and genuine, but cleverly concealed, apostasy as exists in the churches today? The answer, of course, is found in Scripture. Acts 17:11 spells it out most succinctly. We are to do as the Bereans did, for "*. . . they received the word with readiness of mind, and searched the Scriptures daily, whether those things were so.*" How many today in this final church period actually search the Scripture to verify what is preached or otherwise expressed to them regarding God's Word? Not many. Without faithful and dedicated study of Scripture, how can anyone know truth? How can anyone even know whether or not he or she is providing genuine spiritual fruits, the kind for which Jesus hungers, or are simply scattering leaves while believing it's fruit? Through prayerful study of God's word, the Holy Spirit will help anyone who but asks Him to reveal the difference. Again, the beloved Pastor Spurgeon has an inspired remark to say about the professing Christian who provides only leaves.

> *And can it be, that when he hungers after fruit, to call thyself a blood-bought child of God, and yet to live unto thyself! How darest thou, O'barren tree, professing to be watered by the bloody sweat, and digged by the griefs and woes of the wounded Savior—how darest thou bring forth leaves and no fruit? Oh! Sacrilegious mockery of a hungry Savior! Oh! Blasphemous tantalizing of a hungry Lord! That thou shouldest profess to have cost him all this, and yet yield him nothing! When I think that Jesus hungers after fruit in me, it stirs me up to do more for him. Does it not have the same effect on you? He hungers for your good works; he hungers to see you useful. Jesus, the King of Kings, hungers after your prayers—hungers after your anxieties for the souls of others; and nothing ever will satisfy him for the travail of his soul, but seeing you wholly devoted to his cause.*

Don't his words reverberate in the very marrow of your bones and shame you as to the inadequacy of your Christian walk? They do me! But to the world, this kind of talk is not only foolish at the very best, but to most it's offensive and dangerous. So they will, not if, but when, they can, have it completely silenced.

Perhaps we might conclude with this summary observation. Jesus likened the fruitless fig tree to the state of Israel. Their Rabbis and other religious leaders preached hollow and false doctrine and useless rituals, thus providing only decorative leaves. These could not possibly be viewed as acceptable spiritual fruit, for which He hungered and had every right to expect. In cursing the tree, Jesus was saying, enough! It's over with! Nevertheless, through His grace and mercy, He gave them forty more years to repent before He destroyed their temple. Today we find that He has already spewed the present day so-called Christian church out of His mouth, there being nothing in it worthy of His acceptance. But again His grace and mercy have prolonged its existence in order to allow all who would, to hear His knock and come individually to the faith (Revelation 3:20). The rapture will end this current church period. Then finally, His grace and mercy will again manifest repeatedly during the seven plus years after the rapture and before His second coming. During this period, He will restore the opportunity for the Jews to again be fruitful and to finish what He has ordained for them to do, as outlined in Daniel 9. Certain divinely selected of the descendants of the twelve tribes will now profess and evangelize the true faith throughout the world, bearing much fruit by bringing millions of both Jews and Gentiles to salvation. But as Satan through Antichrist, will proceed to destroy the world and kill all converted believers, leaving progressively a hardened population of those who simply will not choose to believe, no matter how compelling the evidence. Then Jesus will again say, "enough," after which the end time will come quickly.

I pray that all who are willing, will achieve a true saving faith, and satisfy Jesus' hunger for fruit so that they will be able to watch these end times proceedings from box seats in God's heavenly mezzanine, instead of fearfully hearing about them much later when they are brought out of Hades to face the final judgment and to be told why their earthly show of only leaves was simply not enough.

—49—

The Bema Seat Blues

In biblical Christian circles, we often hear of the bema seat, the place from which Jesus will judge the lives and works of the redeemed as they enter heaven. The word "bema" does not appear in Scripture. The word was used to identify a raised platform from which Greek orators would speak. It also was a place on which a bench or seat would be placed where an official might sit as judge presiding over, say, the Olympic Games, or other contests. This designation was also used to indicate the place where other types of judgments were rendered. It is said that Pilate sat on a bema seat when he judge Jesus. The Hebrews had such a platform, which is pronounced the same, as is bema, but they spelled it bimah. It was the raised platform in the synagogue on which the rabbi would stand and speak. Jesus probably spoke from such a bimah when He read from Isaiah 61, as recorded in Luke 4:18.

As I have mused about this judgment that will take place in heaven as Jesus sits there on the bema seat, I picture a long table in front of Him, and the newly arrived soul/spirit standing there in humble awe, and in eager anticipation of what Jesus will say. As I visualize it, laid out before Jesus on the table will be the record of every thought action and deed that ever occurred from the moment that person was justified until he or she let out their last breath of mortal life. In this picture, I see Jesus examining every item and judging its quality. Scripture tells us that all of our works will be tried by fire because each will have either a sustaining or a perishable quality. {See 1 Corinthians 3:12–15} The analogy used is that it will be either gold, which can withstand the fire of judgment, or it will be hay and "stubble" which will burn to worthlessness. Those thoughts, actions and deeds that survive Jesus' judgment, the golden ones, will benefit the "winner" throughout eternity and be a determining factor regarding one's position in the eternal hierarchy. Scripture refers to these as crowns or prizes. That image is carried even further when it speaks of some of the "winners" as being kings and priests in the heavenly realm.

All of this can be very exciting to the saved souls, those persons who muse regarding their manner of eternal service to our Lord. However, there are a few things to be aware of before we let our expectations soar too high. First, there is that issue of the quality of our "works." How many of what we ourselves have considered gold worthy, will He judge the same way? Our deceiving and desperately wicked natural hearts do not go away just because God has given us new hearts along with the Holy Spirit to guide us. We very easily quench the Holy Spirit and when we do, the restraint on that natural heart is removed and deception reigns. We don't necessarily rediscover all truth when we allow our new hearts to again dominate. This is especially true if our knowledge of Scripture, God's Holy and inerrant Word, is less than it needs to be to have a clear understanding of just what constitutes the gold verses the hay and stubble kind of works. I believe that even the most astute observer and analyzer of the heart, one who is exceedingly well versed in Scripture will stand in tearful regret and disappointment as to what Jesus will declare regarding his or her works. Scripture tells us there will be tears in heaven. While it does not speak of tears in this context, surely at least a tearful countenance can be expected in the hearts of many who will stand there before Him. Why should there be tears or sadness at this momentous event? We are saved souls! As the body died, the soul entered heaven not Hades! Here we are in front of our precious wonderful Lord and Savior, the one in whom we believed and who delivered us to His eternal presence. How can we possibly ever again have a sad or tearful moment? Perhaps we have here the reasons. There are at least five reasons why we may shed tears:

1. As Jesus' examines our many thoughts, actions and deeds, He will reveal to us what was in our hearts and what motivated us. Works

done out of guilt or out of a desire for earthly praise and recognition, or any other reason that did not come through the empowerment of the Holy Spirit will not survive the fire of judgment. We will see every fault and weakness of our own assessments of our deeds.

2.   Among the "notes" that Jesus has taken, as He observed our lives, will be a list of lost opportunities. How many times did He present us with chances to glorify His name by helping the needy, comforting the sick, and witnessing to seekers, and potential seekers? These were times when we could have earned golden crowns that would have been, but will never, be ours. Surely these will be tearful moments when we see how many opportunities to serve Him, we actually lost.

3.   How often have our prayers been hallow and worthless because they were rote, or hurried, or were offered up to avoid guilt, rather than soul searched expressions of worship, gratitude and a sincere desire for loving communication with Him. Here shame will be mixed with tears.

4.   We are likely to hear a list of unconfessed sins, not only those we carelessly "forgot" but also unknown sins, sin about which we could have and should have known and avoided had we studied and better understood His Word. The Hebrews of old had a special sacrifice just for such sins. They had far more excuses to be unaware of the full spectrum of sins than we have today, given that we have copies of the whole Word of God readily available to everyone in this country.

5.   Then also Jesus will call our attention of the many misappropriations of our money, time and efforts, which we believed, were righteously utilized but instead supported useless causes. The world has assembled innumerable "causes" wonderful sounding agencies to which we are most cleverly induced to contribute out of a sense of decency righteousness and compassion. The professionals who promote these causes are masters in the psychology of guilt. Lacking it is made to seem like sin, and participation, a great virtue. When we respond in great sincerity and love, to these seemingly worthy causes by supplying time, effort and or money, aren't we setting up crowns

for ourselves? Perhaps, if the cause can pass this simple test. Is there clear evidence that Jesus is involved and that His purpose is being served? If He is not involved than neither are there any golden crowns to be had, no matter how sincere and dedicated the effort. For these efforts, hay and stubble is all one should expect to find displayed on the "bema table." Giving to a cause should not be on the basis of need, but only on the basis of Jesus' presence in the activity. We must be extremely careful to discern whether or not the Creator God Jesus is the God that is involved. Many "causes" claim to have Godly merit. One must remember however, that in this world there are many gods being served, and these often are cleverly disguised as God, or even as Jesus. We must be certain that the real biblical Jesus is the God of the cause. This discernment comes only from the prayers and the biblical knowledge of a saved soul.

When we think about this cannot we already feel like crying as we recall and recognize how often we have already failed in these ways?

Scripture also provides another bit of caution regarding this matter when in Revelation 3:11 Jesus tells the people of the church of Philadelphia to "*. . . hold that fast which thou hast, that no man take thy crown.*" Here is evidence that crowns can be lost. This is not speaking of any hay and stubble crowns for these were never real crowns, but it speaks of genuine golden crowns, rewards that have eternal benefit to the soul. Paul speaks of the crown of rejoicing in 1 Thessalonians 2:19 and crowns of righteousness in 2 Timothy 4:8. The crown of life is spoken of in James 1:12 and Revelation 2:10, and Peter speaks of the crown of glory in 1 Peter 5:4. How does that work? If you have genuinely earned an indestructible crown, how can it be lost? Such a crown is real; it may have past God's most severe and righteous test. To say we can lose it is to say that God will take it away, discredit it from our inventory of earned crowns. Why? How can anyone loose a genuine golden crown that one has earned and that belongs to that saved soul?

To put the importance of this into proper perspective, if Jesus' warning didn't do it, look at what Paul says in 1 Corinthians 9:26, 27.

> "*I therefore so run, not as uncertainly; so fight I, not as one that beateth the air; but I keep under my body , and bring it into*

subjection; lest that by any means, when I have preached to others, I myself should be a castaway."

What does Paul mean, becoming a castaway? The Greek word is *adokimos*, which can also mean unapproved, rejected, and worthless. Could anyone such as Paul be judged by God as worthless, rejected, a castaway? Yet we see here that this is exactly what he feared could become of him! In 1 Corinthians 9:24 *"Know ye not that they which run in a race run all, but one receiveth the prize? So run, that ye may obtain."* He speaks of running the race for the prize. He does this also in Philippians 3:14 *"I press toward to mark for the prize . . ."* In Hebrew 12:1 Where he says, *". . . and the sin which doth so easily beset us, and let us run with patience the race that is set before us,"* he again speaks of running with perseverance. Paul is speaking of crowns! He fears loosing his crowns! It's all about crowns! If loosing crowns was that important to Paul, than we should all sit up and take notice! It's not a trivial matter, or the Holy Spirit would not have infused Paul's heart with such concern, nor would He have inserted these admonitions in Scripture for our learning and for our eternal benefit, if only we will understand and appreciate these things.

Realize again that this has nothing to do with salvation. This discussion and Paul's concerns have to do with heavenly rewards for good works. It seems likely that the answer as to how one can loose crowns centers primarily around one word: backsliding! Backsliding I believe can take place under a variety of conditions that result in the loss of a crown or crowns. One such situation might be call pride of grace. There is great vulnerability to this when one has been greatly blessed, such as was Paul. While the only proper response to blessings should be humility and sincere gratitude to our wonderful God, His grace sometimes becomes a source of pride. Perhaps that was what Paul may have feared, given how much he was revered and praised by converts wherever he went. Only God knows just how disastrous this is to ones crowns score, but surely pride and self-esteem, depending on the duration and intensity, can work toward the negating or losing of crowns. In Isaiah 39, chapter 38, we read of Hezekiah's folly. He was a good God-fearing King who was dying of a terminal cancer; God heard his prayers, healing him and granted him fifteen more years. It appears that his humility and gratitude soon tuned into pride of grace and for a short time pride was able to consume him and override his humility. Only God knows what the penalty was in terms of lost crowns.

Weakness in the knowledge of God's Word can lead down many precipitous paths, such as following and being influenced by false teachers whereby crown-loosing backsliding thoughts, actions and deeds can occur. Jesus and each of the writers of the New Testament warned repeatedly of how in the last days there would be false teachers, pastors, and prophets who would deceive with half truths and lies. They would be exceedingly persuasive and able to lull the souls of many to spiritual sleep, or into false beliefs. Some of these would unintentionally do so out of simple ignorance of Scripture. With others it would be deliberate. These evil ones quote Scripture and have the appearances of wisdom, honesty and pious demeanor, yet their messages never ring of a true presentation of what God's word is all about. Those of us who fail to steep ourselves in His word, and fail to discern between truth and half-truth, or cleverly disguised pseudo-truth will surely suffer great loss. If, by virtue of God's infinite mercy and love, such, victimized persons have the faith through which the grace of salvation is confirmed, they are most certainly potential losers of the crowns they may have acquired. It's likely that this is some of what Jesus has in mind when He cautioned the Church of Philadelphia.

The persuasiveness of false teachers combined with exposure and acquiescence to carnal temptations can lead the spiritually weakened into a falling away, a backsliding into any number of thoughts and activities contrary to God's will. This I believe is also what Jesus had in mind when He cautioned His own as He spoke to the Church of Philadelphia. In today's world of abject decadence, Satan seems to be more successful than ever before in bring down in these manners, even the strongest most fruitful saints. I saw this happen to one whom I believe was one of our Lord's most fruitful selfless and dedicated disciples. After being weakened from long days and years of exceedingly faithful service to our Lord, cleaver deceivers surrounded her with many subtle temptations initiating a backsliding that gained momentum, and became almost precipitous. Our Lord in His mercy took her home early, just short of her fifty-first year of life. I believe she acquired a large number of gold crowns, but lost so many in her short period of backsliding that He hastened to take her home, while she yet had a few left.

I could ramble much more on this topic and many good sermons could and should be preached about the subject of crowns, how to earn them and how to lose them, but I doubt that you will ever hear them from the modern pulpit or hardly anywhere else. Instead I'll now complete this paper with some thoughts that Dr. Chuck Missler recently mentioned in one of his weekly discussion regarding the book of Romans. He spoke of the different categories of our earthly conduct that Jesus might consider as we stand before Him at that momentous judgment. To presume that we understand the mind of God sufficiently to know all of His thoughts in this matter is not even remotely suggested. However, Scripture docs give us some clues as to what He will consider of importance. Here are what may be twelve of them:

1. How faithfully persistently and zealously did we apply our God given spiritual gifts in His service? All saved souls have spiritual gifts, which we are to discover and utilize in glorifying His name. We are not speaking here of talents such as musical, oratory, or writing skills. These of course are God-given in the sense that everything we are is from Him. These are not the gifts of the spirit Scripture mentions. As noted earlier, in 1 Corinthians 12, and 1 Peter 4 we find some of these gifts identified. These are the gifts of wisdom, knowledge, healing, prophecy, interpretation, hospitably, charity, administration, and others not as easily identified. We are to search out which of these gifts we have been given and then apply our talents to deliver them up to out Lord through their application.

2. How did we treat other believers? Did we respect and love even those we considered to be the lowliest, weakest and most backslidden? Have we supported them in loving humble friendship, unselfishly, and generously administrating to them and to their needs during their times of great stress?

3. How did we exercise our authority over others? When placed in such authority, did we maintain appropriate Christ-like humility, compassion, generosity and fairness, absent the air of dominance or superiority?

4. How did we use our money? We are accountable for our stewardship of all of God's gifts. The tithe already belongs to Him. Only that given our Lord beyond this constitutes giving. Did we waste our money on trinkets, excessive pleasures and other needless pursuits? Did we carefully determine whether it was a genuine Christ-centeredness in the cause to which gave?

5. How did we spend our time? We are accountable for trivial and nonsensical waste of our time. How vital really were those excursions that preempted or subordinated church attendance, Bible study, serious prayer time, expressing gratitude, worship and communion with Him, and the pursuit of our calling. Our time here is short and He has called each of us into service. He has given us the correct amount of time to do what we have been given to do. If we have wasted it, then we will go before Him with an embarrassing and unconscionable deficiency, about which we will be very ashamed.

6. How much did we suffer for Jesus? That's not just suffering, but suffer for Him? Did we avoid revealing our faith to avoid ridicule, exclusion, abuse or punishment? The world hated Him, and as He said they would also hate His own. This is a difficult task. It seems appropriate that we should not deliberately seek pain and suffering in this cause, but on the other hand, we must not compromise our faith, or our assertion of faith, regardless of the consequences. Daniels' friends did not seek the furnace, but they faced it and chose to suffer it rather than in any way compromise their faith. They should be our role models regarding this matter.

7. Have we chosen the right race to run or the ladder to climb as our life's work, avoiding that which deep down we realize was not the one God chose for us? Did we choose our own path without first seeking His guidance, or did we avoid asking for fear of that to

which we might be directed? This is not about paths chosen before we are saved. However, after having been saved it may very well be that we may be redirected by God, if we will but listen to Him. And listen we must, if we are to truly be His disciples. Not all callings would necessarily require abandoning an established career. It might mean simply re-ordering our after-work priorities into a greater application of our Spiritual gifts.

8.   How effectively have we been in controlling our old nature? It doesn't go away. It remains to tempt and torment. Only through the power of the Holy Spirit, if we will but allow Him, can this old nature be controlled. Satan and the world are continually on the attack cajoling and tempting our souls, seeking to cause backsliding and reducing our effectiveness as disciples. We need the whole armor of God to resist this relentless attack. This armor is not made for attacking, but for standing firm in the faith. We are also to avoid temptations, and when necessary, run from them. The old nature will want to stay and play where deadly covetousness, lust and other temptations surround us. None of us are strong enough to withstand such heat for very long, so run we must!

9.   How many souls have we witnessed to and tried to bring to Christ Jesus? This isn't a "body count" but an effort count. We are not responsible for the result, but only for the effort. But that simple little observation does not get us off the hook entirely. We are responsible for the quality of that effort as well. It's our duty to seek through prayer, Scripture and the Holy Spirit, God-given wisdom, discernment, knowledge and understanding in all matters, so that our efforts will be of the best quality of which we are capable. If we have this, the visible "body count" will not matter as much as will the legacy of future converts that can result from these efforts.

10. How effectively have we reacted to temptation? This is covered fairly well in #8. To reiterate however, we must avoid as much as possible, situations where temptation lurks, and if we stumble into them, we must run away as quickly as possible. Sustained

temptation is almost completely irresistible to the carnal person and we are all carnal as long as the old nature, that deceitful, wicked heart remains. It is with what I believe to be extremely rare exceptions that the old nature ever quits as long as one lives. Avoid and run, and pray every moment as we do so!

11. How faithful have we been to the Body of Christ? In one sense, it is a question of faithfulness to oneself, in that all of the redeemed are part of the Body. We are called to be living active members of the Body of Christ, not just weekly pew warmers or simply participants in church activities. As members of the Body, we each have tasks that must be attended to faithfully. As with the human body, if one of its parts in not fulfilling its assigned tasks the whole body suffers from this deficiency. If your heart, liver, kidney or some other body part isn't working, then we are sick. So it is with the Christian Body. We must each be faithful, active, participating, and persevering members of this Body of Christ if it is to be healthy. Even a cursory look around will tell us, the Body is quite sick in these end times. Let none of us be contributors to that sickness.

12. How faithful have we been to the Word of God? To be faithful to the word of God one must know the word of God. Serious extensive study of Scriptures is the only way to know His Word and thereby become faithful to it! Faithfulness to the Word of God means obedience to His Word. A prerequisite to obedience is to know what constitutes the Word to which we are to be obedient. That requires a strong working knowledge of Scripture. Once a week exposure to pulpit sound bites, and here-say knowledge of scriptural fragments won't do it! It is evident as one fellowships with Christians, that biblical illiteracy is rampant throughout the whole body, with most people not even knowing what essentials there are that they have never even heard of. How can one be faithful to the Word of God when one can't even recognize what it is that one doesn't even know about? Serious Bible study has become almost extinct in many so-called Christian Bodies to the extent that one must fear greatly that the "body" is not a Body at

all, but merely a churchianity club. With this observation, we have crossed over to the professor-possessor issue, that is the problem associated with those who merely profess to have the saving faith as compared to those who actually has such a faith. Where God's Word is not well understood, or erroneously understood because of false or half-truth teachers, doubt confusion and great personal tragedies are inevitable. Without beating on this issue any further, it will suffice it to say that here will be another level of tearful response on the Day of Judgment. This is because there are two judgment seats, the bema seat where Gods own will be judged as to their position in the heavenly places, and the post-millennial placed of judgment, where the lost, who will have been residing in hell, will be assigned their places in the lake of fire, which is in the outer darkness. (Revelation 20:13–15).

Well that is about it. The Bema Seat Blues. Every human being will one day stand before Jesus in judgment. Will it be the Bema seat judgment, or the post-millennium judgment? Will you be receiving your assignment in a heavenly place, or a fiery place? If it is from the Bema seat, will your accumulation of crowns warrant Jesus telling you "Well done my good and faithful servant?" Or will it be from the other place of judgment, from which all will be told something like "Depart from me. I never knew you." It is all up to you. God's grace, and a heavenly place are available to all who genuinely believe in Christ Jesus and His work on the cross.

—50—

Belief Without Salvation

The Bible tells us in many places that belief provides salvation. Here are a few of them:

1. Mark 16:16 *" He that believeth and is baptized shall be saved"*

2. John 1:12 *"But as many as received Him, them gave the power to become the Sons of God even to them that believe on His name."*

3. John 3:15 *"That whosoever believeth in Him should not perish, but have eternal life."*

4. John 3:16 *"God so loved the world that He gave His only begotten Son, that whosoever believeth in Him should not perish but have eternal life."*

5. John 3:36 *"He that believeth in the Son shall have everlasting life . . ."*

6. John 6:47 *"Verily, verily I say unto you, He that believeth on me hath everlasting life."*

7. Romans 10:9 *"That if thou shalt confess with thy mouth, the Lord Jesus, and shall believe in thine heart that God hath raised Him from the dead, thou shalt be saved."*

In Ephesians 2:8, 9 we find another and perhaps the most salient and singularly comprehensive of all explanations of how salvation is provided. It tells us, *"For by grace are ye saved through faith, and that not of yourselves: it is the gift of God: not of works, lest any man should boast."* According to Greek linguists, the "and not of yourselves" as written in the Greek clearly refers to grace only and not to faith.

Therefore, salvation is a gift of God's grace, which can be received only through faith.

Relating this to the seven other Scriptural references above, we see that faith and belief in the biblical sense are so closely related to God's intended meaning that they are interchangeable. In fact, they come from the same Greek word *pisteuo,* which means both to have faith and to believe. Therefore, our salvation is seen to rest on the reality and genuineness of what within us we call our faith or belief. What each of us has which represents our faith or belief is valid from a salvation perspective *only,* if our definition is in strict conformance with God's definition. This is not negotiable. It is not a matter of your opinion being as good as mine. God's opinion is the only relevant one, and can only be found by a Spirit-led search of His Word. What I write here is only of consequence to the degree that it stimulates a need in you to do this, and that it helps you find what God wants you to know, to practice, and to be, if you are to have certainty that you are one of His. You can hope, feel, dream, rationalize, and believe anything you want, but nothing counts except God's definition and your genuine application and adherence to it.

Jesus, and later the apostles, warn us many, many times, as recorded in Scripture, to beware of lies, deceit and false professors of the faith who will, if possible, lead you away from God's truth and into damnation. Remember Satan is the greatest of all deceivers. All false religions are the expressions of his great innovative power to deceive. Every variety of these religions has as its head at least one of the fallen angels or evil spirits. These are the principalities and powers as spoken of in Scripture. They have the power to perform miracles, to a limited but sufficient degree, to impress and keep under control those who succumbed to their particular lie.

But I believe that Satan's greatest achievement, the one for which he is most proud and pursues with the greatest vigor and delight, is the misleading of the would-be genuine Christian believers from a true and saving faith. He does this in a number of ways, but primarily by means of perverting Christian doctrine through his insertion of slight doctrinal deviations and falsehoods into the visible church. Examine church history and you will find that denial, avoidance, discouragement, or prohibition of the study of the Bible has been a major element in his strategy to prevent those seeking the Way from obtaining salvation. Without biblical literacy, one becomes easy prey for his army of deceivers and false teachers. Those who prevent salvation are everywhere; their spiritual poison and half-truths are being spewed on radio, TV, in books and magazines, and from many pulpits. Their versatility is boundless and has but one goal, to cause one to believe that he or she has a saving faith when, in fact, it is a false faith. The "white washed" persona and demeanor of those who lead souls away from the truth, and their clever, learned, pious, and articulate delivery of Satan's deceit, are very persuasive to the biblically ignorant or naive, as it well must be to be effective for Satan's cause. They are personable, intelligent, eminently believable and sometimes even humble in appearance. They are extremely clever and disarming when they quote Scripture, which they know, but don't really believe. This is where they score most, that is, in the subtleties of those slight twists in the context of the Word. This, by stealth, leads the victims into false understanding and tragic consequences. The outbreak of new "easier to understand" and "dynamically equivalent" but cleverly modified versions of the Bible only add confusion and serve as additional entry points for even more deception. The only defense there is against this onslaught is prayer and Scripture. Pray that the Holy Spirit will be your guide to the genuine truth found only in Scripture. Through Paul in Acts 17:11 the Holy Spirit tells us to receive the Word with readiness of mind, but to *search* the *Scriptures* daily to see if these things were so. In other words, don't take anyone's word for it but find out for yourself. This isn't easy, but your eternal destiny depends on it.

There is one more aspect of Satan's strategy, which is outstandingly effective in these latter days of the "lukewarm" Laodicea church. It is blatantly evident that DIVERSION is its name. Jesus points this out in Revelation 3:17 where He describes exactly who we are today as a society and as a "Church." He says, *"Because thou sayest I am rich and increased with goods, and have need of nothing; and knowest not that thou art wretched, and miserable and poor and blind and naked."* There is a great deal that could be said about this particular observation about our times which Jesus shares with us, but in terms of the issue at hand, the following will suffice. Although true in this country as compared to the rest of the world, it is doubtful that anyone reading this considers himself or herself rich. But actually, we are all "rich" in the availability of diversions which have been especially provided by Satan's agents to tempt us and keep us, to the fullest extent possible, diverted from Jesus and His Word. Twenty-four hours a day, amusement and entertainment face us wherever we are. Who can resist attractive, all persuasive diversions? Only those who have decided that eternal salvation, and a life of gratitude and obedience to Him who saves, can overcome such a snare. Through the power of the Holy Spirit residing within "just say no," and instead choose minimal involvement in what the world offers.

Now back to this issue of belief as it relates to salvation. First, we must note that in accordance with Romans 15:4, *all* things found in Scripture are for our learning. It is nice to find simple Scriptural verses we like and apply them to our lives. But it is vital that they be understood and applied in the context of the entire Word. Otherwise, we risk misapplying them. Picking and choosing what we like in Scripture and discarding or ignoring what we don't like, or what seems unfair, difficult, or unpleasant—is not a choice for one who is redeemed or is seeking redemption. If achieving salvation is your goal, then taking any or all of the seven verses listed on the first page—and adopting them as your main basis for believing that you're saved without knowing the full extent of what they signify and what is inferred in them, is an extremely dangerous path to follow. With that in mind, what else is relevant to achieving the salvation, which Scripture tells us, is there to aide us in understanding and biblically applying the message given in the eight references noted at the beginning of this paper? Here are a few such verses to ponder and learn from:

1. Matthew 22:14 is where Jesus tells us *"many are called, but few are chosen."*

441

2. Philippians 2:12 *". . . work out your own salvation with fear and trembling."*

3. 2 Corinthians 13:5 *"examine yourselves whether ye be in the faith, prove your own selves."*

4. James 2:26 *"For us the body without the spirit is dead, so faith without works is dead also."*

5. John 14:23 *"Jesus said unto them, 'If a man love me, he will keep my words; and my Father will love him, and we will come unto him, and make our abode with him.'"*

6. 1 Corinthians 15:1–2 *". . .I declare unto you the Gospel which I preached unto you which also ye are saved if you keep in memory what I preached unto you unless ye have believed in vain."*

7. Hebrews 3:6 *"but Christ as a Son over His own house; whose house we are if, we hold fast the confidence and rejoicing of the hope firm to the end."*

8. 1 Corinthians 1:23 This tells us we are saved, *"if ye continue in faith grounded and settled and not moved away from the hope of the Gospel"*

9. 2 Peter 1:10 *"Wherefore the rather, brethren, give diligence to make your calling and election sure-"*

10. Luke 13:5 *"I tell you, 'Nay', but except ye repent, ye shall all likewise perish."*

11. 2 Peter 3:9 This verse tells us that the Lord is *". . . not willing that any should perish, but that all should come to repentance."*

*All emphasis is mine

Now what do we do with this? Here are eleven references relating salvation where the word "belief" is not even mentioned, except for one reference to non-belief. Of the eight references cited on the first page, only Ephesians 2:8–9 mentions faith. The remaining seven speak only of belief as the way to salvation. There is *nothing* in the Holy Bible, as it was given to the writers in the original languages, which is not God-breathed and inerrant. The eight statements are, therefore, true but so also are the eleven referenced above. Therefore, the eleven in no way contradict the eight, so the latter must be there to add clarity and to amplify what God means by "belief." Let us see how to apply this by taking each of the eleven verses individually.

Matthew 22:14 *"Many are called but few are chosen"* That should be disturbing to all of us because we know that Jesus died so as to take away *all* the sins of the world. However, this verse tells us that while many are called, not *all* are called. Some are so hardened of heart that God, in His foreknowledge, finds it pointless to make this specific call.

Romans 1:24–32 speaks of a variety of incorrigible sinners and irreconcilable believers of Satan's lie. It says, *"God gave them up unto their sins."* Of course, because of God's mercy, the door was and is always open to repentance, but it may be concluded that a large percentage of these "given up unto their sins" were among those not called. Then we have the many who are called but are not chosen. Why? It is because they do not come to a saving faith. They are numbered among the many professors of the faith who heard the call but who never become possessors of the faith, even though they believe they are saved. Perhaps some are among what has been estimated to be 90 percent of those who simply repeat the sinner's prayer of belief in church, or answer the "altar call" at some service or revival meeting, but are never again heard from in terms of showing any trace of a changed life or other evidence of a saving faith. There are also those who have heard and accept the theme of the seven verses listed on the first page, but who have never sufficiently probed their depth of meaning to determine just what a saving belief really is. This verse simply attests to the fact, as Scripture reveals in many places that saved souls are only a remnant number of the total population, even of those "called." The army of false teachers, half-truth purveyors and other agents of the great deceiver make certain of this.

Philippians 2:12 *". . . work out your own salvation with fear and trembling."* This verse is a bit controversial. It doesn't mean that we can obtain salvation through any work of our own. I believe it means to look deep into ourselves, our belief, our conduct, and most of all our motives for what we think, speak and do, and to carefully examine them to see if they are spiritually genuine. We are to do this with "fear and trembling" because what we might find may not be what we expected or wanted to find. Of course, if we are ignorant of the true nature of what we are looking for, the knowledge of which comes only from knowledge of His Word, we may not even be able to correctly assess what we do find. So how can we know if we really believe?

2 Corinthians 13:5 *"Examine yourselves whether ye be in the faith, prove your own selves."* This is essentially the same message as in Philippians 2:12, except that it now urges us to prove to ourselves that we have saving faith or belief. This obviously implies some relevant knowledge of Scripture, along with a willingness and ability to apply it, because without such knowledge and action, where else and how else can there be any genuine proof of anything, especially the effectiveness and quality of one's belief?

James 2:26 *"For as the body without the spirit is dead, so faith without works is dead also."* Here we are introduced to another element essential in determining the means of salvation. If we are to take, for example, the John 3:16 verse of the seven "believe verses" and apply James 2:26, we must conclude that somehow "works" is buried in, or implied in, the word "believe." Otherwise, James 2:26 is only pointless rhetoric, which of course, it is not. Works, if they are in accordance with God's will—done for His sake, out of love for Him, and totally without desire for any personal credit or reward—are evidence of a saving belief. Works of any kind that have any less purity of thought or purpose are not works of a living faith. Those who consider themselves true believers must always look carefully into the motives which govern their actions to see if they are that pure. James' message is that works don't save, but righteous works are an integral part of our salvation "package" and express evidence thereof.

John 14:23 *Jesus said unto them, if a man love me, he will keep my words: and my Father will love him, and we will come unto him, and make abode with him."* WOW!! Here is another ingredient that must be added to the broth that we must drink to be saved. Therefore, love is not a separate ingredient but an integral part of belief. Why must this be so? Because Scripture tells us, at least seven times as indicated on page 55 that we are saved through belief. To have heard it but once from God's inerrant Word would have been enough to know this. But now Jesus says that if you *love Him and keep His Word*, He and the Father will love you and live in you in the Spirit. We know from many scriptural verses that at the moment of salvation, the Father and Son, through the Holy Spirit, come to permanently dwell in the saved soul; and that without the indwelling of the Holy Spirit, there is no salvation. Notice also the phrase, ". . . and will keep my Words" in this verse. What is His Word? It is the Holy Bible, *every* word of it. What does "keep my Words" mean? It means not just having a Bible on you table or simply carrying it around Bill Clinton-style. It means obeying; and "keeping," means to trust and obey. How can you possibly do this unless you read it, study it, and then live by it? So here we have another facet of the precious gem of belief revealed to us. By the way, this verse is specifically an elaboration of Mark 16:16 which states, *"He that believeth and is baptized, shall be saved."* Baptism here does not relate to sprinkling or dunking into water, because this is not a requirement for salvation. This baptism refers to the moving in, the indwelling, of the Holy Spirit which accompanies a saving belief (Acts 2).

1 Corinthians 15:1, 2 *". . . I declare unto you the Gospel which I preached unto you which also ye are saved if you keep in memory what I preached unto you unless ye have believed in vain."* Here again is another facet of understanding of that precious jewel we call belief. The Gospel! Believing in Jesus means believing the Gospel with absolute and uncompromising certainty, and with every fiber of our being. What is the Gospel? It is the "good message." It is the fact that Jesus died for our sins, was buried, and rose again on the third day, all according to the Scripture (1 Corinthians 15:3). This is the entire foundation on which Christianity is based. It represents and makes possible the entire purpose of God's creation. Absent this truth, there is nothing worth believing from a spiritual perspective. Absent this truth, all belief is in vain and the Bible is nothing but a weird history book. However, the Gospel is truth, and belief in it is a requirement for salvation.

But what is the "believed in vain" part all about? The clue here is the preceding phrase, "if you keep in memory what I preached unto you." This is very important because it speaks precisely to the tragic failure by many who will take the belief verses on page 429 as the major basis for assuming they are saved, without ever pursuing Scripture to really understand the full meaning of a saving belief. Here, Paul speaks to the Corinthians' need to first understand fully what they believe and then to hold firmly to their belief in truth. Otherwise, if that initial acceptance gives way to unbelief, they have believed in vain. This is a tremendous problem in today's lukewarm church.

Heb 3:6 ". . . *but Christ as a Son over His own house, whose house we are if we hold fast the confidence and rejoicing of the hope firm to the end.*" This tells us that we are of His house that is, saved *if* we hold fast to the end. This is similar to the "keep in memory" phrase we found in 1 Corinthians 15:1, 2, and is again a conditional statement often repeated in Scripture, such as in Hebrews 2:1, 3:14, 4:16, 7:25, 10:34–38, 12:1–4 and 12:14. It is also emphasized by Jesus in John 8:31, as well as in the context of "overcoming" as stated in Revelation 2:7, 11, 17, 25–26 and Revelation 3:5, 11–12, 21. All of these should be telling us loudly and clearly that a saving belief is intimately and conditionally involved with continuance, perseverance and overcoming. This verse makes it clear that being part of God's household (being saved) depends on having a living, persevering faith. Further development of this issue may be found in the verses which follow, that is, in Hebrews 3:7 and 4:13. From the perspective that the "belief verses" on page 429 can stand alone, this should provide serious cause for concern regarding how many more "conditional clauses" there are in our Savior's contract with those He would save.

1 Corinthians 1:23 tells us we are saved. "*. . . If ye continue in faith grounded and settled and not moved away from the hope of the Gospel . . .*" This verse is a reinforcement and punctuation of Hebrews 3:6 and several other Scriptural verses that carry the same message. A genuine believer is one who is born-again and, as such, necessarily carries the human responsibility to be and to continue to be, grounded in the faith. That is, the believer is to remain unmoved

in his or her dedication to the Gospel. If one is a believer, it is the Gospel in which he or she believes.

2 Peter 1:10 *"Wherefore the rather, brethren, give diligence to make your calling and election sure."* Here Peter is speaking to brethren, to those who are already saved. Therefore, the validity of their belief is already established. While not specifically related to our subject, it is sage advice to those who seek confirmation and perfection in their spiritual journey. This wisdom is developed in the preceding verses 4 through 9 where Peter describes the believer's attributes and virtues that demonstrate the sureness of one's calling. We are not to take our faith and salvation for granted. We must continue to the end and to evidence it by working persistently to perfect our spiritual qualities toward the likeness of Jesus.

Luke 13:5 *"I tell you, nay, but except ye repent, ye shall all likewise perish."* Finally, we come to what may be the most avoided and disturbing word in the whole lexicon of Christian verbiage. REPENT! That was John the Baptist's message as the herald for the coming of Jesus the Messiah. Of itself, as defined in common language, it is by no means scary or offensive. It simply means to change one's mind or turn around a belief. But it is far far, more than that in the biblical sense. It means to turn away from evil ways and to turn towards Christ, and through Him, turn to God the Father. But to do that, one must fully realize that he or she is a hopeless sinner, incapable of self redemption and, therefore, in dire need of not only a savior, but of the one and only Savior, Christ Jesus. Repentance is a decision to turn from sin, to seek salvation through the total unequivocal acceptance of Christ as Savior as well as Lord, and to thereby strive to be obedient to His teachings. Repentance is a change of lords, for there are only two: the lordship of Christ or the lordship of Satan. There are no other choices, no matter how vigorously one might protest that fact. All beliefs other than Bible-based Christianity are under Satan's lordship. Repentance is a free decision of the will on the part of the sinner, and sinner is a category in which we all exist. The decision to repent is made possible by the enabling power of grace given to anyone who hears, turns from sin, and believes the Gospel. In light of this, to believe that a saving belief is merely some dubious form of trust in Jesus as Savior is clearly inadequate. Jesus *demands* repentance. To define a saving faith in any way that does not require a radical break with sin is a tragic distortion of the biblical meaning of redemption. For there to be a saving faith, there must be repentance. This is confirmed in Mark 1:15, Luke 13:3–5, Acts 2:38, Acts 3:19 and Acts 11:21. One would be well advised to study these verses to confirm the biblical meaning and importance of repentance as it relates to salvation.

2 Peter 3:9 tells us that the Lord is *". . . not willing that any should perish, but that all should come to repentance."* Notice that here, as well as above in Luke 13:5, one's choice is simply to repent or perish. From this we must conclude that repentance is no less a requirement for salvation than is belief, faith, trust, obedience or love. In fact, in the biblical sense, repentance may be said to incorporate each of these. Otherwise, how can a genuine repentance, the turning completely toward Jesus, be lacking any of these attributes? The word "perish" here is the alternative to repentance. It is, of course, also what happens to one who is not saved. Perish does not mean ceasing to exist. It means spending all of eternity in Gehenna, the lake of fire, which is in the outer darkness (Revelation 20:13–14).

To summarize what this paper's title indicates and has attempted to convince, there can be belief without salvation. In fact, it is most likely that belief without salvation is far more prevalent than a saving faith. Belief, which results in salvation, is a belief that has a definition that includes many more specific conditions than most people who claim a saving belief ever realize. There is no salvation unless one believes the Gospel that is that Jesus died for our sins was buried and was raised from the dead exactly as Scripture says it happened. There is no salvation unless one's belief includes the fact that we are all hopelessly sinful and cannot be cleansed of sin in any other way but through Jesus. Jesus said on the cross *tetelisti,* which means not only "it is finished" but also means "paid in full." Good works and a seemingly immaculate life can do nothing towards salvation beyond that which Jesus has already done. These good works and spotless life can only enhance one's position in the eternal order. For those saved, it means greater blessings in Heaven. For those unsaved, it reduces the severity of Hell to some degree. Repentance must be of the heart as well as of the mind. Repentance, and all that it implies, must begin in the mind and move down toward the heart. But because "the heart is deceitful above all things and desperately wicked" (Jeremiah 17:9), it cannot take root there but only in the new heart which is given to everyone the moment he or she truly receives that saving faith. Absent the new heart, what may seem to be repentance can never settle in and will soon dissolve, leaving an even more strident heart.

Obedience to God's Word as He told us in John 14:23 is also an essential manifestation and evidence of salvation. It makes no sense for us to believe that we have obtained salvation as long as we choose to continue in sin, contrary to His commandments to "sin no more." Of course, with that hopelessly deceitful heart remaining in competition with the new heart, we will continue to sin, but to an ever lesser degree as we continue to gain strength from the new heart and from the Holy Spirit who dwells therein. John 14:23 speaks of keeping His Word. Do you know His Word? How well do you know it? How well you keep it necessarily depends on how well you know it. How well you know it depends on how well you sincerely study it *directly* from the source, the Holy Bible. Remember, false teachers abound *everywhere and are eager to mislead.*

Salvation of one's immortal soul is infinitely more important than anything else to be accomplished during this physical life. Ephesians 2:8 tells us that it is a gift from God, given by His grace through our faith. But nowhere does Scripture say that salvation is free. Of course, there is nothing we can do to earn it, much less pay for it, but most certainly there is much we must do as our part in the process. What we are obligated to do is found in the word "belief," which is the same as faith. This word is loaded with far more meaning than most people realize. To be secure in our salvation, we must know all we can about what that "load" consists of. I beg you not to presume or assume, but to know that your salvation is secure. Only through genuine study of His Word, under the guidance of the Holy Spirit, will you ever really know what a genuine saving belief is, and whether or not you have it.

There is no doubt that almost as many who read this will take issue with at least some of what is written. If I have stretched meanings or misinterpreted God's Word, I sincerely welcome correction. If what is written is slightly more strict than a reasonable interpretation, it is deliberate because it is far more beneficial to err in that direction than to err the other way, especially when one's eternal future depends on it. I pray that if you err, it will be in that same direction by giving our Lord 200 percent of what you believe He expects of you, and then pray that that is enough.

—51—

Making a Case for Salvation

As I begin to write, I look at this title and ask myself what and why? At this moment, I have no ideas about what to write. The "why" I think I do know, but the "what" is not yet clear to me. The "why" is because I believe that I have been instructed to do so. I got up at 3:00 A.M. this morning as I always do every Monday, Wednesday and Friday in order to pray, discuss things with my Lord, and to do some of the natural protocols which I started more than nine years ago and through which He healed me from a rapidly growing terminal cancer, which was to have ended my life in less than a year. This morning the very first thought to enter my mind was clear as a bell. It was simply, "Make a case for salvation."

I pray continually for His wisdom and discernment and am often rewarded with answers regarding many issues, and especially those regarding biblical questions. The answers come to me often days and sometimes weeks after I have asked them. Many of my previous papers have been written through similar persuasions as this. However, this seems to be the first time that His prompting came without a clue as to what He wants me to write.

Perhaps it was foolish of me to reveal this very precious and personal part of my life. We all, as Christians realize that God, through the Holy Spirit speaks to His sons and daughters, but we believe so more in the abstract than the actual recognizable events. When someone we know tells us that God speaks to him or her, and here is what He said, we look askance and tend to doubt the validity of the claim. We conclude that surely, it must be all in his or her heads. I pray in this case, as with all that I write about, you judge the message, whatever it will be, and not the messenger, or how he came by the message. The truth is always in Scripture, and there only. Please go into it to confirm or refute what follows if you question, doubt or seek to know more about this supremely vital subject.

What is salvation? It is what you have as a result of having been saved. Saved from what? It's not saved from drowning or any physical circumstance. It is strictly a spiritual matter. If someone saves you from drowning or from a fire, you don't consider yourself as now having salvation. It is only when we speak of lost souls being saved that we call the result salvation. Many don't believe that there is such a thing, or that it is even needed. Others believe that they have it because they are more "good" than "bad." Still others "feel" they have salvation in that they decided to call themselves "Christians" even though they have only the vaguest notion of what it means. Also, there are some who believe that somehow souls move on to "higher or lower levels" until they achieve some permanent status, having nothing to do with salvation, but instead with repeated reincarnations.

As one examines various religions and beliefs, it's amazing how many different ones there are. Yet all of them that believe in an after life, excluding biblical Christianity, share a common theme, and that is, that a life of good works will get you to "that better place." This also applies to the many variations of "Christianity," again, except what must be called biblical Christianity, that is faith, which is derived from a direct understanding of Scripture with nothing added or taken away.

Salvation in accordance with Scripture in the true Christian faith, results in an eternity in the heavenly places with our Creator. It can be obtained in only *one way*, and that is by His grace through faith in Jesus. This faith must be an unshakable, unqualified belief that Jesus suffered on the cross for our sins, died, was buried, was resurrected, and ascended to heaven, all in accordance with Scripture. This salvation is the free gift from God available to everyone, who by such faith accepts Jesus as Lord and Savior. It is *not* the result of any good works. However, the act of acceptance includes far more than acquiescence, or an intellectual acknowledgement of His deity and the truth of the Gospel. There are many who claim this alone is adequate evidence as to the achievement of salvation. But this is false teaching! Until this Gospel truth penetrates the heart, and the very marrow of every bone, it must remain suspect! Until one's heart and soul has repented, confessed every known sin and having done so with a contrite heart and broken spirit, nothing has been accomplished in the way of salvation. Many "violently" disagree with this, but Scripture tells us "that the heart is deceitful above all things and desperately wicked: who can know it?"(Jeremiah 17:9) This is true of yours as well as mine, whether we like it or not, or believe it or not. Because the heart is so deceitful, that none are capable of knowing it, how can anyone know even his or her own heart? Therefore to know with certainty that the true salvation providing faith is surely in the heart, one must be watchful and circumspect of ones heart and soul and mind over a period of time, and especially through testing situations in order to be certain that it be so.

The thief on the cross is invariably the "great escape" from this time and evidence dependant premise. Because there was no recorded accumulation of time dependant evidence from which one might draw any conclusions as to the thief's faith, this episode is often used to justify the adequacy of a "just in time," just before death sufficiency of an expression of faith. This seems to prove, at least to some, that simply mouthing the sinner's prayer, and at that moment feeling a belief, is sufficient for salvation. Let us examine the situation of the thief for a moment to see if this is a safe conclusion. Only in Luke do we learn of this event. Here in chapter 23 verses 39–43, we read the following: "And one of the malefactors which were hanged railed on him, saying, If thou be Christ, save thyself and us. But the other answering rebuked him, saying, Dost not thou fear God, seeing thou art in the same condemnation? And we indeed justly; for we receive the due reward of our deeds: but this man hath done nothing amiss. And he said unto Jesus, Lord, remember me when thou comest into thy kingdom. And Jesus said unto him, Verily, I say unto thee, Today shalt thou be with me in paradise."

Here we find in these few short words from the thief:

1. A fear of God

2. A recognition and confession of his sinful justly condemned life.

3. An admission that Jesus is God

4. An acknowledgment of Jesus as Savior who had the ability to forgive, and of his own need for deliverance from sin.

5. A solid understanding that Jesus was innocent, that this was innocent blood being shed on the cross

6. An acceptance of physical death along with recognition that there was another "life" to come

7. A belief that even through this was God beside him, and therefore had the power to save His physical life if He chose to, did not do so for reasons the thief may not have understood, but did not question or challenge, but accepted through faith

All of these obviously heartfelt thoughts were converted into spoken words while the thief was dying in excruciating pain, worse than any of us can imagine. It was hardly a time when one would casually reminisce or engage in intellectual discussions or even think to connive. It was a time when only what is truly in the heart cries out. Furthermore, we are not told of what may have gone on in this thief's life before he was caught and sentenced. He may very well have heard about Jesus and perhaps knew of his miracles and teachings, and may even have been coming around to believing on Him much earlier. The fact that he so firmly attested to Jesus' innocence seems to suggest some prior knowledge of Him. Lastly, this was *Jesus* next to him, the only one who can judge any heart, and He judged him both by his confession, and the heart from which it came. Based on the above, it would seem that anyone who uses the story of the thief on the cross to justify, rationalize, or excuse themselves from any other portion of scriptural instruction as to the nature and means of salvation is on very dangerous ground.

No case regarding salvation could possibly be considered adequate without a discussion of its most important element and strongest evidence of its genuineness. That most precious ingredient is love. Jesus tells us that the greatest commandment is that, "Thou shall love the Lord your God with all of your heart and with all thy soul and with all thy mind" (Matthew 22:36). In John 13:34 and 15:12 Jesus adds, "A new commandment I give you, that ye love one another as I have loved you." In John 4:19 we learn that "We love Him, because He first loved us." And in 1 John 4:16 that ". . . we have known and believed the love that God hath to us. God is love; and he that dwelleth in love, dewelleth in God and God in him." Also in 1 John 4:7, 8 we are told simply to ". . . love one another; for love is of God; and every one that loveth is born of God and knoweth God. He that loveth not knoweth not; for God is love." Paul devotes all of chapter 13 in 1 Corinthians to describing love and how without it we have nothing. In the last verse of that chapter he says, "now abideth faith, hope and love, these three; but the greatest is love." To quote the Holy Spirit through John again we find in 1 John 3:10 ". . . whosoever doeth not righteousness is not of God neither he that loveth not his brother," and in verse 14 ". . . we know that we have passed from death into life, because we love the brethren. He who loveth not his brother abideth in death." So what is the theme here? It is simply that without a genuine love for God and for fellow Christians *there is no salvation*! This doesn't mean that this love is fully manifested at the instant one receives salvation, but the trail of the truly born-again Christian, that is one who has salvation, will be unmistakably marked with ever growing evidence of this Godly agape love. Just as the moon's light exists only in so far as it is able to reflect the sun's light, so is our love a mere refection of God's love. That is part of what is meant by "We love Him, because He first loved us." Any real love is but a reflection of His love. There exists only one real love, that is God's love. We are incapable of generating real love from within ourselves. We, at best, are only capable of reflecting the love that God provides us. That is why He had to love us first before we could love Him. The dross on silver does not reflect. Remove the dross from the silver, and we have a perfect mirror. The dross (sin) on our souls causes that lack of reflectablity of love. Through faith our sin (the dross) is wiped clean. This now allows the cleanliness, the shining reflectively of the transformed souls to receive and reflect back God's love toward Him and towards each other. It would seem therefore, based on the referenced Scripture that this love is the greatest manifestation and evidence of a changed life and the saved soul.

We should not confuse this genuine Godly love with the so-called love within our human nature. This love is, for the most part, a conditional or an erotic love, not a Godly love. Even so, our Creator did impart into every soul a limited capacity for some measure of His love. This is most strikingly manifested in a mother's love. However, God's love in the redeemed heart far exceeds this love, because it necessarily expresses itself even to one's mortal enemies. No human love absent of God's input can possibly attain that quality.

Some additional evidences of the attainment of the new heart that ushers in salvation are first, the acknowledgement that one is a hopelessly condemned sinner whom no one but Jesus can save. There must be this admission along with repentance, a total change of mind and heart regarding one's belief and how life is to be lived. Also, one must grow more and more to hate sin. What is sin? It is everything contrary to God's word. What is God's word? One must read and study the whole Scripture to truly know. Next, one must confess to God all known sins and be ashamed and deeply regret them because they have offended our Creator. One must pray to God for forgiveness and strive to sin no more, although the very best anyone can do at first is to sin less and less. God commands in Matthew 5:48, "Be ye therefore perfect, even as your Father which is in heaven is perfect." Therefore, this *must* be our goal and nothing less. Throughout this process there should be a growing awareness that the Holy Spirit is working within the heart, that there is an increasing faith in Jesus, and that there is a growing love for God and for others. There must also be an ever-growing increase in a sensitivity to sin, along with a strengthening of a resolve to overcome one's sinful ways. A personal commitment to, and an on going relationship with Christ is an essential by product of salvation.

All of this is not to say that salvation did not enter the soul immediately upon ones acceptance of the truth of the Gospel. But if it did, then the things noted above must by necessity have followed, and are continuing. If not, then one should not let the matter rest, but examine one's faith and heart to see what is wrong. This is a profound point! Complacency where salvation is concerned should never be acceptable! To continue in ignorance and apathy can literally be the kiss of death, eternal death!

These are not pleasant words, but neither is hell. We have all grown up in a society that shuns unpleasantness and avoids difficult situations. We have been conditioned to always choose to see "the bright side of things" to be positive, optimistic, and to "see the cup half full not half empty." All these things are fine "in the world." If you are seeking to be not of this world, but only temporarily in the world while Jesus prepares a place for you in heaven, then *real* reality must be faced, and it exist *only* in the spiritual world. The way to become part of it is revealed to us only in the Holy Bible, and through its prescription for salvation. Anyone seeking it elsewhere, regardless of how logical or persuasive it may have been presented, is doomed to disappointment, as well as just doomed, as in not going to heaven.

Above, I said that real reality exists only in the spiritual realm. This may sound crazy, but, even "cutting edge science" today recognizes that we live in a "virtual reality," in a simulation of some sort. This becomes less than ridiculous even to the layman, when we recognize the nature of atoms, the particles of which all matter consists. We know that every atom is made up of a "solid" sun-like nucleus surrounded by planet-like electrons. Each atom, therefore, has a ratio of millions-to-one of empty space as compared with a "solid" substance. So we can rightly say that there is far more of "nothing" than of "something" in every substance, even our own bodies. If we add to this the fact that "science" now realizes that there exist at least ten dimensionalities of which we know only four, with time being the fourth, we can see how they might conclude that we live in a "virtual" reality rather than in a reality of actual substance. With this in mind, we can also imagine how Jesus, in His resurrected body, now in control of all these other dimensions of the real reality, could walk through walls and ascend "weightlessly" into the clouds. Hebrew history tells us that the great twelfth century sage Nachmonides somehow deduced the existence of these ten dimensions simply from the first verses in Genesis. This seems incredible, yet was well documented centuries before "science" even remotely considered such a thing. This is just another small attestation to the super natural origin of Scripture. Consider one more thought. How does, say seventy compare with a seven having a billion zeros after it? It is evident that the seventy is comparatively infinitesimal, truly negligible. Yet the seven with a billion zeros after it is infinitesimal compared to eternity. So then, how does eternity compare to a normal human life-span of seventy years?

Does all of this seem to be one of my excursions away from the main topic? Perhaps, but here is my point. "Science" has stumbled onto a legitimate fact. We do live in a virtual reality here on earth. It is a temporary simulation which God created for His own sovereign purpose some six thousand years ago, and which He said He would end some time in the future. The only real reality is God and the spiritual world in which He exists and which was from eternity past to eternity future. He created this earthly proving ground for us, this simulation where our fleshly bodies exist to house the only real reality that is our individual immortal souls. The seventy years or so we have here on earth in a virtual reality is infinitesimal compared to the eternity that is before us. As noted, Scripture tells us that this earth is temporary and will one day be discontinued. Immortal is that which will continue on forever into eternity. But God has also told us that He will create a new real heaven and earth, which will continue forever, and in which those "made in His image" will eternally dwell. Here, finally is the point! NONE, not one of us is made in His image unless and until we receive SALVATION! Salvation can be said to be that "peace which passeth all understanding," for in the Greek, the word for peace in this verse is *eirene* which can mean being at one again with Him! God cannot, will not accept sin into His reality, His eternity. Salvation is the condition of the soul-spirit that is free of sin, and it is arrived at in only ONE way, through the cleansing authority of the blood shed at the cross by Jesus Christ our Lord and Savior. While salvation opens the gate to eternal heaven, God has prepared another place for those who choose not to receive salvation by this singularly ordained means. It is also an eternal place, but one which no one in his or her right mind, and capable of understanding, would choose. Most who will go there will not go by his or her choice to do so, but by his or her failure to accept salvation, as God, through the Word, has offered it.

The dictionary tells us that salvation is defined as a source of preservation or rescue. In terms of God's plan as manifest in Scripture, this definition applies equally well in the spiritual context. One who has received salvation has been rescued and preserved from an otherwise inevitable and eternal damnation. Salvation brings the blotting out of all of one's sins and transgressions of the past, present and future. It brings acquittal from all guilt and criminalization in the court of heaven. On the Day of Judgment, all who have received salvation will be judged clean and pure.

But Salvation means even more than that. We are all naturally fond of, and hopelessly committed to sin. Salvation, through the power of the Holy Spirit, delivers us from the power of sin if we are responsive to His presence in our hearts. Having received salvation, we do have the power of the Holy Spirit within our new hearts to help in the battle against those propensities to sin. As Spurgeon says "be assured, this emancipation from bad habits, unclean desires, and carnal passions is the main point in salvation." Then he goes on to point out, that if emancipation is not progressing within you, neither then is the *ultimate* purpose of salvation working for you. In other words, you are not actually saved!

This is pretty hard stuff for this soft, easy does it, comfort and pleasure obsessed generation to accept, especially where Hollywood and Washington determine our moral values, and where most pulpits preach user-friendly platitudes rather than soul saving biblical truths. No one wants to hear these things, or believe that there is anything more to salvation than saying, I believe, and then trying to be a nice person, while hoping for the best. That won't cut it! Not nearly! Not ever! Again, salvation requires *repentance* and a conversion to a belief, faith and trust, ONLY in Jesus' accomplishment on the cross followed by a life expressing the consequences of that conversion.

Jesus does want each saved person to know with certainty that he or she is saved. But the knowledge must be based on a firm foundation of evidence not ill informed assumption or presumption. The existence of salvation may be detected through the sincere profession of faith in the achievement of Jesus on the cross as accompanied by a truly contrite heart which has confessed and regretted all past sins, and a soul which has repented, that is turned from its acceptance of its evil ways, and perseveres in a firm resolve to live in the ways taught by Jesus.

Scripture in the context of its whole demands each of these elements as evidence of having achieved salvation. Furthermore, Scripture is replete in this respect with admonishments such as to "work out your salvation," "examine your faith" and the "need to persevere to the end," "if you continue in My word . . ." etc., etc. These and many similar passages can be found which add essential dimension to that simple and most beautifully promising of all verses, "Believe and be saved." It's this word "believe, that is exceedingly loaded with meaning far, far beyond anything we normally attribute to it. That is the issue and the basis of often-tragic misunderstanding. Jesus also said that one must be "born-again" What does that mean? Clearly it means starting a new life! In this case starting a spirit centered rather than the flesh centered life into which we are all born. It is evident that the requirement that one must be born-again in order to be saved adds a whole new and far more complex meaning to the word "believe," in the simple instruction to "believe and be saved." One should meditate long and deeply on this before one accepts as evidence of salvation the common meaning of "believe."

How do we receive Salvation? Of course it's by grace through faith as we learn from Ephesians 2:8. It is a gift from God offered with only one condition "through faith" in Jesus and His work on the cross as already alluded to. But again, how does one get it? If one gets it at all, it comes instantly, faster than the twinkling of an eye. Because God knows everything, He, of course, knows your mind and your heart and exactly what you feel, think, believe and will do every second of your life. Once He sees a true sustaining belief forming, accompanied by a faith even as "small as a mustard seed," BINGO you have it! But remember, He knows what you don't know yet, and cannot know with certainty until some time has elapsed and recognizable evidence of that salvation actually manifests. Perhaps that's why Paul says in Philippians 2:12 "work out your salvation." Of course, he doesn't mean work to get it. That is impossible, as we all know, for work won't do it. He is telling us to look inside and work it out, dig or drag it out into the open where we can clearly see that which can only be found in the heart. He says to do so with "fear and trembling." Why? Perhaps it is because of the possibility that we may discover that there is nothing there to work out! In the context of His admonition, how else will you know? Is an assumption good enough, or should we do some confirming investigation as Paul suggests? We'll all know for sure one second after the last heart beat, but by then the course will have been unalterably set as to where we'll spend eternity. Is anyone offended by this suggestion that one should seek to confirm the existence of his or her salvation? Spurgeon would tell you, that anyone who is saved is never as haughty as to object to the admonition and not wish to re-examine themselves. He views those who would be thus offended as being ones who really need such advice.

Just as we compared time in terms of life span vs. eternity, now let's examine priorities. Whose matter is this, this matter of your salvation? It yours and yours alone! No one, not your Pastor or your parents or anyone else, no matter how much they love you, can substitute or arrange in any way for your salvation. God is "not willing that any should perish, but all should come to repentance" (2 Peter 3:9). Implicit in this expression from the Lord is that He *wants* to confer salvation on everyone, but He is willing to do so only for those who repent, that is change their minds, their ways and their priorities, or to conform to the Gospel message and all it contains. With eternity at stake shouldn't repentance with all that it implies, and all it thereby promises, be by far the top priority in this life, miles above any worldly priority? I'll close this "Case for Salvation" by quoting a few words from page 1376 of a five volume expository commentary on the Gospel of John by James Montgomery Boice. It's an observation about Judas which we should all take to heart if we look with too much comfort at our own perceived position in Christ.

> *Again, there is this final lesson. It concerns Judas, who was so close to Christ and yet unsaved. Think how close he was. He had been with Jesus for at least three years. He had heard his teaching. He had even understood his teaching; for although he had not understood the meaning of Christ's death, he had at least understood*

Christ's warning that he was to die. Judas was that close to Jesus. He understood his thoughts. Yet he was unsaved. I put it to you: It is possible to be quite close to Christ, to sit in a Christian church listening to good sermons, to hear good Bible teaching by radio, even to understand what you hear, and yet fail to make that personal commitment to Christ, that is the necessary human response to God's work of salvation. How foolish it is to come that close yet be lost.

—52—

The Price of Salvation

The price of Salvation? Why it is priceless! There is no way to buy it! Every real Christian knows that it is a free gift from God that cannot in any way be purchased or earned. Although many who believe themselves to be Christians are certain that one must do good works in order to be saved. But those who know even a little bit of Scripture realize that Ephesians 2:8, 9 clearly tells us otherwise, as do a number of the other Bible verses. Ephesians 2:8, 9 says, "For by grace are you saved through faith; and not of yourselves; it is a gift of God, not of works, lest any man should boast."

So it's very clear from Scripture that you cannot get to heaven through good works, that is through good deeds, clean living, dedication, sacrifice, pain and suffering, self denial, payment in goods, money, gold, penance, prayers, confessions or anything else under the sun. God's grace of salvation is a free gift, which absolutely no one deserves, for we are ALL hopelessly wicked. God Himself tells us so through His spokesman Jeremiah in chapter 17 verse 9. Here God says, "The heart (that is *every* human heart) is deceitful above all things, and desperately wicked: who can know it?"

Having said all that, there is, nevertheless, a price to be paid for salvation, that is for the blessed privilege having received eternal life in heaven.

When one becomes saved, that is redeemed, born-again, he or she becomes the son or daughter of God. Much of the world that believe that there is a God, think that everyone is a child of God, but this is not true. Scripture, God's inerrant Word, makes it clear that only those who possess the genuine saving faith in Jesus Christ and the purpose for which He shed His blood, become the children of

God. Again, no amount of virtue or good deeds or prayers can make you a son or daughter of God. But once you have believed in Jesus, unto a repentant saving faith, you do have a Father, who is our blessed God in heaven. As any good father, He takes special notice and care of His own children. Surely He knows all people and cares for them, and would want that none be lost, but all come to repentance (2 John 3:19). But His principal concern is for His own children. As a good father, He guides, educates, reprimands, punishes and rewards, He does not do these things to or for those who are not His. They, in many instances, may do better in worldly ways than His own, for there is another father mentioned in the Scripture, the prince of the world, a highly enabling spirit who delights in spoiling his own, feeding them with carnal pleasures and guiding them in any and all ways which might keep them from knowing the heavenly father, and from believing in His only begotten Son Jesus. So what is this price of salvation? Scripture tells us, in Jesus' own words, in Matthew 10:22 that "You (the redeemed) shall be hated of all men for His (Jesus) sake." That is surely a severe price to pay for accepting the free gift of salvation, for this hatred can and does manifest in many painful ways, ranging from rejection to torturous physical death. Over the centuries tens of millions of the faithful sons and daughters have suffered painful deaths for nothing more than their faith in Jesus and their refusal to renounce it. This manner of persecution continues unabated today across much of the world. We don't see it because it isn't reported by the official media. The extreme reprisal for the faith has not yet arrived on our shores. But reprisal does already exist here in many less violent forms. Of course, if you choose to hide your sonship for fear of reprisal, and avoid claiming your faith and allegiance to Jesus, if fear of rejection or worse brings about your silence or timidity, what kind of son or daughter are you? Could it be that you have taken His name, Christian, in vain and are not really His son or daughter after all?

If you are truly His son or daughter, the Father teaches, reprimands and punishes as He fine-tunes His own in preparation for their position in eternity. This can also be most painful and severe even though applied with genuine Fatherly love. Scripture describes these preparations as intended to cause spiritual growth (Romans 5:3–5), to build faith (1 Peter 1:6, 7), to prevent us from falling into sin (1 Peter 4:12), to provide just earthly punishment for known sins (Hebrews 12:5–61, James 4:17, Romans 14:23, John 1:9), to teach obedience and discipline (Acts 9:15, Philippians 4:11–13) and to equip us to comfort others (2 Corinthians 1:3:4–4). Compared to, and along with the normally difficult condition in common with most of the rest of the world of the unbelieving, these are a few of the additional prices which the redeemed must pay as a consequence of their saving faith.

Let there be not a moment of thought that these payments are unnecessary, unfair or to be feared or avoided. If they were, our Father would not permit them. If we have salvation by grace through faith, that faith cannot doubt, or it isn't faith. If there be the true saving faith, that faith will be evidenced by our reactions to these tests, punishments, teaching, etc. A saving faith will accept these as the just, righteous and loving workings in our Fathers in His personal and intimate dealings with His elect family, dealings which are a necessary part of His conditioning us for the place He has prepared for us in His eternal home. From both a practical and biblical perception, it seems logical to assume that the more appropriately one responds to these workings, the more quickly and less painfully, this maturing and preparation process might be completed.

Thus in conclusion it would seem that the moment of salvation does not necessarily, if ever, bring us out of the stressful, painful and sorrowful aspects of life. In fact, the more committed we are to Jesus as our Lord, the more intense are the adversities likely to become. However, along with genuine redemption, that "peace which passeth all understanding" begins to develop deep within the new heart. Along with it, comes an inner supernatural strength, a strange kind of strength, one that grows out of the weakness of self as the Holy Spirit slowly replaces ones self with Himself. One way in which this inner peace and strength might be described, is that one who is genuinely redeemed knows and rests his or her whole being on the rock solid foundation of knowing that whatever adversities befall us here, it is but a tiny momentary prelude, to the eternal perfect life ahead.

Not only is it a prelude, but a tempering and preparing process most beneficial to the soul. From this, it is evident that genuine salvation extracts a high price during this short earthly portion of one's life. At times it may seem grossly unfair when the redeemed son or daughter of God experiences pain and suffering and complete failure from an earthly perspective, while the unsaved deniers of Jesus prosper and seem to enjoy this life in far more comfort and material success. But the redeemed must always keep in mind that theirs is the most precious, longest lasting gift conceivable. They are infinitely wealthier than the riches most powerful monarchs ever could be. They have obtained that for which God created life in the first place. They have His love and His presence for eternity. This, indeed, is the priceless gift, which no one who has ever surely received it would ever consider not worth the price it cost either in the consequences, or the commitment to obedience, which followed its receipt. The millions of martyrs who died horrible deaths rather than renounce Jesus as their Lord and Savior bare powerful witness to this greatest truth.

—53—

Can Salvation Be Lost?

Those of us who call ourselves "born again Christians" and genuinely are, know, and rightly so, that it was through God's graces that we came into the faith, and that through that Faith we are saved, that is destined for eternal life in heaven. We find comfort and assurances in this fact, because the Lord in His own words told us so. In John 3:3 Jesus tells Nicodemus that ". . . except that a man be born again he cannot see the kingdom of God." In John 3:6 Jesus continues, ". . . that which is born of the flesh is flesh, and that which is born of the spirit is spirit." Then in Ephesians 2:8, 9, Paul says, ". . . for by grace are ye saved through faith; and that not of yourselves, it is the gift of God: not works, lest any man should boast." There are many other passages in the Bible that add clarity and confirmation to this fundamental fact. Therefore, in essence, there is a moment when if we *truly* accept Jesus as our Lord and Savior, knowing with certainty that He died for our sins and was resurrected, we *are* born again forever, and irrevocably. That rebirth gets us a new spiritual heart, which becomes the permanent home of the Holy Spirit We are thus saved, and nothing can, under any circumstances, take away that salvation! If salvation could be lost, then God could not be omniscient. He would have been unable to see the future event, attitude-changed belief, that caused the soul that He saved to no longer be in a state wherein it was qualified to remain saved. This, of course, is absolute foolishness. He is omniscient, and can see all future aspects of one's life. The real issue is not the possibility of loosing salvation, but of never having it at all!

But is that all there is to it? Yes, in response to the question. However, the answer given hereinabove begs further clarification in

467

order that no one misunderstands the full extent of how salvation is assured. The tragic fact is that there are many millions of souls who believe they are saved but are not, because through false or inadequate preaching, teaching or evangelism, they have failed to understand all that is involved in the process that causes one to be saved.

The essence of it all came from our Lord's own mouth when He told Nicodemus that one must be born-again if one is to see the kingdom of God, and to be saved to eternal life. Born again! This is the perfect and most beautiful description, encompassing everything involved. When one is physically born, he or she enters the world as a totally helpless innocent, unknowing creature who needs the most basic elementary care and nurturing. But the newborn grows and learns and matures eventually to adulthood. With a comparatively few unfortunate exceptions, this process is inevitable and irrepressible. With adulthood should come ever-increasing understanding, responsibility, dependability and accountability. All of this is the natural process of the flesh, the physical body. This we know is the process of birth, growth, life and death of all flesh.

However, being born-again as Jesus taught is to be born of the spirit and to have a wholly different, yet similar growth process. The newborn spirit, that which comes into being once a genuine acceptance of Jesus as both Lord and Savior occurs, is also totally helpless, innocent and unknowing. However, the difference is that the Holy Spirit indwells in the infant's new heart, and is ready and willing to care and nurture this new born. As inevitable as it is for the newborn baby to grow, so also must the newborn spirit grow and mature. If evidence of this growth is not apparent, a tragic situation may exist which needs to be dealt with. If that growth is not evidenced, it is highly likely that there has been no re-birth, no indwelling of the Holy Spirit and therefore no salvation. Because a *sincere*, *genuine* commitment to Jesus was lacking, a saving faith did not manifest. That is the tragedy of pandemic proportion in these last days when so many false prophets and false teachers, along with half-truth preachers and evangelists, flood the airways, pulpits and literature. Because there is so little bedrock knowledge of Scripture in the populous, these misleaders convince many to believe that they can obtain salvation through ways other than through the strict biblical truth.

The only test or clue we seem to have of the vitality of the new-born is the nature and extent of the changed life, which only the indwelling Holy Spirit could orchestrate. Even this, however, can be exceedingly deceptive, because of the rampant counterfeiting, which is occurring in these end times. Will this life remain changed in the desired way? Does this changed life carry with it a uniqueness characteristic of only a born-again faithful follower of Jesus? This is not always easy to discern, because there are many truly virtuously behaving people whom, by all superficial evidence, could surely typify the ideal Christian virtues, yet have greatly divergent beliefs. The fact is that one can lead a very Christian like life, yet not be a Christian and therefore not saved. However, I doubt that one can be a Christian and not diligently and sincerely pursue a Christian life. Also there are many truly sincere people. However, sincerity is of no relevance unless it is associated with faith in the one and only triune Godhead and His fleshly manifestation Jesus, as our one and only Lord and Savior.

Clearly, there must be more to this then is commonly understood. If there is, it is vital, to anyone truly seeking salvation, that there remain no question or doubt as to the sufficiency of their faith and their Christian walk. A reliable source of this truth can only be found in God's own words, The Bible. Perhaps, those verses on which the Armenians rely for their interpretation can add an additional dimension through which a clearer understanding can be found.

In Matthew 15:9 and again in Mark 7:7 Jesus says, "But in vain they do worship me, teaching for doctrines the commandments of men." This tells us to always search the Scriptures for the truth and to not rely on the words of men, which can be false or misleading into vain or false faith. Paul's message in Acts 17:11 cautions us against the same mistake. This is not necessarily relevant to the topic issue, which is whether or not we can lose our salvation, but it clearly focuses on the related issue as to whether we are saved at all through our chosen interpretation of how salvation is achieved. It suggests that one can be in grave danger of totally missing salvation if one's faith is built on words of others, which are not wholly verified and confirmed by Scripture. One must, as the Bereans did in Acts 17:11, ". . . search the Scriptures daily to see if these things be so." I believe that many Catholics, as well as those of other "faiths," are in this danger in that they rely wholly on the interpretations and words of others as their sole basis of faith and hope for salvation. This problem can be solved only if we pray sincerely and often and seriously study, learn and understand as much as possible the *whole* Word of God as presented in the Scriptures. Casualness or being 'lukewarm" here is not a satisfactory option.

In 1 Corinthians 15:2, Paul says, ". . . by which also ye are saved, if ye keep in memory what I preached unto you, unless ye believed in *vain*." This suggests that one can know the truth, "keep in memory," as Paul related it directly from divine Authority, but a vain faith can still result. How can that happen? Perhaps we may find the answer in His own words as Jesus relates a parable and then explains it in Matthew 13:5–7 and 20–22 were He speaks of seeds sown and ". . . some fell upon stony places, where they had not much earth: and forthwith they sprang up because they had no deepness of earth: and when the sun was up they were scorched: and because they had no root, they withered away. And some fell among thorns; and the thorns sprang up and choked them." Then Jesus explains as follows: "But he that receives the seed into stony places, the same is he that hears the word, and with joy receives it, yet hath he not root in himself, but endureth for a while; for when tribulation or persecution ariseth because of the Word, by and by he is offended. He also that receives the seed among the thorns is he that hears the Word; and the cares of this World and the deceitfulness or riches, chokes the Word and he becomes unfruitful."

Here the Lord gives two examples of what He may have meant by vain or non-saving faith. The first one might be called the "drop out" faith, where the Word of God is received and it sounds great, truly inspiring, but the soul doesn't have sufficient depth of soil in which faith can grow strong. With the advent of adversities this faith shrivels and dies. The second example of vain faith, which might be called lukewarm or cooled off faith, is that which also starts out vigorous and in sufficiently deep soil, however, the cares, temptations, responsibilities, successes, pleasures etc. of the world assume even greater importance in the believer's life, taking priority over, and choking out or fatally weakening our worship, faith, prayers, and true fellowship with Jesus.

Aren't we all, those who believe ourselves to be true Christians, vulnerable to this form of vain faith? How much do we rationalize that we live in sufficiency of these essentials of a true faith, when in fact we may have fatal deficiencies as we find ourselves struggling amongst the distractions of daily life?

How many of us are of the Church of Ephesus (Revelation 2:4) and have left our first love, our priority love, Jesus, perhaps in a misdirected zeal doing so much work *for* the King that we have forgotten to sufficiently *worship* the King? The Lord Jesus' letter to the seven churches in Revelation 2, 3 contains much insight into how easily sincere, well meaning Christians can live insufficient and misdirected lives.

Of those of us who critically examine ourselves regarding the sincerity and sufficiency of our faith, many discover that we are too deeply immersed in the world and hindered in our Walk by the dense "thorns" that surround us. If so, we should be greatly concerned and alert to the potential of this "vain" worship.

It's easy to say: "once saved always saved. I committed myself to Jesus, I pray often; I attend church faithfully; I read the Scriptures daily; and I see my changed life proving my salvation." Maybe that's all there is to it. I can't say that it isn't. However, I'm continually troubled by thoughts expressed in such words as sufficiency, sincerity, intensely, sustainability, intellectual vs. spiritual etc, as I contemplate my status with Jesus and with eternity. While the Scripture is very gratifying in terms of its assurance of salvation through grace, it also, like it or not, imposes certain conditions beyond the simple commitment to Jesus as a prerequisite to salvation. Consider Hebrew 3:6 "... but Christ as a son over His own house; whose we are *if* we *hold fast* the confidence and rejoicing of the hope *firm unto* the *end*." (note what I've underlined) Again see Hebrews 3:14 "For we are made partakers of Christ *if* we hold the beginning of your confidence steadfast unto the *end*." Then again in Hebrews 6:4–6 "For it is impossible for those who were once enlightened, and have tasted of the heavenly gift, and were made partakers of the Holy Ghost, and have tasted the good Word of God and the powers of the world to come, if they shall fall away, to renew them again unto repentance; seeing they crucify to themselves the Son of God afresh and put Him to an open shame."

From these verses it is evident that it is a day-by-day, moment-by-moment, continuous commitment to, and fellowship with, Jesus that remains strong and uncompromised to the end, which is a demonstration of the true saving faith. It is a once and for all irrevocable done deal the moment we truly, by the above definition, accept Jesus. However, only the Lord knows whether or not our individual commitments are of such sustaining quality, because only He knows the beginning from the end. I believe it is not for us to know the certainty of our salvation until we have drawn our last breath and heard the loving voice of Jesus calling us each by our name to come and join Him in our eternal home.

How can it be otherwise? Faith, which does not endure to the end, was never true faith. Because we can not possibly know at this time what will be in our minds and in our hearts ten, twenty or thirty years from now, what trials, tribulations and temptations we will encounter, how stifling will be the sea of "thorns" that surrounds us or how committed the devil may be to pervert and subvert our faith. It seems clear to me that without perseverance to the end we achieve nothing, and because we have no way to know when or how the end will be, we can not know until then whether or not we are saved. We can only continue in our prayers, strengthen our understanding of His word and *Trust* Him to deliver us safely through whatever trials and temptations may make difficult our remaining days.

I know that many who read this may rage with indignation at my claim that absolute assurance of salvation is not discernable until we have finished the race. That may not be an axiom. There may be many people who are rightly convinced of their salvation early, after, or even at the moment of its occurrence. I pray that this is so for those who so believe. For me, however, based on my understanding of God's Word as I have studied it most seriously for almost nine years now, I find the need to be most critical of myself and my opinion of where I stand in this most important of all possible circumstances. As I see the diabolical workings of the great deceiver in the hearts of millions, my heart aches and I pray greatly for them. These are those who have spoken the right words, felt some twangs of emotion and now believe they have salvation, but do not. Satan can fill most any mind with apathy, self-satisfaction, compliancy and anything else that will deceive him or her into believing a lie. No one is immune to such attacks. From my reading and study of Scripture, I prefer the far conservative side of its interpretation, its directions. I believe, as Paul advises to periodically examine my faith. A backsliding saved soul is still a saved soul. But how about people like Charles Templeton? (See his story in the paper called: How to loose your Salvation. For twenty years he was one of the world's greatest evangelists, preaching to many thousands at a time throughout North America and Europe. It's been said that during his evangelical career, he was even more effective than his contemporary Billy Graham. Then suddenly he no longer believed that there even is a God. He spent the later half of his life lecturing on his new religion, atheism. Should he not have checked his faith once in a while? Could this be simply a backslid saved Christian, or someone who was never really saved? If we didn't know better, we might conclude that here was a case of salvation lost! The issue of salvation is far too important to take casually, with compliancy or with presumptions. Most people believe that it is a good idea to have an annual physical examination for the sake of physical health. Given the far greater importance of ones spiritual condition, should that also be the object of a periodic examination?

—54—

How to Lose Your Salvation

This is written to professing Christians who have "accepted" Jesus and who believe Him to be their Lord and Savior and, therefore, consider themselves as having eternal security and ever-lasting life in heaven.

Have you checked your faith lately as the Holy Spirit tells us to do in 2 Corinthians 13:5? Within what is called the "Christian" community, there are probably as many subtle differences and degrees of "faith" as there are people professing to be of the faith. I suspect that somewhere across this spectrum is a dividing line between what a saving faith is and what isn't quite good enough to get one through that "narrow gate" into heaven. I'm persuaded that within all of that favorable part of the spectrum, there needs to be that quality that "continues to the end."

There was a man who died just a few years ago, whose life expressed the very issue that I've chosen to be the title of this paper. He was a brilliant man. He claimed to have no faith in his early youth, although his mother was apparently a believer. Then one night, when he was about nineteen years old he but let's let him tell it to you in his own words.

> *"She began to talk about God, about the happiness her faith had brought her, and about how she longed to see me with the other children in church. I heard little of what she was saying; my mind was doing an inventory of my life. Suddenly it seemed empty and wasted and sordid. I said, "I m going to my room."*
>
> *"As I went down the hall, I was forming a prayer in my head, but as I knelt by my bed in the darkness, my mind was strangely vacant; thoughts and words wouldn't come to focus. After a moment, it was as*

though a black blanket had been draped over me. A sense of enormous guilt descended and invaded every part of me. I was unclean."

Involuntarily, I began to pray, my face upturned, tears streaming. The only words I could fin, were, "Lord come down, Come down, Come down . . ."

"It may have been minutes later, or much longer, there was no sense of time, but I found myself, my head in my hands, crunched small on the floor at the center of a vast emptiness. The agonizing was past. It had left me numb, speechless, immobilized, alone and tense with a sense of expectancy. In a moment, a weight began to lift, a weight as heavy as I. It passed through my thighs, my belly, my chest, my arms, and my shoulder and lifted off entirely. I could have leaped over a wall. An ineffable warmth began to suffuse every corpuscle. It seemed that a light had turned on in my chest and its refining fire had cleansed me. I hardly dared breathe, fearing that I might end or alter the moment. I heard myself whispering softly, over and over, "Than you Lord. Thank You Lord. Thank you. Thank you . . ."

"After a while I went to mother's room. She saw my face and said, "Oh Chuck . . .!" and burst into tears. We talked for an hour."

"When I went back to my bedroom, dawn was just breaking. I undressed, drew the shade, climbed into bed, and lay motionless in the diminishing darkness, bathed in a radiant, overwhelming happiness. Outside, the birds began their first tentative singing and I began to laugh softly, out of an indescribable sense of well being at the center of an exultant, all encompassing joy."

Could there be a much stronger indication of a supernatural experience than this? To him as it might be to anyone, it was a life changing experience. A few months later he resigned from his position at the newspaper office in order to prepare for the Christian ministry. His name was Charles Templeton. If you are old enough you may have heard of him, because in the 1950s he was the greatest evangelist of that period. As a contemporary of Billy Graham, he was at that time, far better known than Graham. For a while he and Graham, when they were in their early thirties, traveled together all over the U.S. and other countries taking turns at the pulpit. He was a cofounder of Youth for Jesus, an organization that grew very rapidly and soon became international. Even in the early years, he often drew crowds of as much as 30,000 at a time. In one town having a population of 128,000, during a two-week campaign, his audience totaled 91,000.

He had no formal education or training for the ministry. He simply read everything he could find and said the he "learned to preach by preaching and aping others." After a while he managed to get into Princeton Theological Seminary. Only because of his incredible success as an evangelist was he allowed in as a special student. He could not receive a degree because he had not met the prerequisites, having only gone through ninth grade in high school. He did graduate and later received an honorary doctorate of divinity.

He functioned as an internationally known and respected evangelist for twenty-one years. However, during the last seven years of his ministry he had increasingly strong doubts as to the validity of what he preached, until he felt compelled to resign and completely forsake the faith. In 1995 after many years of proclaiming himself to be an agnostic, he wrote a book called, "Farewell to God," which tells the story I've only touched on herein.

Here we have a man who had a very strong spiritual experience that changed his life and for a large part of twenty-one years caused him to be an ardent believer, and motivated him to become a world-renowned professor and communicator of the Christian faith. Is there anyone in the world who knows, or believes he knows the prerequisites qualities of a born-again, saved, redeemed Christian? Who knew or knows of Charles Templeton, who would have doubted that he was so blessed? Yet for most of the last half of his life, he wrote and lectured agnosticism! From what I've read, I would call it more correctly, atheism. The book "Farwell to God," is for the most part, a synopsis of the Bible, in which he attacks nearly every precept, making a mockery of nearly everything true Christians find sacred. There is nothing original in his arguments. They are nothing different than what "science" and secular theology have used ad nauseam to discredit God's Word. I'm tempted here to cite a few of his more sophomoric denunciations of Scripture, but it should suffice to say for this present purpose that he was provably "dead" wrong in every criticism of the Bible.

So what happened? Was Templeton born-again during that supernatural event at age nineteen and so remains saved in spite of decades of total denial of God's existence and of the resurrections of

Jesus? Did he lose his salvation, or was he never saved? The answer is obvious. It is one, or the other of only two of the three choices. The remainder of this paper will consist of possible clues to the answer, and what we can learn from this tragic example.

First the clues. Note, in his description of the supernatural event. His mind was "strangely vacant," and it was as though a "black blanket had been draped over me." It should be noted that mediums and others who engage in occult practices use the techniques of vacating the mind in order to consult with the "spiritual world" to let these spirits enter them and guide them. This is *not ever* the Holy Spirit, but evil spirits who operate in this manner. Obviously, this is only speculation in terms of what may have happened to Templeton, but the technique is real and one of Satan's very effective devices. Other significant factors in his life were the circumstances before and after his "conversion." Prior to that fateful moment, he had shunned church and everything connected with it, even though his mother was of the faith and kept urging him. He had no knowledge of the Scripture, or of its meaning, or the intricacies of the Christian faith. Yet after some reading of the Bible, he jumped deeply and completely into evangelizing, into preaching, and into advising thousands on spiritual matters. Applying his gifts of eloquence, enthusiasm, fervor, articulation, and personality he was propelled almost instantly into fame and power over a spiritually hungry, seeking populous. He was like a person who never had a flying lesson, but who got into the pilot's seat of a 747 filled with passengers. He has figured out how to get the plane off the ground, but now has no ability to fly it or land it safely. How many of his "passengers" died unnecessarily because he failed to land in their hearts the full meaning of the Gospel? How many souls are lost today because of a similar half-truth, "lite," comfortable and misleading Gospel emanating from the lips of modern day "evangelists"? He never became grounded in Scripture. He seems to have been able to grab a few truths, though he never really apprehended them into himself. Nevertheless, he ran with them most impressively, but with no depth of understanding. He said that he chose to ape others. Perhaps parroting without understanding would have been more accurate. But we must not underestimate the power of such actions. In today's amusement-addicted culture, who are the heroes, the most persuasive, and the most honored? Its actors! Those who "ape and parrot" scripts written and directed by others. Society tends to credit the actors with the bigger than life qualities they portray. This in turn tends to convince the actors that they are in fact "as gods" and not subject to mortal (or moral) limits. Can't you see Satan's handiwork through this same process both in Templeton and throughout our present world and its systems?

Templeton personifies the man in the parable of the sower in Matthew 13:20, who ". . . received the seed into stony places, the same is he that hears the word and with joy receives it, yet he has no root in himself, but endures for awhile . . ." With Templeton, it seems to have loosely endured for the better part of twenty-one years. He had no real sustaining roots. What little roots he may have had seemed to have been pulled up quite easily as we shall see. He calls to mind a period where he was evangelizing in a "dreary Michigan town" where he spent his spare time in reading Thomas Paine's, "Age of Reason" and the works of other atheists such as, Voltaire, Bertrand Russell, Robert Ingersol, David Hume and Thomas Huxley. After reading Thomas Paine, he says in his memoirs that, "In a few hours, nearly everything I knew and believed about the Christian religion was challenged and in large part demolished. My unsophisticated mind had no defenses against the thrust of his logic or his devastating arguments." Had he been steeped in Scripture, as one must be to *know* God's truth, had the Holy Spirit opened the eyes of his heart to God's Word, he would have had an immutable "defense" against any of man's logic. He would have known that even the "foolishness of God" is wiser than the wisdom and reason of any man. He had no roots; his foundation was built in sand, and, therefore, the first rain, or wind of human reason washed away the sand and with it his faith.

There is one last clue as to his chronic weakness of faith. This is a difficultly all loners face. I wrote about this extensively in a previous paper called "Spiritual Stumbling." He lacked a spiritually strong "faith partner." In his book he says:

> *The old doubts were resurfacing. I would cover them over with*
> *prayer and activity but soon there would be a wisp of smoke and a*

flicker of flame and then a firestorm of doubt. I would banish them only to have them return. Part of the problem was that there was no one to talk to. How does a man who, each night tells ten to twenty thousand people how to find faith, confess that he is struggling with his own?

There seems to be no evidence in his writings that Templeton ever returned to believing or even tried to reexamine the "evidences" that led him away. How could anyone so seemingly strong in his profession of belief, so stellar in his expressions of faith, and so convincing to so many, lose his faith so easily? Faith and salvation are inseparable, for we are "saved by grace through faith." Does that mean that when he lost his faith he lost his salvation? Of course not! Although in such an extreme case as this, anyone with less than the rudimentary knowledge of Christian teaching might conclude that here was just such a situation. Based on the evidence it appears that he never did have a saving faith. His, appears to be a false faith and I suspect that he also preached false Gospel. Perhaps it was not false in what it said, but false because of what it omitted, and, therefore, false in the sense that it led many to a pseudo salvation.

This thought stems from another clue gleaned from his book. In it he quotes a news article about his ministry that included the following:

> *I have just seen the man who's giving religion a brand new look; a young Canadian by the name of Charles Templeton. Passing up the old hell-fire and damnation oratorical fireworks, he uses instead an attractive, persuasive approach that presents religion as a commodity as necessary to life as salt, and in the doing, has set a new standard for mass evangelism.*
>
> *Dispensing with such props as the "sawdust trail" the "Mourner's Bench" and other tricks from the old-fashioned evangelist's repertoire, he is winning converts at an average of 150 a night and what is something new in modern evangelism, they stay converted.*

The question is "stay converted" to what, a false shallow belief such as his own? Who knows? Apparently the writer of the article knew nothing of significance regarding Christian faith, or this idea of religion as a commodity would not have been so favorably reported. Nevertheless, in that respect he was correct. That is exactly what Templeton did. He was simply an early practitioner of the "New Evangelism," which is more like a worldly business seeking its "market share" of a "religious commodity" than it is a faith based ministry seeking to bring repentant sinners to salvation.

The important thing here is what we have learned, or can learn from Templeton's experience. I believe there is much of significance here for anyone who takes salvation seriously, and especially one who is weak in scriptural knowledge, and complacent about their faith.

1.   First the title of this paper. It was meant to be provocative; Scripture makes it abundantly clear that if you are saved you cannot lose your salvation. There is no such thing as losing it if you have it. Knowledge of this fact is basic, and requires no significant amount of biblical study. Simple common sense will tell you that an omniscient Creator God will not save and then unsave or resave anyone. Only a God who could not know the future could be so limited as to see some saving condition of one's heart today, but later have to change his mind or remove the gift because he later saw a changed heart. The Creator God, knew before the beginning of time every aspect, every thought and emotion and act in each of our lives. Because of this He also knew who would come truly to a saving faith through which His irrevocable gift of salvation would be appropriately received. Only God knows what was in Templeton's heart when he died. However, if one is to judge by the evidence of his own words and deeds, one would conclude that he was not saved.

2.   What about the impressive "spiritual" experience Templeton had at age nineteen? Surely it was life changing in a way that would seem to have been positive in terms of how it changes his life, at least for a while. Yet what fruit did it bear? Perhaps, from the short-term perspective of the time of his heyday as an evangelist, one might have said that his response to this "calling" bore much fruit. But did it? It's difficult to know. The secular columnist said, "they stay converted." This was only because church attendance increased as a result of his sermons. But does church attendance have any direct relationship to salvation? Doesn't it depend a great deal on what a particular church *offers*, and what is *received* into one's heart? False gospel is not necessarily false words. A false gospel can be false simply by omission of certain elements that are essential to the understanding of what

constitutes a saving faith. The "New Evangelism" that now seems to be dominate within the "Christian" church is precisely that! It attracts or calls many, but does it plow the ground in such a manner as to facilitate a saving faith? No! It just makes a great many think they are saved, when they are not, because they are not told enough to even know that they don't know what it is to have a saving faith!

Back to the "spiritual" event. As he described it, and based on the rest of his life, there is ample reason to believe that it was Satan who orchestrated the event and who guided him the rest of his life. The whole process is not at all inconsistent with what Scripture tells us regarding how Satan works. We know him to be the great deceiver. His compelling ways never appear to be evil. Who would be persuaded by evil? All of his evil is coated with good so as to hide the evil. What better way to achieve his purpose, then to convince someone that he is saved when he is not. How better to do this than to convince someone of great talent that he has a sincere calling to preach the Gospel, and to then motivate him to preach a false gospel that can lead thousands to a false faith or to a faith too weak to warrant salvation? How diabolically clever to then later cast such heavy doubts in him so as to have him renounce his beliefs, his ministry, and even God! Think of how many who heard him, and heard of him, he may have "taken down" with him as he proclaimed with much notoriety that Jesus is not God, that there is no God, and that Scripture is a fable! Satan scored big in two ways with this agent. His cleverness is *almost* boundless!

3. Back again to the "spiritual" event. How does one come to believe that one is born-again? Often it seems to have been the result of some sort of spiritual event, not too different from the one Templeton experienced. But his experience should give pause to anyone who has had such an event and claims it as the basis of his or her salvation. It would seem that Templeton's story should cause one to most carefully reexamine such an event and what has followed over the years in terms of a changed life. It took Templeton most of twenty-one years to finally fall away, concluding that there could be no salvation because there wasn't even a God!

From this we may conclude that not all spiritual events are of God, (although some, no doubt, are), because Satan also has the power to cause such things and to make them so real and believable as to almost "fool the elect." Consider the apparitions of Mary for instance. How many millions "swear" by these as godly messages, yet nothing in Scripture remotely indicates that such manifestations derive from the Holy Spirit.

4.   The Templeton story should remind us of what Scripture tells us repeatedly regarding the validity and nature of a saving faith. Absent a contrite heart, the recognition of our sinful nature, an on-going confession of our sins, a sincere repentance, and the continuance of a much changed life, any claimed faith is not likely to be a saving faith.

5.   In the same vein but with specific references, his story should bring to mind a number of Scripture verses such as:

Philippians 3:12 ". . . work out your own salvation with fear in trembling." Apparently Templeton finally did this and found that there was nothing there to work out.

2 Corinthians 13:5 "Examine yourselves, whether you be in the faith: prove your own selves." He did this eventually and realized that he didn't even believe, let alone have faith.

1 Corinthians 15:1, 2 "Moreover brethren, I declare unto you the Gospel, which I preached unto you, which also ye received, and wherein ye stand. By which also ye are saved, if ye keep in memory what I preached unto you, unless ye have believed in vain." Whatever Templeton believed, or thought he believed, was obviously in vain.

Hebrews 3:6 ". . . but Christ as a son over his own house; whose house are we, if we hold fast the confidence and the rejoicing of the hope firm unto the end." Here is that huge terrifying word, IF, which occurs many times in a similar context. IF we hold fast ". . . firm to the end." Obviously Templeton didn't, because there was never anything of substance on which to hold fast.

Oh dear God, how many professing Christians there are today, who are like Templeton, and many of those he influenced, have nothing but an abstraction where they believe there is a saving faith. I pray the Holy Spirit will lead each of them into your precious Word and thereby complete the process of redemption, which "New Evangelism" so miserably fails to do. Amen.

—55—

Work out Your Salvation

The apostle Paul tells us in Philippians 2:12 to "Work out your own salvation with fear and trembling." Many who first read this verse are confused because it seems to suggest that "work" is somehow a necessary element in salvation. However, a little study reveals that what Paul mean is that we are to look very carefully, digging deep into our hearts, to work out, that is bring up out of the depth of our souls, the evidence of our salvation. In some very rare instances that evidence is so irresistible that it flows up to the surface by itself as a beautiful aura, revealing the presence of the indwelling Holy Spirit. I was blessed to have known such a person for a while. She is now at "Home" with our Lord.

The disconcerting part of Paul's instruction, and one about which I've never read a commentary, is the "fear and trembling." Often in the scriptural translation, the word fear is used to express what the original language refers to as "reverential awe." But here, "fear" means fear. This meaning is amplified and compounded by adding the "trembling," which in the original means just what it means in English. Nothing in Scripture is superfluous or without purpose. It is all there for our learning (Romans 15:4). So Paul did not add that phrase "with fear and trembling" just to take up space, or for us to simply glance over and forget. It is my belief after much prayer and meditation, that perhaps the Holy Spirit through Paul is saying to us, something like this:

> *"You had better dig down into your souls and bring out what you find, so that you can examine it in order to prove to yourself that you are saved. Just because you said the sinner's prayer and "accepted" Jesus, and now "feel" saved, doesn't mean you are.*

Until you actually do this "work out," you have no real reason to believe that you are saved. The matter should be of such profound importance to you that you cannot help but fear and tremble until you know with certainty, having sought the evidence, which is in you. 'For if salvation is yours, you will find Me residing in your heart.' (1 Corinthians 6:19)

Thus, it is more than simply bringing the evidence of your salvation to the surface for the world to see, and by which it may be favorably influencing as you witness, but rather for *you* to see and to *know* that it is real. Have you followed this advice? Have you actually looked carefully inside of yourself and tried to "work out" your salvation? Have you done so with "fear and trembling"? I spent a larger part of these seven years since I first "accepted" Jesus, trying to "work" it out. I did so with fear and even experienced "trembling" during times of intense prayer regarding the matter. If you have never followed this advice by Paul, isn't it time you did? Perhaps, you have not done so because you believe that your faith is most certainly a saving faith, and, therefore, you need no further evidence. But remember, Paul was speaking to an assembly of those who believed they were saved, just as he is speaking to us today through the Scripture. This was not his only message in this vein. In 2 Corinthians 13:5, he tells us again to "Examine yourselves, whether ye be in the faith; prove your own selves." There are millions who have "accepted" Jesus and, therefore, believe they are saved. We also know that many, perhaps most, have *not* been accepted by Jesus because their faith is not a real and saving faith. I pray you will *work out your salvation*, and *examine yourself*, in order to find that *absolute* assurance before it is too late.

—56—

Salvation

Let us analyze the manner in which we receive the grace of salvation and the inheritance it represents. Perhaps it may help some to better understand the awesome reality of this blessed gift.

Suppose we view this in the earthly terms of a last will and testament of an extremely wealthy benefactor who, it has been said, has named us, as beneficiaries in his will. His only stipulation is that we pledge to believe that he has done this as a no-strings-attached free gift, and that we truly believe in the truth of a particular historical event. What a strange provision! But we must remember he is quite eccentric, for his ways are not our ways.

We study the historical record, and we determine that it is true. (It's actually in a book called the Bible, of which we have proof that He Himself wrote.) Therefore, upon pledging that we believe in the truth of the historical event and in the fact that this is truly a free gift, we become bona fide beneficiaries of this incredible wealth, you might say a wealth so great that it will outlast everyone of us, undiminished, throughout eternity! Now again, we did nothing to earn this; we simply have been selected because we unequivocally believe. In fact, trying to earn this gift could be grounds for disqualification, because of our pledge. We are, however, expected to express gratitude through love, repentance and a changed life as evidence of genuine belief.

As we mull this over, we realize a couple of sobering facts. First, a will is of little value to anyone until the testator dies! We know this from both man's law and even more assuredly from God's law as in Hebrews 9:16, 17, wherein we read "for where a testament is there must also of necessity be death of the testator. For a testament is of force after men are dead: otherwise it is of no strength at all while the testator lives." That's a bummer! The gift giver must die before we can claim the promise and before we can receive the gift. Suppose He lives longer than we do?

We must also be greatly concerned as to the integrity and faithfulness of the executor of the will, the one who opens the document, reads it and then proceeds to implement its provisions. The executor must be above all possible temptation, immune to corruption, pure and ever truthful. Unless he is all of these things he could easily cheat us out of the inheritance. So, therefore, must we be concerned as was John in Revelation 5:3, 4 as he wept because there was no man in neither heaven nor earth or under the earth worthy or able to break the seals and open the book, to reveal, and implement its content. But just as John was relived from his fears, when the "lion of Judah" the "lamb as He had been slain," our blessed Lord Jesus Christ broke the seals and opened the book, so also do we have Him as our Executor to assure that we will receive the full measure of our inheritance, this blessed grace of salvation. He was and is our Testator, the Man Jesus, who already died so that His will could come into force. But having arisen from the dead as only He could, our honorable Executor lives and will deliver to all believers His incredible promise.

If He has accepted you, if you are named in His last will and testament, rest assured, everything has been accurately, precisely and irrevocably arranged for your eternal security!

—57—

The Foolishness of God Is Wiser than Man

Paul, in 1 Corinthians 1–25 remarks that ". . . the foolishness of God is wiser than man . . ." What a provocative statement! Who was Paul? Paul was perhaps the greatest of the apostles, at least in terms of the amount of the New Testament attributed to him and his influences on the early church as well as on the Evangelical beliefs to this day. He was not one of the original twelve but was a short time later chosen by the transcended Jesus. Originally named Saul and of the tribe of Benjamin, he was a Pharisee of the ruling class called the Sanhedrin. He was extremely bright, articulate and zealous in that faith until his conversion by Jesus. He was from a well-to-do Hebrew family, schooled in Greek and the classics, as well as by Gamaliel, the foremost Hebrew religious scholar of his time. As a most ardent foe of Christianity, he was probably the most zealous of the hired guns working for the establishment to root out all Christians and bring them to justice. It is noted that he even presided over the stoning of Steven, Christianity's first martyr.

The context of this Pauline remark centers on the fundamental tenant of Christianity, the identity and fate of Jesus. Regarding this, he profoundly observes in 1 Corinthians 1:18 that "for the preaching of the cross is to them that perish, foolishness; but unto us which are saved, it is the power of God." Read that again, because it is the summation of all that is Christianity! Then he quotes from Isaiah 29:14 God's declaration, "I will destroy the wisdom of the wise and will bring to nothing the understanding of the prudent." In 1 Corinthians 1:21 Paul goes on "For after that in the wisdom of God the world by wisdom knew not God, it pleased God, by the foolishness of preaching to save them that believe." Finally in 1 Corinthians 27, he makes the observation that, "God has chosen the foolish things of the world to confuse the wise."

These quotes reveal a fundamental aspect of the Scriptures, both the Old and the New Testaments. They make clear that the highest level of man's wisdom is both trivial and ill conceived compared to the wisdom of God. God demonstrates this vast disparity by even fashioning some of His interventions in ways that are divinly effective, but yet so strange and convoluted to the natural human mind as to be considered utterly foolish. There are several places in the Scriptures where the analogy of the pot to the potter is used to demonstrate this. As the pot has no wisdom through which it can comprehend the workings of the potter, so does man himself lack the wisdom to understand the Lord's ways. Understanding comes only after belief and faith have become manifest in the human spirit. Thus, the Lord in His wisdom has deliberately chosen ways that human wisdom finds foolish. In so doing, God is able to separate and easily distinguish the believer from the non-believer. The believer accepts the fact of God and of Jesus as the Scriptures proclaim. This belief opens the way for the Holy Spirit to enter the soul and spirit of the believer. Once there, the Holy Spirit unlocks the secret of God's wisdom revealing the unfoolishness of His actions.

Meanwhile, the unbeliever saturated in the pride of His own wisdom, sees only foolishness in what God has chosen to reveal to us. He is incapable of seeing the truth because he lacks the light of the Holy Spirit. God sees us as we truly are in relation to Him, that is, His children. As His children, He rightly expects us to believe and obey Him. As parents, we expect the same thing from our little children. What we do and require of them may seem foolishness and unfair to them. If we are wise and fair and loving as parents, we know that our wisdom is superior and that theirs is not yet even formed sufficiently to be called wisdom. Clearly the wisdom of God, our Father and Creator, our potter, is infinitely greater than even the brightest most wise of us, His children. How can we then, once we accept the premise of this God-man relationship, ever presume any capacity to comprehend His ways unless He chooses to reveal them to us? This He surely does for all believers, through the Holy Spirit.

Thus, we have a very important message here. God, through the Scriptures, is telling us that no matter how wise we are or think we are, we are no matches for Him. To prove His point, in the context of what I have just written, where He has intervened or directed events as recorded in the Bible, He has often chosen methods, which neither the so-called intelligent man nor any non believer, the natural man, considers anything but foolish. Hence, we get the absurd title of this paper. Here I've chosen but four examples as illustrations of this presumed foolishness. These are, the use of Adam's rib for the creation of Eve, then the Noah and the Ark story, followed by the story of the Ten Plagues of Egypt and Exodus, and finally the culmination of them all, the advent of our Lord God Jesus Christ as a man and our Savior.

Before I begin my attempt to describe these few examples of God's "foolishness," I want to offer a note of encouragement to the beginner Bible student to whom this paper is dedicated, because I was there only three and half years ago, and can, therefore, appreciate the fears frustrations and disillusionments that grip every concerned beginner. I pray that the insights and elaborations with which I've tried to surround the following biblical events will not only reveal His "unfoolishness," but will also illustrate the depth, the fullness and the beauty of God's Word in a manner that will give encouragement to the reader to seek for his or her self, similar soul edifying jewels from this glorious adventure. In reading this or any other human words, one should always remember and apply Peter's admonition in Acts 17:11 where he cautions everyone to have ". . . received the word with all readiness of the mind, and searched the Scriptures daily, whether those things were so." That means don't take my words as truth until you have checked them out yourself in the only reliable source of the truth, the Holy Bible.

For the beginner, the Bible can be very intimidating, confusing and at the very least, extremely difficult to understand in some areas. The simple fact that it is a translation from Greek and or Hebrew necessarily causes some ambiguities and loss of original meanings. Also, it was written thousands of years ago in the vernacular of the ancient world, and is filled with what now seem to be strange expressions, analogies, idioms and allegories. These along with a host of other unfamiliar forms of expression and manners of conveying ideas, greatly compound the difficulty. Nevertheless, it is by far the most read, most studied, most analyzed and most written about book ever to exist. Therefore, there is a world of assistance available by means of which the serious student can enhance his or her understanding as well as gain an appreciation of its richness, its accuracy, its wealth of profound knowledge, and its authenticity as the Word of God. It is one continuous integrated divine message penned by more than forty writers over a period of thousands of years. It is a consolidation of sixty-six books, all of whose author is God Himself.

To the non-believer, the Bible can never be more than a quaint, suspect version of ancient history filled with mystical fantasies and events too absurd to have actually happened, let alone having been divinely orchestrated. To the believer, of course, it is the inerrant Word of God, accurate in every respect, the only problem being, how to understand it all. My advice, beyond careful reading and rereading and reference to the many available aids, is to pray to the Author to guide you through the difficult parts. If you are serious, so He will be also in His assistance.

Why should there be such great disparity of views regarding this great book? If it's truly God's word, shouldn't its message be crystal clear to everyone? Wouldn't an all-knowing, omnipotent God keep His word updated, understandable and fully convincing to everyone throughout all the ages? How could a God so all knowing and all-powerful as the Creator of the universe, publish a book with so much ambiguity and foolishness as the Bible seems to contain? Not that believers have all the answers, but there are questions that only the non-believer feels it necessary to ask. I have chosen the following examples of what may seem to be the foolishness of God because they are well known stories, and, therefore, may be useful to describe and to discuss in this context. Perhaps in examining some of this "foolishness" we may find in it some divine wisdom or purpose that the author included in a manner deliberately too subtle for the casual or skeptic reader to discern, but which deeper study may reveal insights with which even the non-believer can identify. Now let us examine some of these "foolish actions" of the Lord, which He recorded for our scorn or for our edification, depending on where our faith and sentiments lay. Here, I've chosen to give a synopsis of each event from what might be considered a secular perspective. Following this, I've tried to offer my personal understanding and beliefs as obtained from the Scriptures and from other writers to whom I've been blessed to have been exposed. Forgive me when I wander off on to tangents and peripheral thoughts. There is so much in the Scriptures that I wish to shout to the world, that I cannot help but get side tracked when I think of something that I consider profound and feel compelled to share.

1. Adam and Eve and the Rib

From the dust of the earth God made Adam. That's sensible. What else should He have used? But Eve, He made her out of one of Adam's ribs. That doesn't make sense! Why a rib? Why not make her out of the same dust? Using natural wisdom the whole thing sounds foolish. But let's see if we can dig a little deeper into the Word to see if God gives us a clue to His wisdom. First, it is known that portions of some ribs have the capacity to regenerate. That is the part of the rib that God took from Adam, and that grew back, making Adam whole again. I used to wonder why I wasn't short a rib if this story was true. Other bones would not have done that. Now Eve, generated from his rib, had his genes and was, therefore, at the very least a very close blood relative. Thus, there was naturally a close kinship, a unique compatibility and a sameness that God wanted them to have and that He could most readily achieve in this manner. That this was achieved is evident in Genesis 2:23 where Adam said, "This is now bone of my bone and flesh of my flesh: she shall be called woman because she was taken from man." It seems clear that by using a part of Adam to create Eve, and thus giving her his genes, God made certain that there would be an immediate and permanent physiological as well as psychological bond between them that otherwise could not have been. And yet, this was essential under the unique circumstances associated with the role that they were ordained to play as the parents of all mankind.

The next verse is as profound as it is revealing in that it further explains the foolishness of this rib issue, and it is prophetic as well. Even so, to a casual reader it could easily slip by unappreciated. In Genesis 2:24 we learn "Therefore shall man leave his father and his mother and shall cleave unto his wife: and they shall be one flesh." What father and mother? There weren't any yet! Why did God put this verse here, instead of somewhere down the line where one might believe it to be more appropriate? This verse, of course, anticipates the future and establishes the priority of relationships and the importance as well as the permanence of marriage. It's such an important message that God couldn't wait any longer to tell us! As you read the Scriptures notice how often God uses marriage as the major idiom by which to teach us about our relationship to Him as well as to our mates. Adam and Eve being literally of the same flesh were well able to successfully "cleave" (cling to, adhere to, stick). This made them the ideal prototype of all future men and women in marriage who are to "cleave" and be as one flesh."

Thus, in this convoluted foolishness of the rib story, God demonstrated foresight and wisdom that the natural man would not have considered, and in doing so, established at the very beginning, what He prescribes and requires of all marriages, which to Him, except for our union with Him, is the most sacred of all unions. You might counter all of this rib explanation by observing that God could have instilled these sameness qualities in Eve without using Adam's rib, if He had wanted to. Well, not exactly. God made Adam and Eve as He has all of us, with a sovereign will, a freedom to make choices independent of His will, choices that He does not micromanage. He certainly intervenes in events of the world as He sees fit, and to those who believe, He answers prayers. However, on a day by day, moment by moment basis, we pretty much choose our own thoughts and actions as influenced by our surroundings and by our individual personalities. Although we are not all stamped out of the same mold, but are instead unique individuals, we, nevertheless, carry choice influencing qualities in our genes derived from the composite of all of our ancestors. Adam had no ancestors. However, to insure compatibility and agreement in this choice-making realm, God wisely (of course) plucked out this replaceable rib full of compatible genes and made Eve in the manner in which she would be best suited to spend a happy eternity with Adam. This was a sort of required "jump start" to assure compatibility of the first couple who had no past, no history, no inheritable qualities which, clearly all subsequent generations would have. Of course, shortly thereafter they got started; she made a bad choice, and he made the choice to go along with her bad choice, so they only got to live together a little more than nine hundred years. Unfortunately, that bad choice gene has been carried down through the generations, as evidenced by history as well as the present condition of the world and of each of us, their children.

2. Noah's Ark and The Great Flood

This is a short story that, to the non-believer can also be entertaining from the viewpoint of its fairy tale qualities. Here we have Noah, who ". . . walked with God . . ." (Genesis 6:9) given by God the chance to build a barge or ark as they called it; He wants to save Noah and his family and samples of the animal kingdom, while He floods the entire earth in order to kill all other land based life on the planet. Faithful to God's direction, Noah spends the next 120 years building this thing according to God's specifications. It has three levels plus a roof and is three hundred cubits long, fifty cubits wide and thirty cubits high. A cubit was the length of a man's arm from the elbow to the tip of the longest finger. This obviously varied with the size of the man. However, historians conclude that eighteen inches was probably a good average and may have been standardized around that length, just as the foot later became standardized in England, based on the length of the king's foot. My cubit is twenty inches so eighteen inches seems to be a reasonable value to use in converting cubits to feet and inches. Based on this, the ark was 450 feet long, 75 feet wide and 45 feet high. That is one and a half football fields long, almost a half of the width of a football field wide, and as tall as a five-story apartment building. This volume was one and a half million cubic feet. Can you imagine the jokes going around the neighborhood about this old coot that was building a barge the size of a stadium in his back yard because it was going to rain and flood the land? What's rain? There had never been any such thing as rain.

When the ark was finally finished Noah was six hundred years old and his three sons were by then about a hundred years old. Then, as the story goes, God told him to take with him his wife, his three sons and their wives and get into the ark along with a male and female of every species of animal, bird and creeping thing, plus seven pairs of "clean animals." Once they were all tucked in and settled down, God shut the door and commanded forty days of solid day and night rain. This plus some "fountains" flooded the whole earth killing every-thing and everyone on all the land, except for those on the ark. They stayed in the ark for more than a year, 371 days to be exact, and then came out to begin populating the earth all over again.

To the non-believer or casual reader, all of this sounds pretty difficult to swallow. A six-hundred-year-old man with three one-hun-dred year-old sons starting a whole New World population! That kills it right there! A flood over the entire world, even five-mile high Mt. Everest? Collecting two of every species on the planet including ele-phants and rhinos, cobras, lions, sheep, dogs, spiders, etc.? All of these living together sealed in this barge for over a year? All coming out alive and well, redistributing, and propagating across the whole earth? No way! Could it happen? Too foolish to believe any part of it! We are supposed to believe that all of this actually happened when it's even more absurd than Greek Mythology? How could Noah build such a gigantic complex structure in such primitive times? How could he collect and corral every species of animal, bird and creepy thing? How could he control them and feed them, care for them, dispose of their wastes in such limited space for over a year? Where could all of the water come from? For a local flood maybe, but the whole earth— no Way! It's a fairy tale from beginning to end, OK for kids who believe in Santa Claus but not for us reasoning, thinking adults!

Well, that's probably how the majority of natural man, the non-believers, might view this major episode in the history of the world. Now let's see how the believer, one imbued with the Holy

Spirit, one who has studied the evidence, might interpret and understand God's word as it was recorded. We'll try to examine each of the absurdities and the impossible elements of the story applying clues from the Scriptures along with available and relevant scientific information. Lastly, we'll apply the observations of other students of the issues along with our hopefully inspired thoughts, theories and conclusions.

a.   Pre-flood people lived a very long time, around ten times longer than people do today.

For instance Adam lived for 950 years, which means that he lived from 4046 B.C. as the Bible records the year of His birth, to 3096 B.C., therefore, he was alive for 163 years after Methuselah was born in 3424 B.C., while Methuselah was around for 98 years after Shem, son of Noah was born in 2038 B.C. It is also of interest that Noah lived for 950 years and died only eight years before Abraham was born. There were but ten generations from Adam to Shem and ten more from Shem to Abraham, however because of such long lives, there were only two generations separating Adam from Abraham in terms of direct memory trail. Methuselah had potential exposure to a living Adam for 163 years, while Shem had potential exposure to a living Methuselah for 98 years and to Abraham for 150 of Abraham's 175 years. Why do I mention this? Because, while not directly relevant to the subject, this should be of interest in terms of how easily it could have been for history, knowledge, wisdom, and culture to have been preserved and handed down with little loss because of so few generational transfers from the very beginning of time to outside the great flood. It may be the answer to a question that baffles historians and archaeologists, which is, why do all of the earliest known civilizations seem to have had advanced cultures and technologies at their very beginnings, with no evidence of any transitional or evolutionary growth.

b.   Why did people live so long?

The short answer is because that is the way God made it. The longer answer involves clues both scriptural as well as scientific, and includes a sprinkling of logic and reasoned assumptions. From the

Scriptures we know that it had never rained before until the forty-day and night deluge. That means that there may have been a greater amount of water vapor floating around in the atmosphere than there is now. It is also likely that other, since removed, protective atmospheric layers were present to block cosmic rays and other extraterrestrial bombardments that shorten life. There were probably no varying seasons, only one perfect year-round Hawaii type, ideal climate everywhere, given evidence of a past lush green world both under and north of the tundra, as well as all across Antarctica and every other part of the world. The atmosphere, the ground, the water, were all, most likely, free or nearly free of toxins, harmful bacteria and virus—a pristine environment, with only the most health-providing food, air and water. Human genes in this ideal environment no doubt contained fewer, if any, mutations of the type that limit us today and that result from generations of exposure to diseases, radioactivity, toxins and other biological assaults. There is evidence that the earth's electro magnetic field gets weaker each year and that it may also be linked to diminishing health-providing conditions. I sleep with a magnetic pad under the mattress for that very reason. The resulting magnetic field is measured to be equivalent to what existed naturally two thousand years ago. This field was probably closer to optimal in earlier times, thereby providing benefits about which we know very little. Fossil evidence indicates that there were birds that, because of their structure, could have only flown if the atmospheric pressure and been considerably greater than it is now. Perhaps this also contributed to longevity. There is very convincing evidence, based on more than sixty precise measurements, taken over many years, that indicates that the speed of light is slowing down and is certainly not a constant as has been generally accepted. Calculations based on these measurements suggest that the speed of light several thousand years ago was most likely several times faster than it is now. This, of course, based on Einstein's calculations, would have had a profound effect of entropy and the movement of electrons and atoms, and thus on all matter and life forms. There may have also been other conditions, about which we cannot even imagine, that were of great benefit at that time. However, those already mentioned suggest to me that the biblical assertion of such longevity is far from absurd and quite defendable even if it were not the word of God.

c.   The preflood civilization was quite advanced.

We know from the Bible that the preflood people populated cities, worked with iron and brass, and made complex musical instruments such as harps and organs (Genesis 4:21, 22). The 450-foot long boat with a volume capacity of 1.5 million cubic feet and probably 20,000 tons displacement was also no small task for a primitive people. I have read where science has a problem with the fact that archaeological evidence indicates that prehistoric man, these "early people," had larger brains than we do today. Yet, larger brains are known to equate to greater brainpower that is greater intelligence. This may have been the case in these "prehistoric times." Combine a greater brain capacity with a life span ten times longer than ours, which continues in good health and vigor to the end, and what might you logically conclude? Think of how much more Newton or Einstein might have accomplished were they able to sustain their health and sharp brain activity for seven or eight hundred years rather than the thirty or forty years they actually had. I have no doubt that the civilization and technology of that time was far more advanced than is commonly assumed today, and that the flood and related upheavals destroyed nearly all traces of it. Noah and his family, however, would have brought much of its knowledge over into the "New World." Once again, I suggest that this accounts for the archeological evidence everywhere of the "sudden appearance of a surprisingly advanced level of civilization at about that time."

d.   The ark was wholly adequate for the job it had to do.

The dimensions previously noted along with the following, clearly attest to the fact that the Ark was adequate and appropriate for the tasks. First, it has been estimated that there are or were approximately 18,000 species to deal with. It has also been estimated that the mean size of the composite of all species, say from dinosaur to elephant to mouse to spider, would be the size of a sheep. Taking this average size times 18,000, times two of each kind, one can approximate the space requirements.

The standard cattle car carries 240 sheep. Thirty-six thousand sheep "equivalents" would fit in 150 cattle cars, while the ark had volume capacity of 553 cattle cars or well more than three times as much space as required to physically ship them in this hypothetical manner. Of course, supply space and human living quarters were also required. If one insists on dealing with this issue in natural, humanistic terms, issues such as food and water storage, elbow room, waste collection and disposal, care, and feeding, dealing with the sick, births, deaths, unruly behavior, etc., on a year long journey, the project is confronted with insurmountable problems. However, it must be remembered that this was God's gig. He set it up and He provided. Just as there is no way that Noah and his three sons could have rounded up and held together 18000 species and led them into the ark, so also was it impossible for them to provide the animal husbandry that would have been necessary for a year on the ark. God obviously directed these animals to and onto the ark and placed them in suspended animation or some form of hibernation for the duration of the trip. Thus, very little food or water was required, none mated, none died, and they all made the trip quietly and uneventfully. God may have also induced some form of hibernation on Noah and his family to help the time go faster.

The non-believer may consider this last explanation a cop out. I don't agree. Once you know as I do that God authored the Bible, you know that it speaks only the truth. It is evident from the Scriptures that God prefers to accomplish tasks using humans and natural means wherever possible. However, He never hesitates to use His supernatural power when no other means is feasible. There He uses the available Noah, the available animals, and the physical man-made ark. However, the very complex task of collecting, controlling, moving, storing and safeguarding the animals under the described circumstances is not one to be given to man or to nature. He had to do it Himself. It's as simple as that.

Before we leave the ark, there are a few other points of interest here regarding the "foolishness of God." In His instructions to Noah, He directs him in Genesis 5:14 ". . . and shalt pitch it within and without with pitch." When a boat is "pitched" it is done on the outside only to fill cracks and joints and to preserve the wood from the ravages of water. Pitching the inside makes no sense, is a waste, and makes the interior surfaces smelly, sticky and difficult to deal with. Why then would God require this internal pitch unless He had in His mind a long-term preservation well past the short-term use for which the ark was made?

There seems to be considerable evidence that the ark still exists. It has been observed from satellites, by radar, from airplanes, by telescope from nearby vantage points, and by mountain climbers who have been there and taken pieces of it. It sits at an elevation of 16,946 feet above sea level on the mountain of Ararat just where God had made a special point of telling us it would be. It is snow covered eleven months a year and rests on the side of the cliff where access is difficult, dangerous and even breathing is a problem. This high, dry and difficult-to-access location is, of course, ideal for its preservation, especially with its preservation pitch "within and without."

Given where He put it, how He ordered it to be preserved, and the fact that it apparently does still exist, suggests that the Lord may have had some as yet unfulfilled use for the ark. Perhaps it will be one of the certain evidences of the literalness and truth of Scriptures to be brought forth in the final days as one way to convince the unconvinced. Its more recent history seems in some ways to support this premise. It was mentioned as seen by Marco Polo and much later Tsar Nicholas of Russia formed an expedition to survey it. However the communists, who have restricted any examination of it for obvious reasons, deposed him. Being in Turkey near the Russian border, even the Turks have been hostile to its exploration. By all reports, the object in question on the side of Mt. Ararat is of the size and general description outlined in the Bible.

Based on what happened to the earth during the flood, Ararat probably was not nearly as high when the ark landed and was emptied. The upheaval of that region and elevating of those mountains could have occurred later as God chose to raise it up to where it would be safe, preserved and difficult to get to. This, along with the political turmoil that has existed for centuries in this region, seems to me to be all part of God's plan for deferring its verifiable and generally accepted discovery.

e.   We know that God was really "fed up" with the way His creation had developed.

Genesis 6 speaks of the "wickedness of mankind." It also tells of angels mating with women and having children, which were giants. ". . . the same became mighty men which were of old men of renown. And God saw that wickedness of man was great in the earth, and that every imagination of thoughts of his heart was only evil continually." With that, He decided to clean house and destroy the whole thing, except that, "But Noah found grace in the eyes of the Lord." Noah was just a man and perfect in his generations and ". . . Noah walked with God." These giants were also called Nephilim, the "fallen ones," and were the real live titans of Greek, Roman and other mythologies. The wickedness of man was, of course, compounded and probably even increased by the presence of Nephilim who, while probably superior physically and intellectually, were spiritually demonic as sons of Satan and his followers. At any rate, we know that God chose to wipe out the whole population and start all over again with a new Adam in the person of Noah who was "perfect in his generations." Why didn't He simply kill everyone some other way and rapture Noah as He did Enoch and then create a new Adam and Eve? I don't know. As He said in Isaiah 55:8, 9 ". . . for My thoughts are not your thoughts, neither are your ways My ways, saith the Lord. For as the heavens are higher than the earth so are My ways higher than your ways, and My thoughts than your thoughts." As noted, He saw in Noah a man "pure in his generations," that is not contaminated with Nephilim ancestors, a just and faithful man worthy, of continuing the race. Incidentally, while there is nothing in the Scriptures to suggest that anyone else survived, it seems likely to me that God may have also raptured a sizable remnant of the faithful just as will occur just before the world ends again for the second and last time, as clearly predicted in the Scriptures. Also the abomination of this angel-woman union returned for a while after the flood as is evidenced by Anikan, the Amorites and other tribes at the time of Joshua and even later in the persons of Goliath and his four brothers. These, however, were also killed off eventually.

f.   Where did all the water come from to flood the entire world?

There appears to be archeological evidence that there was a world-wide flood. There is also evidence that the earth topography has undergone severe convulsions in the past. This is a very plausible theory that can explain many things and answer the question. Given the lushness of the world's vegetation along with other evidence, it is likely that the world topography was more gently rolling than it is today, i.e.: there was no Mt. Everest or Rocky Mountains. Genesis 7:19 tells us, ". . . and all the high hills that were under the whole heaven were covered." Then Genesis 7:20 says, ". . . Fifteen cubits upward did the water prevail; and the mountains were covered." Both "high hills" and "mountains" are a translation of the same Hebrew word *har*, which is in the singular "mountain" or "range of hills." Thus, it would seem to be literally translated as range of hills and not mountains. With an even climate, and little temperature differences, there would be little or no wind and no seasons. Given that the Bible speaks of "fountains of the great deep water" there probably did exist large Great Lakes sized subterranean water lenses. These would be necessarily under great pressure as are oil deposits today, which release as "gushers." If released by, say an earthquake, these vast reservoirs of water would have burst upward and risen to great heights as fountains. This along with the first ever opening of the "window of heaven" would have provided enough water to well cover the entire gently rolling topography of the earth. This great displacement of these huge underground reservoirs of water would have also ensured major distortion of the earth's crust, including displacement earthquakes and volcanoes, all capable of contributing to the deepening of the oceans and the raising of the mountains. It should be noted, that the amount of stored moisture in the atmosphere was probably not much more than it is today, and therefore its contribution to the flood was probably very minimal. It was the vast underground source that provided nearly all of the floodwaters. These "fountains" probably shot up thousands of feet into the air and would have been widely dispersed coming down as torrential rain. For more information on this intriguing concept, see the book, "In The Beginning" by Walt Brown (Center for Scientific Creation, Publisher).

Perhaps related to this great upheaval is the recently revised theory regarding the Grand Canyon. Until recently an axiom of the geological sciences was that the canyon eroded to its mile deep condition over millions of years. The current theory is that somehow the edge of a gigantic lake opened up and the water burst forth at great velocity scouring the canyon very rapidly. Another exploding theory concerns fossils. An animal caught and buried in mud would necessarily decompose in a short period of time leaving no fossil, unless tremendous heat and pressure were applied very quickly, not through slow layer-by-layer depositing over eons. All of these conditions, the flooding of the entire earth, the formation of fossils, the tropical food still in the gut of quick frozen mastodons, the rapid rise of mountains and deep oceans etc., find plausible explanations in the aftermath of the opening of "window to heaven" and "the fountain of the deep."

We know that the world into which Noah stepped out of the ark was not the same as the one he left a year earlier. God gave him the world's first rainbow because this had been the world's first rain. The atmosphere was lighter, the sky cleaner, there were now variable seasons, winds and different climates in different places. More of the earth was covered with water and there were great rivers and great oceans and great snowcapped mountains as well as deserts, green valleys and plains. Given that all these things exist today, it takes a "leap of faith" as well as scientific evidence mixed with a good deal of studied speculation, to feel comfortable with the acceptance of the fact that things were vastly different a mere four thousand years ago, especially when "science" tells us it took millions of years. Those who "believe" because they have been so inspired, and because they have dug deeply into God's word, find no difficulty in reconciling the evidence of nature with the Word of the Lord, for He has included within His word all that is needed to explain these mysteries.

g. Why such a long time in the Ark?

According to the Scriptures the ark rested on the "mountain of Ararat" 280 days after Noah got in it, and it took another 91 days before God let them out on a generally dry earth where some considerable vegetation had returned. Note that the dove came back a week earlier with an olive leaf. ". . . the waters prevailed on the earth for 150 days" (Genesis 7:24). My interpretation is that there was probably no dry ground anywhere until then, which is at least five months after the rain came. One reason for that long duration of total inundation may have been to assure that there were absolutely no other possible survivors. We don't know but we can assume with some confidence that there was water-borne commerce, that there were boats and even ships of substantial size. I suggest that Noah probably wasn't the only one who ever built a boat during that era. If that is true then it can be assumed that some people managed to get into boats with some supplies before their area was inundated. Five months on such a craft, however well fitted as it may have been, was simply too long to allow survival, especially with forty days of rain or spraying fountains filling the craft and thereby requiring around the clock hand bailing of the collected water.

The fact that the flood was coming was known by at least some for more than 969 years, just as our era has known that there again would be final days "as in the days of Noah." Our era has known of the coming end for more than 1900 years, or since John wrote the book of Revelation. The signs of the times are known now as they were then. Back then Enoch had prophesied it and even named his son Methuselah as a living prophecy. His name in the original Hebrew means, "his death shall bring" which was meant to identify the date of the end of time, or the predicted flood. The flood did come the very year he died. Of course as it is today, so it was then; few if any took it seriously and believed the Word even when they saw Noah, a prophet and a man "who walked with God," working for 120 years building the ark. The Scripture also clearly describes the events immediately preceding the coming end times as it did then. In the book of Daniel can be found the prediction that the Jews would be back in the Promised Land on the very day that the State of Israel was proclaimed on May 14, 1948, 1878 years after the beginning of the Diaspora in 70 A.D. It also predicted that Jerusalem would be back in Israel's control; it is; that Babylon was to be rebuilt; it has been under reconstruction for more than twenty years; that the Temple would be rebuilt; more than two hundred priests are being trained, and temple furniture is being constructed along with other appropriate religious equipment and vestures, all with the firm expectation that the temple will be reconstructed also as prophesized and as evidence of the final days.

h. One more "foolishness of God"

This isn't really foolishness, but it clearly is of God, because no one else could have pulled this off. It is clever, far beyond any human contrivance. I've noted it in previous papers, yet it fits so well here, I must repeat it. Below is a list of the direct line of descendants from Adam to Noah. To the right of the list are the root Hebrew meanings of those names.

Adam	Man
Seth	Appointed
Enos	Mortal (frail, incurable)
Kenan	Sorrow
Mahalaalesh	Blessed God
Jared	Shall come down
Enoch	Teaching (teacher)
Methuselah	His death shall bring
Lemoch	Despairing (from which we get Lamentations)
Noah	Comfort (to bring relief)

Now let's put that into a sentence.

"Man (is) appointed mortal sorrow; (but) the Blessed God shall come down teaching (that) his death shall bring comfort to the despairing."

WOW! That is a one-sentence summary of the whole history and purpose of mankind! Through the original sin, that opening of Pandora's box in the Garden of Eden, man was appointed mortal (subject to death) sorrow, but God (Jesus) shall come down teaching, that His death (crucifixion) shall bring the comfort to the despairing (salvation and eternal life). End of story.

I got this, as well as so many other marvelous insights, from the writing and tapes of the truly blessed Chuck Missler.

What does that tell you about God's Authorship of the Bible? I guess it must tell us that somewhere along the way those who wrote the Torah, or some latter rabbis, got together and composed that list of names so that it would read as a prophecy of a coming Messiah whose death would bring comfort to the world. No? Not likely? Then maybe our Lord Himself, in His clever foolishness left us a lightly coded message about His son, who would come and die for us. You have to keep a sharp eye on this Author and His book, because He has planted dozens of these little gems throughout both the old and new sections of His masterpiece.

There are two sides or perspectives to every story. There is the perception of the spirit and the perception of the flesh that is of natural man. This paper regarding Noah and the event surrounding the flood begins with a short summary as it might be viewed by the casual, uninspired skeptical reader. I've tried to dissect the story into several components with the attempt in a cursory manner to apply the subtle clues found in the Scriptures along with relevant scientific thoughts and evidence liberally sprinkled with plausible conjecture and hopefully spiritual insight. In this way, continuing for the most part from the perspective of the flesh, I have tried to explain the cause of the longevity of early man, the reason for the flood, the manner in which the flood was physically possible, its consequences relating to the character of the earth, and the physical adequacy and feasibility of the ark in fulfilling its purpose as well as its possible future purpose. With the exception of the final item, the prophetic nature of the names of Noah's ancestors, I have refrained from reporting the wealth of spiritual insights and messages with which the Lord has blessed this portion of Scripture. These would include such things as Noah being a type or model of Jesus, the pre-levitical evidence of levitical law, the long-term significance of Nephilim, etc. In this paper, I've tried only to inspire the lukewarm reader to aspire hopefully to a burning need to read, to search, to learn and ultimately to know the blessed word of God as recorded in the Scriptures.

3. The Ten Plagues, The Passover and the Exodus

Here we have a series of events about as far fetched as any good fiction writer could imagine. To the non-believer, this story is more like a fairy tale fantasy full of foolishness, magic and wizardry, rather than the orchestration of an omnipotent God. We have the Pharaoh, ruler of the most powerful nation of that period, having a slave labor population of between one and two million people. These are the children of Israel whom he has making bricks and constructing cities. Then we have this eighty-year-old man, Moses, coming into the court and demanding that the Pharaoh release the whole population of slaves because his God says so. Now the Pharaoh considers himself a god, as well as the Nile River, frogs, snakes, cattle, and a number of other creatures and things that he and his people worship. Therefore, he is not too impressed when Moses shows him how his God can turn a stick into a snake; the Pharaoh's, magicians can do the same thing. Then He turns the river into blood, which the Pharaoh's boys can do also. The next plague is frogs, which again both parties seem to know how to do also. Now Moses, or God, starts turning the screw tighter with a plague of lice, which the magicians can't do; they are very upset, and finally admit to the Pharaoh that Moses' God is the real one. With that, they disappear from the story.

The Pharaoh stays stubborn even as Moses plagues him with flies, kills all his cattle, inflicts everyone with boils, drops big hail stones that ruin the crops, brings in locusts that eat everything that is still green, and then shuts down the sun for three days. Finally, when every first born of all people and animals dies as Moses said they would, Pharaoh is really impressed and lets them go. Throughout all of this, the plagues affect everyone except the children of Israel. Their water doesn't turn to blood; they don't get the frogs, lice, flies, boils, etc. However, they have to do something to avoid the first-born problem. They have to smear sacrificial lamb's blood on their doorposts and stay inside for the night. All of those who do this are spared this tenth and last plague.

After they have all left, bag, baggage, carts, cattle and everything, Pharaoh has second thoughts, and goes after them with his army and all six hundred of his elite chariot corps. In the meantime, they take the worst possible escape route, one that leads to the shore of the Red Sea where escape is impossible, and where the chariots catch up to them and trap them. Pharaoh is thwarted, however, by a wall of fire that keeps him away from the people. In the meantime, Moses lifts his rod, the sea parts and the whole entourage travels safely between these walls of water to the other side of the Red Sea. Once they are safe, the wall of fire disappears so Pharaoh sends his whole force in pursuit only to be completely wiped out when the water engulfs them as the sea returns to normal.

The fame of this debacle spread throughout the ancient world, and Egypt never recovered its former greatness. It's political, social, economic, and spiritual structure was decimated, and its army destroyed. Yet, there never was a tangible physical enemy or any battle. It was just a bunch of slaves led by an old man and the foolishness of God confounding the wisdom of the wise and the power of the powerful. Now let's go back and examine the story a little more closely, paying attention to some of the subtitles and edifying clues that the Author left scattered around in his book. This alone could fill a volume, however, we'll try to limit it to the foolishness of God aspects, and as best as I can, how these tell us some not so foolish truths.

First, who were these people, these slaves? Why were they there in Egypt and why did God intervene in their fate? These were all descendants of Jacob who 430 years earlier had moved there during the seven-year famine when Egypt, through the grace of God, had stored enough food to feed everyone during the entire period. This is another one of those "foolishness of God" stories where Joseph, one of Jacobs twelve sons, had been sold into slavery and ended up number two man in Egypt, and the architect of the famine survival program that made Egypt the most powerful nation of the period. In the ensuing four centuries, this family of seventy grew to an estimated one to two million people. At first, as the family of Egypt's hero and savior Joseph, they were welcomed and given the very best land by the Pharaoh. However, as time passed they grew in number and a new Pharaoh came into power ". . . which knew not Joseph" (Exodus 1:8). He feared that these people who ". . . are more mightier than we" (Exodus 1:9) might fight against him in a war, and so he decided while he could, to enslave them. How could this comparatively limited number of slaves ever be mightier than all of Egypt?

Here we have one of these wonderful opportunities to discover a hidden pearl, a clarifying bit of information, the clues that are in various parts of the Bible waiting to be found, to be savored and to be added to the thousands of other clues that prove the integrated wholeness and supernatural Authorship of this book. Here we are told that the Pharaoh didn't know Joseph. In Acts 7:18, Steven is recounting this historical period when he mentions ". . . until another King arose, which knew not Joseph." This is not much of a clue to anything unless you turn to the particular Greek word for "another" in the original Greek text. In the Greek, there are two words meaning "another." They are *allaylone,* meaning another of the same kind, like another apple, and *heteros* meaning another of a different kind, like another fruit, but not the same as the apple I just had. Here the latter is used. This suggests that perhaps this Pharaoh was not of the usual kind but of a different kind, that is not an Egyptian or whatever "kind" the last one was. Perhaps it seems absurd to reach that far from so little a clue, until we turn left and go back in to the Old Testament to Isaiah 52:4 and read ". . . for thus saith the Lord God, My people went down afore time into Egypt to sojourn there; and the Assyrian oppressed them without cause." WOW! Doesn't that give you goose bumps? The oppressing Pharaoh was not an Egyptian! Something happened to the dynasty of Joseph's time and it was apparently replaced by foreigners, in this case an Assyrian. Somehow this guy got control, probably with a relatively small cohort of Assyrians, which would explain why he feared this tribe of Hebrews. It must have been much smaller than the whole Egyptian population, yet probably was of a threatening size compared to those Assyrians who at the time were running the place.

Once the slavery was instituted and economy grew accustomed to it and dependent on it, no one wanted or could afford to see it ended. To add some additional credence to this, as if the Word of God needed any such thing, Manetho, the ancient Egyptian priest/historian, recorded that non-Egyptians ruled the country at the time of the construction of the great pyramids. Also, Moses himself, some forty to sixty years before the Exodus, as the Pharaoh's daughter's adopted son, had been a likely successor to the then Pharaoh, had he remained in the palace and assumed the role for which he had been groomed. Josephus, the first century historian, tells us much more about the early Moses than does the Bible. From him we learn that Moses was extremely handsome, strong, and intelligent, schooled in the best and most that Egypt had to offer its nobility. He was highly esteemed by the Egyptians for his intelligence and noble ways, as well as his many military and diplomatic exploits. He even conquered an impregnable city in Ethiopia, partly because of his handsomeness and regal manner, when the princess of the city fell in love with him just watching him from the city walls as he rode around directing the preparation for the siege. I wonder why Cecil B. DeMille didn't include this scene in his movie, *Moses*.

Now we have some important background as to why slavery, and why the great reluctance on the part of the Pharaoh to end it. But why did it happen in the first place, and why did the Lord choose to end it the way He did? We don't know all that happened, but those who have faith know the Lord had good reasons. My view is that He used the four hundred years to grow a nation out of this one family to whom, through Abraham, He had promised certain land, which in His scheme of things couldn't be turned over yet as He said to Abraham in Genesis15:16 ". . . for the iniquity of the Amorites is not yet full." Also, it would seem that this move would not happen until they had grown sufficiently in number, had been tempered through servitude and tempted through exposure to pagan gods. Throughout this period they had preserved their ethnic purity and identity as well as a memory of their God. They had, however, succumbed to the paganism and idol worshiping as is evidenced numerous times during their forty years in the wilderness. This is, in part at least, understandable because of their servitude wherein they were forbidden to worship their God in accordance with His earlier prescribed ways. This even extended to the matter of circumcision, which was forbidden to them because in the prevailing Egyptian culture, circumcision, for different reasons was allowed to be practiced only by the elite. Nevertheless, they were God's chosen, and so He chose this time to remove them toward this "Promised Land."

But why all this hocus-pocus with the plagues? Here God deliberately toys with the Pharaoh and rubs his nose in his own pride before he inflicts His retribution for the bondage of His people, for the pagan worship, and for the audacity of Pharaoh believing himself to be a God. These first few tricks, the snakes, the water to blood and the frogs weren't tricks at all; they were supernatural acts by both God through Moses and by Satan through the so-called magicians. These weren't magicians in the same sense as we think of magicians. This was not slight of hand or illusion; this was real. These magicians were actually priests, pagan priest, priests who had limited supernatural powers provided by Satan through what we might call evil spirits. When Moses did the lice bit, they knew that they were out-matched and that God was really behind Moses. A vital part of the pagan (Satanic) ritual practiced by these priests required extreme body cleanliness and thus abhorrence of such things as lice. That is why the Egyptian priests always kept their heads and bodies shaved. The lice infestation was God's way of mocking them and thwarting any further comfort that they or Satan might be to the Pharaoh. In turning the Nile red, God defiled it, one of their major items of worship. With the frogs, He made these particular items of worship so numerous as to make them sickening to everyone. He did so also with the locusts, the killing of cattle and demonstrating His power by hiding the sun, another major center of worship. Thus, God was demonstrating His power and the weakness of their gods as He progressively inflicted greater pain and retribution on this prideful head of an evil empire. Killing the first born was in remembrance of the number of male babies that Pharaoh had ordered killed, and from which order Moses had escaped through divine intervention and planning for this, then future, event.

Even though the plagues and the parting of water were spectacular evidences of God's supernatural power, the Passover, the sparing of all of the first-born housed where the doorways were marked with blood, is His greatest most remembered and revered act in this Exodus scenario. To this day, Jews celebrate the Passover on the fourteenth day of the Jewish calendar month of Nisan as one of the greatest of holidays, the day the Lord delivered them from bondage. Three days later they celebrated the Feast of First Fruits, also called the Feast of New Beginnings, which is associated with the actual beginning of Israel as a nation, the day they crossed the Red Sea. This is truly an interesting day, because in Genesis 8:4 the Lord chose to make particular note of the exact day that the Ark landed and a New Beginning for the earth also began, ". . . and the Ark rested in the seventh month, on the seventeenth day of the month, upon the mountains of Ararat," again the seventeenth of Nisan! That's not all! Remember our Lord Jesus, the sacrificial Lamb of God, was crucified and shed his blood, which was smeared on a cross, the doorway to eternal life, on Passover the fourteenth of Nisan. Three days later on the Feast of First Fruits, the day of New Beginning, the seventeenth of Nisan, He arose from the dead to assure us a new beginning for all who believe in Him.

As I learned of this series of events, I couldn't help wonder and marvel at the logistics and the incredible supernatural aspect of this particular event, the crossing of the Red Sea. So far I have not found any detailed commentary on this event, and, therefore, the following is entirely my own amateurish conjecture. I picture this great mass of people, between one and two million, pressed against the shore of the Red Sea frightened and more likely expecting slaughter than a miracle. Then the waters part and they stream across to the other side. How wide was the spreading of the waters that allowed them to walk on the dry bottom and cross to the other side? How deep was it? How far between shores? The Scripture says that they crossed on the third day. Therefore, they must have done it in one day. From a very small map, I scaled a narrow point along the shore where the sea appears to be approximately eight miles wide and at a location where they might have traveled in that short three days time. At three miles per hour, a very fast pace for such a multitude with children, pregnant women, and cattle, carts, etc. it would take the first person almost three hours to cross the eight miles. If they were traveling at fifty abreast, and say, four feet, one behind the other, the people alone would create a column approximately twenty-three miles long. Again, ignoring cattle, carts, etc. the last person to arrive on the far shore would get there, assuming no stopping along the way, approximately ten hours after the first person started to cross. It is impossible to make any defendable allowances of time for the delaying factors not here considered. However, under any "natural" scenario where hundreds of delaying circumstances would be inevitable, such as stopping to eat, or drink or rest, sickness, broken wheels, accidents, lack of 100 percent control of pace and behavior, etc. this idealized ten-hour time could easily have become days. The fact that it was completed in a "day" attests to the fact that the wall of fire and of water were not the only supernatural manifestations at work that day. Just as it took supernatural orchestration by God to lead the "two of each kind " to and on to Noah's ark in a timely manner without incidents, so must have God also personally strengthened, fed, protected and guided each individual across that chasm and onto safety. Logistically it seems impossible to have happened otherwise. My simple calculation was based on an idealization of the conditions and the discounting of the many variables and conflicting factors that would have necessarily confounded, delayed, and probably foiled the whole operation. The fact that this event could have successfully occurred only through the idealization of all factors clearly proves to me that God did far more than spread the waters and hold the chariots at bay.

Playing a little more with the numbers and assumptions, I'm intrigued with how wide and how deep the parted waters might have been. I assumed people were moving along fifty abreast. There is no basis for this but only as a starting point from which to estimate other dimensions, such as the twenty-three miles long column of people and the resulting time it might take to cross. These merely offer orders of magnitude from which to better comprehend the problem. At fifty abreast in random order as civilians and not as regimented soldiers, the width would have to have been at least 150 feet. If it was that wide, probably the chariots could have averaged at least four abreast as they raced to catch up. Assuming the ground was irregular and so they averaged only ten miles per hour and were say, one hundred feet apart in the direction of travel, they would have created a line three miles long. At that speed, they could have, had God allowed it, crossed the eight miles in less than an hour. It would be my guess that the depth of the water at this crossing may not have been more than fifty to one hundred feet. More than that and it would seem that the climb down and back up would have thwarted the use of wagons and chariots. On the other hand, too much less than fifty feet might have made it possible for some of Pharaoh's soldiers to have survived the sudden inundation and swirling of the returning waters. And yet, if the sea was eight miles wide and the slopes relatively gentile and smooth, the depth in the middle could have been several hundred feet. The four abreast chariot scenario seems plausible, and if close to fact, the sea must have been well over three miles wide in order that all chariots would be without exception, caught and destroyed.

To summarize this episode as it relates to the "foolishness of God" theme, I've already noted that though this series of supernatural acts, planned and unfolded in the manner recorded, the Lord accomplished several things.

a. He rescued His chosen from slavery where they had grown into what could now be called a nation.

b. Through Moses, He provided the leader they needed both physically and spiritually.

c. Through the selectively inflicted plagues, He demonstrated to them, as well as to Pharaoh, just whose God He was and how great His power was, all in terms that were impressionable on even the most "stiff-necked" people.

d. He demonstrated to the Pharaoh and all his people the impotence and true foolishness of their gods.

e. He repaid Egypt in full for the years of slavery and the killing of the male Israelite babies.

f. He demonstrated to the world at large that He was The God, and that these were His chosen people.

This final point is documented in Joshua 2:9 when Rahab tells the two spies (who forty years later went into Jericho) all about their God, and the destiny of their people. She knew all about the plagues and the parting of the waters, as did the whole city who were all in great fear of what they knew was coming. As I read her description of that fear, I almost wonder if God didn't use the vibrations caused by the Amorites shaking in their boots, and the chattering of their teeth, as well as the trumpets and yelling of the Israelites to cause the walls to crumble. Apparently the forty-year-old news of the Lord's work in Egypt was, as He planned, disconcerting enough to totally traumatize these Amorite giants, rendering them defenseless. This Jericho story, how the walls collapsed as a result of the Israelites walking around them for six days in silence, and walking around yelling and blowing trumpets on the seventh day, is certainly another worthy "foolishness of God" story in itself. By the way, when it came time for the Israelites to cross over the Jordan and occupy the Promised Land, God provided an encore to the "parting of the waters" event by actually holding back the waters of the Jordan while the whole nation crossed. This also happened to be in the spring when the river was flooded and as much as a mile wide. If you are intrigued by coincidences, the Scriptures make note of the fact that the location of this crossing is the very place where John the Baptist baptized Jesus about 1440 years later. However, do not be fooled! There are no coincidences in the Bible! Whatever appears to be such is actually God's way of showing us that this book and the events He chose to include in it are His work, His orchestration, His planning. This is strikingly evident as previously noted by His use of the seventeenth day of Nisan, the day of New Beginnings, to celebrate the landing of Noah's Ark, the Israelites reaching the east side of the Red Sea, and Jesus' resurrection. The Jews proclaim that coincidence is not a kosher word. They are correct. There are no chance happenings as the Scriptures illustrate.

4. Jesus, His Life, Death and Resurrection

How does one, a born again Christian, approach this event, which is the foundation and totality of one's belief, and do so in the context of the "foolishness of God," without appearing to be hypocritical and even blasphemous? I write this with sincere reverence and love for the Lord Jesus, and also with love and concern for any and all who might read this. I pray that my words will in some way ignite in the unbelieving, or the lukewarm, an interest and an increase in understanding of this, the most momentous event ever to occur in the history of the world. As with the previously narrated biblical events, I'll begin with the non-believer's view of the story and then try to analyze and elaborate, as far as my limited knowledge will take me along the study path that the believer might follow in trying to understand the meaning and purpose of it all. I am well equipped to tell the story from the nonbeliever's stance because that is where I spent most of my life. I'm far less qualified to tell it from God's perspective; however, with His help I'm sure the result will surely be better than if I had not even tried.

As everyone knows, the story begins just about two thousand years ago, when a son was born to this old man Joseph and his young bride Mary. She was already several months pregnant, but not by him, when they were married. He would have scrubbed the deal if an angel hadn't convinced him that the Holy Spirit had caused this virgin's pregnancy and that he was chosen by God to be the child's adopted father. The angel also told Mary the same story, and that her son would be the promised king through the line of David, who just happened to be an ancestor of both Joseph and Mary.

Of course, a son was born on Christmas Day (what a coincidence) and they called him Jesus as they had been told to by the Angel. His birth had apparently been foretold centuries earlier by the prophets, so it wasn't much of a surprise to some people. The nearby shepherds knew, as they saw this big star move across the sky and stop right over the stable where the family was staying. They followed it there, found the baby, and worshiped Him, knowing who He was. Also, some Magi from another country who knew about where and when of the birth from old time prophecy even in their country, came by and gave him gifts. The news got to King Herod, who saw this as a threat to his own throne, so when he couldn't find the kid he played it safe and ordered every child under two in the whole nation to be killed. In the meantime, however, the angel warned Jesus' parents and packed them and their Son off to Egypt until things cooled down. Later, when Herod was dead, they came back and settled in Nazareth raising the Boy, as well as several of their own conceived in the usual manner.

We don't know about His youth except that on one occasion at age twelve He preached most impressively in the Temple in Jerusalem. Then around age thirty, which is the earliest that a Rabbi can preach, he began his preaching and healing and miracle business. He seemed to know the Bible by heart, preached it with inspiration, and elaborated on its Commandments in an awesome way, preaching for instance that an evil thought is the same as the evil deed. For instance, looking with lust is the same as the act of fornication, and anger could be considered the same as murder. He also taught love and many other uplifting things. His miracles and preaching upset the "spiritual" hierarchy and they too felt their structure and power threatened as his fame spread and more and more people followed him, calling him King and Messiah. Because of this, the chief priests conspired to kill him and finally got the Romans to do it by crucifixion.

After he was dead his friends put him in a nearby tomb. For some time later he was seen by many, especially his apostles and close friends, alive and well, yet with nail holes in his wrists and feet and a big gash in his side. Now he was able to enter a closed room out of nowhere and leave the same way. Later a few of them saw him ascend into the air and disappear.

Well, hardly any of the story makes any solid sense other than the fact that there was a nice guy named Jesus and that He had a nice warm philosophy about life and dealing with others. But changing wine to water, feeding five thousand with only a few fish and loaves of bread and having more left over than He started with, bringing a man back to life who had been dead so long that he already stunk of rot, walking on water, driving out evil spirits, being himself brought back to life after that decisive kind of death, then appearing and disappearing at will, and finally visibly ascending to heaven? Then you add to all of this His claim that He was God, this man who died on a cross of wood, actually claiming that He made the hill on which He stood? That's all pretty hard to swallow. It defies logic, common sense and all areas of science. Are we supposed to believe that he was God and/or the Son of God and that he came here to do all of this just to free us of sins that we can not help committing, and that we have no other way of purging from our evil souls, but that must be purged if we are to avoid eternal hell? Let me get this straight. My flesh and bones will pass away, but my soul, my center of pain, pleasure and memory will go on forever either in heaven or hell? And without God Jesus having become a man, and his human aspect having deliberately died for the sole purpose of taking away my sins, that my only possible destination would have been hell? Am I to believe that my destination is really hell unless I believe in Him and in the truth of his mission? You're saying that He did it all, and that there is nothing that I can do to save myself except simply love and believe? That's even harder to swallow!

What about all of the other faiths in the world, and all the good people who do good things and live good lives but just don't buy this stuff? Are they doomed? Why do I need to believe anything else as long as I lead a good life, behave myself, harm no one, live by the Golden Rule, contribute to charity and do good works? Why should I end up anywhere bad, if there even is such a place? All other religions that I know offer some manner of salvation or reward for a good life. No god had to come down and suffer and die for them; these people can rely on their own good conscience and various observances to assure themselves eternal reward. You're saying I can't do it alone or any of these other ways no matter how good I am unless I also believe this story and put my faith in Jesus? None of this makes sense, this God must be a strange one because this is downright foolish; other religions make more sense because they have more clearly defined causes and effects, things within the individual's control and effort from which one can derive just and fair reward. If you want me to believe this stuff you have some powerful convincing to do. When you talk about the foolishness of God, you've hit a home run here!

As may seem evident, what I just wrote summarizes a true story, my debate with myself not too long ago. Having said all of this, now how can I get God's point of view across convincingly? Only if he lets me, and if he considers me ready to do so. I have to allow for the possibility that this isn't the time or place yet, and that He is not guiding me in this. I pray for His guidance before I do things. Sometimes I think I have his blessing, sometimes I don't know. My ability at two-way communications with Him is yet at the Marconi level of development so I don't always hear his response. I just know that it's all true and that I must express this truth as best I can.

Perhaps, before I get into the main theme here, it might be appropriate to digress a little and relate some of the major milestones along my way to this belief and faith in Jesus, much of which I have written in detail elsewhere. My first reading of the Bible, the New Testament, about four years ago was the result of a curiosity regarding Christianity stemming from some other ideas that I was studying and writing about, and that required some knowledge of this belief. I read the entire New Testament understanding very little, in fact far less than I thought I did at the time. But I did get the main point, although believing it was another thing. Then I read several other commentaries such as *More than a Carpenter* by Josh McDowel and *Mere Christianity* by C. S. Lewis. Lewis was another latter day convert who struggled mightily to resist the faith, but was finally forced to capitulate, as was I, because of the weight of overwhelming evidence as to the true identity of Jesus. I truly believe that it was only this researched evidence and no other "earthly" reason that brought me to faith and belief. (Of course, there had to have been intervention from above.) This is because I had none of the typical motivations such as fear of dying or imminent danger, nor was I aware of any emotional emptiness or need for a crutch with which to support any perceived psychological weakness. In fact from early youth I developed an obsessive compulsion to be totally self-reliant. I needed no one or nothing that I could not do or earn for myself. Habits such as smoking, drinking, or religion, or dependence on others for anything, were disgusting crutches needed by only the weak, sick and lazy. My acceptance of the Gospel, as best as I can discern, was strictly the result of the recognition that the evidence was irrefutable and there was no defendable alternative except to believe that Jesus was exactly who He said He was. Once I became convinced of the deity of Jesus, his birth, life, death and resurrection, the next vital step was to recognize the divine inerrant nature of the Scriptures. It contains its own proof of divine origin once it can be viewed in the light provided by the Holy Spirit. This light is made available the moment one accepts Jesus as his or her Lord and Savior. This is *God's Word*, every word!

In it He reveals all things worthy of knowing. To learn this well, I was blessed with yet another discovery, the books and tape recordings of lectures by Chuck Missler, one of, if not the most, knowledgeable, sincere and effective Bible scholars and teachers in the world. The result of all of this is that the heavens have opened up, revealing themselves to me little by little, filling me with profound gratitude for every moment of my life, especially these last few years since my awakening and second birth. I also know that He was there with me from the beginning, suffering my ignorance, my arrogance, my mistaken belief, and my pride, waiting for that right moment when that faint pre-dawn hint of light was able to penetrate the lifelong darkness that I had mistaken for life. From there He commanded the sun to rise in my soul so that I could finally behold His brilliant truth. As I look back at these last three sentences, I can't help thinking that the non-believer reading this might be persuaded to suspect that God's foolishness is not the only foolishness being here described. I know that all of this was a side trip, away from the stated theme. However, for anyone who is seeking a path to understanding and faith, and may be interested in how someone else found it, the manner of my journey, I pray, might be of benefit.

Probably the first and most important question to be answered is why did God choose to become man and be killed in order to convey His message and to purge us of sin? Doesn't this seem to be an absurd and foolish way for an omnipotent God capable of any and all things to deal with this issue? Why didn't He choose from a limitless supply of more sensible, easier and painless alternatives instead of this strange cumbersome and "seemingly" foolish procedure? When viewed from today where we can see its history, it appears to have been a failure both from the pain and suffering that has occurred in the "name" of Christianity, and in the dwindling number of its real believers. Again, I've entered the role of non-believer for just a moment in order to better focus on the main question of Christian credibility, which I will now try to address.

Let's look at it this way, skipping the issue of creation, the fall from Eden, and the existence of angels, and just examining God's problem, which He chose to solve through His walk on earth followed by His crucifixion. God created mankind it would seem, in order to have a population of loving subjects whom He could love and care for. Why else should He bother to go through all the trouble of creation in the first place? Remember, that He is a profoundly loving God. You could say He *is* love. Furthermore, as God and King, He not only rules but he also makes the rules. As far as I can see for a Christian, all of His prerequisites for getting into His Kingdom boil down to just three. First, you must love him with your whole heart, soul and mind. He wants His love reciprocated; that's a fair enough requirement. Second, you must believe in Him, have faith in Him, and trust Him in all things, choosing to have His will be your will no matter what seems to be the consequences. If He is truly God, you must expect to spend eternity with and under Him; you can never become a happy camper unless you do have complete faith in the leader. He needs to know before hand that you aren't going to be another Satan and rebel once you get to heaven. Third, you must be sinless when you enter His Kingdom. He is a stickler for cleanliness. Sin is dirt. There is no dirt in heaven. Note that the earth is not now His Kingdom. It will be His fairly soon, after the end times, but right now for some reason it belongs to Satan, whose job seems to be to make it ever more difficult for anyone to qualify for God's eternal kingdom. (Oh, You don't buy this business of Satan's world? Believe it! I'll show you later where the book tells you so). Examining these three requirements, it is evident that the second follows without difficulty if the first is lived with sufficient intensity. As long as we live in the flesh, however, number three is impossible to achieve without divine assistance.

Now lets look a little closer to the first problem. How do you *make* someone love you? You can't; even God can't! Love is a choice, a commitment of a totally unencumbered free will. It cannot be forced or programmed, or contrived or purchased at any price. In Greek, the language that Jesus and his apostles often spoke, there are four different words for four different kinds of love. We need an adjective in front of our one word "love" in order to distinguish them. There is erotic love, brotherly love, conditional love, (I love you because, or if) and then there is unconditional love. We all experience the first three many times. These can often be motivated, influenced or dominated by emotions. But unconditional love is that pure choice love, the only kind having real substance and value in God's Kingdom. This is what He demands of us if we are to be one of His.

But how can God orchestrate this? How does He get us to completely and permanently commit to an unconditional love? He had to create us with free will in order for us to freely choose this love for Him. This, of course, leaves us also free to choose *not* to love Him. There was/is no other way even for God. Had He in any way stacked the deck in His favor, the resulting love would not be that pure, freely chosen love that he demands. Do you see the problem? There is no way that God comes out the winner in this situation. I mean He loves us all and wants us all in heaven, but the rules must stand. What kind of heaven would it be if they didn't? Therefore, He can't get us all because we won't all choose what He requires. Of course, He could change the rules, lower the standard, but then what kind of a God would he be? This sort of thing, this escape from accountability, has become common in our permissive society, but God is God. He never changes, never breaks his word and is 100 percent reliable yesterday, now and forever. Compromise is not a Godly quality. We must play by His rules if we are to play in His ballpark.

So now what could God do to cause us, of our *own free will* to love Him, believe in Him, and have faith in Him? This is a very sensitive situation. Too much force or persuasion could obviously compromise the free will condition, while too little evidence from which a positive free choice could be made would be just as unfair. So, for the long haul, He did what we humans can easily relate to when we want to tell a story or get a point across. He wrote a book!

However, in the early years after creation, God did stack the deck a little by getting chummy with some folks. That's because there wasn't yet a book or other evidence to which He could refer. But even with this He didn't bat 1,000! Look at Adam and Eve! Even with His frequent presence, they failed. Cain blew it. Enoch walked with God and was so perfect that God took him directly to heaven. Noah made it, as did Abraham. Isaac and Jacob left much to be desired, as did David and many others, but their faith and love were real; they properly disposed of sin, as it was dealt with on those days, and that was all that was needed. One thing that the Old Testament clearly tells is that this free will in the presence of worldly temptation presents a very difficult challenge for any human to overcome and to choose God and His way, unless the God choice is adequately publicized and evidenced. The history told in volume one of God's books can be fairly characterized as the saga of just one group of people, the one that God chose to personally shepherd and with which to directly communicate. He appropriately calls them a stiff-hearted people, because in spite of His often evident presence, and His clear directions as to behavior, they would over and over apply their free will to grossly deviate from His way, receive punishment, and then behave for awhile, revert back to sin, get punished again, etc., etc.

To the non-believer, all of this would once again certainly suggest an impotent God, a God repeatedly failing His mission, a Shepherd who could not properly tend His sheep. Fortunately, God makes clear throughout the Scriptures that He *is* in charge, that He has a program and knows exactly how events will progress and how it will all end. That is the beautiful thing about His book. As God, He knows from His position outside of the time dimension, everything that will happen and what He will do about it. He knew from the beginning of the world that at this moment I would be writing this. He knew who would choose Him and who wouldn't. While He orchestrated events, He never compromised anyone's free will as to how he or she would respond to these events. The choice to do things His way or another way was always available and unencumbered.

But now, finally, the crux of the matter. He had in the early times dealt with His creation simply and directly. He gave them laws and rules; he gave them direct cause and effect, rewards and punishment; he showed Himself to his chosen leaders and prophets, and thus provided enough evidence from which everyone could intelligently but without coercion choose his or her fate. But he knew, for the long haul, with the advancement of civilization, the spreading and increasing of population and the stiff-necked nature of His creation, that a universal statement, a demonstration, a compelling and everlasting recognition of his omnipotence, His incredible love and His iron-clad clear and simple formula for salvation, must be provided for the many future generations of *all* people. In the past, He had walked personally with a number of men; He had talked directly with many others; He had personally spoken to the people from Mt. Sinai; and He had occupied the tabernacle and the Temple. He had always been a down to earth personal God throughout these early centuries. Could it now be time to make one grand appearance, a most compelling demonstration of His humility and great love, a love of which only He could be capable? Could there really be any other way to affect such a climax than to have God Himself appear personally and humbly among the common people and live and breathe and eat among them? But how could He do this without stacking the deck and without being so compelling as to compromise the free choice rule that He had originally established?

When examined in this context, it becomes far from foolish that He chose to come Himself to deliver His message. Not only that, but He also had to solve this sin issue, the number three condition for salvation. Had He come as a powerful transcendent God, or the all-powerful king of the line of David, which the prophets also predicted would come later. He certainly would have had everyone's attention and immediate belief and worship. However, this surely would have been a violation of the free will precept to which we have repeatedly referred. Being born through the womb of a woman, a virgin, all as clearly prophesied, and raised in a human manner, becoming a meek, nondescript man, yet a biblically well versed rabbi, an able preacher, an incredible miracle worker, He, nevertheless, established His true credentials, but not so powerfully as to preclude any from disbelieving. Of course many did, particularly the religious leaders of that time. The legacy that He did leave, however, through his miracles, His death, resurrection and ascension provided the perfect balance for this free choice issue. What He did, and said as recorded by some of His apostles, as well as what others of them wrote through His inspired direction, provides all that one needs to be compelled to believe. Yet, unless approached in a sincere, seeking-the-truth manner, His whole message can be dismissed as unbelievable, again a demonstration of the sanctity of His free will pledge.

In case you have any doubts about who was in charge all this time, or think that perhaps God played it by ear all the earlier years, and then, when all else seemed to fail, decided to try something different, don't! He knew *exactly* what He was going to do! That's why He wrote the book, so we would know that He knew! There are more than three hundred prophecies, history before it happens, that predicted His coming, the time, the place, and many details exactly as they happened. These are irrefutable proofs of His precise, before the world began, planning and His detailed implementation of that plan.

Perhaps by now, the sharp edges of the word "foolishness" as it pertains to God's program for physical appearance here as the Man Jesus, have been scraped off. But there yet remains the issue of a torturous crucifixion, death and then the resurrection to deal with where the word "foolishness" may still seem sharp and appropriate. The key to this aspect of His sojourn here is the sin issue, requirement number three for opening the gate to heaven. As has been said, no sin can enter heaven. But, we all sin. None of us has the ability to at all times, and under all conditions, go through life having not sinned. So we love God as He wants to be loved and we place our absolute faith in Him. We try our very best not to sin, but we are of flesh, therefore, we sin. How does one get rid of sin? Various cultures and faiths deal with this in different ways, some actually by denying that there is such a thing, the ultimate in rationalization and denial of accountability! But we who have studied God's book and *know* that He wrote it, also know that there is no escape from accountability and no way through our own efforts to wash away our sins.

From the very beginning God provided skins for Adam & Eve to cover their newly recognized nakedness after the first sin. Then there was all that business with Cain and Abel. Here God instructed that the shedding of innocent blood was the only way to deal with sin. The whole Levitical system as it was set up had as a central theme animal sacrifice, or the shedding of innocent blood as atonement for sin. Only the most perfect, unblemished of the "clean" animals were worthy of this task. All of this wasn't as easy and as depersonalized as it may seem. Keeping God's rules and getting purged of sin was probably more difficult then, than it is now. The whole tribe of Levi, essentially one twelfth of the people, were non-producers who had to be subsidized by the other eleven tribes. A large portion of the accumulated wealth had to go to God for building the Tabernacle and the Temple, and to fill God's treasury. The many feast days with mandatory attendance put a strain on productivity, as did the Sabbath. Perhaps the major drain on the economy was the continuous donation of the very best of every herd for sacrifice, that is, many thousands of animals each year. Even then all sins were not covered in this manner. Some were not washable and required immediate capital punishment or other nearly as drastic measures. Just as circumcision was a "token" of a covenant between God and Abraham, so also, I believe, that the people knew, at least those who heard and believed the prophets knew, that this animal sacrifice was an interim ritual, for covering, not removing sin, and that one day a Messiah would come who would end this and "take away the sins of the world," that is all who would believe in Him.

But how would He do this? It couldn't be an easy matter. Sin is a serious issue with God, so serious that it absolutely cannot in any shape or form enter heaven. Yet, there had to be a way that was available to, and within the capacity of, every human being to achieve. If you are a father or mother and your little child gets seriously hurt or sick, would you not gladly take that wound or that sickness onto yourself and away from the child, if you could? That's because you have that fourth kind of love, that agape love, the unconditional love for your child. You would even die to save your child. God loves us the same way. Only as God He cannot die, and it's good for us that He can't! However, if He came here as man, He could accomplish two things at once! He could personalize and amplify, fulfill and validate Volume I of His book, and at the same time the human aspect of Him could die so that we might be cured of our wound, our sickness, and our sins. Now, any of you fathers or mothers tell me that's foolish! Would you do anything less for your children?

Jesus was the Lamb of God who came to take away the sins of the world through sacrifice of His own blood, the last and final and complete forever cleansing of sin. Was there any other way? Do you care to offer a scenario superior to the one God chose? The night before the crucifixion when He, of course, knew what was coming, Jesus' human aspect appealed three times to the Lord above ". . . Father, all things are possible unto thee; take away this cup from me: nevertheless, not what I will but what thou will," (Mark 14:36). Here Jesus, the physical man, the one who must suffer, asked the Lord if there was any other way to wash away the sins of mankind, to please spare Him the incredible pain and suffering and indignity that was to come. Notice that He quickly adds that the Lord's will must prevail, not His. He literally sweat blood that night as He contemplated what He knew He must allow to happen the next day, that He would be mocked, ridiculed, tried unfairly, beat unmercifully, have His beard ripped off, disfigured, dragged through the streets, stripped and nailed to a cross and finally pierced by a spear six hours later when His mortal self died. You parents, to whom I referred earlier, would you go that far out for the love of your children? Our father, the Lord Jesus, did!

There are several other things in the Jesus story that, on the very surface from a simple reading of the Bible, might appear foolish or at least strange. Having been blessed with some great teachers, I have learned a few things that the new student may not find for quiet a while and that can greatly enrich his or her understanding of the book and hopefully stimulate excitement and desire to learn more. I'll do this by elaborating on a few highlights of His life on Earth.

a.   His birth, When was Jesus born?

There is one thing for certain. Jesus was not born on December 25. While the correct date of His birth does not seem conclusive from any available evidence, we can be certain that it did not occur during the winter months. Two clues in the Scriptures make this evident. First, the Shepherds with their flocks were known to have been in the fields as they followed the directions of the angels to the manger. It is known that the climate in the area includes fairly severe winters, such that all flocks are out of the fields and in winter quarters by the first part of October. Second, Augustus Caesar had ordered the world to be taxed. This meant that all subjects had to return to their tribal homes, which in the case of Joseph and Mary, was the city of David, because they were of the lineage of David. This city was Bethlehem.

The fact that they went when they did, with Mary ready to give birth, meant that this was a compulsory time imposed by the administration of Judea. Because Judea was all but impossible for traveling during the winter months, no competent administrator would have imposed such a requirement knowing that compliances would have been impossible for many where such travel was required. The Romans were, if nothing else, competent and efficient administrators and tax collectors. To needlessly schedule this event in winter and suffer the consequences inherent therewith is extremely unlikely.

There is another clue to the date of Jesus' birth. This is found by tracing the apparent date of birth of John the Baptist, and the known relationship between the date of birth of John and that of Jesus. This bit of scholarly detective effort is fascinating to follow, yet beyond the scope of this paper. Suffice it to say, this effort, which is quite convincing, suggests that Jesus was probably born on September 29, 2 B.C. September 29 is arrived at strictly from known dates related to the conception of John and the age difference between the two. The 2 B.C. is confirmed from several directions including the tracings of John's birth date. These include known relationships between the year of His birth and the death of Herod, and also the year of the accession of Tiberius. Furthermore, there are reliable historians such as Eusebeus (264–340 A.D.) and Iremaes (130± A.D.) who, apparently from other bits of evidence, confirm this year of 2 B.C. I have seen the year 5 B.C. and 7 B.C. also referred to as the year of our Lord's birth. These seem to be based on some calendar mistakes made centuries later and to me are less credible then the evidence for a 2 B.C. date.

b.   How then did December 25 get to be the official date?

Apparently the first recording or mention of the December 25 date was on the calendar of Philocatus in 354 A.D., which indicated His birth to be on a Friday, December 25, 1 A.D. Perhaps one of the worst days in the sordid history of Christianity was the day in 312 A.D. when Emperor Constantine declared Christianity a legal religion in the Roman Empire by issuing the "Edict of Toleration" that ended the official persecution of Christians. While it ended physical abuse and persecution, it prepared the way in one giant leap into apostasy in its many forms, which was to evolve into the so-called Christian church. This may seem to be a much too strong condemnation of what evolved from the Edict, and perhaps it is given the many true martyrs in Jesus who continued the true faith. However, some of the results of this union of pagan Rome and the Christian church were for its day, as insidious and destructive as is the ecumenical movement of current times in terms of true Christian faith.

While early Christians apparently didn't celebrate Christ's birth, this December 25 date came to be accepted and celebrated under Constantine, and was later, in 440 A.D. made by the church as the official date of His birth. Why December 25? This was a pagan holiday insidiously slipped into the Christian calendar. Its origin can be found in the Bible from the days of Nimrod and continued into the Babylonian period, adopted by the Persians and then the Romans. Tammus, the son of Nimrod and queen Semiramin, was memorialized in association with their sun god. The religious tradition associated with him was that he died as the sun approached the shortest day in December. This death was symbolized by and paid homage to, through the burning of a log called the "Yule log." His rebirth the next day, as the days began again to lengthen, was celebrated by cutting a tree, mounting it and then trimming it. Thus, we have to this day in the name of Christ a celebration of an ancient pagan holiday in place of His birthday.

Even His resurrection, which Christians celebrate on Easter Sunday, has more relevance to a pagan observance than it does to the resurrection. "Easter" is the anglicized "Ishtar," the mothers' goddess of Babylon and of the fertility rites of spring. Also Easter eggs commemorate the goddess Astarte and other fertility symbols such as the prolific rabbits. These are only two of many rituals, celebrating observances and beliefs that bore their way into the Christian faith system, polluting, confusing, diluting and perverting the original purity strength and even credibility of the Christianity.

c. Who were the wise men, or kings, or magi who brought gifts?

These were not kings. However, one might say that they were kingmakers, for they were of a powerful group of what might be called magistrate/priests from Parthia, a neighbor of Judea and adversary of Rome. They were more commonly called Magi or magicians (not what we today think of magicians). More specifically, they were a heredity priesthood the likes of which could be found in many ancient cultures such as Egypt and Babylon, Persia and Media. One could also compare them to the Levi's priesthood of Israel, except for the false nature of their various gods. The prophet Daniel after being carried away into captivity by Nebuchadnezzar became the head of that king's Magi around 604 B.C.

The particular group, and there were many more than just three, there were probably a dozen or more along with a strong military guard, all came from Parthia. They apparently knew from some handed down prophecy that a "king of the Jews" was about to be born, but they didn't know where. Their King Phraetes IV was on in years and their job was to select a new king to take his place when the time came. A king such as described in prophecy, even a Jew would have been satisfactory to them, and thus they had come to see for themselves the nature of this potential king. However, it appears that God warned them in a dream that this was not for them, so they dropped the matter and returned to their own country. Nevertheless, this whole affair alerted and frightened Herod, this non-Jew who had contrived and bribed for himself the position of king, and who feared the truth of the prophecy of which his own Magi were well aware. For in their search, the Magi had paid their respects to Herod and asked him where this king of the Jews was to be born. He, of course, didn't know but his priest did. They simply quoted Micah 5:2 (700 B.C.) wherein the prophet said ". . . but thou Bethlehem Ephratah, enough thou be little among the thousands of Judah, yet out of thee shall he come forth unto me that is to be ruler in Israel; whose goings forth have been from of old, from everlasting." This clearly is a prophecy of the Messiah, because it referred to His eternal preexistence. It is not difficult from this to see why Herod was shaken and fearful when his own priests offered this answer to the Magi.

d.   Now, what's all this foolishness about Satan?

Except for the quiet hidden legions of people who actually worship him, and the few Christians believers who know and believe the Scriptures, to the world Satan is merely a figure of speech, a synonym for evil, but surly not a real being. The Scriptures depict him clearly as a powerful, intelligent being, capable of miracles and many supernatural things. It describes him as a liar, a master deceiver, and in essence, the fountainhead of all that is evil. There is no good to be found in him. The Old Testament finds him in the Garden of Eden orchestrating the first sin (Genesis 3:1), behind the throne of Tyre (Ezekiel 28:11), provoking David to sin (1 Chronicles 21:1) and in (Isaiah 14:22) where his goals and his fate are described. He is also identified in Job 1 and in Psalms 109. From the references we learn much of what is known about him and it clearly is not allegorical. He is real!

The New Testament has much to say about him and is mostly an amplification of what is already found in the Old Testament. Between the two, it is evident that he is, in fact, the power influencing governments past and present. For reasons yet not clear to me, he is the "prince of the earth," he controls the earth. Apparently God gave it to him, perhaps before Adam; and God hasn't yet taken it back. The proof of this is not only strongly implied in the Old Testament but also made very clear in the New Testament, especially in Matthew 4:89, by the temptation of Jesus. Here Satan shows Jesus ". . . all the kingdom of the world, and the glory of them, and said to him, all these things will I give you, if you will fall down and worship me." Obviously he could not give them if they were not his to give, and Jesus in no way refutes his ownership or authority to make good his offer. He thus validates Satan's claim of ownership. Given all of this biblical evidence, it is amazing to me that so very few Jews, as well as those who consider themselves Christians, continue to disbelieve in the existence of a real live Satan. This fact surely attests to the incredible power of the great deceiver. Is it not the epitome of deception that he can so cloud men's minds so that they almost universally believe that he doesn't even exist? He is the ultimate invisible man, unknown, unseen and in effect unheard of, except by his own human and spirit disciples. What an incredible advantage this gives him in his quest to corrupt our souls! The Scriptures prove their Authorship

531

to those willing to seek the proof. Those who believe in its Authorship must accept the presence and role of Satan. Picking and choosing from the Scriptures what one wishes to believe is exactly what
Satan thrives on. Once this is begun, the entire structure on which salvation is based, crumbles, and Satan wins.

From what I've here written it is evident that this Satan issue is
not in the context of this paper, for I find nothing in this issue from
which to extract any unfoolishness from some seemingly foolishness
of God. In fact, the real foolishness here is mankind's general refusal
to believe in Satan's existence. I can't, at this time anyway, understand God's tolerance of Satan or of his devastating powers. Perhaps
this antithesis that he represents, is the substance of which our alternative choices are made. If so, it would seem that Satan today has a
clear advantage in terms of the number of souls he is able to collect.
In the meantime, I trust the Lord and His Word, and know that what
I can't understand or explain is my deficiency, not His.

e.   The crucifixion—The rest of the story.

Virtually everyone in the civilized world has heard of Jesus and is
aware of the fact that He lived a long time ago and was crucified. The
highlights of this story are also known to most merely as a result of the
holiday traditions that refer to the event. Those who have read the
New testament whether believers or not, know about the highlights of
the event, while the true believer for whom it is also an emotional as
well as spiritual issue knows and feels even more. But I wonder how
many of even these, really know the whole story, the whole extent of
the pain and suffering that our Lord went through in order that we
might be spared eternal hell. I don't know; perhaps most do know. I
am too young in my faith and too inexperienced in association with
other believers to know what the depth of understanding there may be
regarding this matter. However, because of the momentous significance of the event and the fact that the New Testament does not tell
the whole story, I feel compelled to tell the rest of the story so that all
may know just how much pain and suffering our Lord endured that day
for the love of His children, you and me.

Picture if you can, this humble, non-descript man bound and dragged before pompous priests and magistrates. "He hath no form nor comeliness; and when we shall see him, there is no beauty that we should desire him" (Isaiah 53:2). His captors were Roman soldiers, a special breed, trained for dealing with condemned prisoners, but in ways that we today cannot and do not even want to imagine. This particular prisoner was especially appealing to the sadistic nature that their particular work encouraged. He was accused by "holy men" of being an enemy of their Caesar as well as a man who claimed to be God. Remember, they saw Caesar as their god. Therefore, surely this was a just subject on which to demonstrate their best technique in the art of punishment and torture. In keeping with the claim of the accused, they fashioned a crown of thorns. These weren't little prickers found on raspberry bushes. These are long, sharp, and tough and needle-like thorns, found on the acacia bush, the thorn bush of the desert, a Hebrew symbol of sin. When smashed down on His head they tore straight through to the skull. Before this, He was beaten about the face by the temple guard. Then His face was covered and He was beaten again causing severe bruising. Sometime, as part of this ordeal, His beard was ripped off His face. Thus, He became unrecognizable. Then He was flogged. The usual Hebrew inflected flogging consisted of no more than thirty-nine blows on the back. The Romans used a whip containing several thongs about twenty-four inches long. At the end of each thong were attached bits of metal, glass, and bone. These would rip the skin off along with muscle, exposing raw bone and causing much bleeding and often death. Given the hate that seems to have prevailed among His tormentors, the flogging most likely exceeded thirty-nine blows, for the Romans had no such limit. "I gave my back to the smiters and my cheeks to them that plucked off the hair: I hid not my face from shame and spitting" (Isaiah 50:6). "As many were astonished at thee: his visage was so marred more than any man and his form more than the sons of man . . ." (Isaiah 52:14).

Dramatizations and renderings generally depict Jesus struggling to carry the cross on the way to Gethsemane. Most likely, however, it was only the crossbar or patibulum as it was called. The vertical portion was most likely already in place at this usual spot of crucifixion. Even today there can be seen rectangular holes carved in the rock into which these vertical timbers may have been set. The patibulum weighed about 75 to 100 lbs. and could have readily been carried by a healthy man. However, Jesus was no longer able to manage this as the Scriptures records.

Crucifixion was invented by Persians around 300 to 400 B.C. and perfected by the Romans as the most painful extended torture imaginable. We get our word "excruciating" from that form of torture. It was far more than simply being nailed to a cross. It was scientifically designed to cause the maximum amount of pain over the longest period of time before inevitable death. It was the wrist, which was nailed between the ulna, radius and carpal bones. Thus, no bones were broken and the wrist structure in that area was strong enough so that it would not rip apart and fail to support the body weight. The feet were spiked between the second and third metatarsal bones, again where body weight would not rip it out. The spiking was done in such a manner that the knees were bent, causing the victim to "stand with bent knees," an impossible and painful stance for anyone to endure for more than a few moments even with his feet on the ground. In this position one could neither stand the pain of raising the body up against the spike in the feet nor letting the body sag and resting with the weight on the wrist spikes. Yet, both were necessary intermittently in order to breathe. At best, exhaling completely was impossible. This would result in hypercarbia, while the efforts required to breathe caused severe titanic-like muscle spasms and eventual death by asphyxia. This could all last for hours or days, depending on the strength and health of the individual. "I am poured out like water and all my bones are out of joint: my heart is like wax; I melted in the midst of my bowels. My strength is dried up like a potsherd and my tongue cleaveth to my jaws; and thou hast brought me into the dust of death. For the dogs have encompassed me: the assembly of the wicked has enclosed me: they pierced my hands and my feet. I may tell all my bones: they look and stare upon me. They part my garments among them, and cast lots upon my vesture." (Psalms 22:14–18).

Note this incredibly graphic description of the agony of one dying on the cross (pierced hands and feet) and of what the soldiers are doing nearby. They are dividing of His garments and casting lots for His vesture. This vesture was an expensive seamless robe too valuable to tear apart and divide among them so they cast lots to see who would keep it. The last observation is the same as recorded in the New Testament by an eyewitness (John 19:24). However, Psalm 22 was written at least 970 years before the crucifixion and approximately 600 years before that form of punishment had been invented! Also, Isaiah wrote this detailed description of the event 690 years before Jesus was born!

Read carefully Isaiah 52 and 53. It defines as eloquently and understandably as any version in the New Testament, exactly why Jesus died!

From what has been briefly summarized above, it is most evident that this event, this torture and death, was extraordinarily vicious and violent and clearly meant to extract the maximum of pain and suffering. Our dear Lord knew this and could have ended it at any moment and in any way He wanted too. Yet He suffered in silence and even begged for forgiveness of His tormentors saying that they didn't know what they were doing.

Was all this foolishness of a fool or was it the ultimate sacrifice of a loving Father willingly submitting Himself to the ultimate of pain and suffering and physical death in order to rescue His children from an even worse fate? Your heart must answer this question. Please, I beg you to consider it carefully because your answer will decide your eternity.

Now as I have reached the end of this, my latest labor of love, this reporting of divine foolishness that our dear Lord put forth to confound the self-styled wise and knowing, there is one more aspect of this that I am compelled to report. I know that I have already touched on this, but it is too important to be only touched on. It deserves deep consideration.

"For by grace are ye saved through faith; and that not of yourselves: it is the gift of God not of works lest any man should boast" (Ephesians 2:89). What's this all about? Does this mean that this is a free gift from God and there is nothing I can do to earn my own salvation? Is Paul trying to tell us that faith alone can save my soul from damnation and there is nothing on this earth I can physically do to influence my fate? Is he saying that all my kindness, good works and efforts to be honest, honorable and good are of no consequence? The answers to these last questions are, yes, yes, and not exactly. Isn't there a bit of foolishness here somewhere? It sounds like this may be a license to sin, because if my attempts to not sin don't help buy my right to heaven, then why not sin?

The only way out of this snarl is to look more closely at God's Word and see it from His perspective. While not necessarily easy to believe or even fully understand, Jesus died on that cross as the one and only means by which our sins are cleansed away. Even the Old Testament told us this. Isaiah 53:5, written about 690 years before Jesus was born, tells us, "... *but he was wounded for our transgressions*, he was *bruised for our iniquities*, and with his *stripes we are healed*." Then in verse 6 "... and the Lord *has laid upon him the iniquity of us all*." Verse 8 reaffirms that "... he was cut *off out of the land of the living*: *for the transgressions of my people* was he stricken." In Isaiah 53, verse 10 continues, "Yet it pleased the Lord to bruise him; he has put him in grief: when thou shall make *his soul an offering for sin* ..." And finally the Lord through Isaiah says, "... because he has poured out his soul unto death: and he was numbered with the transgressors: and *he bares the sins of many*, and *made intercession of the transgressors*." (Emphases mine.) It would be difficult to find a more clear statement of purpose than this, which was written more than seven centuries before the event. Of course, Jesus and His apostles reiterated and amplified this message. However, when that same message is conveyed centuries in advance of the event, it makes it more difficult for the skeptic to claim any self-serving motivation in a first person narration or in the reporting by close friends regarding the same event.

Now then, if Jesus died for our transgressions, that is for our sins, this was God's solution to the problem, the means by which we can be cleansed, that is become free of sin. When Paul says that by faith alone we are saved, he is simply amplifying Isaiah by pointing out that God did the job, the whole job on the cross. If God did the whole job, do you believe that your participation could ever contribute in any way to improve or complete His work? Nowhere do the Scriptures say that you have any power or authority to forgive or wash away your own sins or the sins of others. God did it all on the cross; there is nothing left to do. God finishes what He starts, so this job is done, finished, just as Jesus said on the cross, *Tetelestai.* It is "finished" or otherwise translated with equal accuracy, "paid in full." To believe that you can or must do anything is not to believe God or the Scriptures. Thus, by simply believing in Jesus, wholly embracing as truth who He is and what He did on the cross, and why He did it, your sins are forgiven and forgotten and eternal life is yours.

This all sounds so easy. There must be a gimmick here, some fine print that isn't mentioned. Actually there is, in a way. The belief has to be real, and the faith sincere and lasting. Also as John Calvin affirmed, ". . . we are saved by faith alone, but faith is never alone." This is where our good works, honesty, charity, etc. come in. They are gifts we offer to God in *gratitude, not in payment* for His gift of salvation. He wants us to be all and do all virtuous things, but they cannot be payments for which He becomes indebted to us. Our efforts to live a virtuous life are only *evidence* of our love and gratitude for our salvation, *not payments* for which we can feel entitled to a reward.

All of this is a prime example of the fact that God's reasoning, His logic, His wisdom are far removed from our own. Our logic leads us to believe the opposite, that when we work we earn and should get paid accordingly. If we behave ourselves and refrain from sin, do good works, somehow God owes us one, and if He is a fair God, we will get our reward, our owed payment. God doesn't think that way. A good deed doesn't cancel a sin. A sin is a mark on your soul that only He can remove, and He did it for all time and for all sins on the cross; it is done, paid in full, *Tetelestai.* But now, once you believe, you must show evidence of that belief through your voluntary adherence to His laws. He knows that you're only human and will break some of them, but He also knows what is in your heart and how you feel about having done so. How you respond to these occasional failures reveals the sincerity and depth of your professed faith.

Over the past three years, I must have tried to report this message of faith and salvation at least a dozen times in different ways. I have yet to feel that my efforts are convincing to anyone but believers who already know the truth. However, the issue is too profoundly important to leave alone. Are you a gambler or do you value what you have too much to risk it? If you were a gambler, would you bet on a trillion to one odds? Surely not! Yet those are better odds than you have betting your soul against an uncertain eternity. If you play it safe, save for your retirement and hope for a few last years of good health and comfort, what are these compared to the health and comfort throughout the eternity of your *final* retirement? Are you willing to take the risk of not knowing where you're going until you get there? If you don't know for sure where you are going to spend eternity, and I guarantee that you will consciously spend it somewhere, isn't it time that you looked into the matter? If you do look into it, remember that the Holy Bible is the only book that contains absolute proof of its supernatural and divine Authorship and that gives you God's solemn promise of eternal salvation. It can't get any better than that!

—58—

Spiritual Stumbling

Because we are all human and contaminated with the original sin, we are all capable of spiritual stumbling or backsliding from time to time. Apparently it is even possible under some circumstances for God's most loyal and faithful and dedicated apostles to stumble, to lose control, to be charmed or mislead. Clearly there are conditions or influences that can cause even these elect to make tragic mistakes through the flaring up of their old natural selves or through other even more subtle influences. Often this happens as a result of long enduring stress, weariness, disillusionment over work and sorrow, pain, depression, or even loneliness or feelings of being unappreciated. These can each manifest in rationalized solutions not of the Spirit but instead from one's own thoughts, emotions and desires. The danger of this, of course, is always present, especially because it is Satan himself who often adds to, or causes the burdens, and then orchestrates the temptations and the natural ungodly, and soon regretted actions. *None* of us ever completely escapes from the inherent evilness of our old selves, such as pride, arrogance, hypocrisy, and especially self-will as expressed in these thoughts, emotions and desires. Taking the easy way and choosing to do what seems right in your own eyes, are always tempting options during moments of spiritual weakness. The potential of this always lurks beneath the thin skin of our own souls no matter how certain we may be that our old selves are safely chained and inoperative. The old self as well as Satan are always alert to possible weak links in the chain, or in the spiritual armor that protects the new self. The more highly esteemed, the more successful one is in our Lord's service, the greater seems to be the danger of some form of backsliding or deflection from the narrow path.

Scripture is rich with examples provided precisely for our understanding that these things can happen. A perfect example is Moses, the greatest of all prophets, and a man whom our Lord "knew face to face" (Deuteronomy 34:10). For just one act of disobedience, that is, striking the stone rather than speaking to it (Numbers 20:8), our Lord punished Him by denying him the privilege of entering the Promised Land. Here was our Lord's most faithful and enduring servant, who spent forty years, from age 80 to 120, in the wilderness guiding, serving, and suffering a million plus band of rebellious people, obeying our Lord under the most difficult imaginable conditions, and who was then denied his most cherished dream. Who knows what stresses, fatigue, anguish and pain he may have been enduring at that weak moment when he ignored and thus failed to obey God's instructions. After all, sometime earlier our Lord did instruct him to strike the stone to bring forth water. Now our Lord said, "speak" to the stone. Why the difference in instructions? Doesn't the difference seem trivial and unimportant? Not in God's view. His will was subordinated by Moses' will.

While it is not relevant to the subject, this seemingly innocent violation is a good example of how seriously God views His instruction to us whether we like them or not. To understand the significance of this act we must recognize the symbolic nature of what God was doing. The rock is symbolic of Jesus throughout the Scriptures while the water symbolizes His Word. The first time they sought relief from thirst, God ordered Moses to strike a certain rock to bring forth the life giving water. This striking symbolized His death (crucifixion), and brought forth His Word and His promise of salvation and eternal life. But for the second miracle of bringing forth the sacred water from the rock, striking was no longer the way. At His second coming, Jesus will not be struck but will be spoken to, prayed to and worshiped, as He then sits on the throne of David. From there the flow of living water, His word, will forever satisfy everyone's thirst. Through Moses' faulty response to God's instruction, God's plan for a prophetic analogy or symbolic representations of the first and second coming of our Lord Jesus Christ was thwarted. In our daily efforts to serve our Lord as we encounter temptations or stresses or grow weary, how often do we miss or misinterpret His prompting or even choose to avoid or thwart His will, as our natural selves gain even momentary control? Are we then failing our Lord in some action he would have performed through us, or putting ourselves into unfortunate or tragic future circumstances? When it comes to choosing to avoid or thwart God's will, we should all remember the lesson our Lord is teaching us in the book of Jonah. As we know, Jonah fled in the opposite direction after God gave him his marching orders. In order to set him straight, God was obliged by means of the storm and the whale to impress on him more clearly, exactly what his job description really was! We can learn much about how to please our Lord from this as well as from the failings of the other great characters of the Bible. Their stories are included precisely for that purpose if we will but study them.

Samson is another scriptural example of where man's own weakness and/or Satan's involvement can seduce even the most favored of God's chosen. Sampson's was a prophetic miracle birth to a barren woman. He was preordained to become a Nazarite and to ". . . deliver Israel out of the hands of the Philistine" (Judges 13:5). Clearly the "Spirit of the Lord" was in Sampson, yet for twenty years, instead of delivering Israel, he merely played the champion but not the leader God had chosen him to be. He was a faithful man but hardly a man of faith. In spite of his faith, he violated every Nazarite vow. Then he met Delilah, whose charms awakened his natural desires, which then clouded his vision and completely thwarted his mission. Clearly, here was one ordained by God, but whose good work was negated and essentially brought to a halt, his life destroyed, all through his yielding to his ego and pride as well as his own pent-up self centered desires aroused through the enticements of both her charm and beauty as well as by Satan's deceptive powers. Again, we don't know what stresses, sorrows, loneliness and other forces or difficulties may have been at work in his life up to that point or how momentarily powerful may have been these natural emotions and desires that may have led him to lower his guard, to rationalize, to ignore, or to not hear clearly God's promptings. Thus, it was that another agent of our Lord paying dearly for letting his human nature subordinate his God given supernatural nature and mission. Variations of this theme appear throughout the Scripture in characters such as Kings Saul, David and Solomon where the natural man's ego and desires are allowed, for whatever reasons, to overwhelm their Spiritual selves.

So how did Saul stumble? He was ordained by God to be the first King of Israel for ". . . there was not among the children of Israel a goodlier person than he" (1 Samuel 9:2), and ". . . God gave him another heart" (1 Samuel 10:9), and finally ". . . the spirit of God came upon him" (1 Samuel 10:10). From this, one must conclude that he was a true man of God when he began his reign and surely did very well initially by following God's instructions to defeat Israel's ene-mies. But then he broke God's sacred ordinance and provided a burnt offering to God. This, of course, was a gross violation of law, which he must have known for only priests could offer sacrifice; Kings could not. There are three official positions in God's ordained hierarchy, they are Kings, Priests and Prophets and they are always distinct, individual and not combinable, with but three exceptions. Scripture tells us that both Jesus and Melchizedek, were Kings, Priests and Prophets, while 1 Corinthians 12:10, Revelation 1:6, 5:10 tell us that born-again Christians also have these qualities.

Next, Saul clearly disobeyed God's directive through Samuel to "utterly destroy the Amalekites but instead spared the King Agag and also took the best of the sheep and cattle for future sacrifice to the Lord. Here again, Saul's great transgression was that he too often chose to do what was right in his own eyes, but not as the Lord had commanded. It is the way of the world for man to do what is right in his own eyes rather than to seek the Lord's way. Here we have a perfect, though somewhat obscured example of man's will versus God's will, and of God's permissive nature, which often allows His will to be thwarted. Because Saul acted contrary to God's will, the Amalekite bloodline continued. Haman, the villain in the book of Esther, was a survivor of that bloodline. Because of Haman's "bloodline" hatred of the Hebrews, divine intervention was required these many generations after Saul, otherwise the entire Hebrew race would have been eliminated.

This is a perfect example of how, while man has the power to choose his actions, right as well as wrong, only God has power over the consequences. As an aside, it is also revealing of God's nature and His perfect way, that Mordecai, the man who was responsible for exposing and causing the failure of Haman's plan, was a descendant of the man Shimel whom King David spared from death. Thus, one could say that had Saul obeyed God, the whole story of Esther would not have been necessary. However, God allowed Saul to assert his own will and the resulting consequences, in order to demonstrate the merits of His own perfect will and how, by His love and grace, He so often chooses to intervene in order to "bail us out" of the consequences of our own sinful ways. Saul's failure to eliminate the seed of the Amalekites as God had decreed, resulted in the existence of Haman. So God put it in David's heart to spare Shimel whereby his progeny, Mordecai would, in that later generation, be there as God's agent to prevent the otherwise inevitable destruction of the entire Hebrew race, which Saul's disobedience would have caused. After that, the Holy Spirit left Saul, and after many other transgressions, his reign as King ended. The life of Saul as narrated, is rich with lessons for all of us who seek to know the nature of God and to learn how to better walk His way. We see in Saul, a man of many attributes and much early promise as an affective agent of our Lord. Yet this availed him little in the long run. Here we see evidence of how great sins can evolve from little matters. We see incomplete obedience growing into irreverent presumptions, willful impatience, and deceit. We see excuses being substituted for confession. If we are truly honest with ourselves, it should not be difficult to see variations of these same weaknesses being manifested in our own souls at various times.

Prior to Pentecost, the Holy Spirit could enter and leave the heart depending on the spiritual condition of the individual at any given time as it did several times with Saul. Today, however, we are greatly blessed, for since Pentecost, once we are born-again the Holy Spirit dwells in us permanently. He never leaves us, because once we are saved we can never lose our salvation. If it were possible to loose our salvation, which we receive by the grace of God, it would be necessary for us to conclude that God didn't know what He was doing when He first so blessed us. We cannot lose our salvation once we have it. However, our transgressions can and do cause us to lose any crowns or rewards our good works may have earned (2 Timothy 4:8, James 1:12, 1 Peter 5:4, Revelation 3:11). Also these transgressions (sins) quench the Holy Spirit and until they are purged, they prevent or severely limit His activity in us and, therefore, also our fruitfulness for our Lord.

The story of Saul should also point each of us to another level of concern. Was Saul saved or not? Only God knows. But the evidence presented does not seem strong enough to confirm him of being one of God's eternal family. Does your life contain sufficient evidence to confirm you of being God's own? Are you sure?

Taking a quick glance at David, we see one whom God called "a man after his own heart." Yet, what did he do instead of tending to his duties as King? As such, he should have been off to war; instead, he remained idle at home, where he was tempted into adultery, and then murdered in an attempt to cover up his own sins. He surely paid dearly for these sins during his lifetime, as did each of the others. Even earlier when he was being chased by Saul, he sought sanctuary with the priest Ahimelech in Nob. There, rather than seeking God for help, he lied to the priest as to his relationship with Saul in order to receive the priest's help. This lie by David cost the lives of Ahimelech and his eighty attending priests, because, even though they were innocent of deliberate treason, Saul had them all executed for helping David. What was in David's mind and heart as he so seriously transgressed? Who knows, but most certainly he allowed self will to subordinate God's will in his life, as did all the others.

The lesson to be learned here applies to all dedicated born-again Christians, but most pointedly to those who are the most fruitful and dedicated to our Lord. This is because it is these in particular who are the most attacked by Satan. He waits patiently for moments of vulnerability when they are tired and weary, and often stressed to the limits of physical and emotional endurance. He also delights particularly when his victim succumbs to what we perhaps can call "clinical depression," where rational reasoning, decision-making and even the recognition of reality become compromised. It is during those times when the great deceiver attacks. Perhaps his most effective methods are using our own weaknesses inherent in our natural selves to foster doubts, confusions and disillusionments in order to compromise our faithfulness. If he fails in this, he has many other ways to direct us down diverse paths along which we can no longer be as effective servants to our Lord. He will do anything and everything, use any device to compromise our Lord's fruitful agents.

Remember Satan is desperate. He knows his days are numbered and the end is growing near. He knows the Scriptures better than most of us, probably better than anyone. He knows that the count-down to his ignominious end starts when the "fullness of the gentiles be done." He knows, therefore, that there is a specific number of born-again Christians who represent this "fullness of the gentiles" after which Jesus will come to collect His own (the rapture) and that this will signal the final days of Satan's control of this earth. Obviously, he wants to delay this as long as possible. Therefore, whenever he can foil God's plan by preventing someone from coming to Jesus it's very important to him. How better to affect this than to attack and suffer our Lord's best and most faithful apostles? What better way than to appeal to their human weaknesses at their weakest moments. We each live our entire lives with a natural inborn free will. When we are born-again in Christ, we each receive new hearts indwelt by the Holy Spirit. From that moment on we each have two wills, the natural one and the Spiritual one, that is, the will of God. The one we feed the most is the one that will be strongest and will dominate our lives. As our faith grows, we tend to subordinate the natural in favor of the Spiritual. However, the natural will always remains, for only the Son of Man, Jesus, was able to totally eliminate the natural will. It could be said that as we grow in faith, we starve the natural will and feed the Spiritual will through prayer, scriptural knowledge, church, fellowship, etc. However, earthly temptations, trials and inherent weaknesses even in the strongest do tend to keep the natural will alive and always available to facilitate backsliding. This then is always Satan's favorite point of entry, that natural will, which is so full of propensities for those damaging natural thoughts, emotions and desires. Even some measures of spiritual pride, arrogance, and hypocrisy can subtly worm their way into the hearts of the most gifted and blessed apostles.

Paul says we fight the devil by putting on the "full armor of God." In Ephesians 6:15, Paul says we have our feet shod with the "gospel of peace" knowing God is with us, so we can stand firmly without spiritual backsliding or emotional slipping. But this isn't even about backsliding in the sense of any loss of faith, or righteousness, or innate goodness, or even salvation. In most instances it is simply a temporary, but regrettable reversion to, or welling up of the natural self, a temporary blindness or clouded visions causing a slipping away from the very straight and very narrow path that these pillars of spiritual strength did so faithfully follow. Those who were already saved could not lose their salvation but they most likely did lose their crowns and also paid dearly in earthly suffering.

So what is the answer? Why do these great pillars of faith stumble and sometimes fall, and how might this be prevented? From evidence available, I believe that they overwork, become overtired, perhaps neglect themselves and thus compromise their health as well as their mental stability. But even more important than that, they often have no one to discipline them but themselves; they lack a spiritual fellowship, a faith partner, someone of similar spiritual status to help them stay on the narrow path by pointing out the little transgressions before they become big ones. They, as do we all, fail to take each thought captive and take time to discern and put to flight those that are not of God. Satan, the world, and our old selves are always seeking opportunities to reset our compasses ever so slightly off course. This adjustment can be so minute as to escape detection until it is too late. It is far more difficult for the affected individual to see this than it is for a sensitive, loving faith partner of equal yoking. Once even tiny bits of spiritual pride and arrogance have set in, it becomes even more difficult for the individual, especially one who is highly esteemed, to see these things in themselves or even to accept any such rebuking from others. Unless such a faith partnership is long established, who would even dare point out these flaws much less rebuke the great? Who could effectively rebuke Billy Graham, even though rebuke is sorely needed based on some of his recent writings and public statements.

When one sits in an exalted position, and adulation is a constant occurrence, Godly humbleness tends to slowly give way to spiritual pride and arrogance. Paul urges us to put on the Spiritual armor of God to protect us from Satan, our ego and the world. Unless this armor is constantly maintained and kept in good repair, chinks are bound to form through which these enemies who are all masters of finding even the slightest weak points, will enter and corrupt even the purest of God's chosen. Jimmy Swaggert and Jim Bakker were both thieves and adulterers, and Martin Luther King was a plagiarizer and adulterer. Yet, our Lord used them for some good and they were, no doubt, fruitful for Him. I suspect that they too may have stood high, virtuous, and alone, before they fell. As has been seen, a greatest of dangers lies in doing what seems to be right in our own eyes, rather than what is right in God's eyes. Without a constant affirmation of what is surely God's way, we are in constant danger of slipping unknowingly onto our own way and to one of the worst of the ultimate darknesses.

Having said all this, what is the message? It is simply this. None of us can or should stand alone in our faith and spiritual walk. Scripture tells us we are part of the Christian body through Christ Jesus and each has specific spiritual gifts to contribute to that body. Only the Christian body has the strength to effectively resist the common enemies. Yet, to be effectively protected even within that body, each member must have at least one spiritual partner of equal yoking whereby each can keep vigil against the other's personal enemies, where each will faithfully keep examining the other's armor, and seeing to it that it remains strong and in good repair. Does anyone really do this? The most glorious condition where this works best is in the loving marriage partnership of the equally yoked, though not necessarily endowed with the same spiritual gifts. Perhaps this is another reason why our Lord uses this, His most sacred institution, as an analogy for so many important precepts He presents to us. Thus, it is evident that any apostle or disciple of our Lord who is without a companion of "equal yoking" is one who is *very* vulnerable to the pressures of the world, of his or her natural self, and of Satan.

Looking to the New Testament we see something quite different and potentially more supportive of this premise than the examples from the Old Testament. After the Pentecost, when the Holy Spirit came to dwell in them, and the apostles took on their ministries, Scriptures suggest that the apostles were seldom alone. In Acts, we find that first Paul had Barnabas as a companion, then Silas, then Timothy. Later in the book of Romans and Corinthians it would seem that throughout his journeys, Paul had Timothy or someone else accompanying him. Even in prison he had worthy companionship; Peter had Luke. Where there is no direct evidence of an "evenly yoked" companionship, it should be able to be inferred that it might have been reasonably so from the precedent Jesus Himself set in Luke 10:1 where it is said, ". . . after these things the Lord appointed other seventy-two also and sent them *two* and *two* before the face of every city . . ." Thus our Lord Himself decreed faith partners for His apostles, surely for reasons at least in part as has been here suggested.

It is evident that the higher and mightier usually carry heavier burdens and have greater temptations than the rest of us, and, therefore, need more powerful checks on themselves, which only spiritually competent faith partners can provide. Those of us who have fewer demands, and who may not be as stressed and as attacked, do nevertheless also need faith partners, or some certain means of being held accountable so as to be kept from straying off the narrow path. For Jesus said, "Be ye therefore perfect, even as your father which is in heaven is perfect" (Matthew 5:48). Only the perfect, that is the spiritually clean and holy can enter heaven. All Christians become clean and holy and thereby eligible for entry into heaven at the moment of their rebirth. This holiness is verified through an ever growing and strengthening faith as confirmed by their love of Him, by their obedience to Him, by their love of their fellow Christians, and by their Christian walk as expressed by their works performed in gratitude to Him. This is true even though the residual remains of the old self will occasionally sin, as long as these sins tend to diminish with time, are completely confessed, and sincere repentance is made. That's the problem, to be able to recognize the seemingly minor applications of sins such as, pride, hypocrisy, dishonesty, omission, etc, which our minds are so adept at not seeing but instead insist on rationalizing or excusing out of existence, unless there is another trusted competent soul to point them out! Also it must be noted here, that holiness means living to please God alone, not man or self, and that it must be *from* God to be genuine. It is impossible to imitate true spirituality. Sentimental religious feelings, zeal, church attendance, scriptural quoting or even writing these tomes are no assurance that we are pleasing God. There are many elegant counterfeits both in and out of the places of worship as well as at the pulpits. There is no growth in holiness except through *close* fellowship with our Lord and Savoir Jesus Christ. From Matthew 5–7, the Sermon on the Mount, we learn the law of intent that is of the heart. This law that governs the Christian walk is much more severe than one could possibly conclude from the Ten Commandments. And we also find that we learn of God from His Word, but our fear (awe) of God is from a devotional life. Clearly it's evident that there is danger in individual Christianity. Believers simply *cannot* go it alone without risking this danger. So what can one do if in this sense one *is* alone?

While no doubt there are better ways perhaps for starters, one might consider doing as I try to do each day. When I first awaken each morning, I praise God, pray to Him in very sincere gratitude, seek His council and commit to living out the day honoring His commandments. Then I used to try to pass through the day conscious of His presence and asking at every turn, what would Jesus do? But because so often I found that Jesus would never have gotten Himself in this circumstance, I now ask instead what would Jesus have me do, and then I attempt to do that, as I perceive I must, and as the Holy Spirit prompts me. At night I pray again in gratitude for having been allowed this day, and for having received so many blessings, after which I try remembering all thoughts, emotions, desires, and actions of the entire day to see if they conformed to scriptural teachings and were of God. After that, I ask Him to reveal to me how I could have done better, and to remind me of any transgressions I may have forgotten. Then I try to confess all thoughts and actions that were not of the Lord, and sincerely resolve to not repeat them.

Clearly nothing can be as effective as a true, loving, trusted, bornagain faith partner who is well grounded in Scripture. However, absent that, the daily process as described above is, I believe, the very least one can do in trying to avoid the pitfalls of going it alone. It should be noted again that frequent and close fellowship with members of the Christian body is very important and often capable of keeping us in line as far as gross, clearly evident transgressions are concerned. However, what is of greater concern as has been already noted are the seemingly little, more subtle transgressions that only a close intimate loving faith partner can see and proceed to "nip in the bud."

In this regard, and also *very* important, I have learned to ask our Lord for His precious wisdom to help me understand His plan for me and what I should be doing regarding the major issues in my life. In James 1:5 He has promised us His wisdom if we ask with *singleness* of mind, that is, a mind and a heart that are both free of our own self-centered agendas, and if we ask with a strong faith that He *will* answer us. While I shouldn't be, I am always amazed at the clarity, relevance, and righteousness of the responses I receive when my heart is right and when these requests are sincere, consistent with His purpose, and centered on a faith that He is true to His promise. I believe that 1 Chronicles 16:11 gives us the same message as James, but in Old Testament semantics, when it says, "Seek the Lord and His strength, seek His face continually." That is exactly what we *must* do if we are to remain steadfast in the faith and not stray from the "path." Always remember that the world, and our old selves, and Satan continually seek to gang up on each and every one of us, both large and small, whenever they can and wherever our armor is weakest. They want us to falter, fail and fall from that precious narrow path. We must battle them continually, fight them and though they may win battles, we must never let them win the war.

Is It Stumbling or Foolishness?

Almost five years ago, when I was but two years into the "faith," I wrote a fifty page paper titled "The Foolishness of God," where I cited a number of God's earthly interventions as recorded in Scripture, and which the "world" considers to be foolish myths. The inspiration and title for the paper came from First Corinthians chapter one, and in particular, verses 25 and 27 where the Holy Spirit, through Paul, has blessed us with a most precious pearl of information that can serve as a key to the understanding of God, His ways and, His purpose. Verse 25 tells us that the foolishness of God is wiser than men, and verse 27 explains that "God has chosen the foolish things of the world to confuse the wise." In essence, He toys with those who think they are wise by deliberately achieving His purposes through what the "wise" can only see as utter foolishness, while those who admit their ignorance and nothingness compared to Him, are blessed with true understanding. Of course, the ultimate absurdity from the world's perspective is the Gospel, which tells us that Creator God Himself had to enter His own creation so that He could suffer and die, it being the only way in which we could be cleansed of our sins. Through the wisest of worldly reasoning and logic, it can't get any more foolish and ridiculous than that! Yet, those of us who have admitted our ignorance and helplessly sinful nature, the Holy Spirit has seen fit to bless us with a deeper insight and understanding that opens our eyes to the sublime beauty of His supernatural love centered wisdom.

In that same vein, the purpose of this paper centers around verse 23, of First Corinthians, where we learn that the idea of Christ being crucified for our sins is to the Jews a "stumbling block" and to the Greeks it is "foolishness." At first it may be difficult to find any modern-day relevance to this observation. But all Scripture is for our learning and application, if we will but pray for and receive from Him, His blessing of understanding and discernment.

First, let us see what this "stumbling block" is all about. As the Apostles began their missionary teachings their audiences were made up almost exclusively of Jews. These were of course, quite well versed in what we now call the Old Testament, it being at the time, the only expression of God's Word. They knew that there was but one God, the Creator God of Genesis, the God of Abraham, Isaac and Jacob. His many predictions through the Prophets were also well known. They knew the commandments, the nature and significance of sin, and the cleansing power of the shedding of innocent blood, as well as the much-prophesied assurance as to the coming of the Messiah. Their main area of confusion was the nature, purpose, and manner of His coming. They knew well that He would come and one day rule the world from David's throne. They also knew from Isaiah 53 and other scriptural references that a Messiah would also come as a Suffering Servant. The problem, among other smaller issues, was that they desperately wanted and, therefore, expected the King to come first to liberate them.

So here was the "stumbling block," the idea that the Suffering Servant had already come, not only in a ceremonial sense, but also as the true final sacrificial Lamb of God to take away the sins; that the Messiah the King had not yet come, and that the same, not another Messiah would come later to be the King. Thus, we can see that the Jews had a well-grounded knowledge and understanding of the Scriptures that allowed them to at least comprehend the Gospel message once the "stumbling block," was removed. The evidence of this is found in Acts 2 when Peter preached the Gospel to the Jews at the first Pentecost and three thousand of them were saved. Peter spoke their language in terms that they understood. This is not referring to Greek or Hebrew, but to the language of the Scripture. He cited words of the prophet Joel, and of David, who both pointed to Jesus. He reiterated the words of Jesus as He preached of His divine purpose. Peter did not mince words when he reminded them as indicated in verse 36 ". . . know assuredly, that God hath made that same Jesus, whom ye have crucified, both Lord and Christ." His evangelical success was because those to whom he spoke were well grounded in God's word. They may not have previously caught the full significance of Jesus, but when it was explained to them from Scripture, they had this solid foundation on which could be built, first understanding, then belief, and finally a saving faith. It should be noted that even though they were well steeped in the ways of God as revealed in the Scripture of the times, this "window" of opportunity to receive the Gospel soon closed to the Jews as this truth became hidden from their eyes even as Isaiah predicted, and as Jesus, during His triumphal entry, most clearly stated in Luke19:42. This time marked the beginning of the age of the Gentiles and it will end with the Rapture, after which God will again focus on the Jews, and come back to rule from David's throne.

Now let us examine the Greek view of the Gospel as foolishness. In order to do this, we need to examine Paul's ministry to the Greeks as recorded in Acts 17:16–32. In Athens, Paul found that the Greeks knew absolutely nothing about the Creator God, but instead worshiped numerous idols and false gods, one of which they called the "unknown god." It was probably thrown in among their thousands of gods to make sure they didn't miss any. How does one introduce the Gospel to those who have no foundation in which to build such a seemingly foolish doctrine as a Creator God becoming man and then allowing Himself to be tortured and killed for the remission of sins? They had no concept of sin or repentance, no actual history regarding creation, or knowledge of prophets, or the accurate and precise fulfillment of every one of their many prophecies. They knew nothing of God's many early miracles or of those performed by Jesus. To start out preaching the Gospel without first establishing this foundation could only be, and was seen as foolishness by those who first heard it, and who would not accept it blindly. Think about it, if you knew nothing about God and the history leading up to Jesus, is there anything more ludicrous than hearing that the Creator God entered His own creation as a man and chose to be tortured and to die, and in that manner suffer the punishment due us for our own sins? Sins? There are four Greek words that have been translated as sin or sins. They relate to "missing the mark, ignorant, willful error, or offense." The concept of sins as defined by Scripture was completely unknown. Notice that the Greeks started out referring to Paul as the "babbler" (Acts 17:18). To even get their attention, he had to refer them to their "unknown god" and suggested to them that this was He, the Creator God who they worshiped ignorantly, the God who ". . . made the world, and all things therein, and who dwelleth not in a temple made with hands neither is He worshiped with hands." In other words, he wisely began by preaching Genesis, the essential foundation of Christian faith, without which a strong, solid, lasting, real saving faith is extremely difficult and, I believe, rarely achieved.

Now we can see that as Peter preached the Gospel to the Jews, it was a "stumbling block" until it was explained to them that it was consistent with their biblical background and that it filled in the gaps as well as completed, that is, brought to a closure, what they could now understand had always been God's plan for salvation. The "stumbling block" was readily removed because they had the background required to understand and were thus capable of being enlightened. However, Paul was preaching to those absent any such background, those who could only find the Gospel to be foolishness, unworthy of serious consideration. Therefore, Peter was enormously successful numerically in converting those early Jews, while Paul had much less success with the Greeks.

It is my understanding that theological seminaries teach this distinction of methods and their relative success, but fail to recognize the subtleties of why, and, therefore, misapply the message. So they continue to teach that to effectively preach the New Testament with its Gospel is sufficient to bear fruit, and that there is relatively little need or value to spend much time in the Old Testament. Perhaps up to fifty or seventy-five years ago, this may have been true and, therefore, appropriate and effective, because in those days, this was a Christian culture. Most homes had a Bible and it was read daily, both the Old and New Testament. This, along with serious prayer, dedicated church attendance, and convicting sermons, was a solid part of family life. Preaching the Gospel was, for the most, commonly understood. "Stumbling blocks" remained impediments for some, but inspired preaching and witnessing could readily remove them for many others. By comparison, and used here as an analogy, most Americans were Jews, in the sense that they had a foundation on which the Gospel could more readily be set in their hearts. Today, this is no longer a Christian culture. We are for the most part "Greeks" without that foundation, and the Gospel is, therefore, seen as foolishness to most people. So, continuing to preach the Gospel to "Greeks" will continue to be but foolishness until the Church recognizes this and begins to take seriously the dire need for real basic *Bible study*, study of the foundational Old Testament, as well as the Gospel. Overcoming foolishness is much more difficult than guiding someone over a stumbling block. Until the "churches" realize the nature, as well as the gravity of the problem, it will continue to succeed only in drawing entertainment seekers and "graduating" multitudes who are absent of any saving faith, but filled with false, vain and very fragile beliefs that do not meet the criteria for salvation.

In the 1800s, men like Wesley, Whitefield, Bunyan, and Spurgeon, and even up to around 1940, men like Ironside and Barnhouse could rightly claim thousands of true conversions, because they powerfully preached the foundation as well as the Gospel, the whole Word of God, the unpleasant along with the pleasant. And when they preached, their words were not just superficially accepted, but they were foundationally understood by audiences who had a basic knowledge of Scripture. They were speaking mostly to "Jews" in this sense. The process was, therefore, a matter of removing "stumbling blocks," not first needing to overcome biblical illiteracy and the perceptions of "foolishness."

Today, in our "Greek" culture, perhaps through the mass marketing techniques, many are coming to churches to hear, and some tend to stay, at least for a while, and others keep coming back as long as the "feel-good Gospel" doesn't take too long, is sufficiently entertaining, *not too heavy*, and above all *not convicting*. "Guilt trips" are the kiss of death to the goal of simply filling pews. But what are the results? What is the fruit? Is there a deep rooted, firm belief followed by real lasting conviction, confession, remorse, repentance and faith unto salvation? Or is it a shallow acceptance of a fanciful image without any depth of knowledge or understanding, an image that will easily fade when the "going gets rough?" If it's a faith at all, it may be a blind faith based on a faith and love for a certain pastor who says what they want to hear, and not necessarily a faith based on a belief in the infallible Word of God as personally understood and proven through the study of Scripture. Will this "faith" survive when its professor is thrust out into the world of mass denial, attractive false gods, humanistic logic, temptations, and tragedies? Polls tells us that seven out of every ten young people from "solid" Christian homes, after a year out in the world, renounce their faith! Why? Was it ever real? Had it been based on a solid in-depth learning and understanding, starting with a lateral belief in Genesis:1–11, along with pulpit messages expressing the *whole* Word of God, rather than just some comfortable niceties, this statistic would be much different. How can a superficial faith not founded on the rock foundation of the whole Word of God possibly survive the prevailing government school's indoctrination of evolution, "billions of years" scientific "proof," and the "great" philosophers of the "age of enlightenment," all of whom were atheists? Add to this the multitudes of alternative faiths, temptations and pleasures of the world thrust upon the hormonally excited, curious, and still moldable characters, how can anyone without the solid rock foundation of the entire Scripture possibly even hope, let alone expect faith to survive?

In today's basically non-Christian culture, it must be understood by those who preach, teach, and witness, that one is dealing with "Greeks" not "Jews" and all evangelizing must deal with that fact or it is doomed to failure. Saving souls must be the goal, and not merely filling the pews. To think "if we just get them in here, we can lead them to salvation" is like chasing rainbows, unless the *whole* Word is preached, both sweet and sour, and unless Paul's strategy with the Greeks is applied.

—60—

Pride

Pride is a sin because it constitutes a theft of glory, or credit for achievements that belong to God. We are nothing beyond that which God created. What ever we as humans achieve is by His grace, by the attributes that He gave us, and nothing more. Can pottery take credit for its beauty or its utility, or the watch for its accuracy? These are the works of their craftsman who have been blessed by our Creator with abilities that permit these accomplishments. Thus, there is no legitimate basis for even the potter or the watchmaker to feel pride. Instead there is an obligation to give prayerful thanks for the endowment to them, of these capabilities by the Creator.

When we work hard and accomplish some significant task it is quite *natural* to feel a sense of pride to be proud of our achievement. However, pride is another one of these natural or things of the flesh that the Lord is not pleased to see us exhibit. He created every aspect of our individual beings. Being strong or handsome, or intelligent or talented or persevering, are God-given attributes that He provided, along with the spark of life and all other faculties that allow any and all accomplishments. Thus, it is gratefulness and prayers of thanks rather than pride that should be our reactions to our achievements, for only God the Creator is justified to feel pride; only to Him can credit be properly assigned. This is not easy. Pride is one of the greatest of all temptations. It was Satan's original and fatal flaw. From his experience, it can be seen that it is a most dangerous and damaging character flaw; it leads to many other sins and can thus be viewed as the father of all sins.

As has been noted, pride usurps some of God's eminence and thus implicitly suggests that one, who is proud, perhaps even subconsciously, believes he has a God-like quality worthy of pride. This was Satan's problem, and is also the problem inherent in most of humanity, except those few who recognize this error, practice humility, and give credit where it is due. For those seriously and diligently pursuing the Christian walk, the replacement of pride with gratitude and humility is an essential effort. Whenever personal success in any form occurs, human pride is there seeking to soak up any and all glory and credit. It is human to crave recognition and praise, and there is nothing wrong with seeking these rewards for honest, praiseworthy achievements. What is wrong is the belief that one is anything more than the blessed implement through which the Lord allowed the praiseworthy achievement. Once this becomes an established pattern of thought, many obstacles in the way of the Christian walk will become less difficult to deal with or may even disappear.

Our built in propensity for pride, that is our ego, can only be subdued through our belief in the Lord and our prayers to Him. If at the moment that pride rears its head, we bring God into our consciousness with all that implies, knowing what we know as to where credits are due, pride by necessity of definition must and will disappear and be replaced by praise for The Lord and transference to Him of all credit.

The more accustomed we become to making this transference, which really should be public as well as personal, the more humble we will become, the more in tune will we be with the Lords desires, and the more will flow peripheral blessings and diminished temptations.

The devil was captivated by his own beauty and talent, and as chief angel in heaven. He failed to appreciate from whence his blessings came and believed that he could be as God. It was the arrogance, this overbearing pride that got him in trouble. On earth, to which he was banished, his pride-spawned hatred of God and his creation. Therefore, when he saw Adam and Eve, he at once sought to blemish and damage the Lord's finest and most precious work. He sought to achieve this through an outgrowth of pride, that is deceit. Because of their innocence and naiveté, it was not difficult for the great deceiver to convince Eve and through her Adam, to disobey God's command regarding this one issue, for he said to Eve, "No you shall not die the death. For God doth know that in what day so ever you shall eat thereof, your eyes shall be opened: and *you shall be as God*, knowing good and evil." That certainly is a tempting thought through which anyone, without the strength and the Truth of the Bible as armor, could easily be severely wounded. The power of that offer has, even today, not lost its effectiveness as evidenced by the many "New Age" beliefs that offer the same illusion as that part of his lie that is here underlined. It was this arrogance, this audacity, this pride, this belief that they could, with impunity, ignore God's commandment, and further that they could be as God, that set the course of the world from that day on. Notice the cleverness of the great deceiver's words, ". . . you shall not die that death." What death? She didn't ask. He didn't say that they would not die, but they would not die *that* death. Technically, he was correct in terms of what he had in mind but deceptively avoided saying. They didn't physically die at that moment but they did die spiritually. At that moment, entropy was introduced and also the process of physical aging and eventual physical death, to which they had been previously immune. Notice also the other deceptive and misleading statement "You will be as God." The fact is they already were to some high degree as God. They were made in His image, they were totally innocent of sin and they had eternal neverending life in Eden, a place as close to heaven as earth could provide. As I write this, especially the technically correct but grossly deceptive statement about dying by *that* death, I'm reminded of Clinton's technically correct but totally deceptive public statements regarding his scandalous behavior. It would seem that he learned the technique well from his mentor.

The Bible contains many references to pride and the Lord's condemning response to it. The following are a few random references to the point.

Psalms 73:6 "Therefore pride is the necklace; they clothe themselves with violence."

Proverbs 11:2 "When pride comes, then comes disgrace, but with humility comes wisdom."

Proverbs 16:18 "Pride goes before destruction, a haughty spirit before a fall."

Proverbs 21:4 "Haughty eyes and proud heart, the lamp of the wicked, are sin."

Proverbs 29:23 "A man's pride brings him low, but a man of lowly spirit gains honor."

In John 2:16 "For everything in the world—the cravings of sinful man, the lust in his eyes and the boasting of what he has and does—comes not from the Father but from the world."

If we need more evidence, consider Acts 12:23 where the Lord teaches Herod the final fatal lesson about pride, and for accepting for himself credit that was due the Lord. ". . . and immediately the angel of the Lord smote him because he gave not God the glory: and was eaten of worms, and gave up the ghost."

Often in the Bible the word leaven is used as an idiom describing pride. It is the "puffing up" capability of leaven that makes it appropriate in the sense that pride is a puffing up of one's self. Leaven is mentioned thirty-six times in this context. The basis of the traditions surrounding unleavened bread has to do with the Lord's admonitions against pride. Whenever we feel pride we are, in fact, puffing ourselves up. The Lord's idioms are, of course, perfect in every way, because leaven causes bread to expand, to puff up through the generation of air bubbles. However, it does not add to the substance of the loaf. It just makes it easier to be devoured. Pride likewise has no substance or worthiness in man, and is spiritually abhorrent. It is of value only to the great deceiver who delights in its use and propagation. This is exceedingly evident in our secular world, where pride takes on the trapping of a virtue and is an emotional reward for any achievement. It is the fleshy feel good product of almost anything from winning a contest to outwitting an opponent, to having superior strength or intelligence, or "good luck," There is no such thing as good luck, only blessings from our Creator, or rewards that Satan is capable of providing and uses very effectively to deceive, seduce and reward his own, or those he is seeking to be his own.

There is one other very important, yet quite subtle and truly devastating form of pride that the Christian believer must always guard against. That is spiritual pride. It is very natural for us as born again

Christians to see ourselves blessed with a condition superior to those who have not received the grace of faith, or who may have not progressed as far in their spiritual growth. It is tempting and difficult not to allow this sense of superiority of condition to become a source of pride and thus a feeling of personal superiority and impatience, which can in fact undo much or all of what the Lord would have for us. It is evident that the attitudes of the Pharisees, which Jesus so rightly rebuked, are clear examples of spiritual pride. Regardless of the strength and power and sincerity of our Christian walk, it should never be the source of pride, but only humble gratitude to our Heavenly Father who gave this ultimate blessing. If we are indeed saved, if we have that saving faith, it is 100 percent the work of the Lord through Jesus on the cross as Paul in Ephesians 2:8, 9 makes clear. Where then is there any cause for pride? Anything we do in concert with, or as a result of, that faith must be nothing more than an expression of gratitude to our heavenly Father!

These things that I have written are relatively new discoveries for me as I try to progress in my spiritual growth as a fairly recent born again Christian. In the past, I was always seeking something of which to be proud. I was addicted to praise and sought it as an essential nutrient without which my ego, my self-esteem, my whole reason for being, could not survive. I have yet to fully "kick the habit" as I even now find myself at times searching for praise to feed my weak ego. However now, praise the Lord, I usually see what I am up to and immediately proceed to transfer the recognition of achievement to its rightful place. That transference has progressively become easier to do as I have learned what pride really is and how good it feels to sincerely give all credit to the Lord. This paper was written for a two-fold purpose. First, to summarize and articulate to myself what I have learned in order that it may be better absorbed into my soul. Second, it was written in the hope that others might find it of benefit in their own spiritual search.

—61—

Satan

J esus is, without a doubt, the primary theme of the entire Bible. However, there is an important sub-theme that begins in Genesis 3 involving Satan and continues throughout the Scripture all the way to Revelation 20:10. Satan "owns" the earth (Matthew 4:9) and through his "principalities and powers" (fallen angel and evil spirits) controls the governments and most other institutions, (Daniel 10:13, 20). With his considerable powers, he has been able to fashion an enigma of himself. Only in the Holy Bible do we find him exposed for what he is. Most of humanity denies his existence as a real being, while some see him under every bush and the cause of everything evil, thereby denying their own fallen nature. Jesus Himself speaks of Satan and evil spirits much more than He does of heaven.

As Christians, we should learn all we can about Satan, because he knows a great deal about each of us, and uses that knowledge against us. Most of his efforts are directed to promoting false beliefs, any beliefs or religions; it doesn't matter to him, as long as faith in Jesus is not involved. He also delights in duping and promoting complacency in those who think they are saved, but are not. His hatred and attack is especially venomous against those who are saved. He knows that he cannot "unsave them," but the more effective they are in the faith, the more he will attack them, in order to distract, discredit and neutralize them.

Since Jesus' victory over death, Satan's principal area of focus is to discredit and destroy Christianity and also to eliminate all Jews. He knows Scripture and, therefore, knows that there must be a Jewish remnant if Christ is to return and fulfill prophecy. For those who wish to better understand Satan, his purpose, his history and methods, the following is a brief and far from complete outline of his attempts to thwart God's plan. These are the more obvious and blatant ones. There are many more subtle ones, such as, the false teachers and prophets, the corrupted New Bible versions, promoters of moral decay, ecumenicalism etc.

1. Satan deceives Eve, thus brings sin and death into the world.

2. He instigated the Nephilim, which so polluted the generations that God flooded the entire earth to eliminate these abortions.

3. He orchestrated repeated famines, which led the Hebrews to Egypt and four hundred years of slavery.

4. He directed Pharaoh in his attempts to extinguish the race by killing all first born.

5. He directed Pharaoh in his attempts to extinguishing the race by his pursuit in Exodus

6. He caused numerous attacks against David and his family, through Saul, through temptations and through indiscretions.

7. He guided the perversions of most of the subsequent kings and kingdoms all in order to prevent the continuation of David's royal line.

8. He orchestrated various captivities and dispersions in an attempt to obliterate the race.

9. He put forth Haman, his agent, who almost succeeded in killing all the Hebrews.

10. He directed Herod, killing all male babies in Bethlehem.

11. He caused two supernatural storms on the sea of Galilee, trying to kill Jesus and His Apostles

12. He enticed Pharisees to stone Jesus.

13. He entered Judas to cause Jesus' betrayal.

14. He directed his agents in the destruction of Jerusalem in 70 A.D. and the great Diaspora

15. He caused the Roman persecution of Jews and Christians.

16. He directed the Crusades

17. He set up the many and continuing pogroms blaming Jews for the crucifixion.

18. He set out to the killing of millions of Christians and Jews by the order of Catholic Popes, for nearly one thousand years.

19 He nurtured Hitler.

20. He brought about the rise of Islam (the cult of death) dedicated to the death of all Jews and Christians.

21. He will take his last shot at Bozrah {Isaiah 63:1–6; Revelation 19:11–21}

Because God is omnipotent, it is difficult to understand why He has allowed and continues to allow Satan to do these many awful things. This in itself is an enigma, the answer for which we may never know with certainty. However, I am certain that man's free will, and his willingness, for the most part, to choose any way other than God's way, is a major ingredient in the answer.

—62—

Self-Love

The world seeks unceasingly to convince man that he needs more self-love and self esteem. It claims that the problems of the world, and one's lack of success in it, stem largely from a lack of these "attributes." Courses are given to strengthen self-esteem. It has become a credo of education and modern psychology. Commercials are ever hawking the mantras of "you owe it to yourself" or "you deserve this or that." After a while, all of this becomes quite convincing if one doesn't have sufficiency of knowledge of God's Word and *His* love in ones heart to resist this most persuasive temptation. The obvious danger here is that the pursuit of an increase in self-love can, and inevitably will casily lead to pride, envy, covetousness, greed and other forms of selfness, which is radically contrary to biblical teaching.

Much of this perceived need for additional self-love seems to have gained momentum about fifty years ago in what might be called the study halls of psychology. Some credit an Erick Fromm, a blatantly anti-Christian humanist psychologist, for this modern emphasis on self-love. He expounded on man's innate goodness, which, of course, is wholly contrary to Scripture (See Jeremiah 17:9). He seems to have sought to apply Matthew 19:19, which says that "thou shall love your neighbor as yourself." To support this false thesis, that because we are all inherently good, we must naturally esteem and love ourselves first before we can love others, and that most of us don't appreciate or love ourselves enough. Therefore, self-love must be taught, nurtured and encouraged as a prerequisite to any progress in relationship with others. This nugget of man's human wisdom, so contrary to God's wisdom, is now one of the cornerstones of modern psychology, even so-called Christian Psychology that isn't Christianity at all; its roots are 100 percent secular and have no basis in Scripture. Fromm was correct in his premise that there is not enough love in the world. However, because he could only apply a human wisdom to the problem, he naturally arrived at a humanistic conclusion, and one contrary to the wisdom of God, for "has not God made foolish the wisdom of the world?" (1 Corinthians 1:2). What is so sorely lacking is NOT love of ones self, but the love of God and of others!

The Humanist Manifesto 1 declares *"Man is at last becoming aware that he alone is responsible for the realization of the world of his dreams, that he has within himself the power for its achievement."* This of course is Godless selfism. We could call it the religion of selfism. It is nothing new, because it started in Eden when Satan turned Eve away from obedience to God, toward her own interests, even to achieving godhood. Today it is being advanced by the godless New Age movement and will culminate in the man who is coming, Satan's son, whom we call the Antichrist. What religions are there, except Christianity that don't look to self in order to obtain some form of self-styled "salvation"? They rely, at least in part, on their own efforts, such as sacraments, mediation, rituals, sacrifices and good works. It's no wonder that this preoccupation with love of self is so attractive and convincing as "the way to go." The problem, however, is that the way to go, will take them to where they wish they weren't!

These psychological constructs of selfism self-esteem, self-love, self-image and self-actualization are predicated upon the assumption that man is innately good by nature, a premise totally contrary to Scripture, God's inerrant Word. The strategy and goal of this whole movement can be nothing more than Satan's way of conditioning and preparing man for his brief end time rule of the earth. A study of the book of Revelation can help make this very clear.

Nowhere do the Scriptures tell us we have insufficient self-love. If we inherently lack sufficient love, would Jesus command us to love our neighbors as ourselves, if we don't already love ourselves enough? Nowhere does it say that we are to first see a psychologist or some other self-love instructing guru to prod us into a greater love for ourselves. Surely, we must already love ourselves enough or His command would be foolish. This is evident from Ephesians 5:29, which tells us empathically that "no man ever hated his own flesh, but nourishes and cherishes it . . ." Humanist psychology recognizes that guilt is a major factor troubling man. It therefore seeks to eliminate guilt through various palliatives, such as more self-love, never admitting that guilt is rooted in sin, and that it is sin that must be removed before guilt will go away. Because the humanists avoid the concept of sin, they can never "cure " the patient any more than the surgeon can "cure" a cancerous body by cutting out the cancer, while denying and not addressing its underlying cause.

Again it is love for God and for others that is severely lacking in the world, not self-love. And this love only comes *from* God himself, for Scripture tells us that we love Him because He first loved us. This means that our capacity to love as God loves is possible only when God's love is in us. This kind of love can only be found in the true born-again Christian, because only he or she has the true love for the true one and only God, Christ Jesus, the God of the Holy Bible, for there is no other god or other genuine love. But how do we deal with the Scripture verses such as Ephesians 5:28, which say that "men ought to love their wives as their own bodies," and "He that loves his wife loves himself. For no man ever hated his own flesh, but nourishes and cherishes it even as the Lord loves the church"? Here Paul is using an analogy to describe the importance and magnitude of what a man's love for his wife and others should be. In order to understand this, we must examine it in the context of the whole Scripture. Jeremiah 17:9 tells us that "Mankind is deceitful above all things, and desperately wicked. Who can know it"? With such a heart no one can have or reflect God's genuine love. However, the born-again Christian with his or her new heart can have this love, and should have as the order of priority, to love God first, all others second and self third. That means that when we can, we are to always subordinate ourselves for others. We are called to humbleness, to lowliness, to meekness, to humility (Colossians 3:12). This is hardly a call to any increase in self-love. Remember that the scriptural meaning of meekness is not a form of weakness. It is simply the power of the Holy Spirit in us keeping the self under control. The world would have us have self-esteem or self-adulation rather than meekness. Humbleness is not having a poor, but a proper estimate of oneself. The world would have us proud of self and teaches that pride is essential to a successful life. But the Holy Spirit in Philippians 2:3 tells us to "let nothing be done through strife or vainglory, but in lowliness of mind let each esteem other better than themselves."

In Luke 14:26 Jesus Himself says, ". . . if any man come to me and hate not his father and mother and wife, and children, and brothers and sisters, yea and his own life, he cannot be my disciple." Hate here is not what we normally mean by that word, but instead it is to "set aside, reject or discount." Here Jesus is speaking of priorities, that is Who must be first on our love list.

We are to maintain self-love only to the extent it is necessary for the taking of reasonable and appropriate care of our bodies and for the future of our immortal souls. This is the sole purpose and extent to which we are to self-love. This self-love of our bodies is a fleshly love. As Christians, the love we are to offer to our wives, as well as our Christian brothers and sisters is a spiritual, God centered love, which is also a sacrificial love. Thus, we are commanded to two kinds of love, that is, our natural and limited self-love, and also Christ's kind of love whereby He gave His life for His bride, the church.

Of course, one must love one's wife as one's own body, because even back in Genesis 2:23 God tells us that man and wife "shall be one flesh." The one flesh in the Christian sense surely must love its combined self as it does its individual self. When Scripture tells us to love others as one loves oneself, it means that one is never to do less, or treat others with any less love and respect than one would have for one's self. In fact, as noted, Scripture calls us to a higher standard when dealing with others.

God's commandment to love must be acted upon as a commitment, not an emotion. It is a decision, a resolve to obedience to His Word, to His sound irrefutable doctrine. This must become our very life, for it validates the assurance of our eternal life. Lacking this, we are in great danger of deluding ourselves and to be practicing a *false* Christianity.

Now if there is any doubt as to the source of this apostasy regarding the need for more self-love, consider 2 Timothy 3:1–3. "This we know also, that in the last days, perilous times shall come. *For man shall be lovers of their own selves*, covetous, boasters, proud, blasphemers, disobedient—without natural affections . . ." How prophetic this is! How appropriate that it's in these end times that the preaching of self-love should so universally manifest! Notice that the lovers of their own selves is the first on the list and is probably listed that way because as stated earlier, it is the precursor to the rest of the list of sins. Consider each one. Isn't it evident that covetousness, boasting, pride, etc. really emanates from selfishness, which is nothing more than *too much* self-love? It is quite difficult to boast and have pride if you are truly meek and humble and fully recognize who Scripture says you really are!

Those who know even a little of the Scripture, realize that we are in those "last days." As noted above, the world is conditioning everyone to be "lovers of their own selves" just as the Holy Spirit through Paul here tells us. Through psychology, even Christian psychology, and even through some speaking from the pulpit, many have been duped into believing that we need more self-love. Those who have an ear let them hear what the Holy Spirit has said.

—63—

Why Did Satan Do It?

Have you ever wondered what caused Satan to rebel and throw away his number one spot in heaven, just below God Himself? Until I asked myself, I had never heard the question asked, nor any theories offered. What follows is not a theory, but a mere conjecture, which was intended to be short, light and simple. But as I got into it, it grew both in length and seriousness. It is still pure conjecture, but to me at least, it has a plausible ring to it. Therefore I must say, although it is based on a true story, any similarity between actual persons, places or things, living or dead, is purely coincidental. Isn't that the way Hollywood says it?

Billions and billions of years ago, well anyway, sometime in eternity past, an event occurred in a place somewhere else called Heaven. There exists, and always did, an omnipotent One whom we call God. He lived alone in a vast expanse. Well actually, He wasn't exactly alone. He was, and is, a Triune God, there being three aspects of Himself. He chose to describe this three-in-one person to us as the Father, Son and Holy Spirit. Perhaps He only chose to describe Himself this way so that our simple, limited minds could relate to His awesome Self in terms with which we happen to be familiar. They are all really one Triune Godhead, equally all God, each having all power and omnipotence, doing all things both as equal, complete individuals and at the same time collectively as a single entity. I know, this is very confusing and unbelievable to most mortals, and I mention it only because knowing of His triune nature is necessary if we are to understand who He is, how He operates, and the "atmosphere" within which Satan "did it."

Anyway a long, long time ago, He, They, God, were all that there was. They had a wonderful loving relationship and often talked among themselves (Psalms 2) But one day, it appears that they decided to "increase their borders" in a sense, by creating some beings, some living things to love and care for, to govern, and with which to fellowship. That Thought became reality, and low and behold, (that's Scripture lingo for WOW!) what God now called angels, suddenly came into being! We don't know how many He created, perhaps many thousands or even millions. In creating them, God also created an organizational structure, a sort of angelic hierarchy, consisting of "principalities and powers." Some angels were stronger than others, some more intelligent, and some even more beautiful than others. Some were eventually assigned specific jobs, such as messengers. One of these, we know as Gabriel, and others were assigned other known roles such as warriors. We know from God's "Diary" that He named one of these, Michael. There were also *sarafin* and *cheribim* angels. These two categories of angels were assigned places of duty close to God Himself. There was also a chief angel, the leader of them all. God made him the most powerful, most intelligent, most talented, and most beautiful of all of these "Sons of God" as He chose to call His new Family.

So now God had a family to love, to teach and to fellowship with. In this "heavenly realm" they were spirits, for as yet, God had created nothing of substance; there was no earth, or stars, only an eternal, timeless, spaceless, hyper dimensional existence beyond our pitifully, limited ability to comprehend. Can anyone imagine how wonderful "life," as an angel must have been, being one of His creations, living perpetually in His presence, free of the stress and troubles that inflict us? How long this situation lasted cannot be understood, because we are incapable of even imagining existence without time and three-dimensional space and substance. We are limited to thinking only in terms of some sequential chain of events, measurable in terms of time, that is, minutes, hours, years, etc. We cannot imagine existence that is timeless anymore than we can imagine a multi dimensional world beyond our four dimensions. Even our relatively primitive "cutting edge" science is now aware that there are at least ten dimensions, six of which are inferred and not directly knowable by our senses.

Anyway, a point occurred when God chose to introduce into being, a whole new system of existence that scientists call the space-time continuum. This turned out to be a finely tuned array of stars and other substances, one of which was the planet earth. On this planet, He introduced, for the first time, physical life forms along with a life-sustaining environment. It was at this point, when God, speaking to and of themselves, revealed the pinnacle of their plan when He said, "Let us make man in our image." (Genesis 1:26) Thus came into being the first man, Adam, and shortly after, the first woman, Eve. God's plan was to have these two procreate and then populate the earth with others of their kind, and all of them in His image. These were all destined to become joint heirs (Romans 8:17), and to rule this newly created universe with Him. The angels were happy with God's new creation. Out of love for Him, they were pleased to realize that God now would have others, more of His kind then they were, beings with whom He could fellowship and share in ways that they could not. They looked forward to this whole new creation, to observe God's incredible work, and saw new opportunities to serve Him as this new world progressed.

Yes, all were happy, except one. He was the chief angel, the number one being of all creation up to that point. For eons, he had been in charge of everything that had ever existed, until then. Now, out of the blue, God has announced that He brought into existence a whole universe and that this new being, Adam, and his descendants were to jointly govern it with God. Adam was the first in a line of persons, who were to be over everything, even Satan and all his brother angels as well! Where would this leave Satan? He was the super angel. Aside from God Himself, there was none other more powerful intelligent beautiful and talented than he. He was perfect! Even God said so. (Ezekiel 28:15) Now, God had pulled the rug out from under him. He was to be relegated to second class, below this physical walking klutz and his offsprings! How awful he must have felt! Let us see if we can imagine what went through Satan's mind as he observed all these happenings and grew more concerned about his future.

Prior to this, Satan ruled the whole show. He had no peers. God had given him full authority to run things pretty much as he pleased. This wasn't right! How could the "old man" do this to him? He had always done a good job; there were no complaints! Before this he had never had even a single bad thought. Why should he? There was nothing but happiness in his heart, nothing to think badly about. Now, Satan would be subordinate to some upstart who didn't have a fraction of his power, knowledge, beauty, and talent. Suddenly, added to this anguish, he realized that he felt justifiable pride in who he was, knowing that he was better than any other angel, and surely better than Adam. He felt anger because of what God had done, and he felt envy, because this Adam, in spite of his obvious inferiority, was what Satan could never be, a likeness of God! Is it any wonder Satan felt these things? Just how much put down, how much humiliation could one angel stand? Especially the super angel!

Well, he would show God! He simply wouldn't stand for it. The "old man" couldn't do this to him. He had great powers too; from his perspective, they were almost as great as the Fathers. But what to do? He knew he couldn't attack the Father, nor could he get Him to change the plan. God had already put it into action. But perhaps, he could mess it up by somehow compromising this simpleton, this still wet-behind-the-ears fool who didn't yet know anything. As he looked down, Satan could see Adam there in the garden, this strange looking creature, and his even stranger looking companion, the likes of which of course, he had never seen. Actually, there was something about her he thought that was rather attractive and even captivating, he mused. "But look at that fool Adam" he thought, "all he can do is to go around naming animals (Genesis 2:19, 20) and in the meanwhile, all she is doing is prancing around sampling fruit and berries. How could Adam, or a million like him ever be able to do what I can do, let alone *judge* and *rule* over *me*! No way, it won't work and I won't allow it"

The more he thought about it the angrier he became. In his thoughts, he said, "I'm through being Mr. Nice Guy, carrying all of

God's burdens of leadership and decision making, doing all the work here in heaven, and them doing nothing but sitting on their thrones figuring out ways to do me in. Their plan isn't going to work; I'll see to that! Sure, I'm upset at being subordinated by some new putz they decided to create. Who wouldn't be? When I get finished with that jerk, God won't even recognize him. Then, when God sees that their "image man" is not what They thought They had created, They will quit this foolishness, reinstate me, and all will be right again."

Well, we know from God's Diary how Satan tricked Adam and Eve to sin and thereby lose their made-in-His-image status. With this Satan, thought he had won because he knew that God could not countenance sin. He believed that God would simply toss Adam out of the garden and end this farce.

How proud he was to have exposed the frailty of this facade. This failure by God to have created an in-depth likeness of Himself. Surely now God would see His mistake, and praise Satan for reveal-ing it to Him.

How delighted Satan was as he watched the two of them, after they had sinned. How poetically just it seemed to him as he saw the cloak of God's light and righteousness that he so envied, and that had clothed them, suddenly disappear. He knew that this "made-in His-image" aspect of God's new creation was gone, and that he had done it! It was like the end of a great performance, when the spot-light moves away from the stage. How pathetic, weak, and fright-ened they looked, as they sought to cover themselves. These sniveling, cowardly excuses for life were now no better, he thought, than the lowly beast Adam had been naming the day before. In fact, they were worse. They didn't even have fur, or feathers or scales to cover their very ugly exposed skin!

Then came that great moment he was waiting for, when God saw Adam's nakedness and knew that he had sinned. Why didn't He blast Adam? Why didn't He end this foolishness and let us all get back to the tranquility and peace we had before God got on His made-in-His-own-image kick? Why didn't God turn to him and thank him for showing Him His error? But look at what happened as a result of

Adam's sin! Satan could see that the whole universe "groaned," that pain and suffering, sickness and death entered the world and infected all living creatures and caused the whole decaying process of entropy to begin throughout both the heavens and the earth. Wow! This was something he had never expected. He was more than a little disturbed by that part of the scene!

But what did God do? Instead of dumping them as rejects, and admitting the project to be a failure, He expressed infinite love for these vile creatures, and great enmity toward Satan! He thought to himself, "What did I do? I just exposed the weakness and imperfections of God's recent handiwork. Now, He has sworn enmity against me and eliminated my rank and position! That's not fair." he thought. "I'm just a messenger, the revealer of God's mistake! Sure, I tempted them, but look how easy it was! He should realize that sooner or later their lack of character would lead them to sin anyway. I just exposed the inevitable a little sooner. Actually, I did Him a favor, by revealing the weakness of this whole new creation sooner instead of later."

Poor Satan, he never did figure out that nothing was wrong or left out of God's plan. There was no weakness or imperfection that God didn't intend or plan on allowing. What Satan couldn't comprehend was that this "weakness" was in fact, the manifestations of God's most intricate and precious ingredient, which we call choice or free will. Strength, as Satan imagined it, would have been strict, unyielding, unquestioning, never failing, adherence to God's will as in a stringed puppet or a robot. Little did he know, and probably still can not understand that he, Satan, and his actions were all part of God's perfect plan. Satan represents the alternate choice to God, which makes free will a living fact, rather than a sham. Of course, it has brought about much pain and suffering, entirely because of wrong choices, but that is the price that had to be paid for the filtering out of those who would not chose correctly, and therefore would not enter His eternal kingdom.

God's response to his actions sorely angered Satan even more. But fortunately for him, he thought, "God did not take away my powers, only my position, and I am left to roam the earth and even to rule it from behind the scenes." God allotted him the freedom to hassle, tempt, and wreak havoc to a limited degree over the whole earth. But only for a certain amount of time would he be allowed this freedom. For God, in banishing him from heaven, told him that his ultimate destination would first be the bottomless pit, (Revelation 20:1–3) and then after a thousand years of an even more limited freedom, he would be cast into the lake of fire, forever! (Revelation 20:10)

When Satan heard this he was extremely distraught and filled with fear. How could this be? It was unreal; it had to be just a bad dream. Just for a simple little trick whereby he exposed the faultiness of God's creation, he, the greatest of the them all, would be banished and forced to suffer throughout eternity? He begged for an audience with the Father, and on his knees, (figuratively speaking, because he had no body or knees) he pleaded for mercy and forgiveness. But God would have none of it. For any angel to sin was an unforgivable act. But this was also a sin of the highest order, one that had literally shaken the whole universe and heaven as well. Because of this one act, God would eventually have to create a whole new heaven and earth. (Revelation 21:1) (Of course He had always intended too.)

Having received no relief by his pleas, Satan went away and sulked for a while. Slowly as all of this sank in, anger and hate and vengeful thoughts against God filled his mind, and his now thoroughly evil heart. He had been top angel from the day he was created. He knew no other "life." As he calmed down, he took inventory of himself and began thinking of what, if anything, he could do about his situation. He didn't have the power to know all things in advance of their happening as did God, but he did have a large intelligence network and many friends within the angel community to inform him of what was going on. God had not stripped him of any of his powers, only of his angelic authority. He had the power to observe on a moment-by-moment basis all that was actually happening on earth and even in the minds of men. He had many other latent powers, which he was only now discovering. The most intriguing of them, he mused, was the power to deceive. How easy it had been to manipulate Eve into believing that she could be "as God," if she would do the only thing that God had forbidden her to do. Deception! That was a new power, a new force that had never before been applied any-where, *ever*! These feelings of pride, envy, hate and anger, that he had only recently come by, were also new to the cosmos, and he was the first to express them! He had invented them! These were powerful new tools! With these, he reasoned, he could easily manipulate these simpletons. He could continue to deceive and to tempt them into sin and thereby to rebel against God's will. This would surely thwart Gods plans, including the one regarding his own ultimate destiny. As his hopes grew, so also did his pride increase to where he began to believe he could not only thwart God's plans, but also eventually, even usurp His authority and become "as God himself!"

God had allowed him domain over the earth. This was God's big mistake he, reasoned. With this he would surely be able to alter what-ever the divine plan might be. But one thing worried him, because he didn't understand it. In condemning him God had said, " I will put enmity between you and the woman, and between your seed and her seed, and it shall bruise your head and you shall bruise his heel." (Genesis 3:15) What was that all about? Even his intelligence sources could tell him. The woman? There was only one, Eve. Surely she couldn't do anything? And seed? What's that? Bruise my head? It didn't make any sense, but because of its source, he had to take it seri-ously and stay alert to everything that was going on with these two wenches God had created.

It wasn't long before Cain and Able some along. Now he could see how these earthlings were able to propagate, that is create to like-ness as of themselves from within. This was astounding! God had surely created a new type of being, one with a built-in ability to bring forth more of his own kind. Did this have anything to do with the seed of the woman, he wondered? Well if it did, he would nix that before it got out of hand. Satan had observed God's insistence on animal sacri-fice as some form of penitence and worship of Him. Seeing that Cain farmed while Able shepherded he saw an easy way to toss in a "mon-key wrench" by simply getting Cain to reason that vegetables were as good as lambs to be sacrificed. He knew that this would not please

God. Throwing in a touch of envy into Cain's heart, because God looked more favorably at Abel's offering, and then add a bit of anger, and bingo! Mr. Good is dead, and Mr. Bad would never have God's favor or produce that head bruising seed! Score one for Satan!

But later Seth came along, Cain multiplied, and so did Seth. Adam and Eve also had many more "unreported" offspring. Now the problem was getting complicated for Satan. He realized that by himself, he couldn't possibly handle all the work involved in perverting all of this growing population. It was easy to do, that is to deceive and to tempt these weak-willed, pleasure-loving humans into sinful behavior, but now he needed help! With that ever-expanding population, he needed his own army of angels if he was going to be able to control this rabble. He knew that some of the angels, those that still communicated with him, were a little weaker in their allegiance to God than were the others. Was it possible that he could convince any of them to join him? Why not! Deception was his name, and control was his game! He knew them better than they knew themselves; after all he had spent billions of years as their boss. These select ones he had in mind already had a soft spot for him. All he had to do was to convince them that he had something better and more exciting to offer them than God did. What would do it? Truth didn't matter; perception was the only thing of value. First, they already knew how great he was, how powerful and how valued he had been in heaven. They saw how easily he had manipulated Eve, and they also had witnessed the Cain strategy. If he could convince them that they had more exciting and rewarding opportunities with him than with God, he would surely be able to develop the means of thwarting God's plans. He could promise each one a powerful place behind each throne on earth whereby they would, under his authority, become the principalities and powers, influence every king, governor, president, emperor, bureaucracy, and governing body on earth. They could even officiate and have control over all false religions, which he planned to create. Most importantly, he would convince them that they would share in his glory as he became "as God." That's when God would finally admit failure of His divine "experiment" and agree to move over and give him his rightful place along side of Them on the heavenly throne.

But too much of this was promises that he couldn't fulfill immediately, and couldn't as yet convincingly guarantee. He needed something very tempting and immediate in order to seduce them out of heaven. If he could just get them out of there, he knew that they would be his forever, because God would never let them come back. They would be all subject to the same fate God had decreed for him. Of course, he wouldn't tell them that! He'd only speak of the good stuff, the power, the activity, the glory and the excitement that would be theirs. Then he had the answer. He remembered that "feeling" he had when he saw Eve. It was something very strange, nothing he had ever experienced before. He had thought her to be "attractive." But what did that mean. He didn't know, but it was potentially seductive, and seduction was his *middle name*! Then, in this context he began looking around and saw that many of the women were "fair" and exuded something that seemed tempting to him. "Temptation. That's what I need," he said to himself. "I need something that will tempt them, something to weaken their spiritual strength. Women, that's it!" He knew that all of the "sons of God" had the capacity to take on a human forms and bodies as he did, even though most of them hadn't as yet experienced this strange ability. He himself had taken the form of a serpent in the garden with Eve, so he knew how these transformations worked. This would be demonstrated many times later in history as God sent his faithful angels in human bodies to perform many specific tasks here on earth.

After briefing his angel friends on all the glory and excitement that could be theirs if they joined him, he simply suggested that they ought to take a moment and look down and observe what had been going on, and in particular, to take a long hard look at the women folk. When they did, "the sons of God saw that the daughters of men were fair, and they took them wives of all which they chose" (Genesis 6:2). How Satan strutted and praised himself over his brilliant achievement! Now, he had them! Only God knows how many. Scripture tells us it was a third of all of the angels in heaven! With such a large army, he believed he now had all he needed to eventually become "as God" and not only avoid hell, but also be able to force his way back into heaven! At the very least, he now had the means to effectively rule the earth, and to a large degree control, to their detriment, the workings of all mankind whom he so hated.

As an aside, it should be noted that in God's recording of this event, as quoted, He used the Hebrew word *ishahah,* which the English translators called "wives." The word actually means "women" although wives is an acceptable translation in certain contexts. However, here it clearly means "women." Therefore, the verse really says, "they took them women all which they chose." It seems evident that they didn't go through any such formalities as marriage; they just took!

This coup that he scored by tempting angels away from God, turned out to be "a hat trick," that is a triple whammy, a victory even bigger than had he imagined, or so he thought. Not only did he now have his army of angels, but with this affair between the angels and women, there was now a race of super evil beings that would so pollute the human race that God, later, was forced to destroy the whole world with a flood, in order to erase the corruption that it caused. And additionally, as these "Nephilim" died, their spirits, not being of human origin, were unacceptable anywhere in the after life of souls, and thus became the so-called: "evil spirits" remaining here on earth as another formidable asset to Satan's arsenal of weapons to be used against humanity, and therefore also against God.

With the advent of the Nephilim polluting much of the human race, and man's natural sinful nature inherited from Adam, the early world became an abomination to God, ". . . and it repented the Lord that He had made man, and it grieved Him at His heart, and the Lord said, I will destroy man whom I have created from the face of the earth . . ." (Genesis 6:7). We might conclude from this statement, that He regretted creating man, as the word "repent" would seem to indicate. The Hebrew word, however, which is *ahahh,* means, "expressing pain exclamatorily." Of course, God felt pain! He loves His creation and it grieved Him whenever we dishonored Him by sinning, but surely He does not regret! To regret would be to have insufficient foreknowledge of the consequences of ones act. God is and always has been in charge and knows all things past, present and future. That He has and does allow Satan to continue to exist and to do his evil is consistent with His plan and must be accepted as such, even though we cannot fully comprehend its divine purpose. In this paper we are conjecturing and describing what might have been the situation from Satan's perspective. But one should remember, God knows and controls everything. He expresses His will as it pleases Him to do so, but He also allows others to express theirs. Because He allows things that are contrary to His will, to that which He does not prefer, only proves the genuineness of His gift to us of free choice. He pays the price of this gift to us many times over, as evidenced by Genesis 6:6, and in many other verses throughout Scripture, all culminating in the sacrifice of His own Son, so that the accumulation of all the bad choices of those who truly believe in Him according to the Gospel, will be forgiven and their souls saved. That is, of course, the essence of God's plan and the purpose of all that has or ever will transpire.

As Satan realized the great tragedy he had inflicted on the human race, he could sense victory approaching as he saw God preparing to wipe out all that He had created by flooding the entire earth. Now, surely he would be vindicated by having proven God wrong in His assessment of this frail and faulty generation that was now so evidently far, far from being "in His image." But then to his astonishment, and what he perceived to be God's desperate attempt to salvage His hopeless plan, he saw the one small family of eight rescued by God for the purpose of repopulating the restored earth. Satan could see that he had let one slip through his cordon of temptation that had perverted the entire population, for God said to Noah ". . . for I have seen righteousness before me in this generation" (Genesis 7:1) Certainly Noah was a sinner as we all are, having the seeds of sin in our genes as transmitted to us from the first one so infected in the garden. But here perhaps is the first documented, demonstrated act of real faith and saving grace through faith, if one excludes Abel and then Enoch, who "walked with God" and was taken directly to heaven. (Genesis 5:23, 24). Our Lord told Noah to build the ark, a task that he struggled with faithfully for two hundred years, and completed just as God had commanded. Can you comprehend how difficult this was, to build out of wood, a ship as long as a football field and as large as a modern tanker? Can you imagine two hundred years of such painful persevering struggle amid the jeers and ridicule of all who witnessed his efforts to build a ship far from water in a world where it had never rained? And when asked, he would say that it was to save his family and animal life from the coming flood. Who among us here today, would not have been one of those jeering him to scorn? Here alone was faith, very long enduring faith, as great as any to be found anywhere in Scripture, or in life.

To Satan's disappointment, as would happen over and over again into the end times, here God had snatched victory from the jaws of what seemed to him would be God's certain defeat. But Satan was far from daunted. He saw this as a pathetic act of desperation by God to try to salvage His "experiment." He now had over 1650 years of experience, learning the fine arts of deception, temptation, and perseverance. He surely could destroy the souls of a measly eight who had slipped through his net!

By now this saga of "why did he do it?" has gone on long enough to bring boredom to even the hardiest of those who might be willing to read it. But the story of the "war" has continued on throughout the ages, and has become personalized to those of us now living, as we see the prophesied end times at hand, with the final battle and the evil ones defeat not too far in the future. The history of this war would fill large volumes, but then God has already written it. Scripture identifies literally hundreds of events directly attributed to Satan's efforts as he has learned of, and responded to Gods redemptive plan for man and for the universe.

Even though this paper has become longer than I had intended, I feel compelled to note the following few additional evidences of Satan's involvement in world history as he has tried to control, condemn and eliminate as much of the human race as he possibly could.

Nimrod: The first would-be world dictator and hater of God. One major strategy Satan employed repeatedly was to try to unify mankind under one government and one religion, which he would then control. Nimrod was his first recorded attempt. When God destroyed the tower of Babel, He also segregated and caused the scattering of man by instilling in them a wide variety of languages where communication between various linguistic people groups became very difficult. This caused them to separate rather than to continue to grow in a single cluster, and it was thus the beginning of the different cultures and nationalities as they spread across the earth to establish their individual "countries." God did this in order to make it more difficult to create another stable, controllable "one-world government," which Satan could fully control. However, as we look around today, we see a one-world government and a single world religion being formed before our eyes! This is no surprise because God has told us that this would be the condition in the end times.

Abraham: The "Father of God's chosen people." It was from here in the Scripture that Gods plan for the redemption of mankind was "formerly" revealed. Oh, it had been alluded to in a number of ways, but so subtlety that it is doubtful that Satan even caught it. His "bruising by the seed of the woman" was one, and even that prophetic sentence that is formed by the definition of the names of the first ten men from Adam to Noah tells of His plan. (see *Is God really the author of the Bible?*) But through Abraham, God would form a nation, a chosen people, through whom the Redeemer would come. Satan has hated all mankind from the very first two in the garden for reasons already given. But now he had a particular people on which to focus his hate and destructive powers. Satan could see that these were the particular people on whom God was relying, and through whom He intended to redeem a remnant, a people who would retrieve that "made-in His-image" quality, and thereby qualify to become joint-heirs in the rule of the universe. If he could but destroy them, he would have demolished God's purpose! Thus began the narrowing of Satan's focus and his campaign of "anti-Semitism," which has continued to this day. This war against God has been not unlike a chess game in many ways, literally, involving kings, queens, knights, bishops, and pawns, and "popes" with moves and counter moves. What Satan cannot admit is that God is the ultimate player and that He in the end, will produce the checkmate.

Pharaoh: It's likely that Satan controlled the hearts of most Pharaohs, for one of them put the Hebrews into bondage and later another one established a program of annihilation by having all Hebrew male babies killed. We see God's intervention in this plan as the mothers improvised to save their sons. Then we see God miraculously intervene as He parted the waters of the Red Sea so as to provide for the Hebrew nation to escape and for the destruction of Satan's agents.

Judges: After the inspired leadership of Joshua, it didn't take long for Satan to seduce the Hebrew tribes into idol worship as he had all other people groups. During the period of about three hundred years until the time of Samuel, the Hebrew tribes were loosely governed by what Scripture calls "Judges," which were simply strong tribal leaders. In these times of the Judges we see the seesaw struggle among good and bad leaders between a few trusting in God, but mostly those whom Satan managed. It was a time much like today when "every man did what was right in his own eyes" (Judges 17:6, 21:25) rather than obey God.

Saul: Here we have the "double minded" man initially good and endowed with the Holy Spirit, only to be repeatedly attacked and influenced by Satan, whose primary focus was to remove David. This is because by now it had become evident that the "seed of the woman" would come through the line of David. Here we see again the seesaw struggle this time within Saul. First he was endowed with good and then with evil, this being repeated over and over again. We must remember that today, beginning with the Pentecost the Comforter that Jesus sent (John 14:16) enters permanently in the hearts of the redeemed. Prior to Pentecost however, the Holy Spirit could both enter and leave one's heart depending on the condition of the heart. Here Scripture tells us that this was the on-again, off-again condition of Saul's heart. It also informs us that the Holy Spirit entered and never left David's heart, as He does today with every redeemed Christian.

The Kings: Starting with David, the first of God's chosen bloodline of Kings we see clearly the titanic struggle between God and

Satan. Throughout the life of David we see Satan trying to kill him, first through Saul and then through others, even David's own son Absalom. Satan was also creating circumstances whereby David would be tempted by Bethsheba and thereby commit adultery and murder. Then with Solomon, we see his initially strong virtuous nature eroded by the temptation and opportunity resulting from wealth and fame, and, of course, the influence of Satan-controlled "principalities and powers." Solomon's reign is followed, at Satan's instigation, by a division of the tribes into two kingdoms, Judah and Israel, each of which went from bad to worse, with a few good kings scattered along the lines of succession. Finally God's patience came to an end in Jeroboam's reign over Judah when He cursed Jeroboam and "cut off" his royal line. With this seemingly rash act of God, Satan believed that God had "shot Himself in the foot." This is because God had said that the redeemer, "the seed which would bruise the head" would come from the bloodline of David, which God had now severed. It took Satan a while to realize what we know from the genealogy of Jesus, as recorded in Luke 3:31, that the blood-line from David to Jesus came not through his son Solomon, but through Nathan another son and down to Mary, which, even though being a woman, she was a qualified heir by virtue of God's ancient decree regarding the daughters of Zelophehad. (Numbers 27) Thus Satan was "checked" again, but not "checkmate" yet!

Haman: As found in the book of Esther, Haman was the equivalent of a Prime Minister, under the Persian King Ahasuerus, son of Darius, also known in secular history as, Xerxes, or Artaxerxes. This was around 535 B.C. as the Hebrew exiles had returned from Babylon to rebuild the temple. By fiendishly clever manipulation, orchestrated by Satan, Haman was given the absolute authority to kill every Jew on earth, and he formulated a foolproof plan to do so. It was only by the grace of God, as it was imparted to Esther and her uncle Mordecai, that this was prevented. This episode also presents a wonderful example of God's omniscience, power and divine presence in the affairs and workings of this world. Haman was a descendant of Agag, King of the Amalekites, an agent of evil whom God had told Saul to slay. But Saul disobeyed and spared him, thus permitting this line of

585

Israel's enemies to continue and to produce Haman and his plan. Also however, King David, who was, according to God, "a man after His own heart," spared the life of one of his enemies, named Shimei, from whose line came Esther and Mordecai! So Satan was foiled again, by our wonderful Father and Master Strategist!

Herod: Here we have the second recorded case of infanticide as Herod tried to kill Baby Jesus as he ". . . sent forth and slew all the children that were in Bethlehem and the coasts thereof from two years old and under . . ." (Matthew 2:16) Here again by divine fore-knowledge God had already sent Mary and Joseph with Jesus to Egypt until after Herod had died.

The Crucifixion: This to Satan was his finest hour! Over the centuries he had tried, whenever opportunities occurred, to eliminate the entire Jewish race, or at least the line that would lead to Jesus. Somehow, God had always out-foxed him. Now, through his devious ways, he had arranged for the execution of this One who would "bruise his head," this Son of God, this incarnation of God Himself! God had failed and he had won! Now the world would really be his, and heaven would be within his reach! It would seem that Satan still didn't understand the full extent of God's plan. But when our Savior had risen from the dead, had defeated death, and had thereby obtained victory over him, Satan was taken aback and realized that *he* had won nothing! Previously his pride and arrogance had caused him to pay little attention to God's whole Word as it is written and where God's divine plan for redemption is so clearly laid out. He had preferred to use his own power of reasoning, to use terrorist hit-and-run tactics, and to respond to whatever he could learn from on-going events, as the means of thwarting God's will. Now he had to study God's revealed plan if he was to ever checkmate Him. Also, with Jesus risen, another whole dimension to the battle had been created. There was now in permanent full-time residence here on earth, another extremely powerful force whom Jesus had called the Comforter and the Restrainer. He was an indwelling spirit of salvation who would enter the heart of anyone who faithfully believed and trusted in Jesus as his or her Lord and Savior.

Previously Satan had used his army of evil spirits to contaminate souls and thus recruit for his own purpose nearly any human he chose. Now, with those who had become "Christians" and thus received the Holy Spirit, he could no longer recruit them. He could not displace the Holy Spirit with his evil ones. He could cause them mental, physical and emotional pain and suffering of every kind, but he could not penetrate their souls, for they forever belonged to Jesus. He also learned from the "New Scripture" that this Comforter, this Holy Spirit would continue to immunize souls until some point in time when ". . . the fullness of the gentiles be come in," (Romans 11:25) after which Israel would be saved by Jesus as He returned to the earth. After that, God would deal with him personally. "Ah, Ha," he thought, "So that was God's plan. When He has enough, a certain number of these "born-again Christians" in heaven to rule over the angels and the universe, that will be the moment when he plans to capture me and end my rule here on earth. Then, having saved the Jews, he plans to assume David's throne from which He, Jesus, will rule the world with the Jews. How foolish it is of God to advertise His moves," he thought as he digested all of this, and then he said to himself, "Now I know how to play out the game and checkmate Him! First I'll extend that time that it will take for Him to collect His own, and somehow during that time, I will eliminate all the Jews so that there won't be any here for him to save and rule over. No Jews, no throne, no return of Jesus and to rule by Jesus, translates to, no threat to me! Checkmate! The game is over, and I won! Sorry God, now you'll see that I am like the most high. It will be time for you to move over."

So now we see here in our own lifetimes, the final moves of this end times game being played out. We see the rise and rapid proliferation of many false religions and even many false gospels within the so-called "Christian denominations" These are all ways to thwart actual salvation and to deceive the vast majority into believing they are saved when they are not. This is part of Satan's strategy to at least slow the rate of salvation and to delay the day when that secret number of saved souls is reached, and the father says to His Son, "go get them." This will be the rapture. We see throughout history, millions of real Christians being persecuted, tortured, and killed for their faith from the time of Caesar to now and beyond. These are also all parts of the same delaying tactics to prolong the time until "the fullness of gentiles."

Satan and his hosts never sleep, and never cease to wage their corruption to subvert, pervert and convert souls into false beliefs. Not only have they been successful in growing the popularity of pagan religions, but they have also subverted the many "Christian" denominations through the tempting logic of ecumenism and the casting of doubts and confusion regarding Genesis and the Gospels. Combining these with the promotion of "easy," "quick" or "manip-ulative" prayerism within even the evangelical's churches, they have converted legions to a false Christianity and even more dangerously to a false belief that they are saved. Having learned what I have regarding this travesty, I no longer consider myself to be an Evan-gelical Christian, but instead a Fundamentalist Christian. Even in this last bastion of real Christianity there is much evidence of Satan having made significant in roads in this respect, I am but a messen-ger. Before, you "hang" the messenger, "check these things to see if they be true." (Acts 17:11)

As for the Jews, and Satan's plan for their elimination, he has always sought this, but now it had become imperative. History shows us evidence of his activity throughout to the present "A.D." era starting with the slaughter in 70 A.D., the Roman persecutions in the first, second and third centuries A.D., "Crusades" ordered by the Popes, and other atrocities and slaughters directed by papal authority over the centuries "in the name of Christianity." Perhaps the most notable of all efforts was through those agents of Satan namely Hitler and Stalin. And now after a brief respite, we see anti-Semitism returning in Europe, and of course continuing in the Middle East where it has always been. It is less evident, but is surely rising here in the United States and elsewhere in the world and will continue to do so until all nations of the world will rise against Israel in the final days, as prophesied

Those of us, who have read the book and believe, know who checkmates whom, and how He does it. Praise the Lord! As prefaced, this paper is pure conjecture as to what Satan thought and why he did what he did. But it is laced securely, I believe, with defendable Scripture, and historical evidence in order to give it a plausible base. Surely, Satan had to have had a reason for his actions. He had, for God knows how long, being a good and faithful servant who suddenly expressed what must have been his prerogative all along, to go against God's will, and exercise his own free will. That others joined him, suggests that God had given all angels free will as He did to those He made in-His-own-image.

If you, hate, scoff, ridicule, or like what I have written, it doesn't matter. The only thing that matters is that it moves you to think about God, about His eternal plan, about sin, salvation, and repentance, and then, that it causes you to search the Scripture, and come closer to knowing God-Jesus. If it does this, praise the Lord, and may He bless you exceedingly through His incredible Word!

—64—

Sincerity

In the shallow, superficial, overly permissive society we live in today, the word "sincerity" is over used, misapplied and trivialized. But that is the way of the world. This paper, however, is not intended to be a discussion regarding the world, or how it works, but about sincerity as it applies to the Christian Body.

Webster defines the word sincere as "free of hypocrisy, deceit or calculation, honest, genuine; honest of purpose or character." The substance of that definition should be an important component of every Christian soul. But in any meaningful discussion regarding sincerity the word has no value until it is applied to some defined belief. To say one is sincere necessitates an answer to the question, sincere about what? Sincerity carries with it no inherent virtue, for one can be sincerely wrong as well as sincerely right. Can anyone doubt the sincerity of faith of the 9–11 bombers as they crashed into the World Trade Center Towers? Likewise, can anyone question the sincerity of faith of the millions of Christians who suffered horrible tortures and death rather than renounce their faith? Who doubts the sincerity of the Jehovah Witnesses as they go door to door demonstrating the sincerity of their beliefs knowing hatred and verbal abuse most likely lies behind almost every door? Were not Stalin, Mao and Hitler sincere in their beliefs as they each killed tens of millions of people in order to advance their individual causes? We can even credit Satan with sincerity in his dedication of purpose to take as many as possible with him to eternal damnation.

In recent times, the secular world, surely with Satan's help, has "discovered" that there are no absolute truths that everything is relative, that my truth is as valid as yours, and that truth changes with time and with changing situations. We might even add that truth, from the worldly perspective, can even change moment by moment to accommodate one's comfort, convenience and carnal desire. So where does sincerity fit in this world? This answer seems to be, anywhere that it's convenient, or anywhere that an expression of sincerity serves to advance one's cause. It's been said that the most important aptitude for a politician to acquire, if he or she is to be successful, is to be able to convincingly fake sincerity. This seems to apply to essentially all other "successful," worldly endeavors. Consider what television, the theater, and Hollywood represent: feigned sincerity! Isn't that what acting is all about? A great actor, as with a great politician, is nothing more than one who postures the most convincingly and thereby convinces the largest number of people that he, in all sincerity, personifies the belief he professes. One might correctly observe that the vocation of acting is nothing more than acceptable, institutionalized, false sincerity. We can accept and enjoy the entertainment it provides when we know what is going on. Therefore, we all know this when it is in the theater, but what about when highly perfected false sincerity is the principal tool employed by educators, politicians, clergy, and the talking heads that shape rather than report the news on TV? Even Shakespeare, five hundred years ago, observed that each of us is but a "poor player who struts and frets his brief hour on the stage and is heard of no more." As players, or actors, by that very definition, we all fake a sincerity when we project ourselves to be better than who we know we really are. How all too common and tragic it is, for example, when the perspective bride and bridegroom, throughout their courtship, project with false sincerity, only their "best side." Is it any wonder then, that when the true whole nature of each is later expressed, as it inevitably must, that there is so often such great disillusionment, suffering, and finally the breaking of the sacred bonds? Genuine sincerity and honesty from the very beginning would have prevented many such mismatches. While not usually expressed, this bluntly, faked sincerity is today a well respected and admired ability. It's essential not only for success in politics but also for salesmen and anyone wishing to "climb a corporate ladder," or to advance almost anywhere in this world.

Also, consider the demonic monster called "political correctness." This is legally mandated false sincerity, because any one having sincere views contrary to what has been decided as politically correct, is legally muzzled, or expected to compromise his or her beliefs. They must not speak or write their beliefs, for fear of loss of their jobs, or even imprisonment for committing a "hate crime." For instance, in Germany, Canada, Austria, and several other countries, there are people in jail whose only crime was to publicly state or write that they believed that somewhat fewer than six million Jews were executed by the Nazis. If this is hard to believe, check it out; it is true! An internationally respected historian of the World War II era named David Irving was just recently released from prison after serving one and a half years of a three year sentence as a hate criminal for simply having challenged the claim that this many Jews died in concentration camps. The sentence would have been much longer but was reduced because he "retracted" his early and sincere contentions. In other words, at age sixty-seven he lied in order to avoid spending most, if not all, of the rest of his life in prison. You don't have to go to another country to find such satanic absurdities. Here, it is unlawful to teach of God and creation. Only the lie of evolution is allowed in public schools. The absurd lie has been proven to be just that, many times over, yet all such proofs are ignored and the godless, Satan-controlled state demands that it is to be believed.

Why go into all of this, when the stated purpose here is to examine the meaning of the word "sincerity" as it applies to the Christian Body? It's simply because "the world" and way too much of what it stands for, including political correctness, has entered into and become part of the Christian church. Think about this for a while. Can sincerity live comfortably with hypocrisy? And isn't tolerance of wrong a clear expression of hypocrisy? We live in a world where this has become the norm rather than the exception.

The meaning and effectiveness of sincerity, as with almost everything else, has greatly suffered as a result of its "marriage to the world." Christians today live much of their lives surrounded by, immersed in, and greatly influenced by the world and nearly all of its ways. Scripture tells us that we must live *in* the world but must *not* be *of* the world. Many Christians have no idea of what that means. As a result, the world has taken up full residency in the so-called Christian church. Because of this, I suspect that very little remains in the "church" that Jesus, or even the Apostles, would find tolerable. The prophesied "Laodcicean" church of this age (Revelation 3) fits current conditions perfectly. The more we have allowed these influences into our lives and into the church, the more each has become like the world, until now there is little or no distinction between "the world" and the "Christian Body."

Tolerance and compromise are two words not found in the Holy Bible, yet they are the cornerstones of that tragic heresy called ecumenicalism, which has seduced major portions of every formerly genuine Christian denomination. This merging of world and church is so extensive today that much, if not most, of the so-called Christian Body is composed of "nominal Christians" and merely dabblers in the faith, rather than genuine and uncompromising committed adherents to Jesus and His truths. As a result, we have what has been called the visible church that which is made up of all who even vaguely claim to profess the faith, and the comparatively small hidden church composed of the truly saved remnants, who actually possess the saving faith.

When one is born-again, he or she is "sanctified" in the Lord. Sanctified means set apart. Set apart from what? Set apart from the world! If you consider yourself a Christian, look deep into your soul and answer to yourself this question: are you sanctified, that is, set apart for Jesus? To be set apart, there must be something to be set apart from. Scripture tells us that we are to be set apart from the world. That means that we are to have as little as possible to do with the world, its ways, beliefs, activities, attitudes, amusements, and immoral behaviors. In many ways the Amish people are living examples of a very serious application of this doctrine.

Scripture also tells us that there are only two categories of people in the world, those who are saved and those who are not, that is, those who are sanctified, and those who are not, those whose destiny is eternal life with the Creator and those who will spend eternity in hell. Determining which category you belong to is not necessarily as simple as most preachers and teachers of this age indicate it to be, when the Whole of Scripture is taken into consideration as your basis for determination. Here, sincerity plays a vital part, but as stated before, of equal importance is, to what is that sincerity applied? To that should be added, how really sincere, or how watered down by world influences is that sincerity? The way the world has tossed around, twisted, and misused the meaning of the word; we must be very circumspect before we accept fully even the sincerity of what we believe to be our own sincerity. It is sincerity of belief in what Scripture tells is the way to salvation, which we must fully understand and properly apply, if we are to confirm that we are truly saved. To this must be added repentances and obedience if we are to examine the whole of available evidence in the matter. I know! Scripture tells us we are "saved" by grace through faith. And "believe and ye are saved" and "confess with thy lips and believe in thine heart that Jesus is Lord and thou shall be saved," etc. These are certainly God's prerequisite instructions for salvation and are therefore, true and complete. However, the issue is, what do "believe "and "faith," which have the same definition, really mean? It could be said that sincerity, belief, repentance, and obedience are the awesome foursome that deal with genuine, evidenced, eternal salvation. But as previously noted, sincerity is meaningless until it is somewhere applied in order to add a quality to some idea or belief. Then it becomes an essential part of that idea. Thus there must be a sincerity of faith, and that faith must be in *Jesus* and in strict accordance with the *whole* of Scripture.

Now let's look at repentance. To the world, the definition is that it's simply a change of mind. In the biblical context, it is far more; it is a complete turnaround from wherever one is, to a singular fully dedicated focus on Jesus. The validity of such repentance is dependant on the sincerity with which it manifests. Repentance, which lacks the slightest measure of sincerity, is not real repentance, and, therefore, has no place in the genuine Christian Body. Repentance and belief /

faith are inexorably bound, for how can a sincere and complete faith manifest without a sincere and complete turning toward Jesus? Faith, therefore, must be sincere by the strongest meaning of the word, or else the faith cannot be a saving faith. Lest the seeker, and anyone who is new to the faith become disillusioned by such a seemingly unattainable standard, one should recognize that the Lord is patient, loving and long suffering for those who sincerely seek Him. Scripture tells us that a saving faith can be as small as a mustard seed. That speaks to its size, but not to any weakness of its sincerity. The described qualities do not necessarily all come at once. God knows where you are, and if you are sincerely seeking. If it is really Jesus you are seeking, you *will* find Him because the Holy Spirit will lead you to Him! We need only to see that there is a continuous evidence of growth in the right direction. God's assistance in these matters is always available for those who ask in sincerity.

Then we come to obedience. That is the tough one that most of us would rather not know much about. Yet obedience is part of the salvation package although it is not a *pre*requisite. It is a very important part of the evidence of salvation, evidence of a growing faith and submission to the Lordship of Jesus. Of course, we are all sinners and to some degree will continue to sin to our last breath. Obedience is implicit in the meaning of true repentance. We are commanded to be perfect as our Lord is perfect. That *must* be the goal and the sincere work-in-process of every redeemed soul. Continuous sincere effort at obedience to God's Word is that work-in-process. If that is not the primary goal and also one's heart's desire, then perhaps one should look most prayerfully into the soul to determine whether or not God's redemptive grace is really there.

This brings us to the final thought regarding sincerity. Having briefly discussed the awesome foursome of sincerity, belief, repentance, and obedience, there is a fifth, very important, yet most highly neglected component of every genuine practicing, obedient Christian, and that is intimate, in depth, knowledge, and understanding of God's inerrant Holy Word, the Holy Bible. Many will tell you that this is not a prerequisite to salvation. Technically, that is true, and was probably much more frequently manifested in earlier simpler times. However, today with heresy, apostasy, ultra clever weavers of lies and half truths, and a myriad of other satanic devices all seeking control of every soul, *knowing* the real truth, which is found only in the Holy Bible, has become ever more essential, if one is to escape these snares. There is no other way to be certain that we have the real saving faith. Are you willing to stake your eternal security stumbling along some poorly lighted path, equipped only with biblical igno-rance, ineptness or apathy as your principal sources of guidance along your way toward eternity? God Authored that precious book just for us, so that we would be able to find our way with assurance, to that narrow gate, and also so we could actually get to know him, to know His purpose for us, and to know specifically just how we are expected to serve Him along our way to our permanent home. The Bible is a bright beacon of truth-light that can not only guide us most surely along that narrow path to heaven, but can also expose and steer us away from those many other false paths so cleverly designed to tempt us away from what God has provided. You cannot effec-tively discover these things through weekly thirty-minute sermons or by occasional reading of His Word.

When I first knew that I had come to believe in Jesus as my Savior, which was about nine years ago, I chose to read the whole Bible so as to learn all I could about Jesus. I read it through three times, as well as dozens of great Bible commentaries, before I ventured out to meet the first Christian and to attend what I hoped to be a real Christian church. I felt quite pleased then, with the seemingly "vast" knowledge of Scrip-ture that I had acquired. It was all so wonderful that my heart surged with desire to spread this word to all who would hear. But who was around to hear, who cared, or wanted to hear? No one! Therefore, I resorted to the only outlet I could find, and which I believe the Lord led me to, that is writing these things in essays such as this one. How-ever, as I began to write, it quickly became a very humbling experience when I found that my "great understanding" was mostly superficial and that if I was to actually "know" His truth and to write anything meaningful and scripturally defendable, I had to pray immensely, and of a single mind, for wisdom and discernment, knowledge and deeper understanding. Then, with His help, I needed to dig deep into every verse, seek the Greek or Hebrew meaning of the key words, and also determine the narrow as well as the broader context of every presented thought and concept. It was also important to me to try to understand the history and culture of the times of the Scripture writers so as to better understand to whom and why they were writing. The more of this that can be learned, the greater is the potential to understand the present day applications of their messages.

I know that this manner of biblical study is just my own particular calling, and is surely not a prerequisite to salvation, nor is it necessary for finding the particular ministry He has chosen for other saved souls. But some significant level of biblical knowledge, I believe, is essential if we are to know what He expects and has the right to obtain from each of us. Pray intensely for His wisdom and understanding and if you are His, He will give it to you! He will at first give you a little light, that is, some wisdom and understanding of what He has written. If you use it well, He will give you more. This is the ultimate case of use it or loose it. If you fail to use what He gives you, He will take away even that which you have. This precept is expressed many times in Scripture; the classic case is found in Matthew chapters 12 and 13. This is where Israel was given the magnificent light of Jesus' presence and failed to use it. Therefore, the light was removed. No more light was given. That's also how it works for each individual.

Notice earlier I mentioned how I realized that Jesus was my Savior. Only after a considerable amount of prayer and study did I fully apprehend His other role that He necessarily plays in the life of every saved soul. He is also our Lord in every sense of the word. Everyone conscious of his or her hopeless condition in sin wants a Savior. But we can't have one without the other. Jesus saved us by His sacrifice on the cross, thereby becoming qualified to be our Savior and is the Savior to all of those who believe in Him. But by doing so, He also purchased us with His blood; He purchased all of those who are willing to submit to His authority as Lord. In order to claim His saving grace, we must also accept His rule as Lord over our lives. One cannot be saved by being only a "half Christian," that is, accepting Him only as one's Savior. To be a whole saved Christian one must have Him as both Lord and Savior. As a so-called "free people," it is not our nature to accept a Lordship, or any autocratic authority. Scripture tells us all that we need to know in order to be His loyal subjects, those who are worthy of His name, Christian. If we are to give this scriptural information a title we should call it OBEDIENCE.

How often do you hear the word obedience mentioned from the pulpit? If the frequency of its use was a fair measure of it importance, we could easily conclude that obedience is merely a figure of speech or surely something to be treated causally, as so many do. Jesus often spoke of obedience to His Word. Look at John 14:21 for instance, where Jesus says, *"He that hath my commandments and keepeth them, he it is that loveth me; and he that loveth me shall be loved of my Father, and I shall love him, and manifest myself in him"* Then in verses 23 and 24, just so that there can be no doubt as to what He means, He repeats the idea in reverse saying, *"If a man love me, he will keep my words . . ."* and *"He that loveth me not keepeth not my sayings . . ."* These verses firmly tie together the love of God with obedience to His commandments, His Word, His sayings, and, therefore, everything our Lord Jesus has revealed in the Holy Bible. He commands that we love Him with all of our heart, soul and mind. This is a genuine *sincere* love. This kind of love cannot ever exist in any heart not wholly dedicated to obedience.

One final note. Notice how often the word "fundamentalists" is used to describe modern terrorism. Having thus repeatedly identified the word with a group having evil intent, it is now more and more frequently being used to paint Christians with the same brush by referring to them as "right wing fundamentalist Christians." If you are a sincere believer in Jesus as your Lord and Savior and believe that the Bible is the inerrant Word of God, you certainly *are* a fundamental Christian. I suppose the word "right wing" is there to be certain no one is ever to consider a Christian as having "liberal" qualities. Liberal, of course, is being on the side of "good," and right as being on the side of bad. But now the world has established through this one word, a hate filled connection between genuine Christianity and terrorist evil. The effect of this connect is presently in its infancy, but rest assured the monster will grow. But even more timely and equally insidious, is the confusion wrought by the world as it has invaded the very soul of Christianity by means of false teachers, prophets and pastors who convey false, or half Gospels as well as many other altered doctrines and compromises. This is probably the most insidious and successful device used today to deprive a seeker of salvation. Those who are seeking salvation seek the truth. But these servants of Satan are like sentries lined up along the path to the "narrow gate" availing themselves of every opportunity to point the seeker to other paths, all of which lead to hell.

So what is the answer? The answer is in the Word of God and nowhere else. Trust no one's opinion, until you have confirmed its truth based on the whole Word of God. Don't even trust a true quote from Scripture until you have examined it in the context of the whole Scripture. A most relied on ploy of false teachers is to piously and with cleverly disguised insincerity, quote Scripture and to apply it in a manner deviant from its God-given intent. Through this and similar devices Satan is able to produce legions of professors of the faith who sincerely believe they are saved, but who are not, because they relied only on human counsel and instruction without referring to God's Word adequately, if at all. Don't deal in presumptions or rationalizations formulated out of earthly desires. The world teaches us to, "go with your heart," and "to do what is right in your own eyes." This sounds like the voice of wisdom, but it is advice straight out of hell, because it's the exact opposite of what God has written. God tells us through Jeremiah in chapter 17:9, *"The heart is deceitful above all things, and desperately wicked; who can know it?"* In Deuteronomy 12:6 and Judges 18:6 God is critical of the people for doing what was right in their own eyes rather than living by God's Word. Prayerfully read and *study* God's Word, read and listen to biblical expositors and teachers, who faithfully explain without modifying God's Word, and carefully examine and confirm all that they say as it is revealed in the Holy Bible. Then pray for God's guidance. If you are saved you have two hearts, the dirty old wicked one that wants always to "do it its way" and the new one that came into you along with the permanently indwelling Holy Spirit that would, if it knew how, do it God's way. Through sincere prayer, the new heart aided by the Holy Spirit, will lead you always, to and through God's Word, to the right path. Absent this effort, the old heart is always waiting to send you down the carnal paths and away from God and from the eternal home it offers. All of this must be in a genuinely sincere quest for Godliness. This may seem like a great deal of work, but it isn't, not when compared with how much your eternal salvation is worth.

—65—

A Lesson in Humility from Job

A few weeks before I began to compose this essay, I had a very painful, non-life threatening but yet severely debilitating and prolonged physical problem. During the most painful moments, I cried out to God for mercy. Other times I simply cried out WHY! Our Father chose to take a while to answer my mercy petition. After awhile, He allowed the intensity of pain to lessen considerably, as for the basic affliction, He chose to let it continue. I'm persuaded to believe, however, that with this pain, this was a clear enunciation that, as with Paul and his "thorn," He was telling me that His grace was enough. My thorn remains, but through His blessed grace He has given me the strength to deal with it calmly and with acceptance. My "why," however, was quickly and simply answered by a single word that came to me with unmistakable clarity, "JOB."

How wonderful is the Lord to those who rightly call themselves by His name, Christians! He faithfully answers all prayers of all who are His. Jesus made this commitment several times during His earthly ministry. Prayers are not all answered promptly as was this one, nor are they all answered in a manner that the petitioner would like to have them answered. But they are all answered in strict accordance with God's will, in His perfect timing, and in the way most beneficial to the one who has petitioned. With this in mind, what is the substance, the message, the lesson that I am to understand, give thanks for, appreciate, and learn from this very severe personal ordeal?

Before I can come to a firm understanding and answer to this question from the place my Lord has led me, I must first examine the several messages to be found in the book of Job, because the answer I am to receive may or may not be self evident and very likely will require considerable spiritual insight as well as much self-examination.

What is in the book of Job that is the answer to my question? Job is a book rich in many insights of great value for those who seek better understanding of some of the ways in which God often deals with individuals, as well as what goes on in the spiritual realm. In a more comfortable condition, and under different circumstances, I would probably have been persuaded to do a more extensive study than this, and write a more detailed interpretation of this precious book. However, right now my purpose, as already noted, is to seek and find the answer to my "why" from the source that I believe my Lord has provided. I also believe that I have been persuaded to write about this search for the benefit of anyone who happens to read it and may be seeking an answer under similar circumstances. If this topic interests you, and unless you are very familiar with the book, it would be beneficial to read at least those portions that relate to what here follows.

In Job we first see an informative and very surprising dialogue between God and Satan. It tells us:

1. God and Satan are on "speaking terms."

2. Satan was man's accuser from the earliest days, just as Revelation tells us that he has continued to be throughout the ages.

3. Satan has great powers to hurt.

4. His use of these powers can occur only by the permissive will of God and then only to a divinely authorized degree and for God's own divine purpose. This is extremely difficult for our very limited human minds to understand. But we must understand it, or at least unconditionally accept it. We must because that is the way it is.

Satan asserts, on a seemingly casual inquiry by God, that Job is being only superficially righteous, that because God has allowed him a fine family and great wealth, that he can afford to be pious because he has not been tested. Therefore, Satan claims that if Job were to be deprived of these things, he would no longer worship God but instead curse Him. The Scripture seems to suggest that God accepted this challenge as to Job's innate righteousness by allowing Satan to kill all of his children and eliminate all of his wealth but not hurt him physically. As a result of this colossal tragedy, Job's faith never faltered for he accepted the fact that God has the power to give and also take away.

Then Satan again appeals to challenge Job's faith by pointing out that he suffered only emotionally and economically but had not suffered physically. God responded by allowing Satan to plague him with boils and other maladies over his entire body but does not allow him to be killed. To add to this already horrible suffering, three of his friends come to "console" him, but only suggest that he must have been an awfully sinful person to have been punished so severely. On top of that, his wife urges him to curse God and die. How bad can it get? Yet Job, although he wishes he had never been born, does not forsake or curse God at any time throughout what must have been many months of intensely cruel and unusual punishment.

A dialogue between Job and his friends goes on for about thirty chapters during which Job masterfully and in faith defends his righteousness and God's supreme authority. However, as yet the "whys" of Job's predicament are not explained. Then, as the three friends complete their discouragements, a fourth observer, Elihu, comes on the scene with some far better council and the beginning of a real explanation. He apparently heard the earlier dialogues and expresses wrath against the three for being completely ineffectual and lacking in love and wisdom that should have been theirs at their advanced ages. Then he analyzed Job's view of God. Here we begin to get to the root of the problem. First Elihu sees Job's view of God as One who is capricious, that is a God who changes, who acts out of feelings like people do, according to His mood. He points out that Job seems to believe that God mistreated him without justification in a capricious way. The second problem Elihu sees is that Job sees God as silent, not saying anything to him, let alone not answering his prayers. Job finds this silence disheartening, a sign of abandonment. He fails to take into account God's timing and style in dealing with us, as we so often do as well. Elihu observes several ways in which God speaks to us. One of them is through pain. Now we are getting somewhere! He tells Job that his very suffering is God speaking to him!

C. S. Lewis's book "The Problem with Pain" points to this manner of God's voice most powerfully.

> *We can rest contentedly in our sins and in our stupidities, and everyone who has watched gluttons shoveling down the most exquisite foods as if they did not know what they were eating, will admit that we can ignore even pleasure. But pain insists upon being attended to. God whispers to us in our pleasures, speaks in our consciences, but shouts in our pains. It is his megaphone to rouse a deaf world.*

Then Elihu continues to examine Job's view of God and points to his erroneous belief that God is unjust, unfair and unwilling to explain what is going on. In chapter 34:9 Elihu speaking of Job *"For he hath said, it profiteth a man nothing that he should delight himself with God."* In other words, one might as well do as the wicked do because it now seems clear that trying to follow godly ways provides no benefit. This is a serious departure from Job's earlier expressions of understanding, where he made note of the righteousness of God to give and take away. It would seem that Job is slowly backsliding in his faith, due to the continual extreme pain, the reason for which seems to be unexplainable. But Job has not yet cursed God, although one might conclude that he is not far from it. However, Spirit-filled Elihu now takes up the truth about God's character starting with the next verse. He assures Job that God cannot be unjust, but also that He is above any accountability to man. We must know without doubt, if we are genuine believers in our Creator God that He is infallibly just. How or why should He be otherwise? We know that He is all knowing, and all-powerful, and we realize that He created man in His own image for His expressed purpose of having a family of faithful believers to be with Him throughout eternity. Therefore, why should, or how could, He play games, be distrustful and needlessly punish or deliberately hurt without cause? This could not possibly be the God of love, the Triune Godhead of which our blessed Jesus, our Lord and Savoir, is a part! But Job had no knowledge of Jesus and His mission on earth as we do. He, nevertheless, had the essence of Jesus' purpose on the cross when he was able to speak with great conviction of his own ultimate resurrection in chapter 19 verse 25, 26.

In chapter 34 verse 10 through 29, Elihu establishes the fact that God is a just rewarder as well as a just executor of punishment. Therefore, he says in verse 31 that God's chastisement is just, and that one should not be offended by it. But Job believes that he has been treated unfairly because he has been a righteous man, that his heart is right, and that he has tried to serve God. However, as we can see, he has erroneously believed he could do it by his own efforts, by his own righteousness. Perhaps now we begin to see more of the problem. The most difficult lesson God tries to teach us is to recognize evil where by our selves we see nothing but good. Whether we realize it or not most of what the world teaches as good is evil, and what it teaches as evil is often that which is good. Our best efforts to do even that which is good are but filthy rags in God's sight until there occurs a severe change of heart. It is our dependence on, and only on His gift of salvation, and *His* gift of righteous direction that has any lasting value. This is expressed through our work in humility and gratitude, and only by these means can our work bear righteous fruit. In believing in his own self-earned righteousness, Job expressed what can only be considered pride, rather than humility, in his dealings with God.

It's important here to distinguish the difference between self-righteousness and the righteousness imparted to the believer through his or her faith. Self-righteousness is the I-did-it-myself kind. "I take my righteousness most seriously; I read the Bible and believe it; I go to church; I help the poor and needy; I refrain from all the evils spoken of in the Ten Commandments. I'm not perfect, but I'm far better than most around me." It's the "I this" and "I that" that puts the "self" in self-righteousness. Scripture tells us of two genuine forms of righteousness, that of the law and that of faith. Righteousness under the law, the "I did" kind, would be genuine, if one kept the entire law, never sinning even once, that is keeping every single nuance of the law over one's entire life. Only Jesus was able to do this. No human can. Therefore, there can be no benefit to the soul from any attempt by man to achieve this form of righteousness. A single sin, no matter how small, would completely cancel that attempt at righteousness. Righteousness under the law is self-righteousness, its man's doing God's commands without God's help. The beginning of humility comes when we realize we are totally helpless within ourselves in this endeavor, and begin to seek God's grace through faith in Jesus. Thus genuine righteousness is the result of faith and the act of divine grace. In Romans 4:3 we find that "Abraham believed God, and it was counted (imputed) unto him for righteousness." Verse five goes on to say that works don't bring righteousness, only faith can do that. We know from Ephesians 2:8 that we are saved only by grace through faith, and that is God's gift that no amount of work can achieve nor in any other way be obtained. Righteousness flows from that saving faith. If we have that quality of faith, we may know that we have God's righteousness in us, but we have absolutely no claim to it as being of our own doing. It should be the prime focus of our gratitude and not in any way held up as indicative of any self developed quality by which we can feel or claim as making us superior to any other human being. More blessed, yes, but not better. Job was of the same dispensation as was Abraham. But Abraham's faith had been thoroughly tempered and then proven by the test God chose when He commanded him to sacrifice Isaac. The book of Job tells us of another way in which God tempers and then tests His own. Up to the recorded portion of Job's life, it seems apparent that he had not been so dealt with. Therefore, Job had imputed righteousness to himself as a result of all of his pious behavior, good works, and his own interpretation of what he believed was God's law. Job and Abraham lived before the law was given to Moses.

We might now reconsider what may have seemed like a charade between God and Satan at the beginning of the book. It was God who initiated this contest, not Satan. God was, of course, well aware of the superficial condition of Job's presumed righteousness. But as Satan observed, it had never been tested. Therefore, neither its spiritual depth nor its sustainability could be known, that is to either Satan or Job. Our all-knowing God, of course, knew the works orientation of Job's righteousness and what the outcome of this test would be. But His love for Job and the greater purpose He, no doubt, had for him required a purification that could only come from the severe lesson that He was allowing Satan to implement. This is an extremely important lesson for all of us.

That's why this book is part of sacred Scripture! The lesson for all of us is the ugliness of self-righteousness. Job was honorable, honest and upright by God's own testimony as recorded in verse eight of chapter one where God describes Job as *"there is none like him on earth, a perfect and upright man that feareth God and escheweth evil."* However, he was yet absent of God's righteousness.

How many of us can claim such a report by the Creator of the universe? However, where spiritual growth is concerned, Job obviously had some distance to go and a change of course to get there. His self-righteousness was a blockage to spiritual growth into God's righteousness. Therefore God chose to advance that growth through what appears to be the only way it could happen. Just as iron must be tempered through extreme heat, so must man be tempered in the spirit by some form of adversity. Much later, Jesus said in John 15:2 *". . . every branch that beareth fruit he purgeth it that it may bring forth more fruit."* Job was being purged.

Now we begin to see the crux of the matter beginning to manifest. Righteousness is an essential quality for all who enter God's eternal realm. However, only God is qualified and has the only power and right to convey and to judge one's righteousness. Man is not qualified to do so, especially regarding himself. Where self-righteousness dwells in the heart, Jesus will not. Self-righteousness by Webster's definition is "to be filled with or showing a conviction of being morally superior or more righteous than others; smugly virtuous." This was Job's problem and it is a problem that plagues all of humanity. The only antidote is its opposite, humility, and this only through our emulation of Jesus.

After Elihu's expressions of wisdom and sage advice, God finally answers Job's prayer by appearing to him to finish the task of setting Job straight in this matter of self-righteousness. God begins by rhetorically asking him where he was when God created the earth. He continues on, in the final four chapters, to ask seventy-seven questions of a similar nature, each attesting to God's power, glory and omniscience. These serve as examples of the infinite difference between God and all mankind. They hammer home with great force the fact that any form, or the tiniest amount of self-righteousness, is nothing less than self-esteem that is nothing different than pride by another name. And we all know that pride is the sin most hated by God. Based on God's comparison between Himself and Job, how can he or anyone claim himself or herself any amount of self-righteousness, when all righteousness belongs to God and only God? What qualities can the most exquisitely molded pot claim, as it's own doing and not that of the potter? Remember the conversation between Jesus and a rich young man in Matthew 19:16, 17? The young man called Jesus *"good teacher"* and Jesus responded with *"Why do you call me good? No one is good but One, that is God."* Had the young man known whom he was calling good, he would have reaffirmed that statement! But here is an admission by Jesus Himself, that no one is good except God! The rich young man claimed that he was already obeying all of the laws of Moses. But that was not enough, as it was not enough for Job or for us. What does that say to those who feel justified in claiming any good in themselves, that is, claiming to have any self-righteousness? In order to grow in the faith and goodness in God's eyes, only an ever-growing humility will suffice. We must decrease so that He can increase in our hearts.

As noted earlier, God spoke of Job as unique among mankind, a *perfect and upright man who feared God and turned away from evil."* How blessed would any of us feel to receive such a report card from our Creator? But God, of course, saw far more than we could recognize. Man in his fallen state is far from perfect at his very best. Reference to the original Hebrew word, translated here as "perfect," indicates that it might have been better translated as "usually pious, gentle, plain, undefiled, or upright." Nevertheless, Job was about as good as a man could get by his own definition, a man to whom God had given much and from whom God had the right to expect much, apparently more than Job was providing or could provide in his self-righteous state. Job, impeded by his pride in his own virtue as are we all, perceived that he had reached a fairly high level of adherence to God's ways and sought no greater height of godliness, although it was certainly in him to rise higher, had it not been for that self-righteousness, through which he deemed himself already quite "good enough" to meet God's standard. He lacked humility, the prerequisite virtue for fruitful service to God. Self-righteousness had to be purged from him as God purges even those who do bear any fruit so that they can bear even more.

We have here in this book only a small part of Job's biography. From this, however, it seems safe to conclude that God may have had a greater purpose for Job, and we were privileged to see only one aspect of God's grooming of him for that purpose which may have been here on earth or somewhere in the heavenlies. We have witnessed God's similar grooming of Joseph as he went into the pit, then into slavery, then to seven years in prison, all of which prepared him to be the prime minister of the greatest empire of that day, as well as the savior of the tribe that became the Hebrew nation. We also see such grooming by God of Moses in his forty years as heir apparent of the kingdom of Egypt, then forty years as a lowly shepherd followed by a quick crash course in how to twist the tail of the serpent Egypt, followed by bringing the whole nation Israel out of Egypt, and for another forty years being God's "walking companion," spokesperson, mediator, and ruling representative to that nation.

Out of all of this, what is God's message to all of us and to me personally, since He led me to Job for the answer to my cry, "why." I'll not attempt to speculate on what the Job story may mean for you. I'll do well if I can sufficiently fathom and articulate what I believe its purpose is for me. This, I believe, can be summarized in one simple phrase: an abundance of self-righteousness and a dearth of humility. Until I examined this message to Job as also a message to me, I would never have accused myself of these severely debilitating faults, much as Job never saw them in himself until God used the "megaphone" of pain and suffering to get his attention, as He also did mine, although in a much milder manner. As noted earlier, self-righteousness is nothing less than self-esteem, which is simply pride by another name. Satan was the epitome of pride as Jesus was of humility. Humility and pride cannot peacefully coexist in the same heart, or decorate the same soul at the same time. While the Holy Spirit may dwell in a genuinely saved soul, He cannot function effectively in a prideful heart, but only in one that has given itself over to Jesus in full humility. In 1 Thessalonians 5:19 we are told not to quench the spirit, that is the Holy Spirit. There are a number of ways in which our sinful nature tends to do this. Each in some way can be traced to pride, to a lack of humility. Only through the activity of the Holy Spirit guiding our efforts can there be any fruitfulness in our works, fruitfulness that will survive God's judgment in that final day of accounting.

Worldly values highly promote self-esteem. In one sense the cornerstone of modern physiological teaching that pervades all advice related to one's human development, consists of building up one's self-esteem, rather than addressing the core issue of all difficulties—sin. Isn't there something quite ironic in this observation? Man's principal construct, his cornerstone of faith in dealing with human relational difficulties, is in developing self-esteem, and thereby, in effect, shrugging off the fact of his sinful nature and by this means diverting blame from himself. Jesus, our cornerstone, our great healer of all ailments, was humble, and taught, humility as the way toward genuine righteousness, eternal peace and spiritual security. Think about this in the context of the evil one who has been temporarily allowed power over this world. It's the great deceiver Mr. Pride himself. To influence mankind to take on this, his principal characteristic is the easiest way for him to assure for himself a very large family with which to share hell!

All who claim to be Christians and know somewhat about what Jesus taught realize that humility is an important virtue. Many of us are quite "proud" of how great is our humility, much like the Pharisee who thanked God that he was not as lowly as the publicans praying next to him, as shown in Luke 18:11. Often outward expressions of humility are just that, outward expressions, premeditated and originated in the head, not from the heart. If humility is not from the heart and placed there by the Holy Spirit, it is not Christian humility.

From what we read about Job, he was a good man, one generously endowed with wealth and a good family. He prayed and sacrificed to God, and no doubt he was honest in his dealings and generally an upright man. Absent of any trial, temptations or serious trouble or grief, it is human nature to become more and more complacent, self-satisfied and self-righteous. Worship becomes more of a ritual than a heart-felt expression of gratitude for God's generosity. Prolonged generosity in any form or from any source becomes an entitlement. After awhile, there develops a complacency that can degenerate into apathy as well as a growing belief that we posses an intrinsic goodness, otherwise why should we be so blessed? That inevitably evolves into self-righteousness. It would seem that that is where Job was at the point his story begins and God set up the process for his rehabilitation and spiritual advancement. God recorded it all as an example from which we *all* need to learn. He might very well have ended the book of Job with what He told us so many other times, when a profound message had been delivered, *"He who hath an ear to hear let him hear."* Only those who are born-again have ears equipped to hear these words and understand their meaning. Those of us, who have such ears and a heart willing to receive, should gain much from the example, if we will but examine ourselves in this context.

This biblical example has touched me deeply because I know that I was directed to it. It was written for me. The steps from complacency toward self-righteousness, as outlined above, represented what I now see as having been my own. And our dear Lord expressed His love for me by calling them to my attention by way of His "megaphone" of pain. I suspect that He probably tried gentler ways to get my attention, but I was probably too wrapped up in myself to hear them! I pray that now I have the message. I pray that I will have the good sense and willingness to meaningfully apply it. But who can be sure? My heart is no better than any other heart. It is deceitful above all things and desperately wicked. Such a heart can deceive even the most well intended soul. But because of the grace of God I also have a new clean heart, as do all who are born-again. The Holy Spirit within us has the power to conquer that evil, self-righteous heart if we will only let it. My "thorn," as with Paul's, seems to have become a permanent fixture, a continuing reminder that God's grace is enough, and indeed it is!

As I reviewed what I had written above, it became apparent that I should try to elaborate more on the importance of humility and to deal more thoroughly with the issue of self-righteousness.

Regarding humility, we must, as Christians, take our cue about this, as with everything else, from Jesus. On that basis here are a few thoughts on the subject that He Himself preached. First, however, we do well to realize that with just one single act, the Creator of the

Universe defined the ultimate expression of humility by becoming man, one of His own creation of creatures. In Philippians 2:5, 6, Paul reminds us of this: *"Let this mind be in you, which was also Christ Jesus; Who made Himself of no reputation (to have made Himself empty of His Godness) and took upon Him the form of a servant; he humbled Himself and became obedient to death . . ."* If you seek Christlikeness, here was humility personified! Now let us see what He preached:

- *"I am among you as he that serveth"* (Luke 22:27) This is God Himself telling us He came to serve. That's humility.
- *"He that humbeleth himself shall be exalted."* (Luke 18:14) Humility leads to exaltation.
- *"The Son can do nothing of Himself . . ."* (John 5:19) If the Son of God could do nothing of Himself as man, that is nothing of spiritual value, what does that say about our own puny self-efforts?
- *"I can of mine own self do nothing; My judgment is just, because I seek not my own will"* (John 5:30). If the Son of God, in His position as Son of man, would not apply His own will, how can we, those corrupted sons of the first Adam, have the audacity to presume that any will of our own can have the slight amount of merit?
- *"I receive not honor from men"* (John 5:41) It doesn't matter what man thinks of you, only God's assessment matters. Walking in humility may offend man, but God delights in those who do.
- *"For I came down from heaven not to do mine own will"* (John 6:38) Jesus admits coming down from heaven, but not as a free and separate agent of God but one who is in total spiritual unison with the Father and was a full-strength reflection of His divine will.
- *"I seek not my own glory."* (John 8:40) Jesus goes on and on stating in effect that He is nothing and the Father is all. This, of course, was true in His position as the Son of man. In heaven, before and after His visit on earth, He was and is part of the Triune Godhead, equal in every way with the Father. His over-riding message in these verses was of His comparative nothing as man. With that as His assessment of His role as man, how can we believe that we are anything more than

beings of even less than that amount of nothingness? Jesus goes on to teach His disciples (that is us, if we are in Christ) about humility.

► *"Learn from me, for I am meek and lowly in heart."* (Matthew 11:29) (Lowly, low in rank as in a military order.) Meek is not weak. Jesus, though meek, showed Himself strong and forceful when He overturned the money changer tables in the Temple, and when He repeatedly called the Pharisees, the spiritual leaders of the day, hypocrites and sons of Satan for their self-righteousness, their twisted beliefs and their attitudes. Here He taught that those having spiritual humility must, nevertheless, rise in justified indignation and action to every occasion where God is being blasphemed, and make known God's truth.

► *"And whosoever will be chief among us, let him be your servant, Even as the Son of man came not to be minister unto, but to minister."* (Matthew 20:27, 28) How forcefully He demonstrated this humility of a servant when He washed His disciples feet at the last supper! If Christ is in us, we also must have a servant's heart and so minister to our brethren and sisters in Christ. Washing their feet was symbolic of that humility and servanthood that must characterize our moment-by-moment, heart-felt Christian walk.

► *"Whatsoever therefore shall humble himself (express his own humility) as this little child, the same is greatest in the kingdom of heaven."* Matthew 18:4 *"He that is least (showing greater humility) among you all, the same shall be great."* (Luke 9:48) Again the promise of eternal benefits from a heart full of humility having no room for self.

► *"he that is greatest among you shall be your servant."* (Matthew 23:11) Jesus was the very greatest and accepted the role of servant, the ultimate of humility. How can we who are inherently so much lower than Him have the audacity to think more of ourselves! As His bondservants, we are to gladly accept that role of servanthood in all humility. Humility must not be limited only toward God, that's the easier part, but it must be a deeply, heart-felt humility toward all mankind as He so clearly exemplified.

Scripture continues to advocate this humility as an essential element in a genuine Christian life. The message is found throughout the Epistles, as evidenced of how well Jesus taught His apostles. They each lived exemplary lives of humility and taught the same wherever they went.

Now, regarding this matter of self-esteem. This worldly cancer seems to have even metastasized throughout the entire Christian body. Speaking ill of it as I have here, may be quite upsetting to those who have had their lives steeped in its alleged virtue and importance from the worldly perspective. After all, a lack of self esteem is synonymous with always feeling depressed and bad about yourself, isn't it? How can one succeed in life with that attitude? We must feel good about ourselves and love ourselves before we can love others, right? Like everything else Satan promotes, there is an element of truth masking his evil intent. In our discussion about Job, the evil side has been reasonably well examined. It's become evident that self-esteem is simply another way to express pride, the sin most detested by God. In the secular world, Satan's domain, pride and self-esteem are deemed to be essential characteristics of a well-adjusted individual. If one's efforts result in an outstanding achievement, isn't that justification for self-esteem? The world lauds an achiever, such as a great actor, or sports figure, a successful politician, or an accumulator of wealth. If the world esteems them, then why shouldn't they esteem themselves? It's all very natural, sensible and appropriate. To have it otherwise would be to discourage extraordinary effort and practically eliminate advancement in all fields of endeavor. Is it possible to separate pride from self-esteem and from self-righteousness? One can rationalize anything, and most of us do. But these three words are so closely related in meaning that we do our intellect a grave injustice if we try to do so from the Christian perspective

So what is the answer for the Christian, the genuine born-again, redeemed, ardent follower of Christ Jesus? Doctrinally, it's quite simple. From an applicational viewpoint it is much less so. It's been wisely said that if we don't have a clear understanding of the question, it's not possible to appreciate the answer! I pray that the question is quite clear, and the answer begins with humility. The genuine born-again Christian has gone through several spiritual modifications before he or she has reached that most precious state. First there must be repentance, a turning away from the world and toward Jesus. This turning must result in a sincere heartfelt acknowledgement of who Jesus is, what He achieved on the cross, and what it means for every individual who will accept Him in faith. But before this acceptance can have any real substance, there must be a full recognition of the fact that one is a hopeless, condemned sinner for which there is no escape, except through Jesus. The result of this, when fully understood, can only bring forth a great personal shame and humility and a sacred commitment of love and obedience to our Lord Jesus. There are some who will take issue with the need for each of the steps to salvation as here noted. There is a widespread belief that there are adequate short cuts to salvation, and we need not necessarily involve ourselves with these more difficult issues of repentance, conviction, obedience and humility. After all, there is seldom even any mention of these things from the present day pulpit, therefore, how can they be so vital? Only ignorance or avoidance of God's whole Word can explain such a view. Trivializing these necessities of salvation is to do the same regarding one's eternal destiny, which is not a trivial matter.

Now how did we get back to humility? Didn't we cover that adequately already? YES, but not in the context of the self-esteem dilemma. It's been rightly said that humility is the first duty and highest virtue of man," and that "humility is the only soil in which graces take root; the lack of humility is sufficient explanation of every defect and failure." These words are from the great nineteenth-century Christian teacher, Arthur Murray. Those who have a full measure of the spirit-given quality of humility have neither the need nor the capability for having self-esteem, self-righteousness or pride, or any other form of self-aggrandizements man is capable of devising for himself. Humility is what can empty the soul of self, and before the Holy Spirit can have full reign in the new heart of a saved soul, that "self" must be gone. With the "self" gone, how can there by any self-righteousness or self-esteem? Does that now mean that we must mope, feel bad about ourselves, and make no effort to achieve, or rise in our chosen profession, trade or vocation? Not in the least! We are to use all of our God-given attributes to the fullest! As born-again Christians we are the earth's most blessed and should be the most joyous of all people for that reason. The key to it all is to know fully and continually who is responsible for any and all of our achievements and to give full, unrestricted credit to Him, our God.

If we have been emptied of self, then we are nothing and He who is in us is our everything, and, therefore, all we achieve is His doing, not ours. All credit, all praise belongs to Him, not us. With self out of the picture, self-esteem is likewise, and only gratitude to our Lord remains as our response to any and all achievements. In one sense, our desire to excel and to achieve should be even greater than those who are of the world, because what we do is for our Lord and not for ourselves.

Removal of all self from our souls is a most difficult task. It's one that we have absolutely no ability to accomplish. Only Jesus can do it through the Spirit. It's a grace accompanying salvation, yet its one that even the Holy Spirit cannot accomplish, unless we let Him. It's our inherited sinful nature to resist, to cling to self, to not want to let go of who we are, for it means letting go of the world and the many forbidden delights we have grown to enjoy. Thus it is an on-going process. It's what is meant in Philippians 1:6 where the Holy Spirit through Paul says, *"Be confident of this very thing, that He which hath begun a good work in you will perform it until the day of Jesus Christ."* What a great promise! If we can only let go of self, He will do all the rest! Here we learn that it is a continuing process; we need not become discouraged when the result isn't as fast as we may wish it to be. God will not forsake His own, but will continue molding them, removing the self from them until either physical death or the rapture, for that is our "day of Jesus Christ." That is the day we will meet Him at His heavenly throne of judgment where crowns will be confirmed, when our earthly conduct will be judged, and our eternal assignments given.

Those who are saved souls would do well, when they witness one of their brethren having received the blessing of some achievement, to not praise the person, but instead praise the Lord in gratitude for having used that person as His instrument of achievement. This act of not praising the person, but instead praising God, will help that person to avoid any thoughts or feelings of self-accomplishment. If we can only learn in our hearts to *always* have gratitude toward our Lord for using us rather than attributing any credit to ourselves, we will soon be seeing solid evidence of Philippians 1:6 working in us.

In summary, the full, mature, born-again Christian needs no self-esteem and should be repulsed by even the thought of it. That Christian knows who is doing the good works. He or she knows that they are but conduits through which the Holy Spirit accomplishes His purpose. Then, gratitude for the privilege of being so used will become their treasure, far exceeding any petty and fleeting feelings of pride that it has replaced. Pursuing that blessed state of Christian maturity takes one along a treacherous and difficult road, the end of which few will ever reach in this lifetime. I believe that it will be the sincerity of effort, and not the final result, that God will judge.

There is one more point I am persuaded to make at the risk of being accused of beating this thing to death. It is another message that seems to have resulted from this ordeal. That is, that unless we are continually diligent in our worship and prayers, and are ever self-examining of our spiritual condition, we are bound to have lapses into some level of complacent, self-satisfied righteousness. This was Job's problem and is endemic throughout the Christian world. I certainly have been no exception. This, I believe, is also what God wanted me to see through His dealings with Job. As we move on, believing that we are fully in the faith, there is a tendency to reach a plateau, a comfort level, and then to stay there, complacent and self-satisfied. This is not appropriate for any true Christian. God wants continuous growth and we dearly need it, because at our very best we fall far short of where we want to and ought to be, if we but examine ourselves critically. It seems that for those who love Him and are called according to His purpose, He has the right to expect considerably more for having given them so very much. I believe that unless we voluntarily "raise the bar," that is continue to increase our commitment by growing in faith, worship, obedience and fruitfulness, we risk the possibility that he may in some persuasive way "raise the bar" for each of us as He did for Job, and in a much less painful way, for me. Is there really any amount of gratitude and evidence of that gratitude, large enough to suffice for His gift of eternal life with Him in the heavenly places? Are any of us who are so blessed, giving of ourselves all we really can, and ought to, in the way of worship, prayer, obedience and fruitfulness to His glory? Who can honestly say yes? I know that I can't.

God's message made that much clearer to me, and I pray that this, and the message to be found in the book of Job, will cause you to increase your awareness and sensitivity to your own position on the ladder to eternity.

—66—

Forgiveness

This simple little noun carries a meaning that, I believe, is of far greater importance to mankind than any other word to be found in English or any other language except, of course, God, Christ Jesus, Holy Spirit etc. This is because it is only through its application that eternal life is possible. Given that man is a hopelessly depraved soul before God, with absolutely no chance of redemption by his own efforts, his fate is dependent entirely on God's grace of forgiveness. Without that incredible act of love whereby our Father God gave His only begotten Son to be the sacrificial lamb through whom there could be forgiveness, there could be no salvation.

Webster defines "forgiveness" as to give up resentment against or desire to punish; stop being angry with; pardon; to give up all claims to punish or extract punishment for an offense, to cancel or remit a debt." God's forgiveness is expressed by every nuance of that definition.

But that's not the end of the story! Over and over again Scripture demands that we forgive others as God has so lovingly forgiven us. Read the sample prayer that Jesus suggested to the apostles. A major element of that prayer was asking God to *"forgive us our debts, as we forgive our debtors."* Then in Matthew 6:14, 15 Jesus tells them / us *"For if ye forgive men their trespasses your Heavenly Father will also forgive you; but if ye forgive not men their trespasses, neither will your Father forgive your trespasses."* There are many other passages in Scripture that make this point, but who needs any more than what our Lord Christ Jesus said here so plainly?

Nevertheless, we'll look at one more, just to illustrate how exceedingly important our acts of forgiveness are to our Lord. Consider the parable of the unforgiving servant as found in Matthew 18:23–25.

The gist of this parable is that Jesus is expressing a particular aspect of the Kingdom of God by describing a "certain king" who was owed a huge debt by one of his servants. It suggests that it was one who had been guilty of great offenses against the King's divine government. There was no way he could ever pay off such a huge debt. He was morally bankrupt. This symbolizes the fact that neither he, nor anyone else, could ever pay, that is make up to God, (who is symbolized by the king in the parable) for the wrong he had done. The king commanded him to be sold, which would be for some period of severe punishment. But the man begged for mercy and for patience to allow him to "pay thee all." Of course, no man could ever do this, yet the attitude of the debtor seemed to be one of penitence and repentance. Because of this, the benevolent king forgave him of his debt even as our Lord forgives man when he comes to repentance.

However, as soon as this servant had been forgiven, he went out to brethren who owed him a very small amount and demanded full payment under threat of prison. He who had been greatly forgiven was unwilling to forgive even a small transgression. Of course, this exceedingly unforgiving act was contrary to how the king had treated him. When the king heard of this, he withdrew his forgiveness and ordered the servant to be punished in full proportion to the size of his debt. The final verse of this parable brings us to conclude that all of this was not about salvation but simply about earthly punishment for lack of a forgiving nature. Note, here Jesus speaks of forgiving *"every one his brother their trespasses."* (Matthew 18:35) Those involved here in the parable were all already saved, as are those who speak authentically in the example of what is commonly called the Lord's Prayer. The prayer begins with "Our Father." That is not a salutation legitimately expressible by anyone other than one who is a son or daughter of the Father through faith in our Lord and Savior Christ Jesus.

The message of this parable as with the cited portion of the Lord's prayer, is that all genuine Christians are instructed to be at all times forgiving of their brethren. To what extent are we obligated to forgive? The verse preceding the parable tells us, we should forgive not seven times, but seventy times seven times, that is as many times as necessary, I assume until the offender no longer offends. We must always keep in mind that if we have been saved, all our sins have been forgiven spiritually, forever. However, there are always earthly consequences to our sins, and the sin of unforgiveness is no exception. Also, the need for a Christian's forgiveness goes beyond the church community; we are to forgive nonbrethern as well. We are required to even forgive our most offending enemies. The Sermon on the Mount made that quite clear as do many other passages in the New Testament. Here is what Jesus said regarding your enemies as found in Matthew 5:43–48.

> *Ye have heard that it hath been said, Thou shalt love thy neighbor and hate thine enemy. But I say unto you, Love your enemies, bless them that curse you, do good to them that hate you, and pray for them which despitefully use you, and persecute you; that ye may be the children of your Father which is in heaven; for he maketh his sun to rise on the evil and on the good, and sendeth rain on the just and on the unjust. For if ye love them which love you, what reward have ye? do not even the publicans the same? And if ye salute your brethren only, what do ye more than others? do not even the publicans so? Be ye therefore, perfect, even as your Father which is in heaven is perfect.*

A very important message exists under the surface of these verses, and that has to do with anger. Think of what Jesus is telling us we must do under extremely trying circumstances regarding our enemies. How can one possibly obey in these ways in a state of anger? Can you love the offender in anger, or pray for him in anger? As humans we are all susceptible to anger. But anger must not rule our lives, but must be dissolved as soon as it begins to manifest or else how can we possibly obey these commands? Paul in Ephesians 4:26 makes a vital point when he tells us *"Be ye angry, and sin not; let not the sun go down on your wrath."* This tells us that a justified moment of anger may not be sin, but becomes sin when it remains in the heart for any extended period of time, like overnight. This is confirmed in the next verse *"neither give place to the devil."* An anger held on to is an invitation to the devil. He loves such a condition of the heart. Here Paul is admonishing us to not give the devil any place, any opportunity to amplify the backsliding that anger can initiate.

Again, if you have come to the faith and are truly a son or daughter of God, you are saved; your sins have been forgiven. Therefore, you now have the power of the Holy Spirit in you, which includes the power to forgive any and all trespasses. If for any reason you have been, or are being hurt by someone, and you cannot genuinely forgive, or to continue to forgive, but feel compelled to remain unforgiving, you have a problem, and potentially a very serious problem. If you are early in your faith, it may be that your old nature remains in control; you have not yet sufficiently subordinated your old nature to that new nature in you as represented by the indwelling of the Holy Spirit. Of course, you still have, and will continue to have free will to choose either one. However, if your unforgiveness persists and or repeatedly flares up, there may be an entirely different issue involved. This is because, as noted, the Holy Spirit who represents the result of God's forgiveness has given to your soul that essential propensity for the forgiveness of others. If that seems to be lacking, perhaps it is time to apply Philippians 2:12 and dig down deeply into the inner recesses of the soul and "work out your own salvation with fear and trembling," and pray to God at the same time, that what is found there is in fact salvation, and not just a veneer of pious pretentious platitudes pretending to be a genuine saving faith.

Primarily, it is forgiveness of severe hurts with which we are dealing. There are two kinds of these hurts; those we acknowledge that we deserve, and those we believe we ought not to suffer. The first kinds are generally resolved quite easily, because even the totally natural man can eventually forgive these once he has recognized that they are of his own doing. But the hurts we have determined are unwarranted, unprovoked, exceedingly mean, and totally unfair are the most difficult, if not impossible, for the natural man to forgive. It's in the same vein with some other things our Lord Jesus said while on earth, like *"love your enemy,"* "turn the other cheek," etc. These are all total absurdities to the natural man. But if one is saved, one is no longer a natural man! That sinful nature is still there, but it has been subordinated, or is in the process of being so by the power of the indwelling Holy Spirit. Therefore, these words of Jesus are not absurd, but are of primary importance, and should be most evidenced in your daily Christian walk. We should never squelch the Holy Sprit, but allow Him free reign over our lives. If we do, God will greatly bless us because of this expression of our trust in Him.

If we have been trespassed against and cannot forgive the trespasser, we are thrice damaged. First, there is the pain of the trespass itself. Second is the temporary denial of the comforting benefit provided by the Holy Spirit. And third, we have the festering painful cancer of unforgiveness eating away at our souls. The first may fade a little with time and prayer. But prayer and a repentant heart will restore the authority of the Comforter, who will then provide all of the power necessary to totally forgive, and thereby destroy the cancer. With this, the forgiver comes out the winner, because the soul is clean, and the Comforter is again in control, while the trespasser has God to deal with, under circumstances most unfavorable to him. Remember, "vengeance is mine; I will repay saith the Lord." (Romans 12:19) It is not meant for any of us to get even or to even fight that battle. That is the Lord's prerogative as He so clearly stated, and in saying so also commanded us not to take revenge ourselves. The natural man takes delight in applying vengeance, but while that may, for a moment, gladden his depraved natural heart, it often will lead to a counter measure and then is a counter-counter measure thereby accomplishing nothing but adding pain to both sides. Simple forgiveness will very soon, if not immediately, end all pain except that which God will in some just way impose on the guilty one. Who knows, your spirit-led forgiveness might even cause this person to repent.

If one is truly saved and a situation occurs where a trespass of such a horrendous nature occurs that it seems impossible to forgive, what happens? I don't know. But I do know that we are told as cited above, that for God to forgive, we must forgive. On that basis I must conclude that there are highly negative earthly consequences to this manner of disobedience as there are to other infractions of His laws. Salvation is not lost, but the earthly portion of our lives may get much more difficult in ways that may be far worse than the pain of the original trespass.

Finally, it probably all gets down to the matter of trust, trust in our Lord and His Word. Do we really trust Him? Dr. Missler likes to express this idea by observing that most likely God asks us in some way every day, "Do you really trust me?" It may be through temptations, "unforgivable" transgressions, afflictions, or any number of situations whereby we must make a choice between His way and the world's way. It is Missler's opinion, and one I share, that most of the time we fail the test. Unforgiveness is but one of many such ways, but His love and patience is infinite, and if we truly seek His way, these failures will become less and less frequent. Genuine forgiveness of those who hurt us, for whatever reason, is a splendid way of eventually earning a "passing grade" in this test of genuine trust. This is not in any way related to salvation that is already owned, but simply toward a more certain, loving, and devout Christian life, which surely is the desire of every sincere Christian.

How very blessed we are, those who have come to the faith, that through the Holy Bible, Christ Jesus has provided everything we need to know, if we will but apply it to serve Him as He wants to be served. All of this present life is simply a short period of learning and love growth in preparation for our eternal heavenly service. Forgiving when there is no earthly justification or natural desire to do so is an important part of that preparation.

—67—

Gratitude and Forgiveness

Gratitude is a wonderful condition of the heart. As far as I can see it is one of these truly warm, feel-good attitudes that contain no negative side effects or regrets. It's a close relative of forgiveness in that respect. Since gratitude and forgiveness both have somewhere within their operational structure a strong element of love, and just as love "covers a multitude of sins" so do these precious responses provide a multitude of blessings to both giver and receiver. This holds true to varying degrees even in the secular world, as is self-evident. This is so even though the words of gratitude and forgiveness are often over used and spoken absent of sincerity. Prolonged generosity inevitably converts gratitude into entitlement, which can even devolve into resentment and then into covetousness. Gratitude is thankfulness. A simple thank you as an expression of gratitude is often enough of a response to some favor. However, the term has been so watered down as a rote response to almost anything, that it is now nearly meaningless as an expression of sincere gratitude unless expressed with ever increasing exclamation.

Sincere forgiveness in the secular world is far less prevalent than gratitude. Gratitude involves the receipt of some benefit, which makes that response almost mandatory, superficially at least. But forgiveness involves putting aside an affront or some emotionally or physically hurtful conduct or action by the one to be forgiven. It's human nature to rail against such a response unless some perceived form of compensation or vindictive retribution has been provided in full measure. Exceptions, of course, are to be found among close friends and family, but they merely confirm the rule. Often even retribution is not enough to elicit forgiveness. Torture, murder and even wars have been considered just responses to affronts, rather than simple forgiveness. Probably, as often as not, a false expression of forgiveness has been given by the lips, while the heart continued to seethe with intended revenge as soon as an opportunity was made possible. In this respect, we find a perfect example of false forgiveness followed by an excessive act of revenge described in Genesis 34, which followed the rape of one of Jacob's daughters. Natural man has not changed at all for the better since that incident. In the world, trespasses are seldom forgotten even if forgiven. This remembrance, this keeping track is such as to place a limit on how many times one is willing to forgive a repeated infraction. With a loved one it can be many times, with a friend perhaps several times. But with an enemy, probably not even once. That would be totally contrary to nature.

In the community of redeemed Christians, things are *supposed* to be quite different. In the mature Christian's heart, all gratitude belongs to God. But all mankind saved or otherwise, has in his very nature a craving for praise in order to increase his self-esteem, otherwise called pride. The world extols self-esteem. It is advocated from the pulpits and especially from the largest "Christian church" in the U.S. But we are all, everyone, fallen beings, having absolutely no intrinsic goodness. Remember, what Jesus said when the rich young man called Him good Master.

> *"And behold, one came and said unto Him, Good Master, what good thing shall I do, that I may have eternal life? And He said unto him, Why callest thou me Good? There is none good but one, that is God: but if thou wilt enter into life, keep the commandments."*
> (Matthew 19:16, 17).

If we have no goodness within our selves, how can we honestly, in good conscience, feel any pride or accept gratitude to ourselves for anything? If such is aimed toward us, we ought to be obliged to acknowledge, through our lips as well as in our hearts, as being nothing more than conduits through which the Holy Spirit has directed His blessings. If anything good results from anything we do, it is through the power of the indwelling Holy Spirit, not in any intrinsic good that we possess. Any conclusion different than that becomes the leaven from which a puffing up of pride begins to grow. We must not allow even a speck of this to enter our hearts less it grows like the mustard seed into its grotesque ugliness where Satan's birds will inevitably begin to gather, as in the parable (Matthew 13:31 and 32).

Regarding this matter of doing good, how can one reconcile this apparent difference between the "good' works of a redeemed person from the good works of the natural, unsaved person? Let's say that the two of them work side by side equally feeding and clothing the poor, tending to the sick, living clean, honest lives, and achieving the same beneficial results. What is different between them and the effects of their endeavors? On the surface there is no difference; as far as the world is concerned, the same works yield the same results. But what is behind these works in the heart of the worker? First, in the heart of even the atheist or agnostic there is a God given conscience that is placed in the hearts of all mankind. It may manifest as a civic duty or a form of social obligation felt toward the less fortunate. Such good works may also be preformed as a form of posturing for the purpose of generating praise or position. Whatever the motive, it is strictly earth-bound, and earth-centered, and wholly humanistic. They do not acknowledge God, and God does not recognize them or their works. Then there are those who believe there is a god or a force of some kind. Many of these persons see good works as a way to impress their god and score "brownie points," believing that good works can open the gates of whatever heaven is, if their good works can on balance score higher than their "bad works." They may even sincerely think that they believe in the Creator God, but unless the evidential basis of that belief is the Holy Bible with Jesus as the Cornerstone, that belief is fatally flawed.

Ideally, these same works provided by the redeemed Christian believers are motivated by a different and supernatural dynamic, namely gratitude. It is gratitude to our Creator God, the Triune Godhead of which Jesus is an integral part. This gratitude stems from the blessed grace of salvation and eternal life received through faith in Jesus and His work on the cross. That gratitude is a moment-by-moment, day-by-day continuous and eternal gratitude that fills the heart and continually seeks opportunities to manifest itself in ways pleasing to God. Such works are never considered obligatory, or self-benefiting. They are the outflowings of divine love imparted to the saved soul by the indwelling of the Holy Spirit. If this aspect of Christian behavior seems to you to be idealistic, you are right, it is. But it should be the achievable goal of every faithful, fruitful believer. The degree, to which it will be achieved, is proportioned to how much of the world is removed from the heart's desires and how much of this is replaced by God's Word and a willingness to submit to it.

The conscience is an inherent supernatural implant placed in the hearts of all mankind. I wonder how the atheists, when they recognize they have the sense of right and wrong, can rationalize it as having resulted from any evolutionary process. It is totally contrary to any random selection or survival-of-the-fittest scenario.

All cultures and religions have laws and morals, which at least early on, are patterned after the Ten Commandments. These are all the result of governmentally codifying, in some form, what God places in every heart. However, man's conscience becomes seared and callused to varying degrees as these cultures atrophy, as they all do. Look at one hundred years ago in this country. It would have been "unconscionable" to consider abortion to be a moral or legal right, along with the many perversions, which today are considered as perfectly normal, legal and even taught in schools as simply alternative life styles. This moral decay was the condition of God's people of Israel, when they sacrificially roasted their babies in the red-hot bronze arms of the pagan god Baal, just before God destroyed the nation. Thus the seared consciences are capable of accepting and ever glorifying and worshiping actions abominable to our Creator God, as is evidenced almost everywhere we look today.

So what is the point of all of this? Gratitude and forgiveness are characteristics indigenous to every human soul to various degrees. The purity and quality of these God-given qualities have tended to deteriorate and become manipulative the further man has drifted from the One true God. Although they remain in the secular culture, they no longer have the spiritual benefits to the soul that they should have. In His teachings, Jesus brought back into conscious understanding the true godly meanings of gratitude and forgiveness. Through God's most precious and profound gift, His grace of salvation through faith in Christ Jesus, He endowed its recipients with new hearts capable of understanding and applying these attributes in accordance with His way. Those who are truly redeemed have an obligation, as evidence of their saved status, to apply most vigorously and sincerely what Jesus taught. While it's obligatory as evidence, the true Christian believer will never consider it an obligation, but instead a precious privilege, to give all thanks and gratitude to God and to sincerely forgive all others as our Lord said we should.

—68—

The Lord's Prayer

Do you know the Lord's Prayer? If you are a professing Christian, of course you know the Lord's Prayer, and perhaps the very question may, to you, seem condescending and demeaning. Please believe that it is asked only in the spirit of love and concern, and in having been strongly persuaded that I should share my experiences, along with the thoughts and understanding that have been revealed to me in these latter years since I received Jesus as my Lord and Savior.

I "learned" the Lord's Prayer in my earlier years, during which time I was forced to go through the motions of being a Catholic. Of course, I also learned the Hail Mary prayer and memorized the catechism. During those years I recited both prayers many thousands of times. I would recite them whenever I was in fear or in want. They became so in-grained in my mind, that I could then say, with some amount of pride, that I could think through the Hail Mary at the same time I spoke aloud the Lord's Prayer. Did God hear these prayers? Of course not! First because, they were simply meaningless rote, and second because the Holy Spirit was not in my heart as He must be if one is a redeemed child of God. And this comes only through that grace through faith in the blood of Christ, as the *completed* means of salvation. Had I been persuaded to read the Scripture or thought to do so on my own, I might have discovered the futility of such prayer well more than a half-century earlier. For in looking up the prayer in Matthew 6, I could not have missed Jesus' admonitions in verse 7 where He says "But when ye pray, use not vain repetitions, as the heathen *do:* for they think that they shall be heard for their much speaking." Where prayer is concerned, talk from the head, which isn't "born" in the heart, simply doesn't count with God.

Although today, I pray a great deal, I seldom recite the "Lord's prayer." When I do, it is only during Sunday services, when the pastor asks us to do so, and as he rightly refers to it as the prayer Jesus taught the apostles. So it isn't really the Lord's Prayer but a beautiful and suggestive outline of how one should approach and speak to God. Jesus Himself couldn't pray it, for it includes forgiveness of sin of which He had none. A genuine Lord's Prayer may be found in John 17 where our Lord Himself is praying to the Father. This, of course, is not a prayer any of us could pray. It is a God-to-God prayer. However, as with all Scripture, it is there for our learning and, therefore, it contains a number of elements we would do well to incorporate in our own prayers of worship.

Because the prayer He taught the Apostles is so deeply etched in my mind, it's difficult and almost impossible to say it with the reverence and deep conviction deserving of being called a real prayer, or conversation with our Creator. To say it by rote is to say it without heart-felt reverence, especially when recited at the speed customary during services. For it, or any recitation of a previously composed prayer to be meaningful and acceptable to God, and for it to be spiritually nourishing to the one praying, it can not be simply gulped down, but it must be carefully chewed, phrase by phrase, both in the mind and in the heart, so that all of its intended meaning and purpose can be extracted, digested and assimilated. None of this is to in any way diminish the value of this prayer, which we call the Lord's Prayer. My purpose is to suggest that the Lord's Prayer value as an element of worship can only come from sincere and deep thought, understanding and reverence for each of its components as they flow from our lips. Having said all of this, let us examine it phrase by phrase from the KJV of Matthew 6 and Luke 11, in order to see what this divine example of earth-to-heaven communication is telling us.

Our Father

Right from the first words, we have a potential issue. Scripture makes it very clear, that this prayer is only for the redeemed, the born-again, those who have received Jesus as their Lord and Savior, and have thereby become sons and daughters of God by adoption. The world speaks of the "brotherhood of man" and most who believe in a god or believe that there is a God, believe that "we are all children of God." Not so! According to Scripture, Jesus gave this to His apostles as an example of how *believers* should pray. Only the redeemed are children of God, and Scripture refers to them mutually as "brethren" Therefore, this prayer is relevant only to Christian brethren, for only they have a right to call Him, 'Father."

Who art in Heaven

It is the Father to whom Jesus taught the apostles to pray. He is the one person of the trinity whom Scripture indicates "stays at home" in heaven, while the personages of Jesus and the Holy Spirit also inhabit or visit the world of time / space.

Jesus is recorded in Scripture as having, on numerous occasions, visited earth and walked in an assumed physical form among people. He walked with Enoch (Genesis 5:22); He ate and conversed with Abraham (Genesis 18). He wrestled with Jacob at Peniel (Genesis 32); He met Moses at the burning bush (Exodus 3); He met Joshua before the battle of Jericho (Job 5) etc. All of those earlier visitations were by Jesus prior to His incarnation as human born flesh and blood. They were all only temporary manifestations of God the Spirit taking on a physical human form in a manner similar to how angels are able to come and go out of space/time. Jesus, however, in this one-time event, became man in the natural manner of all mankind so that He would be true man in all physical respects, being of flesh, blood and bones, even though He was also God through His spiritual being. In John 14:10, he tells us that "he that has seen the Me has seen the Father." Confusing? It shouldn't be if you understand and believe in the Triune (Tri-une, three in a single unit) God. Here Jesus is telling us that He and the Father are ONE. If they are one, then, they are as we would say, one in the same. So when the Lord's Prayer speaks to the Father who is in heaven it speaks also to Jesus (as well as the Holy Spirit), because they are all one with the Father in what we call collectively the Godhead. Because Jesus became man, in no way did it diminish the fact that He was also God. Thus He called Himself the "Son of Man" and He also called Himself "Son of God" (John 5:26). He had to be man in order to be our savior, our kinsman redeemer, and He had to be God in order to be our Lord and our avenger of blood. Thus He is our Lord and Savior!

Hallowed be thy name:

This is an expression of worship and adoration. God's name is Holy, and does He ever take it seriously! Scripture speaks very emphatically to us that God Himself attaches great value to *His* name and requires that His children do so also. For example, in 1 Samuel 12:22 we are told that "God will not forsake His people for *His great name sake*." In Psalm 23:3 we hear, "He leadeth me in the paths of righteousness for *His name sake*." We see, "*For Thy name sake*" in Psalm 25, 106, 109 and 143. In Isaiah 48:9 our Lord says, "For My *name sake* will defer my anger." In Jeremiah 14:7 and again in verse 21 we find "for *Thy name sake*." In Ezekiel 20:9 and again in verse 22, we see "I wrought for My *name sake*." And in Ezekiel 36:22 God says, for "*My Holy name sake*." This type of exhortation occurs as least twelve times in the Old Testament making it very clear how God feels about *His name*. Therefore, it should be no surprise that the third Commandment, right after the two about not having any other gods and not making idols, attests to the importance to Him of *His* name. The third Commandment reads: "Thou shall not take the name of thy Lord God in vain, for the Lord will not hold him guiltless that taketh His name in vain" (Exodus 20:7, Deuteronomy 5:11).

Remember this! By having called Him Father, you have claimed that you have the right to do so by virtue of having been redeemed. Therefore, you have also claimed the right to call yourself *by His name*, "Christian," a member of Christ's (God's) family. In doing so you have an awesome responsibility. You are claiming His name, but when you fail to think and behave appropriately as one of His, you are *defiling* His Holy Name. When you say in prayer, "hallowed be thy name" you are acknowledging that holiness *and* your responsibility regarding it. If you have chosen to be called by His name, Christian, and are, therefore, in the family of Christ, you have a sacred duty and responsibility to uphold and represent your family name in the highest possibly manner. That is the meaning and purpose of the third commandment!

Thy kingdom come thy will be done on earth as it is in heaven

Thy kingdom come:

This is God's kingdom as spoken of by John the Baptist in Mark 3:2. It is the kingdom that will soon banish Satan and take over from him the rule of the world that is when Jesus physically, as well as spiritually, returns after the tribulation to govern from the throne of David. This is when *His will* is to prevail here on *earth as it is*, and always has been, *in heaven*. For He will "rule all nations with a rod of iron." (Revelation 12:4, 19:15). Here on earth, self-will has prevailed ever since Adam and has caused untold misery. We know from Scripture that this kingdom is to surely take place, so here, in this prayer, we express our eagerness for its fulfillment. This is not the universal and eternal kingdom of God we are praying for, but the millennial, Messianic, Divine kingdom so clearly prophesied in Luke 1:31 and elsewhere that will be established here on earth for a thousand years. In essence, we pray for that great moment, the time of the rapture of which Paul spoke in 1 Corinthians 15:51, 52). "Behold, I show you a mystery; we shall not all sleep, but we shall all be changed, in a moment, in the twinkling of an eye, at the last trump: for the trumpet shall sound, and the dead shall be raised incorruptible, and we shall be changed." This is the prerequisite to the seventieth week of Daniel 9 and the second coming. At the time of the rapture, all of the redeemed, both those who have died and those who will be raptured, will be gathered together in heaven to celebrate, and to await the completion of that seventieth week. That is when Jesus, along with all the redeemed, those who escaped the second death, will descend from heaven to the Mount of Olives and make the triumphal entry into Jerusalem. Then Jesus will sit on David's throne, having cast Satan into the bottomless pit for a thousand years (Revelation 20:11). Those who descended from heaven with Him will be "priests of God and shall reign with Him (Revelation 20:6). This is what the sons and daughters of God pray for when they petition the Father, asking that "Thy kingdom come, thy will be done on earth as it is in heaven."

Give us this day our daily bread (Matthew 6:1)

Give us day by day our daily bread (Luke 11:3)

Here the prayer is a petition to the Lord to feed us. It is the expression by the faithful, of their dependence upon the Father for all things including their daily necessities. This would seem to be a double entrendre, a request that most, especially the sick and hungry throughout the ages, would consider as a request for bodily nourishment. However, it is evident from many scriptural applications of the word "bread," that it means more surely a request for spiritual food that is nourishment for the soul and the spirit. Hunger for "The Word of God" is a super-naturally acquired characteristic of the redeemed Christian. And why not? Having been adopted into God's family, into the body of Christ, how could one not hunger to learn all that is possible to know about one's Holy Father, about Jesus with whom one is now "joint heir." And what about the Holy Spirit, who now dwells in the Christian's new heart? If you are a born-again Christian, there is someone, a Person in spirit form living in your heart! That is awesome! Incredible! If He is living in me, I want to know all I can find out about Him!

As Christians, when we ask for our "daily bread," we are asking for genuine communion with God, both personally and through His Word; we are asking for His guidance, and His fellowship; we are asking for Him to reveal the meaning of the different verses we encounter as we read daily His precious Word; and we ask for this "bread," not to fill our stomachs, but to fill our hearts that hunger for these things. To hunger for the Word of God is to hunger for Christ Jesus because Jesus *is* the Word of God. (Revelation 19:13).

And forgive us our debts as we forgive our debtor (KJV Matthew 6:12)

And forgive us our Sins as we also forgive everyone that is indebted to us (KJV Luke 11:4)

And forgive our trespasses as we forgive those who trespass against us. (KJV Matthew 6:14, 15) (Not part of the sample prayer)

Have you noticed these variations of the prayer and wondered about them? Are there any serious differences between sins, debts, and trespasses worthy of concern here? Why are there differences, and is there one choice that best represents what Jesus actually said? Let us see what we can find out from the Greek words:

Debts—debtors: *deneion*: a delinquent transgressor. (as against God, a sinner, under obligation)

Indebted—*opheilo*: idea of accruing, to owe, to be under obligation, to fail in duty.

Trespass—*paraploma*: sideslip, deviation, lapse, offense, sin

Trespass—*hamartano*: to sin, do wrong, contrary to God's will

Sin—*hamartia* (*hamartano*): sin, offense, wrongdoing, anything contrary to God's will & law, an absolute moral failure.

From these definitions it seems evident that no matter which variation of the prayer we choose, the petition to God is to forgive our *sins* as we forgive those who, for whatever reason, do some form of wrong toward us. It's probably of little significance whether we are forgiving debts or trespasses. However, I would submit that what we are to forgive is not sin, whether we choose "debtors," "those indebted to us," or "those who trespass against us." To say that we forgive those who sin against us is to suggest that we have the power to forgive sin. Of course, only God can do that. In Psalms 51, David is lamenting over his sins regarding Bathsheba, which involved murder, lies, and on-going adultery. Yet in verse 4 he says to God, " Against thee, thee only have I sinned, and done this evil in thy sight." While David may have asked forgiveness of Nathan the prophet and others to the extent they were hurt by this harmful action, he acknowledges to have sinned *only* against God. So which of these words do we choose to use in this prayer? It appears to me that we should ask forgiveness of our sins as we forgive those who in whatever way have hurt or wronged us or owe us in someway. We can't forgive their sins, but we must not hold on to condemning feelings against those who offend us. We must forgive hurtful offending words and actions at the physical earthly level, and leave it totally to the Lord to judge and to condemn or forgive the spiritual nature of the offence.

I have found no Scripture version that asks forgiveness of our trespasses as we forgive those who trespass against us, even though this is the way that this verse is often expressed. Perhaps as noted, it stems from Matthew 6:14, 15 immediately following the example prayer, when Jesus says, "For if ye forgive their trespasses, your heavenly Father will also forgive you: but if ye forgive not men their trespasses neither will your Father forgive your trespasses." Also in the Epistles Ephesians 4:32 and Colossians 3:13, we are told to forgive as we are forgiven. H. A. Ironside in his "Notes on Matthew" provides an eloquent closure to the issues regarding the significance of verse 12.

> *"In the government of God as Father over His own children our forgiveness of daily offenses depends upon our attitude toward those who offend against us. If we refuse to forgive our erring brethren, God will not grant us that restorative forgiveness for which we plead when conscious of sin and failure. This, of course, has nothing to do with that eternal forgiveness which the believing sinner receives when he comes to Christ. It is the Father's forgiveness of an erring child, which must of necessity take into account the attitude of the failed one toward other member of the family."*

In this same vein, it is essential to realize that we *do* get punished here on earth for many, if not all, of our sins even though we are saved from eternal punishment by His grace through our faith. Isn't that the divine role of any loving, righteous, attentive father, to punish transgressions as well as to reward outstanding behavior and achievement?

And lead us not into temptation, but deliver us from evil

Lead us not into temptation? Why would Jesus suggest that we pray to our loving God not to lead us, into a place where we are certain that He would not, under any circumstances, want us to be? There are probably at least two ways in which the phrase may be understood. H. A. Ironside suggests, " It is a recognition of our own acknowledged weakness, a cry to God to preserve us from being placed in circumstances where we might be overpowered by the voice of the tempter." This is certainly a very sound explanation of the meaning in that it is clearly in context with everything Scripture tells us about our Father.

And now, let us try a closer look at the Greek word for which the KJV translated as "lead." This gives a precious nugget, which once again reveals God's divine wisdom and love. It also demonstrates again, how when Scripture verses seem strange, difficult to understand, or in conflict with other messages, we should examine most closely the original language for the true meaning. There are no errors or conflicts in God's Word as originally given to us. It's only the limitations of the language translation and the fallibility of the translators where the conflicts arise. It is through diligent loving and faithful attendance to His Word that the Holy Spirit will, in His time, reveal the truth of all things.

The word "lead" comes from the Greek word *eisphero,* which means to carry forward or lead into. However, reaching back to the root word from which it is derived, we find the word, *eis.* It defines a number of related action verbs and phrases, among which is to "set at one again!" How beautifully consistent is in this thought with what we know is our dear Lord's desire and intent for His children! When we insert this expression instead of "lead," we can convert this rather confusing petition into what I choose to believe is its actual intent. Instead of "lead us not into temptation," I believe a more appropriate translation might be, "don't let us be at one again with temptation" (as we were before, when we were hopelessly lost in sin.)

The next part of that verse, "but deliver us from evil," requires no analysis. However, the word "evil" is a translation of the Greek word *poneros,* which means evil, but can also mean both sin and the devil. Some versions of this phrase say, "but deliver us from the evil one." It would appear that either ending is appropriate.

For thine is the kingdom and the power and the glory forever, amen.

This is found in Matthew 6:13 but not in Luke 11:4. Research has indicated that it is also omitted in the most reliable manuscripts. It seems that it may have been added later as the prayer came into common usage as part of ritualistic services.

This prayer, as beautiful as it is and as it has to be, because it came directly from our Lords lips, is nevertheless a *sample* prayer. He clearly tells us so in its preface when He says, "After this manner therefore, we pray . . ." It was composed in order to instruct through example, what the components of a Christian prayer to God should be. There doesn't seem to be any valid reason to believe that it should have taken on the prominence it has as an often-repeated prayer in religious services. There is no mention of it as having been used in early Christian assemblies nor can it be found in the book of Acts or in any of the Epistles. As a "pattern" prayer it would appear that it was not intended to take on the extensive usage it has among Christian faiths. Note that it predates the advent of the Holy Spirit. He came at Pentecost to dwell permanently among and in the redeemed. He also came to guide all believers in their worship, prayers and petitions. I believe that when we wish to converse with God, it is our own personally composed prayers from our own hearts that He wants to hear. It is prayers patterned after the example He gave us, rather than the rote repetition of the sample prayer itself that He wants to hear.

—69—

The Power of Prayer

Earlier this week, a situation was resolved that had caused me much stress, grief and sorrow for more than three years. In more recent times, perhaps for the past year, I have prayed to God for this problem to end, specifically that the Lord would soften the hearts of the two individuals who wrongly perceived some of my actions and my motivations, and were thus undeservedly hostile and suspicious of me. It seemed as though there was nothing I could do or say that could change this. As a result, for the first time in my entire career as an engineer I did not enjoy going to the office, nor did I find my daily presence there anything but stressful and depressing. The situation was all the more unhappy because I love these people and have great respect for them, both as human beings and as professionals. Further, I had continually shared with them most generously and to a fault, from a business viewpoint, the fruits of our collective efforts, sharing that seemed to be neither appreciated nor in any way mitigating, in terms of the ill feelings that they seemed to have.

Then suddenly, through the grace of God, I sensed that this great burden had been lifted. That is, this long-held distrust, or whatever it was, seemed to float away. This change, this sudden release of tension didn't just happen. It was the result of a process that, in turn, was the culmination of a series of other events through which, it would seem, I was pushed and over which I felt little control. At this writing however, it is too early to tell how beneficial or how sustaining will be this new direction and this changed atmosphere.

To a non-believer, this would be clearly a coincidence, a logical series of causes and effects. However, the Jewish Rabbis have an expression that concludes that coincidence is not a "kosher" word;

that there is a reason for everything. In this particular case, it is the culmination of two years of prayer wherein I asked the Lord for a resolution to the problem. In these last few months, as I have continued to learn more of what it means to be a true Christian, I revised my prayers from those where I asked Him to help me with the problem, to where I handed it over to Him entirely and asked Him to solve it in any way He saw fit. Jesus wants us to do just that. He made it very clear, in John 14:14, when He said, "If you ask anything in My name, I will do it." Not I will help you, but I will do it. That is not quite as all-encompassing as it sounds on the surface, however. The "in My name" is a very significant qualifier. Its meaning is much deeper than the words would seem to suggest. It does not apply to everyone, but only to true believers, to those who have placed their complete faith and trust in Him totally, without reservations or equivocations, and even under the most adverse and painful circumstances. Even to those of this level of faith, it does not mean that He will abide by a request in the manner in which it is desired or expected, because His reasoning and judgment, His vision and plan, are each infinitely superior to ours and thus His response may be much different than we expect or even think we want.

Chuck Missler has a great example to make the point about God's answer to our prayers. He notes how careful we should be in what we pray for, and cites the example of a boy hopelessly in love with the prom queen and praying for the fulfillment of his desires. God seemingly ignores these prayers and does not allow for the desired union. Then, twenty years later at a class reunion, the boy again meets the object of his first love, and realizes how blessed he was by God's superior judgment in the matter.

There is only one overriding purpose for our lives here on earth, and that is to qualify for, and to prepare for, eternal life in heaven. The true believer tries with all his might to live that purpose, and his every request to the Lord is, I believe, judged in that context and acted upon in a manner appropriate to that purpose. When the prayers of even the most sincere believer seem not to be answered, it may be a matter of timing or it may be that the request is not consistent with God's greater plan, which, when implemented, will prove superior to the intended purpose of the prayer. Even Paul, certainly one of the most saintly and complete believers in Jesus, and who had a severe affliction, possibly blindness, asked the Lord three times to remove this affliction. The Lord later told him no, that his grace was enough, and indeed it was, because Paul gratefully accepted this highest of all rewards, his assurance of a place in heaven, and continued to do God's work here on earth, probably even more effectively because of his affliction.

I am convinced that the chain of events referred to above was divinely orchestrated and was the direct result of my prayers. This does not mean that I have achieved any state of worthiness, whereby my prayed for requests should be granted. It simply means, to me, that my prayer in this instance was not inconsistent with God's plan. It may also have been a token of encouragement to a novice, an old and confused but doggedly determined novice, who is eagerly seeking to understand and to apply His requirements, to become one of His chosen.

To break away from a life-long obsession with self-reliance and to ask for help, even from the Lord, has been a very difficult transition. However, as I have learned more about what He wants from and for us, I realize that even this is not enough. He wants *faith*, absolute unqualified faith. Faith that reserves nothing, or that retains any form of hesitation, exception or doubt. This is where the going gets really rough. This ultimate state of faith is extremely difficult to achieve. God knows this and does not expect it overnight. He does require, however, that we continually strive earnestly toward that state of total submission.

He doesn't want us to ask Him for help. He isn't a helper. He is the creator, the doer of all things. He wants us to dump our problems on Him for Him to take care of in the way only He can. Again, however, He will only accept these chores if they are given with the full confidence of the giver that He will attend to them, and whatever way He chooses to do this, and whatever the result, will be accepted with love and gratitude and complete faith in its rightfulness.

Because He wants us to dump our problems on Him does not mean that we are free to walk away and do nothing. He doesn't need our help, but He nevertheless wants, in fact He insists, on our involvement, our concerted effort and our righteous concern. In one way, just as a good mother doesn't need her four year old to help prepare supper, she appreciates her involvement and effort and the learning process it provides. While the Lord wants us to hand Him our problems, I believe nevertheless in the old saying that God helps those who help themselves. The seemingly conflicting views here are readily reconciled if one recognizes that we are probably more often than not the instruments through which the Lord solves many of our problems, as well as the problems of others. If you have a financial problem, for instance, the Lord may soften your boss's heart so he gives you a raise, but you have to be worthy of it and do the improved work that justifies it. When Joseph knew that there would be seven years of famine after seven good years, he didn't sit around for seven years hoping that God would take care of the coming problem. Yes, he prayed and had unswerving faith in the Lord and the Lord took care of the problem by giving Joseph the good sense, the managing skills and the authority to increase and store the over-abundance of the first seven years in preparation for the next seven years. God solved the problem but did it through Joseph. When problems cannot be solved using intervention through human agency or natural events, God will use supernatural means such as the ten plagues against the Pharaoh and finally the parting of the Red Sea.

Examples of this true, complete and saving faith are provided throughout the Bible. Look at Abraham, who, at the direction of the Lord, proceeded toward, and intended to, sacrifice his only beloved son, and would have done so had the Lord not stopped him at the last minute. He had complete faith in the Lord and he knew that the Lord had the problem. The Lord told Abraham that through Isaac he would be the father of many nations. Therefore, if he proceeded to kill Isaac as he was told to do, the Lord would have to resurrect him in order to fulfill His promise. The fact is that Abraham was really acting out a prophecy, because two thousand years later, on that same spot, another father did sacrifice His son, and then resurrected Him.

So, what is the point of all of this, and why do I keep writing about this "stuff," you may ask. The point is that prayer and faith in Jesus is where "it is all at! When you reach that conclusion and truly believe it, there is nothing more of any importance that you don't already know, because along the way toward reaching that conclusion, you already picked up everything else worth knowing about life and its purpose. Fundamental corollaries to this conclusion regarding prayer and faith are the following:

1. God the Father, the Son, and the Holy Spirit are real; They are alive and well, as is Satan.

2. Jesus was and is God and He was also man. He lived, preached, was crucified as man, died, and was resurrected to return to Heaven.

3. Both the Old and the New Testament are the inspired Word of God, although written by some forty authors over a period of several thousand years, they are one integrated message, actually "ghost" written by the Holy Spirit. They convey the ultimate truths and are, in the original texts, accurate in every detail.

4. There is but one purpose for all life and that is for the glory of God. For mankind, this purpose is fulfilled by loving Him, striving to live in accordance with His commandments, and most of all by having complete, unqualified faith in Jesus, our Savior.

I say all of this very empathetically, and believe it sincerely. However, at this point in my life I fear that it is more believed intellectually than spiritually. That does not mean that I believe it less fervently than I should, it just means that placing *total* faith in the Lord, under any and every circumstance, without hesitation or exception, is a tall order and one that I doubt I have achieved. How can one know unless one has been tested in some manner equivalent to the lion's den, as was Daniel? Putting my thoughts in writing in this manner is my way of searching myself and trying to make clear, in my own mind, just where and who I am.

—70—
Some Thoughts on Prayer

One of the unique privileges given to a redeemed Christian is the right to answered prayer. God has promised that He will hear the prayers of those who are His, and live a genuine Christian life. In John 16:24 Jesus tells His Apostles "... *hitherto have ye asked nothing in My name, ask, and ye shall receive that your joy may be full.*" So what is the catch? Surely there is one, or else every real Christian would be rich, never be sick and live for centuries. The catch is in the phrase "in My name." It is loaded with meaning that can only be obtained from deep study of God's whole Word, through the guidance of the Holy Spirit.

There are two thoughts that must first be dismissed. One, although God is all powerful and nothing is beyond His ability to provide, He isn't a genie in a bottle waiting to grant our every wish. And second, He answers prayers in accordance with His will, not ours. Furthermore, He is not in the business of granting frivolous wishes, but only those that in His judgment are responses to genuine needs and unselfish hopes. Through James 4:3, we are told not to ask unreasonably, for He say, "Ye ask and receive not, because ye ask amiss." Asking amiss means asking unreasonably, beyond your actual needs. We should pray according to our need. Prayer should not be offered recklessly.

To simply end a prayer with "I pray these things in the name of our Lord Jesus Christ, amen," is meaningless unless what proceeds is from a sincere, redeemed, contrite, worshiping and *trusting* heart. It's not enough to just want. We must want what He wants for us, if our prayers are to be answered affirmatively.

There is another "catch." Sin must be dealt with! If one has a known sin in his or her heart, it must be confessed and there must be sincere repentance. Sin standing between God and man is a basic hindrance, a barrier between them. How can, or why should, God answer the prayers of anyone in a state of sin even though that person is actually saved? But you say Jesus died for our sins, and those who truly believe have had their sins forgiven. That is true. But where ongoing prayer and petitions are concerned, sin can still get in the way, shutting down communication. Any known unconfessed sin is a big obstacle to true communion with God and to His willingness to hear His children's prayers. In Psalm 66:18 we read, "If I regard iniquity in my heart, the Lord will not hear." That makes it pretty clear. Iniquity is simply sin. If anyone has a known sin in his or her heart that one clings to, will not give up, the Lord will not hear that person. Confession of that sin while knowing that we still desire it in our hearts and will continue in it is of little value. This is more than a weakness of outward conduct; it is an iniquity of the heart that must be corrected.

Now one last "catch" (that I know of), and that has to do with the word trusting, which is underlined above. Let us read Mark 11:22–26.

> *And Jesus answering saith unto them, Have faith in God.*
>
> *For verily I say unto you, That whosoever shall say unto this mountain, Be thou removed, and be thou cast into the sea; and shall not doubt in his heart, but shall believe that those things which he saith shall come to pass; he shall have whatsoever he saith.*
>
> *Therefore I say unto you, What things soever ye desire, when ye pray, believe that ye receive them, and ye shall have them.*
>
> *And when ye stand praying, forgive, if ye have aught against any; that your Father also which is in heaven may forgive you your trespasses.*
>
> *But if ye do not forgive, neither will your Father which is in heaven forgive your trespasses*

I called this the last "catch," but as we read the above, there are two parts to it. First we must "have faith" and "believe," and "not doubt in his heart" that one's requests "shall come to pass" and "he shall have whatsoever he saith" (asks for). Second, we find in verse 25 that we are to have forgiven all whom we have something against, or God cannot forgive us. So, if we can't forgive, He won't either, and then again, that is an obstacle to His responding to our prayers.

From these verses, we get the clear message that in order for our prayers to be answered, we must *believe* that they *are being* answered. This is empathetic in verse 24, where it says, ". . . when ye pray *believe* that ye receive them and ye shall have them." That's where *real* faith and a *trusting* heart come in Big Time!

Notice that in verse 24, it says, "believe that ye receive." It doesn't say, believe and ye *will* receive, but that ye receive! It's a done deal! God is in the process of dealing in some affirmative manner with your petition. Assuming all is right with you, in God's eyes, you are redeemed, you've confessed all known sins, your prayer is consistent with His will, and you believe He has heard and answered your prayer; then it's finished, done; He has given His ok; it's in the works. If your faith is that complete, that true, you know it is done, and need not, you should not even pray for that matter again, except only in profound gratitude for His presence, His love and graciousness.

How many of us can become such cleansed vessels? How many of us can know that we have dealt with all of the above noted "catches" so that our Lord can hear us. How many can generate such a faith as to know that their prayers *are* answered before there is evidence of the fact. For the truly redeemed soul who is mature in the faith and knowledgeable of the Scripture, becoming a cleansed vessel need not be very difficult. But this is why we find in Luke 18:1 ". . . that men ought always to pray and not to faint." This verse tells us to pray and continue to pray without weakening. If our prayers are petitions and we don't have faith that God has heard or is yet willing to respond, we must continue to pray until our faith is strong enough to know that we *have* received. In this context one may say that Luke 18:1 tells us to pray repeatedly until Mark 11 "kicks in," that is that our faith is finally sufficient to believe, to know that it is done, that what we prayed for, whether already manifest or not, is in the process of being accomplished.

I thank brother Watchman Nee, a great twentieth-century evangelist, expositor, and martyr, for having shared these insights, which the Holy Spirit gave him, and which now He has allowed me to elaborate and share as well.

—71—

Prayer

In the Christian faith, prayer is a direct spiritual communication with our Father, wherein we take the opportunity to worship, praise, express gratitude, love, petition, and make requests of Him, all in the name of our Lord and Savior Jesus Christ. We are close to Him, and most God-like when we are praying to Him appropriately. Jeremiah 29:3 says ". . . ye shall seek me and find me when ye shall search for me with all of your heart." And Hebrews 11:16 tells us that God is a ". . . reward of them who diligently seek Him." While careful, dedicated, inspired study of the Scripture can reveal much *about* the character and nature of God and what He expects of us, only prayer is capable of actually *finding* God and having the fellowship He wants to have with us. In these two passages we hear essentially the same message. Prayer is implicit in each case. The Holy Spirit tells us that we must express our prayer diligently and with all our hearts. How do we pray diligently? We do so with fervor, sincerity, love, humility and passionate perseverance. How do we pray with all our hearts? We do so with the full measure of our entire inner being, which is the sum of our intellect and our emotions, all in *willful*, loving *subordination* to God's perfect will. This is prayer, the kind God loves to hear and to which He likes to respond. He wants this quality, not quantity of words. He knows all our thoughts, needs and desires better than we do. But He won't waste His time and effort considering prayers that lack full commitment, are half hearted, mindless, selfish or rote.

The key factor in all prayer, if it is to have standing with God, is that it represents a subordination of *our* will for *His*. He isn't impressed by our advice or our persuasion based on our own wills; the only prayers that count, are those in which we condition our requests to His will. Because He knows all things, He knew before the beginning of time even what we would be praying for, and how serious and compassionate we would be, and has, therefore, already judged the merits and decided what is best for us. Thus it is by His sovereign will and His alone in both His perfect love and judgment that all requests of the believer are answered.

Then why pray at all you may ask? If things have all been decided or predetermined, we are merely a pawn in a grand chess game without investment or influence in our own future or anything else. Wrong! God gave us freedom of choice and we do have control of our destinies, subject, of course, to the many outside influences of other wills, wills in conflict with ours, that seek to dissuade and impose on us. God does not do violence to our wills as does the world, nor will He become an active participant in effectuating our own will. God's influence is fully evidenced and expressed in the glory of His creation and in His Word, which He gave us in the Holy Bible. We always have the choice to either seek Him or to go the way of the world. He simply happens to know what our choices will be long before we make them. Of course, He also knew the nature of our prayers, how much of our heart we would put into them and exactly how consistent to His will and plan for us they would be. Those who are truly born again, who are His sons and daughters, must never forget that He does have a divine plan for each of us, even during this short remainder of our visit here. Everything in our lives is Father filtered, our joys and victories, as well as our sufferings and defeats.

Diligent, fervent prayer is a process through which we grow to know Him and what He wants of us. Prayer is more than asking, it is how we worship Him, how we praise Him, how we show our love for Him, and how we thank Him. Because prayer is how we communicate with our Creator, shouldn't there be something very special about the conversation? If we were given the opportunity to speak to the Queen of England or the President of the United States, wouldn't that be a special and momentous event? Yet, here we have a twenty-four-hour open line directly to our Creator, a personage infinitely greater and more important than any President or Queen. Why should we then treat that opportunity as less momentous and with less awe and importance? True, diligent prayer is the essence of our fellowship with Him. He loves nothing more than to hear from us in this loving, sincere and awe-filled manner. Remember, we all have the potential to "walk with Him as did Enoch (Genesis 5:21), to be considered His beloved as was John (John 21:20) to be personally "sent by Him" as was Abraham (Exodus 3:10), or to be "a man (or woman) after God's own heart as was David (1 Samuel 13:14, Acts 13:27). This tells us that we have a very *personal* God, one who *really wants* to have fellowship with each of us as individuals. Scripture gives us no evidence that any of these blessed individuals were worthy, quite the contrary. Nevertheless, they each found favor with Him, and through His grace with their love and humility, along with their sincere and fervent prayer faith and worship, there was provided them that blessed fellowship. As His sons and daughters, we are far better positioned to attain such an exalted place then were these men of old, if we will but fully commit ourselves and our ways to Him through obedience, love, faith, humility, and prayer. Scripture tells us many times to pray and thereby we will receive. The passages that allude to this are perhaps among the most troublesome, difficult and misunderstood in all Scripture. In the Gospel of John 14:14 Jesus says, "If you ask anything *in my name*, I will do it." In Mark 11:24, Jesus again offers, "What things so ever ye desire, when ye pray, *believe* that ye receive them and ye shall have them." Again in John15:7 Jesus assures us that "If ye *abide in me* and *my words abide in you*, ye shall ask whatever ye wish and it shall be done unto you." Jesus also tells us in Matthew 21:22 "Whatsoever ye shall ask in *prayer, believing* ye shall receive." In John 5:14 the Holy Spirit tells us "And this is the confidence that we have in Him, that if we ask anything *according to His will*, he heareth us: and if we know that He hear us, whatsoever we ask we know that we have the petition that we desire of Him." Furthermore, in John 16:23 we hear that "what so ever ye ask the Father in *My name*, He will give it you. Even Psalm 37:4, 5 gives rise to such expectations when it says, "*Delight* thyself also in the Lord and He shall give thee the desires of the heart. *Commit* thy way unto the Lord; *trust* also in Him; and He shall bring it to pass."

This is but a sampling of the many verses that offer similar messages. It is not what they actually say in the *whole context* of the

Scripture, but what they seem to say, that is so troubling. If they say what they *seem* to say, than all who are born again would be rich, never sick, never suffer, never grow old, and always be happy. Who wouldn't pray for, and thereby expect to receive these blessings? But we all know that that's not the way it works. Lack of understanding of the true meaning of these verses has caused not only many who only thought they were saved to utterly reject God because of 'broken promise," but even those who are saved, love Jesus and believe in the inerrancy of the Scriptures, also wonder, are troubled and even question their own salvation when the objects of their petitions are not granted.

Perhaps we may learn something useful by examining these verses one at a time and applying them in the context of the whole Scripture. In doing this, it will be useful to read what is, figuratively speaking, the "fine print" as in an insurance policy. For that reason certain of the key words in those verses have been underlined. In each of these verses the underlined words express or imply the conditions, the "fine print" associated with the promise. In John 14:14 and 16:23 the words again are " *in my name*" in Mark11:24 it's *believe*; in John 15:7 it's "*abide in me*" and "*my words abide in you*," its ". . . *ask what ye will, and it shall be done unto you.*" In 1 John 5:14 its ". . . *according to His will*, and in Psalm 37:4, 5 its ". . . *delight yourself* . . ." and "*Commit thy way* . . ." and also, ". . . *Trust also in Him* . . ." In Examining these one at a time, I pray we will reveal the patterns of conditions that bring this awesome promise into its true perspective.

First, "*in My name.*" Surely, we all realize that we should pray always to the Father, but in His name, in the name of the Lord and Savior Jesus Christ. For in 1 John 2:1 we learn that ". . . we have an advocate with the father, Jesus Christ the Righteous." Also in John14:6 we learn directly from Jesus that ". . . I am the way, the truth, and the life: no man cometh unto the Father, but by Me." However, it should be evident that "in the name of Jesus, or "in His name" is not in itself an accomplishing magical phrase or formula any more than is "open sesame" or the rubbing of a bottle to bring forth a wish granting genie. Jesus is our Lord, our Savior, our God. If simply calling on His name would grant wishes or answer prayers, He would have to be more like a genie and we would be the gods. So it is evident that there must be something much more involved. Surely one's whole life, heart, will, prayers and other significant factors must accompany our requests in the name of our blessed Advocate, our Intercessor with the Father, who is our grantor of all blessings. Prayers in His name must be for the furtherance of His will and glory. Dave Hunt says, "His name must be stamped on the character and engraved on the heart and life of the one praying in His name."

Then there is "believe" as in Mark 11:24. We must believe that we will receive answers to our prayers. This is not calling on some mysterious power of the mind that will make God acquiesce or that can produce results apart from God's will, as the so-called power of positive thinking would seem to suggest. To believe requires faith that He heard you and will respond. As Christians, we know He hears His children. But I suspect that only a very mature faith, a very committed and totally subordinated will, can muster unto itself such assurance. It must be the embodiment of a faith that has gone very far into self-denial, humility and acceptance of God's sovereign will as the only will in that life. It's believing, because the prayer request represents the believer's knowledge of the will of God and seeks nothing for himself or herself but *only* the will of God. It is the result of that rare and wonderful state where one finds more and more that one's desires coincide with His will. It comes from knowing Him and His Word, as He wants us all to know Him, His Word, and His will. This will tend to grow in each of us as grow our submission, humility and love of Him.

Next there is the doctrine of "abiding" as a condition of granted petition as in John 15:7. Abiding means dwelling, a place where one is residing. What a wonderful home He is suggesting! We are residing in Him and His word is residing in us! If, or when, we achieve that place of abiding, when we and His words are fully moved in, we have little need to wonder or to be concerned about answers to our prayers. But surely these "abidings" are not easily attained, for it seems evident that again, the prerequisites of unconditioned submission, humility, worship, and love of a mature believer steeped in the Word are necessary for this move to take place.

Then we have, "ask in prayer," "believing," from Matthew 21:24. This is essentially the same as Mark 11:24 and warrants the same comments. Perhaps it might help here to also

point to some additional advice Jesus gave us in John 18 in the parable of the widow and the judge. The message is that we should "always pray and not give up" (NIV). That is of course, when the cause is just or consistent with His will. We should persevere in prayer for ". . . will not God bring about justice for His chosen ones, who cry out to Him day and night?" (Luke 18:7) Thus He encourages us to keep asking, seeking and knocking at the door. Of course in this vein we must also keep in mind James 4:3 where the Holy Spirit reminds us ". . . ye ask and receive not because ye ask amiss (that is, not to Gods glory) but that ye may consume it upon your lusts." This again is caution to the wise, to carefully examine what they pray, to be certain that it is appropriate in God's eyes. This must not be in vain repetition, which Christ condemned.

John 5:14, 15 speaks of prayer *"according to His will."* Now, here we are at the root of the issue, the real answer to the dilemma. This has already been alluded to a number of times hereinabove. All prayer, if it is a petition, if it is to be answered in some favorable manner, must be in accordance *with His will*. Bottom line! Think about it. Could it be otherwise? Is God going to do anything *not* in accordance with His will? What kind of God would He be if we, such lowly sinful creatures, could do or think anything to change His mind or to convince Him of anything He didn't already know or was already intending to do? Surely not the omniscient God we know Him to be. Yet we must at the same time remember, as stated earlier in this paper, that because God foreknew everything, He knew all about our prayers and petitions. He knew the conditions of our hearts, and knew from every conceivable perspective the merits and ramifications of our petitions. Thus, He made His righteous judgment way back then and set down His divine will in each matter to await its appropriate application and answer to us. So all our prayers made responsibly are, or have been judged in advance and properly dealt with by our loving, righteous and all-knowing God. Would we, should we, want it any different, nor could it possibly be otherwise? When we finally stop to think, to apprehend in any degree the wholeness of His word and the nature of His being, we must realize that "in accordance with His will" is implicit and essential in every promise, in every message Scripture gives us. Even Jesus Himself prayed in this manner in Matthew 26:39 saying, ". . . nevertheless not as I will but as thou wilt."

Lastly, in Psalm 37, we hear the key words, "delight," "commit" and "trust" all in or to the Lord. Delight in the Hebrew is *anag,* which also means soft and pliable. Thus, it suggests that we let Him mould or sculpt us to His way and purpose. "Commit thy way." That is clear and appropriate as is "trust in Him." While this verse is simply another way of expressing the same idea, as has already been delivered in the other messages, it is interesting and comforting to note that our unchanging God was giving similar assurance well before Jesus formally entered His creation.

One final and very important observation. When we pray unselfishly, with sincerity and with all our heart, a prayer where we truly mean ". . . nevertheless not as I will but as thou wilt," we are offering the highest form of worship, as did Jesus at Gethsemane. When we pray in this manner, we are petitioning our Father to have His will prevail and to not allow His will to be thwarted by other wills. Scripture clearly indicates that our God has a permissive will so that at times He does allow His will to be thwarted by other wills, as when Jesus wept and lamented as He rode a donkey into Jerusalem (Matthew 23:3) and in the desert when Moses struck the rock instead of speaking to it as God told him to do. These are also good examples of how we have, through our own free will, authority over our actions but not over their consequences. When we pray ". . . thy will and not mine be done," we are saying that we don't want our will to be in conflict with His will, and we are also asking Him to disallow or override all other conflicting wills so that only His will be done. Herein would seem to be the greatest power of prayer, our petitions to God to disallow other wills that conflict with His.

In summary, there are three points of importance here regarding prayer, and God's response that we must keep in mind even when we think we have reason to believe that our prayers are worthy, that they therefore surely reflect His will. First is *timing.* He knows better than we do, not only if, but also how, and when our petitions should be granted. Second is *patience* for His timing, which is a virtue in short supply in me, and I suspect in many others. But it is His timing that determines when all things are to occur. We must wait patiently without grumbling or despairing. This, of course, implies trust as well, for patience is built on trust, trust in Him. Thirdly, we must recognize that *"His ways are not our ways,"* and the "... the foolishness of God is wiser than man." Therefore, His answers to our prayers may be quite different from what we expect, but they will always be appropriate and exactly right because they reflect God's way and His infinite and omniscient perspective.

We all know how grateful we have been at times when He didn't respond as we had prayed, that is, when we later discovered the error of our wants. God's answers or non-answers are never in error. Remember that! And never forget to pray in gratitude and awe no matter what happens, because as His sons and daughters, He has guaranteed to us our ultimate victory when we shall no longer want for anything, when in eternity our prayers will never again be as requests, but only prayers of worship, love and gratitude.

—72—

Does Prayer Accomplish Anything?

Prayer is to some degree a component of nearly every religion. But does it benefit the one who prays? The answer is that it depends on who is praying, to whom one is praying and for what one is praying. It should be clear that the writer is a biblical Christian and, therefore, this analysis is unabashedly from that perspective. There are many religions and beliefs in the world today, and adherence to most of these include some form of prayer or other evidence of reverence to a "higher" authority, or "deity." In many of these religions, that higher authority may or may not be the true Creator God, the author of the Holy Bible. However, the so-called Christian leadership of the current world-wide ecumenical movement, while claiming belief in the One Creator God, would have us believe that all faiths lead to heaven, as long as they are truly believed. In effect, they would have us believe that the God is able to manifest Himself in each of the many worshipped "deities." This is blatant HERESY and contrary to biblical teaching! But, of course, if you accept this, your path through this life will be made easier. It is the classic earthly adage that one must go along in order to get along! If that's biblical, why didn't Jesus go along with the establishment? He could have saved Himself a great deal of suffering!

Does prayer and worship of any of these various deities bring forth benefits to the faithful of these religions? It would seem so, otherwise why would anyone continue in these various beliefs? All religions that continue to attract worshipers must provide some amount of comfort and answered prayer or they would soon be abandoned. History, both secular and biblical, is replete with evidences of many forms of idol worship, which had to have been very attractive and

656

rewarding. Scripture describes various forms of idol worship so enticing that even God's people, the Israelites, repeatedly and knowingly abandoned the true God who miraculously saved them out of Egypt and fed them for forty years in the desert. The power of the idols was such that even though the people retained the God of Abraham as their main God, there were long periods when they also worshipped the idols acquired from neighboring tribes. Even many of the temple priests, the ordained descendants of Aaron, kept figures of idols for secret "after hours" worship.

In order to offer an opinion regarding the topic question, it may simplify things if we divide those who pray into two different categories. For purposes of this discussion, we will put all those who worship and pray in accordance with all belief systems other than biblical Christianity, into one category, and those who worship Jesus and pray in strict accordance with the Holy Bible, into the other category. This category of belief is as the Bible states, that Christ Jesus was born of a virgin, lived, died on the cross, was buried and rose again on the third day. In having done so, He made possible the forgiveness of sins, and thus Jesus is our Lord and Savior, and only through faith in Him and *Only* in Him are souls saved to eternal life. That, as stated, is Christian doctrine given to us through the Holy Bible, which was authored by God in its entirety. Furthermore, God's Word commands in Deuteronomy 4:1 not to alter His Word, and Revelation 21:19 tells us that anyone who adds to or takes away from the book will have his or her name removed from the Book of Life. That means they are not saved but are condemned to hell. From this overly brief description of Christianity, it is evident why it must be a faith completely separate from all other beliefs, even in the manner and effectiveness of prayer.

With these two categories identified as sources of prayer, we can now discuss the effectiveness of prayer. As noted above, there must be something beneficial in every one of these religious beliefs or they would not attract followers to prayer. Now we might pose a secondary question in order to help answer the first. What kinds of benefits, if any, are derived from prayers, first with reference to all non-Christian faiths? In order to answer this question, we must understand that from a biblical perspective, these are all false religions, originated and propagated by false teachers. Scripture also makes it very clear that Satan is a real personage and by the permissive will of the Creator God, Satan rules the world and is the father of all lies and all false religions as set forth by the false teachers. Our Creator God has permitted this because He has given man his own sovereign will, or freedom of choice, which God will not violate. Man must come to Him through Jesus willingly, through his own choice. What choice would man have if God had not allowed Satan to formulate these "alternative beliefs? In the Holy Scripture, God has provided ample evidence to convince anyone genuinely seeking the truth, to believe in Jesus as Lord God and Savior. To any who are seeking Him, God will provide as much of the Light of Truth as is asked for with sincerity. The initial basic evidence of the existence of the Creator God is all around; it is all of creation itself. Beyond that, if one will simply and sincerely ask for further evidence, it will be given.

There is a spiritual head behind every false religion. The fallen angels and evil spirits are Satan's army who officiate in this capacity, as well as the behind-the-scene influences of every government and worldly organizations on earth. They each have substantial, though limited, directive and spiritual powers. It is through these powers that they are able to not only corrupt governments but also to answer prayers and grant benefits to the adherent of the false religions. His or her mission is to keep every believer of a false religion or any other type of false precept, satisfied that theirs is a sacred beneficial belief system. There is no end to Satan's innovative powers. He will formulate and place one of his agents over whatever new belief that will comfort and satisfy any and all groups, circumstances, persuasion, desires, or preferences, so long as none can lead to a true Christian faith. His favorite creation must surely be a religious system that so closely resembles genuine Christianity that only the very elect can recognize it as false. This is amply evident by the great variety of religions and pseudo Christian cults that have risen to popularity over the past century. Again, given that there are satanic powers behind every one of these belief systems, these powers are eager and capable of answering prayer requests to the extent they are able. Some

answers appear quite impressive and beneficial from a world perspective regarding wealth and fulfillment of carnal desires. These
spirits even follow closely the lives of their victims, and when a loved
one dies they can even mimic the departed one's voice and convey
some very convincing "messages from the dead" that seem quite
authentic. This power appears to manifest in the séances and other
necromancy types of sorceries. Through these evil spirits, there is
often even the promise of some form of eternal life. Of course, these
spirits all know Jesus and the True Way to eternal life, and they know
that their promises are lies, but *that* is the *whole* of their purpose, to
offer false hope while preventing salvation. By "faithfully" answering
prayers for carnal benefits, they achieve intense loyalty from their
adherents, most of who remain with them to the "bitter" end.

In summary, it may be said with a large degree of assurance, that
every non-Christian religion, belief, or faith on earth has adherents
who derive some persuasive amount of benefit from their choices. If
this be true, than either our Creator God answers these prayers or
some other entity capable of such doings is responsible for that work.
Our God is not in the business of answering prayers prayed to idols or
prayers originating out of false religions. Scripture makes it clear that
Satan and his agents have that power and use it in fulfilling God's
commitment to providing man with the choice to choose eternity
with Him, or with Satan.

Now what about Christian prayer? Everyone who has even cracked
the book knows that God says that He *does* answer our prayers. Those
who have read and believe His Word know that He does. In the earlier
years of my short life as a believer, I felt compelled and did write two
other papers on prayer, both, of course from the Christian perspective.
With this in mind, I'll try not to be more repetitive than necessary in conveying some additional observations that have since come to me. Also, if
this seems to be less than what is deserving of such an important Christian blessing, I invite you to the previous writings, which can be found on
the web www.christianmusings.com.

What has prompted this third paper on prayer is the relatively
recent resurrection and proliferation of the false pharisaic belief
that wealth is a validation of faith, and, therefore, evidence that

eternal life has also been provided. How natural and human is this wishful thinking, that anyone who has obtained wealth, must have been blessed with it by the Lord as a reward for whatever has been the nature of his or her faith and works. At the time of Jesus, it had been a long established part of the Pharisaic belief and teachings that wealth was a blessing from the Lord, and along with it came the blessing of eternal life. That is why the disciples were so amazed when Jesus spoke of how difficult it was for a rich man to enter heaven. They had been taught that only the rich were blessed enough to qualify for heaven.

Today we have the "blab it and grab it" preachers who say that if you pray for wealth God will give it to you. If He doesn't, then you have not prayed in true faith. Sending these frauds some money is claimed to be helpful in expediting God's delivery. These radio and TV spinners of lies are very persuasive to tens of thousands of gullible souls who haven't the slightest understanding of God's Word, but assume that because those charlatans call themselves pastors and quote Scripture, their messages must be valid. For several generations the public educational system has had great success in diminishing education and advancing indoctrination, with evolution as its cornerstone and Christianity as a forbidden word. As it has been with public education, so it has been also to a large degree with what is called "Christian education." The world has entered the so-called Christian education curriculum just as effectively and pervasively as the world has managed demonized biblical Christianity. Putting all of this into a relevant perspective, it is not difficult to understand how even relatively sincere professing Christians can fall for such perverted preaching. What's called the Christian church has also been dumbed down through lack of sound, honest, competent biblical teaching. Proverb 29:18 tells us, "*. . . where there is no vision, the people perish.*" The Hebrew word for vision also means revelation. What is the source of all truthful vision or revelation? It is the Holy Bible! Can you not see a great deal of "perishing" going on today? Pray and prepare so that you will not be one of its victims.

Scripture assures us that God answers the prayers of those who are His own. If you are indeed one of His own, your prayers are answered whenever you pray a prayer that is in accordance with His will. It will, however, be answered in *His* way, and in *His* appointed time. He knows what is best for you, far better than you do. Therefore, His answer may not even resemble or be the exact opposite of what you prayed for, but it will be what you needed in His eyes, not necessarily in yours. Prayers to false gods are answered more quickly and in accordance with one's desires. That's what makes them so insidiously more attractive. It's because Satan sees profit for his agenda by catering to one's natural desires; however, he will never answer a prayer in a manner that is in one's spiritual best interest. He knows we all want instant gratification and we want it our way. His answers will generally be of that nature. This keeps His own coming back to him and farther from Jesus. If you pray and your prayers are answered as you hoped, Praise the Lord! But before you glory in your success make very certain that you have sound biblical Christian doctrine under your belt and deep in your heart, with a faith focused fully on, and only on, Christ Jesus. That is the only way to be sure that it is not that other power who is answering your prayer. If that is your true spiritual state, Father God will always answer your prayers in accordance with His will and your very best interest regardless of what you prayed for. Remember that Romans 8:28 guarantees this.

—73—

Peace

Peace is freedom from, or cessation of war or hostilities; that condition of a nation or community in which it is not at war with another. Concerning the individual, it is by definition the freedom from perturbations, a condition of quiet tranquility, or an undisturbed state. We speak of peace of mind, or of soul or of conscience. These are worldly dictionary definitions. But what is the peace spoken of in Scripture, especially by Jesus and the Apostles? What does Jesus mean in John 14:27 when he says, "Peace I leave you, my peace I give you; not as the world gives, give I unto you." This is the same peace referred to in John 16:33, 20:19, 21, 26, and in Acts 10:36, as well as eleven times in Romans and a total of seventy-one times in the New Testament. In each of these it is the Greek word *eirene* (i-ray'.nay), which means "one, peace, quietness, rest, *set at one again*." What a treasure there is here in this word when understood in the fullness of the glory in which Jesus meant to convey it! Listen to His words again with what, I believe, is the fullness of his meaning! "Peace I leave you, My peace, My rest, My father's accomplishment through me of having you *set at one again* with me!" How weak and non-descript by comparison is the word "peace" as a translation of the wonderful word *eirene* in its fuller and here more appropriate meaning, to be *"set at one again!" This* is the peace of God, which "passeth all understanding" (Philippians 4:7). It passes all understanding because it is a spiritual change that can never be understood by the natural man.

When we read John 14:27 as it is translated, we comprehend little more than the current dictionary meaning of the word "peace." The interpretation indicated above is, I believe, a much more accurate and profound statement from our Lord. Simply applying the word "peace," provides us only a tiny fragment of the real meaning that our Lord chose to convey. Here, and seventy more times, the Holy Spirit is saying to us that Jesus has "set (us) at one again." This is the divine promise of Ephesians 2:8, 9 repeated over and over again! He is saying to us who are born again that we are *one again with Him*! We are no longer children of Adam, but are now children of God! Before we were born again, we were a house in ruins; body, soul and spirit were in disarray. Before he sinned, Adam was governed by the spirit, in direct communication with the Holy Spirit of God. He was spiritually at one with God. The human spirit, under the guidance of the Holy Spirit, directed the soul that controlled the body. Then came the fall, the result of the original sin. That "fall" was when this arrangement with Adam and Eve crashed and came to ruin. The spirit was no longer in control of the soul, nor was there any communication between the human spirit and the Holy Spirit. The sensuous creature, that is the body along with the ego or soul, were now in control, with the human spirit remaining in a subordinate position. The man who was made in the spiritual image of God lost that image (1 Corinthians 15:15–50). As his own God-connected spirit separated from the Holy Spirit, so did the light with which he was clothed, and he was no longer "at one" with God, but instead a creature at war with God, filled with sin and the uncontrollable propensity for sin. This took on the nature of a genetic defect in the ruptured spirit, soul-body-trinity, a defect transmitted to all future generations. In effect, the spirit-Spirit communication network was totally severed. But here, giving us His "peace," Jesus says to believers that He has *set us at one* again with God; He has restored the original order of the structure of man; He has put the spirit back in control of the soul and restored spirit-Spirit communication. Even though we retain that generic defect we call sin, it can no longer cause us death or to remain separated from God. For having received the second birth and thus having been *"set at one again"* with God, we become the children of God and thus are immune to the second death, for from the second birth is eternal life.

This peace of John 14:27 and the peace that "passeth all understanding" of Philippians 4:7 is the second peace. It is the peace *of*

God as compared with the peace *with* God. When we accept Jesus as our Savior, that is, when we receive the grace of salvation through faith in the Gospel, we are no longer at war with God. But the ultimate peace, that peace that "passeth *all* understanding," that peace *of* God, is that most inner and blessed peace that comes only when we yield to Him and accept Him as our Lord. It is when we place our trust in Him for *all* things, not worrying about anything, but are prayerfully thankful and accepting of all things. That is the true peace of God, when we are *set at one* with Him. Jesus again expresses this incredible condition of the redeemed soul in John 17:21–23, using, in essence, this definition, but not calling it "peace." Listen to this starting with verse 20.

> *"Neither pray I for those alone, but for them also which shall believe on me through their word; that they may be one; as thou Father, art in me, and I in thee, that they also may be one in us: that the world may believe that thou hast sent me. And the glory which thou gavest me I have given them; that they may be one even as we are one. I in them, and thou in me, that they may be made perfect in one, and that the world may know that thou has sent me, and hast loved them, as thou has loved me."*

Three times Jesus includes the phrase "that they may be one." Think about what He is saying; "that they may be one in us"! Isn't that the condition of "the peace that passeth all understanding?" If we are in God and God in us, are we not set at one again with Him as was the first Adam before sin entered the world? This is "the peace that passeth all understanding!"

Perhaps it can also be expressed this way. The war ends. That is, we stop fighting Him with our disbelief in His Truth and become at peace *with* God as we receive Jesus as our Savior. However, it is when we also become one with Him as our *Lord* that we receive that peace *of* God, that peace that passeth all understanding. All of us, who are born from above, call Jesus our Lord and Savior, but how many live the full measure of the role wherein He *is our Lord*? For Him to be our Savior is the result of our acceptance through faith that He is our Savior. But acknowledging Him and having Him as our *Lord*, is a day-by-day, moment by moment, continuing process of surrender and subordination of self to His will even when it is difficult and inconvenient. It is characterized by our daily conviction, confession and *repentance* regarding our weaknesses as applied to our obedience and faith. It is a continual seeking to give back to Him our own will and accepting His as the only will in our lives.

Making Him truly our *Lord* does not just happen. It is an on going, ever developing process as we pray and seek Him as our Lord and Master in everything we do, think and feel. Only then can grow within us that second peace that "passeth all understanding," that is, when we are fully *set at one* with Him.

It is interesting and somewhat confirming to note that there is no such definition for peace in the Old Testament Hebrew. How could there be? The spirit-Spirit reunion could not come about until Jesus' act of love on the cross-washed away the sins of all who were in the faith. Prior to that, the sins of all of the Old Testament saints were merely covered, not erased, and when they died, their spirits, though destined eventually for heaven, had to descend into the paradise side of Sheol to await Jesus' incredible act of redemption. They could not be "set at one again" until He provided the way, that only way.

How incredibly wonderful it is that He came, and hereby did provide the way to set us at one again with Him!

—74—

Love

What is Love? Does any of us really know? Of Course we do! Most of us use that word many times each day. But it seems to have almost as many meanings as there are people using the word. From a Christian perspective, however, there are only two real categories of Love. God love and human love.

God Love, agape love is always unconditional. It is one-sided in that it doesn't have to be returned in order to be kept alive, or to be kept being initiated (I will love you no matter what you do to me).

Human love is conditional. It is based on what we think, feel and desire. It is based on some particular circumstances, and it is based on the other persons response to you.

Human love is two-sided, because it must be returned in order to be kept alive.

God Love is a freeing love, because it frees the lover from expectations and presumptions.

Human love is a bondage love because it puts the lover in the bondage of expectations, and also forces the one loved to respond from his or her defenses and not the heart.

God love is other centered love, because it puts the other's interests before it's own.

Human love is always self-centered because it always puts itself above everyone else even though the lover may not be aware of it.

As we can see, and would expect, God operates from a plain far above that of man and the manner of His love clearly reflects that difference. Yet God's love is available to everyone who is willing to strip him or herself of all thoughts, emotions and desires that are contrary to God. In this way we become open vessels and conduits through which He wants to pour out His love through us to others. Once this state is achieved in the one so blessed, there is an unimaginable joy and peace and oneness with Jesus as that love not only flows through to others but also permeates every fiber of our own being. As humans, we are not capable of sustaining such a state but continually let it slip away as our self asserts itself. However, once this agape love, the love that Jesus makes available to us, is expressed, nothing less is ever again sufficient in our lives.

—75—

The Fifth Love

Many, many years ago I read a book called "The Fifth Wave." I can't remember what it was about except that every fifth wave or breaker rolling into the seashore was supposed to be bigger than the previous four or the next four. I believe it had to do with surfing and trying to catch the biggest waves. Every time I've gone to the seashore since then I've always counted and observed the wave characteristics, but I've never been able to verify this claim of any specialness of the fifth wave. Because I like to body surf, I still hope to find the "wave formula" and always try to find the very best one to catch and ride into shore.

In the Scripture, in the New Testament, we find a fifth love, which is very real and very special, and if we grab onto it we are guaranteed a wonderful ride to the very shore of Heaven. In the English language we have but one word for "love" to express a number of mental, emotional, spiritual conditions. In Greek, as many of us have learned, there are four different words that express more distinctly four kinds of conditions that in the English we lump into one word "love." These are as follows:

1. *Eros*—This is an erotic, sensual or sexual love.

2. *Phileo*—A friendship love that consists of kind feelings, or natural affection. This is the kind of love Peter said he had for Jesus when Jesus repeatedly asked Peter if he loved Him as told in John 21:15–17.

3. Storage—A filial love, the kind one finds within a family, such as a mother for her child.

4. *Agapao*—Strong's concordance simply translates this as a verb to love (in a special or moral sense). This is not God's love as is evidenced in John 3:19 as opposed to Luke 11:43 where it is used clearly to describe anything but a God's love.

4a. *Agape*—This is the noun love, as compared with the verb *agapeo*, to love. I call this 4a because it is very similar in meaning to its root *agapeo*. Strong's translation is "affection or benevolence, a love feast, charity, dear, love."

In studying Scripture there is nothing special in any of these translated definitions to qualify them to represent God's love. Neither in the Hebrew translations of the word is there any special meaning of sufficient power to qualify it as God's love. Thus there is a *fifth* love, God's love, the definition of which we find most complete in 1 Corinthians 13. Here the Holy Spirit actually coins a new meaning to the noun agape as being God's love. God's love flows into and through the hearts of His sons and daughters, a love lavished on others without a thought as to whether or not they are worthy. It comes from the nature of the lover, not from the attractiveness in the beloved. It is a *commitment* not a feeling. It is the seed of this fifth love that God tucks into the new heart He gives to everyone who is born again. As a true Christian grows in faith, this seed germinates and grows within the heart. I call this Agape, with a capital "A" because it is God's love. It's Agape, the noun, meaning God's love.

The four categories of love listed above, are earthly perceptions of love. Actually, from a heavenly perspective there is only one real love, God's love, Agape. The others are merely human emotions having little or no spiritual quality and certainly nor eternal durability. They all will die with the flesh. Only Agape is eternal, Agape is what God wants in Heaven. It is the love He has for us, and that He wants us to have for Him as well as for His other children. The whole purpose of creation was to create an environment wherein those created in His image would be free to or not to have fellowship with Him, and with Agape being the underlying goal of that relationship. Agape as it grows must become Sovereign in the heart, in the intellect, and in the will.

Now let us examine just what Agape is as the Holy Spirit has revealed it to us in 1 Corinthians 13.

1. Agape—Suffers long—Even though wronged, it is patient, silent and forgiving.

2. Agape—Is kind—It seeks no triumph in obstinacy, but only the triumph of grace. It seeks to be kind beyond any normal impulse to do so. It tries to say words and perform acts that will make life happier for those with problems.

3. Agape—Envies not—How can it when it only desires the best for others?

4. Agape—Wants not itself—It never brags, for it knows that what ever is good is the works of God and His grace in us.

5. Agape—Is not puffed up—It is not arrogant or prideful. It is instead an expression of genuine humility.

6. Agape—Does not behave unseemly—It is not boorish, rude inconsiderate, or inattentive.

7. Agape—Seeks not its own—It does not grasp for its own rights, but is totally unselfish, it seek to serve, not to be served.

8. Agape—Is not easily provoked—It never retaliates or is vindictive. It is kind in the face of unkindness.

9. Agape—Thinks no evil—It keeps no record of wrongs, it is devoted to kindness not to suspicions.

10. Agape—Rejoices not in inequity—It is never glad that others are wrong, nor does it expose the weakness of others. It does not gloat, it is gladdened by goodness.

11. Agape—Bears all things—It always protects, never retaliates, is active, not passive, as it endures and forgives.

12. Agape—Believes all things—It always gives the benefit of a doubt. It is not gullible but loyal and charitable without suspicions or cynicism.

13. Agape—Hopes all things—It never takes failures as final, or despairs, even where there is ingratitude. But this hope is based on truth not vague dreams

14. Agape—Endures all things—It cannot be conquered. It endures not passively, but actively, the key being *perseverance*.

Can there be any doubt that Agape as defined in 1 Corinthians 13 is of a supernatural nature, something that cannot even be understood, let alone become manifest without God's intervention through His grace? The capacity for this fulfillment of love is like salvation itself, a gift from God that cannot be earned or obtained in any other way. Just as faith, through which salvation is given, occurs at various levels of intensity in the newly born again Christian, so does this Agape also come initially in various degrees of perfection, although always far from perfect. Only Jesus had the totally perfected Agape, but just as with faith, Agape at any level of perfection, in order for it to grow, must be continuously nurtured through prayer, through His Word, and through subordination to God's will. Jesus was Agape in the flesh, as He is now also in Heaven. God is love, according to John 4:16. He is, therefore, the personification of those fourteen aspects of Agape. That is why when we are born again and receive the Holy Spirit (God) in our hearts, we have Agape, although again, not a perfected Agape. Yet, praise the Lord, we are assured that Agape in us will continue to grow toward perfection through His promise in Philippians 1:6. "—that he who began a good work in you will carry it on to completion until the day of Jesus Christ." It just can't get any better than that!

—76—

The Third Commandment

Thou shall not take the name of thy Lord God in vain, for the Lord will not hold him guiltless that taketh His name is vain" (Exodus 20:7, Deuteronomy 5:11). Taking the Lord's name in vain, do we really know what that means? Of course, who doesn't? It simply means cursing or swearing and using His name Jesus and His title Christ as part of a vocabulary of profanities, whether it is disparagingly or in anger, hate, frustration, despair or just casual or habitual vulgarity. Surely such utterances are sinful as are all things contrary to God's will. But is that what God had in mind when He carved that commandment on the stone tablets He gave to Moses? I think not, at least not the principal meaning.

The ancient Hebrews took this commandment most seriously, so much so that they would not even speak His name under any circumstances, both out of great reverence and out of fear that somehow God would interpret it as having been spoken in vain. It has been said that in some of their writings, they would even leave a blank space instead of writing His name. Or as was more common, they substituted a tetragrammaton in the text instead of His name. Thus, by never speaking His name, its pronunciation was lost. All that is left are these four letter equivalents of His name, in Hebrew transliterated as JHVH, IHVH, JHWH, and YHVH & YHWH. Adding vowels to these, they became pronounceable and became equivalent names such as Elohim, Yahweh, and Jehovah etc. But we now know Him by His new name Jesus Christ, which is quite pronounceable, yet no less sacred.

In order to get a better understanding of what our Lord meant by the commandment, let us examine the Hebrew meaning of a couple of key words, "take and vain." The word "take" appears 587 times spelled out in the King James Version of the Old Testament of which there are thirty-five different Hebrew words that have been so translated. The applicable one here in Exodus 20:7 is *nasa*. It has a variety of related meanings with the first listed being "accept," with "take" being effectively the last meaning, just before "wear" and "yield," which obviously do not fit the context of the message. The word *nasa* can also mean, advance, arise, suffer to, extol, etc. Only one other of the thirty-five words for take includes the word "accept." That is the Hebrew word *lagach*, which is identified as having a very wide application, such as, "bring, buy, carry away, seize etc." All of the other thirty-five Hebrew words translated as "take" have meanings such as "seize, gather, join, fetch, plunder, catch, consume, pluck, pull off, capture, chase, rob etc." From this analysis and for reasons developed herein after, it seems reasonable to conclude that this particular word *nasa* is used because of its first and prime meaning "accept" in the sense of taking. I believe this most closely relates to what our Lord intended, "Thou shalt not *accept* the name of thy Lord God in vain." At this point, this subtlety may seem like nit picking, but read on, it may not be.

The word 'vain" appears eighty-six times in the King James Version of the Old Testament, and there are fifteen different Hebrew words that have been so translated. The applicable one here is *shav*. According to Strong's concordance, it means, "desolating, evil, ruin, guile, and idolatry, as false, deceptive, lying." The other words translated as vain have meanings such as, "come to naught, lead astray, employer, devoid of cost, reason or advantage, deceive, hallow, wind empty, untrue, worthless etc."

As we can see, the Holy Spirit chose appropriately which of the many related words He would use in composing this commandment so that it could be understood as was intended. It is the unfortunate choice of the translations along with the limiting capacity of the English language to convey the nuances, the subtle distinctions of certain words that cause many of the difficulties associated with really understanding God's Word. Knowing that this would happen, our Lord took good care to carefully preserve, with great accuracy, the originally inspired writings of the Scripture in the original Hebrew and Greek language.

The Three Thieves

A few weeks ago I completed a paper called "Making a Case for Salvation." In it I mentioned the thief on the cross whom Jesus took with Him to paradise, and how that event has so often been used to illustrate the "just in time" adequacy of coming to the faith, and for not necessarily having to provide evidence of faith through repentance obedience and works. As soon as I had finished that paper, it came to me that Scripture had something more to reveal to us if we would but examine the narrative regarding the thieves more carefully. What it was did not come to me until I prayed and pondered the matter for quite some time. What follows is the result.

There were really three thieves with which Jesus was involved during those last hours of His physical life. There were three crosses erected that fateful day. Jesus was in the middle cross and an unnamed thief was on each side of Jesus. In spite of the incredible agony they were suffering, they managed each to converse with one another right past our suffering Savior, with one of them also railing against Jesus. How strange it was that the other defended Jesus. Listen to the conversation as recorded in chapter 23 verse 39–43 of Luke.

> *"And one of the malefactors which were hanged railed on Him, saying, If thou be Christ, save thyself and us. But the other answering rebuked him, saying, Dost not thou fear God, seeing thou art in the same condemnation? And we indeed justly; for we receive the due reward of our deeds; but this man hath done nothing amiss. And he said unto Jesus, Lord remember me when thou comest into thy kingdom. And Jesus said unto him, Verily I say unto thee, Today shalt thou be with me in paradise."*

Here we find in these few short words from the second thief:

1. A fear of God.

2. A recognition and confession of his sinful justly condemned life.

3. An admission that Jesus is God.

4. An acknowledgment of Jesus as Savior who had the ability to forgive sin, and of his own need for a Savior to deliver him from the eternal consequence of his sins.

5. An understanding that Jesus was innocent, that this was innocent blood being shed on the cross.

6. An acceptance of physical death along with recognition that there was another "life" to come.

7. A belief that even though this was God beside him, and, therefore, had the power to save His physical life as well as theirs if He chose to, He did not do so for reasons the thief may not have understood, but did not question or challenge, but accepted through faith.

All of these obviously heart-felt thoughts were converted into spoken words while the thief was dying in excruciating pain, worse than any of us can imagine. It was hardly a time when one would casually reminisce or engage in intellectual discussions or even think to connive. It was a time when only what is truly in the heart cries out.

Now let us examine what the other thief had to say, "If thou be the Christ save thyself and us." The NIV translates his words to be "Aren't you the Christ?" Save yourself and us." Scripture says he was railing against Christ, but quotes only this part of the tirade. Why should he be railing against this other poor recipient of Roman justice? Clearly meanness rebellion and anger had not left his heart, and so he found it necessary to strike out at whom ever was nearby. There apparently was no hint of repentance or acknowledgment of guilt in him. All he wanted was to preserve his mortal life. There is no hint of any concern for his eternal life as there was in the words of the other thief. Did he believe that Jesus was the Messiah as He claimed? He probably had heard the same rumors about Jesus, as had the other thief. He may have even believed them. He spoke as if he did, but the difference was, that if he believed, it was all head belief, but he had no heart belief, or anything that could be called faith. Romans 10:9, 10 tells us:

> *"that if thou shalt confess with thy mouth the Lord Jesus, and shalt believe in thine heart that God hath raised him from the dead, thou shalt be saved. For with the heart man believeth unto righteousness and with the mouth confession is made unto salvation."*

The saved thief believed in his heart, and with his mouth he confessed that Jesus would be raised from the dead, and was thereby saved. The other thief seemed to express a belief with his mouth, but his heart was empty of any faith. How many who call themselves "Christians" are head believers, but not heart believers, believers who merely profess with their mouths but do not possess in the heart the saving Christian faith?

What about that third thief, the one who may have been scheduled to hang on that middle cross, that most fateful day ever to occur on earth? Most likely it was Barabbas. Scripture tells us that Barabbas was scheduled for execution and that it was by demand of the Jewish leadership that Pilate freed him instead of Jesus. Scripture also tells us that Barabbas was a murderer and an insurrectionist. Would he, therefore, not also have been a thief, at least in the sense that he took someone's life? How ironic it is that Pilate, for fear of Caesar, although he found Jesus innocent of *any* crime, condemned Him on the basis of His being an insurrectionist in that He called Himself the King, yet he released Barabbas, a genuine convicted insurrectionist, merely at the urging of the Jewish leaders. Is this evidence of the cunningly deceptive power of Satan, ruling the hearts of his own? Yet here, with this monumental and seemingly victorious decision from Satan's perspective, this was, in fact, a procedure exactly in accordance with God's plan regarding the means by which God would save man.

Try to imagine Barabbas' frame of mind when the jailer came for him that day. He had every reason to believe that he was about to be taken to Calvary to be nailed to a cross. Yet, when the chains that held him to the cell wall were removed, what did the jailer do? He simply handed him a small document and said "get out of here, you are free."

Huh? Free? What do you mean free? You mean I can just go? No punishment? Perhaps the jailor even explained that someone else was to die in his place. Nevertheless, we can be sure that Barabbas wasted no time leaving that place. Scripture tells us nothing more about him or what became of him. Curiosity very likely caused him to seek a fuller explanation. Perhaps he even came to realize that his life was saved by God Himself who died on the cross in his stead. Could he have realized that he was the only one in the history of the world, past, present and future, that was saved from earthly punishment by the substitutionary death of God Himself? Probably not! Although something must have stirred his heart if he thought about it at all, most likely having witnessed the three hours of daytime darkness, along with the earthquake, and heard that the "veil of the Temple was rent and torn from top to bottom." (Matthew 27:51). Unless he took off to a far unknown place or died soon after, he must have heard stories about this Holy Substitute by whose death, he lived. He must have been aware that something extremely special had occurred of which he was the most fortunate beneficiary. Perhaps he even heard that among Jesus last words was *tetelesti* translated "it is finished" or more appropriately, "paid in full." This may have triggered in him a most profound connection with Jesus as he reexamined that little document the jailor gave him as he left the prison. On it was stamped *tetelesti*, "paid in full" the evidence he would always carry with him to prove to the world that his debt to Caesar had been paid in full, and that he could never again be convicted or imprisoned of that same crime. But *had* he paid in full for his crime? Of course not, and he well knew it. It was Jesus who paid in full, just as our precious Substitute paid in full for all of the sins of those who believe on Him. Although those who believe, and through faith are saved to eternal life are eternally grateful, and live lives that demonstrate that gratitude, isn't it possible that the witnessing and partaking of this incredible event led Barabbas to a condition, whereby he too might have been saved eternally?

Scripture causes us to believe, such as through Matthew 7:22, 23, that many of us will be surprised on that fateful day of the Lord, surprised as to where we end up, as well as the fate of others whom we thought would have had eternal destinies different from what will then be revealed. I urge you to look with great concern to your own destiny, so that you will not be tragically surprised.

—78—

The Bulls of Bashan

What an exciting title. Reading this paper looks to be about as exciting as sitting and watching your faucet drip. But what if you were to discover that Jesus' suffering on the cross was added to by the bulls of Bashan? If you are a believer, no doubt the title has suddenly become a little more interesting.

The Holy Spirit through David, in Psalms 22:12, 13 quotes our Lord Jesus as saying "many bulls have compassed me, strong bulls of Bashan have beset me around. They gaped upon me, with their mouths, as a ravening and roaring lion." This was written a thousand years before Jesus died, and seven hundred years before crucifixion was invented by the Medes, and later perfected by the Romans as the ultimate means of inflicting a most torturous death. Even so, there can be no doubt as one reads the whole Psalm that it is autobiographically composed in advance, telling of His tortured thoughts as He would experience them while hanging on the cross. Those who are committed to Jesus, who love Him and who seek to know more thoroughly His Word as He gave it to us for our learning, are no doubt eager to understand the significance of these verses.

As I began researching for their meaning, I intended to write only a short paper on the results of my efforts. I had hoped to merely "connect a few dots," that is, to search the Scripture and other sources for relevant allusions, connect them into a coherent verbal picture, and then simply report my findings. However, there seems to be a bigger picture composed of many "dots," some directly and some indirectly associated with the subject. Some are very weird and even so spooky that they run way counter to common sense and generally accepted beliefs. Therefore, as components of a larger picture they defy being explained in a few simple sentences. Some "dots" risk being dismissed, avoided, or somehow rationalized into more palatable conclusions, as some early expositors chose to do. Some of these rationalizations and misinterpretations of Scripture remain as accepted parts of Christian exegesis and are especially a very staid part of Roman Catholicism. To have written here of the bigger picture, as I started to, reporting on all that I found, would have resulted in a paper so lengthy, and so complex and seemingly so absurd, that the simple answer to the subject question might well have been obscured. Yet, to write less is to be almost assured that the reader, absent all of the background, may be left unconvinced that he or she has been exposed to enough evidence from which to find agreement with the following conclusions. After prayer and reflections on the matter, I chose to write this relatively short version in both the hope and belief that those who do not accept the validity of what I've written will do as the Bereans did (Acts 17:11), and check the Scripture to see if these things be so. I believe that to do less will leave a large and potentially dangerous gap in a "believers" understanding of what really happened "behind the scenes" in the past, what is happening here and now, and what will be the great and final deception, the foundation of which is now being laid, as we continue into these end times. Scripture tells us much about this if we are willing to listen and to search. Wise observers have noted, and now even science is discovering, that we actually live in a simulated world much like a hologram, and that reality is actually in the unseen, multi-dimensional realm of the spirits. God, through the Scriptures, made this known a long time ago as He repeatedly said, "for those with ears to hear." Now, having gone through all of the "Fifth Amendment" rhetoric, let us see what we can find out about the "Bulls of Bashan."

Believe it or not, Bashan is mentioned sixty times in the Old Testament. It was the name of the region east of the Jordan River, which is, in part, today called the Golan Heights. It was known as good cattle grazing land and was the very land into which the tribes of Reuben, Dan and Manasseh chose to settle (Numbers 32:1–5). It was not the land west of the Jordan that God had sent them into, but He did allow them their wish, something their descendants, to this day, would deeply regret. (Numbers 32:33). Bashan was a kingdom and its king was named Og. We hear of him twenty-two times in the Old Testament but learn little about him, except that he and his people were the Rephaim, a remnant of the giants, also known in Hebrew as the "walking dead." These can be traced to Genesis 6:4 where Moses tells us:

"That the sons of God saw the daughters of men that they were fair, and they took them wives of all which these chose . . ." "There were giants in the earth in those days, *and also after that* when the sons of God came unto the daughters of men, and they bare children to them, the same became mighty men which were of old, men of renown."

It is popular belief today that this verse means something much different than a simple forthright exegesis clearly indicates. Somehow, the "sons of God" has been twisted to mean the "sons of Seth." To believe that angels can procreate is very strange and difficult to accept. But that is precisely what Scripture says. " Benc Ha Eloheim" *always* means *angels* in the Old Testament and this clear and obvious meaning was believed throughout the earlier ages as also recorded in such esteemed, non-scriptural literature as Josephus's writings, the book of Enoch, and "The Testimony of The Twelve Patriarchs." In Job 38:7 God himself says as He speaks of His initial creation ". . . and all the sons of God (Bene, Ha, Elohiem) shouted for joy." He didn't say some of His sons, but *All* of His sons. He spoke clearly of this event, which, of course, was long before Seth or his sons came along. Because God is truth, if the sons of Seth were somehow later included as some of His sons, He would have had to qualify that statement to make clear that all didn't mean *all*, but only those He created first.

It was in the fourth century when Julius Africanus, for political reasons, invented the Seth theory as a "comfortable" explanation for this strange event. He claimed that these sons of God were actually the faithful believers of the sons of Seth who inappropriately married the unfaithful daughters of Cain and then produced these giant monstrosities. For some reason, perhaps again political, Augustine embraced this clearly unbiblical stance, and it thereby became established in Roman Catholic dogma. Remember that it was also Augustine who chose to accept, for political reasons, origins, spiritualization or allegoricalization of the prophecy that Jesus would sit on David's throne.

Even Luther failed to recognize these false beliefs, and so they and others remain incorporated even in much of Protestant theology.

The word giant in King James Version comes from the Greek Septuagint *gigantes,* which does not mean giant, but "earth born." The Hebrew word is *Nephilim* from *nephal* meaning "to fall, be cast down, to fall away, desert," and also from *"Ha Gebborim"* "the mighty ones." They did happen to be giants, super human in size (fifteen to thirty feet or more in height, based on archeological finds and historical writings such as by Plutarch). They were also very violent and sinful. Every recorded ancient culture from Sumer, Assyria and Egypt, to those of the Mayans and Incas, along with the famous story of Gilgamesh, contains legends about half God and half man giants. The Greek Titans, such as Hercules are well known examples. Based on Scripture, one must conclude that much of this so-called mythology is more fact than fiction in its essence.

The Seth fallacy is easily demolished simply because there is no biblical evidence to substantiate it, and much to refute it. How and why, for instance, could simple human beings regardless of their faith or faithlessness, produce en masse, such monstrosities. No human mix regardless of the difference in ideology, color, size, or other diverse characteristics ever produced anything close to such beings as, "the mighty men of old." Of course, within any human groups we have considerable size ranges (4± feet to 7+ feet) but nothing close to what those things were. If the lines of Seth were so virtuous, why did they die in the flood? With only Ham and Shem and Japheth left to procreate, where did the Nephilim / Raphaim, who existed after the flood, come from? They were the sons of fallen angels as Genesis 6 clearly tells us! Why torture and twist these simple clear verses into totally unsupportable and false meanings! Some point to Matthew 22:3 as evidence that angels cannot have sex, because Jesus said "they neither marry nor are given in marriage, but are like the angels of God in heaven." This says nothing about the *capabilities* of angels, and Jesus also chose to limit His comment to "angels of God *in heaven*," not the fallen ones. Who knows, it might even have been the temptation of having sex with earth women, which is what Satan used to initially lure one third of the angels out of heaven. This type of mass luring into sin, is not without precedent in Scripture (Check out Balaam). Finally, let's look at Genesis 4:26. "And to Seth, to him also there was born a son; and he called his name Enos: then began men to call upon the name of the Lord." Why is the time of Enos, son of Seth, singled out as the time in which men began to "call" upon the name of the Lord? We see earlier Adam talking to the Lord and even Cain discussing his punishment with the Lord. Are we to assume that neither Adam nor Eve, nor any of their children until the grandson Enos, ever "called on the name of the Lord? There is something strange about this verse as translated. What we have here, some careful scholars recognize is a mistranslation, or as I see it, an unfortunate, out of context, choice of possible meanings of the word "call" from the Hebrew word *qura*. Rather than "call," *qura* can also mean accuse, quarrel, act in a hostile manner, the idea of accosting, berate, etc. It has been observed that this verse would have been better translated "Then men began to profane the name of the Lord." (Call something by the name of the Lord). Missler provides several venerated Hebrew sources that verify that more appropriate meaning of the verse.

Targum of Onkelos: ". . . desisted from praying in the name"; Targum of Jonathan: "surnamed their idols in the name . . ."; Kimchi, Rashi & other ancient Jewish commentators agree; Jerome indicates this opinion of many Jews of his day; Maimonides, Commentary on the Mishna, (a constituent part of the Talmud), A.D. 1168, ascribes the origin of idolatry to the day of Enos.

Let us also look at the root meaning of "Enos." It can mean mortal, desperately wicked, incurable, or woeful. This is not a very flattering or stalwart name, but it fits well with what appears to be the correct message of Genesis 4:26. Why all this emphasis on Genesis 4:26 and Enos? It is simply to further demolish the foolish and wrong idea that the "sons of God" in Genesis 6:4, could in any way be the "sons of Seth," the "good guys" who married the "bad daughters" of Cain to produce the Nephilim. It was with Enos and his generation where idolatry began! We know it began somewhere and spread across the whole earth, because only two chapters later "God saw the wickedness of man was great on earth" Genesis 6:5. It is in Gen 4:26 where God chose to tell us how it got started.

Hopefully, we have established the fact that the residents of Bashan were the Rephaim and that they were the remnant of the sons of fallen angels as Genesis 6 clearly tells us. We can now also see why God ordered them and other tribes of similar lineage such as the Anakins (Numbers 13:33) to be utterly destroyed as He Himself destroyed those who polluted the earth before the flood. These were called the walking dead, because their souls after physical death had no place to go. Jesus died for all mankind, not these satanically caused beings. Scripture records that Jesus dealt a great deal with demons. The area in which He did as part of His ministry was heavily populated with them, there being as many as two thousand in the one man called Legion. All of the demons knew Him and knew His mission (Mark 5:7). They also knew their ultimate destiny, as they complained to Him that their time had not yet come. (Matthew 8:31). The area in which He was ministering, was at that time called Gadara, and the ten-city region was then called Decapolis. This was the area formerly called Bashan. Given that demons seem to tend to be territorial, it's not any surprise that He found them there in great numbers, because that is where their bodies perished at the hands of the Hebrews many centuries earlier. Could the troubles that inflict that region even today, be in any way related to the continued presence of the Bulls of Bashan? Remember also that it was through the tribe of Dan, who lived there, that idolatry first entered the nation. What is idolatry? It's worshiping idols. Does a wooden or stone figure in itself inspire worship? Of course not! It is the principalities and powers behind it who have the powers to do signs and wonders and limited powers to answer prayer that give the figure the illusion of divine power, while in fact it's the devil's power.

Scripture doesn't tell us much more about demons. We know they exist and that they seek to occupy human bodies, unlike angels who are capable of appearing in human form without invading human bodies. We know that Satan and his angels are the "kings, principalities and powers" behind every world power as well as all false religion and idols. We learn this from Daniel 10, and Isaiah 14, Ezekiel 28, and other references. Why is this fact revealed in such a strange manner? It speaks of multiple levels of governance behind the scenes. Perhaps each principality and power consists of a fallen angel and a host of its offspring demons, the dead disembodied spirits of the Nephilim and Rephaim, dead because they have no hope, and no redemption, their fate being the same as that of their spiritual father, Satan.

Recognizing that these demon spirits exist, and that some of them originated from the Raphaim who populated Bashan, it's not difficult to safely conclude that Jesus was describing these demons, when He called them the "bulls of Bashan." Why bulls? Why not? Of course He could have called them the demons of Bashan, but the area of Bashan was known for its cattle, and Jesus many times used locally identifiable items, places or circumstances as metaphors through which to add a timely clarity to His message. Probably their actions were very bull-like, or perhaps He used this expression simply to get us to search out its meaning. All seven letters to the seven churches in Revelation 2, 3 contain such "local color" of that time. The subject verses here suggest that these roving demons, agents of Satan, perhaps even the ones Jesus purged from their former hosts, saw our Savior, their sworn enemy, seemingly helpless and defeated hanging on the cross, and sought to increase His agony by taunting Him and doing whatever was in their power to hurt Him. Praise God, what they saw as His ignominious defeat was, in fact, His victory over Satan, over sin, and over death and, thus, it became our blessed salvation!

I mentioned at the beginning that a broader understanding of this episode at the cross goes well beyond that moment, and may profound ramifications regarding what is happening in this world right now and what will happen in the near future of these end times. These are issues about which I have pondered as to whether or not to discuss in this paper. I'll not delve into them anymore than to refer to another strange scriptural passage as a clue, and then present it without any further substantiation of my suspicions. Those interested can add to the above and connect their own dots from these references and from an understanding of what is available from news articles and science journals that frequently, though unknowingly, allude to these end time events. It is my contention that, especially in the unseen world, Satan is preparing his last and greatest deception, and all of the principalities and powers, fallen angels, demons and evil spirits are being trained, programmed, and lined up to put on the show that might even fool the elect as he continues to set up his counterfeit kingdom. Is it possible that the U.F.O.'s and all that is related to them are manifestations of these beings as they deceive and prepare to deceive? As one digs deeper into the matter, there seems to be compelling evidence that abductions by U.F.O.'s are real. Could this in some way be related to Satan's grand and final deception? In this prophesy of the final days, Daniel 2:43 mentions a very strange thing regarding the final days. ". . . and where as thou sawest iron mixed with miry clay, they shall mingle themselves with the seed of men; but they shall not cleave onto another, even as iron is not mixed with clay." What can that possibly mean? Mingle themselves with seeds of men? Who are themselves? The seeds of man is clearly either mankind itself or perhaps more literally the male sperm. Scripture makes no allowance for any space aliens but it does as mentioned above, point to fallen angels and evil spirits are having these "mingling" propensities. Could this have anything to do with the presumed present day activities of U.F.O.'s and Satan's final grand deception?

It is evident that the Holy Spirit scattered numerous clues regarding all of this in the Scriptures for us to find, to connect, and to arrange into a coherent picture of how this deception might take place. Proverbs 25:2 tells us that "It is the Glory of God to conceal a thing, but the honor of kings to search out the matter." It is doubtful that this is referring to kings as rulers of the nations. Except for David and Solomon, there is no evidence that any of the Hebrew kings, much less any pagan kings, did much searching out of God's concealed things. However, in Revelation 1:6 it seems to provide clarity to this proverb. It tells us that those who have been redeemed, He "hath made us kings and priests unto God and His Father . . ." If you are born again, you are one of the kings God whom expect to search out what He has concealed. I urge you to try it. The quest is exciting and discoveries exceedingly rewarding.

—79—

Was It Murder He Wrote?

The crucifixion of Jesus of Nazareth is no doubt the most widely publicized death ever to have occurred in the entire history of the world. Yet from the viewpoint of who did it and why, it may well be the most misunderstood act of all history. The fact that there was a historical Jesus and that he was crucified seemed to be universally accepted as evidenced in numerous secular historical writing as well as the Scriptures. However, who did it and why, are subjects of considerable misunderstanding that has directly resulted in almost two thousand years of the most tragic and painful aspects in history.

True Christians, well versed in the Scriptures, know with certainty the answers to these questions and are entirely comfortable with their understanding of them. Sadly, however, to the nonbeliever, the real answers seem either mythical, naive, stupid or foolish, and certainly not logical or believable. Even less informed Christians have difficulty with the issue. Were it otherwise, if blame had not been so wrongly placed, the many tragic flows of history might have been averted. The New Testament narration of the crucifixion and the events leading up to it, as well as those immediately following, are found clearly described in the four Gospels. It may come as a surprise to some, but they are also recorded and described in Old Testament books written hundreds, if not thousands, of years earlier than the actual event! Therefore, in order to really understand the issue, there is only one reliable source, and that is God's own words, the Holy Bible. In using this divine source, context is of paramount importance. Many of the worst tragedies of history have been the result of taking the Lord's words out of, or in the wrong, context. It is only through the ingestion of the *whole* Word of

God, the entire Scripture, that it is possible to draw any safe and sure conclusion regarding God's plans and where we are in them. God's words, as recorded in the Scriptures, must have been taken in the context of the whole Scripture. Anything less is very risky and, as history illustrates, potentially tragic. With this in mind, let us see what the Bible tells us about why He died.

1. Was this an execution? Yes!

All four Gospels tell us that Pilate gave the order, though reluctantly, to have Jesus executed (Matthew 27, Mark 15, Luke 23, John 19). Pilate saw no guilt in Jesus, and much preferred to release Him, however, he bowed to what seemed to be political expediency; today we would say he chose to be politically correct, rather than right.

2. Was this premeditated first-degree murder? Yes!

The Gospel cites numerous occasions when certain of the Jews tried to kill Him and failed (John9:58). In (John 11:50, 53) the chief priest, Caiaphas, speaking of Jesus, reasoned "that it is expedient for us, that one man should die for the people and the whole nation perish not." "Then from that day forth they took counsel together for to put him to death." The evidence clearly indicates that they wished to and intended to murder Him. Because "the scepter had departed from Judah," they lost the legal right to administer capital punishment. Therefore, murder, or some manner of subterfuge, or murder by proxy, was the only way to be rid of Him. Why did they want to be rid of this man, this great healer, this wonderful messenger who was totally free of sin? For several reasons. First He claimed to be God (John 8:58). "Verily, verily I say to you, before Abraham was I Am" * This claim to be God was blasphemy and punishable by death. Second, the people were beginning to follow Him in great numbers and believing in Him. This posed a serious threat to the whole priestly class, who valued their status, more than their faith. And third, rapidly expanding legions of His followers were seen as a growing threat to the political stability of the region as well. The main policy of

Roman rule was maintaining law and order, peace and stability. Anything that threatened to disrupt this was dealt with harshly. While they deeply resented the Roman yoke, they feared its power and the wrath that would be readily dispensed on them, should unrest and sedition by the people begin to spread. This, of course, is how they finally prevailed on Pilate, when they said in John 19:12. "If you let this man go, you are not Caesar's friend: whomsoever makes himself a king speaks against Caesar." Clearly, Jesus had also admitted to Pilate that He was the King, certainly at least of the spiritual realm.

Scriptural evidence indicates that Pilate believed Jesus, yet with insufficient moral strength to overcome the curse of expediency and "political correctness." Thus we see that a conspiracy to murder Jesus did exist. The murder was planned and executed in the only way the conspirator could safely and legally achieve it. That is, to conjure up a false scenario as to His guilt in order that the Roman authority would perform for them this evil act. In doing so, they violated almost every precept and rule of both Roman and Jewish law.

Among the great tragedies that a gross misunderstanding of this biblical account has caused is the conclusion that the "Jews" killed Jesus. While a casual and narrow reading of the Scriptures might lead to such a conclusion, in the context of the Whole Scripture, this can be seen as extremely misguided. As we have seen, the Jewish leadership alone sought to kill Him because of His popularity and great following, which although not yet spread much beyond the local region or into Gentile country, was growing rapidly among the Jewish population. He healed thousands, and on two recorded occasions, He drew crowds of many thousands who marveled at His words and His miracles (Mark 8, Luke 9:10–17). Where, therefore, would this "multitude" have come from who sought to kill Him? His blessed fame, which had spread throughout the regions, was built on His goodness and His reputation as a healer, a worker of miracles, a true man of God. To a growing number in and around Jerusalem, He was being revealed as the Messiah Himself. The fact is that there was no "multitude" seeking to kill Him. Both Matthew 26:47 and Mark 14:43 speak of ". . . great multitudes with swords and staves, from the chief priest and the scribes and the elders . . ." came to arrest Jesus at Gethsemane. "From the chief priest and the scribes and elders" suggests that the multitude was made up of this leadership class and their immediate agents, employees and followers. Luke 22:52 elaborates with ". . . and captains of the Temple" while, John in 8:18, describes them as " a band of men and officers from the chief priest and Pharisees." Thus it is evident that this was a select group of the ruling hierarchy along with what was most likely the Temple guard and others of the ruling cadre, and not "the people" or "the Jews." Some very credible scholars believe that along with their immediate followers and some "paid" false witnesses, the total number of Jews who called for His crucifixion could have been as few as thirteen members of the Sanhedrin. This might have constituted an adequate number of that ruling class counsel, and would, therefore, have been able to officially speak for the whole. Thus contrary to common belief, it seems clear that "the Jews," the multitude as is commonly believed, were not the ones who called for His death, but instead a very small hierarchy of the threatened religious ruling class who were responsible.

3. Was it Manslaughter? Yes!

How can this be if, as noted above, it was first-degree murder? Manslaughter is defined as the unlawful killing of a human being without express or implied malice. However, the term is also applied to the act by someone not in control of his or her own faculties or not aware of what they are doing. In Luke 23:34, Jesus said from the cross, "Father, forgive them, for they know not what they do." If you take the Lords Word seriously, as I do, then enough has been said. The case for manslaughter has also been confirmed by the highest authority, both by the Victim and by God Himself.

4. Was it Suicide/Deicide? Yes!

Now we are getting down to the meat of the real cause and effect of this memorable event. One only needs to read psalm 22 and Isaiah 53 written five hundred to a thousand years before the event, to realize that the Lord told us very clearly that He had this whole act in mind and for a specific purpose, even before the beginning of time. The whole issue here was articulated with remarkable insight by Socrates to Plato when he observed to the effect, "Perhaps a just and righteous God can forgive sin, but I don't see how." Surely that was a seemingly unsolvable dilemma. God, whose very nature is pure love and righteous, as well as justice, cannot be other than righteous and, therefore, cannot tolerate sin in His heavenly domain. Neither can His just nature let sin go unpunished, yet all mankind is sinful. Not one is, or ever was, free from sin, except Jesus (Roman 3:9–20).

Man's sins had to be punished and righteousness appointed to Him before he could possibly enter God's presence. But who or what on earth could provide this? Surely animal sacrifices could not, nor could any man by his own works or "goodness" do so. How many good deeds could cancel a bad one? How many truths could cancel a lie? How many whatevers could cancel murder or rape or theft or any other sin? Who would keep score and decide? Could keeping seven out of the Ten Commandments give us a possible passing grade into heaven? Obliviously not. If one thinks long and seriously about this dilemma, one must eventually arrive at the same conclusion, as did Socrates. There is no earthly answer. Yet somehow, the vast majority of mankind blissfully tend to conclude that somehow as long as the balance of good deeds during their lives exceed the bad deeds, God will welcome them. *Nothing* is further from the truth!

God, however, in His infinite wisdom and love, had solved the problem before the beginning of the world by choosing to enter His own creation and pay once and for all, for all the sins ever committed or ever to be committed by those who believe in His earthly manifestation, Jesus, and believe that He *did* die for our sins, was buried and rose again, ascending back to heaven. How perfect the solution! How profound this act of love! How incredible the reward for such a simple acknowledgment of His magnificent act! Here is the evidence, that this was in fact deicide, God Jesus clearly arranged for His own death. He took on all sins of the world and then deliberately died on the cross that all who believe on Him could be cleansed by His blood and have eternal life. Careful reading of the events reveals that Jesus was in charge throughout the whole process leading up to and including the crucifixion. He chose the very time and process by which it would take place. That it was all preprogrammed is evidenced by this fact that in doing what He did, He fulfilled more than three hundred Old Testament prophesies, predictions authored by the Holy Spirit from outside of time and space before the world began, detailing every aspect of that momentous occasion and the events leading thereto.

In summary, we can see that the world's most well known individual death was, in fact, from an earthly perspective, an execution, as well as first-degree murder, manslaughter and suicide. Those who are born-again Christians, however, know with certainty that it was deicide, the ultimate expression and proof of God's love. This was, in fact, the purpose and cause of all history, the crescendo of the greatest orchestrated symphony the world has ever known, the opening of the gates of heaven for those of faith. To the world it was an unfortunate tragedy, the death of a great teacher, perhaps it was a "day of infamy." But again, to the believer, it was the most blessed event of all blessed events. To explain it properly would take volumes, volumes already written many times over. To the world, no suitable explanation is possible and to the faithful none is required. All that matters is that He died and rose again! Praise the Lord!

---

*In the vernacular of the day, especially in the Scriptures when Jesus speaks, when a statement started "I say unto you," it was meant to be an important statement of fact. When "verily I say unto you" preceded, it was a profound fact. And when "Verily, verily I say unto you" was the preface, this was an exceedingly profound, undeniable fact. Here our Lord is triple exclaiming that He is God, the I AM, the God of the burning bush (Exodus 3:2). The Pharisees, in fact all Hebrews, knew that "I am" was, in fact, the true name of God as He had revealed it to Moses in Exodus 3:2.

—80—

The Crucifixion—The Rest of the Story

Virtually everyone in the civilized world has heard of Jesus and is aware of the fact that He lived a long time ago and was crucified. The highlights of this story are also known to almost everyone, as a result of the holiday traditions that refer to the event. Those who have read the New Testament, whether believer or not, know even more about the highlights of the event, while the truc believers, for whom it is also an emotional, as well as spiritual issue, know and feel far more. For they have both agonized and celebrated over our Lord's most glorious sacrifice. But I wonder how many of even these really know the whole story, the whole extent of the pain and suffering that our Lord went through in order that we might be spared eternal hell. I don't know, perhaps most do know. I am too young in my faith and too inexperienced in association with other believers to know what the depth of understanding there may be regarding this matter. However, because of the momentous significance of the event and the fact that the New Testament does not tell the whole story, I feel compelled to tell what I believe I know of the rest of the story so that all may know just how much pain and suffering our Lord endured that day for the love of all who would believe in Him.

Picture if you can, this humble, non-descript man bound and dragged before pompous priests and magistrates. *"He hath no form nor comeliness; and when we shall see him, there is no beauty that we should desire him"* (Isaiah 53:2). His captors were Roman soldiers, a special breed, trained for dealing with condemned prisoners, but in ways that we today cannot and do not even want to imagine. This particular prison was especially appealing to the sadistic nature, which their particular work encouraged. He was accused by "holy men" of being an enemy of their Caesar as well as a man who claimed to be God. Remember, the soldiers saw Caesar as their god, not some lowly Jew! Therefore, surely this was a just subject on which to demonstrate their best technique in the art of punishment and torture. In keeping with the theme of the accused, they fashioned a crown of thorns. These weren't little prickers found on raspberry bushes. These were long, sharp, tough and needle-like thorns found on the acacia bush. When smashed down on His head, they tore straight through to the skull in a number of places. Before this, He was beaten about the face by the temple guard. Then His face was covered and He was beaten again, causing severe bruising. Sometime, as part of this ordeal, His beard was ripped off His face. Thus He became unrecognizable. Then He was flogged. The usual flogging consisted of thirty-nine blows on the back with a whip containing several thongs about twenty-four inches long. At the end of each thong were attached bits of metal, glass, and bone. These would rip the skin off along with muscle, exposing raw bone and causing much bleeding and often death. Given the hate that seems to have prevailed among His tormentors, the flogging most likely exceeded the usual thirty-nine blows, because this was a Hebrew limit, not a Roman one. *"I gave my back to the smiters and my cheeks to them that plucked off the hair: I hid not my face from shame and spitting"* (Isaiah 50:6). *"As many were astonished at thee; his visage was so marred more than any man, and his form more than the sons of men . . ."* (Isaiah 52:14).

Dramatizations and renderings generally depict Jesus struggling to carry the cross on the way to Gethsemane. Most likely, however, it was only the crossbar or patibulum, as it was called. The vertical portion was most likely already at this usual place of crucifixion. Even today there can be seen rectangular holes carved in the rock into which these timbers may have been set. The patibulum weighed about seventy-five to one hundred pounds and could have readily been carried by a healthy man. However, Jesus was no longer able to manage this as the Scriptures record.

Crucifixion was invented by Persians around 300 to 400 B.C. and perfected by the Romans as the most painful long-lasting torture imaginable. We get our word "excruciating" from that form of torture. It was far more than simply being nailed to a cross. It was very skillfully designed to cause the maximum amount of pain over the longest period of time. It was the wrist that was nailed between the ulna, radius and carpal bones. Thus, no bones were broken and the wrist structure in that area was strong enough so that it would not rip apart and fail to support the body weight. The feet were spiked between the second and third metatarsal bones, again where body weight would not rip it out. The spiking was done in such a manner that the knees were bent, causing the victim to "stand with bent knees," an impossible and painful stance for anyone to endure for more than a few moments even with his feet on the ground. In this position, one could neither stand the pain of raising the body up against the spike in the feet nor let the body sag and rest with the weight on the wrist spikes. Yet, both were necessary intermittently in order to breathe. At best, exhaling completely was impossible. This would result in hypercardia, while the efforts required to breathe caused severe tetanic-like muscle spasms and eventual death by asphyxia. This could all last for hours or days, depending on the strength and health of the individual.

> *"I am poured out like water and all my bones are out of joint: my heart is like wax; it is melted in the midst of my bowels. My strength is dried up like a potsherd; and my tongue cleaveth to my jaws; and thou hast brought me into the dust of death. For the dogs have encompassed me: the assembly of the wicked have enclosed me: they pierced my hands and my feet. I may tell all my bones: they look and stare upon me. They part my garments among them, and cast lots upon my vesture."* (Psalms 22:14, 18).

Note this incredibly graphic description of the agony of one dying on the cross (pierced hands and feet) and what the sufferers are saying on the ground. The dividing of His garments and casting lots on His vestige, which was an expensive, seamless robe too valuable to tear apart and divide among them. The last observation is the same as recorded in the New Testament by an eyewitness (John 19:24). However, Psalms 22 was written at least 970 years before the crucifixion and approximately six hundred years before that form of punishment had been invented! Also, Isaiah wrote this detailed description of the event 690 years before Jesus was born!

Read carefully Isaiah 52 and 53; it defines exactly why Jesus died as eloquently and understandably, better than any other version in the New Testament!

From what has been briefly summarized above, it is most evident that this event, this torture and death, was extraordinary, vicious and violent and clearly meant to extract the maximum of pain and suffering. Our dear Lord knew this and could have ended it at any moment and in any way He wanted too. Yet, He suffered in silence and even prayed to the Father for forgiveness of His tormentors saying that they didn't know what they were doing. What has been described is only the physical pain our Lord suffered. Having been made sin, the accumulative sin perpetuated by all mankind past, present and future, the spiritual pain of this horrid burden on the soul of Him, who had never known sin, must have been beyond all possible understanding.

Note: For a very important additional insight regarding our Lord's most horrible of all suffering in order that our sins might be cleansed away, see paper entitled: Biblical Myths, Myth #4.

—81—

Walking Out the Door

This message is only for Christians who are truly born-again. John 3:36 says, "He that believeth on the Son hath everlasting life." It doesn't say will have, but has right now, and from the very moment he or she received the Holy Spirit by God's grace through faith in Jesus Christ our Lord and Savior. One who is born-again is in a non-stop continuum of everlasting life. It doesn't begin when the body stops functioning, it exists now and forever!

After the heart sends its last surge of blood through the arteries, when the tabernacle in which one has been housed begins its final decent into the dust from which it came, it will be like walking out the door into a glorious new world. It will be like the butterfly finally leaving its cocoon and soaring out into the incredible expanse of the heavens. Nothing of consequence will be lost or missed. All that will disappear is that old, sinful, fearing, pain racked, aching and apprehensive confinement called the body. Good memories and feelings, joys and love will all be intact and even sharpened. But filtered out of the now free soul/spirit will be all of the worldly cares, troubles, sadnesses, angers and anxieties.

As the saved one moves through that last doorway, that narrow passage through which only a few can pass, there will be a greeting of joy from an angelic chorus, and loving congratulations from those souls who arrived earlier. Then, just beyond the congratulators and the angels, will be the Great bema seat judgment. From there it will be our Lord and Savior who will provide the official greeting as the saved one gratefully kneels before Him, receives his or her crowns if any, and then places them at His feet. For here will be the climax of all that is precious and worthwhile when He is heard to say, "well done my good and faithful servant."

Again, "He that believeth on the Son hath everlasting life:" There is no death for those who receive the grace of salvation, for salvation means having been saved from death. This is what Jesus' death and resurrection already accomplished. At some point, the ones who are "saved" simply walk out of the confinement of the body and into the limitless Godly expanse of eternity without missing a beat. Paul, in 1 Corinthians 15:55 exclaims rhetorically with the questions, "O death, where *is* thy sting? O grave, where *is* thy victory? There is neither sting nor grave for the saved. Oh, the flesh will stop being a living organism and revert to dust. But even so, God has a file on every genetic code, and one day He will simply recall the numbers and recreate each body as it was at its prime. At His appointed time, He will return each soul/spirit to its original, but then perfect body. However each body will be eternally incorruptible clothed in God's light as it was with Adam and Eve at the very beginning. Each will be transcendent and multi-dimensional as is He. All will see Him as He is, and will be with Him forever in the New Eden.

So from now on, and especially as you are headed for the "door," remember the words of the Holy Spirit as recorded in 2 Timothy 1:7, "For God hath not given us the spirit of fear; but of power, and of love, and of a sound mind." This we know, that through faith, we are saved, and through salvation, the need to fear "the door" has been vanquished.

—82—

Transcendent Love

Does love transcend physical death? Many who experience intense love for another ask this question and pray that it does. For the born-again Christian who will spend eternity in the ultimate loving atmosphere of heaven, it is perhaps a most uniquely relevant question. This is because love, God's unique divine love, exists in the heart of every true believer in Jesus. It is God's love reflected off the regenerated soul back to God and to all whose lives are touched by His grace. It is this returned love of His children for Him that is the principal purpose of His having created mankind in the first place. As His children, we also love each other, again with His love, the only real love.

However, in the most blessed of His children there is a very special love between husband and wife. The Holy Spirit through Paul in Ephesians 5:24, 24 directed thusly: "Therefore women should love their husbands as the church is subject unto Christ, so let wives be to their own husbands in everything. Husbands love your wives even as Christ also loved the church and gave Himself for it;" When this kind of love truly manifests, it is of course a supernatural unconditional love. This love is expressed and detailed most exquisitely in 1 Corinthians 13. It is when this love exists in a heart that the question of its transcendence becomes of greatest concern. The thought that it may end at the grave is disconcerting, and we seek assurance that this very special love will continue throughout eternity.

In Matthew 22:30 Jesus tells us "For in the resurrection they neither marry nor are given in marriage . . ." This must be a very important message because the Holy Spirit has chosen to repeat these words in Mark 12:25 and again in Luke 20:35. Thus it is evident, that marriage, as one experiences it here on earth, does not exist in heaven. However, neither this verse, nor any other that I am aware of, speaks one way or the other regarding the transcendence of this love. Although the blessed union where the ". . . two shall become one flesh" (Ephesians 5:31) is broken due to the death and corruption of the flesh, love is *not* of the flesh, but of the soul and spirit. We are led to believe that we will retain our memories, and that even our bodies will be returned to us in incorruptible perfect form. Surely love, which is the purest most perfect form of Godliness anyone can have, must be the most deeply etched aspect of our memory and of the substance of our soul. Therefore it must *also* cross the barrier into heaven. We know that in heaven we will be united with, recognize and have memory of, those friends and loved ones who are also there. (2 Samuel 12:23, Luke 16:22, 30) Because of this, one could conclude that this special love, in fact all Godly love, which we now carry in our hearts, will be part of us forever. We can also expect that in our perfected eternal state, we will feel more powerfully and gloriously the love others have for us, as will our love be ever more profoundly felt by those we love. Why should it be otherwise? How could it be otherwise? Heaven's very atmosphere is love. God is love; God is in us here on earth, and will be in and around us forever. From the moment we committed to belief, faith, trust and obedience to our Savior, and we were born-again, His love has been in us. What we have done with that love, where and how we have used it, is an expression of the principal substance of our eternal being. How can it be otherwise than that we carry this into eternity?

—83—

In Defense of Jacob

While it was Abraham who was called from the idol worshiping people of Ur to be the first of God's chosen line leading to David and then to Jesus, it was his grandson who sired the twelve sons who became the twelve tribes. These then were the ancestors of those, who four hundred years later became the nation bearing his God given name, Israel. With the exception of Moses, Scripture records as much or more detail about the life and person of Jacob than any other Old Testament character. However, as these details are narrated it seems more often than not that an image is formed in the mind of the reader that this was a truly unsavory character, very unworthy of his position in the Messianic line. Superficial reading of his actions seem to depict a sly, unscrupulous bargainer when he gets Esau to trade his birthright for a bowl of red pottage, and a deceiving scheming liar when he receives from Isaac the blessing meant for Esau. He is again branded as a cold heartless and faithless bargainer even with God when he is at Bethel. Then when Laban tricks him into marrying Leah instead of Rachel, the reader cheers this apparent bit of retribution. Then again he appears to connive and cheat Laban out of his herd as he prepares to leave Haran. This is followed by what seem to be acts of defiance as he wrestles with an angel, and evidences of cowardice as he runs and fears retribution first from Laban and then Esau.

Thus, at least from my limited exposure to commentaries and the opinion of others, Jacob is popularly viewed, to varying degrees as a hardhearted, unregenerate, liar, coward and schemer, as well as a selfish, covetous, self-absorbed opportunist. There is but one exception that I know of and that is found in "The Genesis Record" by Henry Morris. It is from this book from which I have drawn a number of the items of defense that are herein presented. I've heard it said that perhaps the Holy Spirit has included these "insights" into his character in order to give us all hope. Because as it is said, that with Jacob as bad as he was, if God can forgive him, He surely can forgive anyone. Perhaps after reading what follows, some may conclude that there is a totally different message here. Perhaps it is that we tend to be too hasty in making moral judgment that is in condemning others long before we have sufficient evidence and facts on which to base such conclusions. We may also find it somewhat humbling, as it well should be, that our quick condemning conclusions about people are often wrong and that it is our own of-this-world nature that is more faulty than is the subject of our scorn.

So why would God choose Jacob to father the nation and the line from which our Savior would enter the time and space of His own creation? Of course, the same question could be asked regarding Judah, Rahab, David, etc. on down to the entire Messianic line. Yet for some reason as noted above, Jacob seems to stand out in the minds of many as one of, if not the lowliest, of characters. A closer examination of the Scriptures will, I'm certain, shed a more favorable light on this father of nations. In so doing, we are likely to find not just what has already been suggested above, but also a number of other valuable lessons for ourselves, which of course is the principal purpose for studying the Holy Bible. Based on what I believe the Holy Spirit has put in my heart and shown me through His Word, it seems about time, nearly four thousand years after his passing, to more closely examine what Scripture *really* has to say about Jacob. I suspect that the ancients knew him better and had a much more favorable perspective of his life than do present-day pastors, teachers and expositors. This defense of Jacob will seek to expose the unwarranted biases, misunderstandings, and translational errors that have combined to slander and darken the name of a truly great and honorable man of extraordinary faith. While it may not seem so by the length of this paper, in the interest of brevity, I have only referred to, and not quoted most of the Scripture verses relevant to the discussion, except in special cases. I trust that the reader knows the story well and/or will read along in the Scripture as I try to make this long overdue defense of Jacob.

Scripture tells us that after being barren for twenty years, God's promise was fulfilled in that Isaac's wife Rebekah conceived. We are informed that she had twins, and that they fought while in her womb so violently that she asked God why this was so. To this He replied that there were two nations in her womb and that the younger would be over the older (Genesis 25:23) At birth Esau "the hairy one" came out first, followed by Jacob "the heel catcher," clinging to Esau's heel. From Genesis 25:23 it is clear that God intended that Jacob the younger be preferred rather than the first born, Esau. It was the custom that the oldest son should inherit a double portion of the estate and also become the head of the family when the father died. In this role, he would have full authority as well as responsibility over all political, economical, educational, spiritual and social matters. In this case, however, God intervened by choosing Jacob. Clearly this was due to the extremely important task that God had assigned this family, the carrying on of the Abrahamic covenant.

Thus we see that even before they were born, God had already chosen Jacob to carry on the Messianic line and had made this known to Rebekah. We are told that God loved Jacob and hated (loved less) Esau before they were even born (Malachi 1:1–3, Romans 9:10–13). Why? How could He make such a strong conclusion before they even had a chance to prove themselves? By now we all know that God is outside of time. Past, present and future are all known to Him. He knew from before the beginning of time exactly what each would think, feel and do every moment of their lives. He knew then, as it is with all things, that you would be reading this at this very moment. Therefore He knew which one of the brothers would be better qualified for His purpose, and on that basis made the choice as He revealed it to Rebekah. One may make the case that both were poor choices and that He seemed to have been stuck with choosing the least inadequate. That is true not just in this case but in everything God does through mankind. For we are all hopelessly corrupt, weak and inadequate for anything God has in mind. "There is none righteous, no not one" (Romans 3:10) On balance, Jacob was no worse than any of us, but God selects whom He will and molds them into what they must be so that He can work His will through them. All of Scripture, as well as our individual Christian walk, is but one continuous example of God's molding the hopelessly inadequate into doers of His purpose. On this basis, Jacob was no worse than any of us. In fact, as this paper will reveal, contrary to popular opinion, he was considerably more righteous and honorable than most.

It is evident that Isaac greatly preferred Esau to Jacob from the beginning to at least well into his old age. Esau was a strong, virile man's man, a great hunter and active outdoorsman, while Jacob stayed close to home and to Rebekah, perhaps cooking, doing household chores and tending to the herds. Genesis 25:27 calls Jacob a "plain man." Plain in the Hebrew is *tau*, which also means perfect, or undefiled, complete, pious, or mature, the same word God uses to describe Job as, "a perfect and upright man, one that feareth God and escheweth evil" (Job 1:8). As part of our case for Jacob, this is a most important clue, one completely missed due to what appears to be a broadly unfortunate translation into the English versions of the Scripture. The King James translates *tau* as "plain," the new American Standard as "peaceful"; The New Living Translation refers to Him as "the kind of person who liked to stay at home"; the NIV calls him the "quiet man," the Douay Rheims Version says, "Jacob, a plain man dwelt in tents; and the Catholic St. Joseph Edition describes him as ". . . a settled man who stayed among the tents." How strange that none of these versions give Jacob credit for what I believe God wants us to know about him. Couldn't they even have more correctly translated *tau* as "undefiled, pious or complete" instead of "plain"? It would seem that they all had drawn conclusions about him that prevented them from focusing on anything but the most negative or bland interpretation of God's very complimentary word *tau*. Surely this one point by itself does not justify such an assertion. However, before we are through, I believe that the case will have been made both for the translator's bias as well as for the fact that Jacob was far more righteous and of higher moral character than that with which he is credited by most biblical teachers and expositors.

Esau on the other hand, seems to fare much better in terms of how "history" views him. He is depicted as a strong macho man, the "apple" of his father's eye. Yet also, he has taken on a victimhood status, with Jacob as the victimizer. This somehow seems to negate the fact that Esau was an unrepentant profane person and fornicator (Hebrews 12:16) He also took two Hittite wives. Marriage to pagans was expressly forbidden as noted numerous times in the Scripture. In spite of all of this, Isaac much preferred Esau to Jacob and had every intention of giving Esau both his blessing and his double portion inheritance, with all the power, authority, duty and responsibility that it represented. He intended this even though he must have known, as did Rebekah and Jacob, that it was contrary to God's pronounced plan (Genesis 27:7).

It must have been exceedingly disturbing to both Rebekah and Jacob to see and live with this on-going situation, this obviously strong partiality by Isaac for Esau, this blindness to, or acceptance of, Esau's transgressions as well as his obvious unfit nature as Isaac's spiritual successor in the God chosen Messianic line, as promised by the Abrahamic covenant. Under these circumstances, are not their subsequent actions perhaps somewhat more excusable than they might seem at first? Was there not some justification in their desire to see God's will done, and in fearing that without their intervention Isaac would surely thwart God's will and do the wrong thing perhaps even to his own damnation? In our pious hindsight we might say that they should have left matters to God, that it was not their prerogative to take matters into their own hands, but to let God handle it. Anyone reading this, who hasn't done what was right in his own eyes rather than seeking God's way innumerable times, let him cast the first disparaging remark. However, here as in everything, we also know that God knows all things and therefore He knew what they would do. Of course, He doesn't condone lies and deceit, yet in this case, He allowed this to happen and used it for His purpose, as He has shown us He has done many times in the Old Testament.

First there was the birthright. Scripture tells us that Jacob had made some soup and Esau came home after a long, strenuous day hunting, being very hungry. Jacob, in what must have been a somewhat joking manner, offered him a bowl in exchange for his birthright, never expecting Esau would agree. Surely this issue had been discussed between them before. It's very likely that the differences regarding this matter of the birthright where well known as was Esau's disdain for its value to him. It is also very unlikely Jacob would have denied him the soup had he said no, nor that Esau could not have found something else to eat had that been the case. The message here is not one of any trickery or slyness on Jacob's part, but a disdain on Esau's part for the birthright. They both knew that while it provided a double portion of inheritance, it also carried with it not only economic benefit, but also spiritual, political and protective responsibility for the whole family. Esau was obviously the type who had no desire for responsibility, but preferred his freedom instead. Jacob, of a totally different temperament, and knowing that it was right with God, was ready and willing to assume those responsibilities. As far as the economical benefits, no doubt Esau saw himself as fully capable of easily acquiring all he needed by other means. Furthermore, the Scriptures provide no evidence to support the idea that Jacob was greedy and thus sought material gain from the birthright. Jacobs's primary interest in the birthright was the officiation of the duties and responsibilities to him rather than to Esau, as he knew God had ordained.

Next, in Genesis 27 we have the infamous scene that begins when Rebekah plots to get Isaacs principal blessing for Jacob, when she realizes that he is about to give it to Esau. It would seem that at this point, 138-year-old Isaac was blind and ailing. Probably expecting that his death was near, he had decided that it was time now to convey the traditional patriarchal blessing to his sons. These were to be the father's final and prophetic statements having Godly endorsements. We know, as did they, that the Abrahamic Covenant in the form of a blessing had been intended for Jacob, but we see that because Isaac so loved Esau over Jacob, that he had every desire and intention of giving that blessing to Esau. Perhaps because of senility in his old age, he had forgotten God's word when his sons were born. Or possibly being so far removed from his direct involvement with God over the many years, he had forgotten what happened on Mt. Moriah. It could be that he had drifted from his faith and believed that his own judgment was superior to some, now faint memory of divine direction he had once received. Clearly, any pleading to Isaac Rebekah may have made on behalf of God's expressed will in the matter, had no influence on him. At any rate, a horrible event was about to take place and she was bent on preventing it and in making things right.

It is evident that Jacob was a reluctant participant in this deception with Rebekah as she took on the role of planner and expeditor of what she believed was God's will. Of course they both knew that its success would be God's will fulfilled. Jacob may have even tried to dissuade his mother, telling her to let God handle it, while she in turn persuaded him that this means of achievement was God's will. Before one judges the ensuing actions too harshly, one should recognize the urgency and serious nature of the situation. Within a few hours, a profound and irrevocable tragedy was about to occur. All her life she had known of the Abrahamic covenant and its great importance. For seventy-three years both she and Jacob, and surely Isaac had known that God intended that Jacob would be the one to carry it on. Now God's will was about to be thwarted and her dear husband was about to commit an awful hell-assuring sin, the sin of willful disobedience to a personally delivered directive from God! Who of us can say that under these circumstances, they would not believe they were doing God's will, and would be willing, if they even thought about it, to risk God's condemnation for such a single act of deception in exchange for, if nothing more than, the deliverance of a beloved husband and father from a certain spiritual death. Perhaps one may choose to see this differently but one must, nevertheless, give these two the benefit of any doubt that this may be what they saw and believed. If one feels that these deeds should not have gone unpunished, consider this: Rebekah never again saw her beloved son Jacob, nor he his mother. Isaac lived, perhaps better stated, was alive, for another fifty-five years, certainly blind and probably sick and ailing in many ways, which probably made just being alive a punishment. And, of course, Jacob spent the next twenty years under the yoke of a heartless, deceiving selfish master, serving faithfully while being tricked and cheated far more and longer than any earthly sense of justice would have considered appropriate. He also suffered fears of reprisals from both Esau and Laban. Jacob did not get a "free ride" out of this, even though I see him as having done nothing other than being an obedient son to his mother and a reluctant participant in a deception.

Nevertheless, the deception worked, and Jacob received Isaac's blessing. Scripture teaches that such a blessing, like a vow or oath, could not be revoked even though it was given under deceptive circumstances. This is a very serious issue and one worth careful consideration in our own lives. It is a lesson we should all learn. This blessing as with any vow, oath or pledge, which in God's view is a sacred promise, could not, once given, be retracted. It was his binding, irrevocable word. Apparently trickery or ignorance of circumstances under which it was given was no excuse or basis for revocation. Surely, this is an important message for all of us today. Your word should always be your bond, trustworthy and sacred. Scripture tries to teach us this a number of times. For example, in Judges 11, Japhthah, a son of Gideon, became another of the judges over the children of Israel. In order to obtain God's assistance in destroying the Amorites, he vowed to sacrifice to God what so ever came to greet him as he returned from battle. But it was his daughter, his only child, who came forth. He had to keep his vow. Scripture even points to Pagan culture to hammer home the scary significance of vows. In Daniel 6:8 we find King Darius, being tricked into a decree, which is another form of vow or oath, under which Daniel's enemies sought to have him killed by means of the lion's den. Daniel was highly esteemed by Darius who was grieved over the consequences of his decree, but even as sovereign king, he could not rescind his own vow. Another such case is found in the book of Esther 3:8–12, when Haman tricked King Ahasuerus (Xerxes the first) to issue an edict (vow, decree) that all Jews within the entire empire were to be killed. Even he could not rescind his own decree whereby other means had to be found to save the people. These are a few good examples of why we are so forcibly admonished by Jesus Himself in Matthew 5:34–37 to *never* swear to anything when He says, "but I say to you swear not at all, neither by heaven, for it is God's throne: nor by the earth; for it is His footstool: neither by Jerusalem; for it is the City of the Great King. Neither shall they swear by the head because you cannot make one hair white or black. But let your communications be yea, yea, nay, nay for whatsoever is more than these comes of evil."

Now back to the case of Jacob. After things cooled a little, Isaac realized that God had intervened, for he trembled very exceedingly (Genesis 27:33) because he knew, or now remembered God's will. So he repented and called Jacob back, blessed him again with sincerity and told him to go to Padan aram to Rebekah's brother Laban to seek a wife, and not from the pagans as Esau had done. Here again we see evidence of Isaac's backsliding. Just as Abraham had arranged for Isaac's wife, so should he have done for both Jacob and Esau. It was his duty. With Jacob now about seventy-three years old, this action by Isaac was long overdue. Instead, at this later date, he simply sent him off to find his own wife from a family where he could not even be certain that there was an eligible woman. Had he done his duty, perhaps both Esau and Jacob would have married appropriately.

But now, it appears that Esau may have been planning to kill Jacob, so Rebekah, out of fear, sought to hurry him on his journey. Thus, with little preparation he left home alone without companion or beast, with only what he could carry on this treacherous five-hundred-mile trip. It was supposed to be only for a few days' stay there while Esau cooled off. Little did he know that he would remain there twenty years, nor did she know that she would never see her son again. There is no evidence that Jacob ever gained any material benefit from his purchased birthright, or that he ever sought it. Probably, however, some sixty years later when he and Esau went "home" to bury their father, whatever estate there was then, they divided as per custom. Both by then were wealthy and had little need for more. Jacob nevertheless did have the birthright and as such carried with him the political and spiritual power and responsibility, as well as, of course, the all important blessing of the Abrahamic covenant that God had intended him to have and that God later reiterated directly to him more than once.

There is another item of interest here worthy of note that I've not seen in any commentaries. Isaac gave Jacob two blessings, first when he thought he was giving it to Esau, and the other a short time later when he had finally recognized God's intervention and his own failure as a faithful steward. It would seem that when he thought he was blessing Esau, he offered what he intended to be the Abrahamic covenant blessing, but he only gave part of it. As recorded in Genesis 27:28–29, he said, "Therefore God give thee of the dew of heaven, and the fattest of the earth, and the plenty of corn and wine; let people serve thee, and nations bow down to thee; be lord over thy brethren, and let thy mothers sons bow down to thee; cursed be everyone that curseth thee and blessed be he that blesseth thee." This is a very important and prophetic part of what God promised Abraham, as history has surely proven. Yet Isaac left out the vital part of the covenant that he then proceeds to transfer in his subsequent blessing to Jacob in Genesis 28:3, 4 where he says "And the God Almighty bless thee, and make thee fruitful, and multiply thee that thou mayest be a multitude of people and give the blessing of Abraham to thee, and thy seed with thee, that thou mayest inherit the land wherein thou art a stranger, which God gave unto Abraham." Why did God choose to allow His message to be bifurcated in this way; and why did the Holy Spirit describe this episode in such detail if there is not something more and significant for us to learn from it? One might conclude that it was merely the result of a sick, old, confused and wandering mind. However, the Holy Spirit would have no reason to record the detail if that was the case. Perhaps Isaac, who knew from God what the destiny of each of his sons would be, sought to soften Esau's by giving him a little bit of the good that he was supposed to convey to Jacob. What harm would it do to give Esau the fatness of the earth, to have nations and brothers bow, and to be blessed by others while having his enemies cursed. After all, Jacob would still get the Promised Land and be blessed with the seed of Messianic line of Abraham. This is only conjecture on my part, but it has some support in what follows. In Genesis 27:39, forty in response to the bewailing Esau, Isaac gave him the only blessing he legitimately could, that which was truthful because it was God inspired. The King James Version of these verses, however, is flawed, as also is the 1592 Geneva Bible, flaws strangely perhaps to reflect what Isaac wanted to say and what the translators thought he would have said. Where they say, "Behold thy dwelling shall be the fatness of the earth, and of the dew of the heaven from above," it should say, "thy dwelling shall be *away* from the fatness of the earth etc." The St. Joseph textbook edition translates his blessing as "*without* fruitfulness of the earth shall your dwelling be," while the New Living translation says, " you will live off the land and what it yields, and the NIV says "Your dwelling will be *away* from the earth riches, and *away* from the dew of the heaven above." That is not the kind of blessing a father wants to give his favorite son! Should one contest this alternative translation by still favoring the King James, it should be noted, that the land into which Esau actually went later, which was called Edom, was in fact harsh and hilly and clearly *not a fat*, fruitful land. And the Edomites did live by the sword in violence with, and generally under, the subjection of Israel. They would however, at times, "shake off" the yoke just as the blessing foretold. We know that all Scripture, all sixty-six books penned by more than forty writers, is the inspired integrated work of the Holy Spirit as its single author. Therefore, the subject verses in their original Hebrew were also the work of the Holy Spirit. We also know that God as the Holy Spirit was at work in Isaac. But we had here Isaac, momentarily at least, being the earthly man at odds with the Spirit in him, seeking a better deal for his beloved son Esau as he gave the first blessing. It was Esau to whom he thought he was speaking. Later it was the Holy Spirit irresistibly speaking through him as he gave the real Esau his less than desired blessing. Is it possible that this blessing would have been less harsh had he not tried to restructure Gods plan? Surly there were other bountiful lands available had God chosen to assign them to Esau. Again I've digressed.

So again, we see Jacob traveling along on foot with only a backpack with some money, proceeding on a five-hundred-mile journey from Beersheba to Haran across a foreign and dangerous land with "only" God as his guide and protector. Finally, after weeks of travel, he arrives at Laban's home seeking a wife with nothing to offer in exchange but himself. There, God immediately fills his heart with love for Rachel, a younger daughter of Laban. As Scripture reveals he spent the next fourteen years in servitude to Laban for the privilege of being able to marry her. Although, beyond the simple fact that he must have loved her totally and genuinely with God's love, we know little more of this love story. However, the fourteen years of servitude during which he allowed himself to be cheated, deceived, and humiliated all for the sake of his love for her, should make this the signature love story of all times, exceeding even that of Ruth and Boaz, which is regarded as the classic love story. After serving the fourteen years, he still had no material wealth of his own with which to care for his growing family. This led to six more years of servitude under a complex agreement through which a portion of his shepherding efforts were to accrue to his own account. Even here Laban deceived, twisted and modified their agreement to favor himself. A superficial reading of this portion of the story again seems to cast Jacob as the heavy, the schemer, and the bad guy.

But, before we look under the skin of this episode, let's go back to the long trek from Beersheba. Remember it was also to Haran that Abraham had traveled more than a hundred years earlier when he left Ur some six hundred miles to the south. It was there also where he left his family and finally decided to begin obeying God by journeying to the Promised Land. Laban and others there in Haran were the descendants of those relatives Abraham had left. After traveling the first seventy miles out from his home in Beersheba, on probably the third day, Jacob spent the night at a place called Bethel "the house of God"; the same place where earlier, Abram had built an altar (Genesis 12:8, 13:3, 4). It is also where God had appeared to Abram and later to Isaac. That night, Jacob also experienced a theophany in the form of a dream. This is the famous Jacob's ladder dream where he saw a two way stream of angels on a wide ladder that extended from the earth to heaven with our Lord standing at the top speaking to him (Genesis 28:12, 13). Here he heard what he had already known of the Abrahamic covenant. Here God related it to him directly so that there could be no mistake as to whom God had chosen to continue it and the Messianic line. Under these lonely, destitute and frightening circumstances, it must have been exceedingly comforting to hear God say, "I am with you and will keep you wherever you go and will bring you back to this land; for I will not leave you until you have done that and which I have promised you." Contrary to popular assessments of Jacob's spiritual quality, I interpret this to mean that from that moment on the Holy Spirit dwelled in him and remained in him pretty much for the rest of his life. Surely, this promise must have also given him great comfort and confidence, and sustained him and his faith under every trying and difficult circumstance for the rest of his life. Having the indwelling Holy Spirit, explains how he could have such a profound and lasting love for Rachel. It also goes far in explaining how he could remain so patient, diligent and loyal to his commitment to Laban for so many years. Remember, he was already around seventy-three years old when he arrived at Laban's door to begin his servitude, and eighty when he married Leah, and then Rachel and then started his family. Obviously, the sisters were much younger, being yet for some time in their child-bearing years.

Back again to Bethel, Jacobs's response to the theophany was to build a small altar as best he could, and to sacrifice to God what little he had, a drink offering of some oil. He then made a sacred vow to God (Genesis 28:20–22). This vow has been widely interpreted as some kind of a bargain he sought with God. This is because it starts with "If," that is, if God will take care of him, then this will be his God; he will erect an altar of worship and give to this God a tenth of all he receives. This "if" makes it sound like a cold business proposition, a bargain that Jacob is making with God; "If you do this I will do that" It hardly seems like a submissive commitment to God by a worshiping loving believer. Yet this makes no sense in the context of what had just happened to him and to what he already knew quite well since childhood regarding his God ordained mission. Now if we examine the Hebrew word *im* translated here as "if," we find that "it is widely used as a demonstrative," such as lo (see! Behold!) It can also mean, although, while, yet, nevertheless, verily, or since. So if we replace the "if" with an equally valid "lo," or since, the vow now becomes contextually appropriate and expresses a sincere gratitude and a love for God, which I believe, it truly was. What about us? John 4:19 says that we loved Him because He first loved us! Can't we allow Jacob the same privilege? When he said the vow, he was merely repeating what God had just told him, along with a response, which was a life long commitment to God through faith, and through that faith he was made righteous. How different is this from when we, who are born again, first came to believe the Gospel? Didn't we commit ourselves in some similar fashion to Jesus? In John 12:32 when Jesus says, ". . . and I, if I be lifted up from earth, will draw all men to me." Is this some kind of conditional or bargaining statement, because the translators chose the word "if"? Of course not! Neither was it when Jacob said it.

It is interesting also to note that Jacob is here offering to God a tithe, or a tenth of all he will ever receive. At that time we know of no obligation to tithe. Much later there would be under Mosaic Law (Leviticus 27:30). Before the time of Jacob, Scripture mentions such a thing, just once, that is when Abram gave tithes to Melchizedek. Perhaps Jacob even heard that from his grandfather, because he was already fifteen years old when Abraham died. Or, and this is provocative, he may have heard of it from Shem, who didn't pass away until Jacob was sixty-five years old! Many scholars speculate, and a Hebrew tradition claims, that perhaps Shem was the mysterious Malchizedek. It certainly is likely that Shem would be a highly venerated personage having been the son of Noah, one of only eight souls to survive the flood, and the true father of the entire Semitic race. Who better to have been the King of Salem, later Jeru-Salem (Jerusalem)? I believe that here at Bethel, we are witnessing in Jacob a real and powerfully committed faith as well as a loving sincere appreciation and gratitude toward God. At that moment he did all he could do, he made the altar, sacrificed, and gave to God what must have been a significant part of his meager food supply. He then backed that up with the only other thing he had, his word in the form of a sacred promise.

Now we should look at the events that began taking place after Jacob's fourteen years of servitude under Laban (Genesis 30:25, 31:13). This is the speckled cattle episode, where again Jacob comes off undeservingly as the bad guy. During those fourteen years of servitude, Jacob had worked faithfully and loyally, greatly increasing Laban's wealth. Laban knew very well that it was the Spirit of the Lord that had been working through Jacob for his benefit all those years as he freely admits in Genesis 30:27. Jacob also here in Genesis 30:30 gives full credit to God for whatever good his efforts have produced. However, after all these years of servitude, Jacob had nothing of his own in material wealth with which to support his family if he was to leave Laban. However, the Holy Spirit did put it in his heart to leave and to return to his own land; but first he must accumulate a bit of wealth of his own with which to support his growing family, now consisting of eleven sons and an unnamed number of daughters.

When Laban asked what he wanted for wages, Jacob said he wanted nothing heretofore earned. Does that sound like greed, or a cunning soul speaking after twenty years of unpaid servitude? He asked only for a chance to develop his own herd from there on, for he knew that God would supply his needs. He agreed to continue serving Laban, but for doing so he asked only that all speckled cattle and goats as well as brown sheep yet unborn were to be his, while all of the normal animals would be Laban's. By being unwilling to accept any gift or wages, he was refusing to become indebted to this man whom he knew to be an ungodly, cheating, selfish schemer. This deal, however, provided God an opportunity to now bless Jacob materially as he had Laban through Jacob, and to do so in a way that could only be seen as divine intervention. The agreement, that Jacob structured, was ridiculously unfavorable to him and eminently favorable to Laban, in fact Laban well recognized this, at least initially. Here Jacob not only restricted himself to keeping only the off-colored animals yet to be born, but he further limited what was to be his as being only those off-colored animals born of normally colored animals. That is, he would not even claim any of the off-colored cattle born to off-colored animals in Laban's herds. To the world that is to Laban, his sons, and any other, who knew of it, this must have seemed to be the working of a senile old fool. Most likely, Jacob became a laughing stock of all who heard of the agreement, and Laban must have felt secure that he would have Jacobs's servitude for the rest of his days, because under these conditions Jacob would never have enough to leave.

At this point, in the defense of Jacob, it is appropriate to step back and recognize the significance of this particular event. Jacob was no fool. He knew where he stood with God, he knew the ludicrous nature of the agreement; he knew that only through God's intervention could this be turned to his favor. He had faith because he was this "plain" man this *tau,* in reality this "perfect undefiled, complete, pious, and mature man" as God Himself had described him in Genesis 25:27 as previously noted. This is simply another expression of Jacobs's great faith, which somehow seems to again get obscured, this time as a result of a misunderstanding regarding the "striped rods." When we look carefully under the surface of these events, we see a man endowed with the Holy Spirit, which does not seem to come and go, but remains with him to the end of his 147 years, even as he then confers those awesome prophetic blessings on his fourteen sons.

Now regarding this issue of the striped wooden rods. Those already critical of Jacobs's character are quick to again condemn him for some new kind of trickery or deception as he placed the rods in the water troughs. Thoughts turn to the likelihood that this was some ungodly pact with the devil. A kind of hex or marking, or prenatal influence on the cattle to make them somehow by seeing stripes, have more striped or speckled offspring. There is no scientific evidence that supports this as being effective, nor that this was his intention! There is, however, a very compelling explanation that in no way dishonors him. Jacob had been a shepherd nearly all of his eighty-nine plus years and was no doubt a keen and intelligent observer in animal husbandry. He knew from all these years of observation about the reproductive abnormalities that are explained today by what is known about genetics. That is, that although a species may have certain dominant traits, there are lesser traits that will occasionally manifest to produce somewhat modified, in this case, off-colored offspring. These variations, however, are normally far too infrequent to be counted on to generate significant numbers of such mutants. So what possessed Jacob to make such a grossly unfavorable agreement? We need only to look in Genesis 31:7–13 to see that he was not alone in this. God was the planner and Jacob the obedient, trusting and faithful servant. Note here also that he again gave God all of the credit for the miraculous results. It was God and He alone, who influenced the higher than "normal" ratio of mutants!

It is well known today, and as evidence indicates, it was also known in ancient times, that certain woods, such as the poplar, hazel and chestnut, do contain substances that act as fertility promoters or aphrodisiacs in animals. That is just what Genesis 30:38, 39 says, that when the flocks come to drink from the watering trough containing the rods, they did conceive. The word "conceive" is a translation of the word in Hebrew *pacham* meaning "to be hot" thereby suggesting that they more readily came into "heat" and thereby increased their sexual activity. Verse 39 says that they ". . . conceived before the rods and brought forth cattle ring streaked, speckled and spotted." This suggested to the casual reader that somehow the rods caused more mutants. The fact is that the aphrodisiac simply cause a larger number of total births, while as Scripture clearly says, it was God who influenced the genetics to better favor Jacob. Therefore what Jacob was doing from the practical earthly perspective, would normally have benefited Laban far more than himself, absent of course God's intervention. It should be noted that had he been trying to somehow "mark" the animals, that is to cause them to breed mutants by simply their seeing or being near stripped wooden rods, why wouldn't he have scattered them around the whole area and made fence (or fences,) posts and railings out of them, etc.? But instead he put them in the watering troughs where, and only where, the secretions from the wood could be ingested. Clearly, it was the nondiscriminating effect of the aphrodisiac in the wood that he had over the years observed or heard of, which he employed to increase the general herd population, not any underhanded, deceiving, or deceitful scheme of a twisted, morally defunct mind to somehow benefit only himself.

Next we read in Genesis 30:41 that Jacob separated the strong of the herd from the weak and only placed the rods in the water where the strong would drink. The result of this would have been the same distribution of normal to mutant offspring as already noted, again a situation much more favorable to Laban. The difference here is being that he was attempting to strengthen both herds equally by causing only the stronger to proliferate at a faster rate. This, of course, was good stewardship (or shepherdship) on his part, providing absolutely no advantage to himself. Again however, it was God who influenced the gene selectivity that in the end caused Jacob's herd to grow faster with strong healthy cattle. Then in Genesis 30:42 we find he did not apply the rods to the water when the weaker cattle drank. This of course would cause less proliferation of the weaker cattle thus benefiting all of the herds. But here again God intervened, by strengthening Jacob's herd and allowing Laban's herd to get progressively weaker. It seems that now was pay back time for Jacobs's faithful hard labor and honesty, and for Laban's greed and wickedness. When seen in the light of these facts, where is the substance to the allegations that Jacob stacked the deck or did anything dishonorable? It was God, not Jacob, who arranged the cards to give Jacob the winning hand, all in accordance with His own righteousness and justice. The problem here for us as we more informatively read this episode is two-fold. First, is that God's intervention here is more subtle than is often the case in other stories, and the second, that by now our minds have become so prejudiced against Jacob that whatever transpires is somehow construed to be just one more example of his cunning, deceitful nature. We are accustomed to seeing God's work as very compellingly evident such as ninety-year-old Sarah being restored to fertility or Gideon's 300 routing 135,000 Philistines, or a parting of the Red Sea. Here, as in all aspects of Jacobs's life, God as the Holy Spirit in him was clearly at work during these events. But His fingerprints are so faint we must look most carefully in order to see them in all their glory and be less ready to jump to unfortunately wrong conclusions about Jacob.

The next item worthy of examination and discussion regarding this defense of Jacob is his flight from Laban. Here, the general conclusion seems to be that Jacob sneaked away in the night like a thief and a coward. Certainly he did leave without telling Laban, but he did so because God had directed him to leave and he knew that Laban would not have let him go with his wives and his cattle (Genesis 31:1, 2). Laban already coveted his now superior herd and had no intention of letting his daughters and grandchildren leave, even though they did belong to Jacob. Laban had grown sons and many men as well as friends to enforce this stay and would have used them to do so. This is evident from the fact that he did gather a superior force and go after Jacob with every intent of taking everything and probably killing Jacob, until God again intervened while he was en route. God warned him in a dream to not do ill to Jacob (Genesis 31:24).

It is interesting to note that before leaving, Jacob explained everything to Leah and Rachel. It is evident here (Genesis 31:4–16) that they both loved and respected Jacob and saw his righteousness as well as that of his actions and his cause. Furthermore, they deeply resented their father's deceitfulness and selfishness as well as his evident lack of respect and concern for them. We should also note that Jacob was meticulously careful to take absolutely nothing belonging to Laban, both for the sake of his honesty and also so as not to give Laban any legitimate excuse to go after him or to have any reason for retribution. Nevertheless, had God not intervened, Laban surely would have killed Jacob, or at least left him alone in the desert and taken everything.

So it was a frustrated and angry Laban who arrived at Jacobs's caravan wanting to take spoils but fearing the wrath of Jacob's God. Under the circumstances, all he could do was feign hurt feelings and disappointment that he had not been allowed to send them off joyfully and graciously. His one legitimate claim, however, was the theft of his idols, which Rachel had taken, but of which Jacob knew nothing. After searching the camp in vain and then going through the motions of fashioning a sort of non-aggression pact between him and Jacob, Laban left. Later when Jacob knew Rachel had the idols, he removed them from the caravan and buried them.

Even this little idol incident has a message, as does all Scripture, if we can only notice it. There are at least four possible reasons why Rachel decided to take Laban's idols, which were his religious figurines. Perhaps it was to spite her father, a pay back for his ruthlessness and lack of caring for his daughters. Or maybe she thought that the absence of the idols would be a sign or a motivation to lead him to believe in the true God. It could also be that she herself had some residual faith in the pagan beliefs she had been raised under before knowing Jacob. A fourth possibility is the one I lean to because of Genesis 31:14–16 and the following. It's possible that she considered them as symbols of inheritance and property rights that she might later use to claim that which she believed was being denied her and that she was owed. This idea gains some additional credence based on certain archaeological finds in the 1930s called the Nuzi tablets. The inscriptions on these tablets alluded to the idea that certain of these types of terraphim or idols were associated with such rights.

But for whatever reason Rachel may have had, Jacob would not allow them to remain with his family or with those under his control.

In line with this, it is useful to note that most surely Laban and most of the population in Pandonaram had heard of the God of Abraham, Isaac and Jacob, yet there is nothing in the Scripture to indicate that there were any believers. Even after twenty years of close association with Jacob and the power of the Holy Spirit in him as represented by his extraordinary fruitfulness, there is no evidence that Laban or anyone else became a believer. Jacob must have witnessed to his wives and children, but the surrounding idolater's influence must have made it difficult for him to be very effective. The subsequent actions and behaviors of his sons is adequate testimony to these influences and to the weakness of their faith, at least until their later years when they were in Egypt under Joseph. It's confirming to note that the last of eleven sons, Joseph, who was a child when the family left that influence, had by far the highest moral, spiritual qualities.

Looking at this from the other direction, we must give great credit to Jacob and our wondrous God who sustained him. Here was Jacob totally alone in his faith in a world where there were only idol-worshipping people. For twenty years through God's grace, because of the Holy Spirit in him, he resisted the inevitable temptations and remained faithful to the only true God. Only the invincible sustaining power of the Holy Spirit could have caused this. Think about this for a moment. If you are of the faith, consider spending twenty years completely surrounded by idol worshipers. Of course, most of us already live under these conditions. But we have our precious Bible as well as fellow believers, our church, our Pastor, our radio and TV evangelical programs as well as libraries and Christian book stores full of inspirational literature. Jacob had *none* of these. Remember also that these idols were not just benign figurines in the spiritual sense. There were real supernatural powers capable of delivering favors behind every one of them. Had there not been, they would have soon lost their attractiveness and there worship worthy qualities. Of course these powers were and are limited because they are satanic, but nevertheless they did, or did seem, to deliver enough in the material sense to keep the worshipers believing as they did.

Can any of us honestly say that we are certain that we would have been immune to any backsliding under the conditions Jacob endured? Put in this context, is it becoming evident that we are discussing a man whose stature should rightly be described a little more favorably than just "plain"(Genesis 25:27)?

Our next excursion into the heart of Jacob carries us with him through the mountains of Gilead as he continues his journey back to Canaan. As he drew closer to home, he realized that he must soon encounter another potentially very grave danger, that of a possibly very angry vengeful and powerful man, his brother Esau. However, as he began this next leg of his journey after parting from Laban, he was again met by a host of angles, just as he had more than twenty years earlier at Bethel. Here again God was assuring him and evidencing His protective powers. Jacob called the place of this encounter Mahanaim that means "Two Hosts." This would appear to signify the comforting fact that his strength to resist Esau was now greater than that represented by his militarily untrained shepherds and servants. However, he had no way to assess the physical earthly power that these angels could or would provide. He didn't have the benefit we have in these matters, as Scripture so generously provides. He couldn't know as we do that one day some 1200 years later, under King Hezekiah, one angel one night would destroy 185,000 Assyrian soldiers (2 Kings 19:35). This was, of course, but one of God's many protective blessings on Jacob's progeny, his ordained namesakes, and the Children of Israel.

Thus, when he suddenly learned that Esau was rapidly on his way to meet or intercept him with four hundred armed men ". . . then Jacob was greatly afraid and distressed" (Genesis 32:7). This is the first time it's been noted that Jacob feared, and also the first possible evidence of anything but a rock-solid faith in God. We might assume that the appearance of the host of angels and God's repeated promises to him should have precluded fear of anything. Perhaps for himself he had no fear. But he had the God-given responsibility of protecting his family. It would seem, however, that here for a short while he may have questioned his own understanding of God's promise when it came to earthly preservation. God had promised to never leave him until He had done all He said He would do (Genesis 28:15). However, Jacob already had eleven sons, and he had no way of knowing that it would be twelve tribes that were to issue from him. Perhaps he reasoned at that moment that the promise had already been fulfilled, that the promised seed and the nations that would follow had already been provided for, and that therefore his usefulness was over. At any rate, after a very beautiful heart-felt prayer (Genesis 32:9–12) he did what was customary and prudent under the circumstances by dividing the caravan into two parts so as to give one a chance to escape, while the other was engaging the adversary. Realizing their importance to God's plan, he probably put his sons and wives in the one that could escape. He also sent ahead gifts to Esau amounting to 580 animals, not as a bribe, but to show his brother that he was coming in friendship and not himself as a plunderer as perhaps Esau might well have reasoned. That it couldn't have been Jacob's intent to try to bribe Esau so that he would spare him is evidenced by the common sense fact that such a gift offered to an angry vindictive plunderer would only have whetted his appetite and made him realize what a great abundance of spoils awaited him.

Now, having done all that was prudent under these troubling circumstances, he went off, most likely back across the river to be alone, probably to again spend the night in prayer. But instead ". . . there wrestled a man with him until the break of day" (Genesis 32:24). What on earth was that all about? And what did the Holy Spirit want us to learn from His recording of this event? It is evident that this was another and most significant encounter with an angel. But perhaps it was not an angel in the usual sense, but in fact the Chief of all angels, the preincarnate Christ. This is probable because of Genesis 32:30 where Jacob says ". . . for I have seen God face to face and my life is preserved" Even Hosea in 2:3, 5 refers to this as the appearance of both angel and God. It should be noted that this was not an isolated Old Testament appearance of our Savior. His physical manifestation is recorded several times. He was one of the three angels who appeared as men to Abraham when he promised Abraham and Sarah a son, and also when He revealed His plan to destroy Sodom and Gomorrah (Genesis 18); He appeared to Moses at the burning bush (Exodus 3:2–6); He appeared to Joshua as

Captain of the Lords hosts (Joshua 5:13–15); and He was the fourth man in the fiery furnaces (Daniel 3:25).

But why did they wrestle? Perhaps we can get closer to the answer by examining the meaning of the Hebrew word here translated as wrestle. Wrestle appears only three times in the entire Old Testament. It occurs in Genesis 30:8, where Rachel speaks of having wrestled with Leah regarding conceiving children. Here the Hebrew word is *pathal* otherwise used to connote a "struggle," to be "morally torturous or forward, to show self-unsavory," but obviously not some physical activity. The other two times the word wrestle is used are both here in Genesis 32:24, 25. Here the word is *abag* the principal meaning of which is "to bedust, i.e., grapple (wrestle)." Thus to "bedust" or "grapple" are the stronger definitions. Certainly grapple is more in context with the narrative when we see that the meaning of grapple is to "hold fast, seizing or gripping, to grip, to hold close." At he end of this all night engagement the "angel" finally had to wound Jacob to get him to let go, to remove his grip. Here Jacob exhibits great strength, tenacity and perseverance, as he grabs onto the Angel and holds him all night rolling and twisting in the dust of the ground. The word "bedust" according to the Oxford dictionary means nothing more than to cover with dust. This is what they must have had all over them after a whole night of this activity.

What an exhibition of chutzpah by Jacob! What confidence, strength, faith and dogged determination this ninety-three-year-old, tired and weary and stressed man displayed! By comparison this makes Abraham's bargaining with God in Genesis 18, seem like juvenile bantering. Here he is alone in the dark desert intent on kneeling and praying to his God when he sees this figure in front of him. He clearly recognizes him from the first to be an angel of the Lord. He certainly has seen enough of them to recognize one when he sees him. So what does he do? He grabs onto him and tries to extract from him a blessing. From Scripture (Genesis 32:26) we only know the tail end of their all night conversation. However, the blessing was most likely central to it. The "Angel" surely could have ended the matter whenever he chose. But instead He apparently assumed not only a human form but also human physical limitations for their encounter.

It is evident that because of Jacobs's extraordinary strength and tenacity at daybreak, the "Angel" had to apply a bit of supernatural effort in order to break Jacob's grip. This seems to have been to slightly dislocate his thigh joint, which resulted in a permanent limp. Thus, Jacob actually prevailed over the "Angel" as far as the natural physical contest was concerned.

Couldn't it be that the episode was some kind of a demonstrative test much like God imposed on Abraham and Isaac on Mt. Moriah? Couldn't it also be the hand delivered message by God himself in a way acknowledging and rewarding Jacob for his lifetime of faithfulness, and now also validating and announcing his divinely ordained fatherhood of the family from which would spring the chosen nation and later the Messiah? For in the end, God pronounced him to be ". . . Israel, for a prince has thou power with God and with men and hast prevailed." I believe that "prevail" means far more than simply having won a wrestling match. Jacob prevailed spiritually over a lifetime of temptations and adversities and having never lost his faith and trust in God. The Hebrew word for Israel is *Yisrael* meaning "he will rule as God" and is derived from two root words *sarah* (to prevail to have power as a prince,) and *el* (strength, mighty, especially Almighty). Couldn't this also be a prophetic pronouncement relating to Revelation 7, where 144,000 are chosen and sealed, 12,000 each from twelve tribes of Israel, and then in Revelation 14 where they later stand with our Lord on Mt. Zion as He prepares to rule with them, as He will when He finally sits on the throne of David? Thus he was no longer just the supplanter or heel catcher, but he could now be called the "Prevailer, the one who fights victoriously with God," "A Prince with God."

To an observant reader of the whole of scriptural references to Jacob, it is evident that he spent much time in prayer and was a man of extraordinary faith and love of God. While he may not have, for a long time, fully understood all of its ramifications, he was, nevertheless, well steeped in the knowledge of the awesome responsibility God had placed on him regarding the Abrahamic Covenant. Certainly many of his prayers were prayers for guidance as to how to fulfill this responsibility, which must have been his major concern. At this particular moment he was particularly concerned about this, given the grave danger that he perceived may be galloping toward him from the south. Then suddenly here before him is at the very least, an informed and influential representative of God. What better opportunity would there be to settle this matter, to get answers to his questions, which may have been burning in him all his life, and to also go for broke in seeking a powerful, reassuring and lasting blessing that would carry him through to the end of his life? Thus it was that he boldly enlisted that incredible strength of will and tenacity that he had always possessed, even in the womb, as he decided to grab on to this physical manifestation of the One from above and to there settle that which had been unsettling to him all his life. His risky challenge succeeded. He received the blessing as well as a most illustrious immortal name, the name of a great nation, God's chosen nation that was to manifest some four hundred years later.

Beyond this episode, there is little more to be said in terms of "A defense of Jacob." Scripture records several more events in his life but none worthy of mention in this context. It is evident that the Holy Spirit remained in him to the end and that God spoke to him favorably several more times and continued to protect and guide him. He suffered the loss of his beloved Rachel as she gave birth to his twelfth son, Benjamin, and he grieved greatly when he thought he had lost his favorite son, Rachel's first born, Joseph. However, later of course he finds that Joseph is not only alive but prime minister of Egypt, which was at that time, the world's greatest empire. After the "wrestling" episode, Jacob lived another fifty years and died in bed just after pronouncing God-inspired prophetic blessings on his fourteen sons. (He had adopted Joseph's sons Ephraim & Manassas).

Aside from the Scripture narrative, there is one more issue regarding the "Defense of Jacob" that needs to be addressed. That is, all the biblical characters whose names were divinely changed, such as Abram to Abraham, Sarai to Sarah, Simon to Peter, and Saul to Paul, retained only their new names and were never again referred to by their former names. All of those except Jacob. He became Israel, but also remained Jacob in many Scripture references. The popular assumption regarding this only exception seems to be aligned with the common, yet unwarranted, perception of his unsavory character. It suggests that when he is of the flesh, that is being a "bad guy," he is Jacob, and when he is of the Spirit, that is being a "good guy," he is Israel. The name Jacob appears 352 times in the Scripture, while Israel appears 2539 times. A review of each of these, fails completely to establish any correlation regarding this assumption. Yet we know that there is nothing arbitrary, accidental, or coincidental in the Scripture. Every word, every "jot and tittle" has specific purpose and meaning. Therefore, there is a reason why he is sometimes Jacob and other times Israel, but it has nothing to do with any good guy-bad guy condition or action. The answer I have concluded is very simple. When the Scripture refers to him as a man, he is called Jacob. When he is the titular head of the clan or the future nation, or when he is involved in any way associated with these roles, he is called Israel. For instance, in Genesis 48:2 ". . . and one told Jacob and said behold thy son Joseph cometh unto thee: and Israel strengthened himself and set up in bed." Here the man Jacob was told, and the father of the clan, Israel must now assume that role. In Genesis 47:27, 28 "And Israel dwelt in the land of Egypt in the country of Goshen, and *they* had ". . . and Jacob lived in the land of Egypt seventeen years . . ." Here, quite obviously the "Israel" as *they* are referred to is the entire clan including Jacob, but then Jacob the man is noted to be also living there as if he were separate and distinct, but he is so only because this is the way the Holy Spirit chose to tell us the age of Jacob the man. To have called him Israel there, and in that context, would have been confusing and inappropriate. It should be noted also that throughout the Scriptures his progeny is always called the "Children of Israel," or the "Men of Israel," or "the House of Israel." They are never called the Children of Jacob no matter how wicked they were. If this good-bad myth had any substance it would seem that it should have carried over as well into a descriptive punctuation of their character as a people. In Numbers 23:23 we read, "Surely there is no enchantment against Jacob, neither is there any divination against Israel." The Hebrew for enchantment can also mean divine prognostication, or diligent observation, while divination can be determination by lot or used of a soothsayer; this would seem to suggest an "equality of quality" of the two names. It's saying that there is no divine judgment relative to Jacob nor is there any nefarious allegation against Israel. Then again in Numbers 24:5, we read, "How goodly are thy tents O Jacob, and thy tabernacles, O Israel." The Hebrew for tent *ohel* also means dwelling, home or tabernacle, while the Hebrew word here used for tabernacle *mishkawn* can also mean shepherd's hut, dwelling place, and tent. Again it is evident that there is no intent to express a qualitative distinction between the person Jacob or Israel. It is simply equating, yet distinguishing, between man Jacob, Israel and the Tribe, Nation Israel. This is further evident in Numbers 24:2 where ". . . he saw Israel abiding in tents according to their tribe . . ." At this point in history, Jacob is long gone, yet he is here in these verses where we see him lovingly commemorated and equated with his progeny. From all of this it should be evident that he had to retain the name Jacob and to be called such in those cases where calling him Israel would have been confusing, because Israel also became the name of the tribe and nation. It's as simple as that! Why read more into it than the Holy Spirit has intended.

This concludes my "Defense of Jacob"! I pray that whoever reads this will now think a little more compassionately toward him, because I am convinced, as I believe this paper proves, that he has been unfairly maligned. I suspect that our Lord believes this also, because there is not one word anywhere in the Scripture where He condemns or rebukes or criticizes Jacob the person, or his actions or his behaviors. In fact, as already noted in Genesis 25:27, God calls him *tau* that is, not only "plain" but also "complete, pious, gentle, dear, perfect undefiled, upright." Nowhere does He retract, modify or diminish that assessment of him. On that basis, from where do we draw the right to override our Lord's pronouncement and adopt a contrary one? If one looks carefully at the sagas of the other great patriarchs, such as Noah, Abraham, Moses, David, Solomon, etc., Scripture reveals far more blemishes on their souls, and many more growing pains as they groped their way along the pathway toward faith and righteousness, than are recorded about Jacob. There doesn't appear to be anyone innately more reverent, faithful and obedient to the Lord than Jacob, with the possible exception of Joseph, his son. Even Joseph, however, exhibited some spiritual pride in his youth.

I have felt compelled to write many papers during these six wonderful years since our Lord laid his hand on me and adopted me as His son. Often, I have felt inspired and "pushed along" as I wrote. However, this is the first time that I not only felt I was being pushed along, but also that Someone else was actually doing both the steering and the navigation. I pray that the result will be as gratifying for the reader as it has been for me.

Looking back at the above, and the many dozens of hours of effort it represents, I realize from past experiences that some will question the worthiness of this effort. It may seem that it could have been better used to glorify our Lord in a much more meaningful manner. After all what difference does it make in the long run how good or bad Jacob was? I have also pondered this issue myself many times and often wondered whether or not this kind of effort was serving Him, as He would prefer to be served. Surely, there are better ways, and as He prompts me, I always try to obey these as well. Beyond that, all I can say in response is that I know that I am part of the Body, and as Paul says in 1 Corinthians 12:12 "For as the body is one, and has many members and all members of that body, being many are one body, so also in Christ." In verses 14 and 15 he continues, "For the body is not one member but many. If the foot shall say, "Because I am not the head, I am not of the body," is it therefore not of the body? I see myself as perhaps a toe or little finger, of no great importance, yet nevertheless part of the body. I believe that these writings are one of the functions that the Holy Spirit has assigned this toe to provide within the body. I pray for His continued desire to assign me *whatever* tasks He would have of me. Finally I praise you, dear reader, for having the fortitude to have persevered to the end of this long tome, and I pray that it was worth that effort.

—84—

The Mark of Cain

Cain killed Able. He was the very first murderer. It's likely, certainly it was in my case, that most readers of the Scripture assume him to be the most vile and evil of all the characters mentioned, second only to Judas. There is scant evidence recorded about him, but what there is should, when examined carefully, give us pause and perhaps even cause us to question the strength of our condemnation.

First, after he had killed Able, he and our Lord had a conversation recorded in Genesis 4:9–12. Then we hear him lamenting his earthly punishment in Genesis 4:13, 14, and pointing out to God that "*. . . everyone that findeth me shall slay me.*" Of course, death was the decreed punishment for murder, and so God would have been just to have slain him or to have allowed him to have been slain. One could correctly say that the levitical laws, which required this manner of punishment, had not yet been given. True, the laws had not been given formally, but this one along with others that could be cited, had already been given as evidenced by the fact that Cain knew that everyone who saw him would attempt to slay him. Why would everyone feel disposed to slay him unless they already knew that that was the appropriate punishment for murder?

Second, what did God do in response? Read Genesis 4:15. He put a mark on him, some symbol or message that he somehow carried or wore, and that gave him God's protection from being executed. The "Mark of Cain" is commonly thought of as some symbol or badge of evil. But Scripture makes it evident that it was an expression of God's divine protection. But why? Why didn't God do to him, or allow it to be done to him, what His later codified law would demand as punishment? Perhaps, God saw mitigating circumstances and a repentance in Cain's heart as he pleaded his case in Genesis 3:14.

We must realize that this killing of Able was probably the first physical death of a human being ever to have been experienced up to that moment. We know nothing of the circumstances except that, because of God's rejection of his worship offering, Cain was "wroth" (to glow or grow warm, blaze up, jealous, angry, grieve, fret self). Sometime after that, "Cain talked with Able his brother, and it came to pass, when they were in the field, that Cain rose up against Abel his brother and slew him" (Genesis 4:8). It is evident that they had some kind of discussion as they walked to the field, or perhaps it was some-time later, ("it came to pass") that they continued their discussion in the field. From what is written it seems that Cain was somehow pro-voked and struck Able. He may well not have intended to kill him. Going out into the field, an open place is not a likely location for a pre-meditated murder. It likely was accidental, which would explain God's leniency. If Cain's actions led to this unintentional consequence, that is, if his act was what we would call manslaughter, the ensuing punish-ment of exile was appropriate. Premeditated murder, of course, would have demanded the death penalty. Perhaps this, in a way, sets the example of God's later decreed solution for protecting from the "avenger of blood," anyone who had killed unintentionally. For later, God set aside "six cities of refuge" within the land of the Hebrews, to where one who committed manslaughter could run and be safe from the avenger's punishment (Joshua 20). To be an "avenger of blood," one had to be a close kinsman of the victim. Of course, at that time, everyone was a close kinsman of Cain, because there was no one who was not already closely related. That is why Cain could say that every-one would try to slay him. This "mark of Cain" was Cain's refuge, his protection in the land of Nod, the exile "city of refuge."

Also it is evident that for some reason, God chose to give us Cain's genealogy to the seventh generation beyond Cain himself. From this we discover a number of interesting things:

1. He dwelt in exile east of Eden in a land called Nod: Nod means exile.

2. There he built a city named after his son, Enoch, which means teacher. This was the world's first city, which indicates that by then a considerable population had developed. Who were they all? Obviously, Cain had married one of his sisters, or if Able had been married before his death, she may have been one of his daughters, but this is doubtful. Obviously, marriage to close relatives was allowed then, and for a couple millenniums longer, until the genes became so corrupted that God banned such unions to this day. There must have been several generations around by this time when he built the City.

3. Enoch the "teacher" had a son named Irad, which means "fugitive." So something must have been going on there, about which we are told nothing more, except that he had a son named Mehujael, which means "smitten of God" Now this is interesting. Smitten of God, not by God as we might quickly conclude. Smitten of God suggests that he had God in his heart, was Godly! And another son was named Methusael, which means "man who is of God," So here, we have at least one generation of what we might conclude from their names as being Godly men from the line of Cain! Could they have, all down the line, been exposed to godly teachings and an inspired example from the repentant, now forgiven and saved patriarch Cain? Isn't it likely that Cain came to realize the awfulness of his crime and repented? Couldn't it be that he realized gratefully the "mark of protection" that God had given him, revealed a merciful loving God to which he now gave himself, and whom he now worshiped as he witnessed to his grandchildren?

4. Now we come to something else quite interesting when we read about Lamech, the son of Methusael, the sixth generation after Cain. In Genesis 4:23, 24 where Lamech tells his two wives, *". . . I have slain a man to my wounding and a young man to my hurt"* (bruise, mark, strip or wound). *"If Cain shall be avenged seven fold truly, Lamech seventy times seven fold."* Here we see that the "mark of Cain" was remembered for seven generations. We see also that the crime of killing was very serious in that culture, which probably was by then over a thousand years old, assuming that

their life spans were similar to those of the descendants of Seth. What strikes me as very interesting, however, is that Lamech seemed to believe that he himself deserved to be avenged *"seventy and sevenfold."* He seems to believe that God would afflict anyone who chose to be an avenger for his crime much more severely than He would have avenged Cain having been killed. Perhaps Lamech's action had been accidental. This would make his assertion a little bit plausible. It is difficult to conclude whether his comment came from a heart sincerely believing that he did no deliberate wrong, or from one so very self righteous that he felt his worth was many times that of Cain's. Why are given this information regarding Lamech and his crime?

5.   Lastly, we learn that Lamech had two wives. One named Adah (adornment) and Zillah (shade, dark, perhaps darker skinned). Adah's son was Jabal, the father of those who "dwelt in tents and of such as have cattle." He had a brother Jubal, who "was the father of all such as handle the harp and organ." Zillah had Tubalcain an "instructor of every artificer in brass and iron." Just as all of Genesis, especially the first eleven chapters, is foundational to all Scripture, so is this little section regarding Cain, most informational regarding the antediluvian period of history. "Science" would have us believe that very early man, in whatever time frame, was ignorant, lived in caves, and was a wander-gather for thousands of years. Here we see that within seven generations and probably less, brass and iron were in use and there were at the very least, complex musical instruments (harps and organs). These are clearly symbolic of considerable technological advancement. We are told of herdsmen who "lived in tents" and we are told of cities. The distinctions here suggest that cities were collections of some other more advanced and permanent dwelling types than tents. Through the genealogy of Seth we learn very little of significance regarding the history and culture of those times. It is only through these few short verses regarding Cain's descendants that anything of this nature is revealed.

The Holy Spirit chose not to give us any time frame in the eight generations of Cain's descendants. Only Seth's chronology had any time line significance because this led to Noah, the flood, and the continuance of mankind through to the Messiah. But assuming similar longevities of Cain's line, his Lamech would have been a contemporary of Seth's Lamech. It's likely that the various tribes from both lines remained in contact with each other and so exchanged technologies. In this vein it is of great significance to note that Abraham was already forty-eight years old before Noah's son Shem died, and that Shem had been around for one hundred years before Methuselah died, and that Methuselah had been around for 243 years before Adam died. Even Lamech, Noah's father, lived 46 years before Adam died. This makes it evident that Abraham was effectively separated from Adam by only three generations in terms of handed down word-of-mouth information, even if there was yet no written language, although there very well may have been. Of course, much technological development in terms of "stuff" may not have gotten on the ark, but a great deal of accumulated knowledge must have survived the flood in the heads of Noah and his three sons. When one examines the size and complexity of the ark, its construction alone is very compelling evidence of a very high degree of technology of that time.

I suspect that there is more to this Cain story than I've yet been able to glean from these verses. However, there is one thing that my study has led me toward, and that is that when one gets to heaven, one ought not be too surprised to see the brothers Cain and Able residing there in loving fellowship.

—85—

Role Models

It is man's nature to model his attitudes, behaviors and values after someone or a group that he admires or respects. Such role models have tremendous influences on the character development of individuals, and, therefore, on the nature and quality of the society in general. Who were the primary role models of our American society a few generations ago? I believe one would find them to have been primarily persons of high moral integrity and great achievement in terms of their contributions to the well-being, strength and advancement of our nation and of all of mankind. They were the likes of George Washington, Abraham Lincoln, Booker T. Washington, Thomas Jefferson, Florence Nightingale, etc. Emulating such personages and seeking to model one's life after such people was imminently beneficial and uplifting to all of society, both secular and religious.

In the earlier part of my life, these were the popular role models and sources of inspiration for the average person who chose to learn about such people. My favorite literature as a youth was the biographies of these and many other great benefactors of our culture. But who is shaping the values of the present generation? Who are today's heroes, those who stand out as icons of what most people today would like to be like, if they could? Clearly, they are the movie stars, sports figures, so called musicians, and those who have achieved wealth and power by whatever means. Success is no longer measured by any of the previously respected qualities or achievements. In fact, great attempts have been made to empathize or contrive whatever flaws might be laid against these great personages of the past in order to discredit and undermine their worthiness and to thus deprive us of any genuine heroes. This change of role models continues to contribute greatly to the steep moral decline we see in each succeeding generation during this end period of these end times, exactly as Scripture predicts. This decline closely relates to the qualities of the modern day "heroes" being emulated, these moral scum that, like dross, rise to the top in every decaying culture. This characterization is certain to offend many because most have been slowly conditioned to it and cannot see it for what it is. This process is perfectly represented by the heated frog analogy. This analogy depicts frogs placed in a kettle that is slowly heated. The frogs don't notice much difference because of the very slow rate of heating, and so are able to adjust to each increment of heat, and are; therefore, blissfully ignorant of what is happening to them. They continue to adjust and adjust to this slowly changing environment until one day they are cooked dead. Being one who can remember well the 1940s on to the present day, this analogy represents the manner of our nation's decline very well. But none of this is directly relevant to the main point of this paper. It merely describes the pathetic environment in which the Christian community is immersed, and which the surrounding world offers as models for "success" in this life.

As Christians, our one and only genuine role model must be Jesus. It is both our desire and duty to emulate Him. Yet as lowly sinful humans, the very best of our efforts fall far below achievement of that goal, even though we are commanded to seek it, for Jesus said "*. . . be ye therefore perfect even as your Father which is in heaven is perfect.*" (Matthew 5:48) However, in order to even commence such an endeavor, there must be a genuine faith, a strong faith in Him which can prevail even during the most trying times of adversity, temptation and pain that the world is wont to throw at us. But even so, the awesome nature of the task can devour our resolve even before we commence. The answer to this problem is to recognize that it is impossible to do this by our own strength. It is only through His strength in us that can accomplish anything. It is a simple fact that Scripture teaches, yet one we all seem to have difficulties apprehending and holding on to. Again, it is only Him working through us that anything of lasting value is achieved, even this. The bottom line in all of this is to firmly resolve to end our sinful ways. Of course, it is not that simple, because Scripture tells us that everything that is not of God is sin. By that definition there is very little in worldly activities beyond those needed to survive and provide for our families that might not be considered sin.

Jesus, of course, is the ultimate role model. However, through the Holy Bible, God has given us biographical sketches of several personages who had characteristics worthy of serving as role models and to thus inspire us, as all good role models should. Of course, none were perfect but each had attributes worthy of learning from and emulating. In each case, God has also shown us some of their warts as well. I believe that this was to show us that they were neither perfect nor infallible, but were, in some instances, big sinners who overcome, as we are obligated to do as well. The following are a few examples, from which to draw hope and guidance as we seek to live God's Word.

1. Enoch

We know very little about him, and nothing that we can use for role modeling. He is included here as what might have been the ultimate human role model, if only God had given us more details about his life. What we do know from the Old Testament in Genesis 5:24 is that he lived before the flood and *"walked with God"* for three hundred years after he begat Methuselah at age sixty-five. Walked with God for three hundred years! Just try to imagine that! God hates sin, and will not tolerate it in His presence. Can we, therefore, assume that Enoch was absolutely sinless? I believe so, because how else could he have been translated directly to heaven before Jesus paid the price for man's sins? Except for Elijah, who was the only other person Scripture tells us was translated, the souls of all other Old Testament's saints had to wait in Sheol until Jesus, on the cross, washed away their sins. What a role model he should have been! He also was a prophet and must have been told by God of Jesus' future coming for he actually predicted His second coming in Jude verses 14, 15 were we are told,

> ". . . *and Enoch also, the seventh from Adam, prophesied of these, saying, Behold, the Lord cometh with ten thousands of his*

*saints, to execute judgment upon all, and to convince all that are
ungodly among them of all of all their ungodly deeds which they have
ungodly committed, and of all their hard speeches which ungodly
sinners have spoken against him."*

One more thought regarding this walking with God. Of the Triune Godhead, the Father is spirit and, of course, the Holy Spirit is
spirit. Jesus is the only one who ever appears in the flesh. We are told
that no one can see the Father and live. His presence and the presence
of the Holy Spirit are always depicted as a cloud or as fire. We generally conclude that the recorded theophonies such as with Joshua at
Jericho and with Abraham on the road to Sodom, were appearances of
the Son before His earthly birth as the Man/God who was then named
Jesus. Therefore, it seems to me at least, that the God who walked with
Enoch was probably the pre-incarnate son, our Lord and Savior Jesus.
Although it is unlikely that any of us can ever walk with Jesus here on
earth in the flesh, those who are born-again do walk with Him in the
spirit and will do so forever!

2. Noah

Here is a *". . . just man perfect in his generation and Noah walked with
God"* (Genesis 6:8). He too walked with God. What an incredible
privilege and testimony to his righteousness and purity of his ways!
But even though his genes were perfect, God saw something less than
absolute perfection in his character, as we see later in his biography.
We can learn a great lesson in obedience, perseverance and avoidance of ungodly ways from him. These qualities may be seen in his
building of the ark and all that followed through to the end of the
flood. Just imagine his spending 120 years building this three story
barge about 450 feet long and 75 feet wide all out of wood, making it
capable of withstanding the flood, and floating it safely for more than
a year. Of course, he had God's guidance, but the logistics and effort
required to cut and haul timber and construct this monstrous thing
with only hand and possibly oxen labor would, I believe, exceed the
strength, patience and perseverance of any man or men, not supernaturally endowed. Beyond that, can you imagine the difficulties
involved in pursuing this effort in the presence of neighbors? For 120

years he must have been the laughing stock and focus of much abuse from everyone for miles around. They must have come from all over to mock and scorn him, perhaps to even sabotage his efforts. After all, it had never rained. No one even knew what rain was. Therefore, there probably had never been any kind of flood either. And it is unlikely that such a large structure had ever been built out of wood. What can we learn from this that can serve as a model? First, obedience to the Lord as He has decreed to each of us, regardless of what others believe and say, even if you are alone in the entire world in your belief. We belong to God's autocratic kingdom, not too democratic or consensus rule. It doesn't appear that the Lord physically walks with anyone today, but we can each of us walk in the Spirit of the Lord, for He indwells all who have been born again. Obedience does not come easy, for our resolve to do so is tested almost moment by moment as we have to swim daily in this sea of sin and temptation we call the world. We must, all who try to walk in His Spirit, suffer similar scorn and mocking, as did Noah. His uncompromising perseverance under these trying circumstances is also a valuable lesson for each of us. We must thank our Lord that our physical tasks are so small compared to Noah's and that few if any will ever have to endure them nearly as long. To persevere and obey so long and so valiantly is an incredible demonstration of unwavering faith that must have been tested mightily many times.

There are at least two reasons why Noah was not translated along with Enoch. First God chose him and wanted him here for a very specific job, to build the ark, and through his sons to repopulate the earth, as perhaps the only one left who was "perfect in his generation," not having been contaminated by the "Sons of God" debacle. Second, God foresaw a flaw in his character that would eventually manifest and result in a curse on one of his grandsons. Because Noah got drunk and passed out, an awful thing happened that resulted in a curse on Ham's son Canaan, (Genesis 9:20–27). The lesson here is that due to our sinful nature we are all fallible and subject of backsliding regardless of how strong, obedient and persevering we are. Avoidance of all temptation and opportunities to sin must be part of our every day, moment by moment, conscious effort.

3. Abraham

Abraham is known as the father of the entire Hebrew race. He is also called the father of the entire grouping of people who are commonly called Arabs, through his son Ishmael and through his six sons by his second wife Keturah. Additionally, the people from the sons of his great grandson Esau are also considered to be part of the Arab people. God chose Abraham, this idol-worshiping pagan, and molded him for the purpose of carving out for himself a special people, Israel, through which his act of redemption was to be implemented for all mankind. It is in the saga of Abraham's life where much of God's eternal plan is revealed, mainly through the covenants He made with him. It is clear that God found some good material in him, material that he could mold into the man He wanted for His purpose. Abraham seems to be one of a group of people when God has chosen for a great purpose, but in whom at least initially, there seems to be no visible merit or distinguishable evidence that they, in any way, seek Him. However, any and all of us, who come to Him with humbleness of heart and commit ourselves to faith in Jesus, have some amount of material that God will find and work with, if we let Him. He will use that material regardless of how tiny an amount it may be, to mold each of us for some divine purpose.

As we follow Abraham's life, we see his many weaknesses as well as his growing strength, through God's working in him. First, while his name is yet Abram, he was told to leave his family in Ur and go to the land where God is directing him. But he didn't go immediately as commanded, and when he did, he took his father and others northeastward up the Euphrates more than five hundred miles to Harran where he stayed for about five years until his father died. This is not what God directed him to do. Then he headed southeastward through the Promised Land into Egypt and into other areas south of the Promised Land, again not what God commanded. On two occasions during the fifteen years of his wondering in this area, he lied and convinced his wife to lie regarding their marital status. He did this each time in order to save his own life, at the expense of his wife, knowing that as a result of the lie she would appear available for marriage to whoever was in authority and wanted her. These two events occurred about fifteen years apart. First when Sari was sixty-five years old and the Pharaoh, ruler of all Egypt, wanted her, and later when she was about eighty-five years old and chosen by a king named Abimelech. What an incredible beauty she must have been to yet so attract such men of power, men who could have anything and anyone within their reach. However, God intervened on both occasions and preserved their union, which, of course, was vital to the fulfillment of His plan. Not only that, but each of the thwarted monarchs befriended Abraham, giving him great amounts of wealth, making him one of the richest men of the region. In between these two events, he does have his moments of courage and strength along with some evidence of a lack of greed. This is when he takes his own army of 318 "trained servants" to rescue his nephew Lot from a five kingdom army that had conquered Sodom and Gomorrah and three other cities, taking captive all the people along with their goods. After freeing these people and recovering their goods, he refuses any reward or any of the spoils. There is no evidence that he prayed first for Lot's release, or simply acted on his own strength in this matter, although God is obviously allowing or guiding his every move. Also during this period he and his wife, rather then wait for God to act on His promise that he would be the father of great nations, decided not to wait on God, but to act on their own in a strictly worldly way to fulfill that promise. His wife was of course, barren, and because she was incapable of having children, they decided to not wait for God's timing, but to take the matter in their own hands. Therefore, he had a son through his wife's handmaiden. Later, of course, when God was ready, He gave ninety-year-old Sarah the miracle baby whom He had promised.

Beyond this point in time, we see what we might call God's patience with him vindicated, and His work beginning to bear fruit as Abraham began to exhibit strength, integrity and above all faith, the faith that God was seeking in the man who would be the father of many people, especially the father of the one people from which our Lord and Savior, God's Son, would come. With such disobedience at the beginning of his calling, and his protracted record of cowardice and weakness of faith, what a testimony of God's own faithfulness, patience, and loving care it is that Abraham should also become the foremost of the faithful, the standard, the premier example that Scripture uses to portray unquestioning totally committed faith in our Creator. This, of course, was epitomized when Abraham actually proceeded without hesitation to fulfill God's command to sacrifice his beloved and only legitimate son, Isaac.

Abraham is indeed a role model from whom we can all learn and greatly benefit. What makes God's narratives about most of His key players so helpful to us is that He not only reveals their beautiful qualities, but also their warts, that is, their weakness, their failings, and their sins, as well as how they are able to rise above them to become His effective servants. Without this revelation of their flaws, we would find it almost hopeless to even try to emulate their finer qualities, given our own depraved natures. Perhaps the biggest lesson to be derived from Abraham's life is God's patience and perseverance with even the most seemingly incorrigible and self centered among us, for once He chooses to begin His work in anyone, He continues it until His will is done. Human patience would have abandoned Abraham very early in his journey, but God had a plan for him that He intended to fulfill and nothing could prevent it. As noted, Abraham is remembered as the model of ultimate faith in God and in His promises. After what greater attribute can we possibly model our lives, because faith in God, Jesus, is after all, the only contribution we are able to make to our eternal salvation? But that is not all there is to it. As James, Jesus' brother, told us, "Faith without works is dead." Regarding Abraham, here is what else James said in James 2:20–24.

> *"But wilt thou know, O vain man, that faith without works is dead? Was not Abraham our father justified by works, when he had offered Isaac his son upon the altar? Seest thou how faith wrought with his works and by works was faith made perfect? And the Scripture was fulfilled which saith, Abraham believed God, and it was imputed unto him for righteousness: and he was called a friend of God. Ye see then how that by works a man is justified, and not by faith only."*

How do we know we have that saving faith? We know that something happens to us inside. And if that happening inside is a genuine saving faith, it must eventually burst forth outside as works reflective of that faith. I pray that we all read, reread, muse, study, and pray about this observation by James, because I believe it is fundamental to the process surrounding salvation and eternal life in God's presence.

4. Moses

Having been credited with writing the first five books of the Old Testament, Moses is second only to Abraham in stature from the Hebrew historical and spiritual perspective. Scripture makes it clear that he was indeed specially chosen by God for a very great and complex work. As with Abraham, there is much to be said regarding his missions, his efforts and his achievements. However, because this paper is focused on role models, I'll try to limit this to what I consider relevant to the subject. We can see God's loving hand and evidence of a purpose for Moses from the day he was born. Satan had long ago directed Pharaoh's heart so as to put the whole of the family of Israel into slavery. Because this was not destroying them and their heritage fast enough, it was decreed that all male babies were to be put to death. We all know the story of how his mother defied the decree, placing Moses in a floating basket that was found by Pharaoh's childless daughter, who took him for her own; how he was raised by his own mother, because the daughter chose her for his nanny; how he became a highly educated, widely respected prince of Pharaoh's court, and heir apparent to Pharaoh; how through his mother he became aware of his original heritage; how through his compassion for his blood line people, he killed an Egyptian oppressor in order to save the life of one of his own blood; and finally how he, therefore, gave up his Egyptian position and fled into the wilderness to become a simple shepherd for the next forty years. Looking carefully one can see God's loving hand orchestrating every major aspect of his life even before the burning bush event.

There is no evidence that Moses adopted any of the beliefs or practices of his blood line culture, for it appears doubtful that much of any such thing survived the long period of servitude and lack of relevant spiritual leadership among his people. Even circumcision had long ago been prohibited by the Egyptian overlords. All they seemed to really have was that supernatural instinct and tenacity for preservation of their bloodline heritage as children of Jacob / Israel. Although through the miracles of the plagues against Egypt, and God's guidance through Moses regarding the procedures they were to follow in order to be spared the horror of the Passover of the angel of death, they did begin to get some small inkling of God's intervention. It's that next and last forty years of Moses' life where the "payoff" seems to come. During this period God used him intensely. We observe here an almost continuous and intimate relationship between God and Moses, much like a loving father might have with his devoted and committed son. We find them working closely together to nurture, educate and grow their flock of particular people. As if attending to the overwhelming needs of more than a million people during nearly forty years of wandering in a desert was not more than a full time job, Moses, through divine authorship, pens nearly every word of the first five books of the Old Testament. These not only detail the history of the world from the moment of creation to just before these people were to cross into the promised land, but they also lay down God's laws, provide minute details on how to construct the Arc of the Covenant, the Tabernacle and all of the furniture and utensils needed therein, along with very explicit instructions on how to live and worship God until the Redeemer was to come. To many of the Hebrews, even to this day, the content of these five books of Moses are all that they believe is needed to know and to properly worship God, the book of the prophets and other Old Testament writings being useful but unessential fill ins.

From a role model perspective, Moses, as with Abraham, is a tough act to follow. Until the age of forty, Scripture gives us nothing about him to laud or criticize. Then, when he kills the Egyptian out of his sense of righteous indignation, he becomes a murderer. In running away, even though he is leaving a life that offered the very most that the world could provide, we can also consider him to be a coward who ran rather than face the consequences of his crime and to then pursue seriously the liberation of his people. Because of his powerful position, along with the great love and respect that both Pharaoh and the Egyptian people had for him, it is likely that his crime would have gone unpunished and viewed merely as a reasonable expression of authoritative power, which would have been considered acceptable. Instead, I believe, that it wasn't cowardice, but Providence, which guided him to leave, and to thus get down to the business of preparing for God's purpose and in God's way. Preparing how? For forty years he was a prince of Pharaoh's court, educated in all of the best in science, religion, politics and medicine, that that advanced, pagan culture could provide. He was decorated and much admired as a general in Pharaoh's army, distinguishing himself in battles that enhanced the size and stature of the empire. Thus for forty years he was steeped, honed and conditioned in ways hostile and contrary to God's ways. It would seem, therefore, that God led him into the wilderness and to a humble shepherd's life, using another forty years to clean Egypt out of his soul.

> * If these details seem to exceed the scriptural account, it is because Josephus in his writings provides many details about Moses not found in Scripture.

After forty years in Egypt, and another forty years as a wilderness shepherd, at eighty years of age, Moses finally gets the assignment that God had chosen for him. At first, we find him very reluctant and full of excuses as to why he is the wrong man for the job. Isn't it that way with most of us when God gives us a task? It always seems beyond our ability to perform, and it always is. That is because what He is really asking is for us to be vehicles through which He will do the job. Of ourselves we are nothing, nor do we have anything that is adequate for any God-ordained task. He just wants our availability and willing participation. He will then provide us with what we need so that through us His purpose will be accomplished. Our Father is a spiritual being, and it is of spiritual matters that are His priorities and principal realm in which He operates. Things of the flesh, and physical matters are but temporary and trivial in His great scheme of things. After all, what was His involvement in creating the earth, sun, moon, stars, and man? It was merely six thoughts of His over a six-day period. It is the soul and the spirit of man where the Father is most concerned and where His focus is. This earth is merely a temporary workshop and proving ground where souls, willing to love Him and believe in His Son, are cleansed and made ready to be part of His eternal family. This is a difficult time-consuming work for Him in one sense, and He has worked at it now for more than six thousand years. It is difficult because of His self-imposed rule whereby He gave man free will, which God honors and will not override, particularity in the matter of love and faith. Man's choice to worship Him and His Son must be of his own free will, if he or she is to be His son or daughter. There is no other way for anyone to become part of His eternal family.

As we read through the saga of that last forty years of Moses' life, we see an extremely intimate relationship between God and Moses. They seem to be in almost daily conversations as Moses seeks divine guidance and God responds. We see Moses' love for his people, and his responsibility for them, grow. As their leader, he is responsible for more than a million people wandering a desert wilderness for nearly forty years, totally dependant on miracles for their food, clothing, shelter and water. These miracles continue to happen; yet faith in God among them is sorely lacking. They too need forty years to get Egypt out of their souls. Throughout this long sojourn, neither Moses' faith nor his love and loyalty to his people ever wavered. This is expressed most profoundly when Moses interceded for the people and was willing to have his name struck from the Book of Life if only God would spare them (Exodus 32:32). Of what greater love could mortal man offer than his own soul for the salvation of others?

In his role as leader of this huge mob, naturally there were many disputes, as well as questions regarding God, the law, faith, conduct, etc. Moses sat daily for many hours as teacher, judge, and councilor to all who came to him. This, of course, was by itself a daunting, exhausting task, aside from his other responsibilities. In Exodus 18, we learn of Jethro, his father-in-law, coming to their encampment. There he saw how Moses was trying to do all of these tasks by himself. Jethro was a Median priest, most likely a worshiper of many gods. Upon seeing the great miracles the true God provided, and having heard the story of their escape from Egypt, he realized exactly who was the one true God. Jethro was also an able organizer because he immediately recommended that Moses select among the elders a group to share the judiciary burdens with him, thereby leaving only the bigger issues for his personal attention. Moses took this advice, thereby greatly improving the efficiency of his leadership. It is most certain that Moses prayed on this and obtained God's guidance before implementing the idea. I believe Numbers 11:14–17 provides another perspective on this same event where God tells Moses to select seventy men of the elders of Israel and God then proceeds to educate and ordain them for this mission. This council, which always consisted of seventy elders plus a leader, remained as the judicial authority of the people right up to the destruction of the temple in 70 A.D. In Jesus' time, we see them called the Sanhedrin, the ones who tried our Lord and sent Him to the cross.

The point of this, in the context of our topic, is to demonstrate that even though Moses was without exception, the most important leader in Israel's history, he was willing to accept council from others and didn't cling to his prerogatives or to his sense of singular importance. Moses is the finest of role models not only for his outstanding leadership, but also for his obedience and closeness to God, as well as his great love and sense of responsibility to those he had been ordained to both serve and to lead.

Furthermore, Moses is a prime example of what God will do to those He has chosen for a particular purpose. God's hand is visibly on him at every turn of his life, from when he was rescued from the bulrushes all the way to his death, and even beyond (his presence at the transfiguration). I believe that all who have been born again have been called for a particular purpose, and can, therefore, look back at their lives and see with equal clarity how God has molded them for His use. Other than his killing of the Egyptian and his moment of pride and anger as he disobeyed God by striking rather than speaking to the rock, we find little or nothing about Moses that was in any way shameful. What greater role model could we choose for our own lives?

5. Daniel

Here is a man "greatly beloved" by God! (Daniel 10:19). Wow! Can it get any better than that? Wouldn't it be wonderful if we could hear those words spoken about ourselves with God as the source? Well, you may not hear them, but the fact is, if you are born-again, born into His family, you *are* greatly beloved! Your life may not be as near perfect as was Daniels, but if you are truly God's son or daughter in the faith, you qualify for that title "greatly beloved." Could our heavenly Father love in any other way? All He has ever wanted from His creation is to have a family to love, those whom He created in His own image, a family who believes, obeys, and returns that love for Him and His son. If these qualities are representative of what fills your heart, then rest assured that you too are "greatly beloved." Search the Scriptures all you wish, but I believe that nowhere will you find recorded any flaw in Daniel's character or in his faith. Of course, he was a sinner, as are we all, but apparently he committed no sins worthy of mentioning, or that God considered appropriate for our learning. As we can see, as we read God's numerous biographical sketches, He doesn't exclude the negative qualities or actions of those about whom He has written. From a human perspective we might even say that God is embarrassingly honest about the negatives in His portrayal of the lives and deeds of even His most illustrious servants.

Daniel lived prior to, all through, and even beyond the seventy-year Babylonian captivity of Judah, the lower kingdom. Taken captive as a young teenager from the royal house of Judah, he spent the rest of his life in Babylon. It was Babylonian policy to take back to the king's court the most brilliant and useful of the captive people to serve the king. Scripture tells of only Daniel and three others who were so selected. Regardless of how spiritually depraved the nation of Judah must have been for God to have rendered such a severe punishment, some small remnant surely was very strong in the faith and how they raised their children, because these four, and especially Daniel, displayed a rock solid absolutely unyielding and uncompromising faith in their God under the most rigorous testing possible. We all know the story of the three, who rather then even fake paying homage to an idol, chose what had to be certain death in a fiery furnace, and how God protected them even as they were in the furnace. A similar attack was made on Daniel for praying to his God rather than to an idol. This got him into the lion's den where we find a similar demonstration of how God preserves His own until they have achieved the tasks He has given them. Daniel's strength of faith and character were powerfully demonstrated at the very beginning of his captivity when he refused to eat the king's food and insisted on what we might call "kosher food only." This rebelliousness was punishable by death. Shortly after this, when the king was ready to have all the magi killed for not knowing his dream, Daniel claimed that he could interpret the king's dream and did so, even describing the very details of the dream. When making this claim he knew absolutely nothing about it, nor did anyone else, but his faith in God was so powerful that he knew that God would reveal all he needed to know, to save him and the others. This one event launched Daniel on a lifetime career of being what we might call "prime minister," the number two man to king Nebuchadnezzer, the Babylonian king, and also later under Cyrus the king of the Persia Mede Empire. I believe one might say that Daniels' godly witnessing may have led to the salvation of Nebuchadnezzar, who, in fact, was allowed by God to write chapter 4 of the book of Daniel. As the chief of the priesthood of magi under the Babylonian king, some scholars believe that Daniel foretold the coming of Jesus as King, and that this is how the subsequent generations of magi knew to follow the star to Bethlehem seeking Him.

Daniel as a youth had been taught so well, and steeped so thoroughly in the God ordained belief system of the Hebrews, that he never forgot and never wavered in his commitment, trust, love and faith in God. Regardless of his responsibilities and other duties, he always kneeled in prayer at least three times daily at the appointed times of temple worship even though he was hundreds of miles from Jerusalem and there was no temples anymore. He gave his life to God and God gave him a long and glorious life, not only in earthly terms, but also as one of the most blessed prophets in all Scripture.

Daniel is a superb role model to all who would be uncompromisingly servants of God, and who seek examples of that stalwartness, along with an absolute, unquestioning faith, a deep heartfelt genuineness of worship, an agape love of the Lord, and a willingness to suffer and die rather than yield even slightly toward forsaking Him. Daniel's prayer, regarding the liberation of his people as the seventy years of servitude that had been prophesied by Jeremiah was nearing an end, is an exquisite example, and model prayer for all of God's people of all ages (see Daniel 9:1–19). Finally, Daniel's life should serve as an example for all parents in whose heart it is to raise their child to be a true lifetime servant of our Lord. We know nothing of his parents or how he was trained. There was no temple to worship in, and no priest to pray and offer sacrifice for his sins. His only recourse was to remember the law and to live by it to the fullest extent he could remember it, each and every day. But whatever they did, it was indeed impressive, everlasting and right. How many could be torn from their home as a young teenager and taken away to spend the rest of their lives isolated in a cruel, sin-laden, idol-worshipping, pagan culture, and survive a lifetime with their souls unscathed? This is not a hypothetical question, because that is precisely the kind of world into which all parents necessarily send their children today. It is an outstanding Christian parent who can say even four years later, after a college "education" that his or her child's faith survived. Daniels' parents, because of the spiritual training they gave him, along with Daniel himself, should be viewed as valued role models.

6. Esther

Scripture identifies quite a few women who God has blessed by having used them to advance His purpose, and their participation in His divine plan was often pivotal to each of the purposes for which he chose them. He apparently did not think it useful or relevant to say very much about them. Therefore, there is little regarding their character and behavior that might be used to identify them as role models. This is also true regarding most of the men mentioned in the Holy Bible. For instance, we know very little about the majority of the sons of Jacob who were the fathers of the twelve tribes of Israel, or of the twelve apostles. In some instances we know only their names. God's authorship of Scripture is the epitome of succinct efficacy and adequacy for the serving of His purpose. This may not appear evident to our very limited human minds as, for instance, when we read the book of Leviticus and Numbers. They seem to us long, laborious and full of irrelevancy. As we read Genesis, especially the early chapters, as well as the last chapters of Revelation, they seem to only hint at profound principles, and we cry out in our hearts in hunger for more information beyond that which God has chosen to share. Nevertheless, the entire precious book has been finely honed to a perfect balance in accordance with His purpose, as only God could so precisely author. Much of what we may hunger for, and is not evident in a simple reading, can be found through serious study and prayer to the Holy Spirit for His leadership and guidance. Proverbs 25:2 tells us "it is the Glory of God to conceal a thing; but the honor of kings is to search out the matter." Remember, Scripture identifies those who are born-again into the faith as being kings and priests in His future realm. Therefore, to some degree, that capability has been given to us if we will only use it. Note also that Jesus said, *"Till heaven and earth pass, one jot or tittle shall in no wise pass from the law, till all be fulfilled."* From this we can reasonably assume that much more knowledge will become available to us in these end times, and that some of what we now see as irrelevant or superficial in Scripture will be explained and its importance identified. Some Bible scholars have also offered the observation, that from a doctrinal perspective, the Holy Word can be viewed as being shallow enough for a baby to safely bathe in and yet deep enough for an elephant to swim in. That means that Scripture reveals sufficient truth, such that even the most shallow emersion into it can lead to a saving faith, and also that it has such limitless depth that no matter how much evidence an intransigent soul (like myself) might need to find evidence sufficient to generate a saving faith, it can be found, but only through prayer, guidance of the Holy Spirit, and perseverance.

Well, after that diversion excursion let us get back to Esther. There is considerable disagreement among scholars as to what period of history the book of Esther represents, and just who was the Persian / Mede ruler that is referred to in Scripture as Ahasuerus. After reviews of various opinions and chronologies, my preference is that as determined by Dr. Floyd Nolen Jones. This is because of his remarkable scholarship, his truly exhaustive analysis of available literature, and his uncompromising reliance on the inerrant Word of God as the primary basis for his conclusions. From this it appears that Ahasuerus was Darius I Hystaspis, and Esther became his wife in 515 A.D. This was during the period of the rebuilding of the Temple after the seventy years of captivity that

God had imposed on Judah (606 B.C. to 536 B.C.). Actually only about 50,000 Jews returned to Judah and Jerusalem. The others chose to stay where they had been resettled by the Babylonians and were now subjects of the Persian / Mede kingdom. At that time, the capital of the Persian / Mede empire was Susa, a city about a hundred miles from Ur, where Abraham had come from about 1400 years earlier, and about 750 miles due east of Jerusalem. The Jews had been widely scattered by the Babylonians and were now living in many parts of the empire over which Darius I was king. History seems to record Darius as a cruel, greedy, tyrant and among the first to extract tribute from his subjects. Herodotus, the first historian, said of Darius that he "looked to make gain in everything." At that time the Jews were no longer slaves. They were simply living relatively pleasant and lucrative lives where they had been planted generations before. Esther became queen after the king had ordained a nation wide round up of the most beautiful virgins. It was from that group that he chose her. Her moment of great biblical significance came when her uncle Mordecai told her of a plot by the government official named Haman that would have caused the death of all the Jews in the kingdom. The fact that Esther was of Jewish origin had been kept secret. In order to thwart the plan, she composed an elaborate plot of her own, which put her life in great risk. God was surely using her, guiding her throughout, so that her plan would succeed. The Jews were saved and Haman was executed.

What makes Esther a worthy role model? She was the queen, and a very favored queen of the king, who ruled the greatest empire of that period. She had the very best that the world could offer and no earthly reason to do anything to damage her position much less risk her own life. The Jews in question, were not a cohesive interdependent group or community where anything resembling a common bond could be credited to them. They had long ago lost their religious loyalties and customs. If they had had any, they would have been part of that small remnant who did return after the captivity. Those who returned were the ones who restored the Temple and, therefore, their ability to worship as it had been their calling, being sons and daughters of Abraham. That they even retained their identity as Jews was a supernatural circumstance as it has been for the past 2500 years since then. This was surely God's supernatural calling to her, which to her great credit, she chose to hear, and on which to act. How many of us today are willing to do much of anything difficult, much less anything painful, or dangerous in an answer to His call? This one answer to God's call can be viewed as having changed all of Jewish history. In fact, their history might well have ended right there. For Haman's plan, which the king had already signified and was scheduled to be carried out on a certain date, was to kill all Jews within the empire, which at the time included Jerusalem and all of Judea.

Esther's cool, calculated and well-executed heroic act of bravery and self-sacrifice, is well worthy of the historic notation it has received in Scripture. It could be argued that it has been given to us not only to illustrate both Satan's activity as he repeatedly tries to destroy the Jewish race, but also to illustrate God's divine use of women as well as men to thwart him. Here, Scripture also gives us this role model of how we can all, rich and poor, be transformed for use in His greater plan.

7. Other Valiant and Effective Women from Scripture

As already noted above, God has chosen to elaborate on the lives of but a select few, even though He identified many whom He has used to advance His plan. Many of these, although we don't know enough about them to choreograph specific role model images, what Scripture has revealed about them is enough to determine the nature of God's calling and how they responded. The following is a listing of a few others and what they did to warrant their place in the Holy Scripture.

a. Sarah

God chose Sarah to be the patriarchal mother of the entire Jewish race, the one from which our blessed Lord and Savior was destined to be born as God /Man. Sarah's devotion and obedience to her erratic, wandering and sometimes badly compromising husband, Abraham, is a worthy example of God's ordained role of a wife. Being barren until the age of ninety, when she finally had the long awaited "son of the promise," she must have suffered many years of ridicule and condemnation. This is because in that culture, bearing children was a major factor in establishing a woman's stature and prestige among her peers. Becoming a mother at that advanced age must have been not only a great blessing, but a very difficult challenge as well.

b. Tamar

Genesis chapter 38 reveals a sordid, sin-filed story of how God has used even some of the worst of His creation to advance His plan of redemption. He did this even in His choosing the very bloodline from whence Jesus would be born. Of the twelve sons of Jacob, God chose Judah to be the one who would continue the bloodline from Abraham to Jesus. It was also through Judah that the bloodline of the kings of Israel would eventually follow. With the exception of Joseph, none of the twelve sons appear to be of such a fine character that a father could feel blessed. Here God chose the fourth son after Rubin, Simeon and Levi to be the standard bearer. How bad could they have been for God to have had to pass by them and choose such an unsavory character as Judah? Scripture does tell us a little about their iniquities.

In Genesis 30 we learn that Judah took a Canaanite wife. This was wholly contrary to God's long-standing directive to marry only within the ethnic group. Judah had three sons. The oldest one married Tamar, but he died before Tamar could have his son. As per God's ordained Levirate custom, Judah ordered the second son to marry Tamar, so as to provide a son that would then be considered to be of the line of the first son. He refused, so God killed him. (God is serious about these things) Then Judah told Tamar to live in his house and wait until the youngest son would be old enough to marry her. In the meantime, Judah's wife died and eventually this son became old enough, but Judah did not honor his pledge to Tamar. As noted many times in Scripture, a woman without children was a failure both in her own mind and also to the rest of the world. Tamar felt helpless and betrayed. Judah had sole authority over her future, and he was not allowing her to do what she believed she was destined to do. Probably now her child bearing years are approaching an end.

Knowing her father-in-law's sordid ways, and learning that he was to travel some day's journey, she "conceived" a plan that would solve her problem. She changed her garb from that of a mourning widow to that of a harlot, and set up a place along the trail where she knew Judah would travel. Sure enough, he bought her services and the result was twins, Pharez and Zerah. The story is far more interesting and involved than the simple highlights here noted. It would be good to reread and study it. But what is the point of all this, and how is Tamar and her story worthy of taking up space in the Holy Scripture? There are at least three reasons: First, it is another confirmation that God can use, to advance His divine plan even through the most inveterate of sinners. But then aren't we all? If God chose not to use sinners, there could be no plan having man's involvement. In the Old Testament dispensation, sin could not be removed from the soul, because the means, by which sin could be removed, did not exist yet. Conformance to the religious system, which was centered on faith in the law, could only cover sin, not remove it. In the present dispensation, since Jesus made it possible to actually cleanse the soul of sin, which He does for all who are born-again, God is now able to also work through people who, though yet sinful, are, nevertheless, through faith in Jesus, cleaned of their sins.

The second reason the Tamar story may have been included in Scripture, is to show how doggedly determined this woman could be and was, in order to obtain what she believed was right, that is, to continue her husband's line and her own fulfillment as a woman. She put her life and her reputation at risk in several ways in order to accomplish this. Any one could have come to her tent on the trail before Judah arrived. Rape and death could have caught her anywhere as she traveled alone to and from this place. Had she not had proof that Judah was the father, her pregnancy would have been her death sentence. Being ostracized from the community for her action was quite likely the price she did pay for wanting so badly to be a mother and for the way she chose to have her dead husband's line continue. From what we can read it seems fair to consider her to have been a strong and virtuous woman who chose to do a wrong for what she believed to be a greater right.

The third reason is clearly the primary one as to why her story is recorded. We know that God, in His sovereign authority and for His own reasons, chose the line of Judah to be the one through which Jesus would come. From what we read, it seems evident that Judah's line had stopped dead, and it was only through Tamar's initiative that it was able to continue. Of course, we know that had this not happened, God would have orchestrated another way. But it did happen and God used this as the way in which the generational line toward Jesus was continued. We see it over and over again, that God often uses man's errant ways to advance His purposes. Tamar couldn't have known that she was being an instrument in advancing God's plans. She only knew that there was a powerful force in her that was driving her to do what she did. Was it God's doing, or simply His foreknowledge that was at work here? Because God could never be a participant in a wrong in order to make a right, it had to be that because of His foreknowledge whereby He saw the infinitely complex labyrinth-like ways mankind would travel, He could choose whatever sequence of paths that would best serve His purpose. It is interesting to note in passing, that God chose the path through Perez as the one that would lead to the birth of His Son. God's laws, as they were applicable during the dispensation, forbid an illegitimate offspring from being king, and this restriction was valid until the tenth generation of his bloodline. Of course, at that time and until much, much later, it made no difference, for the time was not yet right for kings to be ordained among the Hebrew tribes. It was, about six hundred years later, after the Exodus and into the period recorded in First Samuel, that this issue become significant. We read that at that time the people were howling for a king so they could be like the pagan tribes. It had always been God's plan that they would have a succession of kings, for Jesus himself was to become the ultimate and final king from the line of David. But the time was not yet for God to implement that plan. Nevertheless, God gave them Saul to be their king. But he was of the tribe of Benjamin not Judah. Therefore, he was but an interim king and one whose line could not continue. Only through Judah could the line to Jesus be completed. So why didn't God simply take from the line of Judah to start that royal lineage?

Again, because the time was not yet right. The tenth generation from Peraz had not yet been born. David was that tenth generation man, and he was the one who God had chosen before the beginning of time to be the one to initiate the dynasty, and to establish the throne on which his son, our Lord Jesus, would sit and one day rule the entire world for a thousand years.

Doesn't that give you goose bumps to witness God in action "taking sows' ears to make silk purses," as He wrote each note of the musical score for that greatest of all symphonies that one day will resound throughout the universe so all will know of His glory?

8. David

From a spiritual perspective, I believe that David must be the greatest of all human beings ever to have lived. Scripture has told us a great deal about his life as recorded in First and Second Samuel, First kings, and First Chronicles. Most of the Psalms were composed by David, and they give us broad insights into his thinking and into his soul. Why should I believe that he is the greatest? It is because God called him a man after His own heart (Acts 13:22). This is also a common expression many of us use as we express admiration for someone's exploits or behavior. It's one of the ways we indicate our concurrence or agreement with them in their conduct. But for God to say this about anyone, any created being, elevates the expression beyond human comprehension, beyond mine at least. If we read all that has been written about David in the context of this statement by God, it may be possible to find that God has revealed even more about Himself than He has about David.

Before we dwell further on that thought, let's examine a sampling of some of David's shortcomings that God has allowed us to see. First, he was a liar who lied as it served his immediate interest. He lied to Ahimelech, the temple priest at Nob in order to eat the shew bread from the temple and to obtain a sword, actually, the very one Goliath had owned (1 Samuel 22). Because of this lie, the priest accommodated David in a way that caused King Saul to have him executed, along with his family and other temple priests, totaling

756

eighty-five people. David could have very well known that such consequences of his deceit would result. Also he lusted for another man's wife, committed adultery with her, and then schemed to have Uriah, her husband, killed. Uriah was one of David's most dedicated, valiant and trusted of his generals who was away at war, where David should have been, instead of being at home yielding to temptation. David also had multiple wives, seven we know of, all contrary to long established laws that God had given Moses. Surely all of this must have been horribly offensive to God. Given all this, how could God possibly call him a man after His own heart? This seems to be a very strange paradox, but one from which we can learn something quite important about the mind of God and what characteristics He values most in His human creatures. Is God telling us that someone who is a liar and adulterer, a schemer and a murderer, can also be a man after His own heart? Yes, He is! From the perspective of what Scripture tells us about God and what He thinks about sin, this is something deserving deep study and not a matter to be taken lightly.

David seems to have had all of the human weaknesses of the flesh typical of all humanity. So what was so extremely special about David that it transcends these things? The answer if anywhere, is to be found in his heart, that element within man that expresses the quality of one's soul. This was made evident in 1 Samuel 16:7 when our Lord told Samuel, ". . . *the Lord seeth not as man seeth, for man looketh on outward appearance, but the Lord looketh on the heart.*" In 1 Samuel 16 we find that God had directed Samuel to the house of Jesses to find the one God has chosen to be king. It turns out to be David, the youngest of Jesse's eight sons. Notice in verse 13 that as David is anointed . . . *the Spirit of the Lord came upon David from that day forward.*"

This is a very significant and unusual event. Only after Jesus ascended to heaven, starting on the day of Pentecost, did the Holy Spirit take permanent residence in all saved souls. Pentecost was the momentous event that launched the church age. Prior to that, Scripture indicates that the Holy Spirit, while present among believers, did not normally take up permanent residence, but came and went in accordance with a believer's position regarding obedience to God's directives. But here, God, in accordance with His sovereign will, is making an exception in the case of this young teenage boy. In His foreknowledge, God has waited for this one special person with whom He would establish a dynasty and a throne on which one day Jesus would sit and rule for a thousand years. We read in 1 Samuel 16:18, that David already had a reputation as *". . . cunning in playing (the harp), and a mighty valiant man and a man of war, and prudent in matters, and a comely person, and Lord was with him."* That was quite a reputation for one so young!

Now we come to the very popular Goliath story in 1 Samuel 17. Here, I believe, is revealed a very important part of David's character and faith that sets him apart from all others in such a way that from it we can begin to see why David is a man after God's own heart.

It is evident that as a young shepherd, he spent many days and nights in the wilderness alone with his sheep and his God. He lived with God through those many solitary days musing about and worshiping the Most High. He grew to adore God and felt a familiarity and ever-growing closeness to Him. When he entered the military camp and heard this pagan Goliath pouring out blasphemies against his God, a holy rage came upon him and it became evident that he must put a stop to this evil. In convincing Saul that he should be the one to do it, David cited the occasions where he had single handedly killed both a lion and a bear, when they had tried to take his sheep. He claimed that it was having done this that qualified him to take on Goliath. But notice in telling of his exploits, he gave full credit to where all credit belongs. He told those listening, *"The Lord that delivered me out of the paws of the lion and out of the paws of the bear, He will deliver me out of the hand of the Philistine."* You see, there were two participants in this action, God and David. David slew the lion, the bear and the Philistine. That is the human part of the effort. But as David so states, God delivered; that is the divine side. All lasting achievements, that are not but hay and stubble, occur that way, man's effort through God's strength. There is a great lesson to be learned here. God never meant that faith in Him should be synonymous with sloth. With David's great faith, why didn't he simply go out into the field, get down on his knees, beg and pray and then simply let God slay Goliath? That sounds crazy, doesn't it? But before you scoff at the idea too much, think of how many times each of us has done exactly that! When a problem is difficult, rather than faith, fear grips our heart and we fall apart. Instead of moving ahead to do that which is necessary and what genuine faith in Jesus as our guide and protector would require us to do, we take on the character reminiscent of the sloth. We simply hope that through prayers alone, God will somehow do supernaturally what He appoints us to do, and what we should do in His name through His strength, and in faith in the righteousness of our actions. God never does supernaturally what can be done naturally. He works through man, and in particular through those who are His own, those who are a part of the body of Christ. What is the body of Christ, if it is not His present earthly manifestation through whom He chooses to work good things? Scripture tells us that if we are born-again, we are His; He bought us with His blood. We are His bondservants as well as His Body during this present dispensation. If you think that being saved is a free ride just because it is a free gift from God that we cannot pay for, you need to become better acquainted with God's Word. Look to David to see what the faith that *really* saves is all about.

That is how David's heart was exceptional and most pleasing to God. David never shied away from whatever work God gave him to do. Not only that but he did it happily, without fear, and giving full credit to God for its achievement. One of many general lessons from David's life may be summarized as follows. What you do in the name of the Lord, do as if your salvation depended on it, and then give full credit where it is due, to the Lord, for without His grace, your works would be nothing more than dirty rags. David surely backslid and sinned, but his laundry was absent of dirty rags of either sloth or self-esteem.

We see that incredible, totally committed faith throughout his life. We see it joyous and unabashed as he leaps and dances as he brings the Ark of the Covenant back home. His wife, Michal, hated and was ashamed of him for his unkingly behavior in such matters. He demonstrated his absolute faith when his young son died. He prayed and fasted and mourned for a great many days hoping for his son's recovery while the boy lived, but the minute he died, David immediately resumed his duties as if nothing had happened. In his faith, he prayed for God's will to be done. When that will took his son, he accepted it unquestioningly, telling his aides that while God had ruled that his son could no longer be with him, he accepted that, knowing well that one day he would again be with his son. How often do we see such complete acceptance of the Lord's will, that even a profound grief regarding such a great loss fades completely where genuine faith is present? This son was the result of David's great sin. While it is clear that God forgave him, Scripture shows us here most assuredly through David's example that the consequences of our sins can, and will, in some way and to some degree, plague us for the rest of our lives.

David is, I believe, the best role model for genuine uncompromising life long faith. Jesus, of course, is our ultimate role model for how to live, what our physical and spiritual values need to be, and from exactly where our strength is derived. David, on the other hand, is the model of human applications of these qualities. We see Abraham as an example of an uncompromising faith under a most testing circumstance. But David is an example of a life long, sweet and simple, but absolute and never questionable faith in our Almighty God. Before time began, God saw this shining beacon of what He wanted in His standard bearer, in the one worthy to first establish the throne on which our Lord Himself would one day sit and rule as both the Son of God and the Son of David.

It is important that before we leave our study of David, that we at least examine one or two of his Psalms. David wrote most of the 150 Psalms that are included in the Holy Bible, and we are told that he probably wrote many many more that have been lost to us. The Psalms, even more than his biography, reveal the inner workings of his extraordinary heart and soul.

Looking briefly at Psalms 56, we observe a prayer spoken when the Philistines had taken him to Goth while he was yet running from King Saul. While his enemies sought mercilessly to *"swallow him up,"* he sought mercy from his God. In verses 3 and 4 he says, *"what time I am afraid, I will trust in thee. In God I will praise His word, in God I have put my trust, I will not fear what flesh can do unto me."* This is the trust of a soul that can sing praises to God amidst mortal dangers, a soul that has complete trust in God's decision in all matters, even when death may seem inevitable. It is a faith that can trust when he is afraid, and in so trusting not be afraid. True faith in God drives fear out of man. Skipping down to verse 9, *"When I cry unto thee, then shall mine enemies turn back; this I know, for God is for me."* David is completely confident in God, even in this dire and seemingly hopeless and painful situation. If God is for us, what does it matter who or how many can be against us? In verses 10 and 11, he repeats this declaration of praise and trust. How honoring and pleasing to the Lord's ears it is to hear such commitment, and what an example it is to other seriously tried believers to follow such an example. In truly praising and trusting in our Lord, we are able to put away any fear of what man can do. Then finally in verse 13, David gratefully acknowledges God's grace and mercy for his delivery from his enemies. This he continues to remember in profound gratitude when he again, in Psalms 116:8 and 9, repeats this expression of gratitude. Here is another worthy example to guide our walk in the Lord. Recognize and remember God's great and small workings in our lives, and re-express over and over again our gratitude and love for Him and for His many mercies.

Now, let us look at how David and God dealt with that awful series of sins mentioned earlier. We find that in chapter 12 of 2 Samuel. It appears that David's conscience must have been sleeping for many months, both during and after his most horrendous backsliding into his sins regarding Bathsheba. It was God, through the prophet Nathan, who finally cited to David a parable through which his horrible sins finally pricked his conscience.

In hearing this parable, David was made to condemn himself as he finally saw the true nature of what he had done. In this chapter of Samuel, we hear from David nothing more than the simple confession, a sincere acknowledgment of his sin against God. However, it is in Psalm 51 that David bares his heart and makes his full heartfelt confession and prayer to God. While his great heart is revealed in many of his Psalms, it is this particular one that can serve as a great role model prayer of a truly repentant soul, one that is humbled, contrite and profoundly sorry for its transgressions. I will not attempt to analyze it. It would be sacrilege for me to do so. For even the great Spurgeon spent many months of prayer and struggle attempting and failing to even commence the work. Here is what he said about the Psalm: *It is a bush burning with fire yet not consumed, and out of it a voice seemed to cry to me. "Draw not nigh hither, put off thy shoes from off thy feet." The psalm is very human, its cries and sobs are of one born of woman; but it is freighted with an inspiration all-divine, as if the Great Father were putting words into his child's mouth. Such a Psalm may be wept over, absorbed into the soul and exhaled again in devotion; but, commented on-ah! Where is he who having attempted it can do other than blush at his defeat?*

For anyone seeking understanding as to how to empower their prayerful petitions to God, this Psalm should be seriously studied. It is a public confession as is evident from the fact that it was published to be sung publicly. It is also important to note that nowhere does David at any time offer excuses for his actions nor cite any extenuating circumstances in order to suggest the slightest justification for what he did. We should, nevertheless, realize that throughout his life he had no one but himself to prevent his backsliding. Only Nathan the prophet after the fact sought to correct him. It is also to be recognized that in those days, as it most certainly is today, the world would think nothing of such actions, nor would it even consider these to be sins. Remember that he was a man of very strong passions, a soldier and oriental monarch with despotic powers. No king of his time would have felt any conviction for having acted as he did. This all the more speaks to the greatness of his heart, that he could in the context of the times and in his exalted position, accept the full blame and seek forgiveness from the even higher power that he realized he had profaned. You will notice in the Psalm that David says to God "Against you, you only, have I sinned." Here is a telling example of David's great depth of understanding of the divine. We may ask, what about Uriah and the others? Didn't he sin against them also? No! Sin by definition is against God, since it is only by God's law that sin is defined as sin. A wrong done to others is an offense against humanity. How very close his heart must have been to God's heart for him to have had that distinction so clear in his mind.

At this point in the story of David, there is another very important lesson to be learned about sin and how God deals with it in the earthly portion of the lives of His own sons and daughters. I wrote a paper on the consequences of sin some time ago but here, in the story of David is a very clear and specific example put here for our learning as it pertains to the compounded ravage of sin and how God's chastisement is rendered. Please read chapter 12 of 2 Samuel in order to get the full measure of what is here only highlighted. Note first that David was made to see his sin in its true light before it was forgiven. Moreover, he was made to strongly condemn himself, prior to forgiveness. It was only then that God, through Nathan, told him that his sins were forgiven. But now we read of the awful realization that descended on David, and that we must, all who are saved, hear and know in our hearts as the consequence of our own sins. David was made to see the greatness of his sin by the effect that is produced in the lives of others as well as in his own. Nathan said ". . . *by the deeds thou hast given great occasion to the enemies of the Lord to blasphemy.*" David's Psalms reveal this sad fact several times. There always were, and are today, diverse activities in any court or government body. In his court, there were the very faithful as well as the men of Belial who were ungodly. When the ungodly caught David trespassing this way, it gave them much basis for blasphemy. At the same time, it was a very sad and undermining topic for the faithful to speak of. They must have wept greatly to see their godly hero king so fallen.

But that was far from all of it. Never again was David the same happy and joyous example of God's workmanship. He was forgiven, but from that day onward, "the sword never left him," and the consequences of the sin continued to plague him all the rest of his life, a fate we all should expect for ourselves as the consequences of our own sins. A very sad change overcame David's life from then on. Just read of Tamar, Amnon and Absalom to see how degraded his own family had become. Enemies within his own court, even his own son, sought to overthrow him. Most of this latter part of his life was one of mourning and lamentations. Even his dying testimony, though full of faith, was marred by regret, as he expressed it when he said, ". . . *although my house be not so with God.*" We find that even he, this man after God's own heart, was nevertheless a man of like passions as ourselves and was no exception when it came to having to pay the consequences. Let not any of us believe that because we are saved and our sins are, therefore, forgiven, we are "home free." We should all realize that there is no such thing as being "home free" from sin's earthly consequences. David's story teaches us how bitter and long lasting sin is, and that even though guilt may be removed, the consequences cling to us and continue to be subjects of sorrow until *"God shall wipe away all tears from our eyes."* (Revelation 21:4). We cannot control what is in the past, but with this lesson as foreknowledge, we can, through greater resolve towards obedience to God's ways, greatly reduce the potential for such additional consequences.

Our final excursion here, as we seek to understand David's heart, will be a brief examination of one more Psalm, Psalms 57, where we see some more very worthy expressions of the great heart of David. This Psalm is titled *"To the Chief Musician, Al-taschith, Miichtam of David when he fled from Saul in the Cave."* This is one of four Psalms that are particularly graphic expressions of David's very special heart in which he sings praises to God and expresses his great love, faith and confidence. The word *Al-Taschith* means, "thou shall not destroy" and *Michtam* means "engraving." This would suggest that these prayers were of special meaning to David and he wanted them preserved, as well they were, for God did save them just for us.

As we read the Psalms we see the calmness of David's heart when he was in great peril. Basically he was a man of peace until inspired by God to right some wrong. Here he is being hunted to death as if he were a vicious dog, by the king to whom he had done no wrong and to whom he had complete loyalty. This compounded the pain of the situation, yet with all the sensitiveness of his nature, his faith in his God never wavered. Here is an example of how the more he was afflicted, the more he was strengthened.

In verse 1, he pleads for mercy twice, the circumstances being so very urgent. Then he expresses his faith as that of a little chick being protected under the mother hen's wings. He knows that God will so protect him as long as necessary. In verse 2, he cries unto God in perfect faith, not blind or dumb faith, for that is no faith at all, but in a knowing faith that God will protect him. In verse three, his faith is such that if he cannot be saved by earthly means, God will send the means down from heaven if necessary. In verse 4, he makes note that he does now "lie" among the lions and other enemies armed and ready to kill him. He lies among them, as we must live in this world among some who would do us harm just for our beliefs. But in his case, these are killer enemies, yet he can "lie" among them without undue fear, because he knows God is with him and his faith will protect him. In the midst of all the danger and prayer of mercy, David takes a moment to rise above it, for in verse 5, he again praises the Lord with a calm but passionate reverence. Here the message for us is that there are no circumstances, no matter how dire they may be, that one should not take a moment to praise God. It is in times of such stress that test our commitment and love of God and, therefore, no better time to stop and praise him for all He has already provided, even if it is not in His will to cover us in our immediate circumstances.

They hunted him as wild beast perhaps digging holes covered with netting and leaves for him to fall into as he described the circumstances in verse 6. Then he discerns that they fell into their own traps. This was God's immediate answer to his prayers. Perhaps the message here is to leave them alone who would hurt one of God's own. For sooner or later they will be defeated by their own evil, as God wills it. The remainder of the Psalms is again glorifying God for His great mercy and faithfulness. We should all pray with that same calm praiseful frame of mind and heart that David possessed, even if we are called to endure such trials as befell him. Rest assured, most of us will be called to such trials of faith before our journey here comes to an end. Careful reading of David's Psalms, as he expressed what was in his heart, is where we find the most compelling evidences that it was indeed a Godly heart.

A study of a few others of David's many Psalms would most assuredly confirm what we have already observed about David's exceedingly strong and faithful heart. But was that enough to totally negate the condemning nature of his very serious transgressions? Obviously so, because he does remain for all time a man after God's own heart. Trying to look at the larger picture, perhaps as God saw it, we know that God has a loathing for sin, but also a supernatural love for the sinner. Where genuine faith and love for Him exists, the solution to the sin problem was solved by God before the earth was created. Sin permeated the first man and none have, or ever will, escape its contamination. But, where there is a genuine saving faith, sin is not a primary issue with God. Those who are saved have been given new hearts but they must, nevertheless, continue with the strength of the Holy Spirit to struggle against sin. However, God is more interested in man's new heart and in seeing it perfected in preparation for its greater eternal purpose. David's new heart was considerably perfected at an early age and continued to increase in attributes, as his Psalms clearly indicate. We might say that his sins were on a totally different plane, the plane of that old heart, the one that is *"deceitful above all things and desperately wicked"* (Jeremiah 17:9). For those who have been redeemed, that plane is no longer of relevance to God from a spiritual perspective, other than for determining one's position in heaven. In our present "church age," those who are saved can collect crowns for good works and also lose them through sin. But David, being of the Old Testament dispensation, could not receive such crowns. However, David was given a very special earthly crown and a throne; as the king of God's chosen people. But, it was not just any kingly throne, it was the one our Lord Christ Jesus has a claim to and will one day occupy.

David had a deep, highly developed understanding of God, His way, and what He wanted for His creation. At the same time, David also expressed a life-long, child-like awe, trust and love for his Creator. One would have to say that David was very much in tune with God and His workings, and it is for our learning of these things that God has revealed to us so much of David's life and his thoughts as expressed in the Psalms. In this vein, look also at what God gave David in the way of prophecy. Read Psalm 2. Here David was allowed an ear into heaven where he overheard a conversation among the Father, the Son and the Holy Spirit discussing things that would be going on at the end times just before Jesus would return to sit on the throne of David. Then read Psalm 22. Here David was given ear to the tortured intimate thoughts and observations that our blessed Lord and Savior would have as He would one day, ten centuries later, as He hung from a cross dying for us, so that we might have everlasting life with Him. Could David have had any comprehension of the meaning and significance of what he wrote? This certainly is debatable. However, I tend to believe he did. I don't believe that David was in some sort of trance and simply wrote without knowing what was being dictated to him. I suspect that God gave him these visions along with some degree of understanding, just as He did to the apostle John when Jesus revealed himself and directed John's writings of the book of Revelation.

David's heart was certainly a model for all of us. While he was often emotional in demonstration of his faith, it was not that, but the uncompromising faith, absolute commitment, complete devotion, and full time genuine agape love for God that made his heart so special to God. That's the heart that God chose to compare with His own! Oh, if only each of us could obtain such a heart!

Scripture is replete with other great personages worthy of study and emulation as role models. However, those we have met here give us ample examples for our learning of what God would have of us. I pray that their messages have been as inspirational to you as they have been to me.

86

The Samaritan Woman at the Well

The first forty-two verses of the Gospel of John chapter 4 described how Jesus and His disciples left Judea and journeyed northward through Samaria, on their way to Galilee. Samaria was, for the most part, the land that had been originally allotted to the Tribes of Ephraim and Manasseh, and lies between Judea and Galilee. The events recorded in this first portion of the chapter tell us of Jesus' encounter with a Samaritan woman. As described, it is rich in explaining God's grand purpose and how Jesus was here on earth to implement it.

Verse four tells us that ". . . as He must needs to go through Samaria." There was severe mutual hatred between the Jews and the Samarians. Jews were often harassed and even killed, especially as they journeyed southward through Samaria toward Jerusalem. Therefore, Jews seldom crossed through that province, preferring instead to cross the Jordan and go a long way around that area when they had business to the north. The controversy between these people began when the Jews returned to Jerusalem after the Babylonian captivity, and began rebuilding the Temple. In Ezra 4 we learn that the Samarians offered to help, but the Jews wouldn't allow them to because they were by then a mixed breed, both racially and religiously. Racially, they were a mixture of the Jews who survived the Assyrian occupation and of foreign gentiles whom the Assyrians brought in to occupy the land. Religiously, the Northern Kingdom, even before the Assyrian conquest, had turned to idolatry. Furthermore, the Assyrians brought additional false gods into the culture. Later the Samaritans did adopt Jehovah as God but without repudiating or abandoning the other gods (2 Kings 17:25–41). Nevertheless, by the first century, at the time of Jesus, they again had become monotheistic, and somehow came to believe that they were all descendants of Jacob, through Joseph. However, after not having been allowed to help build the Temple, they made Mount Gerizim their holy mountain in contrast to Mount Moriah the real holy place of Jerusalem. Also they had removed all mention or reference of Jerusalem in their copies of the torah. This, in some perverted way, may have been an additional response to their having been denied participation in the building of Jerusalem's Temple. Sometime during the rebuilding of the Temple, according to Josephus, Manasseh son of Judah, the high priest in Jerusalem, contrary to law, married the daughter of a Sanballat chief of the Samaritans. When the Jews demanded that he either repudiate the marriage or renounce his sacred office, he fled to his father-in-law's, where he hoped to rebuild the faith structure that had been so long denied to these people. They apparently hungered for what they had lost long ago and were seeking its return. Therefore, they embraced Manasseh as their hope for restoring their ability to properly worship God, because he was a genuine, trained priest of the descendents of Aaron. However, Manasseh, although eager to fulfill this need, viewed things somewhat differently than the whole of Scripture demanded. Therefore, he fashioned a religious system to his liking that is described hereinabove. It then followed that Sanballat sought and obtained permission for Alexander the Great to build their own Temple on Mount Gerizim. This stood as their place to worship until it was destroyed by Hyrecanus in 129 B.C., after which they had only this "holy mountain" as their religious center. How easily it is for Satan, through false teaching, to twist truth and to selectively omit or add, so as to totally corrupt the Word of God. Because of this corruption, the Jerusalem Rabbis decreed very limited contact with the Samaritans. Jews were forbidden to ever, in anyway be obligated to a Samaritan. That is why, as we are told, that the Samaritan woman was surprised when Jesus asked her for water without offering payment.

Why did Jesus choose to go to Galilee at his time? First in Luke 3:19–20 and Matthew 4:12 we learn that John the Baptist had been imprisoned. This posed a threat of imprisonment for Jesus who had been the focus of all of John's preachings. Second, it was to avoid a confrontation with the Pharisees as we learned in verse 1. Third, Luke 4:7 tells us Jesus was "led by the spirit." Fourth, He had this preordained ministry to accomplish in Samaria. As we can see, Jesus' route was deliberate, for He had this divine appointment with the woman at the well.

Verse five tells us that they came to a city called Sychar, which means, "purchased." It was located near a portion of land Jacob had purchased and given to Joseph. This is probably the basis of their belief that they were descendants of Joseph. Also this is where Jacob's well is located, at the foot of Mt. Ebal. That well is still in use and is reputed to be more than sixty feet deep. To have hand excavated it was no small feat. To have shored it such that it would remain functional for 2500 years required supernatural involvement.

In this verse we are also told that it was the sixth hour, or high noon, when the woman came to draw water. This in itself is revealing because it was the custom to draw water only in the morning, before the heat of the day made it more difficult, and also when it was most needed for the animals as well as for human use. This woman came at noon when no one else was likely to be there. Perhaps the reason for her choosing this time may have to do with what we learn about her in verse 18.

The woman was surprised at Jesus' request for water, without an accompanying offer to pay. We should recall, as mentioned above, that this was a very deep well. A long rope and special bucket were required to bring up water. Although this was difficult work, we learn from other Scripture passages, such as Genesis 44:43, that this was generally deemed to be part of a woman's duties. In verse 9 we also notice two more things. First, she knows immediately that He is a Jew and second, that He has chosen to speak to her in spite of the fact that it was forbidden. That He was a Jew, she probably determined from the identifying blue threads that were commonly woven into the hems of Jewish outer garments. That He spoke to her at all, being that she was a Samaritan, was a surprise, but further that He spoke to her alone without the presence of witnesses was shocking. It was against Pharisaic law for a man to speak to a woman other than his wife without others being present.

Now we get into Jesus' divine purpose, where in verse 10 He proceeds to tell her who He is, and about the living water that only He can give. She could not understand what "living water" was because at that point, she could think only literal, worldly terms. Living water is spiritual imagery, symbolizing eternal life. Until we can see ourselves as God sees us, as condemned sinners, and thereby understand that we need a Savior, we cannot, as she could not yet, comprehend Jesus' message. But our Lord had now laid the groundwork for her understanding. Then in verses 16–18 Jesus proceeds to point out her sins, which were very evident to her, and which, must have weighed heavy on her conscience as well as having plagued her socially. In pointing out her sins, without any human way of knowing about them, He had proven to her that He was even greater than Jacob, their most revered ancestor.

Here we might stop to notice how her perspective of Him changed as their conversation progressed. First, he was a Jew, then one greater than Jacob, next a prophet, and finally the Christ. Calling Jesus a prophet was a big step for her because in Samarian theology, the next prophet after Moses would be the Messiah. The Samarians had rejected the whole Scripture except the five books of Moses, and in all other writings as previously noted, they had removed all references of Jerusalem. Therefore, she knew of none of the other prophets or of all of the great knowledge and insights that God had provided through them, and through the Psalms and other Old Testament books. Calling Jesus a prophet was calling Him the Prophet, i.e., the Messiah. In verses 21–23, Jesus informs her that their theology regarding Mt. Gerizim was totally wrong and Jewish theology was correct, that is, that the Temple in Jerusalem was the proper place to worship. Jesus also said that the time was coming when worship would no longer be limited to any one place. This came true when the Messiah died, after which worship would be in the spirit of truth during this yet current dispensation of grace. Finally, Jesus revealed the true content of faith, and also unmistakably identified Himself as being the Messiah, a fact she was already strongly suspecting. This excited her so much that she forgot her pitcher of water as she ran home in her eagerness to spread what she had learned. Christ had so satisfied the thirst of her heart that she completely forgot the thirst in her throat.

Near the end of the conversation, the disciples returned with the food they had been sent to bring back. But as they urged Him to eat, He said, "I have meat to eat that ye know not of." Opportunity to do God's work had presented itself. The woman went back, and He knew she would return with many who needed to hear in order to believe. His physical need could wait, because the spiritual fulfillment that that opportunity provided was far more satisfying and nourishing than any earthy food. His time was short and He had yet much to do. Before the woman would return with the many who were aroused by her report, Jesus used the time to instruct His disciples about sowing and reaping spiritually, using the grain harvest as an analogy. Jesus was foreseeing, in the short term, the coming of these Samaritans who were ready to be "harvested" and whom in the long term would sow for others to harvest in the future. Also Jesus was teaching the disciples a long term lesson pointing in a geographically broader sense that the seeds sown through past ages by the prophets and the continually existing remnant of believers, were now as fields of white grain ready to be harvested. It would be their commission and lifelong work to both harvest what others had sown and to sow what others would later harvest. We today, who are the result of the sowing of others and who are thereby His disciple as well, have that same divine duty and privilege, that is to do exactly what He called these first disciples to do. That, I believe, is the principal message to be gleaned from this one precious episode in our Lord's short earthly life.

What else should we learn from this story that might help us to know Him, to better understand His purpose and His ways, and to thereby be able to serve Him better? The following is what has come to mind as I have studied these verses:

1. Jesus chose by divine guidance to reveal His message of salvation to the very lowest, most hated of all people from the Jewish perspective. That His message drew such a big and positive response from the Samaritan is evidence that these despised

people were as eager for, and as responsive to, the truth as one might find anywhere. From what we are shown, it seems that they exceed the Jews in their willingness to receive the true faith.

2. For those who claim that Jesus never said that He was God, verse 26 should be examined. When Jesus says, "I that speak unto you am He." Who is the He to whom He is referring? The woman had spoken of the only prophet, the only Messiah she ever heard of, the One of which Moses spoke as the Eternal One who would reveal all things. Jesus' words are better translated as "The One of whom you speak, *I AM*." There is no he in the Greek version. It was added by the translators. Jesus is the great I AM of the burning bush and it is of Him whom Moses prophesied. Notice in verse 42 the men of the city now believe the truth and know Him to be the Christ, "the Savior of the world." This is the first time in Scripture that Jesus is so identified.

3. In this story, Jesus takes the opportunity to teach His disciples of the great need for "workers," for evangelizers to sow the word and to reap the harvest of salvation through faith in Jesus. Are you one of His? Have you joined His working army, or are you pleading 4F status, that is not even Functionally Fit For genuine Fellowship with our Savior? In verses 34–38 He is speaking to His disciples. That's *you* and *me* as well, if we are truly saved. We are called to sow and to harvest, to spread His Word, to bear fruit for Him, for after all He *is* our *Lord* and *Master*, as well as our Savior. James 2:18 speaks of fruit (works) being evidences of faith. In different words, Jesus was teaching the same thing when in verse 36 He speaks of gathering fruit unto eternal life. Are you gathering fruit so as to assure yourself that you indeed have the faith that provides eternal life? This is something we must each ask ourselves. Complacency, coasting, dormancy, backsliding, these take no effort at all. Certainly they provide no evidence of real faith either. Serving Jesus is work, but it is work that those who are His are most eager to do. Why? Because our hearts are so filled with love and gratitude for having been rescued from sin and called unto salvation, that nothing is more important for us

to do than to do that which He wants from us, while we yet have the time and the strength to do it!

4. This is something not necessarily learned directly from this message, yet it is desirable and applicable for the enhancement of any scriptural message. It deals with context, but not necessarily with what is normally meant by that term. I'm speaking of historical context, a knowledge of the times and places of which Scripture speaks, and what was behind the situations and events with which it deals. The first part of this essay deals with this type of context in order to provide an enrichment and a clearer understanding of what lay behind the scenes, and what historically preceded and influenced conditions, attitudes and behaviors there described. Without such background information we are all too frequently relegated to understanding only superficial portions of a message and not the full rich depth of meaning that such knowledge can provide. For instance, without more understanding than the immediate text offers as to whom the Samaritans were and what they believed, the story may seem somewhat abstract and less relevant to us than it is when we have these additional background details. So here we have a case for greater study of the whole word of God and of what more can be learned from other sources. On this point, many will rush to state that Scripture is everything we need in order to know God and what He wants of us. That is absolutely correct. However, if historians such as Josephus and Herodotus, along with the many archeological discoveries can add background context to God's Word, are they not also beneficial and worthy of use?

I pray that this little story of the woman at the well, as Jesus has chosen to tell it, will fill the reader with another increment of increased or renewed love and zeal for our Lord, and also be an inducement to take up the work He has assigned His disciples, past and present. Jesus admitted to the woman His deity, and this most sinful woman became not only saved but also an ardent follower and fruitful disciple of the Lord. From this one little seed planted in a rich, though initially foul soil, much fruit resulted and caused the planting of many more seeds, which the later disciples harvested. Are any of us less qualified or less capable than that woman whose name we will never even know? Perhaps it is through the subsequent generations of her sowings and plantings that you or I have been harvested. We surely owe it to someone's sowing that we are His. Will your or my conscience allow either of us to do less in gratitude than she did? I pray not.

87

The Parables of the Mustard Seed and of Leaven

These two parables will be discussed together because they both have essentially the same message to convey, that is, the growth of the visible kingdom of heaven and of evil within it. Before we begin to probe the depths of spiritual meaning Jesus is conveying to us through them, let's first try to better understand why He is speaking in this seemingly convoluted manner. Also it is important to better understand just what the kingdom of heaven is, where it is, and in what time frame it exists.

First, it might be useful to end the possible confusion between the kingdom of heaven as spoken of by Matthew and the kingdom of God spoken of by Mark and Luke. They appear to be both the same. Most Bible scholars have concluded that Matthew, whose primary emphasis was on Jesus as the Messiah and was thereby appealing primarily to the Hebrews, would have offended them by using the word God. Throughout the Hebrew history, the name of God was so sacred that it dare not be uttered or even referred to, except indirectly. Because it was never spoken, the pronunciation of His name seems to have been been lost. The closest we come is through the word Yahweh. Thus Matthew called it the kingdom of heaven. Mark and Luke, however, had no such restraints, because they considered their readers to be mostly Romans and Greeks. Their calling it the kingdom of God is probably more literal in terms of what Jesus actually said. The parable of the mustard seed in Matthew is describing the kingdom of heaven while that exact same parable in Luke is said to be describing the kingdom of God. Nevertheless some scholars seem to believe that there is some subtle difference between kingdom of God and king-dom of heaven, but I have not read as to why they believe this.

After speaking such profound and eternal truths with such great clarity that everyone could understand, throughout the earlier part of His ministry, Jesus suddenly ends this aspect of His ministry to the people. After the point in time represented by Matthew, chapter 12, Jesus speaks publicly only in parables. Why? chapter 12 tells us why. In verse 22, we learn that He healed a man who was blind and dumb and possessed by a devil. This was truly a miracle healing, the likes of which had never before been seen. Others had apparently removed evil spirits, but never from anyone who couldn't speak, because such exorcism required the spirit to first identify itself through the spoken word of its victim. This, of course, was impossible when the person was incapable of speaking. That is why some claimed that Jesus must be the "Son of David," the Messiah (versc 23). However, the official verdict as decreed by the Pharisees was that this had to be the work of Beelzebub, which is another name for Satan, and which also means, "dung god" in Greek. Having been thus officially proclaimed by the spiritual leaders, this constituted the national rejection of their Mes-siah. They had been given ample light by means of which they could have known the truth, but they rejected it. Henceforth, there would be no more light given to them; He would speak only in parables, which the people would not understand. Only the Apostles and genu-ine disciples would be given the privilege of knowing more truth. Matthew 13, verses 11–17, tells us this in Jesus' own words. From these verses, we find three reasons why Jesus would continue to speak, but to speak only in parables. First, in verse 11, these truths would be given only to His followers, His true believers, that they would know the mysteries of the kingdom. Second, it was not to be given for those who had rejected Him to know, and third, it was to fulfill prophecy, which predicted His parabolic method of teaching. He refers here to Isaiah, which would be chapter 6, verses 9 and 10. This prophecy can also be found in Psalm 78:2.

So the purpose of these parables is to explain the mysteries of the kingdom of heaven / God. Now then, what is the kingdom? In what we call the Lord's Prayer, we say *"thy kingdom come, thy will be done, on earth as it is in heaven.*" That is not the kingdom of heaven Jesus referred to in Matthew 13. It is the kingdom that will come in the millennium, when Jesus rules on the throne of David here on earth, and in that kingdom His will will be done here on earth as it is in heaven. The kingdom of which Jesus speaks in Matthew 13 is here and now, and encompasses the period from His first to His second coming. We might best call this the period of Christendom. It is the specific sphere over which God rules today. Dr. Arnold Fruchtenbaum offers a very clear and informative explanation of God's overall kingdom program as expressed in Scripture. A compression of his analysis is as follows:

There are five facets of God's overall kingdom program.

1. The external timeless kingdom of universal scope. Here God is always in control, either by His decrees or by His permissive will. There is nothing anywhere or at any time that is not by His decree or permissive will.

2. There is a spiritual kingdom that includes every born-again person from all people of all times.

3. There was the theocratic kingdom where God ruled over Israel through the establishment of the Mosaic laws. This was in two phases.

a. The mediatorial kingdom where God ruled through mediators such as Moses, Joshua, and the judges.

b. The monarchial kingdom that extended from Saul through Zedekiah to the Babylon captivity where He ruled through the kings.

4. The messianic kingdom. This is the kingdom that the prophets began to expound. It is the kingdom that Jesus offered and which Israel rejected. The fact is that it is the millennium kingdom that will begin just seventy-five days after the great tribulation (Daniel 12:12). With Israel's rejection of their Messiah, the offer was taken away for a while, that is, postponed some two thousand plus years until the closing days of the Tribulation at

which time it will be offered again and accepted, as the Israelis see "whom they have pierced" (Zechariah 12:10).

5.   The mystery kingdom. This is best called Christendom, the period between the first and second coming of Jesus. It expresses the condition of the earth now, while He is away. The mystery kingdom is not the same as the eternal kingdom. It is not a theocratic kingdom because it is not limited to one nation, but involves both Jews and Gentiles. It is also not the same as the messianic kingdom, although it is included in it. The mystery kingdom includes both believers and unbelievers. Therefore, it is not the same as the church, but the church, that is, the saved believers, is included in it.

Thus Scripture makes clear that the kingdom of God, as spoken of by Jesus through parables, is, in fact, what now exists and that we must deal with every day. Is it not, therefore, essential, if we have chosen to be His disciples, to learn as much as possible about this period of time in which He has placed us? It was not, as He stated, for the non-believers to know this mystery. And through this parabolic method of teaching, none could accurately decipher His meaning. It is only through the supernatural guidance of the Holy Spirit that His truth can be known. It is through our prayers and the prayers of saints who came before us that the Holy Spirit was, and is willing to reveal what He wants us to know. There seems to be a basic message theme flowing throughout all of these parables, and each presents a particular facet of that theme. At this point, in my quest to understand, I believe that the kingdom of God message, as Jesus is providing it in the parables, has to do with Christian behavior, values and choices, and what the world conditions would be like during these ever increasingly corrupt, deceptive and faith challenging times. Finally let us examine the two subject parables by first reading each of them:

The Parable of the Mustard Seed

31 *Another parable put he forth unto them, saying, The kingdom of heaven is like to a grain of mustard seed, which a man took, and sowed in his field:*

779

32 which indeed is the least of all seeds: but when it is grown, it is the greatest among herbs, and becometh a tree, so that the birds of the air come and lodge in the branches thereof.

The Parable of the Leaven

33 Another parable spake he unto them; The kingdom of heaven is like unto leaven, which a woman took, and hid in three measures of meal, till the whole was leavened.

I pray forgiveness from those who read this and want only the "bottom line" meaning, and feel that they have suffered through too many words here before reaching that point. In order to best understand our Lord's message, it seems important to me that we understand as much as we can about the figures used in the parables and what they represent, in order to be most capable of extracting from them what is hidden. Remember Jesus meant these parables to contain hidden truths, not to be readily understood, except by those who have been given the light.

In the parable of the mustard seed, it refers to the "least of all seeds." If you have seen a mustard seed, you know that there are many smaller seeds such as the orchid. However, it then speaks of it as "the greatest among herbs." Therefore, we may consider it to be the smallest in an herb garden, which in fact it is. The mustard plant most common to the region only grows to about three to four feet in height, surely something that would not be very attractive or even possible for birds to "lodge in." This has led some commentators to conclude that this is a mutation, a perversion that grew to large and grotesque proportions. This is not necessarily true, however, because according to the Oxford English dictionary there is a black mustard plant called the brossica nigra, which grows to the height of eight to twelve feet and can be found in Israel. This would qualify to be the greatest among herbs; however, at this height it still does not seem in my opinion, to express the large stature of the tree suggested by the parable. Therefore, whether Jesus is using as an example the small yellow mustard plant or the larger black mustard seed "tree," the parable is surely referring to a plant that sprung to life from a tiny seed and grew into an exceptionally large tree for that type of plant. Scripture frequently uses a large tree with spreading branches to describe worldly kingdoms as with Babylon in Daniel 4 and the Assyrian dynasty in Ezekiel 31:3. Here Jesus is saying that the kingdom of heaven is like this huge tree. It sprang to life from a single tiny seed, which is to say the Gospel, and grew into the worldwide power, which is Christendom. However, it is not all righteous and fruit bearing as it could be, because it becomes infested with birds that come to occupy its branches and perhaps devour much of the "fruits" as do the birds in the parble of the sower. Birds, of course, symbolize, as they do elsewhere in Scripture, Satan's agents, the false professors, evil teachers and other kindred spirits who seek to undermine, pervert and discredit Christ's way by any and all possible means. This "tree" that began so beautifully, the kingdom, grew rapidly and perversely from the time of Constantine, when it married the world, on through the middles ages, when it reigned supreme over all the power of Europe, and then on into the Reformation age of "branches," that is, the denominations. Surly the "birds" can be seen to having been continuously active to this day, even in the branches, and now more than ever.

In summary, Jesus is describing the kingdom of God, that is the church age, as a tree which grows from a very tiny seed, the Gospel Word as first planted by Him and His apostles, into a great tree, that is, into a large kingdom. Although ordained by God to contain His own, it does, nevertheless, through His permissive will, become contaminated through the agents of Satan. This serves as another warning to those who live in it to be ever alert as to the dangers these agents represent. The mystery as revealed by this and the other parables is that, while this is the church age, the age of redeemed Christians, not all who profess to be a part of it are saved. Satan's agents who are in all of its branches are there to deceive and to thus prevent as many as possible from accepting Jesus as their Lord and Savior. The deceit and resulting departure from our Lord's way will continue to increase "*as in the days that were before the flood*" (Matthew 24:38). Then He will "*in the twinkling of an eye,*" (1 Corinthians 15:52) remove His faithful and end the church portion of the kingdom of God.

With the preceding background, little need be said directly regarding the Parable of the Leaven. Leaven throughout Scripture expresses evil, just as the birds do in the preceding parable. The three measures of meal takes us back to Genesis 18, where Abraham asked Sarah to make ready three measures of meal for the guests who had arrived at his tent on their way to Sodom. These guests, of course, were our Lord and two angels, all in human-like bodies. These three measures of meal have become a traditional fellowship offering in both Jewish and Arabic cultures. A measure in Greek is "saton" and is derived from the Hebrew word *seah*, which is a unit of measure said to be one third of an *ephah*, or seven quarts. Meal in both Greek and Hebrew means flour. It would be finely ground grain such as wheat or barely. Here it was most likely wheat, because barley was viewed as an inferior grain. If indeed a measure was seven quarts, that batch of dough that Sarah made was huge, enough for many meals. Perhaps it was intended to supply the visitors during their several days journey to and from Sodom. In the parable the woman hid leaven in the meal, contaminating all of it. The woman might be viewed as a Jezebel of Revelation 2:20, through whose agency the earthly church was contaminated. She called herself a prophetess and taught unholy principals which were subversive to the faith. This mystery of iniquity began in the times of the apostles and has continued for two thousand years, growing increasingly powerful and evident in these final days. Notice the whole was leavened. That is most expressive of these final days, immediately prior to the rapture, when there is hardly any great doctrine of Scripture that has not been perverted by false teachers. Once the whole of Christendom has become perverted it will signify that moment spoken of when Jesus says in Luke 21:24 *"the times of the Gentiles be fulfilled."* That, I believe, is also the moment Jesus will come for those who are His own.

Dr. Fruchtenbaum has an interesting perspective on the three measures. He likens this to the three world religions that make up Christendom, that is, the Catholic, Eastern Orthodox, and Protestant, which are all contaminated with the leaven. Our Lord's words are always very deep and packed full of profound meaning. Surely no violence is done to His word if this be a part of the understanding of the parable. There is another view regarding this parable as espoused by other Bible scholars which I find difficult to accept. They consider the leaven to be the kingdom and the meal to be the whole earth into which it spreads. Because leaven is so frequently identified with evil, hypocrisy, puffing up, pride, etc. as in Luke 12:1, 1 Corinthians 5:6, 7, 8, Galatians 5:9, Amos 4:5, etc. I don't believe this alternative can be as rigorously defended.

In summary, we again have the message, that during this age of the kingdom of heaven, there is this widespread apostasy. Except for the saved remnant within this age, it is nothing like what God's millennium kingdom will be, nor is it like the subsequent new heaven and earth. The kingdom of heaven is a sin-infected interlude within which a remnant of saints will be found who becomes so because they have believed in Jesus, in who He was, and in what He did. They will be those whose faith is demonstrated by their works. Their works will include total repentance, a contrite heart and a sincere striving for obedience to His Word, in spite of the awesome and powerful worldly temptations. The parable of the leaven might be called a description of the kingdom at its very end. With the meal representing the kingdom, the whole of it is here depicted as sinfully contaminated. Of what use is it to God any longer, when it is incapable of bearing any more fruit, i.e. saved souls? Nothing. So, of course, He will cut it down as with any fruitless tree. The book of Revelation describes this cutting down in very graphic detail.

Knowing all of this, and seeing the evidence that there is very little time left for this kingdom in which we find ourselves, is it not urgent that we put our spiritual affairs in order right now? If we are to be part of that blessed rapture, our house must be continuously in order and ready. We must be among those of the "good ground" (Matthew 13:8). We must be the wheat among the tares (Matthew 13:24). We must be among the good fish found in the net (Matthew 13:48). We must be like the man who found treasure hidden in the field (Matthew 13:44). We must be like the virgins who had the oil, etc . . . We must be spiritually ready now, because He said He could come at any moment. Given what we can clearly see in this world, that moment will not be long in coming. May God bless you with this sense of urgency and a need for sincere devotion to His Lordship and all that that implies.

88

The Parable of the Talents

This is another kingdom of heaven parable, where Jesus is teaching something that, for Christians, is very important for us to know. A good rule to follow is, if He chooses to include something in His book, no matter how strange it is or how difficult it is to understand, it must be of very great importance. Therefore, it is incumbent on each of us to seek an understanding of everything He says.

The first few times I read this I found nothing to grab on to as spiritually relevant. It is simply a story of a rich guy going on a trip and leaving three of his servants in the care of some of His wealth. When he gets back, two have doubled what he put in their trust, and the other buried what he was given in order to keep it safe, so he could return it to his master undiminished. He obviously feared the boss, and wasn't taking any chances. So what is the issue? As I first thought about it, it seemed to me that I would probably have done what the third guy did, keep his money safe so I could give it back without having lost any. But for that, he got sentenced to HELL! What's that all about? Without the assistance of our great Interpreter, the Holy Spirit, that's probably all that many people can get out of it, I suppose. But with Him, God's instructional message can be found loud and clear!

Let us first read the parable and then cast our Spirit-given net into its waters and see what precious truth we can bring up from under its surface.

The Parable of the Talents

14 For the kingdom of heaven is as a man traveling into a far country, who called his own servants, and delivered unto them his goods.

15 *And unto one he gave five talents, to another two, and to another one; to every man according to his several ability; and straightway took his journey.*

16 *Then he that had received the five talents went and traded with the same, and made them other five talents.*

17 *And likewise he that had received two, he also gained other two.*

18 *But he that had received one went and digged in the earth, and hid his lord's money.*

19 *After a long time the lord of those servants cometh, and reckoneth with them.*

20 *And so he that had received five talents came and brought other five talents, saying, Lord, thou deliveredst unto me five talents: behold, I have gained beside them five talents more.*

21 *His lord said unto him, Well done, thou good and faithful servant: thou hast been faithful over a few things, I will make thee ruler over many things: enter thou into the joy of thy lord.*

22 *He also that had received two talents came and said, Lord, thou deliveredst unto me two talents: behold, I have gained two other talents beside them.*

23 *His lord said unto him, Well done, good and faithful servant; thou hast been faithful over a few things, I will make thee ruler over many things: enter thou into the joy of thy lord.*

24 *Then he which had received the one talent came and said, Lord, I knew thee that thou art a hard man, reaping where thou hast not sown, and gathering where thou hast not strewed:*

25 *and I was afraid, and went and hid thy talent in the earth: lo, there thou hast that is thine.*

26 *His lord answered and said unto him, Thou wicked and slothful servant, thou knewest that I reap where I sowed not, and gather where I have not strewed:*

27 *thou oughtest therefore to have put my money to the exchangers, and then at my coming I should have received mine own with usury.*

28 *Take therefore the talent from him, and give it unto him which hath ten talents.*

29 *For unto every one that hath shall be given, and he shall have abundance: but from him that hath not shall be taken away even that which he hath.*

30 *And cast ye the unprofitable servant into outer darkness: there shall be weeping and gnashing of teeth.*

First, it is evident that Jesus is speaking of Himself as the man traveling into a far country. Jesus is referring to His ascension to heaven. He has entrusted His servants with His wealth until such times as He decides to return. He has entrusted some with more than

785

He has with others, each in accordance with His foreknowledge of their capacity to deal with what is given. They all know that one day He will return and require an accounting from each of them.

In verses 16 and 17 He tells us that the first two "traded" with the talents and doubled the value of that which He had entrusted to them. "Trade" is the translation of the Greek word *ergazomal,* which means, "to toil (as a task or occupation), to commit, do, labor for, trade, or work." Because of verse 27 where Jesus speaks of receiving usury it may be concluded that this was probably the nature of the way in which each of them used what had been left for them. But obviously the meaning of the translated word "trade" is far more inclusive and could have involved many kinds of wealth generating efforts. Furthermore, the word talent, in Hebrew, is defined as a unit of weight generally believed to be about ninety-six pounds when it is referring to silver money. I've read that the Babylonian talent was even heavier and that the Greek talent was eighty-six pounds. Generally, however, it is spoken of as a large unit of money being the equivalent of about four thousand shekels, the basic unit of Hebrew money, which was about two fifths of an ounce of silver. But the talent spoken of in the parable could have been ninety-six pounds of anything such as seeds to plant, or oil, or spices, etc. to trade. Therefore, in the context of earthly wealth, they could have been left almost anything where the value could have been increased through their labor and prudent management.

In using the word talent, with its potentially different meaning, as His choice of words, describing what He left them to manage, it could well be that the Holy Spirit is here engaging in a pun, as He frequently does in some of His messages. If it was intended to be a pun, it was a latent one intended to be revealed in these later times when English would become a nearly universal language of the Christian world. Talent, in English, of course, is best defined as a person's special ability. For us today, that is the essence of the parable, and how we, who are Christian, should apply it and learn from it. Christians are His servants in that He is our Lord as well as our Savior. Every servant of the Lord, every saved soul, has been given a special gift, that is, some talent or special ability which he or she is to use to the greater glory of God. The collective application of these abilities by all who are His, is what constitutes and makes dynamic, the living Body of Christ. That is why Christians are called the "Body of Christ." The Holy Spirit, through Paul, in his first letter to the Corinthians chapter 12 verses 1 through 27 lays out with great clarity this miraculous mystery, and how, as various members of the body of Christ, we each have a particular spiritual gift that is a special talent. Each member must use the gift that is given to him or her to the best of their abilities, if the Body is to function properly. Failure by any "part" to function as assigned can cause the "body" to be diminished in its effectiveness, a condition obviously displeasing to the Father.

In the parable Jesus demonstrates the fact that He knows the ability of every individual, and assigns to each, responsibilities perfectly commensurate with their abilities at the time. To those who have a greater capacity to serve Him, He assigns greater responsibilities. Realizing the limitations of the three servants, He gave each according to his or her ability and potential to perform. The first two used their "talents" and doubled His investment, that is, were fruitful to His purpose while the third failed totally, in regards to the very reason for which the talent was entrusted to him.

He made two mistakes. The first was his failure to use his one talent. In burying his talent, he achieved absolutely nothing for his Master, and therefore, violated the trust. Having neglected the opportunity, he was now to be deprived of it forever. His other mistake was his failure to really know and trust in, his Master. Notice that he called his Master a hard man who reaped where he had not sown and gathered where he hadn't strewed. He was unable to see beyond his nose because he had not taken the time to really know all he could about his master. In the Gospel of John, chapter 4 verse 37, 38, Jesus explains this very issue of reaping where others have sowed. Because his Master did not appear to physically sow what he harvested, or to thrash the wheat to separate the seed from the straw, he saw Him as one who simply derived His wealth from the efforts of others. He had no concept of his Master's abilities, or of His work, or of His character. This excuse for his slothfulness exposed not only his ignorance and deficiencies as a servant, but also his unwarranted fear and ignorance. All of this translated into a useless servant, and this is what sent him to the outer darkness. In his reprimand, the Master told him that, at the very least he should have gained something, even interest (usury), from what he had been given. Today we equate usury with an excessive rate of interest. In Old Testament times usury meant interest, not necessarily excessive interest. Charging interest of other Hebrews was forbidden, but was allowed if the lending was to gentiles (Deuteronomy 23:20).

The essence of this parable message may be summarized as follows:

1. All of Jesus' servants, that means all who are Christians, are given talents (spiritual gifts) that they are expected to use.

2. He provides these talents on the basis of His foreknowledge in accordance with each individual's capacity to use them.

3. We are held accountable only for what we have been given, not what we do not have. (2 Corinthians 8:12).

4. He expects each person to use to the best of his or her ability what is given to him or her. It is slothful to fail to act energetically in these matters.

5. Those who use their talent wisely in accordance with His will are generously rewarded.

6. Those who fail to use what is given to them loose even that which they have. Today's secular axiom "use it or loose it" might be said to have its origin right here in God's Word.

7. Some who pose as God's faithful servants are really not. Notice in verse 14, Jesus refers to all three as His own servants. This includes the one who obviously was not one of the redeemed. Our omniscient Lord, of course, knew this from the beginning. Remember, this is a parable not specific to real life situation. The third servant's role is here as a means of delivering a very specific message. It tells us that all of God's servants are not necessarily God's fruitful or redeemed. Some profess the Christian faith but do not possess it. They appear to walk the Christian walk but they are not on the same path that is the one which

leads to the narrow gate. Remember Judas. He was an Apostle, the highest order of Jesus' servants, for more than three years. He went the way of the third servant in this parable.

8. Verse 29 expresses not only here, but in other references regarding Jesus' teaching, a very important principal. Those who have the willingness to serve and to use their God given talents, more of these will be given to them. Those who fail to use what has been given to them will loose what little they have. God will take it from them. The justice of all of this will be understood when we each face the mercy seat in the heavenly kingdom. Most of us will probably be surprised at how much, or how little of our applied talents were of value to our Lord. Their value will be judged by what was in the heart and what motivated the use of these talents.

I believe that there is at least one more important truth to be extracted from this parable, if taken in the broadest context of Scripture. As mentioned above, it was tragic that the third servant failed to use his talent. If he had stopped there instead of imputing his Master's Character and purpose, thus demonstrating his lack of love, obedience and faithfulness, one might have assumed that he was a repentant believer, but one who was merely lazy, fearful and ignorant of his responsibility in the matter. In that case, assuming that his heart was right, he would have been simply rebuked, and perhaps his life shortened, but he wouldn't have been denied salvation. But then the Parable would not have contained the specific message it was intended to provide.

If we are His, He expects each of us to fulfill the purpose for which He gave us our talents, our spiritual gifts, and we *all do* have them! If we fail to do this, of what good are we to Him here as His servants? NONE! Furthermore, recognizing these gifts, and applying them to glorify Him daily, can be powerful evidence of a repentant and obedient heart, which can also be the evidence of a redeemed soul. On the other hand, lack of this, that is, the lack of good use of our God given talents can be evidence to the contrary. It behooves each of us to examine ourselves frequently to be certain that ours is a genuine Christian life that personifies His purpose for each of us.

Postscript

Two years after having written this, and just before it was to be woven into "Christian Musings," I have come to realize that this parable may have nothing to do with salvation. Most, including myself, when studying it conclude that it must be telling us that the third servant was unsaved, because we conclude that he was cast into the lake of fire in the outer darkness, but that isn't quite what it says. It only speaks of an outer darkness, and because the only context we have in our minds is that place where one would find Ghenna, that is the eternal lake of fire, we conclude that is where he was sent. But further and more careful study can lead to a different conclusion. Had I'd been faithful to my concern as expressed in the second paragraph of this study, and in how I'm usually led in my studies to examine the key words in their original language, a better interpretation might have followed even back then. The word "darkness" can be translated as "obscurity." Obscurity is where there is a lack of light, a vagueness, a lack of clarity. The word "outer" means simply, "out doors, or outside." From this we could conclude that where he was to spend eternity was certainly not among the illuminated, not in the clear presence of God. Because hell or the lake of fire is not mentioned, it seems that we should not add it to what is written. Had the translators written "cast the unprofitable servant outside and into the dark place, or into obscurity" we would not as easily choose to believe that the servant was sent to the eternal place of damnation. Furthermore, Scripture is very clear on the fact that only Antichrist and his false prophet are to be cast directly into the lake of fire. There is no one there today, nor will there be until the end of the tribulation when Antichrist and the false prophets will be its first and only occupants for the next thousand years. We should remember that all other lost souls remain in sheol until the end of the millennium. Therefore, might we not conclude that the servant will reside in some remote place here on earth during the millennium, and later in another remote obscure and dimly lighted place outside the gates of the New Jerusalem? (Revelation 21)

It should be remembered that this is a parable describing "the kingdom of God" which is limited in time to the period from Pentecost to the Rapture. If indeed this "servant" is to be cast into the outer darkness, where is this within the time frame of the kingdom? It cannot be the lake of fire. Furthermore, servants in this parable are a translation of the Greek word *doulos* meaning "bond servant or slave." This is a term Paul applies to himself and is used through the New Testament as one totally and permanently committed to their Lord. There are four other Greek words translated as servant, but this connotes nothing of their nature. They are defined as [runner of errands, attendants, waiters] [slave or servant as a boy (beaten with impunity), child] [menial domestic, household servant] [menial servant, attendant]. If this servant was someone of less quality than the other two, why wouldn't his label have been different from the others? It seems evident, to me at least, that they were all equal positionally, that is saved souls. However, they were far from equal effectually as to their use of the "talents" God had given them for the purpose of serving Him and to accumulate "rewards" or "crowns."

My personal belief now is that this parable is more likely about rewards associated with how well we serve our Lord during our short stay here on earth. Those of us who are saved, that is justified have our ticket to an eternal life in a heavenly place, but all places, positions, or levels of service in the kingdom are not the same. Those who serve Him best here with our "talents" will be the nearest to Him, and live brightly in His glorious light. Those who receive justification and do nothing with it (bury it like the servant in the parable) will be somewhere far out somewhere in a heavenly place, but not where there is much of God's glorious light or presence. Isn't this the more likely message Jesus is giving us rather than what I originally wrote?

I believe the same is true regarding the man who went to the wedding feast improperly dressed as described in Matthew 22:11–13. Here Jesus may be offering another example of a justified soul who chose to simply "coast to heaven." During his life, he failed to exhibit the expression or works of gratitude that would have "clothed him" in the

791

pure white linen attire needed in order to attend the wedding feast of the Lamb. There will be great and eternal regrets in heaven for those who fail to live fruitfully during their Christian lives. This condition is expressed in the "weeping and gnashing of teeth." If this isn't your idea of heaven, then get to work (yes, work). Pray that the Holy Spirit leads you to reveal God's purpose for you, to show you your particular "talent" or "talents," and to thus guide you to become an obedient and fruitful servant. Those who do this, will earn, (yes earn) a place on the new earth close to God, rather than somewhere outside of the gates of the New Jerusalem in what one might call "Regretsville."

—89—

The Parable of the Ten Virgins

In Matthew, chapter 25, verses 1–13, Jesus provides us with another of His wonderful parables. Let us read it first, then we'll try to glean out of it what vital truth He is revealing to us.

The Parable of the Ten Virgins

1 *Then shall the kingdom of heaven be likened unto ten virgins, which took their lamps and went forth to meet the bridegroom.*

2 *And five of them were wise, and five were foolish.*

3 *They that were foolish took their lamps, and took no oil with them:*

4 *but the wise took oil in their vessels with their lamps.*

5 *While the bridegroom tarried, they all slumbered and slept.*

6 *And at midnight there was a cry made, Behold, the bridegroom cometh; go ye out to meet him.*

7 *Then all those virgins arose, and trimmed their lamps.*

8 *And the foolish said unto the wise, Give us of your oil; for our lamps are gone out.*

9 *But the wise answered, saying, Not so; lest there be not enough for us and you: but go ye rather to them that sell, and buy for yourselves.*

10 *And while they went to buy, the bridegroom came; and they that were ready went in with him to the marriage: and the door was shut.*

11 *Afterward came also the other virgins, saying, Lord, Lord, open to us.*

12 *But he answered and said, Verily I say unto you, I know you not.*

13 *Watch therefore; for ye know neither the day nor the hour wherein the Son of man cometh*

As one of the Kingdom of God Parables, it is for teaching us the mysteries that are related to that period of history in which we now live, that time that is between His first and second coming. This includes two segments of time, the period from when Jesus ascended to heaven until the rapture, and also from the rapture to His second arrival, when He will literally sit on the throne of David as promised. "Mysteries," when spoken of in the Scripture, are things of God and His workings that are absolutely new and not previously revealed. Some of the parables speak specifically to the period before rapture; others seem to relate to the post-rapture times.

The Parable of the Ten Virgins is one that has generated some differences of opinion as to which event is being used as a benchmark for conveying its message. Is it at the time of the rapture, or is it at His second coming? Perhaps this little excursion into the Word will help us to decide the matter in our own minds. It is important to know, however, that when it happened is not of any great significance; it is the message it conveys in either case that is of relevance. My personal view is that it is a pre-rapture event. The Parable uses ten virgins as the medium through which to develop the allegory. The word virgin in Greek is *pathenia*. It means maiden, unmarried daughter, or virgin. In the culture of the day, all translations would apply to almost every such young woman, because an unmarried maiden would also be a virgin.

Here we have ten such young girls going out to where it has been told they could meet the coming Bridegroom. These words coming from Jesus in the context of the kingdom of God mysteries, makes it evident that He is speaking of Himself as the Bridegroom, with the bride being the raptured church. The question previously mentioned centers around whether this is His coming for the church, that is, His rapture coming, or whether He is coming with His bride after the tribulation.

In either case, these girls apparently reach the place where He is expected, and have to wait quite a while, not knowing just when He will come. After a while, they all fall asleep. Jesus tells us that five were wise and five were foolish, because the wise brought oil for their lamps while the others did not. Throughout the Scripture, oil is symbolic of the Holy Spirit. Scholars like to create impressive names for such things. They call this the Principal of Expositional Constancy, when Scripture uses such symbolism repeatedly and consistently. Oil is the fuel that brings forth light, God's holy light, which is His Word. Only the genuine saved believer has the indwelling of the Holy Spirit, and is, therefore, capable, through the light that the Holy Spirit provides, to understand the spiritual messages found in God's Word, the Holy Bible.

Suddenly the Bridegroom appeared, that moment they had been eagerly awaiting, the moment when they could join Him in whatever was His plan. They immediately got up and trimmed their lamps. Lamp is lampas in Greek and can mean a light, lamp or torch. If these were torches, then the oil would be carried in a separate container to be added to the torch, as it was needed. I prefer to assume that they had lamps because they did exist at that time, and they would be the more likely choice of light source for young maidens as compared to a torch. Oil lamps consist of an oil container into which a long wick is submerged. The outer end of the wick extends out of the container and is held in place just above it. Capillary action draws the oil up to its outer end. The wick probably was made from a piece of twisted or woven cloth, which could be ignited and would continue to burn with the oil being continuingly drawn up serving as fuel. Without the oil, a lighted wick will burn up quite quickly and become a worthless char. When there is oil, the wick is only slightly charred at the end as long as the oil continues to flow and remains the source of fuel.

Before lighting the lamp it is desirable to "trim" the lamp, that is, the wick. This is to remove the small amounts of char from the previous burning so that the flame will be brighter and more efficient. All ten did this and lighted the wicks. It is then that five of them discovered that the flame was short lived and that only the wick burned because there was no oil in their lamps. Perhaps it was only when they saw that the other five had lamps that were burning brightly where theirs had burnt out, did they realize they had a problem. It may have been only then that they realized that oil was needed. Why else would have they brought empty lamps? In the earthly context it is improbable that they wouldn't have known about the need for oil. But remember, this is a spiritual message being expressed through earthly symbolisms.

They asked the five who had oil to give them some, but they wouldn't because they couldn't share it. Instead they suggested that they go where they could get their own. Of course, by the time they got back, presumably, but not necessarily, with some of the *right* oil, it was too late; the opportunity was gone; the door was shut; and the Bridegroom was compelled to say, "I know you not." Notice I said the right oil, which could only have been the Holy Spirit.

The message here is quite clear and profound. Word had gotten around that the Bridegroom was going to come sometime soon, and for them to become part of the wedding party would be a very good thing, a great privilege. Some, represented by the five wise girls, were truly saved believers as revealed by the fact that their lamps were filled with oil, (the Holy Spirit). If we can stretch the analogy a bit, we might say the lamps were their hearts and their hearts were filled with the Holy Spirit, which often expresses His light through the very countenance of the true believers. They were genuine possessors of faith. They couldn't share the oil, the Holy Spirit. We each must seek Him through individual personal faith. The other five were ignorant of the truth, were probably falsely taught or may have been only dabblers in the faith. They saw what these five wise girls were doing and where they were heading and decided that it would be a good idea to join them, believing that the way was easy and that they were "as good as" every one else. They each had heard the "good news" of His coming, gave credence, that is "believed" in their "own way." They were "believers" in that they believed that they were saved! Why else would they have tried to go where only believers were allowed? They had head knowledge, which most likely was the sole source of their belief. They were professors, but obviously not possessors of the faith. To all outward appearances, they were identical to the wise five. The difference was something often not discernable because the oil, the Holy Spirit, is in the lamp, that is, the heart, and not necessarily very evident externally. Often those with "empty lamps" who lack adequate knowledge of the *Word*, may provide a great deal of many outward expressions of "goodness." This gives them reason to believe that they are saved. Those, whose lamps are full, often express their holiness in quieter, less noticeable ways. Who could tell them apart until the moment that TRUTH arrived? Only God Himself knows who really has the "oil." However, He implores us to repeatedly examine ourselves *in the context of His Word* so that we may acquire a level of certainty as to our own salvation.

It was not until all ten were assembled at the place of welcoming that the empty ones discovered their emptiness but then it was too late. The wise ones knew the Word, they had already become genuine believers whose lamps (their hearts),were full of oil (the Holy Sprit) and they knew well the purpose of the Bridegroom's coming and what credentials were needed to join His entourage. The others, the foolish ones, probably had observed the actions of the wise and had superficially emulated them. But you might say it was all in their heads but not in their hearts. They professed very compellingly and even believed that they had all of the qualifications of the wise even though they possessed them not. This is very reminiscent of Matthew 22:11–14, in the Parable of the Marriage feast where one guest is seen to not have on the proper garment and is, therefore, thrown out. The "garment" in that case is also the Holy Spirit. Verse 14 of the same chapter tells us that *"many are called, but few are chosen."* At this point, I'm reminded of Genesis 7:16, when God shut the door of the ark. For 120 years as Noah built the ark, he was probably reported to be the weirdest weirdo of the century. But how many of those who called him that do you suppose came pounding at that closed door and screaming to be let in when the flood came?

We have here within this Parable a very important message for all of us. It's about a relationship. You may be very comfortable in your belief that you know Jesus, but what is far more important, does He know you? That is the meat of this message. Do you spend time with Him? Enough time? He is always available to us, if we seek Him in prayer and gratitude with contrite, repentant and obedient hearts. He is always standing at the door of our hearts, knocking; His gentle knocking expresses Hi hoping we will let Him in so that He and we can get to know each other. (Revelation 3:30) The five wise girls knew Him, and through the indwelling of the Holy Spirit *He knew them.*

Perhaps when Jesus comes for His own at the rapture, it will be midnight as in the Parable. Of course, it can't be midnight every-where at once, but for the sake of simplicity and in order to add another bit of symbolism, let's assume it is. His quest for His own will be easy; His people will all be visible by the spiritual light provided in each by the indwelling of the Holy Spirit. Imagine Him looking down from the clouds at the time of rapture. As His eyes peruse the dark-ness, He will see these many tiny lights, like we see lightening bugs across the landscape. These will be the redeemed, filled with the shining light of the Holy Spirit waving to Him and saying, "Here I am, I'm ready. Take me home"! And He will! But as in the parable, there will be many, many others, not unlike the foolish virgins who will also be waving, calling and believing that they too are chosen, but He will not know them, for again, *"many are called but few are chosen."* (Matthew 20:16 – 22:12). One might wonder how many "foolish virgins," as they represent much of the world at large, might have earlier *"confessed with their mouth the Lord Jesus and believed in their hearts that Jesus was raised from the dead"* (Romans 10:9) and, therefore, believed that they were saved. It seems that for some Christians the head believers, the head believes that the heart believes, because it sensed an emotional moment or two at the time belief came. But that heart belief must be carefully and frequently examined and nurtured lest it turn out to be nothing more than that which affected the "category two" believers Jesus describes in the Parable of the Sower.

Regarding the issue of sleep. Several times Scripture tells us to remain watchful, to not be lax, but to stay alert, because we have no way of knowing when the rapture will occur. This doesn't mean we should not sleep as a normal part of our lives. It means to not be lulled into the sleep of complacency or dullness of our spiritual senses. The wise girls slept along with the foolish ones. However, the wise were ready at a moment's notice. They kept themselves spiritually ready, keeping their lamps filled. The parable makes this very clear, and does not rebuke them for sleeping. It is o.k. to sleep as long as you stay ready and alert for His coming. He merely says in verse 13 to "watch" because no one can know when He will come. (It's this verse that leads me to believe that this symbolizes a pre-rapture event.) In Revelation 3:3 He tells us again through the church of Sardis. *"I will come as a thief in the night and thou shall not know the hour I will come upon thee."* It doesn't mean that we should spend all our time at the window watching to the extent we neglect our daily duties and responsibilities, as did some in Paul's day. This isn't a threat; it's merely an urging to keep clean, pure and ready, as were the five wise maidens.

One more observation regarding the oil. As observed earlier, the lamp oil in the context of the parable, as well as in many similar

Scripture verses, is symbolic of the Holy Spirit. There is, however, another application of the word that can be appropriated, especially in these end times. Satan, the master counterfeiter, has his own brand of oil, which he uses for his own sinister purposes. Is it doing violence to Scripture to suggest such a thing? I believe not. In the very end times, during the seventieth week, prophesied by Daniel, chapter 9, Satan will produce a false, counterfeit Christ we call the antichrist, and also a great false spiritual leader we call the false prophet. He will be Satan's counterfeit holy spirit. Thus he will sell this "trinity" to all "earth dwellers," in those last days. On that basis it seems consistent and appropriate that he has already synthesized spiritual oil, which he uses to fill many hearts, and through which they come to accept his numerous false religions. He even instills it in the form of complacency and a false sense of security in those Christian-like believers who wrongly, through ignorance of God's Holy Word, succumb to the words of seducing spirits. For this oil is nothing more than putrid sludge that cannot be ignited so as to express a flame of righteousness, but can only produce a smoldering hatred for our Creator God and a turning to Satan's numerous substitutes. It can only be used to increase the heat of hell, which is, after all, his intended purpose for everyone he can deceive.

No doubt I've once again used far too many words to express a simple message. In summary, Jesus is telling us here in this parable what is the essence of most of His Kingdom of God messages. That is simply that there will be many who will be tragically deceived in these last days. The ultimate deception is that many will be so deceived as to believe that they have salvation when, if fact, they do not as with the five foolish virgins. This is what bears most heavily on my heart. It is that a great portion of these will be those who believe they are saved because they are calling themselves Christians. But many will have fallen victim to false prophets and false teachers who will sound very "Christian" because they speak of Jesus and quote Scripture. Those will successfully, and some not even intentionally, lead many into blissful, but fatal, ignorance of truth. Jesus warns us of this nearly every time He speaks in Scripture, and the Holy Spirit tells us in 1 Timothy 4:1 that ". . . in latter times some shall depart from the faith, giving heed to seducing spirits and doctrines of devils." Knowing Scripture is the only way certain to avoid these terminal pitfalls.

KNOW! Be sure, that you are a possessor of the faith that true scriptural oil is in your lamp, that you are not merely a professor of the faith carrying an empty lamp.

—90—

The Marriage of the Lamb

God's most sacred covenant, the one with which He blessed mankind from the very beginning with the first man and woman, was the covenant of marriage. This was ordained in Genesis 2:2, where God said, "Therefore shall a man leave his father and his mother, and shall cleave unto his wife, and they shall be one flesh." There probably was more to this conversation than Scripture tells us, because with this alone, it is difficult to see how Adam could have understood the full meaning of this blessed covenant. There was no father or mother for Adam or for Eve to leave. But, nevertheless, it is evident that Adam did understand what "cleave," meant. While the word "love" is not found in Scripture until Genesis 22:2, when it refers to Abraham's love for Isaac, it is evident that Adam loved Eve with a genuine God-given love, as God intends it to be in all men for their wives.

Many who read the verses that follow verse 24, may fail to see the incredible significance of this love, and how Adam loved his bride as Jesus loves His bride, the church. One could say that both Adam and Jesus were made sin out of love for their wives. Adam wasn't deceived. He could have remained sinless, but if he had, the marriage could not have continued, given the great disparity of condition that would have existed between them. He knowingly followed Eve into sin so that the marriage would be continued. Had he not, the "seed of the woman," that is our Christ Jesus, would not have become Man as God had foretold that He would.

Thus we see the institution of marriage between a man and a woman established in the very beginning of God's book of Instructions by which we are called to live. Throughout Scripture, marriage is used as an idiom or an analogy through which to illustrate and help us to understand major precepts. Sadly, the world through Satan's incessant prodding and perverting along with man's inherent sinful nature has, in these end times, made a mockery of this sacred institution, just as prophesied.

However, the purpose of this paper is not to expound on this, but to deal solely with the "marriage of the lamb" as referred to in Revelation 19:7. Of course, we know that this is the marriage between Christ Jesus and a portion of the "church" that is, I believe a select portion of the body of redeemed Christians, that composite of all of those who will have been born-again, up to the time of the rapture (John 3:3). But now let us look at the "marriage analogy from an individual prospective, that is between Jesus and a person who considers himself or herself to be within the corporate body of the church and who is therefore seeking to be part of the "collective' bride. In a marriage, the groom as well as the bride is supposed to agree to that binding covenant until death parts them. Sadly in today's society, even among "Christians," more than half of these sacred vows are renounced through divorce. Vows have become meaningless rituals that are honored only as long as it is easy, comfortable and convenient to do so. But between Christ Jesus and His bride it is inviolate, and for eternity.

In modern evangelical "match making," between a person and Jesus, it has become simply a matter of asking the prospective "bride" whether he or she "believes" in Jesus and the cross, and is willing to accept Him in this union. If the person says, "I do" and repeats what is called the "sinners' prayer," and perhaps some other bit of confirming utterances, the cry goes up "hallelujah!" Chalk us up with another saved soul! For, as the modern reasoning goes, didn't Jesus simply say in John 6:47, "He that believeth in me hath everlasting life"? Therefore, if you believe or "feel" you are saved, end of story! But is it? Perhaps, but it depends on what He meant by "believeth," and how the "believers" belief corresponds to God's definition! Have the purveyors of salvation asked Him or sought, or the whole answer in His Word? In their currently fashionable gathering of souls, do they teach or even know of such prerequisite essentials as a contrite heart, conviction, repentance, commitment, and obedience? Will Christ Jesus even accept into the Body of Christ, let alone a bride absent of these attributes? Without these qualities present in His betrothed is *He* willing to say, "I Do." Revelation 19:8 tells what He expects of His bride ". . . that she should be arrayed in fine linen, clean and white, for the fine linen is the righteousness of saints." Who is a saint? By definition, it is one who is blameless, and thereby righteous (Philippians 4:21). It *takes more than an "I believe" and an "I do" to be righteous*! One can only become righteous by having one's sins forgiven and washed away by the blood of Christ, and thus being born-again. The Holy Spirit dwells in all who are borne again and *only* those who are born-again! But Acts 5:13, 32 tells us "Him has God exalted with His right hand to be Prince and Savior, for to give repentance to Israel, and forgiveness of sins. And we are witnesses of these things, and so is also the Holy Ghost, whom God has given to them that *obey* Him." That's it! Here we have the fine print regarding both salvation and the wedding contract! It is the prerequisite to Jesus' saying His "I do! The bride must be clothed in the white linen of righteousness, which comes only from the forgiveness of sins! First John 1:19 tells us that "if we confess our sin, He is faithful and just to forgive our sins and to cleanse us from unrighteousness." One is forgiven by grace through a true and saving faith, which is always accomplished by the indwelling of the Holy Spirit. Now we have also determined that the giving of Holy Spirit is limited to those who obey Him! Therefore obedience is an essential part of both the entry into the Body of Christ and of course, the bride's premarital condition. Furthermore, in John 14:15 Jesus says, "If you love me, keep my commandments." And in John 14:23, ". . . if a man loves me, he will keep my words . . ." "Keep my Word." That means also means obedience. Notice that these things are necessary conditions without which "love" is *not God's kind of love*! Would you marry someone who didn't love you? It's likely that if you did, it would not be a good marriage. Surely we know that our omniscient God Jesus would *never* take a bride that did not love Him. Because to love is to obey, obedience as well as love are prerequisites, to salvation, and to becoming the Body of Christ.

Jesus said the greatest commandment is to love God (Him) with all of your heart, soul and mind (Matthew 22:37). All of us fall short of that command. But I believe that those who come the closest, are those who leave here with the greatest number of golden crowns and are the one who become the Bride of Christ.

We have seen that these prerequisites do not derive from *anything* less than a contrite, convicted, obedient and repentant heart fully dedicated to service to our Lord and Savior. Anyone who seeks to bring souls to God, without making sure that all of these prerequisites are fully understood, is perpetuating a fraud, a very *evil* disservice to those who unwittingly go on their way believing that they are saved, and destined for an expected future they will never know. I pray for God's mercy for such a "witness," for one day he or she must face the seat of judgment on which will be sitting the deprived "groom."

I pray even more and grieve for those deprived of membership in the Body of Christ as well as for the would-be "brides," who pass through life falsely believing themselves to be His because they had put their trust in those false witnesses, never having sought or understood the whole Truth as provided by Scriptures.

—91—

Putting Words in God's Mouth

Hello! This is God. I have a simpleton here who keeps bugging me with all kinds of questions about things that are none of his business. He is an old fool who spent most of his life faking goodness while consorting with that devil, Satan. Now, finally, at his eleventh hour, he stumbled across some Truth, and so now he wants to know everything. I have given him a little credit, however, because for an old fool, he has come a long way in a short time. In this paper I am going to let him tell you the little bit about Me that he has gleaned from My book and from others who have studied My book. By the way, the flippancy of style that seems to pervade this in no way indicates any lack of reverence for Me or for My Word. It just happens to be the particular way he chose to put some heavy thoughts into a light lunch that may not be particularly nutritious but might be more easily digested, hopefully interesting, and intentionally provocative.

For years he believed that clever nonsense called evolution, which claims that all existence is by chance, an accident of nature; that first there was nothing, and then it exploded becoming the universe including this planet where, again by accident, there was formed some "goo" that later became you. Here is probably the best example of that human expression that points out that if a lie is big enough, and expressed often enough, it will be believed to be the truth. That damned Satan! I should have chained him long ago. One of these days that devil will get his due. But that's another story. Anyway, back to the subject.

Because he knows that his "eternity" is coming up pretty soon, this old fool wants to know more about Me, who I am, what I did, how I did it, why I did it, and what's next. I suppose that is the price of having given these creatures free will, a curious mind, and enough intelligence to think up these questions. I already gave him all the answers he needs; I wrote the answer book! It is not only the formula for life, but is also a history book with all of the past as well as the future all spelled out. It is very cleverly written, if I do say so Myself. For those with eyes willing to see and who seek the simple essence of truth, it is there in simple terms that anyone can figure out. For those seeking greater depths of understanding, that's all there too, but less evident and in ever greater need of study. Actually, I buried a great many secrets in the book, secrets that are revealed only to those who choose to accept My Holy Spirit as their guide and who accept that part of Myself that walked the earth, and whom I named Jesus Christ, as their Lord and Savior. My basic motto here is: If they choose to love Me and to believe, great! I've got wonderful things in store for them! If not, to hell with them! Don't get Me wrong; I love them all, each and every one, no matter how wicked they are. I just can't tolerate their wickedness! Of all My creation, I endowed them, and of course my angels, with many of My own attributes, abilities and qualities. Sometimes it seems as though I gave them too many, especially that devil, Satan!

That free will part is, of course, the vehicle by which most of their troubles are brought into their lives. The troubles they get into are the result of the free will opportunities to do what is contrary to My directives. But think about it. What choice did I have except to give them the power of choice to either obey or disobey? What would they be without it? Rocks? Trees? Monkeys? Machines like those things they call computers? We'll talk about that some more a little later. In the meantime, remember this is his story that he is trying to pass through my mouth. What a father will do for his kids! I'm not saying that any of this is right or wrong. It is merely what his simple mind has come up with based on My book, some commentaries about My book that others have written, and his own imagination. If you want to be sure of anything and want genuine Truth, you will have to come to Me yourself.

Now he wants to start at the very beginning of everything, as if he could have any idea at all of what really happened, although I must say his thoughts on the matter are not all that ridiculous.

Well, at first it was just Me, Me being the Father, Son and Holy Spirit. I've always been. Actually that's not quite right either, because that always suggests some form of time frame. I'm outside of time. Time is but one of many available dimensions, something that I put into prominence after Adam messed up, and something that I will discontinue when my overall program has been completed. Anyway, at one point, way before I created the universe and everything in it, I created a whole population of immortal beings called angels. (You should note that I have to put everything in a time frame or sequential context. Otherwise you won't be able to comprehend any of this.) With them, I created a social structure that gave Me a great deal of satisfaction and an outlet for my love. Actually, I am love itself, but love without someone to love is meaningless, like a word spoken where there is no one to hear it. Your parents know what I'm talking about. I gave them all that Godly capacity that your mother discovered before her child was even out of the womb, and your father felt it soon afterward. I endowed these angels with free will and with other qualities much like My own. Of course, as immortal beings, they too had their existence outside of time and a capacity to be in a variety of dimensions. I should point out that, in the Big Picture, time is sort of a contrived dimension and, by definition, a limiting one. I created it as part of an enclosing envelope that I placed around the physical universe, a finite limit, a beginning and end. No such limits had previously existed.

In the angelic social structure, we were one big, happy, loving family. Everyone had his position, his job, and his area of responsibility. One of these, in fact my chief angel, I had made a little more handsome, more intelligent and more powerful than all of the others. Sadly, however, all of this, you might say, went to his head. This was Lucifer, my angel of light. He became proud and, therefore, committed the first sin. You know how I hate sin. Pride is the mother of all sin. All sin is derived of pride. He admired his superior attributes and took credit for them. That is what pride is, taking undeserved credit for something. Whatever attributes one has, whatever one achieves, it is gratitude not pride that is appropriate and right. Should the pot take credit for its beauty, or utility, or age, or how many beans have

807

been cooked in it? I am the Creator. Everything that is or happens is such because I either instigated or allowed it. By always remembering this and thanking Me, one can always avoid pride and thus the onset of the other diseases that can contaminate the soul.

Lucifer is a good example of the diabolical nature of pride. As his pride grew, so did his belief in himself and that his qualities were inherent, generated from within himself, that he was master of his own fate and could do as he pleased, independent of his Creator. Thus his pride led to arrogance, disrespect, and even jealousy of Me. He believed that he could be equal to Me and even replace Me! This led to his development and perfection of lies and deceit as he tried to compete with Me. He got so good at these sins that he actually persuaded about a third of my angels to cast their lots with him as he mutinied. That's when I kicked the lot of them out of heaven! What could I do? Of course, anything I want to! I am God! Somehow, because of his pride, he never really understood this. To this day he thinks that he can be effective against Me. I suppose that I could have snuffed him out. But I made him and the rest immortal, and I don't undo what I have done nor do I fail to keep promises. When I kicked them out I banished them to the earth, the place that I had just created.

That's also about the time I decided to create man and to give him the same qualities that I gave the angels and even more, such as dominance over all other creatures and living things on earth, and the earth itself. I had in mind that perhaps through man I might bring Satan, as I now prefer to call him, back to his senses. (Now this old fool who is writing this, doesn't know anything about what was on My mind. He is making this all up! Although, from a human perspective, I must say it sounds reasonable.) Anyway, I made this man Adam and then added a whole new wrinkle to My creation; I gave him a wife, and gave them the power to procreate, that is, in a sense, create others of their kind. Thus, I gave man more Godly attributes than I gave the angels. I had created them all directly as full-grown man angels as I had the man Adam. There were no women and thus no "procreation." As a loving Father, I put Adam and Eve in a lovely garden, with everything that they could possibly ever need or want, and with the prospects of eternal love, peace and joy. They would live this way close to Me forever, along with their offsprings, and their offsprings, on a warm, friendly earth populated also with friendly animals and lush vegetation. Of course, I also gave them free will and a few simple rules that I expected them to follow if they wished to keep this paradise. Even you can see that I had to do this. What would be the purpose of the power of free will, or choice, if there wasn't a menu from which to choose? I don't mean a choice of potatoes or pasta. I mean real choice that, in this case, was strict obedience or disobedience regarding a few things. I actually made it quite simple to understand and not very difficult to adhere to. Putting it in the vernacular of the Garden where they lived, I simply forbid them to taste the fruit of a particular tree.

When Satan got wind of all of this, he became very angry, quite threatened, and even more jealous, this time of Adam and of his unique gifts and position. He certainly was also jealous of the fact that Adam was given Eve and the ability to procreate. This was a gift greater than even he, head of all the angels, had ever had or even knew could be.

Well, this is where all of the trouble began, big trouble from your perspective, but not from Mine. To Me, Satan is no more onerous than a fly on an elephant's "butt." But for you, and all of what you seem to like to call mankind, he caused a peck of trouble. Before I go on, let me set something straight, once and for all. Many of you, especially those who have read My book but have learned only enough to be dangerous, seem to believe that Satan and I are adversaries. Can a grain of sand be an adversary to a mountain from whence it washed down into the sea? He thinks he is My adversary, but that's because his hatred, his ego and his pride get in the way of his reasoning and sense of reality. Also, as the master of deception, he has become the worst victim of his own deceptive nature. I hear many of you ask, "If God is so great and so powerful, why doesn't He just eliminate Satan and get rid of all this evil and the pain and suffering that goes with it?" That's easy for you to ask, but you are not God and so you don't know all of the issues involved here, so I'll tell you!

Sure, I created him; I created everything, and I can do anything I choose to. But here is the rub. When I created Satan, as with all of the angels, I gave them immortality! I did the same with you and all man-kind starting with Adam and Eve. Do you understand what that means? I can't eliminate anyone, angel or man! Why can't I? Because that's the condition under which I chose to create you all, and I don't change my mind nor break my word!

That doesn't mean that I can't contain Satan or punch him out. In fact, I already told you in My book that one of these days I intend to put him in chains for a thousand years. I also have a hot place for him, and some of you too, who make the wrong choices. That brings Me to the second irrevocable commitment that I made to them and you, sovereign free will, or the right to make choices through your own volition. Choice is yours to use or abuse. Sadly, many of you have chosen to abuse, and that, dear ones, is the source of all of your pain and suffering, your collective abuse of your free will in its harmful application of it on each other. Oh, Satan is surely evil; he is chief of dirty tricks. But he is more of a facilitator than an instigator. He orchestrates evil doings and sets up many temptations, but it's your free will that ultimately makes the choice of whether or not to go along with him.

It's not that I didn't know what the results of this commitment would be. Of course I knew! But, in order to end up with a few "good men" (and women) as the marine posters say. I had to allow this ying and yang, this good and evil choice to exist. You may not agree or appreciate the problem, but I want in My heaven only those who choose to go there. This choice is demonstrated first by accepting Jesus as their Lord and Savior, trusting Him completely, and then demonstrating these things through repentance, confession of sins and obedience to My Word. Is that asking too much for eternity in heaven? It's your choice. I can't, because I won't force Myself on anyone. You must want me on My terms, otherwise, I cannot accept you. Remember I am God and I make the rules.

Enough of this digression, and back to the story. Soon after Satan heard about Adam and Eve, he wasted no time heading for Eden with the intention of messing things up. He figured that Eve would be an easier mark than Adam, and through her he could get Adam. He knew that I get pretty upset when anyone breaks my rules, so if he could get them to do just that, then I would probably do to them something about as drastic as I did to him. So, as soon as he was able to find Eve alone, he introduced himself and really applied the charm. Remember, he was my handsomest and most intelligent angel and had more than his share of charm. Being the master of half-truth and every other form of deceit, he introduced himself as My chief angel, on leave here on earth, who just dropped in to see how My newest beings were doing. Remember, she was a pretty naïve young thing, never even having seen another talking being except Adam. So it wasn't long before she felt pretty comfortable and trusting of this supposed emissary of Mine. When she told him of the no-no regarding the tree of knowledge of good and evil, he knew he had her. He said, "Come on, Eve, that's no big deal. I've eaten that fruit many times. It's good! If you eat some, you surely won't die! Nobody dies around here! If you eat that, you will be as God, very smart! He doesn't particularly like people being as smart as He is, but it's really no big deal." Well, of course she swallowed that line as well as the fruit, and the rest is history, as you well know.

By the way, a very interesting thing happened next that you might not have caught, even if you read about it in My book. When Adam got back to Eve, Satan was gone, but Eve told him the whole story. Of course Adam was very upset. He knew the terrible consequences of disobedience to Me. What I'm going to tell you is a heavy-duty testimony to the power of two of the most important qualities that I gave to all mankind, love and choice. You see, Adam loved Eve more than he did himself. When he heard what she had done, he had two choices; to step away from her, stay pure and let her take the consequences alone, or to join her in this sin and take the consequences with her. His love and his choice changed the face of the earth and the destiny of all mankind.

You might say that I was very disappointed by all of this but, of course, I already knew that it would happen because I know the future. As I said before, I live outside of time; past, future, they are all the same to me. I even knew eons before you were born that, at this very moment, you would be reading this. Well, of course, I had to punish them both, although I must admit I admired Adam's valor and great love, and felt sympathy for Eve's gullibility. As you know, I kicked them out of Eden, took away the immortality of their flesh, left them with the bittersweet or double-edged sword, if you will, of the knowledge of good and evil. Of course, I also left Satan to roam the earth to make certain that nothing would ever again be easy. Ever isn't quite the right word. It's until My Son Jesus returns for a second time, but that's another story.

Again, I see the need to put in a disclaimer. Remember this is the old fool's story. I'm just narrating it for him. I'm not going to say that he is right or wrong in any of this. If you really want to verify anything, just read My book. If you read it with the right mind and heart, My Holy Spirit will show you everything. Without His light shining on My words, your grasp of the full meaning of My messages will not get to you. Well, I thought that we could end it here, but that crazy old coot is begging Me to continue. So, I'll reminisce a little more and tell you a few things that happened after the fruit episode.

After they obtained this "knowledge of good and evil," a heavy change came over them. For one thing, their innocence was gone. For the first time they saw their own nakedness and tried to hide it with fig leaves. That's when I made for each of them garments of animal skin so as to hide their embarrassment. You see, that's how the shedding of innocent blood all began. Because of their sins, they had to carry the responsibility of the shedding of innocent blood as a symbol of atonement for those sins. I caused them to continue this practice of blood sacrifice of the best of their flocks and herds as a reminder to the mortality of flesh that resulted from their sins. I later imposed a detailed ritualistic process of this type that lasted for the next four thousand years as a prelude to what I would finally do to cleanse all sins, on a cross at Calvary. But that too is another story.

As you know, they soon had two sons, Cain and Abel. Cain became a farmer and Abel a shepherd. You see, now they had to work. No more of that easy life in the Garden of Eden. Physical life became a struggle, as it will continue until the end of time. As I said, I demanded blood sacrifice to Me in the form of a ritual so that they could never forget that original sin, and so they would always remember Me and who I am. When the time came for the ritual to take place, Abel obliged with the sacrifice of a lamb, while Cain brought Me produce from his garden. Thus Abel lived by faith of My direction, while the other tried to please Me with works, the efforts of his hands. Of course, I wasn't pleased with Cain and let him know it. Then he got so angry that he killed Abel in a fit of jealousy. I punished him by denying him his inheritance and banishing him to the wilderness where living was even more difficult.

There is a message here that I'm not sure you get. *Faith* and obedience to My instructions, My Word, are what I value and reward. Abel acted on faith and obeyed. Cain was self-righteous and disobedient and ignored My directives. He thought that he could satisfy Me with work. Let that be a lesson to anyone reading this! Works without faith don't mean "squat" to me. Yes, you say, but Abel died because of his righteousness. What's good about that? I'll tell you. As a righteous man of faith, Abel missed out on some of his mortal existence. But that is only an infinitesimal loss compared with the eternity in heaven that he gained from faith. Cain had many years of hardship, anger and guilt to live with, and very poor prospects for eternity. I could go on and on in this vein, about faith versus works, and the fate of Cain's seed, but the old guy promised Me that if I would tell you about how things were on earth in those succeeding years, until I created rain and flooded the place, he would not ask me to go on further. I didn't get too detailed about this period in My book, although some clever readers did discover some of My more subtle messages and coded meanings that tell more than the casual reader could ever discover, especially in the English translations. Again, I'm not going to admit that they are right or wrong, I'm only going to report on what they determined.

The lineage I chose to follow in My book was through Seth, Adam and Eve's third son, who was born when Adam was 130 years old. Seth, by the way, means, "appointed," because he was a substitute for the murdered Abel. Adam lived to be 930 years old, old enough to have lived fifty-six more years after his great, great, great, great, great, great grandson Lamech was born, who was, of course, Noah's father. From Adam to Noah were only ten generations along this lineage, which is the only one that continued after the flood. Eight of these ten guys lived more than nine hundred years each. Only Lamech died younger, at age 777. And Enoch was such a wonderful man, and a real friend of Mine, that I transferred him directly to heaven at age 365, so he never died.

You find it difficult to believe that these early people lived to be nearly a thousand years old. That's because you have no frame of reference as to what the world was like at that time. I created a different world than exists today. It was a wondrous, generous world where life could be eternal. After Adam and Eve disobeyed, I commenced a gradual modification through the introduction of entropy. The whole world was lush and green continually and there for the benefit of all creatures. The lion literally could lie with the sheep because all were vegetarians. There was no killing, no death, until that first murder when Satan caused Adam and Eve to learn of good and evil, thus causing the eventual death of all flesh.

In those days, rain did not happen. A large portion of the earth's water was suspended in the heavens as vapor and, through nocturnal condensation or dew, I nurtured the earth and supplied all of its needs. This thick layer of vapor filtered out the cosmic rays and other elements detrimental to life. Because of this and other idealized characteristics such as the absence of toxicity and any forms of necrotizing virus or bacteria, aging was extremely slow even after I did introduce it. It was with this massive supply of water vapor along with oceans of pressurized underground water that I caused the first rain that lasted forty days and nights and flooded the earth at the time of Noah. If you read My book, you will see, as a symbol of My promise to never again flood the earth, I created for Noah the first rainbow. You see, the rainbow could only be after the heavens had been purged of their massive layer of moisture and the first clear sky also became possible.

I wanted to end this here, but the old man begged Me to reveal to you just one more thing that he seems to think is incredible and wants you to know about. Well, to Me it's just all in a day's work, that is, I should say, a week's work, if you want to include the whole universe as well. You see, when I wrote the book, it was primarily about Me, so that you could get to know Me, how I expect you to behave, and what the consequences of your behavior would be. I wrote it very cleverly as only I could. It is also a fairly detailed, and I shouldn't even have to mention, precisely accurate history of the world from its beginning to its end. You see, the past, present and future are all history to me, and so I wrote the whole story, including what you call the future. I did this future bit through the prophecies. Those who have examined these carefully have come to realize their truth and accuracy, because so many have already come to pass exactly as predicted. I also include many coded messages, some of which are easy to find while others are quite challenging. Why did I do this, you ask? Couldn't I have spelled everything out clearly and completely without having to play these games of hidden messages? Sure I could, and I did! Are the Ten Commandments that I carved in stone and gave to Moses, ambiguous or unclear in any way? How many of you believe and obey them? Was the Sermon on the Mount difficult to understand? You all, even those of you who profess to believe, have invented ten thousand ways each as to how to get around My Word, how to twist it, re-phrase it, dilute it, avoid it, dismiss it, and/or deny it. I knew that in the latter days these sorts of contrivances would occur, and so I built into the Scriptures codes of varying complexities that could be discovered in these end times by the concerned and the faithful as another higher order of proof, and as a means of absolute validation of My authorship and the truth of My Word. As I clearly stated in My book, in the final days Satan's grip on the minds of men will be so strong and so persuasive, "... and shall show signs and wonders to seduce, if it were possible, even the elect . . ."(Mark 13–22).

I won't go into detail on these codes, except to say that some occur as predictive models such as the episode that I staged for Abraham, per My directive, where he was wholly intent on sacrificing his beloved son Isaac on the exact same spot where I sacrificed Mine two thousand years later. There are many other coded proofs that are only now being "discovered" that cause even skeptics to admit to My authorship. These are through clear messages that can be deciphered by examining equidistant letters within My text. I'll leave you that to explore on your own, because there are now books on this discovery that "those with eyes to see" can find on their own. The one example of another kind of easier code that the old man wants Me to tell you about has to do with the original meaning of Hebrew words in the

Scriptures that spell out messages that are not evident in their translations, nor even in the original text without some degree of faithful and loving examination. The one in particular that I will describe as a good example that I put in Genesis 5 is derived simply from the names of the first ten men within the lineage I chose to write about.

You see, every word I wrote, every jot or tittle, has meaning, and these meanings will become more and more revealed in the end times as I start closing the book on time and corporal existence. By the way, I almost closed the book once before with the flood, but because Noah was "correct in his generation" and thus the only one not corrupted, I spared him and his family and gave man, through him, a second chance. Anyway, I arranged the names of these ten generations to be Adam, Seth, Enos, Cainan, Mahalaleel, Jared, Enoch, Methuselah, Lamech and Noah. Now see what these names mean in the original Hebrew:

Adam	Man
Seth	Appointed
Enos	Mortal (frail, incurable)
Kenan	Sorrow
Mahalaleel	Blessed God
Jared	Shall come down
Enoch	Teaching (teacher)
Methuselah	His death shall bring
Lamech	Despairing (from which we get Lamentations)
Noah	Comfort (to bring relief)

Now add a couple of conjunctions and punctuation and you get "Man, appointed mortal sorrow, but the blessed God shall come down teaching, and His death shall bring the despairing comfort." How do you like that as a clever way of foretelling Jesus and the cross? Right from the get-go of history!

Well, that finally got the old man off my back so that now I can get back to more important business. By the way, before I leave, I'll throw in one more tidbit, just for good measure. You see the name Methuselah that means, "his death shall bring." Well, as you can see, that was my good man Enoch's son. I had him name his sons that because I told Enoch that the year his son dies, I would bring on the flood. That was a thousand years before I caused it to happen. Everyone knew what the name Methuselah meant and what I said would happen when he died. But no one believed Me or Enoch, except Noah. In My book, I've also told you when I would terminate things again, for the last time. But no one believes me this time either, except a very few Noah's here and there who will also be prepared.

By the way, that day isn't very far off. And on THAT happy note, I'll say good-bye, and scc you soon, on Judgment Day!

    Dear God, thank You Lord for sharing with us this little bit of early history and for the early warning preview of coming attractions. I, for one, plan to diligently study Your Word and put on the spiritual armor that will be needed when only that Noah-type faith and fortitude can prevail.

                     Your loving believer,
                     The Old Man

—92—

Cat and Dog Theology

Have you noticed how house cats walk around with a regal air about them? Perhaps it is because they were once, in ancient Egypt, worshiped as gods, and they still remember those good ol' days.

Then there is the witty related bit of humor that compares certain canine characteristics with their feline counterparts. It is said that a dog thinks to itself regarding his master, "He feeds me, he shelters me, he cares for me, and he loves me. He must be god!" The cat makes similar observations but says "He feeds me, he shelters me, he cares for me and he loves me, therefore I must be god!"

This was meant to be merely a humorous illustration regarding the general attitudinal differences between these two animal species man most values as pets. However, it can also serve as a useful, perhaps even very powerful analogy and comparison between Christians and non-Christians, and even between Christians of variant attitudes and beliefs within the Christian community. What follows is not meant to suggest that animals have any spiritual sense, or that they can comprehend God or good and evil. It is merely these differences in instinctual characteristics between most members of these two species that lend themselves to be used as analogies regarding human religious attitudes.

Let us first examine dog theology. Dogs, by their nature, seem to have a capacity for what appears to be a very powerful, unconditional love for their masters. They demonstrate intense loyalty. Most dogs yield readily to training and unquestioning obedience. Dogs will, and at times have, given their lives for their masters. The high point of a dog's life comes when its master gives it attention, whether it is by walking, petting, playing or anything else, as long as it is some form of one on one fellowship. It lives to please, and is heartbroken when it knows that it has displeased its master. As I write this, my heart aches, as I realize how much more Christian-like a dog is to its master than I am to mine. Oh, if I could only have in my heart the completeness, the totality of love, faith, devotion and obedience toward my Master, my Lord and Savior, as a dog has to its master. God must have given us these wonderful creatures to show us, if we are willing to see, what the highest state of these divine qualities can be, and to humble us by expressing them through a mere animal. Even a dog's bark, which we commonly spell as W O O F, provides a descriptive acronym of what should be our own living motto as Christians: W.O.O.F. "**W**e **O**bey **O**ur **F**ather! Or perhaps, **W**orship, and **O**bey **O**ur **F**ather! Can anyone do better than that?

Now, let us examine what may be called the "Cat theology." In essence, it could be summed up in a cat's favorite word, MEOW, when put in the form of the acronym M.E.O.W. **ME O**ver **W**hatever, or perhaps **M**y **E**ffort **O**ver **W**orship.

It is this meow theology, or me-ology, that has taken over the world, and to some extent, and in some ways even Christianity. It seems evident, as far as I can see, that most of the religions on earth, except for real biblical, evangelical Christianity, observe some form of M.E.O.W., My Effort Over Worship theology, in that some *individual effort* must be applied in order to qualify for heaven, or, as many believe, to reach some other higher spiritual state or reality. True Christian faith claims eternal salvation in the sufficiency of Jesus and what the cross symbolizes.

The MEOW theology suggested by the acronym of Me Over Whatever, is quite sadly, and unintentionally symbolic of many Christian's attitudes and of those of others who call themselves Christians. They read the Scripture and almost everywhere find God's love for his creation. He loves us so much that He gave His only Son to die on the cross in propitiation of our sins that we might share eternity with Him. He tells us to ask and we will receive. His Word is a guide to health and long life. One can find any number of verses that suggest that the Scriptures are for each of us individually, For Me, and that God is For ME. Scripture is for *My* knowledge, *My* health, *My* wealth, and *My* salvation-ME, ME, ME, -MEOW!

In one context, all of this is true. It is God's book of promises and instructions for each of us. But let's look a little further into His instruction, because, along with this "for me" aspect of the Bible there is another and preeminently overriding theme and message.

The words glory, glorify, etc. appear in the Scripture more than five hundred times. Mostly they refer to God's glory and His charge to us to glorify Him. He created us *not* for *ourselves*, not for *Me*, but for *Himself*, for *His glory* "according to *His* good pleasure and *His* will " (Ephesians 1:15). Isaiah 43:7 tells us ". . . everyone that is called by my name for I have created him *for My glory* . . ." 1 Corinthians 6:20 Tells us, "For you are bought with a price; therefore *glorify God* . . ." From these and many, many more verses in both the Old and New Testament we are given the clear message that our purpose here is *not* for ourselves but for *Him*, *for His glory*. To glorify means to *Honor*, *Praise* and *Worship*.

So if you want to live and believe and serve as God wants us to and has instructed us to, think W.O.O.F. and not M.E.O.W. But when you think of your pets, neither blame nor credit them for how they act. Just as He created us for *His* pleasure, so also He created them just as they are, for our pleasure. However, perhaps now, after this, we may also see them as another one of God's instruments for our learning.

The Lord is Throwing a Party and We Are All Invited!

And what a party it's going to be! It is a party that will last forever! There has never been anything like it and once you know more about it, you surely won't want to miss it. Although everyone is invited, there is a catch, a prequalification, for admission. You see, it is sort of like a costume party where prizes are given for the best costumes. At this party, however, they will judge the costumes at the gate and only those with appropriate costumes will be allowed in. "Well, you ask, "how does one know what kind of costume will win admittance to the party?"

That's an easy one. This party was planned many years ago, and the Lord wrote a book of instructions at that time and on this very subject. In fact, He wrote two books. The first book of instructions, which told how to dress for the party, seemed to be very strict and didn't leave much room for error. And over time it got so badly misunderstood and poorly followed that He decided to come here Himself, in the body of Jesus Christ, in order to both simplify and clarify these instructions, to give us clues as to what the party would be like, and to officiate most directly over the writing of the second book. He even went so far as to sacrifice His earthly body in order to compensate for some of our weaknesses, as well as to impress on our souls the seriousness of His commitment to us and the depth of His love for us. Then He gave us the ultimate proof of His power and sincerity when He actually came back to life after having been dead for three days. He even walked around for quite a while among His friends, in His resurrected body, demonstrating how the eternally reunited body and soul can transcend time and space. He did this, for instance, by suddenly being in a closed room full of people without entering through any opening. While there, He ate and talked, and some of His friends even touched Him to verify that He was actually there in the flesh. He could even disappear just as easily and quickly as He appeared.

Before He left for the last time, He told His friends that He was going to heaven to get set up for the party. Well, He didn't actually discuss the party at that time, but He did mention it as a parable in Matthew 22. Also, He did, in fact, say that He was heading back to prepare rooms, that is, places where all of us who qualify, will be staying while at the party and forever more. His friends were so impressed and so excited about the party and all that He had shown them, they spent the rest of their lives, some writing parts of His second book, but all of them spreading the Word and telling everyone what they needed to know about how to get the right costumes so that they could get into the party. There were powerful people who didn't want anyone to hear this message and tried very hard to suppress it. In fact, every one of these friends of Jesus were so certain of His message that they subjected themselves to incredible tortures, and all but one were themselves killed rather than disclaim His divinity.

"Well that's great. I'm impressed," you say. "He was quite a guy and His friends really believed in Him, but this costume business sounds too complicated and I'm not much for parties, so I think I'll sit this one out." O.K., you can do that. You can skip this party if you really want to. Certainly your free will allows that choice. However, once you fully understand the significance of that choice, you may feel differently. You see, there are actually two parties going on and you, all of us, in fact, will *have* to go to one of them; there is no other choice.

There is only one gate leading to the Lord's estate and it is quite narrow. This is because He wants to inspect each costume individually and to greet each of us personally. If you are wearing the right costume, you are in. Otherwise, you *must* go to the other party where there is open admission, wide open gates, and no costumes, just come as you are, the more raunchy the better. "Hey, I like that better anyway," you say. "No book of instructions to follow, no costumes, come as you are, that sounds like the better choice, if I have to go anywhere."

That may sound pretty good, but before you firm up that decision, there are a few other differences to consider. If you could view the approaches to the Lord's gate, you would probably notice an orderly column of people. They would appear quite calm, comfortable, and all having tranquil but smiling faces. It would also be difficult not to notice a beautiful aura of intense spiritual love surrounding each of these partygoers. Actually this aura is a major part of the costume. The clincher for admission however, and the part that you probably will not see unless you look very closely, is the underlying garment of spiritual armor each is wearing. The stitching and patches and repatches on these garments are the badges of honor, and victories in battles fought for the privilege of reaching this narrow gate.

There you have it, the whole enchilada. It's easy as 1, 2, 3, Read, understand and believe the Word that is the Bible. Learn who Jesus is and why. After this, faith and love are only short steps away from creating the whole costume and thus passage through the gate.

If you were to visit the approaches to the other party, you would probably see a broad boulevard and a wide-open gate. The boulevard would be crowded with people appearing to have a variety of moods. It would be a "no holds barred" atmosphere, anything goes, no rules, no laws, no restraints, whatever feels good is good. Do your own "thing" and enjoy, no costumes necessary here. Be a good guy if you want, follow the golden rule, be honest, do good deeds, even practice any variety of religions, no problem. But just don't come with any of that spiritual armor stuff, no Jesus freaks are allowed to go through this gate. That is the *only* thing *not* allowed here. *Everything* else is O.K.

"Well, I'm still not convinced that I should change parties," you say. "This other party looks pretty good to me."

O.K., then let's try, if we can, to see what's inside each of these gates. We don't know too much about this because no one has ever left either party to come back and tell us about it. However, the Lord, in little sidebars in the Old and in the New Testament, did give us some clues from which we can get a pretty good idea about what to expect, and what our life at the party will be like in the long term. And the long term it is, because once we pass through the gate, it is forever, and that's a long time. It is a never-ending party we are going to, one from which we can never return, so we had better be sure to pick the right one.

The most that I can tell you about the Lord's party is that it will be great and never disappoint anyone. He is the Host and He will be there making sure that everything is perfect and that you are happy. If you are one of those who chose Him, He already knows it and has a place waiting for you. One thing is certain; you will be in great company with guys like Noah, Abraham, Daniel, Isaiah, and Ruth, Paul, Peter, etc. What stories they can tell! "Who are they? you ask. They are a few of the greatest people who ever lived! If you get into the instruction book, you will learn a great deal about them and many others. Then you will be eager to know them. But, if you choose the other party, knowing them won't be important. I know also that there won't be any pain, suffering, hate, greed, envy, hunger, deceit, lies or crime at the Lord's party. You see, all of those things have been scooped up, put in a container, and shipped somewhere else that I will tell you about in a minute. The most succinct thing that I can say about the Lord's party is that once you qualify for admission, there is nothing that you could conceivably hope for that will not be there waiting for you to enjoy, forever.

Now, let's look through the other gate at the party that is going on there. From outside the gate it is going to look great. Just inside the gate, I'm sure you will see a few smiling faces, because they will be new comers looking at a very impressive façade. But remember this is the *great deceiver's* party. He earned that name and lives up to it every moment. He is the father of all lies. That façade is one of His finest achievements. It is meant to be seen from outside the gate to serve as a lure, to deceive, and create an impression as false as he is. What you can see is the greatest, the mother of all Potemkin Villages, a movie set façade better than the best that Hollywood could ever create. Behind it is the real party, the real place, where everyone who passes through that gate stays throughout eternity. This is also where our Lord took all that pain and suffering and other bad stuff mentioned above. It was dumped and spread around behind the façade where everyone at the party will be up to their necks in it.

You can meet some great people there too, great in the earthly sense, but absent from any spiritual quality. You might like to converse with the likes of Hitler, Mao, Stalin, or even some of the Caesars, and Popes, as well as other religious icons. There will surely be many others of the world's great leaders, scientists, philosophers and most assuredly many American politicians. But that stuff that was dumped and spread around will be keeping everyone there too busy crying, screaming and "gnashing teeth" to be able to hold any kind of conversation. So, if you go there, you can expect plenty of stimuli, but not the intellectual kind, or any other pleasant kind.

Well, that's about all that I can tell you at this time. Many believe that there are other options such as repetitive re-birth into a series of lives here on earth. Others believe that there is nothing, no heaven, no hell, no God, no Satan. The only limit to how many different kinds of beliefs there are is the limit of Satan's imagination and his ability to plant them in receptive minds. He wants to have the biggest party and will do everything in his power to make it so. He knows that the only truth is God's word, as recorded in the Bible, and does everything in his power to discredit it and to limit its acceptance. Once you are able to shed yourself of his influence, and read and understand God's Holy Words, even the devil's most elaborate concoctions, even his Potemkin village will not fool you.

My advice is that you had better start checking this out, and make your choice based on fact, not fiction. Time is of the essence, because none of us knows when we will be hit by a train, a cancer, or get a really bad cold and suddenly find that "default" made the choice for us. We have all been invited to both parties; we must R.S.V.P. to one or the other. Only your choice and commitment will get you into God's Party. Without specific acts in this matter, you automatically end up at Potemkin village.

—94—

The Master Tailor

There is a tailor among us who is indeed a true master of his profession. He customizes the material, color, style and fit of every garment so as to most please his clients. Through his genius, his garments provide enhancements to the wearer's proudest qualities and can even obscure any negativity the tailor chooses to hide. His garments are capable of providing the appearances of beauty, charm, intelligence, wisdom and piety as well as religious fervor and righteousness. He will even customize the very fabric to best serve his goals, using scripturally based material where necessary and appropriate. In fact, in many circumstances this is his favorite fabric. He weaves, cuts and sews this fabric with great care making certain that because of its apparent supreme quality, the world will perceive the wearer to be whatever the tailor has chosen him to be.

When plying his trade with scriptural fabric he is especially attentive to detail, being sure to carefully cut a little here, or add a little there, where such alterations are almost impossible to detect. Thus the garment is not only comfortable and pleasing to behold, but it also conveys the appearance of the true Word. It can be slipped into and out of easily, so as to accommodate any and all circumstances that the owner may encounter or choose to create, especially where the appearance of piety is desired. Most of the world wears his label. Many wear simple earthly garments fashioned by his legion of assistant because he personally attends only to those he perceives to have special qualities useful to him, or to those whose potential he fears and seeks to obscure or destroy.

By now it is evident that the master tailor is the prince of this world, the angel of light, Satan, himself. As with any analogy, there is a limit to its effectiveness in expressing an item of truth. But surely Satan does fashion the images worn by much of humanity. Sadly, however, he often does this, not from the outside, but by boring deep into the individual's soul where he injects his venom of deceit. From there, the poison spreads outward as it forms the external appearances and qualities that become the composite attire Satan has planned for the individual. It manifests in their thoughts, emotions, desires and attitudes as well as their countenance and behavior. As the master of deception and imagery, his handiwork is often very subtle. He can counterfeit almost anything. Many of his garments are so close in appearance to God's own handiwork that they can sometimes, for a while, fool even the elect. His label has been known to be on garments worn by the whole spectrum of humanity from presidents, popes, and politicians, to pastors, priests and peasants. Only those truly born of the Spirit are immune to his cloaking. However, they are far from being safe from his attacks and attempts to control or destroy them.

So far we have spoken only in generalities and through the likeness of Satan as a tailor, fashioning the appearances and actions of those he selects as his clients. These are his chosen from among the unsaved multitude. They are those of the world whom he can use, and who can be tricked or purchased through worldly rewards and the "good life." Many of these are the "great, the rich and the famous" of the world. He doesn't bother with the rest of humanity who are already his by default (John 1:12–13, 3:3, Matthew 12:30, 1 John 3:8–10). However, if he sees any choosing to seek the Lord, toward these he has a totally different agenda and strategy.

I said that only those born of the Spirit are immune to his cloaking. But they are also the ones who get the most of his personal attention. Satan hates Christians with a vengeance. He also fears them! Satan fears Christians? How can one say that this prince of the world who controls all of the principalities and power on earth, this super angel who can produce great signs and wonders, actually fears Christians? He fears them because those who are truly born of the Spirit are sons and daughters of God (Romans 8:14). They have been saved from him, and their souls are immune to his objectives. Therefore, he cannot shape a garment to fit a Christian, in spite of his tailoring genius. While all of this is more a matter of frustration and anger to him, the actual fear is in the fact that each new Christian is like a marble added to a nearly full jar. When the jar is full, when the "fullness of the gentiles (Christians) become in" (Romans 11:25), *his* number is up. The count down to his demise is at hand. Each new Christian is also like another nail poised and ready to secure the cover of his coffin. No one knows when that jar will be full, but we know that when it is, our Father will send Jesus back here to bring His family home. (1 Thessalonians 4:16) This will usher in the seven-year great tribulation, which will be Satan's last hurrah, *his* "last supper" (Daniel 9:27).

Although he knows the Scripture and these prophetic passages as well as or better than anyone, he nevertheless retains the hope, and probably the belief, that somehow he can yet thwart God's plan and change the inevitable. Why else has he struggled so tenaciously throughout history to corrupt, subvert and remove God's chosen? This is evidenced over and over again. First it was in the pollution and wickedness he wrought on mankind through the Nephilim (Genesis 6) that resulted in the wiping out of all but eight by the flood. Then, in an attempt to preclude the advent of Jesus, he enlisted Pharaohs in the killing of all male Hebrew babies and again motivating Herod to do the same thing when it was evident that the child Jesus had come. Then there is Haman in the book of Esther, who was groomed by Satan as his agent through which the entire Jewish race was to be exterminated. The calamity of 70 A.D. and the modern day holocaust in Germany are but two more of many other genocidal attempts by Satan against those chosen to have a destiny in God's plan.

Today, the Christian born of the spirit is the prime focus of Satan's attention for reasons already given. He cannot destroy the true believer, but he is a master at destroying his or her usefulness. I have personally witnessed such destruction. He has had thousands of years to observe mankind, to learn of every category of man's strengths and weaknesses, physical and spiritual as well as mental and emotional. When he sees someone who is being fruitful for our Lord, his attention and study is immediately focused on that individual for the purpose of eliminating that effectiveness. He can use loving strokes as effectively as severe trials, tribulations and adversities to bring him or her down. He can do this with such subtly that his victim is totally unaware of whence or why these things happen. He can even make it impossible to distinguish between cause and effect, thereby so obscuring his involvement that we never even suspect that he played any part in the matter. In sizing up his victims, he knows exactly what their strengths and weaknesses are. While our weaknesses are obviously his favorite areas of attack, he will at times even make a mockery of our strengths in order to exhibit his superiority as he did with Peter. This, the bravest of the Apostles, collapsed into cowardice when he denied Jesus three times after his capture. Look how he humiliated Sampson, and how he made a spectacle of David's high moral standards through Bethsheba.

Satan's favorite being is the false Christian, especially the one who believes he is a real Christian. He delights in *all* of the false beliefs and religions he has so masterfully contrived or has gleefully seen man fashion for himself. But to see a person falsely and complacently believe that he or she has been born again, gives him the greatest pleasure. Perhaps this is because he knows that he doesn't have to keep his eye on them as much as he does others who might somehow see the error of false doctrines and actually seek the true way to salvation.

What is a false Christian? Surely there are several possible responses to this question. But for present purposes, it seems appropriate to mention only two. First, there are those who recognize Jesus for who He really is, and that He did die to save us from our sin, but they also believe that they themselves must do something else in order to earn their salvation. They believe that Jesus' death on the cross was not in itself wholly sufficient. The official doctrines of the Catholic Church, for example, teach the insufficiency of the cross, that we must also do things ourselves as payment for our sins. This kind of false Christian has not studied the Scriptures, or else does not understand them, especially such passages as Ephesians 2–8, Galatians 2:16 etc. Salvation is free, given by God's grace; to receive it we must accept it as a gift through faith, that it is free to us because Jesus already paid for it in full on the cross. You see, salvation is not really free. God's justice demands a payment, but it's a fine much bigger than anyone could ever afford. So because of Jesus' great love for us, He paid our fine in full.

When we acknowledge this through absolute faith in Him and His act as documented in the Scripture, then we are born again and are assured eternal life with Him in heaven.

—95—

Meditation

Psalm 104:34 says, "My meditation on Him shall be sweet; I will be glad in the Lord." Scripture speaks twenty times about meditation. Today when we hear the word "meditation," many of us think of someone sitting on the floor with legs crossed looking straight ahead humming and trying to clear his or her head of all thoughts. That is, I believe, what is called, "eastern meditation" or "transcendental mediation." Scriptural meditation is essentially the opposite. It has been said that meditation is to the soul what digestion is to the body. One can be in most any position, being still and focusing the mind on Jesus or some other truth from Scripture. Meditation is deep, thorough contemplation, or pondering, which also means to muse. As an aside, it would do us well to note that, to muse is seriously "to think." Amusement means not to think; the "a" as a prefix means "no," therefore no thinking. Try to remember that, when you allow yourself or your children to sit for hours in front of a TV or engage in the myriad of other addictive "a-musements," with which so very many seek to fill their lives, or perhaps to somehow compensate for a deficiency of God in their lives. For those who are without Jesus in their hearts, a-musements, non-thinking, may be the only comfortable refuge they can find.

Getting back to biblical meditation, one should cultivate and encourage such activity. But meditation isn't simply thinking about scriptural matters wherever you are, or whatever you are doing. It involves setting aside specific times during which meditation is the only activity. When applied sincerely and personally it is extremely rewarding and restful to the spirit. Spurgeon called it a "couch of the soul" and "rest of the spirit." He also called it "a very profitable exercise" and a way to "extract the most honey from a honeycomb." To be fruitful, meditation must be conducted in solitude, being completely alone where there is quiet and where there are no distractions. It expands in its fruitfulness when it follows shortly after the reading of something of consequence, especially from Scripture, and when that is the focus of the meditation. My favorite and most fruitful manner of meditation is to simply go to my room, shut the door, lie on my bed, and lapse into deep thought. My thoughts usually are about something I have read, or some Bible passage that I don't understand, or it could be, as Spurgeon suggests, simply pondering the "weighty matters of eternity." It may be merely counting and appreciating my many blessings, or it may even be discussing with Him some troubling issues, spiritual or otherwise. Whatever the subject, I usually return to the world more edified and satisfied as well as more spiritually relaxed than I was before. It is during these periods of meditation when I become inspired with most of the ideas that then become the compelling subjects of these papers.

I must warn you, however, that genuine meditation is very addictive! Once you have the habit, you will find that it becomes a necessity in your life. You will hunger for its effects and feel that your day was incomplete without it. Go without it for several days and you may expect to feel a sickness in your soul.

Meditation is what Spurgeon calls "the machine in which the raw material of knowledge is converted to its best use." I know that it's an effective means through which knowledge is often transformed into wisdom. It's how a truth that is comprehended can become one that is apprehended. Psalm 4:4 advises us to "commune with your own heart upon your bed and be still."

You say it is a luxury you can't afford because you just don't have the time. I say that it's a necessity you cannot afford to do without if you value your Christian faith enough to want it to grow and strengthen! Do you watch any TV, read magazines or newspapers? Are there times when you engage in other a-musements? If you say yes to these questions, you have refuted your claim to not having enough time!

Please note, that meditation is not a substitution for prayer. Meditation and prayer should be inseparable, not interchangeable. Prayer, in my opinion, should always precede meditation and also follow it. It need not necessarily relate to your main prayers, but there should, I believe, be a short prayer asking God for a fruitful meditation and another one thanking Him for whatever was the result of this effort.

One last thought. Don't wait to meditate until you are mentally and physically too tired to think deeply. Just as you want to say your prayers when you are at your very best, and can, therefore, give Him your very best, so also should you meditate when your mind is alert. Try it! You'll like it! So will our Father.

Lent

What is lent? It's the annual forty-day period before Easter during which many Christians fast and do penitence in preparation for Easter. This begins on what is called Ash Wednesday, at which time it is the custom to have a priest dab a bit of ashes on the adherent's forehead.

How did this custom begin? From the Christian's perspective it began at the time of Emperor Constantine when he began the "Christianizing" of the highly pagan Roman population. Roman religious beliefs were many and varied, having been adopted from the various cultures they had conquered and assimilated. They worshiped many gods, and when Christianity came into vogue it presented no problem to the pagans. Christ was added as just one more god to be worshiped. Contrary to common belief, the majority of the population did not "convert" to Christianity but merely added its trappings to their pagan beliefs if and as they chose.

However, for the faithful formerly persecuted genuine Christians, this sudden "freedom" brought with it some very serious ecclesiological problems. Immediately there was this incredible pressure to "go along in order to get along." Much of this pressure was to incorporate the trappings of the pagan worshiping ways to the Christian expressions of worship. Festive holidays and celebrations were among the first to be compromised in the liberated Christian Community, along with their morals, manners of prayers and worship. Doctrinal issues took a little longer to become perverted. For instance, there seems to be no evidence that Christ's birthday had ever been celebrated by the early Christians. In fact no one even knew when He was born. What was known, however, is that it was not December 25 or any other winter date. Nevertheless, it wasn't long, as we shall see that this pagan holiday date became celebrated as Jesus' birthday. Jesus' resurrection had always been celebrated on the 17th of Nissan, the third day after His crucifixion on Passover, which was, of course, on the 14th day of Nissan, according to the Jewish calendar. Now instead it was to coincide with the day of worship of Ishtar, the pagan goddess of fertility. However, after the council of Nicaea in 325 A.D., and after several later amendments, it was decreed by the "official Church" that this holiday Ishtar, now called Easter, would be celebrated throughout the "Christian" world on the Sunday after the full moon following the vernal equinox. If the full moon should occur on a Sunday and thereby coincided with the Jewish Passover festival, Easter would be commemorated on the following Sunday. Thus it could never fall on the 17th of Nissan, the date Jesus actually rose from the dead. But who cared? Those who might were so glad to get the Roman yoke off their backs again, that they perhaps viewed this as a minor concession, and, therefore, accepted this as a small compromise of going along in order to get along. So from then on Christians have celebrated both Christ's resurrection by church services, and also Ishtar through the rabbit and eggs rituals that symbolize fertility. His death and His resurrection are not celebrated on their correct anniversary dates, but instead on dates pagans had chosen to celebrate events related to their false gods. As we can see and imagine, many pagan and Christian feasts were reinvented, commingled and merged into a perverted amalgam, eventually having little if anything remaining that related to the doctrines for which millions of Christians had suffered and died.

Regarding Lent, there is nothing in Scripture anywhere calling for a forty day period of mourning (which is the supposed symbolism of the ashes). The custom seems to have originated perhaps as far back as the time of Nimrod, the first "world" dictator, the founder of Babylon, Nineveh and several other cities, all of which became perpetual enemies of Israel. This was less than three hundred years after the flood. Legend indicates that Nimrod and Simeronus had a son Tammuz. Perhaps because he died around the winter solstice, and they chose to deify him, they made him into the Sun god. They are said to have begun the custom of burning a Yule log commemorating his death, at the end of the shortening days of winter. The next day, when the days began to lengthen, as the sun grew "stronger" they cut down and decorated a fir tree to celebrate his rebirth, the "returning" of the sun. This then is one of the explanations floating around as to how this pagan winter celebration began. The "Official Church" under Constantine also "grafted" this pagan holiday unto the church tradition making it Christ's birthday with no scriptural basis what-so-ever.

Somehow, associated with this, is how the ash-on-your-face idea may have started, as we shall see. There is evidence that such a practice was going on in apostate Israel, based on Ezekiel 8:13, 14, which tells of God lamenting to Ezekiel about the degenerate state of his priesthood. God showed him examples, saying "turn thee yet again, and thou shalt see greater abomination that they do. Then he brought me to the door of the gate of Yahweh's house which was toward the north, and behold there sat women weeping to Tammuz." The pagan custom of that day was for there to be a period of mourning and fasting and covering themselves with ashes to show their grief. After this period of forty days was ended, at the time of the Feast of Ishtar, they would again celebrate the "resurrection" of the sun god, as he resumes his life-giving warmth and fertility to the earth.

The ritual of covering ones self with ashes as a sign of lamentation does also seem to have a basis in Old Testament Scripture, but I find no such thing advocated anywhere in the New Testament.* The first mention of such a ritual is by Mordecai in the book of Esther 4:1, then later Jeremiah says, ". . . wallow thyself in ashes, make thee mourning as for one only son . . ." This is a messianic prophecy certainly advocating the use of ashes as a symbol of mourning. Ezekiel speaks similar words in a pagan context of those lamenting the destruction of the sin city Tyre. In Daniel 9:3, he hid himself to do ". . . supplications, with fasting and sackcloth and ashes." I believe that it is evident from all of this that the practice of applying ashes to one's self has a basis in Scripture as well as in pagan rituals. However, nothing of this nature was taught by Jesus directly, nor is it advocated anywhere else in the New Testament teachings.

Am I reaching too far to suggest that this ritual, which evidently has its roots, at least in part, in pagan (Satan inspired) ancient religions, is merely one way in which Satan is "conditioning" many to become familiar, with and thereby more accepting of, the mark that Antichrist will demand on every forehead or hand? I probably am, to those who choose this manner of reverence and who are less sensitive to what Scripture reveals regarding Satan's end time plan (Revelation 14:9). Do what you choose in this matter; I pray you do so fully informed through Scripture and in genuine reverence to our Savior.

    *In both Matthew 11:21 and Luke 10:13 Jesus makes reference to that old custom regarding ashes, but does not in any way promote it for His church.

—97—

Oh Death, Where Is Thy Sting?

These are the words spoken by the apostle Paul as recorded in 1 Corinthians 15:55. *"O death where is thy sting? O grave where is thy victory?"* Paul was a special Apostle who, according to Scripture, was chosen by Jesus a short time after Jesus' ascension from this earth. Jesus personally taught Paul several truths that had not been previously revealed to anyone, not to the other Apostles, nor to the prophets. It was in this context that Paul was able to ask this most famous rhetorical question. It is rhetorical in the sense that from Paul's perspective, death has no "sting," that is, it was no horrible affliction or fearful fate to him, because he *knew* what would follow it, that physical death was nothing more than a release from the confinement of a corrupt flesh into the eternal perfect realm that God has provided for His chosen, those who have accepted Jesus as their Lord and Savior. To Paul, death was preferable than continued physical life, because the "afterlife" was infinitely more desirable than anything this earth has to offer physical man. This is, or should be, the belief and attitude of all redeemed Christians. Unfortunately, this attitude toward death, as Paul expressed, is not at all foreign to many who are not believers in Jesus. Many believe that death is total obliteration, the end of all existence. Others believe in reincarnation, that their souls keep returning as other persons until perhaps they can reach godhood. This, however, comes from a frightening ignorance and rationalization of what follows the last breath. It is especially true of those who are suffering the prolonged agonies of physical pain and have determined that death, which will end the pain, is preferable to continued life as they are experiencing it. Dear God, if only those who are not redeemed in Christ Jesus could know the true consequences of that for which they wish!

I believe that anyone who professes to be a redeemed Christian and lives in fear of death does so out of an unconscionable ignorance of Scripture or a potentially dangerous lack of faith in God's Word. No genuine son or daughter of God the Father should fear death, because they have learned and know the truth that Paul spoke when he said, *"we are confident, I say, and willing rather to be absent from the body, and to be present with the Lord."* (2 Corinthians 5:8). Paul elaborated further on his own personal view that is memorialized in Philippians 1:21–24. *"For to me to live is Christ, and to die is gain. But if I live in the flesh, this is the fruit of my labor: yet what I shall choose I wot not. For I am in a strait betwixt two, having a desire to depart, and to be with Christ; which is far better; nevertheless to abide in the flesh is more needful for you."* What more should any redeemed Christian want? It is not for any of us to determine when to leave, for only God knows when our purpose will have been completed. I expect, however, that He will provide some of us with signs of that completion. I expect that it may be when we perceive that our fruitfulness for Him and usefulness for others is nearing an end. In my personal prayers, I also ask that He guide me to attend to the proper closing of my earthly affairs so that I not leave a mess for those dear ones that I leave behind. If that doesn't happen through no fault of my own, then I know that He will most perfectly attend to the matter for me.

To my personal reconciliation with death, one could reasonably press the issue and respond to me by saying something like "that is fine for you to say. You are eighty years old, you have already lived beyond the full allotment of life and you have no small children dependant on you. But I am only twenty, forty or sixty years old; should I be ready at this time or any other time to accept death and not be subject to any number of negative emotions such as anxiety, fear and regrets?" No, I can't say that. I couldn't even if I knew all about your circumstances. That is why it is a personal issue between you and Jesus. It has to do with the strength of your faith in Him, your knowledge and understanding of His Word, what pain, suffering and neglect your passing might impose on others, etc. If you are a true son or daughter of God, when He calls you, it will be at exactly the moment He has chosen for you to come home to Him. By faith you must believe that whatever "unfinished business" you perceive that only you can finish, will be dealt with by the One who always accomplishes things better than any of us. All that I can say in this respect is that we all should keep earthly affairs as simple as possible, and our souls in such a condition that it doesn't matter at what moment we face Him at His throne, because there will be nothing we will personally regret or wish to hide from Him. We must believe that He will deal lovingly, and in the best interest of all whom we leave behind, no matter the seriousness of any circumstances. Complacency about death comes from one's assurance of salvation; the main business of our lives should be preparation for death and the after life it allows to commence.

John Wesley, the author of the popular hymn, "Amazing Grace," once observed that those who fear death have reason to fear death. From Jesus' perspective it is likely that He rejoices whenever one of His own gives up the ghost and comes home. The homecoming of each saved soul represents a step closer to the day when all of the Lord's work here will be finished and He can gather His whole family into the New Jerusalem for the perfect eternal life He has promised. Spurgeon describes the death of a great Christian man named Baxter. When a friend came to see him moments before his last breath, he asked him, "Mr. Baxter, how are you today?" To that Baxter replied with a big smile, "I'm almost well." That is the kind of faith we should all have who know where we are going.

A Prayer for the Country

I was asked recently at a festive event to offer a prayer for our country. As I look at this nation today, I feel more like crying than praying. I have been a careful observer of this nation for most of my eighty
years, and have seen it go from being a God fearing people to one
who now forbids His name even being mentioned in public schools,
and is being systematically removed from every aspect of public life.
God, that is the God of Abraham, Isaac and Jacob, our Creator God,
is no longer of interest to the majority of the people.

My heart is heavy and cries as did Jeremiah, the weeping prophet,
that great and noble man who preached God's word for forty years to
the very end of David's dynasty, when the destruction of Jerusalem,
and the beginning of the seventy years of captivity in Babylon began.
As it is recorded, God explained to Jeremiah that it was because of
their long and worsening offense against Him that this punishment was
to take place. Not only that, but God then told him, and I here quote:
*"Therefore pray not thou for this people, neither lift up a cry or prayer for
them: for I will not hear them in the time that they cry unto me for their
trouble."* God repeated this admonition to Jeremiah three times.

With this in mind, I find it easier and more fitting to cry than
pray, because I believe that we are today, very close to the condition
that Jerusalem was in when God spoke these words, more than 2400
years ago. However, in the spirit of hope, I truly believe that our merciful God would spare us if we would but learn, even from God's
words to Solomon regarding the manner of response He would consider from an apostate people. God said to Solomon, and I quote:

*If my people which are called by my name, shall humble them-
selves, and pray, and seek my face and turn from their wicked ways; then*

I will hear them from heaven, and will forgive their sins, and will heal their land." As I see it, that is our only hope.

Notice God is calling out to *His* people who are called by *His* name. He is not calling the rest of the world with its many false gods, but only to His people. Who are His people? They are us! They are those who genuinely believe and worship the One and only God, the God of Abraham, Isaac and Jacob. If we, collectively and individually will pray in the manner as He has prescribed, He *will* heal this land!

Our most Holy and merciful God, I pray that you will hear this plea, and soften and humble the hearts of each and everyone of your people, both in the synagogues and churches, so that they will hear and obey, and so that this once great land can be healed.

Amen